Management

Management

Richard M. Hodgetts

Florida International University

Academic Press, Inc.
(Harcourt Brace Jovanovich, Publishers)
Orlando   San Diego   San Francisco   New York   London
Toronto   Montreal   Sydney   Tokyo   São Paulo

Cover photo courtesy of Johnson Wax.

For Nicholas Alexander

Academic Press, Inc.
Orlando, Florida 32887

United Kingdom Edition published
by Academic Press, Inc. (London) Ltd.
24/28 Oval Road, London NW1 7DX

ISBN: 0–12–351060–0
Library of Congress Catalog Card Number: 83–71406
Printed in the United States of America

Contents

Chapter 3:   The Environment of Modern Organizations 52

Part Two: Planning the Enterprise's Direction 87

Chapter 4:   The Fundamentals of Planning 89

Chapter 5:   Strategic Planning in Action 115

Chapter 6:   Decision Making in Action 139

Part Three:

Organizing and Staffing the Structure 175

Chapter 7: Designing the Overall Structure 177

Chapter 8: Coordinating the People and the Work 205

Chapter 9: Recruiting and Selecting the Workforce 236

Chapter 10: **Training and Developing the Organization's Personnel 264**

Part Four: **Leading and Influencing the Personnel 299**

Chapter 11: **Human Behavior in Action 301**

Chapter 12: **Motivation at Work 328**

Chapter 13: Group Behavior in Organizations 358

Chapter 14: Managerial Leadership 387

Chapter 15: Managerial Communication 415

Preface

Every enterprise, regardless of size, faces the challenge of managing operations effectively. In fact, effective management is an objective that organizations have been pursuing for thousands of years, and there is no evidence that this pursuit will cease in the near future. No matter how well a manager carries out his or her job, there are always ways of doing at least part of the task more effectively. Fortunately, over the last half-century, practitioners of management have come to realize that this process of getting things done through others requires more than just experience, intuition, and a genuine concern for the well-being of the workers. It also requires a basic understanding of management fundamentals that is often more efficiently achieved through some formal study than through on-the-job experience exclusively. The purpose of this book is to identify, examine, and explain these fundamentals, or principles, of management. In doing so, I have employed a number of special features.

Special Features

The special features are designed to make this book interesting, useful, and challenging. They have been developed to provide ease of reading and clarity of ideas and to make the book "user friendly."

Overall Model

Managers do many different things throughout their work day. The many tasks can be placed in an overall context of planning, organizing, staffing, leading, influencing and controlling. This is the general model for this book.

Managerial Environment

Management involves more than just a series of functions and does not take place in a vacuum. The manager needs to understand the environment in which he or she operates. For this reason, this book opens with three chapters that examine the nature of management and closes by reviewing the value of management education to the reader. We begin our study of management by looking at the manager's job and the environment in which organizations function, and conclude by putting all of this information into a meaningful and applied perspective.

Objectives and Review Questions

Each chapter begins with a set of objectives and closes with a series of questions for analysis and discussion. The text material is tied directly to these objectives and questions. At the beginning of the chapter there is a preliminary introduction of what will be covered, and at the end there are follow-up questions that can be used to measure reader understanding and progress.

Margin Notes

In each chapter I have written a series of margin comments that appear alongside the text material. The purpose of these comments is to provide a brief summary of or reference to the material that is presented there. For readers who like to make notes as they go along, the comments can be complemented by written personal remarks and summaries that can be used in referring to the text material or studying its contents.

Cartoons, Figures, Exhibits, Charts

Every textbook writer faces the challenge of making the material interesting without sacrificing content. One way in which this can be done is through the use of cartoons, figures, exhibits, charts, and other materials that enhance the readability and flow of the book. In this text I have used these tools to present information in an interesting, informative, and entertaining style.

Photographs

In Chapter 2 the history of management thought is presented. This chapter contains photographs of famous management personalities, making it easier for the reader to associate names, faces, and contributions.

Chapter Summaries

At the end of each chapter, I have written a brief summary of the major points that were presented. The purpose of these summaries is to provide a quick refresher for study and review purposes.

Glossaries

At the end of each chapter there is a glossary of the important terms presented in that chapter. This chapter glossary allows the reader to quickly review the most important terms associated with the material.

End-of-Chapter Cases

Two cases appear at the end of each chapter. The first is a short one that provides the opportunity to apply some of the major ideas in the chapter to a real-life situation. The second is longer and gives the reader a chance to gather together most of the material in the chapter and apply it to a detailed and involved situation. I have called these longer cases "You Be the Consultant." This type of case allows the reader to assume the role of managerial decision maker and apply chapter materials to lifelike situations. I believe this type of case to be unique.

At first, some readers will have trouble analyzing these cases. By carefully reading each one, making notes, and then rereading it, however, the reader will grasp the critical issues and topics. A review of the chapter material will help establish the link between the text material and the case data. Finally, recommendations and answers to the questions at the end of the case can be formulated. The important thing to remember in working with these cases is that your analytical ability will improve with experience. Most readers will find the case analysis approach to be an interesting growth process and one of the most valuable aspects of this text.

Comprehensive Cases

Comprehensive cases appear at the end of each major section of the book. These cases were developed and written by Dr. Donald F. Kuratko of Ball State University and Dr. Norman Gierlasinski of the University of Montana, especially for use in this text. They are designed to be used as a supplement to those that appear at the end of each chapter by providing a basis for discussion and analysis of material found in their respective sections. These cases apply and integrate material from the entire section. They are challenging, stimulating, and fun.

Supplementary Materials

While *Management* is a detailed text and is able to stand by itself, supplementary materials have been designed for use by students and teachers.

Student Resource Manual

A student resource manual accompanies this text. It was written by Dr. Jane Gibson of Nova University, Regina A. Greenwood, and Dr. Ronald G. Greenwood of the General Motors Institute. The purpose of the *Student Resource Manual* is twofold: to reinforce the concepts presented in *Management* and to complement the coverage in the text. Concepts are reinforced by the use of true-false, multiple choice, and matching exercises. The text coverage is complemented by the inclusion of additional problems, application exercises, and several readings for each part of the text.

Instructional Aids

In addition to the student resource manual, an extensive package of instructional aids accompanies *Management.*

Instructor's Resource Manual

The instructor's resource manual contains the following features.

(1) Lecture Review and Organization.   For each chapter in *Management,* the instructor's resource manual provides (a) learning objectives, (b) a brief summary of the chapter, (c) a chapter outline, (d) a set of comprehensive lecture notes, and (e) suggestions on how to teach the chapter.

(2) Class Discussion and Case Analysis.   The questions at the end of the chapter are designed for analysis and discussion. The cases have been developed as a means of reinforcing the important concepts in the chapter. The instructor's resource manual provides recommended answers to all of the questions at the end of the chapter as well as the questions that follow the cases. Suggested answers and strategies for using the comprehensive cases are also provided.

Test Manual

A detailed test bank of true-false and multiple choice questions has been developed for use with *Management.* For each chapter in the book, there are 25 true-false and 75 multiple choice questions. This test bank is the most comprehensive of any in the field.

Transparencies

Approximately 100 transparencies are available to the instructor. Chosen for their pedagogical value, these transparencies are designed to complement the lectures and provide a basis for discussion of key concepts in the book.

Computerized Test Service

A computerized version of the Test Bank is available to adopters. Besides allowing microcomputer test generating, this service also provides options for random question selection and for inclusion of your own test questions.

Acknowledgments

Many people played an important role in helping me write this text. My family, from whom I took so much time, deserves my deepest thanks. I would also like to express my appreciation to the staff at Academic Press who worked so closely with me on this project, including Susan Elliott Loring, my sponsoring editor; Julia Jones, associate editor; Frank Soley, designer; and Mickie Thomason, production assistant.

The reviewers who read the manuscript and offered copious suggestions for improvement played a decisive role in the final output. These include William Biggs, Beaver Evening/Weekend College; Gary Cameron, Washburn University of Topeka; Ed Cavert, Northern Virginia Community College; Martin Gannon, University of Maryland; Robert Gatewood, University of Georgia; Don Gibson, Nova University; Jane Gibson, Nova University;

Joseph Gray, Nassau Community College; Ronald Greenwood, GMI Engineering and Management Institute; Norman Harbaugh, Georgia State University; Durward Hofler, Northeastern Illinois University; A. T. Hollingsworth, University of North Carolina at Asheville; Ron Johnson, Texas A & M University; C. W. Millard; Edward J. Morrison, University of Colorado; George Odiorne, University of Massachusetts at Amherst; John Reynolds, Texas A & M University; Harriett Rice, Los Angeles City College; Maurice Sampson, Community College of Philadelphia; Kenneth Thompson, University of Notre Dame; Father David T. Tyson, University of Notre Dame; Phil Van Auken, Baylor University; John Woods, College Text Research Associates.

Finally, I would like to thank my colleagues both at Florida International University and around the country who have always been available when I had a question or needed assistance regarding what to put into the book or to leave out. As always, Fred Luthans, professor of management, University of Nebraska, has proven to be a wise counselor and a good friend. Don Kuratko and Norm Gierlasinski took time out of their busy schedules to write the comprehensive cases for me. Tim Hollingsworth, University of North Carolina at Asheville; Ron Johnson, Texas A & M University; Henry Albers, former Dean of the University of Petroleum and Minerals in Dhaharan, Saudi Arabia; John F. Mee, Indiana University; and Wayne Cascio, University of Colorado, Denver, have always been helpful with both their time and their ideas. So have my colleagues Steven Altman, Enzo Valenzi, Karl Magnusen, Dana Farrow, and Efraim Turban. Finally, thanks go to Ruth Chapman, Sharon Quigley, and Amelia Rodriguez for their assistance in typing the manuscript.

Richard M. Hodgetts
Coral Gables, Florida
July 1984

ONE

Introduction

The purpose of Part I of the book is to introduce you to the field of management by providing a general overview of the subject. Some of the specific questions answered in this section include: What is management? How do managers spend their time? How did modern management emerge from the contributions of earlier theorists in the field? How does the external environment affect organizations?

Chapter 1 focuses on management and the manager's job. In addition to learning what the term *management* means, you will learn about the various types of managers and the skills required for success in management's ranks. You will also study the four major management functions and learn how together they enable the manager to get things done through other people.

Chapter 2 discusses the evolution of management thought and the people who have contributed the most important ideas to our developing knowledge of management. How do we currently know so much about management? The answer is that both the art and science of management were learned over thousands of years. The Egyptians provided contributions. So did the Greeks, the Chinese, and the people of virtually every other major civilization. Yet it was not until the rise of the Industrial Revolution that a systematic study of management was undertaken on any large scale. In the work of the early scientific managers who sought ways of getting more done in less time, mechanistic principles of management began to emerge. These principles were eventually complemented by ideas about administrative and behavioral management. The outcome has been a wealth of information useful to managers in their dealings with people, with things, and with the environment in general.

Chapter 3 then examines the environment of modern organizations, considering both the internal and external factors with which enterprises today must contend. The chapter identifies, describes, and analyzes these factors, paying particular attention to such environmental forces as the economy, competitors, customers, suppliers, technology, political–legal issues, customs/culture, and international developments.

When you have finished studying the material in these first three chapters, you will have a basic understanding of what management involves. You will also be aware of some of management's challenges and opportunities.

1

Management and the Manager's Job

Objectives

The success of every organization depends heavily on the ability of its managers. This chapter examines the nature of management and the manager's job. It answers questions such as: What is management? What skills are needed by managers? How do managers spend their time? What functions do managers perform? When you have finished studying the material in this chapter, you will know what management entails and how the modern manager carries out his or her job. You will also be able to

1. define the term *management;*

2. explain why management is both an art and a science;

3. describe the criteria of a profession;

4. compare and contrast the three different types of managers;

5. describe the three skills of a manager and discuss the difference between efficiency and effectiveness;

6. tell how managers spend their time;

7. describe the four basic functional areas of management; and

8. explain the importance of the systems concept to the study of modern management.

The Nature of Management

Management is a universal consideration. Almost every problem faced by organizations or nations can be at least partially solved through effective and efficient management practices. Firms in the private sector continually strive to increase their managerial efficiency and effectiveness, as do organizations in the public sector. All can profit from the ideas and concepts described in this book. In beginning our discussion of modern management, let us start with a consideration of the nature of management. The following material addresses six major topics that help describe what management is all about.

What Is Management?

Management defined

Management has been defined in many different ways. In this book we shall be using the following operational definition: **Management** is the process of setting objectives and coordinating the efforts of personnel in order to attain them. Note that by its very definition, management involves getting things done through other people. The manager must be a planner, communicator, coordinator, leader, and controller; and most of all the manager must be a facilitator. He or she must smooth the way for subordinate performance.

The material in this book is designed both to explain and to teach effective and efficient management practices and principles. Before we begin our discussion, we should point out that not every person who carries the title of manager actually *is* a manager. Some "managers" have so little authority—for example, managers who have to check everything with the boss—that they are little more than managerial assistants. Others really do not want to manage. Preferring to let subordinates be in control, they delegate virtually all of the authority to lower-level people who, then, are responsible for seeing that things get done.

Still others who are called managers only manage some of the time. Consider the following:

> Tim Carver is a sales manager. He was promoted to this position four months ago. Tim spends four days a week on the road calling on customers and helping his people sell. During this time his secretary runs the office. On Friday Tim returns and together the two work on problems that have come up during the week.

Is Tim a manager? Yes, but not all of the time. He spends some of the week getting things done through others and the rest of the time doing things himself. In fact, unless it is company policy, he should not be out selling. He should be in the office handling administrative work or helping the salespeople sell. Now consider the following:

> Mary Carren is an associate administrator at a local hospital. Mary spends approximately 20 percent of her day working with the administrator, 40 percent handling administrative paperwork, and 40 percent meeting with department heads to discuss operational problems and ways of dealing with them. Except for the occasional times when she attends national professional meetings or training programs, Mary's time is spent at the hospital.

Is Mary a manager? Indeed, yes. She spends a great deal of her time getting things done through others. In fact, assuming that both she and Tim are doing their jobs properly, Mary has the greater need for management expertise because her job is more managerial in nature.

Management as an Art and a Science

Is management an art or a science? This question is often asked by both practitioners and students of management. The answer is: Management is *both* an art and a science.

Management requires the use of behavioral and judgmental skills . . .

As an art, management requires the use of behavioral and judgmental skills that cannot be quantified or categorized the way scientific information in the fields of chemistry, biology, and physics can be. For example, management involves communicating, motivating people, leading, and using qualitative judgment, intuition, gut feeling, and other nonquantifiable abilities. In this respect, management is similar to another art, acting. Who can say precisely why one actor is a great Richard II and another is merely good? Although theater critics attempt to describe differences in style, interpretation, and movement, their evaluations are subjective and open to dispute. Critics cannot quantify the qualities of a performance.

A manager can be described as an actor in an organizational setting. Just as the actor tries to sway the audience, the manager tries to influence those with whom he or she comes into contact in the enterprise. Both have objectives, both strive to plan and execute their strategies, and both are judged by a group of critics. A major difference, however, is that the actor can go home after a poor performance with the resolve of doing better the next day. The manager often finds that yesterday's mistakes remain and have to be dealt with today and tomorrow.

as well as computers and quantitative formulas.

Management is a science, as well as an art, in that it requires the use of logic and analysis. The manager arrives at a solution by systematically observing, classifying, and studying facts in relation to the problem at hand. The scientific aspects of management have been greatly advanced by the development of computers and applicable mathematical formulas. Today there are quantitative techniques that can be used for dealing with a variety of management-related problems, ranging from the control of inventory to the reduction of customer waiting time. These techniques can also answer such questions as when to repair or replace machine parts and what combination of product lines to manufacture for maximum profits.

When dealing with people, managers approach management as an art; when dealing with material things, they approach it as a science. The approach used most often varies at different levels of the organizational hierarchy. At the lower levels of an organization, managers most often face problems that can be resolved using scientific techniques, for example, problems in work flow, machine replacement, and overall efficiency. At the upper levels, managers most often solve problems using judgment, reflection, thought, and intuition. Successful managers at *all* levels of the hierarchy, however, need to employ both the art and science of management.

Management as a Profession

Profession defined

In addition to being an art and a science, management is a **profession.** By definition, "a profession is a vocation whose practice is founded upon an understanding of the theoretical structure of some department of learning or science, and upon the abilities accompanying such understanding."[1] To

1. Cited by Morris L. Cogan in Howard W. Vollmer and Donald L. Mills, *Professionalization* (Englewood Cliffs, N.J.: Prentice-Hall, 1966), p. 10.

qualify as a profession, an occupation must meet five major criteria. It must accumulate knowledge about the field and require competent application of that knowledge. It must also accept social responsibility, exercise self-control, and receive community sanction.[2] In ways that vary according to the kind of business, management meets all of these criteria.

Knowledge

Management knowledge has accumulated rapidly during the past ten years.

Management meets the first criterion because a large fund of information has been accumulated on the subject. Particularly during the last ten years, the amount of management-related research and writing has risen dramatically. Articles, books, college courses, and degree programs all make this information available to managers.

Competent Application

Competent application occurs on the job.

Management encourages competent application of knowledge, using a system of on-the-job controls. Other professions such as medicine and law ensure competent application by certifying people for practice. Management provides no such preliminary screening process. Screening occurs on the job and those who are unable to measure up are replaced by others who can.

Social Responsibility

Business assumes social obligations.

Today, more than ever, business is aware of its social role. Without neglecting obligations to stockholders, companies are trying to be good citizens. They demonstrate this intent in various ways, for example, by contributing time and money to charitable organizations, by creating programs to train the hard-core unemployed, by developing voluntary ecological programs to protect the environment, and by setting up consumer clinics to help customers understand how to use the company's products and services better.

Self-Control

It employs self-control . . .

Business exercises self-control through both industry codes of conduct and the ethical codes of managers. Industry codes are developed by industry representatives to protect the image and reputation of all the industry's firms. Managers' ethical codes depend on their personal standards, and, according to research, most executives believe that their ethical standards are higher than ever before. Of course, many people argue that managers try to get away with as much unethical conduct as they can. Managers, however, are quick to point out that with today's media coverage and the ever-present possibility of public disclosure, they are not likely to resort to unethical conduct, even if they are tempted to do so. Self-control is now a prerequisite for effective management.[3]

---

2. Kenneth R. Andrews, "Toward Professionalism in Business Management," *Harvard Business Review,* March–April 1969, pp. 50–51.
3. Steven N. Brenner and Earl Molander, "Is the Ethics of Business Changing?" *Harvard Business Review,* January–February 1977, pp. 57–72.

Table 1–1 Job Titles in Different Departments and at Various Hierarchical Levels

Organizational Level	Department				
	Marketing	Production	Finance	Accounting	Personnel
Top	Vice-President	Vice-President	Vice-President	Comptroller	Vice-President
Middle	Division Sales Manager	Purchasing Manager	Credit Manager	Internal Auditor	Director of Training
First-line	Unit Sales Manager	Foreman	Unit Supervisor	Accounting Supervisor	Training Supervisor

Community Sanction

and has community sanction.

Management is now widely recognized as a profession. The public knows of business's contributions to social programs. More generally, it knows how important effective management is to our free enterprise system.

Types of Managers

For classification purposes, there are three types of managers: first-line, middle, and top. These managers have different titles depending on the field or department in which they work. Table 1–1 provides some examples of the titles commonly found at each hierarchical level.

First-Line Managers

Many **first-line managers** are called supervisors, although, depending on their specific jobs, they may instead have other titles such as foreman in a production plant, ward nurse in a hospital, or department chairperson in a university. First-line managers supervise employees and resources at the lowest levels of the organizational hierarchy (see Figure 1–1). Much of their concern is with seeing that specific work assignments are carried out on time.

Most first-line managers find their days continually interrupted by workers who need their assistance and problems that require immediate solutions. These managers spend very little time with superiors or outsiders; instead they concentrate on technical details, work quality, work quantity, employee job performance, and employee coaching and counseling. Robert Guest has reported that more than two-thirds of the activities of first-line managers consist of talking (46.6 percent) and looking (20.9 percent).[4]

First-line managers spend much of their time talking and looking.

Middle Managers

Middle managers function between first-line and top managers (see Figure 1–1). Their jobs vary according to their positions in the middle management

4. Robert H. Guest, "Of Time and the Foreman," *Personnel*, May 1956, p. 482.

Figure 1–1   Management Levels in the Hierarchy

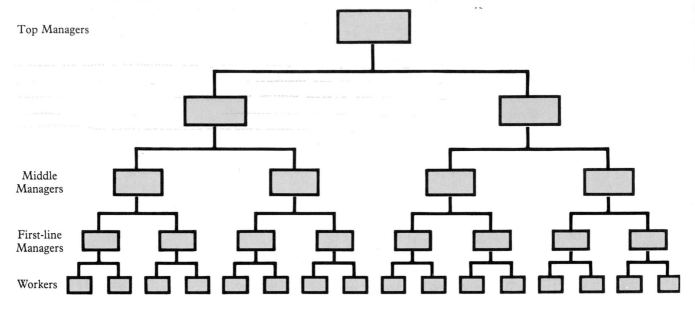

Top Managers

Middle
Managers

First-line
Managers

Workers

ranks. For example, those who directly supervise first-line managers are more concerned with day-to-day activities than are those who report directly to a top manager. The latter middle managers, in fact, often spend as much as 25 percent of their time away from the office working with clients, customers, and other key groups. In this regard, their work is very similar to that of the top manager.

In contrast to the hectic life of the first-line manager, the life of the typical middle manager is slower and more carefully planned. Commenting on the way middle managers see themselves, Lyman Porter and Edward Ghiselli have written that "they seem to describe themselves as stable and dependable individuals who try to avoid making mistakes on the job or elsewhere."[5]

The middle manager coordinates organizational activities.

Much of the activity of middle managers is related to organizing and controlling resources. Middle managers participate in meetings with superiors and other managers, handle paperwork, write reports, and carry out other activities designed to keep the organizational machine moving smoothly. J. H. Horne and Tom Lupton have found that middle managers spend more than half their time giving and seeking information (42 percent) and seeking and preparing explanations (15 percent).[6] These managers concentrate on coordinating organizational activities.

Top Managers

Top managers have many different titles. Some of the most common include chairman of the board, chief executive officer, president and vice-

---

5. Lyman Porter and Edwin Ghiselli, "The Self Perceptions of Top and Middle Management Personnel," *Personnel Psychology*, 1957, p. 402.

6. J. H. Horne and Tom Lupton, "The Work Activities of 'Middle' Managers: An Exploratory Study," *Journal of Management Studies*, February 1965, p. 26.

president in business firms; administrator and director in government and hospital organizations; and academic vice president and dean in academic organizations. These individuals are the chief policymaking people in their organizations.

Top managers are planners.

Planning is an important part of every top manager's job. In fact, it usually takes more of the manager's time than any other function. Top managers chart the overall course of action; the other managers follow through by organizing and coordinating the necessary activities (middle managers) and seeing that the final output is produced (first-line managers).

Individuals who make it to the top usually do so because they have been successful at the middle levels. Do these individuals have any characteristics in common? A *Fortune* Magazine survey found that they do.[7] After surveying the chief executive officers of the 500 largest industrials, the magazine reported that almost half of these managers had a master's or doctor's degree and that another 19 percent had done graduate work. They typically had majored in business in undergraduate school and one-third had graduate business degrees. Most (84 percent) came from middle-class families and reported an average work week of more than 50 hours. Finally, the survey reported that there was no one road to the top in terms of functional area. Marketing, finance, and production all produced top managers, although marketing did produce the largest number, 28 percent, while finance produced 25 percent, and production 19 percent. The remaining 28 percent came from all other functional areas, including the legal field.

Management Skills

Success at the lower levels of management does not require the same combination of managerial skills as does success at the upper levels. Robert Katz has identified three different kinds of managerial skills: technical, human, and conceptual. As seen in Figure 1–2, the requisite degree of each kind of skill varies, depending on the manager's level in the management hierarchy.[8]

Figure 1–2
Relative Amounts of Conceptual, Human, and Technical Skills Needed for Effectiveness at Various Levels of the Management Hierarchy

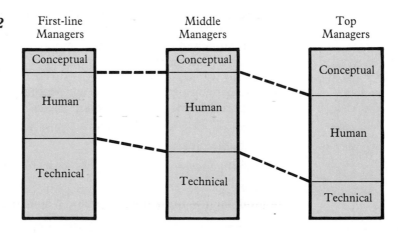

7. Charles Burck, "A Group Profile of the Fortune 500 Chief Executives," *Fortune,* May 1976, pp. 172–177, 308–312.

8. Robert L. Katz, "Skills of an Effective Administrator," *Harvard Business Review,* September–October 1974, pp. 90–102.

Technical skill is the ability to use the techniques, procedures, and tools of a specific field. This skill is particularly important at the lower levels of the organization where the manager needs to know how the work is done. Only in this way can the manager direct subordinates effectively and assist them when they have problems. Many times, in fact, lower-level managers are given their positions because of their ability to do technical work well. Management reasons that if these workers know how to do the job, they will also do well in supervising the work of others. After all, at this level of the hierarchy, the main concern of the manager is to get the work out.

Human skill is the ability to communicate, motivate, and lead individuals and groups. An understanding of human relations and organizational behavior is most important to managers in the middle ranks of the management hierarchy. Because these managers are concerned with directing lower-level supervisors and other middle managers, their jobs are more human than technical in nature. The ability to persuade, negotiate with, and coordinate the activities of others is the key to their success.

Many people like to describe the middle manager as a kind of politician. Situated between upper- and lower-level management, this individual takes top-management directives, turns them into operational plans, and passes them on to the lower management for action. The middle manager must have all the human skills of a politician who is trying to balance the various needs or concerns of groups with different interests. No wonder one researcher has reported that some of the things middle managers want to learn more about include (1) how to relate to people in higher-level positions; (2) how to acquire communication skills on a one-to-one basis, in oral presentations, in listening, and in obtaining information; (3) how to improve their skills in sizing up employees; (4) how to use time more efficiently; (5) how to become results oriented rather than activity oriented; and (6) how to deal with organizational politics.[9]

Conceptual skill is the ability to plan, coordinate, and integrate all of the organization's interests and activities. It is most important at the upper levels of the organization where long-range forecasting and planning are the principal activities. To chart the organization's course, the top manager must be able to balance the demands of the organization's various departments and units with the demands of the external environment. Some other characteristics of the top manager include

- the capacity to abstract, to conceptualize, to organize, and to integrate different ideas into a coherent frame of reference;

- tolerance for ambiguity—the ability to withstand confusion until things become clear;

- intelligence—the capacity not only to abstract but also to be practical; and

- judgment—the ability to know when to act.[10]

---

9. Peter D. Couch, "Learning To Be a Middle Manager," *Business Horizons,* February 1979, p. 37.

10. Harry Levinson, "Criteria for Choosing Chief Executives," *Harvard Business Review,* July–August 1980, pp. 114–116.

Technical skill is the ability to use the techniques, procedures, and tools of a specific field.

Human skill is the ability to communicate, motivate, and lead.

Conceptual skill is the ability to plan, coordinate, and integrate activities.

Notice in Figure 1–2 that as a manager progresses up the hierarchy the importance of technical skill decreases while the importance first of human skill and then of conceptual skill increases. The lower-level manager must be a technician who knows a great deal about one area of operations; the top manager must be a generalist who knows a little bit about many areas of organizational activity. The former has to take a narrow view of things, the latter a broad view.

Efficiency and Effectiveness

Although often used interchangeably, the terms *efficiency* and *effectiveness* have different meanings. The distinction is important because successful managers tend to be *both* efficient and effective.

Efficiency is measured by output/input.

Efficiency is measured by dividing output by input. It is an economic concept. A manager who initiates a cost-cutting program that reduces overall departmental expenses by 10 percent is being efficient. The amount of work being done (output) remains the same while the cost of producing this output (input) declines. Another efficient manager is the one who has new machinery installed so that the number of units produced per hour (output) increases while the amount of materials and labor (input) remains the same.

Effectiveness means doing the right things.

Effectiveness pertains to the manager's ability to choose appropriate objectives and the means for achieving them. While efficiency means doing things right, effectiveness means doing the right things. Of the two, effectiveness is more important. The reason is perhaps best explained by Peter Drucker, the well-known management writer and consultant, who has noted that "The pertinent question is not how to do things right but how to find the right things to do, and to concentrate resources and efforts on them."[11]

It does no good to attain an objective efficiently if the objective is wrong. For example, organizations that produce goods and services for which there is a limited market do not realize high profits. Their major problem is not cost or price; it is market demand. Regardless of price, does anyone but a barber really want to buy a straightedge razor? Is there much demand for shirts that have been out of fashion for five years? Are many people interested in buying an inexpensive, inefficient air conditioner when utility prices are so high? Products such as these have very limited markets no matter how efficiently they can be produced.

Figure 1–3 shows how efficiency or inefficiency and effectiveness or ineffectiveness have been combined in the automobile industry. Notice that efficiency and effectiveness are *independent* factors in that one does not affect the other. A manager can be high in both, low in both, or high in one and low in the other.

A manager who is high in both sets appropriate objectives and is efficient in attaining them. A manager who is low in both sets inappropriate objectives and is inefficient in attaining them. A manager who is effective–inefficient sets appropriate objectives but spends too much time and uses too many resources attaining them. Finally, a manager who is ineffective–efficient

11. Peter F. Drucker, *Managing for Results* (New York: Harper & Row, 1964), p. 5.

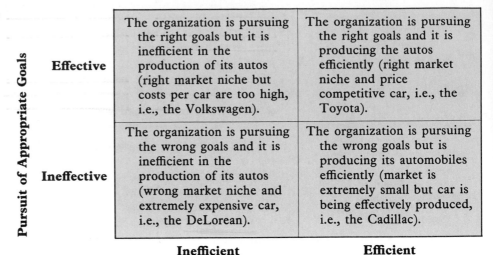

Figure 1–3
Efficiency and Effectiveness in the Automobile Industry in the Early 1980s

pursues the wrong objectives but attains them at a very reasonable cost. Of the latter two combinations, the second is less desirable. More organizations fail because they are ineffective than because they are inefficient.

How Managers Spend Their Time

Over the years a number of researchers have sought to expand our understanding of management by answering the questions: How do managers spend their time? What do they do during their work day?

The Mahoney Study

In one study Thomas Mahoney and his associates studied managers operating at all levels of the hierarchy, from supervisor to president.[12] Their research involved 452 managers from 13 companies. The results are presented in Figure 1–4.

The figure shows that lower-level managers do less planning than their upper-level counterparts. Planning takes up only 15 percent of the lower-level manager's time compared with 28 percent of the upper-level manager's. Notice also from the figure that the need for the conceptual skills of the generalist is much higher at the upper levels than at the lower levels, while the middle manager has to be a coordinator and negotiator. The Mahoney study supports our comments on the skills needed by managers at the various levels of the hierarchy.

The Mintzberg Study

More recently studies have focused on determining whether managers really behave as they are said to by literature in the field. Henry Mintzberg fol-

---

12. Thomas A. Mahoney, Thomas H. Jerdee, and Stephen J. Carroll, "The Job(s) of Management," *Industrial Relations,* February 1965, pp. 97–110.

Figure 1–4
Distribution of Assignments
Among Job Types at Each
Organizational Level

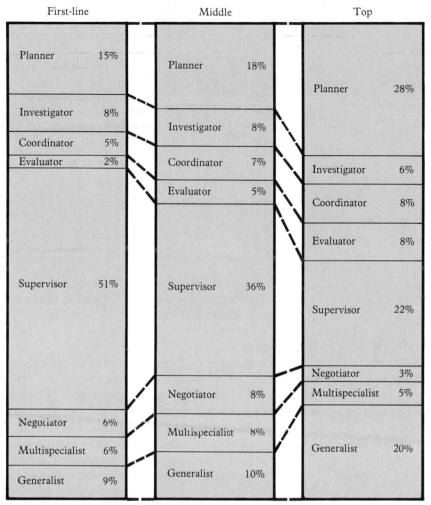

First-line

Planner	15%
Investigator	8%
Coordinator	5%
Evaluator	2%
Supervisor	51%
Negotiator	6%
Multispecialist	6%
Generalist	9%

Middle

Planner	18%
Investigator	8%
Coordinator	7%
Evaluator	5%
Supervisor	36%
Negotiator	8%
Multispecialist	8%
Generalist	10%

Top

Planner	28%
Investigator	6%
Coordinator	8%
Evaluator	8%
Supervisor	22%
Negotiator	3%
Multispecialist	5%
Generalist	20%

Note: Totals may not add up because of rounding.
Source: Thomas A. Mahoney, Thomas H. Jerdee, and Stephen J. Carroll, "The Job(s) of Management," *Industrial Relations,* February 1965, p. 103. Used by permission.

lowed five top managers for one week, analyzing their behavior and attempting to categorize the functions they performed.[13] Basically he found that these managers did not perform *all* of the traditional functions described in the literature. However, he did find that their work activities could be classified into three categories representing types of roles: interpersonal, informational, and decisional. Figure 1–5 lists these categories and the specific roles contained in each.

Managers keep the organization running smoothly.

The manager assumes **interpersonal roles** to keep the organization running smoothly. As a *figurehead,* the manager meets important people, takes customers to lunch, and simply lets people know that he or she is the key person. As a *leader,* the manager is responsible for hiring, training, counseling, and directing subordinates. As a *liaison,* the manager interacts

13. Henry Mintzberg, "The Manager's Job: Folklore and Fact," *Harvard Business Review,* July–August 1975, pp. 49–61; and Henry Mintzberg, *The Nature of Managerial Work* (Englewood Cliffs, N.J.: Prentice-Hall Inc., 1973).

Figure 1–5
The Manager's Role

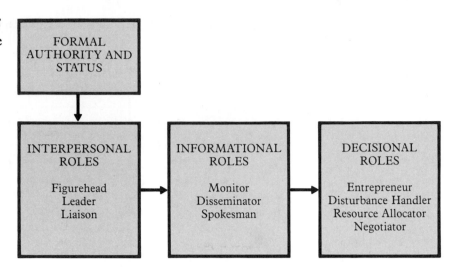

with people at the same level of the hierarchy as well as with others outside the organization.

They gather and pass on information.

Three **informational roles** enable the manager to gather and pass on information. As a *monitor,* the manager talks to subordinates and gathers information that is useful in running the department. He or she is also a *disseminator* who passes information along to subordinates. Without the manager, many employees would have little way of knowing what was happening in the organization. As a *spokesperson,* the manager provides information to people outside the department, either to inform the public about organizational activity or to satisfy influential people who control the organization.

They make decisions.

The four **decisional roles** are the ones through which the manager makes things happen. He or she may act as an *entrepreneur,* or owner-manager, who seeks to improve the unit and adapt it to changing conditions. In this role, the manager looks for new ways to increase the department's effectiveness. The manager may also act as a *disturbance handler,* by trying to resolve problems before they become serious. As a *resource allocator,* the manager decides who will get resources and how much they will receive. These resources include salaries, secretarial assistance, and the manager's own time. In the role of resource allocator, the manager also designs the unit's organizational structure, deciding, for example, who will do what and who will report to whom. Additionally, the manager exercises control by requiring subordinates' decisions to be approved prior to implementation. Finally, the manager is a *negotiator,* a role that varies with the level of the organization. For example, the president may lead the organization's team in negotiating a new contract, while a first-line supervisor may discuss a grievance problem with the shop steward. Negotiating is a major part of the manager's job because only the manager has the authority to make the required decisions and to commit organizational resources.

Every manager performs these 10 roles. Some, however, will be more important to the individual manager than others. For example, sales managers spend the largest percentage of their time in interpersonal roles. Staff managers spend most of their time in informational roles since they are experts who manage departments that advise other parts of the organization. Production managers most often assume decisional roles.[14]

Management Functions

The roles described by Mahoney, Mintzberg, and other researchers provide a basis for the study of management in that they allow the formation of a *functional framework*. This framework helps us to identify and analyze each of the management functions. It shows the component parts of the manager's job.

In this book we will examine four basic functional areas of management: (1) planning the enterprise's direction, (2) organizing and staffing the structure, (3) leading and influencing the personnel, and (4) controlling organizational operations and resources. Before we begin, however, a few introductory remarks are in order. First, some people might argue with our choice of these four specific functional areas, suggesting, for example, that planning and decision making should be considered separately. We realize that arguments can be made for other categories because the four functional areas encompass many managerial duties. For purposes of analysis, however, we have grouped similar duties together.

Second, there is no universal agreement regarding the management functions that every manager performs. If we looked into a large enough number of organizations, we would indeed find some managers who had very little staffing responsibilities and some who were greatly limited in their decision-making power. The four functional areas we have identified, however, are both encompassing and representative of the modern manager's job.

Finally, these functions will be studied in sequence, beginning with planning and ending with controlling, although in practice the manager does not perform them in this way. He or she actually may begin with influencing, go on to planning, then to organizing, and then to controlling. The manager's schedule depends on the problems or issues that arise day to day and hour to hour. It is important to understand that the managerial functions are *interrelated*.

Planning the Enterprise's Direction

Planning defined

Planning is the process of setting objectives and then determining the steps needed to attain them. In carrying out this process, organizations often rely on many different types of plans, such as purposes or missions, objectives, strategies, policies, procedures, rules, programs, and budgets. These types of plans vary in nature and scope, with some being developed at one level of the hierarchy exclusively while others are developed at every level. The planning process itself consists of five steps: (1) awareness of the opportunity, (2) establishment of objectives, (3) determination and

---

14. Mintzberg, "The Manager's Job: Folklore and Fact," p. 59.

choice of alternative courses of action, (4) formulation of derivative plans, and (5) budgeting of the plan.

In large companies the planning process is called strategic planning. The four elements of a strategic plan include the formulation of the basic mission, the setting of long-range objectives, the determination of strategy, and the management of the organization's product lines. Having determined its strategic plan, the organization then begins developing an operational plan that breaks the strategic plan into its component parts, delegates responsibility to the various departments or units, and helps bring the strategic plan to fruition.

Decision making is the process of choosing from among alternatives. Decisions are made under one of three conditions: certainty, risk, and uncertainty. The manager must know under which condition the decision is being made in order to understand how to make the choice. The manager also needs to know what steps form the decision-making process and how this process is affected by behavioral factors such as simplification, subjective rationality, and rationalization. Finally, the manager needs to know how decision making can be improved through the use of management science tools and techniques, through creativity, and through matching decision-making situations with leadership styles.

Planning and decision making are covered in depth in Chapters 4–6.

Organizing and Staffing the Structure

Organizing is the process of assigning duties to personnel and coordinating employee efforts in order to ensure maximum efficiency. Organizing is a natural outgrowth of planning and decision making. Once the organization knows what goals it wants to achieve, it can organize to achieve them.

To organize, the manager must consider both structure and people. In dealing with structure, the manager's primary concerns are departmentalization, job descriptions, organizational charts and manuals, and organizational design. In organizing people, the manager works on the delegation and decentralization of authority, job design, coordination, and overall people–structure fit. The purpose is to meld the structure and the people.

Staffing is the process of recruiting, selecting, training, and developing organizational personnel. This process begins with a forecast of the organization's staffing needs. The manager, for example, may try to determine how many people with what skills the organization should hire during a six-month period. The next steps are recruitment and selection, orientation of the new employees, and then training and development. At this stage, the new personnel who are workers receive technical training, while the new managers receive training that is behaviorally oriented. After the initial training period, some of the new personnel are let go, following performance appraisals; others receive additional training. The manager then starts to fill the empty positions by beginning the staffing process over again.

Staffing considerations are discussed further in Chapters 7–10.

Leading and Influencing the Personnel

As soon as an organization knows what its goals are and has the necessary people to achieve them, leading becomes the manager's most important

Decision making involves choosing from among alternatives.

Organizing is concerned with both structure and people.

Staffing involves recruiting, selecting, training, and developing personnel.

function. **Leadership** is the process of influencing people to direct their efforts toward the achievement of some particular goal. To be good leaders, managers must be knowledgeable about human behavior, the concept of leadership, and communication.

The study of human behavior is important . . .

More specifically, managers must understand the behavior both of individuals and of groups. Personality, attitudes, learning, values, interpersonal relations, and motivation all are important aspects of the individual's behavior. To understand the group, managers should have knowledge of group characteristics, intragroup behavior, intergroup behavior, and the informal organization. With regard to leadership, managers should study both leadership behavior and contingency leadership theory. They must also understand interpersonal and organizational communication. Because **communication** is the process of transferring meanings from sender to receiver, they need to know about communication flows, communication barriers, and ways to develop communication effectiveness.

as is the study of leadership . . .

and the study of communication.

In Chapters 11–15 you will learn how modern managers lead and influence their personnel.

Controlling Organizational Operations and Resources

The **controlling** process consists of three steps: (1) establishment of standards, (2) comparison of results against standards, and (3) correction of deviations. Every organization needs to control both operations and people.

Operations can be controlled . . .

Techniques for controlling operations vary, depending on what needs to be controlled. The budget and the break-even point are particularly useful for handling departmental and divisional control problems. For control of the entire organization, many enterprises have developed key result area control systems. By monitoring performance on these key result areas, they ensure that everything is going according to plan. Additionally, expanding organizations are often turning to operations management tools and techniques and computerized information systems.

as can organizational performance.

Yet control is more than a mechanical process for analyzing quantitative results. Managers must also know how to control people. They must meet the challenge of managing conflict and change, inevitable events in every organization.

The way in which modern managers go about controlling organizational operations and resources is the focus of attention in Chapters 16–18.

Management and the Systems Concept

Managers do not operate in a vacuum. They are continually being influenced by their environment and, in turn, trying to influence it. For example, consider the manager who at noon receives an order from the boss to prepare a special report by 3 P.M. When the manager drops everything and immediately starts working on the report, he or she is being influenced by the environment. When the manager realizes that the report cannot be completed without assistance and orders two subordinates to help, he or she is influencing and leading others. This example shows that the organization is made up of many different interrelated individuals, groups, and forces. These forces can be thought of as systems that affect organizational output.

The Nature of Systems

A **system** is defined in the *Oxford English Dictionary* as a "set or assemblage of things connected, or interdependent, so as to form a complex unit; a whole composed of parts in orderly arrangement according to some scheme or plan." Within every organization there are many systems, from the company at large to the various departments and units within. Each influences the others and, in turn, is influenced by them. Some of the key concepts of systems theory include the following:

1. A system, such as an organization, is more than the sum of its parts. It has to be viewed as a whole.

2. Systems can be either closed or open. When the system has no interaction with its environment, it is closed. When the system receives information, energy, or material from the outside environment in order to function more efficiently, it is open. Organizational systems are open systems since they are continually being influenced by the outside environment and adjusting to new conditions.

3. In order for a system to exist, it must have boundaries that separate it from the outside environment. An organization can be distinguished from its external environment.

4. Closed systems are subject to entropy, a process of increasing energy loss that leads eventually to the system's death. Open systems are able to overcome the effects of entropy because they are influenced by the external environment.

Key concepts of systems theory

5. In responding to the external environment, the organization must contend with two kinds of forces. One kind encourages the organization to continue doing what it is doing and not to take in any new information or material from the outside. The other encourages the organization to change. Effective organizations try to balance the two in order to make necessary changes without creating chaos or uncertainty by changing too rapidly.

6. By using feedback from the external environment, a system is able to achieve dynamic equilibrium. Equilibrium occurs when the organization achieves a steady state and is not in danger of breaking down.

7. Every system is also a subsystem. An organization is a subsystem of the entire industry. Meanwhile, within the organization there are such subsystems as divisions, departments, units, groups, and individuals (see Figure 1–6).

8. Open systems tend to become more specialized as they grow larger. For example, as an organization increases in size, specialized departments will spring up, the organization will expand its product line, and new offices or districts will be created.

Figure 1–6
Organizational Systems

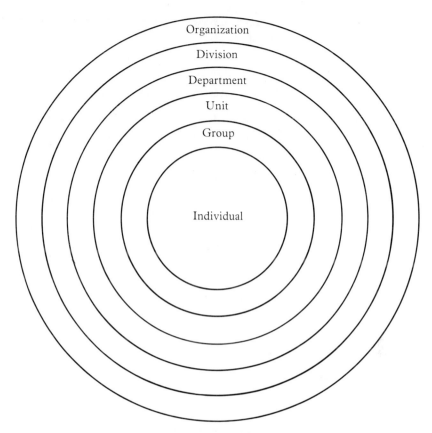

9. Open systems may grow in different ways. For example, one large manufacturing company may produce moderate-price, moderate-quality goods while another turns out high-price, high-quality goods. (As applied to the automobile market, the first organization could be Chevrolet and the second could be Rolls Royce.)

Systems and the Management Job

The systems concept is useful to managers because it helps them understand how their organizations function. Organizations and organizational units continually interact with the external environment. The organization and the external environment are interdependent, and the larger or more powerful the organization, the greater their reciprocal influence. Units within the organization are interdependent, too. Divisions, departments, and individuals all influence each other.

The manager's job is systems oriented.

The manager's job by its very nature is systems-oriented. Managers oversee the **transformation process** through which inputs are transformed into outputs (see Figure 1–7). For example, they supervise new employees (inputs) who produce a certain number of units per hour (outputs).

Figure 1–7
Basic Input-Output Process

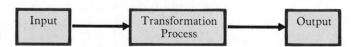

Figure 1-8 Management as a Transformation Process

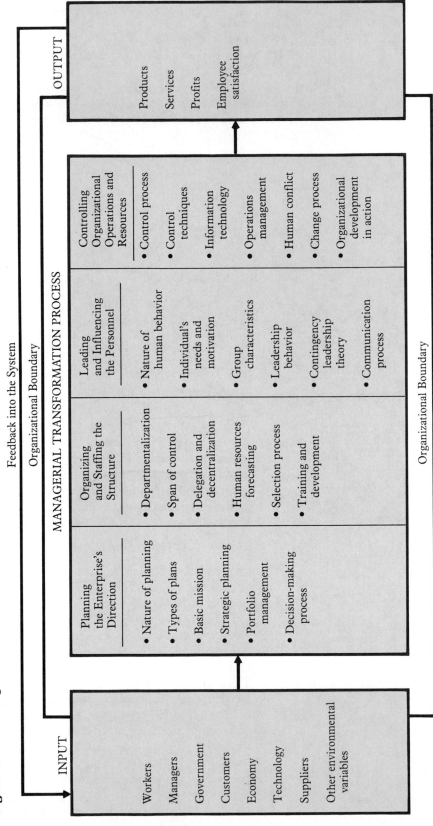

Feedback into the System

Organizational Boundary

MANAGERIAL TRANSFORMATION PROCESS

INPUT

Workers
Managers
Government
Customers
Economy
Technology
Suppliers
Other environmental
 variables

Planning
the Enterprise's
Direction

- Nature of planning
- Types of plans
- Basic mission
- Strategic planning
- Portfolio
 management
- Decision-making
 process

Organizing
and Staffing the
Structure

- Departmentalization
- Span of control
- Delegation and
 decentralization
- Human resources
 forecasting
- Selection process
- Training and
 development

Leading
and Influencing
the Personnel

- Nature of
 human behavior
- Individual's
 needs and
 motivation
- Group
 characteristics
- Leadership
 behavior
- Contingency
 leadership
 theory
- Communication
 process

Controlling
Organizational
Operations and
Resources

- Control process
- Control
 techniques
- Information
 technology
- Operations
 management
- Human conflict
- Change process
- Organizational
 development
 in action

OUTPUT

Products
Services
Profits
Employee
 satisfaction

Organizational Boundary

Managers are responsible for planning, organizing, staffing, influencing, leading, and controlling. To carry out these responsibilities efficiently and effectively, they must understand how the organization interacts with the external environment and how the different parts of the organization work together.

Figure 1–8 completes this chapter's brief discussion of management. In graphic form, it summarizes the material covered throughout the book. As later chapters present the manager's role in more detail, you will learn how to make the process depicted in this figure work well.

Summary

1. Management is the process of setting objectives and coordinating the efforts of personnel in order to attain them. Some managers have a greater need for management training and expertise than do others.

2. Management is both an art and a science. As an art it requires the manager to use behavioral and judgmental skills. As a science it calls for the manager systematically to observe, classify, and study facts in relation to the problem at hand. Management is also a profession because it meets the five requisite criteria. It has accumulated knowledge about the field and requires competent application of that knowledge. It also accepts social responsibility, exercises self-control, and receives community sanction.

3. There are three types of managers. First-line managers supervise workers directly. They are greatly concerned with work quantity, work quality, and employee job performance. Middle managers function between first-line and top managers. They are concerned with organizing and controlling resources and seeing that the organizational machine moves along smoothly. Top managers function at the highest levels of the hierarchy. They are most concerned with charting the overall course of the enterprise.

4. Every manager needs three kinds of skills: technical, human, and conceptual. Technical skill is the ability to use the techniques, procedures, or tools of a specific field and is most important at the lower levels of the hierarchy. Human skill is the ability to communicate, motivate, and lead individuals and groups. It is most important at the middle levels of the hierarchy. Conceptual skill is the ability to plan, coordinate, and integrate all of the organization's interests and activities. It is most important at the upper levels of the hierarchy. In using these three kinds of skills the manager must be both efficient and effective. Efficiency refers to doing things right and is measured by the equation "output/input." Effectiveness means doing the right thing and is measured by market demand considerations such as market share and growth rate.

5. First-line managers spend most of their day supervising, while top managers spend more time planning than anything else. Mintzberg found that managers perform three different types of roles. Their interpersonal roles include figurehead, leader, and liaison person. Their informational roles include monitor, disseminator and spokesperson. Their decisional roles include entrepreneur, disturbance handler, resource allocator, and negotiator.

6. The management process can be broken down into four basic functional areas. The first is planning the enterprise's direction. The second is organizing and staffing the structure. The third is leading and influencing personnel. The fourth is controlling organizational operations and resources.

7. Managers do not operate in a vacuum. They are continually being influenced by their environment and, in turn, trying to influence it. The organization itself

is made up of many different divisions, departments, and individuals. These different units can be thought of as interdependent systems, and the way they work together affects organizational output. The manager who works efficiently and effectively understands how the organization interacts with the external environment and how the different parts of the organization work together.

Key Terms

Communication   The process of transferring meanings from sender to receiver.

Conceptual skill   The ability to plan, coordinate, and integrate all of the organization's interests and activities.

Controlling   The process of establishing standards, comparing results against these standards, and correcting deviations.

Decisional roles   The manager's roles as entrepreneur, disturbance handler, resource allocator, and negotiator.

Decision making   The process of choosing from among alternatives.

Effectiveness   Doing the right thing. It is often measured by market demand considerations such as market share or growth rate.

Efficiency   Doing things right. It is often measured by the equation "output/input."

First-line manager   The lowest level manager in the hierarchy; this individual directly supervises workers.

Human skill   The ability to communicate, motivate, and lead individuals and groups.

Informational roles   The roles a manager plays when he or she monitors information, disseminates it, or acts as a spokesperson.

Interpersonal roles   The manager's roles as figurehead, leader, and liaison person.

Leadership   The process of influencing people to direct their efforts toward the achievement of some particular goal.

Management   The process of setting objectives and coordinating the efforts of personnel in order to attain them.

Middle manager   This individual, who functions between a first-line manager and a top manager, is most concerned with organizing and controlling resources and seeing that the organizational machine moves smoothly.

Organizing   The process of assigning duties to personnel and coordinating employee efforts in order to ensure maximum efficiency.

Planning   The process of setting objectives and then determining the steps needed to attain them.

Profession   A vocation whose practice is founded upon an understanding of the theoretical structure of some department of learning or science, and upon the abilities accompanying such understanding.

Staffing   The process of recruiting, selecting, training, and developing organizational personnel.

System   A set or assemblage of things connected, or interdependent, so as to form a complex unit; a whole composed of parts in orderly arrangement according to some scheme or plan.

Technical skill   The ability to use the techniques, procedures, and tools of a specific field.

Top manager   This person, who functions at the highest levels of the organization, is most concerned with charting the overall course of the enterprise.

Transformation process   The process through which inputs are turned into outputs.

Questions for Analysis and Discussion

1. In your own words, define the term *management*. Illustrate your definition by using an example of a manager and a nonmanager.

2. In what way is management an art? A science? Is it also a profession? Be as complete as possible in your answer.

3. How do the following differ from each other: first-line manager, middle manager, top manager? Compare and contrast the three.

4. What is meant by each of the following terms: *technical skill, human skill, conceptual skill?* Who would profit most from each? Integrate a discussion of the three types of managers into your answer.

5. How does management efficiency differ from management effectiveness? Be sure to define the terms in your answer. Then compare and contrast them.

6. Using Figure 1–4 as your guide, explain how the first-line manager's job differs from that of the middle manager? How does the middle manager's job differ from that of the top manager? Be complete in your answer.

7. Using Mintzberg's research as your guide, describe what the modern manager does when carrying out each of the following roles: interpersonal, informational, decisional. Be sure to describe each role fully.

8. What does the manager do in each of the following four functional areas: (1) planning and decision making, (2) organizing and staffing the structure, (3) leading and influencing the personnel, and (4) controlling organizational operations and resources? Describe each area.

9. How is the systems concept of value to the modern manager? Include in your answer a discussion of the key concepts of systems theory and then relate the use of systems thinking to the use of effective management.

Case

A Great Worker but . . .

In the insurance company where she works, Rosemarie Carillo is considered very efficient. In fact, three months ago she was chosen over 11 others for a promotion to the supervisory level. Rosemarie's performance had been exceptional and, since this is the primary criterion used by management for promotion to the supervisory level, she was the overwhelming choice of the management committee that made the final decision.

Rosemarie initially was overjoyed with the news. However, this is no longer the case. During the last three weeks she has indicated to some of her fellow supervisors that she does not care very much for her job. One of the primary reasons appears to be her inability to get along well with the members of her unit. Rosemarie supervises seven workers, and while she appeared to be establishing a rapport with them soon after her promotion, that is no longer so. Two of the seven have asked for transfers to other units and another has submitted her resignation effective next Friday.

In an effort to understand the problem, Rosemarie's boss has had her in for a talk. He has also talked to three of the people in the unit. Here are their viewpoints:

Rosemarie: I don't really care to supervise these people. They are not very hard working and they resent being shown the proper way to do their job. They seem to think they know it all—but they don't. We could do 25 percent more work if they would just do things the way I show them.

Workers: In the beginning we got along just fine with Rosemarie. However, our feelings have changed. She may have been a great worker but she's a lousy boss. She has very little human relations skill. She tells us what to do, gets angry if we don't do things her way, and is critical of anything less than perfect performance. It's no fun working for her.

1.   In terms of the skills of a manager, which one does Rosemarie have in abundance? Explain.

2.   What exactly seems to be Rosemarie's problem? Why is she having trouble with her work group? Who do they dislike her management style?

3.   If you were Rosemarie's boss, what would you tell her? How would you attempt to help her? Be complete in your answer.

You Be the Consultant

Work, Work, Work

Roberta Sanchez started her own catering service five years ago. At that time she had only two part-time employees. These women worked on weekends only and Roberta accepted only three types of jobs: birthday parties, weddings, and small dinners.

In the beginning, most of Roberta's week was spent planning the menu for each event and getting the food together. After a couple of months, however, she was able to provide the customer with a description of a typical menu and quote a price as soon as she had a basic idea of what the person wanted.

Roberta's good reputation soon began to spread. There were two reasons for her success. First, her prices were at least 10 percent lower than those of the competition. Second, she was an excellent cook and with her assistants could provide fast, efficient service. She seemed to have a knack for the catering business.

A year ago Roberta began expanding her schedule and taking jobs for the middle of the week as well. Since the two women who were working for her had families of their own and could not get away, she hired two other part-time people for this time period. It took a couple of months but these individuals also began to do their jobs extremely well.

When Roberta realized that she could expand her business still further, she decided to hire full-time people and try to generate as much business as possible. She made this decision just four months ago. Since then she has hired five full-timers to supplement the four part-time people. These new people do the same work as the others: they help her prepare the food, purchase any party favors or miscellaneous items that will be needed, transport the food and sundry items to the party's locale, serve the food, clean up afterwards, and return everything to the small store out of which Roberta operates.

Since her decision to go into the business on a full-time basis, Roberta's income has tripled. However, she is not sure the decision was a good one. One of her biggest concerns is that she is now working harder than ever. In the beginning she could set up the menu, order the food, and get everything arranged for that weekend's parties in perhaps five hours. Now she gets up first thing in the morning, begins working, and does not stop until late in the evening. Most of her time is spent seeing that the food is being cooked properly, that nothing is being omitted, and that everyone knows what he or she is supposed to be doing.

Yesterday she mentioned to her husband that she might have overextended herself. "Maybe I should cut back and just handle a small number of parties and dinners each week like I used to do," she said. Her husband disagreed, presenting her with some surprising arguments. The gist of his conversation was as follows:

> You don't need to cut back on the overall business work load. You need to cut down on your own personal work time. You are doing too much. You have to turn more things over to the employees. You supervise and direct everything, yet most of them know almost as much as you do about running this business. You should spend more time planning the operation, talking to customers on the phone, and ordering the food and other things you will need for the party. Turn the busy work over to these other people. Quit killing yourself. You're supposed to be the owner, not one of the workers.

Your Consultation

Assume that you are Roberta's personal friend and that after looking over her operation you find her husband's comments to be accurate. What would you recommend that Roberta do? What skills must she develop? Which does she already have in abundance? Using Figure 1–2 of the text, tell her about the manager's job and where she might be falling down in getting it done. Be as complete as possible in your answer, and be sure that your advice is of a practical (as opposed to a theoretical) nature.

2

Foundations of Modern Management

Objectives

The purpose of this chapter is to study the foundations of modern management. Since the first foundations were laid thousands of years ago, many dramatic changes have occurred. Basically, however, there were three main branches of early management thought: (1) scientific management theory, which sought to increase work efficiency at the lower levels of the organization and served as a forerunner of modern management science; (2) administrative theory, which helped pave the way for modern management theory and the process approach to management; and (3) behaviorism, which helped set the stage for modern behavioral science approaches to management. This chapter explains the emergence, development, and importance of these three sets of ideas. When you have finished reading and studying this material, you will be able to

1. provide a brief review of early management thought for the purpose of illustrating management practices and interests;

2. explain the effect of the Industrial Revolution on the rise of the factory system and the emergence of the scientific management movement;

3. list the contributions of leading scientific managers to American industry;

4. describe the current interests and scope of concern of modern management scientists;

5. explain the contributions of early administrative theorists to management thought and discuss the current interests of these administrative scientists;

6. describe the work of early behaviorists and the emergence of modern behavioral science; and

7. place all three major branches of early management theory in perspective by discussing modern management thought.

Early Management Thought

Management has been practiced for thousands of years. All early civilizations that rose to prominence and power employed management tools and techniques effectively. The Egyptians and Greeks provide representative examples.

Egyptians

The Egyptians had important managerial insights.

The Egyptians are best known for their construction of the pyramids, a massive engineering *and* management feat. From an engineering viewpoint, the largest of these structures, the Great Pyramid in Giza, is almost perfectly square. When intact, it covered an area slightly over 13 acres and was approximately 147 meters high. The sides were accurately oriented to the four cardinal points and, according to modern engineers, the inside is so vast that the Cathedral of Florence, the Cathedral of Milan, St. Paul's in London, Westminster Abbey, and St. Peter's in Rome could all be grouped within it.

To accomplish this engineering feat, the Egyptians had to have important managerial insights into planning, organizing, staffing, leading, and controlling people at work. Stones had to be precut at the quarries, numbered, floated downriver, taken from the raft, dragged to the construction site, and hoisted into place. Much of what is currently known about construction management was undoubtedly known, if only in rudimentary fashion, to the management team that constructed the Great Pyramid.

"Believe me, fellows, everyone from the Pharaoh on down is an equally valued member of the team."

Greeks

The Greeks also had a working knowledge of effective management practices. For example, they were aware that maximum work output could be attained most easily by using uniform methods at a set work tempo. They found this principle to be especially true in the case of monotonous, repetitive, or difficult tasks, and they set the pace with music. This latter approach is still used today, in firms that pipe soft music into their work surroundings to make the environment more pleasant. The Greeks also employed specialization of labor. They realized that great efficiency could be attained if each worker concentrated on just one job or task. In his *Republic*, Plato stated the idea this way:

> Which would be better—that each should try several trades, or that he should confine himself to his own? He should confine himself to his own. More is done, and done better and more easily when one man does one thing according to his capacity and at the right moment. We need not be surprised to find that articles are made better in big cities than in small. In small cities the same workman makes a bed, a door, a plow, a table, and often he builds a house too. . . . Now it is impossible that a workman who does so many things should be equally successful in all. In the big cities, on the other hand . . . a man can live by one single trade. Sometimes he practices only a special branch of a trade. One makes men's shoes, another women's, one lives entirely by the stitching of the shoe, another by cutting the leather. . . . A man whose work is confined to such a limited task must necessarily excel at it.[1]

The Greeks knew about specialization of labor.

While history indicates that early civilizations had already developed important knowledge of management techniques, the writings of select individuals reveal that management philosophy and leadership have been subjects of concern for many centuries. These subjects are studied, for example, in the works of Sun Tzu and Niccolò Machiavelli.

Sun Tzu

The oldest military treatise in the world is the *Art of War* written by Sun Tzu, a Chinese military writer, around 500 B.C. This treatise illustrates that strategy, planning, leadership, and the effective management of people were all basic areas of interest to early military leaders. Commenting on two of these areas, Sun Tzu wrote:

> *On planning:* Now the general who wins a battle makes many calculations in his temple ere the battle is fought. The general who loses a battle makes few calculations beforehand. It is by attention to this point that I can see who is likely to win or lose.[2]
>
> *On directing:* If the words of command are not clear and distinct, if orders are not thoroughly understood, the general is to blame. But if his orders

Planning and directing were areas of interest to ancient military leaders.

---

1. Francis Cornford, *The Republic of Plato* (New York: Oxford University Press, 1959), pp. 165–167.

2. Thomas P. Phillips, *Roots of Strategy* (Harrisburg, Pa.: Military Service Publishing, 1955), p. 23.

are clear, and the soldiers nevertheless disobey, then it is the fault of their officers.[3]

These basic guidelines are of value to military leaders even today.

Niccolò Machiavelli

Niccolò Machiavelli was born in Florence and obtained employment there at the age of 29, eventually serving as an unofficial emissary to every important city-state in Italy, as well as to several outside countries. When the Medici family returned to power in 1512, however, Machiavelli lost his job and was exiled.

During his time in exile, Machiavelli wrote extensively. His most famous book is *The Prince*, which presents broad management principles to which he believed all leaders should subscribe.[4] In particular, Machiavelli set forth four principles of leadership. The first principle was *mass consent*. Every leader should realize that authority emanates from the bottom and that no one is a leader unless the followers agree. Second, a leader must *strive for cohesiveness* in the organization by rewarding friends and supporters and maintaining their allegiance. The leader must also have a *will to survive* to keep him alert and ever-prepared to protect his position should danger strike. Finally, the leader has to *set an example* for the followers so that they can identify with him.

Machiavelli's four principles of leadership

Machiavelli made a systematic analysis of the leader's job and from it derived practical principles that are as useful today as they were 500 years ago. No wonder that one writer has described Machiavelli's works as "bursting with urgent advice and acute observations for top management of the great private and public corporations all over the world."[5]

The Industrial Revolution

The earliest management practices developed in relation to the needs of specific civilizations and countries. When the Industrial Revolution took place in the eighteenth century, however, it affected management practices throughout the entire world. Nowhere was it more fully felt than in Great Britain, where the factory system was in full swing by 1750.

Some of the major developments the Industrial Revolution brought about included (1) a rising per capita income, (2) economic growth, (3) reduced dependence on agriculture, (4) a high degree of specialization of labor, and (5) a widespread integration of markets.[6] These developments occurred in conjunction with the invention of new machinery and the scientific application of job specialization in the workplace. The result was the emergence of the factory system.

---

3. *Ibid*, p. 75.

4. Niccolò Machiavelli, *The Prince* (New York: The Modern Library, 1940).

5. Antony Jay, *Management and Machiavelli* (New York: Holt, Rinehart and Winston, 1967), p. 4.

6. Phyllis Deane, *The First Industrial Revolution* (London: Cambridge University Press, 1965), pp. 5–19.

The Factory System

Before the Industrial Revolution began, many people were employed within their own homes, spinning and weaving textiles. The demand for this output was very high. As a result, attention was directed to finding faster and cheaper methods of production. As technical inventions emerged,[7] the entire textile industry became mechanized.

Technology revolutionized business practices.

This same pattern occurred in other industries, and as it did many small entrepreneurs were gradually forced out of business. The owner-managers lacked the capital to purchase the new, efficient machinery and they could not compete for long with firms that could produce much greater output at a much lower price than they could. When the owners of the new machines realized that it was more efficient to place all of them in one locale and hire a workforce to come to this site to work, the factory system came into being.

The factory system was characterized by strict control of operations. The owners were intent on making the greatest profit possible. Therefore, they focused their attention on streamlining operations, eliminating waste, and increasing output. Their two main areas of concern were production power and standardization of operation.

Power and Standardization

Arnold Toynbee, the great historian, has credited the rise of industrialism to two individuals: James Watt and Adam Smith. Watt provided the power and Smith popularized standardization.

James Watt developed the steam engine.

The power James Watt provided was the steam engine. In 1781 he made his greatest breakthrough in technology with the development of an engine with a rotary, as opposed to an up-and-down, movement. This invention made the machine more adaptable to factory use.[8]

Adam Smith popularized the concept of division of labor.

Adam Smith popularized the concept of **division of labor** in his book *An Inquiry Into the Nature and Causes of the Wealth of Nations* (1776). Using the manufacture of pins as an example, he explained how a group of individuals who specialized their efforts, with one drawing out the wire, a second straightening it, a third cutting it, etc., could make 12 pounds of pins in a day while one of them working alone could not make 20 pins.[9]

While Watt's invention and Smith's concept helped factories increase their output, there was still interest in developing other labor-saving techniques and devices that could further increase productivity. The individuals who helped discover and perfect these techniques have come to be known as scientific managers.

---

7. Some of the most important were John Kay's flying shuttle (1733), James Hargreave's spinning jenny (1765), Richard Arkwright's water frame (1769), Samuel Crompton's "mule" (1779), and Edmund Cartwright's power loom (1785).

8. Daniel A. Wren, *The Evolution of Management Thought,* 2nd edition (New York: John Wiley, 1979), p. 45.

9. Adam Smith, *The Wealth of Nations* (New York: The Modern Library, 1937), p. 7.

Scientific Management

Scientific management was a natural outgrowth of the Industrial Revolution. As the factory system emerged, more and more attention was directed toward increasing output. Managers studied many possible ways to achieve this goal, for example, looking for ways to feed work into a machine at a faster rate, to increase the speed of the machine, and to determine the most efficient flow of materials through the workplace. In every instance, the objective was the same: increased efficiency.

By the middle of the nineteenth century, "efficiency experts" could be found in all large industrial complexes, not only in England, but also in the United States, which was emerging as a giant industrial power. While some of these efficiency experts learned their business through trial and error and on-the-job experience, many of them were trained mechanical engineers. These individuals ushered in the era of scientific management that dominated management thinking until well into the twentieth century. **Scientific management** was a system that attempted to develop ways of increasing productivity and to formulate methods of motivating workers to take advantage of these labor-saving techniques. While many people made contributions to this field, three of the most important American scientific managers were Frederick Taylor, Frank Gilbreth, and Henry L. Gantt.

Frederick Taylor (1856–1915)

Frederick Taylor gained fame through his experiments and writings.

A mechanical engineer by training, Taylor contributed to the field of scientific management by conducting time-and-motion study experiments and by recording his knowledge of management. Taylor's primary objective was to discover the most efficient way of doing a job and then to train the workers to do it that way. Relying heavily on time-and-motion study, Taylor and his associates approached management by breaking a job down into its fundamental operations, determining how each operation could be done quickly and efficiently, and establishing a work quota for the job.

During his career, Taylor conducted many important time-and-motion study experiments. In one case he redesigned the work of individuals who were loading "pigs" of iron (blocks or ingots weighing about 92 pounds each) into an open railroad car. Before Taylor's experiments, the average worker loaded 12½ long tons (2,240 pounds per long ton) a day. After Taylor completed his work, the average individual loaded 47½ long tons a day. In another case Taylor studied the amount of coal a worker shoveled in a day. His experiments led him to conclude that an average scoop load of 21 pounds would result in maximum output. By matching the scoop size and the weight of the coal, Taylor was able to increase the daily number of tons loaded from 16 to 59 and to reduce the average cost of handling a ton of coal from 7.2 cents to 3.3 cents.

In addition to his experiments, Taylor also published articles and wrote books on scientific management. In his best known work, *Principles of Scientific Management,* he set forth what he felt were the four basic **principles of scientific management:**

1. Management should develop a science for each element of the work to be done.

The four basic principles of scientific management

2. Management should scientifically select, train, teach, and develop each worker.

3. Management should cooperate with the worker in ensuring that all of the work is done in accordance with the principles of scientific management.

4. Management should divide work responsibilities between management and the workers with the former studying jobs and determining how they should be done and the latter carrying them out.[10]

By the time he died, Frederick Taylor was already being referred to as the "Father of Scientific Management."

Frank Gilbreth developed a categorization of basic hand motions.

Frank Gilbreth (1868–1924)

Frank Gilbreth passed up the opportunity to attend the Massachusetts Institute of Technology, deciding instead to go into the contracting business. Starting as an apprentice bricklayer, he quickly realized that much of the work was performed inefficiently at best. This realization eventually led him into the area of time-and-motion study.

During his long career Gilbreth made so many contributions to the field that today he is known as the "Father of Motion Study." One of his most significant studies was in bricklaying where, after much experimentation, he was able to increase the number of bricks a man could lay in an hour from 120 to 350. He also pioneered the use of the movie camera for scientific management purposes, filming people in the workplace and then playing back the film to see how the work could be streamlined by eliminating extraneous time and motion. So detailed was his approach to the area that he developed a categorization of basic hand motions (grasp, hold, position) that could be used in analyzing the work. Today these motions are called **therbligs,** Gilbreth spelled backwards with the *t* and *h* transposed.

Henry L. Gantt developed a planning and control chart.

Henry L. Gantt (1861–1919)

Henry L. Gantt was Frederick Taylor's protegé. His most significant contribution was the chart (Figure 2–1) he developed in 1917. Known today as the **Gantt chart,** it shows that scientific managers were not confined to time-and-motion study in their quest to improve worker efficiency. Along the horizontal axis of the chart, work scheduled and work completed are measured. Along the vertical axis are the jobs to be done. In the example given in Figure 2–1, there are five jobs scheduled. The first, order number 94, calls for the production of 4,500 units. The job was begun on January 2 and is scheduled for completion on March 2. The second job, order number 160, was begun on January 23 and is scheduled to be finished on March 16. The *V* at the top of the chart after the week of February 27 indicates the current date, namely March 2. Progress on each order is

10. Frederick Taylor, *Principles of Scientific Management* (New York: Harper & Brothers, 1911), pp. 36–37.

Figure 2–1
A Gantt Chart

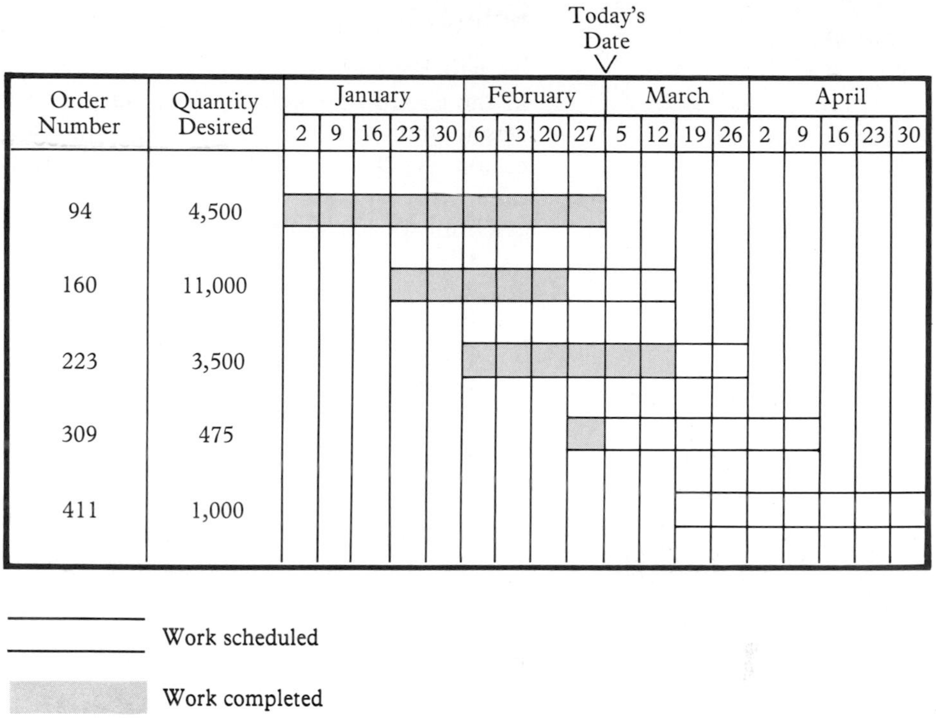

Today's
Date
∨

Order Number	Quantity Desired	January					February				March				April				
		2	9	16	23	30	6	13	20	27	5	12	19	26	2	9	16	23	30
94	4,500	░	░	░	░	░	░	░	░	░									
160	11,000				░	░	░	░											
223	3,500						░	░	░	░	░	░							
309	475										░								
411	1,000																		

──────── Work scheduled

▓▓▓▓▓▓▓▓ Work completed

designated by the dark line bar that extends throughout the bar line. A visual examination of the chart reveals the following:

- Order 94   finished on time
- Order 160   currently one week late
- Order 223   currently two weeks ahead of schedule
- Order 309   currently on time
- Order 411   scheduled to begin March 19

Management Science

The proponents of scientific management made important contributions to the management of work. Their time-and-motion study experiments resulted in dramatic increases in efficiency, and this quantitative orientation continues to the present day. Along the way, however, their work has been complemented by that of other quantitatively oriented people whose interests extend beyond time-and-motion study to encompass linear programming, inventory control, work flow, production planning, purchasing, quality control, quantitative decision making, computers, and systems theory. Today these areas are collectively grouped under the title of **management science,** and modern scientific managers and others with an interest in improving work quantity or efficiency are referred to as *management scientists.* They practice the scientific method, use mathematical tools and techniques, and have a high regard for systems theory.

Scientific Method

As will be seen throughout this chapter, one of the major characteristics of the group that helped establish the foundations of modern management was their interest in the **scientific method.** Today, management scientists emphasize the use of this method because of their interest in solving mathematical or quantitatively oriented problems. The steps they follow in this scientific process are the following:

1. *Identifying the problem:* Here the emphasis is on clearly stating the issue under study. What roadblock or hurdle needs to be overcome? Does the organization need a more efficient purchasing system? An inventory reorder point for certain products? A better work flow design? In other words, what is the purpose of the study?

2. *Obtaining preliminary information:* In this step the management scientist gathers as much available data on the problem as possible. Some of the questions that are addressed include: What is currently known about the situation? What other types of information would be helpful? In this way a link is established between current information and the information needed to solve the problem under study.

Steps in the scientific method

3. *Posing a tentative solution to the problem:* In this step the management scientist states a tentative hypothesis that can be tested and proved to be either right or wrong. The individual, drawing on knowledge of the problem and preliminary information, establishes a problem-solving direction.

4. *Investigating the problem area:* Using currently available data and any other information that can be gathered, the management scientist now examines the problem in its entirety. He or she conducts research, obtains more data, and secures all necessary inputs needed to solve the problem.

5. *Classifying the information:* The management scientist now takes all of the data and puts it into an order that will expedite its use and help establish a relationship with the hypothesis. During this step, he or she analyzes the information and gains insight into how it can be used to solve the problem.

6. *Stating a tentative answer to the problem:* The management scientist now draws a conclusion regarding the "right" answer to the problem. He or she may develop a mathematical formula, set forth a new work flow design, or simply provide a reorder point level for inventory. In any event, a specific recommendation for action is forthcoming.

7. *Testing the answer:* Now the answer or proposed solution is tested. If it works, the problem is solved. If it does not work, the management scientist goes back to Step 3 and continues through the process again, reworking the solution based upon these latest results.

Use of Mathematical Tools and Techniques

A second major characteristic of management science is its reliance on mathematical tools and techniques for decision making and problem solving.

Many of these tools and techniques have been developed and need merely to be modified to meet the particular situation. In some cases, however, the management scientist has to develop a new formula or model that can be tested and modified for use in a specific situation. In using all of these tools and techniques, management scientists often rely upon computers. They have found these machines to be extremely efficient and cost effective in handling the quantitative computations and analyses required for solving modern management problems.

The Systems Approach

Management scientists also have a high regard for the systems approach. This regard is undoubtedly a reflection of their need to understand how decisions affect more than one part of the organization. For example, if they design a more effective inventory control system, they may also have to design a new purchasing system. Of course, the systems concept is not restricted to management scientists. However, they do employ it in their day-to-day operations.

Administrative Management

The early scientific managers had great success at the lower levels of the organizations. As output increased and operations grew, however, organizations began to be confronted with new management problems. Planning and coordinating operations became much more important than ever before, and the organization of people in the workplace became a focal point for consideration. The individuals who were interested in dealing with these problems began to formulate theories of administration. Four of the most famous were Henri Fayol, Mary Parker Follett, James D. Mooney, and Lyndall F. Urwick.

Henri Fayol (1842–1925)

Henri Fayol, a Frenchman, spent his entire career working for a mining combine. By the age of 46 he was president of the organization and remained so for 30 years.

Fayol's interest was in the administrative side of operations. In particular he was concerned about the fact that different abilities were needed as one moved up the management ranks. At the lower levels an individual required greater technical skill in order to supervise workers effectively. At the upper levels the individual required administrative ability in order to get things done through other people. This idea is illustrated in Figure 2–2.

Fayol's experience led him to conclude that there were five basic functions of administration: planning, organizing, commanding, coordinating, and controlling. *Planning* called for the formulation of objectives and an operating program. *Organizing* entailed the effective coordination of resources for accomplishing the predetermined objectives. *Commanding* was the art of effective leadership. *Coordinating,* the orderly arrangement of group efforts to provide unity of action, ensured the harmony necessary

Henri Fayol identified five basic functions: planning, organizing, commanding, coordinating, and controlling.

Figure 2–2
Managerial Skills

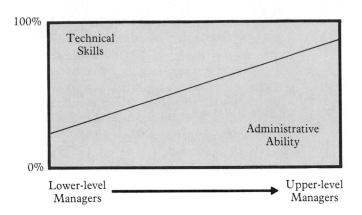

for a smoothly functioning organization. *Controlling* involved seeing that everything was done in accord with the adopted plan.

Fayol also set forth a series of administrative principles. These principles were intended as flexible guidelines for managing both people and work. The 14 principles Fayol felt he used more frequently were

1. *Division of labor:* Efficiency can be increased through work specialization.

2. *Authority and responsibility:* Authority, which is the right to command, should always be equal to responsibility, which is the obligation or duty to carry out assigned tasks.

3. *Discipline:* In its essence, discipline requires obedience, diligence, and a proper attitude on the part of employees and effective leadership on the part of managers.

Fayol's administrative
principles

4. *Unity of command:* Everyone should have one and only one boss.

5. *Unity of management:* For every plan there should be an objective and a manager who is responsible for overall direction.

6. *Subordination of individual interests to the common good:* The goals of the organization and the department must take precedence over the personal goals of individual employees.

7. *Remuneration of the staff:* All staff members should receive compensation that is fair and motivates them to do good work.

8. *Centralization:* Organizations tend to confine too much decision making to the upper levels. Instead, they should seek that balance of centralization–decentralization that provides the greatest overall efficiency.

9. *The hierarchy:* There should be a clear-cut chain of command running from the top of the organization to the bottom.

10. *Order:* A place should exist for everything, and everything should be in its place.

11. *Equity:* Everyone in the organization should be treated fairly and justly.

12. *Stability of staff:* Since it takes time for people to learn their jobs and function at the highest level of efficiency, the long-term commitment of the staff should be a primary concern of management.

13. *Initiative:* Managers need the power both to conceive and to execute a plan of action.

14. *Esprit de corps:* Morale depends heavily on harmony and unity of the organization's staff.[11]

These functions and principles provide an important framework for the study of modern management. In particular, they illustrate that by studying the functions of a manager, one can obtain a high degree of administrative training and insight. Fayol's contributions to the field were so significant that today he is known as the "Father of Modern Management Theory."

Mary Parker Follett (1868–1933)

Mary Parker Follett emphasized the importance of conflict resolution.

Mary Parker Follett was trained in philosophy and political science and from this background made a series of important contributions in the administrative management field. One idea for which she has become well known is the **law of the situation.** Follett pointed out in her writings that the situation itself, not the hierarchical chain, should dictate who has authority. The person giving the orders should be the one who knows the most about the situation and is best able to get the job done, not necessarily the one who is highest in the hierarchy. This philosophy was a result of her belief that people should cooperate with each other for the overall good of the group instead of allowing personal interests to dominate the situation. Follett also believed that if people examined each situation closely they could work out a solution that would be beneficial to all parties involved. This concept, often known as *conflict resolution,* was her second important contribution to the field of administrative management. The third was her writing on the value and importance of *coordination.* Only through effective coordination, she argued, could unity, control, and efficiency be attained. Finally, her philosophy of *community service* by administrators showed that she was aware of the importance of management's social role. She put her belief this way:

We work for profit, for service, for our own development, for the love of creating something. At any one moment, indeed, most of us are not working directly or immediately for any of these things, but to put through the job in hand in the best possible manner. . . . To come back to the professions: Can we not learn a lesson from them on this very point? The professions have not given up the money motive. I do not care how often you see it stated that they have. . . . Professional men are eager enough for large incomes; but they have other motives as well, and they are often willing to sacrifice a good slice of income for the sake of these other things. We all want the richness of life in terms of our deepest desire. We can purify

---

11. Henri Fayol, *Industrial and General Administration,* translated by J. A. Coubrough (Geneva: International Management Institute, 1930) pp. 19–33.

and evaluate our desires, we can add to them, but there is no individual or social progress in curtailment of desires.[12]

In retrospect, we can see that Follett was a management philosopher. She was also ahead of her time. Over the last three decades, her ideas have gained in importance as executives have come to realize the value of conflict resolution, coordination, and the need to temper a concern for efficiency and profit with concern for social responsibility.

James D. Mooney (1884–1957)

James D. Mooney uncovered principles of organizing.

James D. Mooney was a General Motors executive. In 1931, with a coauthor,[13] he wrote a book entitled *Onward Industry!*[14] This book analyzed the organizing function in detail, drawing heavily from Mooney's business experience and studies of military, government, church, and industry patterns. Mooney concluded that the first principle of organizing was coordination, which is the orderly arrangement of group efforts to provide unity of action in the pursuit of a common objective.

While the book was difficult to read and overly complex in presentation, it was an important effort toward uncovering principles of organizing. Most significantly it provided additional insights into administrative theory and helped advance the growing body of knowledge in the field.

Lyndall F. Urwick (1894–1983)

Lyndall F. Urwick undertook a synthesis of management theory.

Lyndall Urwick was educated at Oxford and from 1928 to 1933 was director of the International Management Institute in Geneva. Until his retirement, he was also chairman of Urwick, Orr and Partners Ltd., a management consulting firm in London.

Urwick was familiar with management theory literature on both sides of the Atlantic. This knowledge enabled him to write a book entitled *The Elements of Administration*, which integrated the theories of Taylor, Fayol, Mooney, and other early management writers.[15] In synthesizing the major ideas of these theorists, Urwick discovered that they agreed about many administrative principles. Commenting on their agreement, he wrote:

> The main point [of the book] is that it focuses in a logical scheme various "Principles of Administration" formulated by different authorities. The fact that such "Principles"—worked out by persons of different nationalities,

---

12. Henry C. Metcalf and Lyndall F. Urwick (eds.), *Dynamic Administration: The Collected Papers of Mary Parker Follett* (New York: Harper and Row, 1940), p. 145.

13. The coauthor was Alan C. Reiley. It is widely accepted that Mooney provided the framework for the book while Reiley contributed primarily to the historical analyses of the organizations that were presented.

14. James D. Mooney and Alan C. Reiley, *Onward Industry!* (New York: Harper & Brothers Publishers, 1931).

15. L. Urwick, *The Elements of Administration* (New York: Harper & Brothers, Publishers, 1943).

widely varying experience and, in the majority of cases, no knowledge of each other's work—were susceptible to such logical arrangement, is in itself highly significant.[16]

As a result of Urwick's writings, it became evident by the early 1940s that administrative theory was far more scientific, better researched, and more clearly understood than had previously been believed.

Administrative Science

The contributions of these early administrative theorists helped develop a framework for the study of modern management. The outcome of their efforts, as complemented by current writers and researchers, is known as the **administrative science** or **management process** approach. This approach is similar to the one suggested by Fayol when he set forth the functions of a manager. First, a list of management functions is developed. Then each is studied in detail. A typical list of such functions might include planning, organizing, staffing, leading, and controlling. This approach offers a number of important advantages in the study of modern management.

An Enduring Framework

A framework for the study of management emerges.

One of the primary advantages of a process approach is the enduring framework it provides. Anything new in management can be integrated into this framework. For example, a new development in strategic planning can be made part of the planning material; new contingency organization design research can be added to the organizing material; and a newly developed information system approach can be made part of the controlling material. In this way the process approach offers a lasting framework for the study of management.

Management functions can be systematically studied.

In contrast to management scientists, *management theorists* are not as interested in providing tools and techniques for decision making as they are in developing a model for the systematic study of management. Like the management scientists, however, they recognize the value of a systems approach. For example, while they study functions in a sequential order, they also recognize the functions' interrelationships. Planning affects organizing, staffing, leading, and controlling; the same is true, in turn, for the other functions. This idea is illustrated in Figure 2–3.

Figure 2–3
Interrelationship of
Management Functions

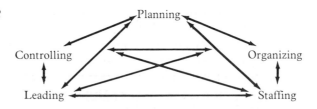

---

16. *Ibid.,* p. 7.

A Focal Point for Study

A second major benefit of the process approach is that it provides focal points for the study of management. The identification of functions helps make possible their systematic study. Individuals interested in becoming more effective managers can determine those functions about which they have insufficient information and can work on improving their understanding of them.

Research findings developed over a period of time can provide additional insights into the way to carry out these functions. Sometimes these insights are provided in the form of management principles, which are general guidelines for understanding and implementing the functions. An example is the exception principle of control, which holds that managers should concern themselves with controlling exceptional cases and not with routine results.

A Generalist Viewpoint

Management theorists have a generalist point of view.

Modern management theorists have a generalist point of view. They are most concerned with studying how organizations function in general and how managers should carry out their jobs. Management scientists, on the other hand, are interested in quantitative tools and techniques. Administrative science, management theory, or management process people are more concerned with macro-oriented topics such as strategic planning, organizational design, and the formulation of key areas of control for the organization at large. Management scientists are empirical in their approach to the field; they want to use the scientific method to formulate problems and obtain results. Administrative scientists are happier using a general approach; and while they respect the need for empirical research, they also place great value on intuition, gut feeling, and the importance of past experience. Many practicing managers like this general approach because they are uneasy dealing with management science techniques. Nevertheless, both are important to the study of modern management. Behavioral orientation, which will now be the focus of our attention, is also important.

Human Behavior

At the same time that the early administrative theorists were concerning themselves with the management of organizations, other people were arriving on the business scene who were concerned with human behavior at work. Some of their work was heavily psychological in nature; some of it was sociological. In either case, these early behaviorists made the first contributions to our understanding of human behavior in organizations. Four of the major contributors during the pre-World War II period were Hugo Munsterberg, Lillian M. Gilbreth, Elton Mayo, and Chester Barnard.

Hugo Munsterberg (1863–1916)

Hugo Munsterberg, born in Prussia, received his Ph.D. from Leipzig where he studied under Wilhelm Wundt, the "Father of Modern Psychology."

Hugo Munsterberg developed screening tests.

Two years later he was awarded his M.D. from Heidelberg University. In 1892 he came to Harvard University as a visiting professor and five years later returned to direct Harvard's Psychological Laboratory.[17]

Munsterberg's major contribution to management came in the field of industrial psychology. Determined to strengthen the bridge between scientific management and industrial efficiency, he wanted to find out why some workers did well on the job and others did not.[18] He was convinced that the scientific managers spent too much time trying to match the physical skills of the worker with those required by the job, and that in the process they overlooked psychological or mental skills. This interest led him into the area of vocational testing.

Munsterberg believed that he could develop tests that would help screen out unfit job applicants and workers. His most famous experiment was conducted among trolley car operators, but he also developed screening tests for other work groups, including ship's officers and telephone operators. Always the central objective was to determine whether or not the person was psychologically fit for the job. Did the individual have the requisite mental skills? Munsterberg was convinced that psychological testing could be valuable in screening people at *all levels* of an organization:

> The results of experimental psychology will have to be introduced systematically into the study of the fitness of the personality, from the lowest to the highest technical activity and from the simplest sensory function to the most complex mental achievement.[19]

Munsterberg popularized psychology by showing how it could be of value in many fields, and heralded the advent of psychologists into industry. He also showed how a scientific approach to the study of human behavior at work could produce effective results. Today Munsterberg is known as the "Father of Industrial Psychology."

Lillian M. Gilbreth (1878–1972)

Dr. Lillian Moller Gilbreth, the wife of Frank Gilbreth, not only played an important role in her husband's work but earned a significant reputation of her own. After marrying Frank, Lillian changed her academic interests to psychology. In 1915, she received a Ph.D. from Brown University and turned her thesis into a book, *The Psychology of Management.*[20] She also played an important role in bringing to scientific management an understanding of the role and importance of psychology. Prior to her time, much of the concern of psychologists was with crowd behavior. Lillian Gilbreth, in contrast, focused on individual behavior. She also examined management styles and concluded that there were three: traditional, transitory, and

Lillian Gilbreth focused on individual behavior.

---

17. *Encyclopaedia Britannica,* 1982 edition, Vol. 7, p. 104.

18. Hugo Munsterberg, *Psychology and Industrial Efficiency* (Boston: Houghton Mifflin, 1913).

19. *Ibid.,* p. 96.

20. L. M. Gilbreth, *The Psychology of Management: The Function of the Mind in Determining, Teaching and Installing Methods of Least Waste* (New York: Sturgis and Walton, 1914).

scientific. The traditional style was typified by the hard-driving manager who believed in unity of command and employed centralized authority. The transitory style fell between traditional and scientific. The scientific style depended on the careful selection of personnel, the use of incentives, and an overall consideration of worker welfare. Each employee was to be developed to the fullest degree possible. These ideas were advanced for their time. Not until the 1970s did the behavioral field turn toward a human resources philosophy in which concern for the development of the employee's total potential became a focal point of interest. Lillian Gilbreth had already presented many of these ideas 50 years earlier. By the time she died in 1972, she was known throughout the world for her contributions to the field of management psychology. In the process, she had earned the title "First Lady of Management."

Elton Mayo (1880–1949)

Elton Mayo was an Australian who taught ethics, philosophy, and logic at the Queensland University and later studied medicine in Edinburgh, Scotland. He then became a research associate in the study of psychopathology and eventually came to America. By 1926 he was an associate professor of industrial relations at Harvard University.

During his early work in American industry, Mayo seemed to have more understanding of scientific management principles than of behavior at work. He gradually came to recognize, however, that output often increased when work patterns and procedures were changed not because the new arrangement was more efficient but because the workers liked it better. Morale and attitude were often more important than work flow and efficiency procedures.

Mayo is best remembered for coordinating the writing and reporting of the **Hawthorne studies.** Today these behavioral studies are regarded as the single most important historical foundation for the behavioral approach to management.[21]

Hawthorne Studies

The initial purpose of the Hawthorne studies (1924–1932) was to determine the effect of illumination on output. The studies, sponsored by the National Research Council, were started in late 1924 at the Hawthorne Works of the Western Electric Company near Cicero, Illinois. Before the studies were completed, they passed through four major phases: the illumination experiments, the relay assembly test room experiments, the interview program, and the bank wiring observation room study.[22]

Illumination Experiments   These initial experiments, designed to study the effect of illumination on output, lasted two-and-one-half years. During this time, numerous experiments were conducted. They were all inconclu-

---

21. Fred Luthans, *Organizational Behavior,* 3rd edition (New York: McGraw-Hill, 1977), p. 19.

22. For a complete description of these studies see: F. J. Roethlisberger and William J. Dickson, *Management and the Worker* (Cambridge, Mass.: Harvard University Press, 1939).

sive and the researchers were unable to determine the relationship between illumination and output. Two conclusions were reached, however: that lighting was only one factor affecting output and that there were too many variables present to allow the researchers to isolate illumination as a causal factor. Greater control of the experiment was needed.

Relay Assembly Test Room   To obtain this control, the researchers decided to isolate a small group of employees from the regular work force and study their behavior. Six women were placed in a room by themselves. After allowing some time to study the effect of the new environment, the experimenters began introducing changes such as rest pauses, shorter work days, and shorter work weeks. Output went up. When these changes were taken away, however, output still remained high. Why were the women doing more work than ever before? The researchers concluded that changes in their social conditions and the method of supervision were bringing about improved attitudes and increased productivity. To gain more information, management decided to investigate employee attitudes through an interviewing program.

Interviewing Program   During this third phase of the studies, more than 20,000 interviews were conducted. The interviewers asked questions regarding supervision and the work environment. They found, however, that the employees gave guarded and stereotyped answers. They therefore switched to a nondirect method of questioning, allowing each employee to choose his or her own topic. The outcome was a wealth of information about employee attitudes. The researchers realized that a person's work performance, position, and status in the organization were determined not only by the individual personally, but by the group members as well. This information resulted in a decision to study group behavior at work more systematically.

Bank Wiring Observation Room   The researchers then decided to study a small group at work, and they chose to study the bank wiring room, where workers were wiring and soldering bank terminals. After studying behavior in the room for an extended period of time, the investigators realized that many behavioral norms affected the workers' actions. Some of these norms were related to the amount of work the workers did, the individuals with whom they traded jobs or to whom they offered assistance, and the way in which they treated the various managers who came by. As a result of this phase of the study, the researchers were able to identify a series of behavioral norms, some of which included: You should not do too much work. You should not do too little work. You should not squeal to a supervisor about a fellow employee.

The Hawthorne studies had a significant impact. In particular, they uncovered important insights into individual and group behavior and focused attention on supervisory climate and leadership research. The studies heralded the advent of the behaviorists into industry. Much of the behavioral work that was to follow had its beginnings here.

Chester I. Barnard (1886–1961)

Chester Barnard was president of New Jersey Bell from 1927 until his retirement. A practicing manager, he found much of the management writing of the day to be incomplete, misleading, or superficial. In 1938 he wrote

The illumination experiments determined that lighting was only one factor affecting output.

In the relay assembly test room experiments, output went up and stayed up.

The interviewing program provided a wealth of information about employee attitudes.

The bank wiring observation room experiments uncovered a series of behavioral norms.

Chester Barnard identified and described executive functions.

Barnard also formulated the acceptance theory of authority.

The Functions of the Executive.[23] This book has proven so influential to the study of management that one writer has credited Barnard with having had "a more profound impact on the thinking about the complex subject matter of human organization than has any other contributor to the continuum of management thought."[24]

Barnard's behavioral contributions fall into two major areas. First, he identified and described the functions of the executive. These he found to be (1) the establishment and maintenance of a communication system throughout the organization; (2) the promotion and acquisition of essential effort by recruiting the best people and rewarding them appropriately; and (3) the formulation of the purpose and objectives of the organization.

Second, Barnard set forth a theory of authority. As a behaviorist, he realized the importance of educating people to cooperate. Giving someone an order is insufficient, he said, for the person might well refuse to carry it out. When will the individual not refuse? Barnard answered the question this way:

> A person can and will accept a communication as authoritative only when four conditions simultaneously obtain: (a) he can and does understand the communication; (b) *at the time of his decision,* he believes it is not inconsistent with the purpose of the organization; (c) *at the time of his decision,* he believes it to be compatible with his personal interest as a whole; and (d) he is able mentally and physically to comply with it.[25]

Today this view is known as the **acceptance theory of authority,** which holds that the ultimate source of authority is the individual who chooses either to accept orders or to refuse to follow them. Of course, as a practicing manager Barnard realized that there were few times when people would refuse to follow orders deliberately. In explaining why, he introduced the concept of the *zone of indifference.* Orders falling within this zone are accepted without question. Other orders either fall on a neutral line or are considered unacceptable. The zone of indifference is either wide or narrow, depending on the incentives management provides for employees and the sacrifices employees have to make on behalf of the organization. The effective executive makes sure that the employees feel they are getting more from the organization than they are giving to it. In this case the indifference zone is wide and they are likely to accept orders. Barnard also hastened to point out that even when one person does not want to follow orders, the other members of the group will pressure that person to comply, if they are satisfied with the organization.

Barnard is important to the study of management because he was one of the first people to describe executive functions in analytical and dynamic terms. He stimulated an interest in behavioral topics, especially communications, decision making, and authority–responsibility relationships. Many behaviorists who came later considered Barnard to be the "Father of Modern Behavioral Science" because of the contributions of his early writing.

23. Chester I. Barnard, *The Functions of the Executive* (Cambridge, Mass.: Harvard University Press, 1938).

24. Claude S. George, Jr., *The History of Management Thought,* 2nd edition (Englewood Cliffs, N.J.: Prentice-Hall, 1972), p. 140.

25. *Ibid.,* p. 165.

Behavioral Science

The work begun by Munsterberg, Gilbreth, Mayo, and Barnard continues today. Thousands of psychologists, sociologists, anthropologists, and social and industrial psychologists are employed in both industry and academia. Their area of interest is now called **behavioral science** and its focus extends from the study of individual behavior, on the one hand, to the study of large groups and organizations on the other. Three of the broadly based areas of interest for behavioral scientists today are individual behavior, group behavior, and organizational development.

Individual Behavior

Some behavioral scientists focus on the individual as a socio-psychological being.

Some behavioral scientists are most interested in individual behavior. These people tend to be psychologists and their focus is on the individual's motivation as a socio-psychological being. What motivates the worker? How does motivation work? Why are some people more motivated by a particular reward than others? These are the kinds of questions that intrigue this kind of behavioral scientist.

Group Behavior

Others study individuals as parts of a social system.

Other behavioral scientists are concerned with studying people as parts of a social system or collection of cultural interrelationships. They see an organized enterprise as a social organism which, in turn, is made up of many social suborganisms. They are interested in studying such subjects as attitudes, habits, and the effects of pressure and conflict within the cultural environment. They are also concerned with the effect that personnel have on organizations and the countereffect of organizations on the personnel. To what degree do people make the organization and vice versa?

Organizational Development

Still others help managers understand and cope with change.

In recent years some behavioral scientists have begun calling themselves *organizational development experts* or *change agents*. These people typically work for large organizations or are brought into companies as consultants. Their objective is to help managers and employees both understand and cope with change. They are also useful in helping employees understand interpersonal and intraorganizational behavioral problems and in developing behavioral change strategies for dealing with them.

Modern Management Thought

In this chapter we have examined the three basic foundations of modern management: management science, administrative science, and behavioral science. As seen in Figure 2–4, each of these three approaches has been seriously modified since its beginning. The scientific managers were interested in the efficiency of operations. Today management science is concerned with the management of work. The administrative theorists were interested in the nature of management and organizations. Today the

Figure 2–4
The Emergence of Modern
Management Thought

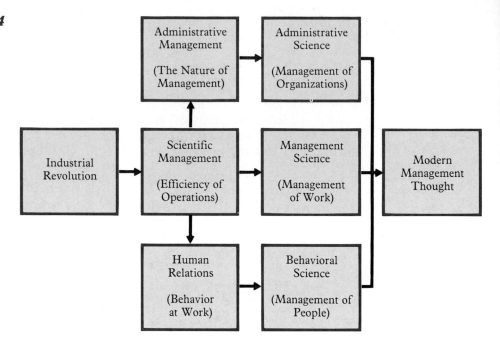

management process or administrative science people concern themselves with the management of organizations. Finally, the human relations orientation of the early behaviorists has given way to a behavioral science approach that is concerned with the management of people.

The management science and behavioral science approaches are much more empirically based than is the approach of the administrative science or management theory group, and this is the way it should be. The first two provide specific information that helps us understand such important management topics as decision making, work flow, inventory control (management science), individual behavior, group behavior, and organizational behavior (behavioral science). The management theory group helps us understand how to use this information in a comprehensive framework for studying management.

All three approaches are important in the study of modern management, and you will see that they are intertwined. For example, decision-making techniques are an important area of concern in management science. In studying them, however, we must also be interested in the way decisions affect organizations and people. The three developments illustrated in Figure 2–4 actually overlap. For this reason, many modern management scholars and practitioners like to think of management in *contingency* terms: The manager must make those decisions and take those actions that will produce the desired results. Fulfilling this responsibility sometimes requires a quantitative orientation; at other times it demands a qualitative approach. To cover both kinds of managerial responsibilities, this book attempts to provide the comprehensive framework of the management process approach while studying too the information provided by both management science and behavioral science.

Summary

1. Management has been practiced for thousands of years. The Egyptians and Greeks employed many of the ideas known to us today, and selected writings of historical figures such as Sun Tzu and Niccolò Machiavelli are as useful now as they were when originally written.

2. The Industrial Revolution brought about the factory system. Two of the men who contributed most to the rise of industrialism were James Watt, who invented the rotary steam engine, and Adam Smith, who popularized the division of labor concept.

3. Factory managers sought to increase efficiency, and this resulted in the scientific management movement. Many of the scientific managers were mechanical engineers who used time-and-motion study to analyze and redesign jobs so they could be carried out more quickly and efficiently. Frederick Taylor's experiments, Frank Gilbreth's studies, and Henry Gantt's chart all contributed to attaining these objectives.

4. The work of the scientific managers has been complemented by the work of other quantitatively oriented researchers. Today these researchers are known collectively as management scientists. Their interests include not only time-and-motion study but inventory control, linear programming, work flow, production planning, computers, and systems theory. They also make extensive use of the scientific method.

5. The success of the scientific managers at the lower levels of the organization resulted in a need to understand more about the overall administration of the enterprise. Four of the people who provided early administrative theory insights were Henri Fayol, Mary Parker Follett, James Mooney, and Lyndall Urwick. Fayol set forth a series of management functions and principles that would eventually serve as a framework for the study of modern management. Follett contributed a philosophy of management that emphasized organizational needs vis-à-vis the individual and the larger community. Mooney made a systematic study of the organizing function. Urwick synthesized the work of early contributors and provided a basis for understanding the current state of knowledge.

6. The contributions of the early administrative theorists helped develop a framework for the study of modern management. Today these administrative scientists use a process framework in studying and analyzing the subject. Their generalist approach is very popular with practicing managers.

7. At the same time that the early administrative theorists were doing their work, behaviorists were arriving on the business scene. Hugo Munsterberg developed personnel screening tests; Lillian Gilbreth was a pioneer in management psychology; Elton Mayo participated in the Hawthorne studies; and Chester Barnard wrote about the functions of the executive and set forth the acceptance theory of authority.

8. The work begun by these four individuals continues today, carried on by psychologists, sociologists, and other behavioral scientists. Three of the latter's primary areas of concern include individual behavior, group behavior, and organizational development.

9. Modern management is an integration of all three approaches: management science, administrative science, and behavioral science. Each plays an important role in helping explain how to manage people.

Key Terms

Acceptance theory of authority A theory, popularized by Chester Barnard, which holds that the ultimate source of authority is the individual who chooses either to accept orders or to refuse to follow them.

Administrative science See Management process.

Behavioral science The study of human behavior in organizations including individual behavior, group behavior, and organizational development.

Division of labor Dividing work into small components so that the workers become specialists in their tasks.

Gantt chart A chart used for scheduling jobs and measuring work progress.

Hawthorne studies Early behavioral studies (1924–1932) that are regarded today as the single most important historical foundation for the behavioral approach to management.

Law of the situation A law of management that holds that the situation itself should dictate who has authority. This law argues against the idea of a hierarchical chain in which the superior always gives orders to the subordinate.

Management process (also known as administrative science) An approach to the study of management that involves the identification and systematic analysis of management functions. Modern management theorists support this approach.

Management science A quantitatively oriented discipline, studying such topics as time-and-motion experiments, linear programming, inventory control, work flow, computers, and systems theory.

Principles of scientific management As set forth by Frederick Taylor, they were that (1) management should develop a science for each element of the work to be done; (2) management should scientifically select, train, teach, and develop each worker; (3) management should cooperate with the worker in ensuring that all of the work is done in accordance with the principles of scientific management; and (4) management should divide work responsibilities between management and the workers, with the former studying jobs and determining how they should be done and the latter carrying them out.

Scientific management An approach to management concerned with (1) studying work methods and processes for the purpose of determining how to increase work efficiency, and (2) developing ways of motivating the worker to use these methods and processes.

Scientific method A logical approach to problem solving that contains seven steps: (1) identifying the problem, (2) obtaining preliminary information, (3) posing a tentative solution to the problem, (4) investigating the problem area, (5) classifying the information, (6) stating a tentative answer to the problem, and (7) testing the answer.

Therblig A basic hand motion (grasp, hold, position) used in analyzing work.

Questions for Analysis and Discussion

1. The Egyptians who supervised the building of the Pyramids had the greatest understanding of management in which of the following three areas: management science, management process, or behavioral science? In which one of these three areas did the Greeks show an understanding of management when they established uniform work methods and used music to set the work tempo?

2. Can the writings of Sun Tzu be of any value to the modern manager? What about those of Niccolò Machiavelli? Explain.

3. How did the Industrial Revolution bring about the emergence of the factory sysem ? How did James Watt and Adam Smith contribute to this development?

4. In what way was scientific management a natural outgrowth of the Industrial Revolution? Explain.

5. Specifically, what contributions did each of the following make to the scientific management movement: Frederick Taylor, Frank Gilbreth, Henry Gantt?

6. Modern management scientists have an interest in the scientific method, the use of mathematical tools and techniques, and a systems approach. What is meant by this statement? Be sure to include in your answer a description of the steps in the scientific method.

7. How did the following individuals contribute to the emergence of modern management thought: Henri Fayol, Mary Parker Follett, James Mooney, Lyndall Urwick?

8. What is the management process approach and what are some of the advantages it offers in the study of modern management?

9. How did the following people contribute to the early study of human behavior at work: Hugo Munsterberg, Lillian Gilbreth, Elton Mayo, Chester Barnard?

10. What are the three broadly based areas of interest for modern behavioral scientists? Describe each.

11. The three basic foundations of modern management are management science, administrative science, and behavioral science. What is meant by this statement? Be complete in your answer.

Case | # Quality Efficiency

The Quality Wholesale Company distributes its products to more than 500 retailers in a six-state area. One primary profit factor in wholesaling is rapid order filling. Retailers need to have their orders filled as quickly as possible and, should there be a breakdown in delivery time, they are likely to turn to other wholesale sources.

The owner of Quality Wholesale, Bert Wilson, finished revamping his facilities last month. A number of major changes have been introduced. First, all merchandise has been rearranged so that the fastest moving items are located closest to the loading dock. Second, a new inventory control system has been installed. Third, all major record keeping has been computerized. Fourth, the main office has been rearranged, new fixtures and equipment have been installed, and music is being piped into the workplace.

Since making these changes, Bert has been keeping close tabs on operating performance. Records show that delivery time has been reduced from four to three days and profitability is up 27 percent. Of course, it is still too early to tell whether this is the beginning of a long-term trend or just a temporary development. Bert believes, however, that much of this efficiency can be tied directly to the changes he introduced in the work environment.

1. Which of the major approaches to management did Bert employ: management science, administrative science, or behavioral science? Defend your answer.

2. Did these work changes have any effect on work behavior? Explain.

3. An understanding of the management process helped Bert make these work changes. In what other ways can it help him be an effective manager? Which of the functions in this process would Bert rely on in determining whether current profitability is a long-term trend or a temporary development? Be complete in your answer.

You Be the Consultant

An In-House Program

A few months ago the president of a large multiline corporation made two major decisions. First, he announced that the company would begin recruiting and hiring graduates from both business and nonbusiness colleges. In the past the corporation had concentrated its efforts almost exclusively on business graduates. Second, he informed the Training and Development Department that he wanted a basic management course offered to all new personnel. He explained his reasoning this way:

> My daughter was graduated from a top-flight liberal arts college last year and immediately came to work for us. Since then she has taken a number of management training programs. All she has gotten, however, is a series of tools and techniques related to subjects such as decision making, communication leadership, time management, and stress management. How do these different training programs make her an effective manager? What she needs is a basic course that will familiarize her with the general field of management. Then she can take training programs to supplement her knowledge of basic concepts.

The head of the Training and Development Department has been working on developing such a basic in-house course. He has asked for input from a number of people throughout the company. So far, however, he feels he has not gotten what he needs. All the people who responded to his request for training ideas stressed the importance of their own areas. The people in sales want everyone to have a sales-management orientation. Those in production feel newcomers to the firm should know about production planning, layout, and inventory control. Those in personnel want the training to emphasize communication, small group behavior, and behavioral techniques. Two of the top managers who responded noted the importance of overall planning and control techniques.

The outcome, so far, is a mixture of suggestions lacking a common unifying theme. The training and development director thinks that all of the ideas are good but that they are still too technique oriented and that there is no broadly based management approach that can pull all of them together. For this reason, he has decided to have someone from outside the organization integrate the ideas of the various in-house people and formulate a well-balanced basic course that will meet with the approval of the president.

Your Consultation

Assume that you have been called in as a consultant to the training and development director. Drawing upon your knowledge of the material in this chapter, broadly outline the types of topics that should be included in a basic management course. Use Figure 2–4 to help you in this process. Be as specific as possible, but remember that the in-house director will refine your answers to comply with the request of the president.

3

The Environment of Modern Organizations

Objectives

Every organization operates within two environments: external and internal. The external environment consists of forces outside the organization's direct control. The internal environment is made up of forces over which the organization has some control. This chapter examines these two sets of environmental forces.

The first objective of this chapter is to examine external environmental forces. These forces can be subdivided into two groups: first tier and second tier. First-tier forces create the general environment in which organizations operate; second-tier forces make up the specific environment in which enterprises function.

The second objective of this chapter is to examine internal environmental forces. In this case, the focus of attention is on managers and workers. When you have finished studying the material in this chapter, you will be able to

1. identify the four major first-tier environmental forces and describe each in depth;

2. identify the four major second-tier environmental forces and describe each in depth;

3. compare and contrast the arguments both for and against social responsibility;

4. identify the two major internal environmental forces and describe each in depth; and

5. discuss the current state of management ethics and worker values.

The External Environment

The external environment consists of forces outside the direct control of the organization. These forces are of two types: first tier and second tier (see Figure 3–1). The following sections examine both tiers.

First Tier

First-tier forces affect virtually every organization.

First-tier forces make up the *general environment* in which organizations operate. Included in this group are the general economy, suppliers, customers, and competitors. An enterprise may not be influenced by all of these forces, nor is it always able to respond to every one of them. It is important to remember, however, that these forces are usually *dependent* on each other, even though they can act independently.

The General Economy

The economy affects organizations both directly and indirectly.

The most dominant first-tier force is the general economy, which affects organizations both directly and indirectly. Automakers such as General Motors (GM) are directly affected when customers either stop buying or start purchasing from competitors. Smaller businesses that supply firms like GM with parts or equipment are indirectly affected by the economy when the corporate giant cancels or cuts back sales orders. However, all industries in the United States economy do not move in the same direction at the same time. Some may do well while others are doing poorly. For an example, we can look at some key U.S. industries during the early 1980s.

At that time, the U.S. auto industry was reeling because of rising prices and because inflation was eroding the purchasing power of the dollar. As a result, many customers held on to their old cars. Others looked for quality-built autos, and foreign automakers took advantage of this development to increase their market share to more than 25 percent. Then as the economy

Figure 3–1
First- and Second-Tier Environmental Forces

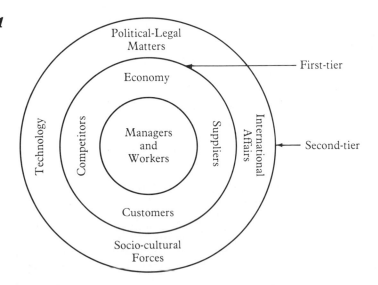

turned around, the Big Three bounced back, with GM and Ford both registering profits of over $3 billion and $1 billion respectively in just one year.

During this same period, the chemical industry's performance was mixed. Fertilizer sales were good, but the plastics businesses were having trouble. And while the manufacturers of pesticides and medical supplies were both doing well, orders for organic chemicals were much lower than expected.

The food industry in the early 1980s found that its profit margins were becoming very thin. Declining consumer buying power, higher inventory carrying charges, and soaring production costs all hit the packaged-food processors at the same time. The processors tried to fight back by increasing their advertising, expanding coupon contests, and making promotional offers. Companies focused their attention, however, on the management of costs, as they sought to preserve their profit margins.

In the area of information processing, prosperous times were anticipated. Annual growth rates of 30 to 40 percent were projected for office automation, personal computers, and minicomputers. Not all of the industry's firms participated in this growth, however. Large mainframe computer manufacturers looked at sales gains of only about 5 to 8 percent annually, and as competition heated up, many of the small firms that had done well in the late 1970s suddenly found their sales growth reduced dramatically.

The machinery industry, meanwhile, was living off its backlog orders. As interest rates rose, the amount of capital spending declined. Fortunately, previous orders kept the machine manufacturers going. Three of the main industries or types of industries responsible for these orders were the petroleum industry, which needed equipment for exploration, extraction, and processing of oil; the transportation industry, which was under intense pressure to build fuel-efficient cars and aircraft; and productivity-minded industries that had the cash to spend on cost-saving equipment such as automated materials storage and retrieval systems. The machinery industry also looked forward to a federal tax incentive program that would encourage businesses to buy more new machinery.

The petroleum industry and the paper industry were also in good condition. Rising OPEC prices had driven revenues for petroleum to new highs before price declines in 1982. Independent refiners were having some difficulty, but the large firms like Exxon, Texaco, Mobil, and Standard Oil of California were grossing billions of dollars. They were also looking for ways to diversify their operations. Because of high energy costs in Japan and Western Europe, U.S. papermakers were now the world's lowest-cost producers. They even began exporting their products into high-priced world markets. Although domestic demand was less than ideal, the international market was greatly helping profits.

On the other hand, steel industry performance was poor. Backlog orders were helping out, but low auto industry sales were seriously affecting steel sales. Imports were also hurting the industry, although American executives were hoping that the federal government would take action to limit their impact.

As developments like these filter through the overall economy, some organizations benefit while others suffer. In one way or another, all feel some impact. For this reason, in recent years, large companies have begun

Figure 3–2
The Corporate Economics
Staff

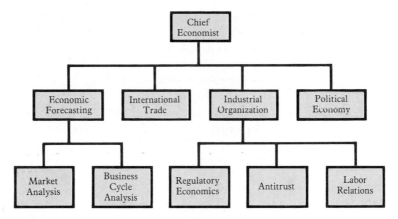

Source: Thomas G. Marx, "The Corporate Economics Staff: Challenges and Opportunities for the '80s," *Business Horizons,* April 1980, p. 17. Reprinted with permission.

maintaining a full staff of economists who specialize in many different areas.[1] As seen in Figure 3–2, these areas include economic forecasting, international trade, industrial organization, and political economy. Such a staff helps the corporation deal with many first- and second-tier forces.

Suppliers

Suppliers provide important materials.

Suppliers provide an organization with those materials it needs for turning out goods and services. Examples include raw materials, parts, equipment, machinery, energy, and labor. Most organizations, realizing their dependence on suppliers, try to maintain multiple sources. If the needed materials or parts cannot be obtained from one supplier, the organization can quickly turn to another. This strategy is particularly important when there is a shortage of materials or when one supplier cannot provide everything the organization needs.

Sometimes business can turn the tables on suppliers and put the latter in a weak position. The metal container industry provides an excellent example. Because of the overcapacity for production in this industry, those who sell metal containers are at a disadvantage. Buyers can demand the lowest possible prices and concessions and get them. If they do not they will simply stop doing business with one container manufacturer and start doing business with another. The threat of the buyer's going to the competition is sufficient to keep each container manufacturer responsive. In most cases, however, this situation does not develop. An organization has to cultivate sources of material supply.

The labor market, meanwhile, is most influenced by the economy in general and business conditions in particular. When the economy is flourishing and businesses are expanding, there is a good chance that workers can get higher salaries and greater fringe benefits. In a tight market, however, firms find it necessary to maintain wages and benefits at a fixed level.

---

1. Thomas G. Marx, "The Corporate Economics Staff: Challenges and Opportunities for the '80s," *Business Horizons,* April 1980, pp. 15–18.

The economic status of a particular company also affects labor. For example, when business was good at the Chrysler Corporation, the unions were able to obtain increased wages and benefits. When the corporation began to run into trouble in the late 1970s, the union went along with the company's request to hold its demands to a minimum. Suppliers of labor want higher salaries, but not at the price of organizational bankruptcy. As the company turned around in the early 1980s, the union again started demanding more wages and benefits.

Customers

The customer is still king.

Ultimately, it is the customers who dictate the success of organizations. If no one needs the services of a particular governmental agency, it will go out of existence. A hospital without patients will soon close its doors. A business without customers will be forced to declare bankruptcy. Customers create the demand for goods and services. America is still a market economy. The customer is king.

Many illustrations can be cited to support this statement. One of the most interesting is provided by the TV industry. Until the mid-1970s, most people bought television sets as receivers for programs provided by the large broadcasting firms: ABC, NBC, and CBS. By the early 1980s many other appliances could be plugged into a TV set, including videocassette recorders, videodisc players, videogames, TV cameras, satellite antennas, home computers, hi-fi sound equipment, cable TV, and two-way communications systems.[2] Today people want more from a television set than just standard program fare.

Cable TV came about in response to the demand for additional TV programming. In fact, cable TV had become so popular with customers by the early part of the decade that firms were racing to bid for cable franchises and buy other companies that had them. For example, Westinghouse Electric paid $646 million for Teleprompter Corporation, the country's largest cable firm, with 1.3 million subscribers to one or more of 112 systems in 32 states. Capital Cities Communications bought Cablecom-General, which has nearly 250,000 subscribers for $139.2 million. The New York Times Company bought 55 cable franchises for $83 million.[3]

In addition to basic cable, pay-TV has also gained acceptance. Many people are also willing to pay for two-way services such as fire protection and overall home security. One cable company conducted a survey and found that while 50 percent of the homeowners in a Houston suburb had pay-TV, 65 percent purchased the company's security system. These survey results illustrate why cable firms have been fighting each other for franchises. Customer demand indicates that the area could be a gold mine.

Competition

Every organization faces competition.

Virtually every organization has to be concerned with competition. Governmental agencies scramble to beat out other agencies for a bigger piece of

2. "TV: A Growth Industry Again," *Business Week*, February 23, 1981, p. 89.

3. "Cable TV: The Race to Plug In," *Business Week*, December 8, 1980, pp. 62–68.

the budget. Hospitals and other medical facilities attempt to justify current services and to add new ones, objectives which can often be attained only at the expense of other institutions in the field. The business arena provides an even clearer example. While governmental agencies and medical facilities are not supposed to compete with each other, business managers are paid for their ability to compete effectively with other organizations. During the early 1980s such efforts seemed to be reaching new heights. The following are examples:

> General Electric has decided to become a leader in color television. Between 1976 and 1981 it doubled its share of this market. The firm intends to capture an even greater share during the next ten years.[4]

> The Adolph Coors Company, producer of Coors beer, used to worry not about selling its beer but allocating it. Demand was so high that every drop was sold. In the late 1970s the firm found itself with excess capacity. Now it is rebounding, fighting the competition. Current plans call for the firm to move to third place (from fifth) in the industry and expand operations from its home base of Colorado all the way to the East Coast.[5]

> Dow Chemical, the nation's second largest chemical firm, has decided to diversify. It wants to obtain at least one-third of all profits by the mid-1980s from end-products and services that are non-chemical-related. These include such well-known products as Saran Wrap, Dow Oven Cleaner, and Vicks Vaporub.[6]

Some industries, of course, are more competitive than others. However, only in those cases where profits or return on investment are low does competition diminish. Conversely, the greater the available profit or return on investment, the more intense the competition. In fact, some researchers seem to feel that competition combines many of the other forces described here and helps shape the organization's strategy.[7] Figure 3–3 illustrates this idea.

Second Tier

Second-tier forces greatly affect large organizations.

Second-tier forces make up the *specific environment* in which organizations operate. These forces more heavily affect large organizations than they do small ones. Included in this group are political–legal, technological, international, and socio-cultural forces, although this is certainly not an exhaustive list. In contrast to first-tier forces, second-tier forces influence an enterprise directly. There is no sidestepping or avoiding them. Their impact on operations is so important that the organization must develop ways of accommodating them.

---

4. "GE's Big Comeback in Color TV," *Business Week,* February 23, 1981, p. 91.

5. "Adolph Coors: Brewing Up Plans for an Invasion of the East Coast," *Business Week,* September 19, 1980, pp. 122–124.

6. Winston Williams, "Dow Broadens Product Lines," *New York Times,* February 11, 1981.

7. For more on this topic see Michael E. Porter, "How Competitive Forces Shape Strategy," *Harvard Business Review,* March–April 1979, pp. 137–145.

Figure 3–3
Forces That Govern
Competition in an Industry

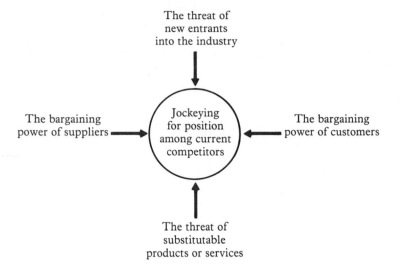

Political–Legal Forces

**Political–legal forces
constrain and direct activity.**

One of the most common second-tier forces is the political–legal force.
Political–legal forces consist of those laws and regulations that constrain
and direct organizational activity. Laws that constrain activity set forth
those things organizations are prohibited from doing. Examples include
laws that prohibit an organization from engaging in unfair labor practices,
from discriminating against employees on the basis of race, color, creed,
sex, or national origin, and from disposing of hazardous wastes in a dangerous manner. Laws that direct organizational activity set forth those things
which must be done. Examples include laws that require organizations to
withhold taxes from employee paychecks, ensure safe working conditions
for all personnel, and abide by all legal contracts that they have entered
into.

During the last 50 years, thousands of new laws have been enacted.
Table 3–1 provides a select sample. Most of these laws both constrain
and direct organizational activity.

Over the years, legislative emphasis changes. In 1935 Congress passed
the National Labor Relations Act, a pro-union law prohibiting management
from carrying out certain unfair labor practices. In 1947 Congress passed
an amendment to this act, the Taft–Hartley Act, which prohibited unfair
labor practices by unions. The legislative pendulum had swung from prola-
bor to promanagement.

As laws change, organizations must adjust to the new political–legal
environment. In most cases this means following the change, not leading
it. Even when organizations expect a change in legislation, they should
not take early action. For example, years ago the automakers knew that
safety equipment such as passive restraints would be advantageous to the
consumer. However, such equipment would also add a few hundred dollars
to the price of a car, making it less price competitive. As a result, no one
automaker wanted to start adding these safety features independently. As
legislation calling for more safety was passed, they all began to do so at
the same time. The changes became "safe" for the industry.

Table 3–1
Government Regulation:
Selected Examples

Year	Act	
1932	Federal Home Loan Bank	Regulated home financing institutions for the first time
1935	National Labor Relations	Promoted collective bargaining and prohibited unfair labor practices by employers
1947	Taft–Hartley	Extended the National Labor Relations Act to cover prohibition of unfair labor practices by unions
1954	Atomic Energy	Opened nuclear technology, under regulation, to private industry
1964	Civil Rights	Prohibited discrimination in private employment because of race, color, creed, sex, or national origin
1972	Consumer Product Safety	Provided for mandatory product safety standards and for the banning of hazardous substances
1978	Airline Deregulation	Loosened control over airline routes and rates—the first major deregulation step

Organizations should try to anticipate the impact of laws already in effect. For example, large companies are always trying to evaluate the likelihood of antitrust action. In the mid-1960s when GM was dominant in the auto industry, it was concerned that the government would try to break it up. More recently, American Telephone & Telegraph (AT&T) was required to divest itself of its operating companies, a move occasioned by government action.[8]

Technology

Technology is a key environmental variable for many firms, especially those in industries such as manufacturing, chemicals, and information processing. If a competitor produces a superior product, the other manufacturers may face a dramatic loss of business. On the other hand, the company with the latest development may not be able to cash in on it, especially if competing companies can improve their products quickly. By using a follow-the-leader strategy, some firms have managed to be second or third into the market with a product and still acquire a very large share of the sales and profits. Others, especially small enterprises, cannot afford to lead. The costs of this strategy are too high. They must be content with a follow-the-leader approach.

Sometimes a follow-the-leader strategy is best.

Technology must be developed in conjunction with the resources needed for capturing and maintaining the customer. Companies usually have to develop effective marketing plans and provide adequate product service in order to sell their technological advances. When Texas Instruments (TI) improved digital technology during the mid-1970s, it was able to reduce

8. For more on this challenge see Joel Bleeke, "Deregulation: Riding the Rapids," *Business Horizon,* May–June 1983, pp. 15–25.

the price of digital watches greatly. Japanese manufacturers, however, were able to follow suit quickly. When the competition for customers came to depend on low-cost production and marketing effectiveness, TI lost sales. By the early 1980s Japanese and Hong Kong manufacturers dominated the digital watch market. The Swiss were in third place, and the Americans were far behind them all.

Other firms have been more successful in blending technology with marketing expertise. GE is an example. At present the firm is trying hard to increase its technological base. In a way, this emphasis marks a return to earlier days. Many of GE's successes can be traced directly to technological expertise, but during the 1970s product quality suffered when the firm tried to control costs and monitor financial performance. Realizing that leadership in the technological arena is a key to its success, GE is now in the process of developing many new research-and-development-based products in such diverse areas as engineered materials, numerical controls, energy storage, medical electronics, and biological research.

International Forces

MNCs operate worldwide.

International forces are a consideration for firms doing business in other countries. Companies known as **multinational corporations (MNCs)** have their headquarters in one country but operate in many different nations. Management views the entire organization as one giant, interdependent system, and the relationships between headquarters and the various subsidiaries are collaborative. Communication flows in two directions. Top management sets directions for the whole organization. Subsidiary managers carry out these plans at their particular locale and report the results to the top. Two-way planning discussions then lead to follow-through activity.[9]

Some of the best known MNCs in the United States include IBM, Exxon, General Electric, Ford Motor, and National Cash Register. Some of the primary advantages of multinationals include their access to natural resources and materials not available to domestic firms, their capacity to recruit and train personnel from a worldwide labor pool, and their ability to capitalize on world markets.

Customs/Culture   In every country of the world there is an established way of doing business. Business customs often reflect the culture or values of the society. For example, in many Latin American countries a manager from the United States finds that 2 P.M. meetings do not get started until well past the hour. On the other hand, in western European countries punctuality is expected. Or consider the entertainment of business executives. In the United States a top manager might take a visiting overseas customer to his house for a home-cooked meal and feel proud when the customer tells his spouse, "You're a terrific cook." However, this scenario would not be reenacted worldwide. In Japan business entertaining is usually done outside the home, while in Latin America, the U.S. manager might be invited to a home-cooked meal but should not praise the wife's cooking. Such praise might be interpreted as a comment on the Latin executive's

---

9. Mark Fitzpatrick, "The Definition and Assessment of Political Risk in International Business: A Review of the Literature," *Academy of Management Review*, April 1983, pp. 249–254.

financial status because it suggests that the wife actually had to prepare the meal herself.

Customs and culture affect organizational activity.

Customs and culture also affect the way organizations are run. German managers expect obedience from their subordinates. On the other hand, labor does participate in the decision-making process because it is represented on supervisory boards in executive committees of large organizations. In Japan many employees (about 35 percent) spend an entire working life with a single organization. Among the large firms, lifelong employment is virtually guaranteed, and a seniority system provides privileges for older workers. At the same time there is a great deal of participative decision making. Many changes are initiated by lower-level employees, presented to the supervisor, discussed, analyzed, clarified, and, after a complete review and approval, sent back for implementation.

Business firms wishing to operate in industrial nations such as Germany and Japan must be aware of their customs and cultures. These businesses must also know how the different countries conduct their economic planning.

Economic Planning Some nations of the world employ an economic planning process similar to that of the United States. Others use a much more centralized approach.

Some planning is heavily market oriented.

Like the government of the United States, the German government pursues a steady, anti-inflationary, macroeconomic policy. The objective of this policy is to create a climate of investor confidence. Corporate managers are free to decide how and where to invest company resources. In other words, the Germans employ the market concept, in which customer demand is allowed to determine which goods and services to produce.

Some is moderately government influenced.

In France the situation is different. The French government sets industrial objectives and encourages businesses to pursue them. It indicates industrial areas, for example, that it feels are promising and offers incentives to firms that develop them. For the years 1981 to 1985, the government has set an objective for the electronic office equipment industry, asking it to acquire 20 to 25 percent of the world market and to eliminate trade deficits. The government has also established an objective for the consumer electronics industry, asking it to create a world-scale group of manufacturers including TV-set and tube makers who will each rank among the top three globally. The government is prepared to negotiate contracts and set specific goals for sales, exports, and jobs with firms that are willing to pursue these objectives. These companies will qualify for tax incentives, subsidized loans, and other official aid.

Some is heavily government influenced.

Japan employs even more control over the economy with its national industrial plan. The strategy is quite simple. The government supports industries that seem likely to develop new technologies and exploit world market opportunities. Conversely, it takes both financial support and workers away from industries that are declining. Table 3–2 shows some of the industries that were targeted for government help during the 1970s and those that will be given special attention during the 1980s.

Socio-Cultural Forces

Socio-cultural forces are in a state of flux.

Socio-cultural forces consist of the attitudes, beliefs, and values of individuals and groups in society. These forces have been in a state of flux since the end of World War II. Values have been changing, largely as a result

Table 3–2   Japanese Government Support for Various Industries

During the 1970s	For the 1980s
Research-intensive industries	**New Products**
• Fine chemicals • Computers • Nuclear power equipment • Semiconductors • Aircraft • Industrial robots	• Optical fibers • Ceramics • Amorphous materials • High-efficiency resins
Industries requiring market promotion	**Energy industries**
• Pollution control equipment • Office copying equipment • Office calculating equipment • Numerically controlled machine tools	• Coal liquefaction • Coal gasification • Nuclear power • Solar energy • Deep geothermal generation
Others	**Advanced high-technology industries**
• Consumer audio equipment • Apparel • Data processing services and softwear	• Ultra-high-speed computers • Space development • Ocean development • Aircraft

of changes in the economic environment. Young Americans have grown up in a more affluent environment than their parents did. They have also been exposed to television, movies, and a faster pace of life. As a result, young people today are apt to question authority, want immediate satisfaction of needs, and feel that more should be done to help the poor and disadvantaged. Their values have helped to promote the practice of social responsibility. Many people feel that business should become actively involved in the social arena.

Some people feel businesses should exhibit social responsibility.

Social Responsibility   **Social responsibility** consists of those obligations a business has to the society in which it operates. How far should these obligations extend? Social responsibility supporters say that business should play an active role in ensuring such things as (1) equal opportunity in employment, especially for minorities and women; (2) protection of the environment from all dangers created by a business's production processes or output; and (3) safe and properly functioning products that provide full value for the purchase dollar.[10]

Others oppose such action.

Opponents of active social responsibility argue that business's primary objective is economic, not social. They maintain that pursuit of noneconomic goals results in a less effective organization. Arguments set forth by both groups are provided in Table 3–3.

While every business exhibits varying degrees of social responsibility, the general trend has been toward increased government regulation in this area. Some examples are the Equal Pay Act, which requires that all workers be given equal pay for equal work, and the Civil Rights Act, which prohibits

---

10. For more on these specific areas see Fred Luthans, Richard M. Hodgetts, and Kenneth A. Thompson, *Social Issues in Business*, 4th edition (New York: Macmillan, 1984).

Table 3–3   The Social Responsibility Debate

Point	Counterpoint
1. Our economic system works best when businesses pursue stockholder interests.	1. Our economic system works best when businesses pursue the interests of society at large.
2. Businesses are economic institutions and are most efficient when allowed to do what they do best—pursue profit. This is socially preferred behavior.	2. Profit alone no longer implies socially preferred behavior.
3. Businesses are prohibited from engaging in socially responsible behavior by both the law and their corporate charter.	3. The courts have continually upheld the right of businesses to pursue socially responsible behavior even when it reduces overall profits; corporate charters also support such action.
4. Managers are not trained to pursue social goals.	4. Managers may not be trained to pursue social goals, but since their actions have social and political impact, they cannot now claim incompetence as a defense against becoming socially responsible.
5. Social responsibility often leads managers to give away money that rightfully belongs to stockholders.	5. In spending money on social responsibility programs, the company is simply paying society back for the social costs of doing business.
6. Social responsibility is a threat to democracy.	6. Social responsibility is not a threat to democracy. Businesses are social institutions and must live up to society's standards. Moreover, if they do not, the government is likely to step in and make them.

Note: For more on this topic see Thomas M. Jones, "Corporate Social Responsibility Revisited, Redefined," *California Management Review,* Spring 1980, pp. 59–67.

discrimination on the basis of race, color, creed, sex, and national origin. In addition, much of the movement towards increased social responsibility can be attributed to the personal values of managers. Raised in an affluent society, these managers are bringing their values into the workplace with them.

The Internal Environment

The internal environment is determined by forces operating within the organization. There are two basic internal forces: managers and workers.

Managers

Managers are an environmental force because of their values and ethics. To some degree these values and ethics are encouraged and developed through organizational influence. Industry codes of conduct establish levels of acceptable behavior. To a greater degree, however, these values are personal. Managers bring them to the job and use them in decision making.

Values

There are a number of ways of examining managerial values. One is to study those set forth by Edward Spraunger and measured by the Allport–

There are six specific kinds of managerial values.

Vernon–Lindzey *Study of Values.*[11] This approach looks at six specific kinds of values:

- **theoretical**—values showing a concern for order, system, and logic
- **economic**—values showing a concern for usefulness and practicality
- **aesthetic**—values showing a concern for art and beauty
- **social**—values showing a concern for people and their welfare
- **political**—values showing a concern for power over people and things
- **religious**—values showing a concern for unity and harmony in things

Research reveals that businesspeople and top managers have the highest concern for economic and political values. If these values are not very high when the manager joins the organization, they become so or the person does not do well in the management ranks. These values are essential for success.[12]

Another way to examine **managerial values** is to look at the way these values have changed over time. Many of the changes have been influenced by society at large, as is evident from close analysis. One of the most popular comparative models is that by Robery Hay and Ed Gray, who have described the three phases through which many businesses have progressed.[13] The model is presented in Table 3–4.

Changes in managerial values have occurred in three phases.

Phase I was in vogue 50 years ago. Except in small firms, however, it no longer accurately describes the values of managers. Phase II is most representative today. The manager is a trustee of the organization's resources and views the job as one requiring a balance between concern for profit and concern for people. Phase III, quality of life management, is not representative of most organizations. However, many people feel that managerial values are shifting in this direction. Perhaps the cliché that best describes Phase III is "we worry about the people and let profits take care of themselves." In any event, values certainly do affect internal organizational operations.

Ethics

Ethics refers to right and wrong conduct.

The word **"ethics"** refers to right and wrong conduct. In recent years, like social responsibility, business ethics have become a focal point of public attention. This is true not only for national firms but for MNCs as well. Elkins and Callaghan have noted that:

> Illegal and questionable political payoffs, bribes, and "grease payments" abroad by U.S.-based multinationals have unfolded as matters of grave

11. Gordon W. Allport, Phillip E. Vernon, and Gardner Lindzey, *Study of Values* (Boston: Houghton Mifflin, 1960).

12. Richard M. Hodgetts, Mildred G. Pryor, Harry N. Mills, and Karen Brinkman, "A Profile of the Successful Executive," *Academy of Management Proceedings,* 1978, p. 378.

13. Robert Hay and Ed Gray, "Social Responsibilities of Business Managers," *Academy of Management Journal,* March 1974, pp. 135–143.

Table 3–4 Comparison of Managerial Values

Phase I Profit Maximizing Management	Phase II Trusteeship Management	Phase III Quality of Life Management
Economic Values		
1. Raw self-interest	1. Self-interest 2. Contributors' interests	1. Enlightened self-interest 2. Contributors' interests 3. Society's interests
What's good for me is good for my country.	What's good for GM is good for our country.	What is good for society is good for our company.
Profit maximizer	Profit satisficer	Profit is necessary, but . . . .
Money and wealth are most important.	Money is important, but so are people.	People are more important than money.
Let the buyer beware (*caveat emptor*).	Let us not cheat the customer.	Let the seller beware (*caveat venditor*).
Labor is a commodity to be bought and sold.	Labor has certain rights which must be recognized.	Employee dignity has to be satisfied.
Accountability of management is to the owners.	Accountability of management is to the owners, customers, employees, suppliers, and other contributors.	Accountability of management is to the owners, contributors, and society.
Technology Values		
Technology is very important.	Technology is important but so are people.	People are more important than technology.
Social Values		
Employee personal problems must be left at home.	We recognize that employees have needs beyond their economic needs.	We hire the whole man.
I am a rugged individualist, and I will manage my business as I please.	I am an individualist, but I recognize the value of group participation.	Group participation is fundamental to our success.
Minority groups are inferior to whites. They must be treated accordingly.	Minority groups have their place in society, and their place is inferior to mine.	Minority group members are people as you and I are.
Political Values		
That government is best which governs least.	Government is a necessary evil.	Business and government must cooperate to solve society's problems.
Environmental Values		
The natural environment controls the destiny of man.	Man can control and manipulate the environment.	We must preserve the environment in order to lead a quality life.
Aesthetic Values		
Aesthetic values? What are they?	Aesthetic values are okay, but not for us.	We must preserve our aesthetic values, and we will do our part.

Source: Robert Hay and Ed Gray, "Social Responsibilities of Business Managers," *Academy of Management Journal,* March 1974, p. 142. Reprinted with permission.

concern. Over a short period of time, over 250 firms have disclosed such payments totaling in excess of $300 million. Such corporate stalwarts (heretofore) as Gulf Oil, Lockheed, 3M, United Brands (Chiquita Bananas), Phillips Petroleum, Goodyear, and Exxon have joined the flock, disclosing payments under the decree by the Securities and Exchange Commission. Exxon alone, for example, has admitted to more than $46 million in illicit and questionable payments made between 1963 and 1972. United Brands' activity ultimately led to the suicide of its chairman. And the SEC is pressuring for still further disclosure by these and other multinationals.[14]

Are business ethics really on the decline? While newspaper stories might suggest that they are, the facts do not support such a bleak finding. Actually, most business executives feel that their ethics are good and getting better. Furthermore, most say that their ethical conduct is higher than that of the average business executive.[15]

What will influence ethical standards in the future? A survey conducted among practicing executives by Steven Brenner and Earl Molander produced the lists provided in Table 3–5.[16]

Many factors affect ethical standards.

Notice from the table that public disclosure, publicity, and the fear of people finding out about ethics violations are of primary importance. Other considerations such as a code of professionals ethics, social pressures, and business's sense of social responsibility are also important. On the other hand, business executives blame society's low standards, social decay, and the rise of materialism for causing low standards in business.

Two other factors, mentioned only indirectly in this study, will most influence ethical standards during the 1980s: the manager's own standards and those of the organization. The two reinforce each other. Corporations that demand the highest ethical codes will get them. Those managers whose personal codes do not meet the standards of the organization will either leave or be forced out. Competition plays a key role in this process. When one business firm offers kickbacks to its customers, it is difficult for others not to follow suit. They stand to lose business if they do not match the competition. This is the reason why public disclosure and government regulation will continue to be important. As long as everyone is playing the game according to the same rules, there is equity.[17] If some are acting unethically, however, they have an unfair advantage. For this reason we are likely to see continued public attention directed to the area of business ethics.[18] People want to know when business managers are acting unethically. So do ethical managers, who feel that this public spotlight will keep other managers on the straight and narrow path.

---

14. Arthur Elkins and Dennis W. Callaghan, *A Managerial Odyssey,* 3rd edition (Reading, Mass.: Addison-Wesley, 1980), pp. 61–62.

15. Steven N. Brenner and Earl Molander, "Is the Ethics of Business Changing?" *Harvard Business Review,* January–February 1977, pp. 57–71.

16. *Ibid.*

17. Glenn T. Wilson, "Solving Ethical Problems and Saving Your Career," *Business Horizons,* November–December 1983, pp. 16–20.

18. Donald R. Cressey and Charles A. Moore, "Managerial Values and Corporate Codes of Conduct," *California Management Review,* Summer 1983, pp. 53–77.

Table 3–5
Factors That Influence
Ethical Standards

	Percentage of Respondents Listing Factor
Factors Causing Higher Standards	
Public disclosure; publicity; media coverage; better communication	31
Increased public concern; public awareness, consciousness, and scrutiny; better informed public; societal pressures	20
Government regulation, legislation, and intervention; federal courts	10
Education of business managers; increase in manager professionalism and education	9
New social expectations for the role business is to play in society; young adults' attitudes; consumerism	5
Business's greater sense of social responsibility and greater awareness of the implications of its acts; business responsiveness; corporate policy changes; top management emphasis on ethical action	5
Other	20
Factors Causing Lower Standards	
Society's standards are lower; social decay; more permissive society; materialism and hedonism have grown; loss of church and home influence; less quality, more quantity desires	34
Competition; pace of life; stress to succeed; current economic conditions; costs of doing business; more businesses compete for less	13
Political corruption; loss of confidence in government; Watergate; politics; political ethics and climate	9
People more aware of unethical acts; constant media coverage; TV; communications create atmosphere for crime	9
Greed; desire for gain; worship of the dollar as measure of success; selfishness of the individual; lack of personal integrity and moral fiber	8
Pressure for profit from within the organization from superiors, from stockholders; corporate influences on managers; corporate policies	7
Other	21

Note: Some respondents listed more than one factor, so there were 353 factors in all listed as causing higher standards and 411 in all listed as causing lower ones.

Source: Reprinted by permission of the *Harvard Business Review*. The exhibit is from "Is the Ethics of Business Changing?" by Steven N. Brenner and Earl A. Molander (January–February 1977), p. 63. Copyright © 1977 by the President and Fellows of Harvard College; all rights reserved.

Workers

Workers also help create the climate within which the organization functions both through their work ethic and through the work values they follow on the job.

Work Ethic

Many employees support the work ethic.

The **work ethic** consists of the beliefs people have about their jobs and about carrying them out. This ethic may have religious overtones, as in the case of the individual who believes a life of hard work will be rewarded in the hereafter. Or it may simply be reflected in the belief that work is desirable because it helps society. Both of these philosophies, as seen in Figure 3–4, are forms of the work ethic.

Some are workaholics. Others support the worth ethic.

Figure 3–4 also identifies some other common attitudes toward work. Some people work long hours, bring tasks home with them, and never seem able to slow up. These people are **workaholics** who represent an extreme form of the work ethic. Other people believe in the **worth ethic** either because work provides them satisfying feelings of competence, job mastery, or self-esteem or because it offers personal rewards such as money and a feeling of accomplishment. One final attitude toward work can be

Still others subscribe to the leisure ethic.

defined as the **leisure ethic.** People who subscribe to this ethic fall into two groups. For the first, work is an unfortunate obligation, although people

Figure 3–4
The Meanings of Work

Work is
highly
desirable

Continuum of Importance

The Workaholic

Person derives satisfaction from continual work. The meaning and purpose of work are distorted. Life is out of balance.

The Work Ethic

Work is a desirable activity, in and of itself. A person ought to work hard.

Work is desirable because it is beneficial to society. Thanks to work, goods and services are produced.

The Worth Ethic

Work increases self-esteem. It develops feelings of competence and job mastery in people.

Work provides personal rewards. The employee can earn a livelihood and achieve the feeling of having done a good job at the same time.

The Leisure Ethic

Work is an unfortunate obligation. Money earned on the job is used to pursue nonwork activities.

Work is undesirable. The individual finds no rewards associated with it.

Work is
highly
undesirable

in this group manage to find satisfaction in the money they earn. For the second, work is regarded as totally undesirable. People in this group work only to survive.

Work Values

Research shows that the work ethic in some degree is still accepted by most workers. There are differences, however, between the age groups. Some of these are shown in the following table.[19]

More Important to Younger Workers	More Important to Older Workers
Money and fringe benefits	Pride in craftsmanship
Quick promotions	Hard work
Enriching jobs	Commitment to the organization
Friendship of co-workers	Service to others
Leisure and free time	Organization's role in the community

Younger workers are more interested in money, fringe benefits, and rewards. Older employees are more concerned with work pride, service, and commitment to the organization. These attitudes represent internal environmental forces that managers must confront. How can a modern organization develop desirable work values among its people? Researchers have suggested that managers should

1. Establish an organizational climate that fosters positive work values and a commitment to excellence.

2. Communicate clear expectations about productivity and high-quality craftsmanship.

3. Teach and explain the value of work, the dignity of labor, and the joy of service.

Principles for developing desirable work values

4. Establish individual accountability through effective delegation.

5. Develop personal commitment and involvement through individual choice and participation.

6. Provide feedback on performance through effective performance appraisals.

7. Reward effective performance with pay and other social reinforcements.

8. Continually encourage employees in their personal growth and skill development.[20]

---

19. David J. Cherrington, *The Work Ethic* (New York: AMACOM, 1980), pp. 65–71.

20. *Ibid.,* pp. 181–182.

Summary

1. The external environment consists of forces outside the direct control of the organization. These forces can be divided into two groups: first tier and second tier. First-tier forces affect virtually every organization. Second-tier forces are of more importance to large organizations than to small ones.

2. The most dominant first-tier force is the economy. The economy affects organizations both directly and indirectly. However, not all industries are affected in the same way at the same time. In an economic slump, some industries are affected earlier than others. Moreover, some are hard hit while others do not show much of a downturn.

3. Suppliers provide an organization with the materials it needs for turning out goods and services. In order to avoid shortages, most organizations cultivate two or more suppliers.

4. Customers, ultimately, dictate the success of organizations. The competition attempts to steal customers away.

5. Political–legal forces consist of laws and regulations that constrain and direct organizational activity. As laws change, organizations must adjust to the new political–legal environment. In most cases this means following the change, not leading it.

6. Technology is an important variable for many large firms. Some, such as GE, must maintain a high technological base because it provides the input for new product development. Smaller firms are often more content to adopt a follow-the-leader strategy.

7. International forces are a consideration for firms doing business in other countries. These multinational corporations (MNCs) must be concerned with two major environmental challenges: customs/culture and economic planning.

8. Socio-cultural forces consist of the attitudes, beliefs, and values of individuals and groups in society. These forces are currently in a state of flux. One development has been the rise of a social responsibility philosophy that is followed by many firms, although there are some who argue against such an approach.

9. The internal environment consists of those forces operating within the organization. There are two basic internal forces: managers and workers.

10. Managers are an environmental force because of their values and ethics. There are a number of ways to examine managerial values. One way is to identify specific values. A second way is to study value changes over time. Ethics refers to right and wrong conduct. Many businesspeople feel that ethical standards are on the rise. Certainly there are factors contributing higher standards, although, as noted in Table 3–5, there are also factors causing lower standards.

11. Workers are another internal environmental force. They help create the climate within which the organization functions, through their work ethic and the values they follow on the job. An organization can develop desirable work values in its workers by following the principles set forth at the end of this chapter.

Key Terms

Aesthetic values   Values showing a concern for art and beauty.
Economic values   Values showing concern for usefulness and practicality.
Ethics   Right and wrong conduct.

First-tier forces   External environmental forces that affect virtually all organizations. They include the economy, suppliers, customers, and competitors.

Leisure ethic   The belief that work is an unfortunate obligation, or that it is totally undesirable.

Managerial value phases   Phase I: A concern for profit maximization; Phase II: A concern for balancing profit considerations with the well-being of personnel; and Phase III: A concern for personnel and society at large with profit given secondary consideration.

Multinational corporations (MNCs)   Firms that have their headquarters in one country but operate in many different nations.

Political values   Values showing a concern for power over people and things.

Religious values   Values showing a concern for unity and harmony in things.

Second-tier forces   External environmental forces that more heavily affect large organizations than small organizations. They include political-legal, technological, international, and socio-cultural forces.

Social responsibility   Those obligations a business has to the society in which it operates.

Social values   Values showing a concern for people and their welfare.

Theoretical values   Values showing a concern for order, system, and logic.

Workaholic   A person who derives satisfaction from continual work.

Work ethic   The belief that hard work is a desirable activity.

Worth ethic   The belief that work increases self-esteem and provides personal rewards.

Questions for Analysis and Discussion

1. The economy affects organizations both directly and indirectly. What is meant by this statement?

2. What types of materials do suppliers provide to an organization? Be complete in your answer.

3. In what way are customers and competitors environmental forces with which an organization must deal? Give an example of each.

4. Why are second-tier forces of more importance to large organizations than to small ones? Defend your answer.

5. In what way do political–legal and technological forces affect an organization? Which is more important? Why?

6. In dealing with international forces, the organization must take two things into account: customs/culture and economic planning. What is meant by this statement? Be complete in your answer.

7. How do socio-cultural forces affect the organization? Explain. Do these forces have a greater or lesser effect on the organization than competition does? Than technology? Defend your answer.

8. Are managerial values changing? Are managerial ethics improving? In your answers be sure to include a discussion of the three phases of managerial values and factors that influence ethical standards.

9. What is meant by the work ethic? The worth ethic? The leisure ethic? Describe each.

10. Are employee work values changing? How? Explain your answer. How can a modern organization develop desirable work values among its people? Set forth at least five practical principles.

| Case | # Work Philosophy and Values |

The backlog of orders at the Shellett Company has been increasing month by month. Six months ago it was $95,000. Three months ago it was $240,000. Currently it is $460,000. In an effort to reduce this backlog, the company president devised an incentive payment scheme. The plan is tied to the hourly wage rate and rewards workers for overtime and Saturday and Sunday work. Overtime pays 150 percent of the hourly rate. Saturday work pays double time. Sunday work pays triple time. In order to qualify for Sunday work, an individual also has to work Saturday.

The average employee at Shellett makes $6.75 an hour plus fringe benefits. The person willing to work an extra two hours a day, all day Saturday and all day Sunday would make $641.25 for the week. The total is computed this way:

Regular 40 hours (40 × 6.75)	$270.00
Weekly overtime (10 × 6.75 × 1.5)	101.25
Saturday work (8 × 6.75 × 2.0)	108.00
Sunday work (8 × 6.75 × 3.0)	162.00
	$641.25

The president feels that this is quite an incentive for those willing to help reduce the backlog. Surprisingly, however, only 35 percent of the workforce takes weekly overtime. Just under 15 percent work Saturdays and 10 percent work Sundays. The president cannot understand it. "These guys are downright lazy," he has complained to his senior vice-president. "The work ethic in America must be dead."

The vice-president agrees, but many of the managers do not. One of them put it this way, "Why do the workers want to knock themselves out with weekend work? Life is too short. The president should realize this. In fact, he himself ought to take more time off. There's a lot more to running a company than just maximizing profits. Quality of life should be a major consideration. I know it is with a lot of us managers."

1. How would you describe the workers' philosophy of work? Use Figure 3–4 in answering this question.

2. How would you describe the president's work philosophy? Explain.

3. Under which of the three phases of managerial values in Table 3–4 do the managers operate? Defend your answer.

You Be the Consultant

A Changing Environment

Harrington Brothers Inc. has been in business for more than 85 years. The company specializes in replacement parts for industrial machinery. Two years ago the firm patented a replacement part that swept the market. Many manufacturers were hard pressed for cash, and profits were at a 10-year low. As a result, most manufacturers preferred to repair their machinery rather than to replace it with new models. The Harrington replacement part could be used in any of 65 major industrial machines and, when compared with the replacement parts offered by the competition, it was both cheaper and more efficient. Within eighteen months Harrington had captured almost 75 percent of the replacement part market. In an effort to ensure delivery of the parts, Harrington went to a double shift in its factory and used five suppliers for the needed materials. The company never had a problem with suppliers. If one was unable to provide the required materials, another would.

Six months ago, however, two competitors came out with a replacement part that is slightly more expensive than Harrington's but offers greater efficiency and longer life. This part allows a machine to be run at a speed 10 percent faster than normal while incurring very little wear and tear. From a dollar-and-cents standpoint, the competitors have a better replacement product than Harrington does.

Harrington has purchased a dozen replacement parts from each of the two competitors and has examined what each competitor did to make the parts. After careful analysis, Harrington has realized that the competitors simply took Harrington's patent and figured out a way to improve it. Employing a follow-the-leader strategy, they piggybacked on Harrington's basic concept. Harrington is now in a game of catch-up trying to figure out how, in turn, it can piggyback on the new developments.

In the meantime the company has run into another problem. Two of its salespeople in Europe have been very successful in selling replacement parts there. The company has now learned, however, that the salespeople have been giving kickbacks to the purchasing managers in some firms. Because kickbacks were paid in the form of "commissions" and charged to Harrington's account, the company thought the salespeople had merely hired additional agents to help with the selling and that the commissions were legitimate expenses. Harrington paid the money directly to the salespeople, who then passed it on to the purchasing managers. Now the Internal Revenue Service has informed Harrington that it wants to make a full audit of the company's books for the last three years.

In the midst of these problems, the company's financial officer has told the president that his analysis of industry buying habits indicates that, with the recent change in the business tax laws, the replacement market will soon start to decline. More and more firms are going to be buying new equipment. Upon hearing the news, the company president smiled and said, "Oh, brother. It all seems to happen at the same time doesn't it?" The financial officer agreed.

Your Consultation

Assume you are the president's primary advisor. Give the individual your advice regarding how to deal with the environmental forces presented in the case. Also, provide the individual with advice regarding other key environmental forces that might affect the firm. Use Figure 3–1 to help you.

Comprehensive Cases

A Student of Management

Background and Facts

With only seven weeks remaining before he receives his bachelor's degree in accounting, there is no doubt in Richard Wheeler's mind that now is the time to be thinking about his future. It is not that he has been sliding his way through college—hitting all the parties, attending all the athletic events, and living for official school vacations. On the contrary, while Richard has been going weekly to a few parties and athletic events, he has also been working part time (20 hours per week) for a bill collection company and earning above-average (B—) grades. And while he has set no definite future goals, he has done some subconscious thinking about entering the business world. For example, he enjoys reading about and studying business. He is also president of the Business Club at his midwestern college and is well thought of by his business professors and classmates, yet he is troubled by the fact that he does not know where he should go in business or how to achieve his objectives.

The Issue

Many of Richard's goals and aspirations regarding his profession are similar to those of other people in his position. Yet in some ways he feels different from other college seniors. Richard wants to command as high a salary as possible, but he really feels that money is not as important as job enrichment and the opportunity for future growth and learning. Furthermore, he wants to remain with his first employer until he reaches retirement age. The traditional view that success results from working one's way up the corporate ladder was instilled by his father, who just celebrated his 27th year as a vice-president of finance for a Fortune 500 firm. Richard wants to be a success like his father. The occupation he would most like to list on his resume is "manager." Yet again, there are the nagging questions: Manager of what? And how does one get there?

Unlike many of his peers, Richard has already decided not to continue in the accounting area and not to earn a CPA. He feels that accounting is too restrictive. He wants a position that will mix his accounting background with the human resource management content from which he derived so much satisfaction during his college years.

The Alternatives

Earlier today, with pen in hand, and his family gone from home for a few hours, Richard sat back and sketched out some of the options available to him. First, he listed the alternatives that would provide immediate and high cash inflow. On the top of the list was a managerial position at a supermarket in the area. Second was a sales job with one of the leading computer manufacturers in the country. His other choice was to begin on the bottom rung as a staff accountant for a company close to home. He has job offers from all three companies.

He also has job offers with little promise of high salary or advancement. His volunteer work with a local scouting chapter has given him many contacts and a job offer in the chapter's finance office. And the college he is now attending has offered him a graduate assistant position.

Evaluation of the Alternatives

Richard is now trying to evaluate each alternative. Work in the supermarket would satisfy his desire to manage both people and money. Once he is given his own store, however, the next rung on the ladder is district manager—a step that the recruiter described as very hard to reach.

The computer company promises to be financially and personally rewarding. But Richard was advised that the step from salesman to manager always requires relocation to an area other than the Midwest. He wants to live in the Midwest, and he is concerned about having to move around too much and never finding a place he can call home.

The staff accountant position looks very good, but Richard knows that the next step is accounting manager, followed by company controller. A CPA is needed for these positions, and both look quite unattainable for at least five more years—a long time for him to be a staff accountant.

Richard recognizes that money is not the root of all pleasure, but he knows that the scouting chapter works on a very limited executive salary budget. His desire to start his own family and begin a savings base for later in life would be sorely limited under this option. The experience would be great, but his feelings about starting a family and the fact that he would no longer have time for contact with the younger scouts weigh heavily on his mind.

The graduate assistant position at his soon-to-be alma mater also has its positive and negative sides. Richard would receive a small monthly stipend which he could just live on, although a tuition waiver for the MBA program would be provided in the contract. The position itself promises an opportunity to study the professors' teaching methods, some of which he could imitate, develop, and use in the possible occupation of teaching. Yet between the lines of the job description Richard senses a certain amount of professorial clerical work, to which, quite frankly, he is not too receptive. In addition, 16 years of formal education and brown bag lunches (17, counting kindergarten) have definitely begun to take their toll.

After putting down his pen and rubbing his tired eyes, Richard releases a heavy sigh and wonders where he will be at this time next year.

1. What is a manager? In your answer, incorporate what you believe are the qualifications of a manager.

2. If you were in Richard Wheeler's position, which alternative would you select? Why?

3. As a student of management, what opportunities do you see in the field of management?

4. What changes do you anticipate in the future for which managers will have to be prepared?

5. What resources should Richard Wheeler rely on as he enters the business world? Explain.

Memorial Funeral Home

History

Memorial Funeral Home began as a small family business, founded in 1947 by Donald Kellen. Located in an upper-middle-class suburb of a large city, the business prospered and gained an excellent reputation. After thirty-three years as director of the business, Donald Kellen retired and was succeeded in 1980 by his son, Kenneth.

Memorial is the only funeral home in the suburb. However, funeral homes in neighboring suburbs offer strong competition. Under the guidance of Kenneth Kellen, Memorial began diversifying its services. Currently, Memorial handles sixty-five funerals a year under its own name. In addition, Memorial supplies removal, embalming, directing, livery service, and rental of funeral vehicles to other funeral homes. While maintaining its primary function as a family-run, neighborhood business (concentrating on personal service), Memorial has successfully diversified its operations.

Recognizing the rapidly changing ideas and expectations of society, Kenneth Kellen is adjusting. Economics are beginning to play a major role in funeral decisions. The client is more sophisticated and informed, necessitating clear-cut definitions of services, costs, and available options.

Fundamental Components

A number of fundamental components are associated with the funeral home business.

Property

Land and buildings must be large enough to meet the demand of visitations and of the funeral service. Owning such property—in a convenient and accessible location where the public can be properly served—constitutes one of the major, ongoing costs of a funeral-home operation.

Facilities

A funeral home must be tastefully furnished to provide a homelike atmosphere and must be easily adaptable for visitation and for the funeral service. Facilities also must be able to accommodate more than one funeral at a time.

Automotive Equipment

Funeral directors must provide the latest in automobiles for transportation between the funeral home and the cemetery. Owning and maintaining this equipment, much of which is specially designed, is costly.

Selection Room

Special facilities house a wide variety of merchandise (caskets, vaults, and clothing) made available by the funeral home for burial purposes. This service requires considerable space and investment in inventory.

Professional Staff

Salaries make up the largest part of the funeral expense. Personnel must be carefully chosen so that families receive both expert and efficient service. To attract qualified personnel, funeral homes must compete with salaries paid by other professions, business, and industry.

Educational Requirements

Funeral directors and embalmers today are required under state law to meet certain college academic standards and pass state board examinations before they may practice funeral directing and embalming under state-approved licensure requirements. This highly specialized training prepares the funeral director to offer expert professional service to bereaved families, and the director must be paid a salary commensurate with his or her knowledge.

Documents

A number of documents must be completed by the funeral director. These are required by law.

Counseling Skill

An intangible factor in funeral cost is that of counseling. An effective funeral director helps families to better accept death, grief, and bereavement. The ability to take a traumatic situation and mold it into a meaningful and impressive service of remembrance for the surviving family is an important part of the funeral director's job and contributes to the survivors' personal health, both mental and emotional.

24-Hour Service

The typical funeral home is open continuously for service. This means the telephone must be attended, and personnel must be available to assist those who have experienced a death regardless of the day or the hour.

Community Service

The funeral director must be a civic-spirited member of the community. He or she must be actively involved in business, civic, and religious organizations.

Public Perception

According to the National Funeral Directors Association (NFDA), there are approximately 22,000 funeral homes in the United States. A major concern of the industry is the new attitudes of the public regarding the disposition of the dead. The executive secretary of the NFDA noted that

1. Many people believe that a funeral does meet many needs, including individual, family, religious, and community needs.

2. Some people feel that emotions can be intellectualized and the quickest possible disposition of the deceased is the best course of action.

3. There are those who as yet have formed no definite view. They have had little, if any, experience with death. They are honestly asking what needs arise when a death occurs, and whether the funeral helps to satisfy these needs.

Recent investigations of funeral homes by the Federal Trade Commission, as well as newspaper feature stories in exposé form, have not helped the image of the industry. The public, aroused by the sensational and emotional nature of the issue, is easily persuaded into the belief that some funeral homes are dishonest. A basic lack of understanding about death and the funeral home business lies at the root of the public mistrust.

Death is not as commonplace as it once was. Millions of Americans have never experienced the loss, by death, of someone close to them. Millions of Americans have never been to a funeral, or even seen a funeral procession, except one that was televised. Millions of Americans have never seen a dead body except on TV, in a movie, on a battlefield, or on a highway. Even where people have been directly involved in the arrangement of a funeral service, there is often confusion or doubt about the role of the funeral director and the cost of his services.

Often the place of the casket in the funeral service is unclear or undefined. Historically, the funeral director has been a provider of goods and some services. A casket was purchased, and all other services were provided "free." Today, on the average, the merchandise amounts to only about 20 percent of the total cost of a funeral service. (*Source:* National Funeral Directors Association.)

Financial Structure

People are probably less knowledgeable about funeral costs than about any other aspect of funeral services. The following provides a general description of pricing and payment in Memorial's section of the country.

Methods

The surviving relatives accepting responsibility for payment may be charged under one of three methods or a combination thereof. The method to be used is the one chosen by the funeral director. They are (1) complete itemized pricing which itemizes every detail, (2) functional pricing which gives prices for major categories of costs, and (3) unit pricing which gives only the complete price.

Complete Itemized Pricing   For a typical funeral, the complete itemized pricing is detailed on a form similar to the one in Exhibit 1. The following is a typical pricing structure:

Professional services

Funeral director and staff	$ 400

Funeral home facilities

Chapel and facilities (one night)	395
Embalming and preparation	215
Preparation room	95

Merchandise

Casket	504
Cards and register book	135

Transportation

Removal	95
Hearse	150

Total	$1,989

The range of services available, and therefore the costs, may vary (see Exhibit 2). In the foregoing example of itemized costs, the total of $1,989 minus the casket cost of $504 equals $1,485, which corresponds to Major Services—B in Exhibit 2.

The price range of the casket may vary as well, from approximately $400 to $10,000. Other services are available at an extra charge. They are as follows:

Item	Price Range
Burial vault	$105 to $1,200
Clergyman	50 to 100
Beautician	50
Chapel organist	50
Cemetery charges:	
Grave opening	295 to 535
Mausoleum	Varies greatly
Death notices (one day, one paper)	75 (average)
Extra funeral cars:	
Flower car	110
Limousine	130
Copies of death certificate	$3 (first), $2 (each additional)
Burial garments	75
Church soloist	50

If cremation is desired, some costs will be eliminated, such as the casket and grave opening charges. Additional costs encountered would include the following:

Item	Price Range
Cremation cost	$ 95 to $120
Cremation container (box)	65 to 75
Cremation urn	116 to 237

Exhibit 1 Memorial Funeral Home Pricing Form

SERVICES FOR:	DATE:
1. PROFESSIONAL SERVICES:	**CASH ADVANCES:**
Professional Care of the Deceased, Staff Service Fee .... $ _____	As a convenience to the family, we will advance payment for the following:
Professional Services of Funeral Director and Staff.......................... $ _____	Clergy Honorarium................................ $ _____
.... $ _____	Beautician................................ $ _____
.... $ _____	Chapel Organist................................ $ _____
	Church Organist................................ $ _____
	Death Notices................................ $ _____
TOTAL PROFESSIONAL SERVICES................................ $ _____	Certified Copies................................ $ _____
	.... $ _____
	.... $ _____
	.... $ _____
	.... $ _____
	.... $ _____
2. FUNERAL HOME FACILITIES:	**TOTAL**................................ $ _____
Use of Chapel and Funeral Home for visitation and services.................... $ _____	**SUMMARY:**
Preparation/Operating Room...................... $ _____	OUR CHARGES................................ $ _____
.... $ _____	SALES TAX................................ $ _____
.... $ _____	CASH ADVANCES................................ $ _____
	LESS CREDITS................................ $ _____
TOTAL FACILITIES................................ $ _____	TOTAL BALANCE DUE................................ $ _____
3. MERCHANDISE:	The foregoing contract has been read by (to) me, and I (we) hereby acknowledge receipt of a copy of same and agree to pay the above funeral account and any such additional services or
Casket................................ $ _____	merchandise as ordered by me (us), on or before _____
Burial Vault................................ $ _____	_____ 19 _____ .
Clothing................................ $ _____	The liability hereby assumed is in addition to the liability imposed by law upon the estate and others and shall not constitute a release thereof.
Printing, Clerical and Sundry Business Expenses................................ $ _____	
.... $ _____	Signature Relationship
TOTAL MERCHANDISE................................ $ _____	Signature Relationship
4. TRANSPORTATION:	Signature Relationship
Removal................................ $ _____	Funeral Director
Funeral Coach................................ $ _____	
Limousines/Family Cars................................ $ _____	NET DUE ON/BEFORE _____ (30 Days)
Flower Cars................................ $ _____	This account will become past due and delinquent if payment is not made on or before the above date. An Unanticipated Late Payment Fee of 3/4 of 1% per month (9% annual percentage
.... $ _____	rate) on the outstanding balance will be charged after that date
TOTAL TRANSPORTATION................................ $ _____	on all accounts in default.

Source: Thomas G. Marx, "The Corporate Economics Staff: Challenges and Opportunities for the '80s," *Business Horizons,* April 1980, p. 17. Reprinted with permission.

Exhibit 2   A Range of Funeral Services (charges listed by categories)

Major Services Provided	A	B	C	D	E
Use of chapel & funeral home for visitation and funeral services	2 nights & services next day	1 night & services next day	1 night & no services next day	Visitation on day of service (max. 4 hrs.)	No visitation or service
Removal of deceased from local home or hospital	Included	Included	Included	Included	Included
Professional care of the deceased, preparation room, and staff service fee	Included	Included	Included	Included	Not included
Transportation of deceased to local cemetery or crematory	Hearse included	Hearse included	Service vehicle	Hearse included	Service vehicle
Professional services of Funeral Director and staff, sundry business expenses	Included	Included	Included	Included	Included
Prayer cards/chapel folders, register book, donation envelopes, and acknowledgment cards	Included	Included	Included	Included	Not included
Total Professional Fee	$1685.00	$1485.00	$1260.00	$925.00	$425.00
Deceased transported to our funeral home from out of town	$1175.00	$975.00	$750.00	$650.00	Direct to interment $195.00

Casket, vault, and other items of choice are left to the further discretion of the family and are added to the above service expenditures.

In the complete itemized pricing method, all costs are known. Included in some of the itemized costs are mark-ups by the funeral director.

A comparison can be made between the costs of Memorial Funeral Home and the average industry costs provided in Exhibit 3. The exhibit also lists the industry's range of costs for each item.

Functional Pricing   A more compressed presentation of costs is provided under the functional pricing method. In contrast to the eight details provided under the complete itemized pricing method the functional pricing method lists only three major categories:

Professional service	$1,105
Merchandise	$ 639
Transportation	$ 245
Total	$1,989

Functional pricing, like detailed pricing, adds all outside charges to the functional total. This method provides more detail than unit pricing does but less than that provided by complete itemized pricing.

Unit Pricing   Unit pricing is nothing more than providing the casket and all associated services under one lump sum. The unit total varies with the casket selected and with any increased services that are provided.

Exhibit 3
The Cost of Funerals

	Average	Range
Funeral Home Costs		
Overhead	$ 440	$ 169 to $ 943
Planning, management, supervision, embalming	237	137 to 422
Staff and salaries	523	276 to 798
Funeral vehicles	196	88 to 655
Casket	584	65 to 7,685
Outer receptacle (grave box or burial vault)	411	101 to 1,475
Burial Costs		
Cemetery burial	582	345 to 1,065
Grave memorial	310	135 to 5,105
Mausoleum entombment	2,520	1,150 to 5,200
Cremation	147	110 to 150
Urn	159	30 to 1,100
Columbarium (place set aside in cemetery for ashes)	336	215 to 580
Funeral director profit	275	Not available
Optional Items		
Death notices	69	31 to 113
Flowers	160	20 to 446
Clothes (for deceased)	72	27 to 104
Donation to church, rabbi, etc.	53	20 to 150
Music, organist, vocalist	38	15 to 220

Source: Funeral Directors Association of Greater Chicago.

Most funeral directors of years ago used a cost method called the *four-by-four method*. It was based on the casket price with the funeral director's fixed costs and profit built into the calculation. An example, using a casket with a cost of $400 follows:

Casket $400
              $\times$ 4
              $\overline{1,600}$
              $+ 400$

Total $2,000

Subsequently, funeral directors used a five-by-six method: $400 $\times$ 5 = $2,000 + $600 = $2,600. However, this method is no longer widely employed either. Rather it is common to simply determine all costs involved and add a percentage for profit. In the main, however, unit pricing is declining in popularity as many states require itemized pricing.

Form of Payment

In order that there be no misunderstanding regarding who pays the bill, someone has to accept responsibility by signing a legal contract. This, along with the signing of an additional release form, allows removal of the body to take place. Full details are then documented on a comprehensive worksheet.

When services have been selected, certain cash payments must be made. A cash advance is also made to the funeral director to defray out-of-pocket costs. Finally, a direct payment must be made to the cemetery to pay all graveside costs in advance.

Future

The emphasis today is on low-cost funerals and relatively inexpensive selections. Two kinds of funeral homes predominate in the industry: independent, family-run funeral homes with one location, and large corporate-run funeral homes with many locations, many employees, and many pieces of equipment.

Automobiles are a major capital outlay for the funeral director. In 1982, a new hearse cost from $24,000 to $44,000 (for deluxe models); a new limousine cost approximately $24,000. The initial outlay and future maintenance are major considerations for the independent funeral director.

As an alternative to owning vehicles independently, three or four noncompeting funeral homes sometimes pool their hearses, limousines, and flower cars, thus reducing the large capital expenditure. When necessary, professional services can be rendered by one director if another is busy. These developments are proving important to the survival of independent funeral homes.

The Challenge

Kenneth Kellen realizes that the economy and environment pose problems for the survival and continued growth of his firm. He knows his expenses will continue to remain high, while a questioning public weighs its traditional obligations against current economic conditions. Mr. Kellen's major concern is the direction that his firm must take in the years ahead. In his view, education of the public and adaptation by his business to meet the changing demands of society are the essential elements necessary to ensure the future existence of Memorial Funeral Home.

In an interview with the casewriters, Mr. Kellen provided the following information about his services and plans.

Grief Counselor: Mr. Kellen has a master's degree and is completing his studies for a Ph.D. in guidance counseling and grief. He believes that his background will help Memorial in the future because of his ability to provide the professional service of counseling during the grief period.

Diversified Operations: Mr. Kellen has begun two service operations for other funeral homes. One provides professional services: embalming, directing, and removal. The other is a livery service that involves the use of his funeral vehicles by other funeral homes.

Cooperatives: Mr. Kellen is not presently engaged in cooperatives with other funeral homes. He does, however, see cooperatives as a viable alternative to vast capital expenditure. Members of cooperatives share facilities, vehicles, and services; their formation allows the small, independent funeral home to compete favorably with the large funeral home that has many locations.

1. Based on the information and background provided in the case, do you feel this type of business (i.e., the funeral business) should be regulated by government (federal or state) agencies or continue its traditional form of self-regulation through its own industry associations (e.g., National Funeral Directors Association)?

2. Which pricing method is best for Memorial Funeral Home? Why?

3. What impact has the change of attitudes and beliefs in today's society had on the small funeral director?

4. What are the alternatives for succeeding in this ever-changing environment? Be complete in your answer.

Planning the Enterprise's Direction

This part of the book begins our systematic study of the manager's functions. Planning is a good topic to begin with because until an organization has a plan, there is really no basis for organizing, staffing, and influencing or controlling operations.

Chapter 4 is devoted to an examination of planning fundamentals. It attempts to answer the question: What is planning all about? In this chapter, you will learn about planning horizons, types of plans, the planning process, and management by objectives. These fundamentals are building blocks that can be used in any planning activity. They are the basics found in both the least sophisticated and most complex projects.

In Chapter 5, the topic of strategic planning is presented. Over the last 10 years, the number of firms that have begun formulating strategic plans has increased dramatically. What has accounted for this trend? Part of the answer is that modern enterprises recognize that effective planning can dramatically increase both efficiency and effectiveness and that companies that do not formulate such plans will be left far behind. In this chapter you will learn the characteristics of a strategic plan. You will also study the four basic elements of strategic plans: the basic mission, strategic objectives, strategy determination, and portfolio planning. The last part of the chapter pulls together these diverse ideas and discusses how to put a strategic plan into operation.

Chapter 6 is about decision making in action. Actually, planning and decision making are intertwined. When an organization formulates its strategic plan, it also chooses objectives; and this is what decision making is— the process of choosing from among two or more alternatives. Nevertheless, because of its importance in the study of management, decision making warrants a chapter of its own. In this chapter, you will learn the nature of decision making. You will also see how the typical rational decision-making process, often used when people try to describe how decisions are made, differs from what is called the bounded rationality model, which takes into account such considerations as simplification, subjectivity, and rationalization. In short, you will be able to compare and contrast the way in which decisions are supposed to be made with the way in which they often are made. You will also learn how managers attempt to improve their decision-making effectiveness through the use of mathematical tools and techniques, creativity, and a matching of decision-making styles with leadership situations.

When you have finished reading the three chapters in this part of the book, you will know how modern managers actually formulate plans and make decisions. You will also have a basic appreciation of both the objective and subjective sides of this process. The material you read in Chapter 1, where management was described as both an art and a science, will become more meaningful.

The Fundamentals of Planning

Objectives

This chapter examines the fundamentals of planning—the ideas and concepts that every manager should know. Its subject matter extends from the nature of planning to the planning process to the methods and techniques that can be used in putting the process into operation. When you have completed your reading and study of the material in this chapter, you will be able to

1. define the term planning and discuss key factors that influence planning time horizons;

2. explain what is meant by a purpose or mission statement and describe its value to a modern organization;

3. list some of the major types of goals pursued by modern organizations and state four general conclusions that can be drawn about these organizations;

4. explain how a strategy differs from an objective and how such approaches as gap analysis and a strategic issues orientation can be of value in strategy formulation;

5. compare and contrast policies, procedures, rules, programs, and budgets, and explain how each can be of value to the modern manager in planning;

6. describe the planning process in detail, including in your description a comparison of strategic, intermediate, and operational plans, a description of forecasting techniques, an explanation of how alternative courses of action are chosen, and a discussion of the value of budgeting; and

7. discuss how management by objectives can be of value in carrying out the planning process.

The Nature of Planning

Planning is the process of setting objectives and then determining the steps needed to attain them. Of course, planning actually begins before objectives are set; it starts with an analysis of the environment for the purpose of determining which objectives to pursue. Then when the analysis has been completed, objectives arc set, and the organization has the direction it needs for developing a plan of action.

Planning Horizons

There are three time horizons: long-, intermediate-, and short-range.

Specific instances of planning can be categorized according to their *time horizons:* **long-range planning** covers more than five years, **intermediate-range planning** covers one to five years, and **short-range planning** covers less than one year. Top managers are typically responsible for drawing up the long-range plan, while middle managers develop the intermediate-

Figure 4–1   Planning Horizons at Different Hierarchical Levels

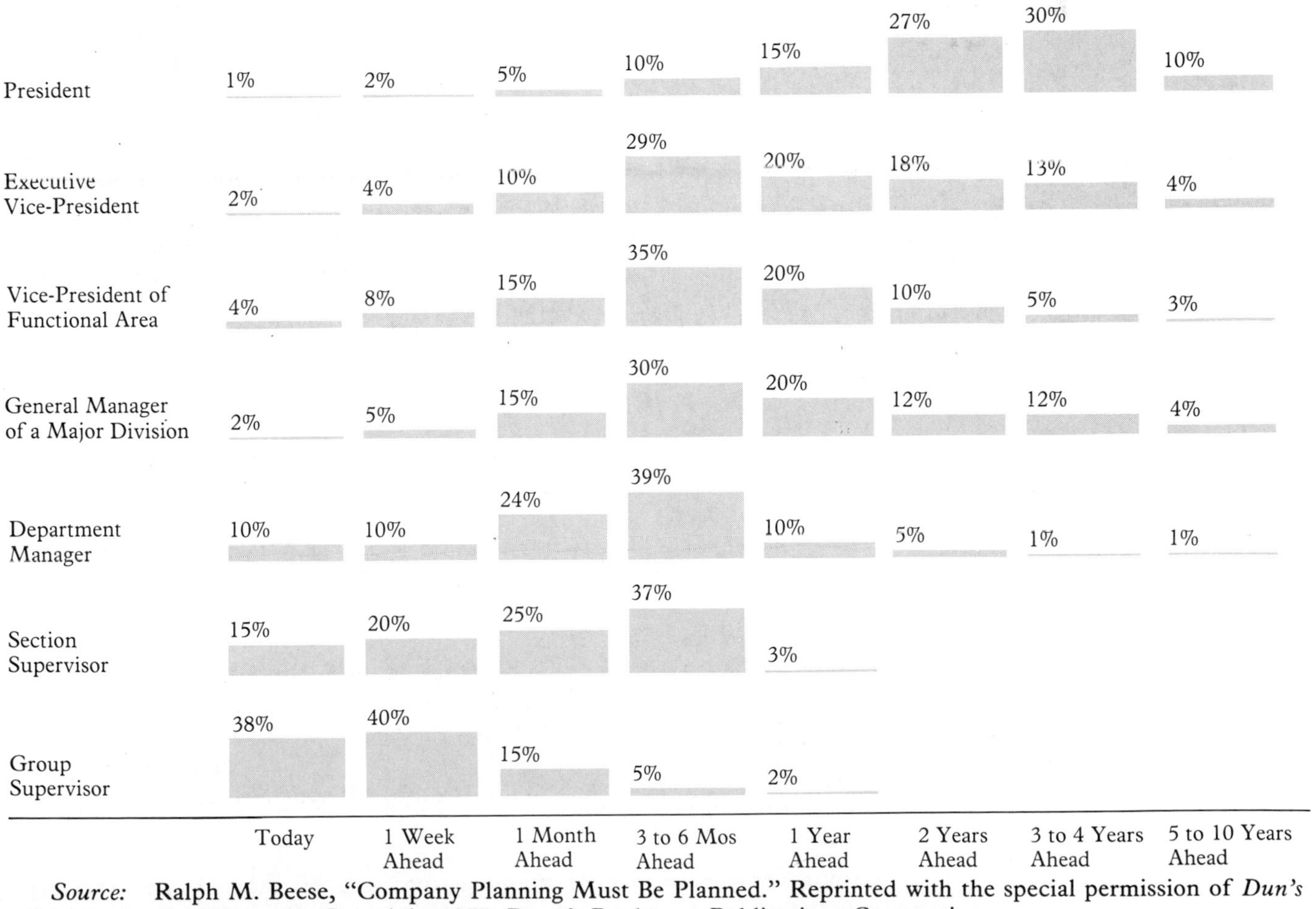

	Today	1 Week Ahead	1 Month Ahead	3 to 6 Mos Ahead	1 Year Ahead	2 Years Ahead	3 to 4 Years Ahead	5 to 10 Years Ahead
President	1%	2%	5%	10%	15%	27%	30%	10%
Executive Vice-President	2%	4%	10%	29%	20%	18%	13%	4%
Vice-President of Functional Area	4%	8%	15%	35%	20%	10%	5%	3%
General Manager of a Major Division	2%	5%	15%	30%	20%	12%	12%	4%
Department Manager	10%	10%	24%	39%	10%	5%	1%	1%
Section Supervisor	15%	20%	25%	37%	3%			
Group Supervisor	38%	40%	15%	5%	2%			

Source: Ralph M. Beese, "Company Planning Must Be Planned." Reprinted with the special permission of *Dun's Review,* April 1957, p. 48. Copyright 1957, Dun & Bradstreet Publications Corporation.

Table 4–1
Types of Plans Developed at
Different Hierarchical Levels

	Top Management	Middle Management	Lower-Level Management
Purposes or Missions	x		
Objectives	x	x	x
Strategies	x		
Policies	x	x	
Procedures		x	x
Rules		x	x
Programs	x	x	x
Budgets	x	x	x

range plan, and lower-level managers work up the short-range plan. Figure 4–1 describes the planning horizons of a typical medium-sized firm. For a large firm these horizons would extend farther into the future, while for a small organization they would move closer to the present.

Many factors affect these time horizons.

Time horizons are affected by a number of factors. In many business firms, one of the most common is the *length of time required to recover capital funds* invested in plant and equipment. For example, if a company buys $5 million worth of new machinery, it should have a plan showing how this money will be recovered. A second factor is the *lead time* for the products or the industry at large. Many firms engaging in research and development (R&D) have five- to ten-year plans, while many retail organizations get by with much shorter time horizons. The R&D company has to take a product through a very long cycle before it gets to the customer, while a retailer is most concerned with seasonal sales and some general long-range planning. A third factor is *competitiveness* in the industry. The greater this competitiveness, the more likely it is that management will emphasize the short- and intermediate-range plans that will help it respond to changing events. A fourth factor is organizational *size relative to others* in the industry. The larger the firm, the more likely it is that the company will have longer planning horizons.[1]

Given the varying nature of organizations and their environments, it is impossible to establish rigid time-horizon guidelines. Except for the very smallest organizations, however, all prepare short-range plans. Many small and medium-sized firms and virtually all large enterprises have intermediate-range plans. Many medium-sized and large organizations have all three time-horizon plans: short-, intermediate-, and long-range.

Types of Plans

There are many different types of plans, each with a different purpose. The most common are purposes or missions, objectives, strategies, policies, procedures, rules, programs, and budgets. These plans vary in nature and scope, with some developed at one level exclusively and others developed at every level. Table 4–1 shows the level(s) at which each type of plan commonly is prepared.

1. Philip H. Thurston, "Should Smaller Companies Make Plans?" *Harvard Business Review,* September–October 1983, pp. 162–163+.

Purposes or Missions

The **purpose or mission** of an organization is its underlying aim or thrust. Large firms often express their aims in the form of mission statements. Small firms do not, although the mission is known to the owner-manager and is often a reflection of the individual's personal values and philosophy.

Missions are usually stated in product or market terms. The following are general examples for different types of organizations:

Type of Firm	Basic Mission
Insurance Firm	To provide personal financial planning and protection.
Airline	To provide fast, efficient, and economic air transportation for people and freight.
Oil Company	To meet the energy needs of an increasing population.
Fertilizer Manufacturer	To improve food production throughout the world through the manufacture of multipurpose fertilizers.
Compact Car Manufacturer	To provide economical, efficient automobiles.

Missions are usually stated in market or product terms.

Mission statements are often broadly based and very encompassing. A bronze plaque on the Lever House in London reads as follows: "The mission of our company, as William Hasketh Lever saw it, is to make cleanliness commonplace, to lessen work for women, to foster health, and to contribute to personal attractiveness that life may be more enjoyable for the people who use our products." Other statements are multidirectional in nature.

> Coleco Industries makes video game computer systems. It also manufactures Cabbage Patch Kids, a line of "adoptable little people," as it calls them. Other businesses include a broad variety of ride-on vehicles for children and aboveground swimming and wading pools. As the firm defines its mission, it is to be a "major manufacturer of entertainment and recreation products."[2]

Mission statements set the stage for planning. They determine the competitive arena in which the business will operate and how resources will be allocated. George Steiner, a leading authority on planning, notes that such statements

> . . . make much easier the task of identifying the opportunities and threats that must be addressed in the planning process. They open up new opportunities, as well as new threats, when changed. They prevent people from "spinning their wheels" in working on strategies and plans that may be considered completely inappropriate by top management.[3]

---

2. Coleco Industries, Inc., 1982 Annual Report.

3. George A. Steiner, *Strategic Planning: What Every Manager Must Know* (New York: The Free Press, 1979), p. 156.

Objectives

Objectives, often called goals, are the ends toward which activity is aimed. In planning, objectives flow from the purpose or mission statement but are much more specific. Most organizations have multiple objectives. Table 4–2 provides an example.

Profitability, growth, and market share are common objectives.

Although business organizations pursue many different kinds of objectives, economic goals tend to predominate. The most common include profitability, growth, and market share. Table 4–3 shows the range of corporate goals in 82 firms in four basic industries. The table reveals that after these three economic objectives, several noneconomic goals, including social responsibility and employee welfare, are the most popular. Then come goals that emerged during the last decade, including maintenance of financial stability, conservation of resources, multinational expansion, and consolidation.

What must be remembered is that these goals vary in accordance with both industrial group and company size. (See Tables 4–4 and 4–5.) Some general conclusions can be drawn, however, regarding corporate objectives during the 1980s. After conducting an interindustry analysis of firms in chemicals and drugs, paper and containers, electrical products and electronics, and food processing, Y. K. Shetty reports:

1.   The dominant goals of corporate enterprise continue to be profitability, growth, and market share.

Table 4–2
Hewlett-Packard's Corporate Objectives

Profit. To achieve sufficient profit to finance our company growth and to provide the resouces we need to achieve our other corporate objectives.

Customers. To provide products and services of the greatest possible value to our customers, thereby gaining and holding their respect and loyalty.

Field of interest. To enter new fields only when the ideas we have, together with our technical, manufacturing and marketing skills, assure that we can make a needed and profitable contribution to the field.

Growth. To let our growth be limited only by our profits and our ability to develop and produce technical products that satisfy real customer needs.

People. To help our own people share in the company's success, which they make possible: to provide job security based on their performance, to recognize their individual achievements, and to help them gain a sense of satisfaction and accomplishment from their work.

Management. To foster initiative and creativity by allowing the individual great freedom of action in attaining well-defined objectives.

Citizenship. To honor our obligations to society by being an economic, intellectual and social asset to each nation and each community in which we operate.

Source: Y. K. Shetty, "New Look At Corporate Goals," *California Management Review,* Winter 1979, p. 72. © (1979) by the Regents of the University of California. Reprinted from *California Management Review,* volume 22, no. 2, p. 72 by permission of the Regents.

Table 4–3
Range of Corporate Goals

Category	Number	Percent*
Profitability	73	89
Growth	67	82
Market Share	54	66
Social Responsibility	53	65
Employee Welfare	51	62
Product Quality and Service	49	60
Research and Development	44	54
Diversification	42	51
Efficiency	41	50
Financial Stability	40	49
Resource Conservation	32	39
Management Development	29	35
Multinational Enterprise	24	29
Consolidation	14	17
Miscellaneous Other Goals	15	18

* Adds to more than 100 percent because most companies have more than one goal.

Source: Y. K. Shetty, "New Look At Corporate Goals," *California Management Review,* Winter 1979, p. 73. © (1979) by the Regents of the University of California. Reprinted from *California Managment Review,* volume 22, no. 2, p. 73 by permission of the Regents.

2. The changing economic environment and poor track record of many organizations have resulted in their moving away from diversification into unrelated industries and toward goals such as financial stability, resource conservation, and the consolidation of activities.

3. Strategic issues facing an industry help determine company goals, so that drug and electronics firms stress R&D while container and paper firms give attention to efficiency and conservation.

Table 4–4   The Five Most Frequently Cited Goals of Corporations in Four Industrial Groups

	Chemicals and Drugs (n = 19)		Paper and Containers (n = 17)		Electrical and Electronics (n = 24)		Food Processing (n = 22)	
1.	Profitability	79%	Profitability	100%	Profitability	96%	Growth	91%
2.	Social Responsibility	74	Growth	94	Growth	88	Profitability	86
3.	Research and Development	63	Social Responsibility	59	Research and Development	83	Market Share	82
4.	Growth	53	Efficiency	59	Product Quality and Service	75	Social Responsibility	73
5.	Product Quality and Service	47	Resource Conservation	53	Social Responsibility	67	Product Quality and Service	68

Source: Y. K. Shetty, "New Look At Corporate Goals," *California Management Review,* Winter 1979, p. 76. © (1979) by the Regents of the University of California. Reprinted from California Management Review, volume 22, no. 2, p. 76 by permission of the Regents.

Table 4–5   The Five Most Frequently Cited Goals of Corporations with Different Amounts of Sales

Greater than $5 billion (n = 19)		$1 billion to $5 billion (n = 16)		$500 million to $1 billion (n = 20)		Less than $500 million (n = 27)	
1. Profitability	89%	Profitability	87%	Profitability	95%	Profitability	93%
2. Growth	84	Growth	75	Growth	85	Growth	85
3. Social		Research and					
Responsibility	74	Development	69	Market Share	75	Efficiency	67
4. Product Quality		Social		Financial			
and Service	68	Responsibility	63	Stability	65	Market Share	63
5. Employee						Financial	
Welfare	58	Market Share	56	Efficiency	55	Stability	55

Source: Y. K. Shetty, "New Look At Corporate Goals," *California Management Review,* Winter 1979, p. 76. © (1979) by the Regents of the University of California. Reprinted from *California Management Review,* volume 22, no. 2, p. 76 by permission of the Regents.

4.   Large firms give relatively more attention to socially oriented goals while small companies focus on economic objectives.[4]

A hierarchy of objectives

After the overall objectives are determined, they are broken down into more specific goals. This is done on a hierarchical basis, with each level translating the objectives of the one above it into more concrete end points. The result is a **hierarchy of objectives** from the top of the organization to the bottom. Such a hierarchy is illustrated in Figure 4–2. The long-range strategic objectives are thus translated into short-range objectives which serve as the basis for day-to-day, operational plans.

Strategies

As used by the military, a **strategy** is a grand plan that is drawn up to reflect the results the unit would like to achieve in dealing with its adversaries. In nonmilitary organizations the term strategy still carries this competitive implication. More important, a strategy sets forth "a general program of action and an implied deployment of emphasis and resources to attain comprehensive objectives."[5]

Strategies flow from objectives.

Strategies flow from objectives. The organization first decides its goals and then formulates a plan of action to attain them. In practice, however, there is often a give-and-take between objectives and strategies. The organization sometimes finds it necessary to modify one or more major objectives in formulating strategy. In recent years, for example, some American auto

---

4. Y. K. Shetty, "New Look at Corporate Goals," *California Management Review,* Winter 1979, p. 78.

5. Harold Koontz, Cyril O'Donnell and Heinz Weihrich, *Management* 7th ed., (New York: McGraw-Hill, 1980), p. 163.

Figure 4–2   Hierarchy of Objectives

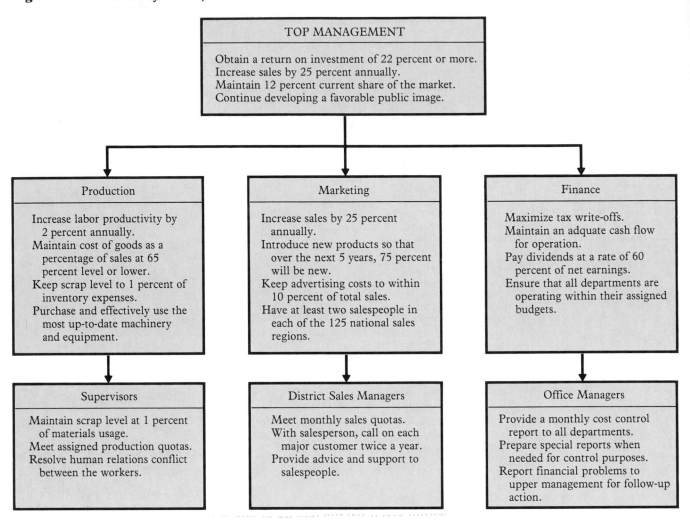

manufacturers have had to alter their market share objectives to more accurately reflect the competitive nature of foreign imports and the need to revise and reallocate resources.

Regardless of the way strategies are actually tied to objectives, two different approaches are popular today. One is called **gap analysis.** Using this approach, the organization compares current performance with desired performance. With knowledge of the gap between the two, the organization analyzes its strengths, weaknesses, environmental opportunities, and threats and then formulates a strategy for closing this gap. (See Figure 4–3.)

Some strategies are formulated by using gap analysis.

The other approach is a **strategic issues orientation.** In this case the organization examines its current strategic profile (where it is now) and reviews developments occurring in the external and internal environments. It then identifies the major issues to be dealt with and addresses them via specific strategies. (See Figure 4–4.)

Figure 4–3   A Gap Analysis Approach to Strategy

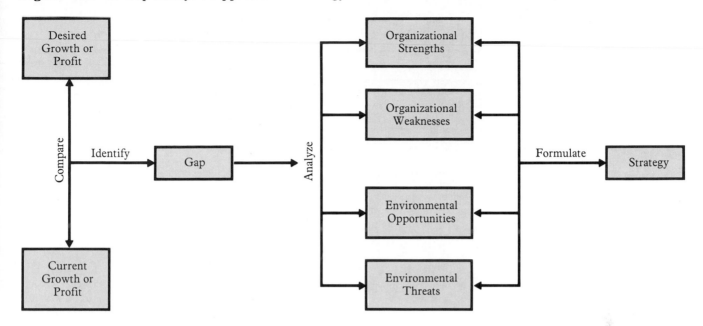

Policies

Policies are guidelines to thinking and action.

Policies are guidelines to thinking and action. They delimit the area within which a decision is made and ensure that the decision is consistent with objectives. There are many types of policies. Some are used to channel decision making at the upper levels, others at the middle ranks, and still others at the lower levels. Figure 4–5 depicts a hierarchy of policies related to the ways in which personnel may go about marketing the firm's products. Notice that in each case the policy provides a guideline both to thinking and to action. The respective manager or salesperson's authority is limited, but within given parameters he or she is free to make decisions. The vice-president, for example, can approve price concessions up to 20 percent.

Figure 4–4
A Strategic Issues Approach to Strategy

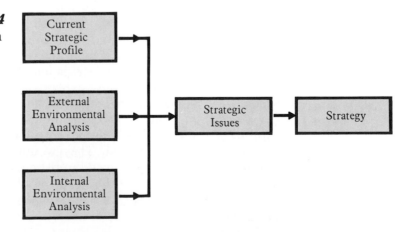

Figure 4–5

Policy and Hierarchical Level

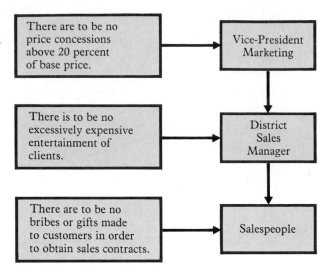

The district sales manager can entertain in any manner that is not "excessive." The salesperson can entertain and attempt to influence customers as long as no bribes or gifts are given. There is clearly a hierarchy of policies just as there is a hierarchy of objectives. The organization develops policies for objectives at each level of the hierarchy.

The purpose of a policy is to provide direction. In implementing policy, however, personnel may sometimes use either too much discretion or too much initiative. To reduce the likelihood of such an occurrence, many organizations encourage managers to talk to their subordinates and discuss how they can stay within bounds. This practice does not always eliminate policy violations, but it can help in reducing the number of flagrant cases.

Procedures

Procedures are guidelines to action.

A **procedure** is a guideline to action that sets forth a list of chronological steps for employees to follow in handling a particular activity. In contrast to a policy, a procedure allows no room for interpretation.

Numerous examples can be cited. One of the most typical procedures relates to the filing of expense accounts when someone returns from a business trip. Quite often the procedure is to attach all receipts to a completed expense form and send them to a designated individual in the accounting department. This person then checks the form over for accuracy and completeness and authorizes payment if everything is in order.

A second typical procedure explains how to deal with merchandise refunds. If a customer returns defective goods to a retailer, the store usually has a policy for handling the situation. For example, employees may be authorized to give a credit refund in the department where the defective merchandise was purchased. They would also be required to record the transaction and report it directly to the computer. For cash refunds, procedures vary. In some cases the money is returned in the department, while in others the buyer is given a receipt and sent to the business office for the money.

Procedures serve a double purpose. First, they provide an orderly system for handling specific types of situations. Second, they establish controls to ensure that money, merchandise, and other assets are accounted for.

Rules

A **rule** is an inflexible plan that requires specific, definite action. Rules are the simplest form of plans and are used by modern organizations in a variety of situations. Typical examples include the following: "No smoking." "Safety glasses must be worn in this area." "Only authorized personnel are allowed beyond this point."

Rules, unlike policies, do not allow for interpretation. In practice managers and other employees often misuse the terms, saying, for example, "It is our policy not to give cash discounts." Since this is a hard-and-fast statement, it is actually a rule, not a policy.

Rules are useful plans because they severely limit action and help personnel decide how to handle specific situations. Of course, if there are too many rules, personnel may have trouble remembering them all. However, to the extent that rules are limited in number and carefully formulated, they can be very valuable in the planning process.

Rules are inflexible plans requiring specific, definite action.

Programs

A **program** is a complex of objectives, policies, procedures, rules, resources, job assignments, and other elements necessary to carry out a given plan of action. Programs typically are supported by the necessary capital and operating budgets.

A primary program is often accompanied by a series of derivative programs. For example, a primary program to replace half of a manufacturing firm's plant and equipment would have derivative programs for maintenance, personnel training, cost and quality control, financing, and insurance. In the case of a private university with a $50 million building program, there would be derivative programs for maintenance, facilities usage, financing, and insurance.

The larger the organization, the greater the likelihood that it has a number of primary programs. Each program has to be monitored carefully because of internal complexity and external interdependence. Within each program there are many activities that must be carried out. At the same time, it is often necessary to coordinate programs since each may influence or affect the others.

Primary programs are often accompanied by derivative programs.

Budgets

A **budget** is a statement of expected results expressed in numerical terms. While often thought of as a control technique, a budget is also a plan since it sets forth objectives to be attained. For this reason, the financial operating budget is commonly referred to as a profit plan. Typical objectives expressed in a budget relate to profit, cost, units of production, labor hours, advertising, promotion, and other measurable goals.

A discussion of many of the specific techniques of budgeting is best left for the chapters devoted to controlling. It should be noted, however, that the construction of a budget is clearly a planning activity. In fact, in

Budgets are statements of expected results expressed in numerical terms.

many organizations it is the primary planning instrument. A budget forces an organization to think through its goals; the budget is an effective control tool only if it reflects the organization's goals accurately.

The Planning Process

The three planning horizons noted earlier (long, intermediate, and short range) provide the basis for the planning process itself. The long-range plan is the *strategic plan*. The medium-range plan is the *intermediate plan*. The short-range plan is the *operational plan*.[6] Figure 4–6 provides an illustration of this model. Note that planning begins before the strategic plan is constructed and continues through tactical planning to the review and evaluation of results. Throughout the entire planning process, feedback and monitoring keep the plan on track. Keep in mind as this process is discussed, however, that Figure 4–6 presents a planning model for a large organization. This is the entire process. It will be reduced or short-circuited in smaller organizations.

Regardless of planning detail there are five basic steps in the planning process, as shown in Figure 4–7. Some of these have already been discussed in detail, while others have not. The five basic steps, in the proper sequence, are (1) awareness of the opportunity, (2) establishment of objectives, (3) determination and choice of alternative courses of action, (4) formulation of derivative plans, and (5) budgeting of the plan.

Awareness of Opportunity

The real starting point for planning is an awareness of opportunity. For this reason, an organization should maintain a continual surveillance of the environment to detect changes in the market and the competition and to determine its own current strengths and weaknesses. In conducting such an analysis, the organization evaluates the external environmental forces discussed in Chapter 3. It also evaluates its internal capabilities. What can it do well? What does it do poorly?

Based on an awareness of opportunity and the organization's ability to capitalize on it, a general plan of direction starts to emerge. The company knows what it should do and how to proceed.

Forecasting

The most common way to identify opportunities is to conduct external forecasts and then decide on the best course of action. Many different kinds of forecasts can be conducted. Four of the most important are economic, technological, social-political, and sales. The first three kinds of forecasts address the general environment while the fourth helps the organization translate its findings into a plan of action.

6. C. Aaron Kelley, "The Three Planning Questions: A Fable," *Business Horizons*, March–April 1983, pp. 46–48.

Figure 4–6   Overall Planning Model for a Large Organization

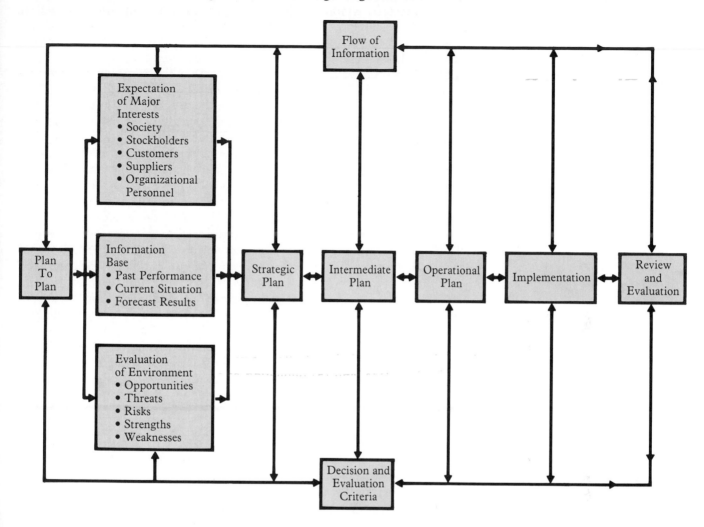

Economic Forecasting   There are two basic kinds of economic forecasts. One, which is quite simple, is known as **extrapolation.** This kind of forecast assumes that the economy will continue to develop predictably and that the future will follow the pattern of the past. Using extrapolation, an organization that has had sales of $2.5, $2.6, and $2.7 million, respectively, during the last three years would forecast $2.8 million for the coming year. Small businesses often use extrapolation or some similar approach because it is both easy and inexpensive.

Extrapolation is a simple kind of economic forecasting.

Figure 4–7
Steps in the Planning Process

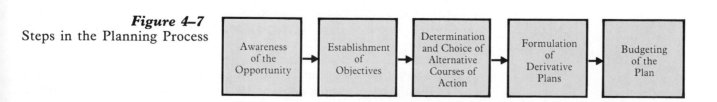

Econometric models are very sophisticated.

Larger organizations are more sophisticated in their approach. Some use **econometric models,** which are mathematical models designed to represent either the economy at large or a select part of the economy that affects the company specifically. By testing various economic scenarios in the model, the company can determine their effect on operations.

Most firms choose a way of forecasting that lies between the two extremes of simple extrapolation and sophisticated econometric models. They examine economic conditions in the general environment and attempt to predict how these conditions will affect their industry and their share of the market. If the firm is large, some of these calculations are done inhouse. In many cases, however, companies rely on studies available through either industry or governmental sources. Most federal government departments with a business interest publish economic material that is useful for forecasting. The same is true of trade associations, trade publications, banks, private research organizations, and professional associations.

Technological Forecasting   In many industries technology is changing rapidly. Comparing the typical business office of today with that of 10 years ago reveals changes in typewriting equipment, photocopying processes, communication systems, and the range of computer uses. Products being offered for sale to the general public have also changed dramatically. A look around an average home or a large department store reveals that the number of electronic and computerized products is larger than ever before. As a result, technologically based companies such as Texas Instruments, IBM, and Honeywell need to forecast changes in their environment continually. A failure to predict developments in the market accurately can result in a severe financial setback, and, in some cases, bankruptcy.

While there are a number of ways to carry out a technological forecast, currently the most popular method is the **Delphi technique.** Assume that a high-technology consumer goods manufacturer is in the process of developing a minitelevision set that can be carried around in a person's pocket. The company expects to have a model ready for the market by 1988, but wants to know when the competition will have a similar product. To answer this question it might use the Delphi technique. The first step in using this technique is to assemble a panel of experts who are knowledgeable about the product and the market. Each is asked to forecast the time when the competition will have a competitive product. The answers are then

Steps in the Delphi process

compiled and the results are fed back to the panel members. Throughout this process all members of the panel remain anonymous to avoid the possibility that they will be influenced by an expert with a prestigious reputation. Finally, based on the answers to the first round, everyone is asked to give a second answer. At the same time those who intend to give answers that are outside of the interquartile range of the previous quarter (the range of answers where 50 percent of all the responses fall) are asked to explain their answers. In this way, those who are predicting earlier or later developmental times than the majority are have to defend their responses.

After four or five rounds, responses tend to converge around a central range which becomes the acceptable forecast. In the case in question, for example, the forecast might be that the competition will have a similar product ready between 1987 and 1988.

Not every firm uses the Delphi. Some prefer alternative approaches. One is simply to extrapolate from the present and ask the question: If

Exploratory forecasting uses simple extrapolation.

technology continues to develop at its present rate, what new products can we expect to be produced in this industry by 1990? This is known as an **exploratory forecast.**

Another approach is to select a future technological development and then determine how long it will take to attain it. For example, how long will it take our firm to develop a miniature portable TV set? In this case the company works from the future back to the present, identifying obstacles that will have to be surmounted along the way. This type of forecast is known as a **normative forecast.**

Normative forecasting works from the future to the present.

Regardless of the approach used by the firm, the results of technological forecasting are estimates regarding future developments. Companies use these estimates to formulate objectives and draw up plans.

Social–Political Forecasting   Social forecasting involves the prediction of social values and their impact on business operations. How will changing values affect business results? Because this question is so difficult to answer, many companies simply wait for values to change and then try to address them. However, the large retailing and consumer product firms have tried to keep up with changing values by providing the new goods and services demanded by today's customers.

Social forecasting involves the prediction of changing values.

Political forecasting has not received a great deal of attention from firms operating solely in the United States. Usually these companies wait until a development occurs and then adjust for it, although in some cases they do draw up a series of forecasts on the amount and type of spending they believe will be done at the local, state, or federal level. The election of Ronald Reagan as President in 1980 was undoubtedly forecast by some businesses which then proceeded to act on the basis of this forecast. Firms in military production keep a close eye on political developments, as do governmental agencies whose budgets can be expanded or contracted, depending on who is elected.

Political forecasting is done by governmental agencies.

Sales Forecasting   Just about every business firm conducts a sales forecast. Some of these are quite simple while others are very sophisticated. In any case, these forecasts often serve as the primary basis for annual planning. Operations are tied to the sales forecast. The most common types of sales forecasting include (1) the jury of executive opinion, (2) the sales force composite method, (3) the users' expectation method, and (4) statistical and deductive methods.

The **jury of executive opinion** method combines the views of top managers to arrive at a sales forecast. This method typically entails having the executives give their opinions about future sales and then having the result modified by the president. This approach can be useful if the executives have a basic grasp of marketing and are knowledgeable about customer demand.

Sometimes executives make the sales forecast.

The **sales force composite method** relies upon the salespeople to provide a forecast for sales. When an organization uses this method, salespeople in each district make forecasts which are reviewed by the regional sales manager and then forwarded to headquarters. Many people feel that since the salespeople are out in the field every day they should have a very good idea of what will sell. It is common, however, to find these sales force forecasts being modified by top executives, in which case the organization actually combines the jury of executive opinion method and the sales force composite method.

The **users' expectation method** requires the company to poll customers and find out their demand for the firm's goods and services. This approach is widely employed among companies that sell industrial goods, although marketers of consumer products also employ such sales or marketing surveys. If a random sample of the market can be obtained, the results can be extremely accurate.

All three of these approaches can profit from the use of *statistical or deductive methods* or both. Statistical methods include trend analysis, sampling, correlation analysis, and other mathematical techniques that can help refine the sales forecast and increase its validity. Deductive methods use judgment, intuition, gut feeling, and experience to modify and adjust the final forecast. Most firms use both of these approaches, objective and subjective, so that the final sales forecast is actually the result of a combination of forecasting methods.

At other times salespeople have primary input.
In other cases a marketing survey is employed.

Usually companies use a combination of forecasting methods.

Establishment of Objectives

The first formal step in planning is to establish objectives. We discussed the value of objectives earlier in the chapter, but you should note again that objectives are established at all levels of the structure, beginning at the top and cascading downward. The hierarchy of objectives begins at the strategic planning level and ends at the operational planning level.

The difference between strategic and operational objectives is very important. **Strategic objectives** are *effectiveness oriented*. They help the organization compare itself with the competition. Typical strategic objectives state what the company would like to accomplish in terms of return on investment (profit/assets), market share, and growth. Operational objectives are *efficiency oriented*. They help the organization control internal resources. Typical operational objectives include plans for cost control, output, and employee turnover.[7]

Strategic objectives are effectiveness oriented; operational objectives are efficiency oriented.

Strategic objectives help the organization operate in an environment in which it has minimal control. Most of these objectives concern marketing and finance. **Operational objectives** help the organization operate in an environment in which it has a great deal of control. Most of these objectives concern production and personnel.

Determination and Choice of Alternative Courses of Action

Having set objectives, the organization must identify alternative courses of action for reaching its goals. Actually in most instances the challenge is not to find alternative courses but to determine which ones are best. This decision requires an evaluation process.

The most effective way to evaluate alternative courses is to establish acceptable criteria. If the organization wants profit above all else, the choice may be quite easy. However, if the firm wants to minimize its outflow of cash, it may have to accept a lower level of profit. For example, a company whose objective is to enter a new industry usually determines the maximum loss it is willing to sustain during the entry period. Entry strategies must

Acceptable criteria must be developed to evaluate alternative courses of action.

7. See for example "U.S. Steel Sees Its Future in Even More Steel," *Business Week*, February 13, 1984, pp. 36–37.

balance market share against operating loss. Firms leaving an industry or abandoning a product line follow the opposite strategy, choosing a course of action that minimizes expenses and maximizes profit. On the way out they do little advertising or promotion, keep costs down, and sell to people who still want the product. The first example describes a firm that is trying to develop a stronghold in the market and is willing to pay for it. The second describes a company that has developed a foothold and wants to milk this share for all it is worth.

Formulation of Derivative Plans

After the organization has chosen alternative courses of action, it can formulate derivative plans. These plans are particularly important in the case of major programs.

Derivative plans help
companies breach the gap
between where they are and
where they want to go.

    Derivative plans help the organization breach the gap between where it wants to go and where it is currently. In the case of a strategic plan, derivative plans take the form of intermediate and operational plans. In this way the organization forges a link between long-range and short-range objectives. Part of this process was illustrated in Figure 4–2 which presented the hierarchy of objectives concept.

Budgeting the Plan

The budget activates the plan.

The last step in the planning process is to budget the plan. Budgeting serves to activate the plan while setting forth numerical targets that can be used for control purposes. Figure 4–8 shows how operating budgets are put together from the operational plan. Notice the flow from income objectives to expense/cost budgets to the financial statements that report operating results. Based on these results, the organization can begin the planning process anew. In this way planning becomes a closed cycle in which current results help to shape future actions.

Management by Objectives

Regardless of their size, many organizations have found they need a simple, easy-to-understand approach for carrying out the planning process. **Management by objectives** (MBO) has proven very useful in this regard. Figure 4–9 shows the sequence of steps used in managing by objectives.

Everything Flows from Objectives

Identifying key result areas

Starting at the top of the organization, each manager reviews the objectives for his or her department. These objectives are then translated into key result areas in which specific performance must be attained, for example, a 25 percent return on investment, a 6 percent market share, an 18 percent increase in sales, a 4 percent reduction on scrap, a 10 percent reduction in turnover.

    Then the manager reviews the organizational structure. What is everyone in the department or unit doing? Will their current responsibilities, if carried

Figure 4–8   Development of Operating Budgets

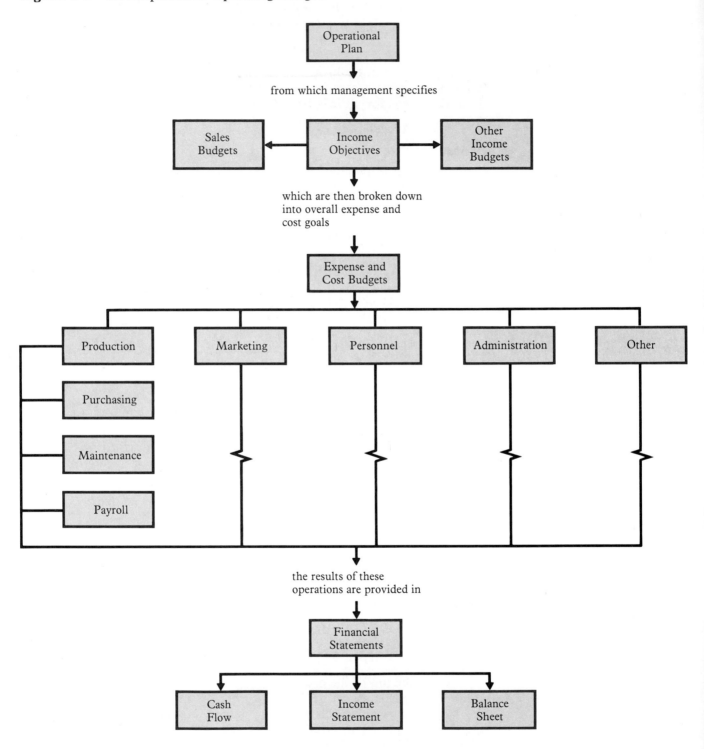

Figure 4–9
The MBO Process

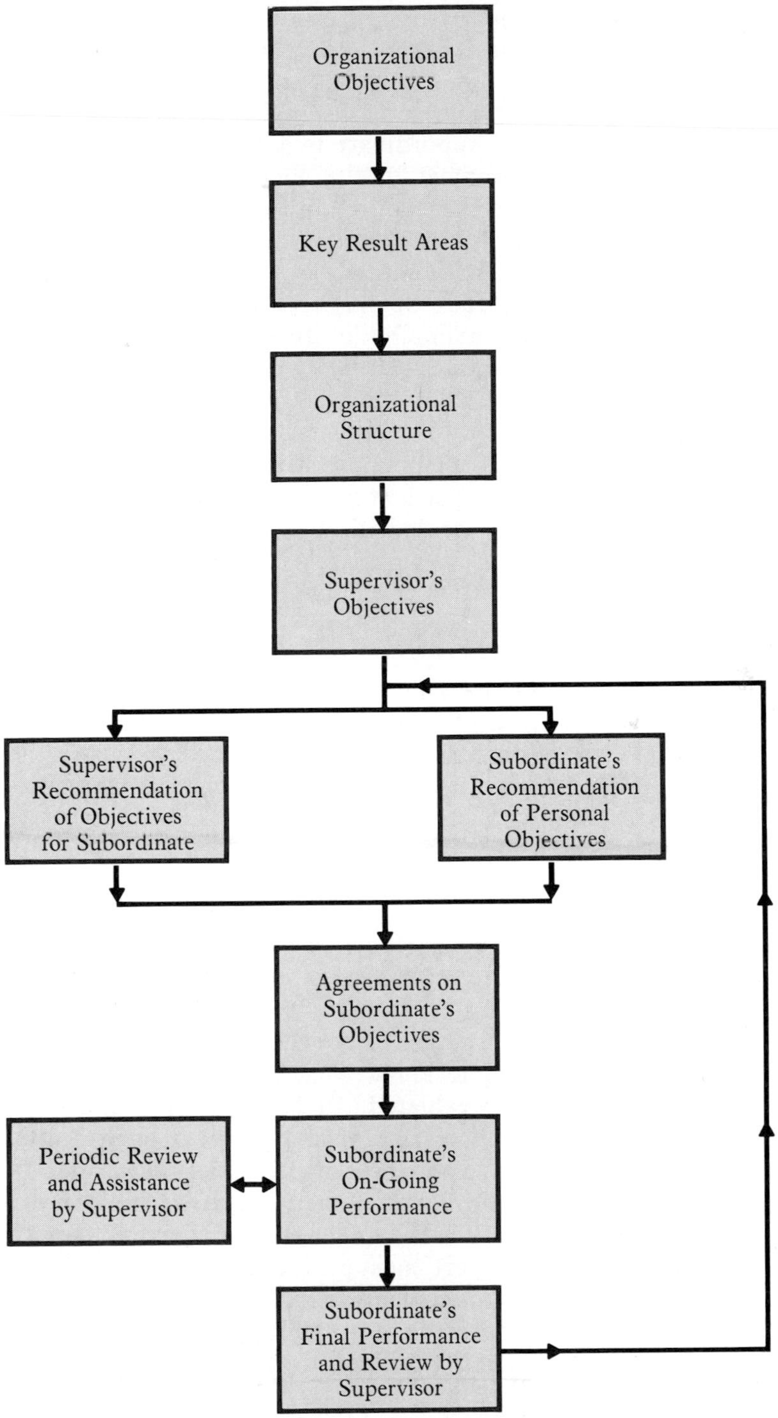

```
        ┌─────────────────┐
        │  Organizational │
        │    Objectives   │
        └─────────────────┘
                 │
                 ▼
        ┌─────────────────┐
        │ Key Result Areas│
        └─────────────────┘
                 │
                 ▼
        ┌─────────────────┐
        │  Organizational │
        │    Structure    │
        └─────────────────┘
                 │
                 ▼
        ┌─────────────────┐
        │   Supervisor's  │
        │    Objectives   │
        └─────────────────┘
```

Supervisor's Recommendation of Objectives for Subordinate	Subordinate's Recommendation of Personal Objectives

```
        ┌─────────────────┐
        │  Agreements on  │
        │   Subordinate's │
        │    Objectives   │
        └─────────────────┘
```

Periodic Review and Assistance by Supervisor	Subordinate's On-Going Performance

```
        ┌─────────────────┐
        │  Subordinate's  │
        │Final Performance│
        │   and Review by │
        │    Supervisor   │
        └─────────────────┘
```

out properly, result in the desired performance? If not, what changes in structure need to be made?

Setting Objectives

Once the supervisor has the organizational structure in order, he or she can turn to the setting of objectives. The first step is to determine how

Goal setting is a mutual process.

departmental or unit objectives can be broken down into subobjectives and delegated to subordinates. This step is carried out through a mutual goal-setting process.

The supervisor sets preliminary objectives for each subordinate, and the subordinate is asked to do the same for himself or herself. Then the two meet, discuss their respective lists, and agree on a final set of objectives for the subordinate. This list usually contains no more than five or six objectives, which are specific and tied to a time frame. For example, it might cite the following goals: (1) to reduce personnel turnover by 6 percent by June 30; (2) to increase work output by 9 percent by August 31; (3) to maintain the current level of productivity for the entire year; (4) to increase the sales force by 20 percent by December 15; and (5) to complete all initial supervisory training by March 30.

As soon as the supervisor and subordinate agree on the goals the latter will pursue, they are written down. Both the supervisor and the subordinate then get a copy. The supervisor uses the list for performance review and to provide assistance. The subordinate uses the list as a guide to developing an action plan for accomplishing the goals.

Review and Performance

Throughout the MBO cycle (often quarterly), the supervisor and subordinate sit down, discuss the latter's ongoing performance, and determine how any problems can be resolved. At the end of the entire cycle, the results of these evaluations are used as a basis for rewards and for setting future objectives for the subordinate.[8]

MBO: An Evaluation

MBO has its strong points . . .

MBO has been used effectively by many organizations.[9] On the positive side, employees often like the participation they have in setting objectives and developing a commitment to them. The communication system that is established between supervisor and subordinate also helps to ensure that people know what they are to do, by when, and how they are going to be evaluated. In fact, by clarifying expected results, the manager often reduces employee anxiety and helps build high achievement drive.

Problems can occur, however, that if not corrected, can result in the failure of the total program.[10] One such problem often develops when subordinates fail to get top management support at the beginning. Without such support, most programs are doomed. Another common problem results from an inadequate explanation of how the program works. If the personnel do not understand the total MBO process, they may not fully support it.

and its limitations.

A third problem is a failure on the part of some managers to set clearly

---

8. For an excellent review and description of MBO see: Mark L. McConkie, "A Clarification of the Goal Setting and Appraisal Processes in MBO," *Academy of Management Review,* January 1979, pp. 29–40.

9. Jack N. Kondrasuk, "Studies in MBO Effectiveness," *Academy of Management Review,* July 1981, pp. 419–430.

10. Charles M. Kelly, "Remedial MBO," *Business Horizons,* September–October 1983, pp. 62–67.

"Gentlemen, I'm afraid we've brought an entirely new meaning
to the term dummy corporation."

defined, measurable objectives with the subordinates. A fourth problem is personality conflicts between superiors and subordinates during the joint development of objectives. A fifth is an overemphasis on paperwork, which can turn MBO into a costly, technique-oriented exercise in filling out forms. Finally, some managers fail to tie rewards to the attainment of objectives.

Overall, it has great potential.

Studying both the benefits of MBO and its potential problems reveals that the process can be time consuming and demands a commitment on the part of all involved. If the organization is devoted to planning effectiveness, however, the approach can be profitable for the organization and rewarding for participants.

Summary

1. Planning is the process of setting objectives and then determining the steps needed to attain them. In planning there are three time horizons: Long-range (more than five years), intermediate-range (one to five years), and short-range (less than one year).

2. There are many different types of plans. The purpose or mission of an organization is its underlying aim or thrust. Missions are usually stated in product or market terms.

3. Objectives are the ends toward which planning activity is aimed, with long-range objectives serving as a basis for strategic planning and short-range objec-

tives serving as the basis for operational planning. In the process, a hierarchy of objectives is created. The most common business goals are profitability, growth, and market share.

4. Strategies set forth general programs of action that are used in deploying resources for the attainment of comprehensive objectives. One way of formulating strategy is to use gap analysis, which involves comparing current and desired performance for the purpose of determining a plan of action. Another way is to employ a strategic issues orientation in which the current strategic profile is examined in light of environmental analysis, and major strategic issues are identified and addressed via specific strategies.

5. Policies are guidelines to thinking and action. They delimit the area within which a decision is made and ensure that the decision is consistent with objectives. Just as there is a hierarchy of objectives, there is a hierarchy of policies that runs throughout the organizational structure.

6. Procedures are guidelines to action. They set forth a list of chronological steps that employees must follow in handling a particular activity. Procedures are not open to interpretation. Rules are inflexible plans that require specific, definite action. They are the simplest form of plans.

7. Programs are a complex of objectives, policies, procedures, rules, resources, job assignments, and other elements necessary to carry out a given plan of action. Primary programs are often accompanied by a series of derivative programs.

8. Budgets are statements of expected results expressed in numerical terms. In many organizations they are the primary planning instrument.

9. The planning process begins with awareness of opportunity. This awareness is often achieved through forecasting. Some of the most common types of forecasting include economic, technological, social-political, and sales. Sales forecasting often uses the jury of executive opinion, the sales force composite method, the users' expectation method, statistical methods, and deductive methods.

10. The first formal step in the planning process is the establishment of objectives. There are two basic types of objectives: strategic and operational. Strategic objectives help the organization compare itself with the competition. They address marketing and finance. Operational objectives help the organization control internal resources. They address production and personnel.

11. The next step in the planning process is the determination and choice of alternative courses of action. The most effective way to evaluate alternative courses is to establish acceptable criteria.

12. The next step in the planning process is the formulation of derivative plans. These plans help the organization breach the gap between where it wants to go and where it is.

13. The last step in the planning process is to budget the plan. This serves to put the plan into action.

14. Some organizations have turned to management by objectives (MBO) to help them implement the planning process. In MBO, the first step is to review the organizational objectives of the department or unit and determine key result areas. Then the organization structure is reviewed. Next the supervisor sits down with the subordinate and together the two establish objectives for the latter. Finally, periodic reviews and assistance are provided by the supervisor, who also conducts a final performance review. Based on the results, the process then starts anew.

Key Terms

Budget A statement of expected results expressed in numerical terms.

Delphi technique A technological forecasting technique.

Derivative plans Plans that help the organization translate long-range goals into shorter-range ones.

Econometric model A quantitative economic forecasting model.

Exploratory forecast A technological forecast based on the idea that technology will continue to develop at its present rate.

Extrapolation A forecast that assumes that the future will follow the trend of past.

Gap analysis An approach to strategy formulation that involves comparing current and desired performance to determine a plan of action.

Hierarchy of objectives A chain of objectives beginning with long-range ones and cascading downward, with shorter-range and more specific goals being formulated from those directly above them.

Intermediate-range planning Planning that covers a time period of 1–5 years.

Jury of executive opinion A sales forecast based on the expectations of managers.

Long-range planning Planning that covers a time period of more than five years.

Management by objectives (MBO) A planning approach that involves (a) identification of organizational objectives and key result areas, (b) a review of the organizational structure, (c) a mutual goal setting process in which supervisor and subordinate agree on objectives for the latter, and (d) a review of subordinate performance by the supervisor followed by the setting of new objectives for the subordinate.

Normative forecast A technological forecast that identifies a future technological development and then determines how long it will take to attain it.

Objectives Ends toward which planning activity is aimed.

Operational objectives Objectives that help an organization control its internal resources. Examples include plans for cost control, output, and employee turnover.

Planning The process of setting objectives and then determining the steps needed to attain them.

Policy A guideline to thinking and action.

Procedure A guideline to action.

Programs A complex of objectives, policies, procedures, rules, resources, and other elements necessary to carry out a general plan of action.

Purpose or mission The underlying aim or thrust of an organization. It is usually stated in product or market terms.

Rule An inflexible plan that requires specific, definite action.

Sales force composite A sales forecast that is put together with input solely from the salespeople.

Short-range planning Planning that covers a time period of less than one year.

Strategic issues orientation An approach to strategy in which the current strategic profile is examined in light of environmental analysis, and major strategic issues are identified and addressed via specific strategies.

Strategic objectives Objectives that help an organization compare itself with the competition. Examples include the company's objectives for return on investment, market share, and growth.

Strategy A general program of action used in deploying resources for the attainment of comprehensive objectives.

User's expectation method A sales forecast constructed on the basis of customer surveys and/or marketing polls.

Questions for Analysis and Discussion

1. What is meant by the term planning? Do all organizations have a need to plan? Explain.

2. Planning time horizons are affected by a number of factors. What are some of those factors? Identify and describe three.

3. How can a definition of purpose or a mission statement help an organization? Cite two examples and explain each.

4. What are some of the major types of goals pursued by modern corporations? Identify and describe five. Then set forth four general conclusions that can be drawn regarding corporate objectives during the 1980s. How can an understanding of the concept of hierarchy of objectives be of value to managers interested in understanding the role and importance of objectives?

5. How does a strategy differ from an objective? How can gap analysis be of value in strategy formulation? How can a strategic issues orientation be of value?

6. How does a policy differ from a procedure? How does a rule differ from a policy? How does a program differ from a procedure? In your comparison, be sure to cite an example of each. Then explain how policies, procedures, rules, and programs help modern managers.

7. In what way is a budget a type of plan? Why do some organizations use it as the primary planning instrument? Explain.

8. How does the strategic plan differ from the intermediate plan? How does the intermediate plan differ from the operational plan? In your answer be sure to include a discussion of Figure 4–6.

9. How are each of the following types of forecasting conducted: extrapolation, technological forecasting (specifically the Delphi technique), social-political forecasting, and sales forecasting (specifically the jury of executive opinion, sales force composite, and users' expectation method)? Which of these is most valuable to a small retailer? A research and development firm? A large consumer products manufacturer?

10. How do strategic objectives differ from operational objectives? Compare and contrast the two.

11. How should an organization go about determining and choosing alternative courses of action? What is the process? Additionally, how can the formulation of derivative plans be of value in the planning process? How does the budgeting of the plan fit into this process? Explain.

12. How does management by objectives (MBO) work? What are the key steps in the process? Use Figure 4–9 to help you formulate an answer. Then, after comparing the advantages and problems of MBO, write a brief answer to the question: How valuable is MBO to modern organizations?

Case | # And Then Things Changed

Things had been very good at Harper Manufacturing. For seven years sales had risen by an average of 26 percent annually. Last year, however, the company encountered a severe slump. Sales dropped 18 percent, and this year, unless there is a dramatic turn-around, sales will decline another 12 percent.

The reason for the sales drop-off is no secret. Harper has had three basic products that accounted for 40 percent of total sales. Two of these products were manufactured under a subcontract with a national retailer. The third was developed in-house and sold to wholesalers under a competitive bidding process. A year ago all three began to nose-dive. The national retailer witnessed a decline in some of its own major products so it canceled a portion of the subcontracting agreement with Harper and began producing these products with its own available machinery and equipment. At about the same time three competitors began selling products similar to the ones Harper had developed and was providing to wholesalers. Since the new products were less expensive, wholesalers began canceling their orders to Harper.

Harper has conducted an analysis of these developments and reached four conclusions. First, the company failed to do substantive forecasting. It assumed that things would continue as before; this was a major mistake. Second, most of its efforts went into production with little attention given to the development of marketing objectives. Third, no contingency plan was developed regarding what the company would *do* if one of its major markets dried up. Fourth, it did not identify new market opportunities and ways to pursue them. As one manager put it, "We were basically concerned with the here and now."

1. In terms of time horizons, what kind of planning did Harper Manufacturing do?

2. Using the information in the case, identify the kinds of forecasting Harper did. What kinds should it have done?

3. Using the planning process as your guide, develop a general plan of action to take Harper Manufacturing through the next three years. What should the firm do? Be as complete as possible in your answer.

You Be the Consultant

Helping To Manage Dynamic Growth

The Harrison Insurance Company has witnessed a tremendous growth over the last four years. Premiums have risen from $4 million to just under $23 million. However, the company now has to step back and evaluate where it is going and how it will get there. No one would have predicted such a dramatic increase in business. On the other hand, the president, Anthony Harrison, carefully identified the firm's target market and concentrated attention on high-profit kinds of insurance that are not offered by many large insurance firms, but that are deemed mandatory by many companies. One of these is kidnap/ransom insurance. Multinational corporations want this protection for their people operating in overseas markets, and since the rates for such coverage are not widely quoted and competition is minimal, it offers an excellent opportunity for high profitability.

Unfortunately, with this dramatic growth has come a need for planning—something the company has not spent a lot of time doing. In fact, up until three months ago the time horizon for planning was 18 months. Now management realizes that it must extend this horizon. Additionally, it needs assistance in a number of planning-related activities. For example, policies, procedures, rules, and programs have been basically ignored. Most attention has been focused on selling. The firm realizes that its growth will be limited if it does not direct attention toward developing these types of plans.

In an effort to formalize planning and introduce some fundamentals to managers, President Harrison has decided to bring in an outside consultant. This person, along with whomever he or she has on the consulting team, will be asked to provide management with planning direction. Some of the specific areas of concern are to be a mission statement, strategic objectives, operational objectives, and types of plans including policies, procedures, rules, and budgets. The president realizes that these consultants may not be experts in the insurance field, but he feels that planning fundamentals are universal. If the consultants can spell out fundamentals, the in-house managers can translate them into an action framework. The company needs to know about basic planning ideas.

Your Consultation

Assume that you have been given the role of consultant. Drawing upon your knowledge of the material in this chapter, what would you tell the company regarding the need for long-range planning? Also, how can the various types of plans be of use to Harrison Insurance? Be as complete as possible in your answer. Finally, can MBO be of value to the firm? How? Explain your reasoning.

5

Strategic Planning in Action

Objectives

The previous chapter examined the planning process. Now we want to study this process in more depth by looking at the area of strategic planning. Virtually every modern organization uses strategic planning to some degree. The first objective of this chapter is to study the nature of strategic planning and learn its value for modern organizations. In examining the uses of strategic planning, we will use specific illustrations from industrial settings. The second objective of this chapter is to study the elements of strategic planning, giving particular emphasis to basic mission, strategic objectives, strategy determination, and portfolio planning. At this point we will consider various ways of handling both successful and unsuccessful product lines. When you have finished studying the material in this chapter, you should be able to

1. identify the major characteristics of a strategic plan;

2. discuss the overall importance of strategic planning;

3. tell who needs strategic planning;

4. describe in depth the four elements of strategic planning: basic mission, strategic objectives, strategy determination, and portfolio management;

5. describe how modern organizations use portfolio management to handle stars, cash cows, question marks, and cash traps; and

6. explain how strategic planning is put into operation.

The Nature of Strategic Planning

Strategic planning draws heavily on many of the ideas discussed in the previous chapter. However, two major characteristics differentiate strategic planning from planning in general.

Characteristics of Strategic Planning

One of the major characteristics of strategic planning is the value system it promotes. When an organization carries out only operational planning, it emphasizes *meeting the budget.* As the organization grows and gives more attention to planning, its value system becomes concerned with *predicting the future.* As the organization grows still larger, it begins to focus on external developments and ways of responding to them. Its value system becomes concerned with *thinking strategically.* A final shift in orientation usually occurs only among companies that have grown extremely large. These companies attempt to manage all resources in such a way as to create competitive advantages. At this stage their value systems are concerned with *creating the future.* So, as an organization moves more and more toward a strategic planning posture, passivity gives way to activity, and the desire to respond to the environment is replaced by a plan to control it.

Changes in an organization's value system

A second major characteristic of strategic planning is the philosophy behind the process. In many organizations when managers have completed a general plan they breathe a sigh of relief and note, "Thank heaven that's over. Now let's get back to work." In contrast, strategic planning fosters a philosophy of "plan now, plan later." Planning becomes a regular part of organizational activity. It is not added on to the top of managers' activities; it becomes an integral part of their job.

A philosophy of planning

Elements of Strategic Planning

As seen in Figure 5–1, there are four elements in strategic planning: formulation of the basic mission, setting of objectives, determination of strategy, and the use of portfolio planning. Each of these elements is briefly described and then elaborated upon later in the chapter.

Figure 5–1
Elements of Strategic Planning

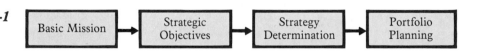

The basic mission was discussed in the previous chapter. However, organizations that engage in strategic planning examine this mission in much greater depth than do organizations that are merely interested in general planning.

The basic mission

The setting of strategic objectives was also covered in Chapter 4. However, it is important to realize that in setting strategic objectives management carries its philosophy down the line, influencing the rewards, leadership, and problem-solving approaches that are used.

Setting strategic objectives

Strategy determination involves decisions regarding how to attain strategic objectives. Strategy depends heavily on the industry or environment in which the organization operates. Companies that are dominant have different strategics from companies that "follow the leader"; companies that serve the entire market have different strategies from those that appeal only to a specific portion of it; companies that are interested in building market share have different strategies from those interested in maintaining theirs.

Formulating strategy

Portfolio management

Finally, organizations with a number of product lines are now turning to what is called portfolio planning. This entails an evaluation of product lines on the basis of the profit or return on investment they earn currently and what can be expected of them in the future. Based on the results, top management allocates resources.

Before turning to a more detailed discussion of these major elements of strategic planning, let us address two preliminary subjects. The first is the importance of strategic planning; the second is the kind of company that needs it.

The Importance of Strategic Planning

Strategic planning is important for two reasons. First, it helps organizations cope with their external environment. Second, it assists them in redefining or reformulating their strategies or both.

Coping with the External Environment

Most organizations operate in a dynamic environment. In the world of business, a firm is either moving forward or it is falling behind; and this statement is more than just a cliché. Research shows that on a year-to-year basis among even the largest industrials, some firms always are improving their position at the expense of others.

One way to obtain a closer look at this situation is to take the 100 largest industrials and examine their relative sales positions at the ends of different decades. How many industrials that were among the largest in terms of sales at the beginning of the 1970s were still maintaining their positions at the beginning of the 1980s? Table 5–1 provides the answer.

Note in the table that these 100 firms have been broken down into blocks of 10. Then their positions in 1972 have been compared with their positions in 1982. Of the first group of 10, only six were still in the same relative positions; the other four had fallen back. The same methodology was used in examining those firms that ranked between 11 and 20 in terms of sales. Two of these firms were still in the same category in 1982 while four had moved up and four had fallen back.

Sales volatility

A close examination of Table 5–1 reveals two things. First, only 74 of the top 100 industrials in 1972 were still in this group in 1982. The other 20 had either been merged, acquired, reclassified, or simply fallen out of the group. Second, of the 74 remaining, 30 moved up, 17 maintained their same relative positions, and 27 fell back. There is indeed a great deal of movement among these firms.

The volatility is even greater for the second 100 industrials; for those not in the top 500 the volatility must be extremely great. In an effort to cope with this kind of external environment, many firms are turning to strategic planning. In fact, William Lindsay and Leslie Rue, after conducting a two-stage survey of 199 corporations in 15 industrial classifications, have reported that firms tend to adopt more complete formal, long-range planning processes as the complexity and instability of their environment increase.[1]

---

1. William M. Lindsay and Leslie W. Rue, "Impact of the Organization Environment on the Long-Range Planning Process: A Contingency View," *Academy of Management Journal*, September 1980, pp. 385–404.

Table 5–1   Changing Positions Among Fortune's 500 Industrials (in terms of sales)

1972 \ 1982	1–10	11–20	21–30	31–40	41–50	51–60	61–70	71–80	81–90	91–100
1–10	6	2	2							
11–20	4	2	3							
21–30		2	1	1			2	1		
31–40		2		2	2	1	1	1		1
41–50			1	2	3	1	1		1	
51–60		1	2		1		2		1	1
61–70				1	1	2	1	1		
71–80							2	1	2	2
81–90				2				2	1	
91–100			2	1		1	1			

Obtaining an Adequate Payoff

The second major reason why strategic planning is important to modern organizations is that it pays off. Many studies support this statement. Hans Ansoff and his associates have found that firms that conducted formal planning outperformed those that did not on almost every one of 21 different financial criteria.[2] Similar results have been reported by Zafar Malik and Delmar Karger, who collected planning and financial data on 38 firms in the electronics, machinery, and chemical-drugs industries. These companies were then divided into two groups, integrated long-range planners and nonintegrated planners, and their financial performances were compared. In more than two-thirds of the categories, the formal planners outperformed the others.[3] (In the other categories, the results were mixed.) More recently, D. Robley Wood and R. Lawrence La Forge examined the impact of comprehensive planning on performance among large banks. They reported the following:

> The relationship between formal planning procedures and financial performance was examined for a sample of large U.S. banks. It was found that the sample banks that engaged in comprehensive long-range planning signifi-

Strategic planning helps to improve financial performance.

2. H. I. Ansoff, J. Avner, R. C. Brandenburg, F. E. Portner, and R. Radosevich, "Does Planning Pay? The Effect of Planning on Success of Acquisitions in American Firms," *Long Range Planning*, December 1970, pp. 2–7.

3. Zafar A. Malik and Delmar W. Karger, "Does Long-Range Planning Improve Company Performance?" *Management Review*, September 1975, pp. 27–31.

cantly outperformed those that had no formal planning system. They also outperformed a randomly selected control group.[4]

Keep in mind that strategic planning does not guarantee success. Nor is there a direct relationship between strategic planning and organizational results; the companies that do the most planning do not always have the best performance. However, strategic planning generally does pay off.

Who Needs Strategic Planning?

As organizations grow, their need for strategic planning increases. For this reason, all industries can profit from such planning, as can specific companies that are concerned with redefining or reformulating their strategies. The following discussion examines both an industry and a handful of firms that can benefit from strategic planning. Keep in mind, however, that this discussion is not meant to provide a comprehensive answer to the above question; it is merely designed to illustrate strategic planning's value.

The Oil Industry in General

During the 1970s the oil giants began diversifying, expanding their holdings to include not only coal and other alternative energy sources but also chemicals, pipelines, minerals, real estate, retailing, and computers. Figure 5–2 shows some of the areas into which these giants moved.

Not evident from the figure is the fact that some of the nonoil holdings did not work out well for these firms. Mobil Oil was not particularly happy with its purchase of Montgomery Ward. Gulf Oil liquidated most of its real estate holdings. In deciding what to keep and what to sell, these firms used portfolio analysis planning, a topic which will be examined in more depth later in the chapter. The oil firms know that the volatility of their environment and the need for successful diversification require strategic planning.

The oil firms use portfolio analysis planning.

Large Businesses in Particular

Many large businesses are also finding that they can profit from strategic planning. Quite often these firms need to redefine their strategy because (1) they are not having a great deal of success with their current one, (2) they have sold away some of their product lines and have to decide what to do next, or (3) they feel they have moved too far in one direction and want to realign their strategy with what they do best. In any event, these companies can find a strategic plan helpful. In the following cases, notice that a great deal of emphasis is given to marketing. In strategic planning, the identification of specific target markets, coupled with a decision about which product lines to keep and which either to sell away or to stop producing, is one of the primary considerations.

4. D. Robley Wood, Jr. and R. Lawrence LaForge, "The Impact of Comprehensive Planning on Financial Performance," *Academy of Management Journal*, September 1979, p. 516.

Figure 5–2
Oil Company Diversification

Oil Company Diversification

Major nonoil investments, by category, of 10 large domestic oil companies ranked by total revenues in 1978.

■ Indicates Investment   □ Indicates No Investment

Company	COAL	CHEMICALS	PIPELINES	URANIUM	MINERALS	ALTERNATIVE ENERGY	OTHER
EXXON — Petroleum Investments: $34.3 billion / Nonpetroleum Investments: $1.3 billion	■	■	■	■	■	■	■
Mobil — Petroleum Investments: $14.4 billion / Nonpetroleum Investments: $2.6 billion	□	■	■	□	□	■	■
TEXACO — Petroleum Investments: $17.2 billion / Nonpetroleum Investments: $692.4 million	□	■	■	□	□	□	□
Chevron * — Petroleum Investments: $12.5 billion / Nonpetroleum Investments: $339 million	■	■	■	■	■	□	■
Gulf — Petroleum Investments: $10.1 billion / Nonpetroleum Investments: $345 million	■	■	■	■	■	□	□
AMOCO ** — Petroleum Investments: $14.7 billion / Nonpetroleum Investments: $110 million	□	■	■	□	■	■	■
ARCO — Petroleum Investments: $9.9 billion / Nonpetroleum Investments: $2.4 billion	■	■	■	■	■	□	□
SHELL — Petroleum Investments: $12.1 billion / Nonpetroleum Investments: $301 million	■	■	■	□	□	■	□
CONOCO — Petroleum Investments: $5.8 billion / Nonpetroleum Investments: $1.6 billion	■	■	■	■	■	□	□
Getty — Petroleum Investments: $5.7 billion / Nonpetroleum Investments: $146.8 million	□	■	■	■	■	■	■

*Standard Oil (Calif.)   **Standard Oil (Ind.)

Notes: Petroleum investments include investments in chemicals. Alternative energy category includes ventures in solar energy technology and synthetic fuels. Other category includes a variety of ventures – computers, real estate and retailing.

The New York Times/Sept. 25, 1979

Source: © 1979 by The New York Times Company. Reprinted by permission.

ITT: Now What?

During the 1970s International Telephone and Telegraph (ITT) expanded vigorously, buying firms in many different areas, including food, heating and cooling systems, wire products, cosmetics, and electrical parts distribution. By the end of the decade the company knew that the returns on investment from many of these acquisitions were too low to justify keeping them. As a result, within a 24-month period ITT divested itself of more than 30 businesses which together accounted for total revenues of $1.2 billion. The company then faced the problem of deciding how and where to reinvest these funds. In groping for a new strategy, ITT relied heavily on strategic planning.[5]

New strategy formulation

Motorola: Changing the Product Mix

Mention the name Motorola and some people may still think of televisions. Actually, by the early 1980s Motorola already had been out of TV production for years, having sold its profitless Quasar line to Japan's Mitsushita Electric Industrial Company in 1974. The firm had also stopped producing car radios, the very business that launched it in 1928. These product lines were replaced with others via a long-range strategy designed to change Motorola's total product mix.

Strategy reformulation

In the 1970s, the firm began an acquisition strategy designed to add computers to its base in electronics. As part of this strategy, the company bought the Codex Corporation, a supplier of computer equipment, and Four-Phase Systems, Inc., a manufacturer of computer terminals and a software supplier. Motorola also began to look into mobile communications that would permit managers to communicate with a home-base computer when away from the office. By 1981, the company dominated the U.S. mobile communications market and was closing in on Texas Instruments, the world leader in semiconductor chip production. As a result of these and other developments, Motorola's sales increased from $800 million in 1970 to $3.75 billion in 1982 and are forecasted to reach $15 billion by the early 1990s. In commenting on the planning for the 1980s, the company's director of corporate strategy stated, "Now we're strategizing. We're thinking about where we want the company to go."[6] In so doing, the company has developed a formal strategy for each of its more than 40 businesses and appears to be well on its way to an average annual growth rate of 15 percent.

Union Pacific: Back to the Railroad

In the late 1960s the Union Pacific Railroad made an important strategic decision: to move into the energy field. This decision led to the ownership of (1) the Champlin Petroleum Company, which is engaged in the exploration, production, manufacturing, transportation, and marketing of petroleum products; (2) the Rocky Mountain Energy Company, which conducts extensive mining operations and owns 25 percent of all the coal reserves in

---

5. "ITT: Groping for a New Strategy," *Business Week*, December 15, 1980, pp. 66–69+.

6. "Motorola's New Strategy," *Business Week*, March 29, 1982, p. 129.

Strategy adjustment

the United States; and (3) the Upland Industries Corporation, a land development and land management subsidiary. The company's strategic plan has two major parts: to maintain the railroad in its best physical condition and to develop natural resources aggressively.[7] By 1982 nontransportation revenues constituted 69 percent of total revenues as energy income increased dramatically, indicating that Union Pacific's earlier objective of obtaining 50 percent of all revenue from railroad operations was probably unrealistic.

Scientific Atlanta: Practicing What They Preach

Present strategy continuation

Scientific Atlanta is an electronics firm that sells scientific instruments and test equipment to the military, manufactures satellite earth stations, plays a leading role in the cable-television equipment business, and is one of a handful of firms providing utilities with communications systems for monitoring and controlling residential electricity use. The company's success came about as a result of a chief executive with a strong commitment to strategic planning. Commenting on the success of the firm, he once noted, "In running a company, you have to continually ask yourself: 'What business am I in? What is the purpose of my company?' Then you develop a business strategy that will make you a leader in that business." From the early 1970s until the end of the decade, Scientific Atlanta saw its revenues increase fivefold. Profits rose from $800,000 to more than $7 million, and by 1982 exceeded $14 million.[8]

Strategic Planning Elements

As seen in Figure 5–1, there are four major elements in strategic planning. The first two, basic mission and strategic objectives, were discussed in some detail in Chapter 4. At this point only key elaborations will be made. The last two elements, strategy determination and portfolio planning, will be examined in detail.

Basic Mission

In determining the basic mission of the organization, top management must ask itself: What business are we in? What business should we be in? Will we need to change this mission over the next five years? Ralston Purina is a good example. Starting out as an animal feed store on the St. Louis riverfront, it began diversifying during the 1970s. By the end of the decade, it was breeding shrimps in Panama, growing mushrooms from Connecticut to California, fishing for tuna in the Atlantic and Pacific oceans, selling cat and dog food in Europe, and operating the Jack in the Box fast food chain, in addition to buying the St. Louis Blues hockey team. A few years later the tuna-catching, mushroom-raising, and European-based pet foods were gone and the hockey team was for sale. The company had gone back

---

7. "Back to Railroading for a New Era," *Business Week*, July 14, 1980, pp. 64–70.

8. Peter J. Schuyten, "Chief Took Company into Cable Systems," *New York Times*, January 7, 1980, p. D1, 4 and Scientific Atlanta, Inc., annual report, 1982.

to its basic markets of agricultural and grocery products. Many firms today are finding themselves returning to their primary lines of business, although many others are expanding. Sears, for example, has recently expanded into real estate and financial services.

When it comes to basic mission, however, companies that are interested in strategic planning must go beyond a simple definition or identification of the basic business. They must examine the relationship between mission and corporate culture.

Corporate culture relates to the values such as defensiveness or aggressiveness that set a pattern for a company's activities, opinions, and actions. This pattern is instilled in the employees by the examples of the managers and is passed down to succeeding generations of employees. The chief executive officer's words and actions, as well as those of the other managers, create this culture, and it may last for years before it is effectively changed by managers with a different culture. When this culture is consistent with strategy, the firm can develop an effective game plan. The following are examples:

Corporate culture affects strategy.

> International Business Machines Corp., where marketing drives a service philosophy that is almost unparalleled. The company keeps a hot line open 24 hours a day, seven days a week, to service IBM products.
>
> Digital Equipment Corp., where an emphasis on innovation creates freedom with responsibility. Employees can set their own hours and working style, but they are expected to articulate and support their activities with evidence of progress.
>
> Delta Airlines Inc., where a focus on customer service produces a high degree of teamwork. Employees will substitute in other jobs to keep planes flying and baggage moving.
>
> Atlantic Richfield Co., where an emphasis on entrepreneurs encourages action. Operating men have the autonomy to bid on promising fields without hierarchical approval.[9]

Corporate culture can help the organization adapt to its changing environment or it can prevent the company from meeting competitive threats, thereby leading to stagnation and ultimately to failure. In recent years many firms have worked to change their corporate culture and become more aggressive. For example, Pepsico moved from being a company that was content to being number two to a firm that was willing to take on Coca Cola and try to beat it out for the number one slot. Another successful corporate culture is promoted by J. C. Penney, although it is quite different from that of Pepsi. At Penney's the aggressiveness that is so evident in Pepsi's culture is discouraged. Penney's believes that building long-term customer loyalty is the most important objective. It tries to do this by ensuring that customers "know they can return merchandise with no question asked; suppliers know that Penney's will not haggle over terms; and employees are comfortable in their jobs knowing that Penney's will avoid layoffs at all costs and will find jobs for those who cannot handle more

9. "Corporate Culture," *Business Week,* October 27, 1980, p. 148.

demanding ones."[10] No wonder that the average tenure of executives at Penney's is 33 years!

A company's basic mission is affected by its corporate culture. Organizations that have encouraged a competitive culture formulate strategies markedly different from those that have encouraged a more relaxed approach. Depending on the industry and degree of competitiveness, either kind of culture can result in the formulation of an ideal basic mission.

Strategic Objectives

The strategic objectives that an organization formulates are external in orientation. They attempt to provide the firm with a means for comparing its performance with that of the competition. As noted in Chapter 4, typical examples of **strategic objectives** include return on investment, growth, and market share while examples of short-range, operational objectives include profit, productivity, and cost containment. Strategic objectives set overall direction; operational objectives provide a basis for short-run progress and control.

Strategic objectives are future oriented.

The focus and problem-solving styles required for strategic planning are quite different from those used for operational planning. For example, strategic objectives are directed toward future profits, while operational objectives are concerned with present profits. Strategic objectives help determine future opportunities and call for a flexible/entrepreneurial leadership style that is willing to accept moderate to high risk; operational objectives are concerned with current opportunities and call for a stable/adaptive leadership style that is willing to accept only low to moderate risk.

Strategic objectives are formulated to help the organization attain its basic mission. Like the latter, they are directional in nature.

Strategy Determination

Over the past two decades there has been a dramatic change in the way strategy is determined. For many firms diversification is now giving way to integration. More important, strategic planning is being used to tailor-make a "fit" between the organization and its environment.

Strategic Planning: Past, Present, and Future

Investment planning is declining.

While more and more businesses are now employing strategic planning, many are changing their approach. During the 1960s, for example, the term strategic planning often meant investment planning. The conglomerates attempted to buy diverse firms and parlay these portfolios into high profits the way an individual investor seeks to buy the most profitable stocks in a number of different industries. In the case of the conglomerates, however, quite often the acquisition did not meld with or complement the business's line, and the company had trouble managing the operation. As a result, profits lagged and real growth declined. These firms soon learned that investment planning was not a substitute for strategic planning.

During the 1970s many firms turned away from the investment planning

---

10. *Ibid.*

Compatibility of basic mission and synergy is sought.

approach and toward growth opportunities within the company itself. Strategies for cost reduction were initiated, reviews of the firm's marketing strategy were undertaken, and efforts were made to develop innovative research and development. At the same time, acquisitions and mergers were examined from the standpoint of compatibility of business missions and synergistic effect. One of the best examples is Pepsico, which acquired Pizza Hut and Taco Bell, two firms that tied in well with Pepsico's rapidly growing soft drink division and helped serve the same group of consumers.

During the 1980s it appears that there will be continued emphasis on strategies designed to help organizations build on what they do best. However, since there is the danger of antitrust action from the federal government should a firm begin acquiring or merging with other companies in its own industry, we are likely to see many companies seeking a balance between growth and market share in the industry. This will be done through what is called **concentric diversification,** which is a combination of integration and diversification. Concentric diversification requires a firm to "develop or acquire new products which have marketing and/or technological synergies with its current products but which are normally not intended for sale to the company's present markets."[11] In this way the firm gains the benefits of its experience and knowledge while avoiding the dangers of antitrust action. An example is found in the case of Philip Morris, which

Some firms employ concentric diversification.

bought Miller Brewing. At first blush, an acquisition like this appears to be a simple conglomerate diversification. However, beer and cigarettes are distributed through many of the same retail outlets, and many of the same people who drink beer also smoke. So Philip Morris really knew a great deal about marketing to Miller beer drinkers when it entered this market. Hence, the purchase of Miller Brewing is actually an illustration of concentric diversification. Another example is found in the case of Texas Instruments (TI), which has relied heavily on internal concentric diversification, with technological expertise providing the major thread binding its diversity. As the 1980s began, the firm's sales were spread over five market segments: digital products, components, metallurgy, government electronics, and services. TI has avoided inordinately high shares in any of these segments while remaining a growth-oriented and integrated single technology firm, concentrating on what it does best.

Tailor-Making Strategies

Today strategic planning is tailor-made to meet the needs of the organization. Keeping in mind that there are far too many situations to address all of them in just a few pages, let us look at three typical strategic planning concerns: (1) building market share, (2) maintaining market share, and (3) surviving in a hostile environment. Each requires a tailor-made strategic plan.[12]

---

11. William L. Shanklin, "Strategic Business Planning: Yesterday, Today, and Tomorrow," *Business Horizons,* October 1979, p. 13.

12. For one not covered here see: Kathryn Rudie Harrigan and Michael E. Porter, "End-Game Strategies For Declining Industries," *Harvard Business Review,* July–August 1983, pp. 111–120.

"Is this any way for a parent company to treat its offspring?"

Building Market Share The Strategic Planning Institute has been sponsoring the Profit Impact of Marketing Strategies (PIMS) since the mid-1970s. Drawing upon information from almost 2,000 businesses, PIMS has found that high-share businesses enjoy above-average profit margins and rates of return on investment, while most small-share businesses have below-average margins and returns.[13]

Strategic factors for increasing market share

How can a company plan strategically for higher market share? What does it need to do? Research to date reveals that the strategic factors generally involved in market share gains include the following: (1) the development and introduction of new products, (2) increases in relative product quality, and (3) increases in the marketing budget for such things as the sales force, advertising, and sales promotion relative to the growth rate of the particular market. When these factors are employed in combination, the result is a balanced marketing program.

A classic illustration of the effectiveness of a balanced marketing program is evident in the experience of L'eggs pantyhose. The Hanes Corporation introduced L'eggs in 1971 with a marketing strategy that included several novel elements: a one-size product to fit most users, a new system of direct-to-the-store distribution, and heavy introductory advertising and promotion.

13. Robert D. Buzzell and Frederik D. Wiersema, "Successful Share-Building Strategies," *Harvard Business Review*, January–February 1981, p. 135.

By 1974, L'eggs was the leading brand in the pantyhose market. While each component of the strategy undoubtedly contributed to the product's success, it also seems clear that the components reinforced each other. For example, heavy advertising and promotion speeded up consumer trial; that facilitated acceptance by retailers; and the system of direct distribution ensured that L'eggs would seldom be out of stock, allowing satisfied buyers to develop steady repeat buying routines.[14]

Most successful share-building strategies are based on the idea that a company should focus on a limited number of segments within a particular market. Most successful firms have achieved their success by concentrating their efforts on selected market segments. Often these segments are relatively small at first. Philip Morris provides an example. The company was successful in promoting Merit, a low-tar cigarette with special appeal for health-conscious smokers, and Miller "Lite," a beer aimed at diet-conscious drinkers. In building market share, a business must select its markets and then work to cultivate and expand them.

Maintaining Market Share   Some companies do not want to increase their market share. They are interested in maximizing their return on invested capital by maintaining the share of the market that provides them the highest return. Recent research shows that a strategic plan for maintaining market share consists of four basic elements.[15]

Segment the market.

The first element is for the company to compete in a limited number of market segments within the industry. The company should focus on market segments in which its own strength will be most highly valued and in which its major competitors will be most unlikely to compete. This type of plan was adopted by Crown Cork & Seal, a company that concentrated on two products: metal cans for hard-to-hold products such as beer and soft drinks, and aerosol cans. By building small single-product plants close to the customers, the company managed to secure a much higher return on investment than the competitors who made a broad assault on the metal container market and built large, multiproduct plants at some distance from the customers.

Use R&D efficiently.

The second element of this strategy is to use R&D (research and development) efficiently. Successful firms spend their money on applied, as opposed to basic, research. If a competitor produces a good product, they try to copy it. If they must do basic R&D, they try to be innovative or unique in some way. Crown Cork & Seal, for example, worked very closely with large breweries in developing drawn-and-ironed cans for the beverage industry. As a result, the firm beat all three of its major competitors in equipment conversion for the introduction of this new product.

Think small.

The third element is to think small. Companies that are successful in maintaining market share limit their growth. Consider the case of Burroughs, a mainframe computer manufacturer that limited its growth to 15 percent per year because its president said that fast growth would not allow for proper employee training or for proper development of the management

---

14. *Ibid.,* p. 143.

15. R. G. Hamermesh, M. H. Anderson, Jr., and J. E. Harris, "Strategies For Low Market Share Businesses," *Harvard Business Review,* May–June 1978, pp. 95–102.

structure. When successful firms interested in maintaining market share do diversify, they diversify cautiously.

The final element of a successful plan for maintaining market share is the strong influence of the chief executive. Influential chief executives often view obstacles as challenges and enjoy competing in unorthodox ways to beat the odds. They also work closely with teams of other senior managers and limit their responsibilities to a few key areas. In fact, as R. G. Hamermesh and his associates have noted, "In successful low-share companies, the influence of the chief executive often extends beyond formulating and communicating an ingenious strategy to actually having a deep involvement in the daily activities of the business."[16]

Have an influential chief executive.

Surviving in a Hostile Environment   Economists and business analysts agree that, compared with the previous decades, the 1980s will be a decade of slower growth, intensified regulatory pressures on business conduct, increasing inflation, and greater competition both at home and abroad. How can firms survive in this hostile environment? After conducting an in-depth study of 64 companies, William Hall has found that success comes to those that achieve either the lowest cost or most differentiated position:

Low cost and a differentiated position are important.

> . . . throughout their modern history . . . leading companies have demonstrated a continuous, single-minded determination to achieve one or both of the following competitive positions within their respective industries:
>
> Achieve the lowest delivered cost position relative to competition, coupled with an acceptable delivered quality and a pricing policy to gain profitable volume and market share growth.
>
> Achieve the highest product/service quality differentiated position relative to competition, with both an acceptable delivered cost and a pricing policy to gain margins sufficient to fund reinvestment in product/service differentiation.[17]

The strategic plan should be developed with this information in mind.

Hall reports that firms that achieve both of these strategic objectives, whether by developing a full product line or by specializing in a limited number of products, have the highest growth rates and returns in the industry and are most likely to prosper. Those that achieve the next lowest costs and the next most differentiated position or both have moderate but generally acceptable growth rates and returns. As the market matures, firms that are less successful in achieving low costs and a differentiated position show little growth and small returns. They can become profitable only by discovering new market segments and focusing on them or by transferring their assets into diversified markets.[18] Finally, in hostile environments, when firms do not achieve either low costs or a differentiated position, they fail.

---

16. *Ibid.,* p. 191.

17. William K. Hall, "Survival Strategies in a Hostile Environment," *Harvard Business Review,* September–October 1980, pp. 78–79.

18. For more on strategies in mature industries see: Donald C. Hambrick, "An Empirical Typology of Mature Industrial-Product Environments," *Academy of Management Journal,* June 1983, pp. 213–230.

Portfolio Planning

Regardless of its strategy, every organization finds that some product lines do better than predicted, some do more poorly, and the rest perform as expected. Based on its findings, the firm decides whether to invest more money in the line, reduce the investment, or do nothing.

In an effort to analyze product line performance systematically and develop a follow-up strategy, some companies have turned to the use of the **strategic business unit** (SBU). Popularized by General Electric in the early 1970s, the SBU concept of planning breaks the company into business units based on the following principles:

> The . . . firm should be managed as a "portfolio" of businesses, with each business unit serving a clearly defined product-market segment with a clearly defined strategy.

SBU principles

> Each business unit in the portfolio should develop a strategy tailored to its capabilities and competitive needs, but consistent with overall corporate capabilities and needs.

> The total portfolio of business should be managed to allocating capital and managerial resources to serve the interests of the firm as a whole—to achieve balanced growth in sales, earnings, and asset mix at an acceptable and controlled level of risk. In essence, the portfolio should be designed and managed to achieve an overall corporate strategy.[19]

Each SBU is a discrete, independent, product-market segment serviced by the firm. Some of the characteristics of an SBU include a distinct mission, its own competitors, the focus of a single business or collection of related businesses, and the ability to plan independently of the other SBUs in the organization. The SBU is a business within a business.[20] Some firms can handle their portfolio planning with two or three such units, while large corporations such as General Electric in the United States and Toshiba Corporation in Japan have more than 40.

The Portfolio Matrix

The business portfolio matrix helps the organization allocate resources among the various SBUs. This matrix is illustrated in Figure 5–3. Two major criteria determine the resource allocation: product-market attractiveness and competitive position.

The Dimensions

The **long-term product-market attractiveness indicator** measures market potential. Two distinct philosophies have evolved about ranking SBUs

---

19. William K. Hall, "SBUs: Hot, New Topic in Management of Diversification," *Business Horizons,* February 1978, p. 17.

20. For more on this see: R. G. Hamermesh and R. E. White, "Manage Beyond Portfolio Analysis," *Harvard Business Review,* January–February 1984, pp. 103–109.

Figure 5–3
Portfolio Matrix Used To
Evaluate SBUs

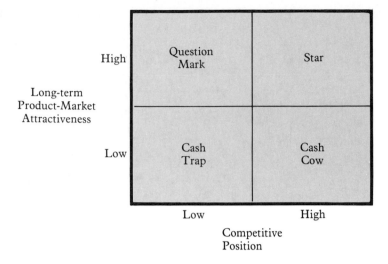

Market potential

on this dimension. The first advocates using the long-term projected real growth rate of the product-segment. When this method is used, the break point between industry high and low growth rates is commonly set at 10 percent, although sometimes it is set at the level of growth for the economy as a whole or the level of growth of a particular sector of the economy. The second philosophy concerned with ranking SBUs according to market potential considers a combination of quantitative and qualitative factors. At GE these factors include segment size, segment growth rate (in units and real dollars), competitive diversity, competitive structure, segment profitability, and technological, social, environmental, legal, and human impacts.

Measuring business strength

Competitive position refers to the firm's business strength. Here again, two alternative philosophies have evolved for ranking SBUs. One considers a single market share relative to the competition. The other considers a combination of qualitative and quantitative factors such as segment size, SBU growth rate, share, profitability margins, technological position, skill or weaknesses, image, environmental impact, and management.

Strategic Handling

Depending on its long-term product-market attractiveness and competitive position, an SBU is either a star, a cash cow, a question mark, or a cash trap. After an SBU has been evaluated, the company can choose the appropriate strategy for handling it. This strategy is then employed until the next evaluation period (usually one year later), at which time the unit is again evaluated and a new decision is made regarding its ranking. A new product line often starts out as a question mark, grows and becomes a star, matures and becomes a cash cow, and then declines and becomes a cash trap. Of course, during this product life cycle the organization can work to move the product back to one of its previous positions, as in the case of a cash cow that, with a dynamic advertising program and some new product design, becomes a star again. Or, if a product line is on its way out, the organization can terminate it before it becomes a cash trap.

Star   A star is an SBU with high long-term product-market attractiveness and a high competitive position. Star product lines are businesses that

A star is to be groomed.   must be groomed for the long run. Right now they are cash consumers.

Resources must be spent to develop their full potential. If this is done, they will grow faster than the competition in this market segment in terms of sales, profits, and cash flow. The strategy to employ with stars is one of building and investing.

Cash Cow   A cash cow is an SBU with low long-term product-market attractiveness and a high competitive position. Since the product line is dominant in the industry, it generates a great deal of cash from operations. The strategy to employ with a cash cow is to preserve market position while generating dollars.[21] Some of the most common strategies that are employed for these product lines include targeting growth segments, stabilizing price, differentiating the product, using selective cost reduction, and employing less creative marketing.

A cash cow is to be held and milked . . .

If things start to turn bad, however, the organization must begin to milk the cow for all it is worth. The strategy to use with strong cash cows is to "hold," while the strategy to employ with weak ones is to "harvest." Unfortunately, there is no single indicator that points reliably to candidates for harvesting; one must rely on a multiple set of indicators. Seven of the most important are the following:

1. The business entity is in a stable or declining market.

2. The business entity has a small market share, and building it up would be too costly; or it has a respectable market that is becoming increasingly costly to defend or maintain.

and sometimes harvested.

3. The business entity is not producing especially good profits or may even be producing losses.

4. Sales would not decline too rapidly as a result of reduced investment.

5. The company has better uses for the freed-up resources.

6. The business entity is not a major component of the company's business portfolio.

7. The business entity does not contribute other desired features to the business portfolio, such as sales stability or prestige.[22]

The fact that a product line has begun to be harvested does not mean that the line will generate cash for only a short period of time. Some companies have found, to their surprise, that harvested products can have remarkable staying power long after their marketing support levels have been reduced or removed. For example, Bristol-Myers sold its Ipana toothpaste brand rights to two small businesspeople who continued to produce it and stock distributors while stopping all advertising. Sales continued for years, and the two made a healthy profit. Lifebuoy soap's market dropped off and Lever Brothers cut most of its advertising and promotional support. Sales continued, however, and because the soap was priced higher than

---

21. See, for example: "Burlington Northern's Cash Cow," *Business Week,* March 8, 1982, pp. 112, 114.

22. Philip Kotler, "Harvesting Strategies for Weak Products," *Business Horizons,* August 1978, pp. 17–18.

its leading competitors were, it produced enough profit to justify its existence. General Electric decided to harvest its artillery manufacturing division because it did not want to risk poor public relations by getting deeper into the arms business. Despite its reduction of investment, failure to maintain high R&D, and raising of prices, the company found demand for these products persisting at a high level. The result was a substantial increase in profits.

A question mark must become a star for the company to keep it.

Question Mark   A question mark is an SBU with high long-term product-market attractiveness and low competitiveness. This SBU poses a major problem for the firm. If its competitive position is not strengthened, its product-market segment will be attacked by the competition. Yet the costs of an effort to strengthen the SBU's position may not be justified. Some firms opt to put money behind a question mark and see what happens. If the SBU develops into a star, everything is fine. If it declines or does not improve enough to justify further support, the company divests itself of the SBU. Question marks must either get into the star category or get out of the portfolio.

A dog must be managed for short-term cash flow.

Cash Trap   A cash trap is an SBU with low long-term product-market attractiveness and a low competitive position. SBUs in this category are clearly unattractive for either the short or the long run. Additionally, even if the organization were to put more resources into the unit to improve its position, the SBU would still have low potential. This is why cash traps are commonly referred to as "dogs." The strategy here is always the same: to manage the SBU in such a way as to maximize the short-term cash flow. Sometimes this strategy is carried out by closing the SBU down or conducting a rapid divestiture. In other cases it is carried out by harvesting cash from operations through cost cutting, short-term pricing policies, and giving up market share and growth opportunities that absorb short-term cash.

Given the fact that SBUs are often changing from one quadrant of the portfolio matrix to another, management must continually assess the progress of each. Moreover, since all of them will eventually be harvested or divested, the company must always be on the lookout for new ventures that will turn into profitable SBUs of the future.[23]

Putting Strategic Planning into Operation

Once an organization has finished its portfolio management analysis, it knows which SBUs to push via further investment and which to prune via harvesting or direct divestment. It can then begin to put the plan into operation. The way this is done was explained in Chapter 4. Sometimes a firm opts for MBO; at other times it prefers a different type of approach, which helps break the overall plan into its component parts, delegating responsibility to the various departments or units. Figure 5–4 illustrates the relationship between the organization's strategic and operational plans.

---

23. For a complementary approach to portfolio planning see Thomas J. Cossé and John S. Swan, "Share Profit: A Planning Model for Product Managers," *Business Horizons,* July–August 1983, pp. 69–73.

Figure 5–4
The Relationship Between the
Strategic Plan and the
Operational Plan

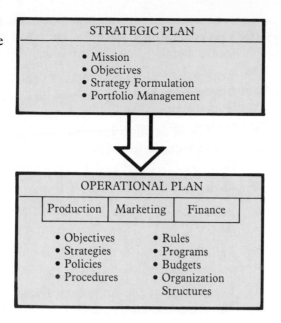

Dealing with Problems

Common pitfalls

One thing that management needs to do is to deal with problems that arise.[24] Table 5–2 reports some of the major pitfalls that have to be avoided in carrying out strategic planning. These pitfalls were identified by managers themselves in a national survey.[25]

Few plans work as anticipated.

Another thing management must realize is that few plans ever work as anticipated. Usually something happens that is unanticipated. This is why many firms have contingency plans that support their primary ones. If something unexpected happens they switch to the contingency plan; if they had not planned for the new development in the contingency plan, they begin to do so immediately. They are flexible.

Strategic plans should be reviewed and revised annually.

Finally, organizations must develop a monitoring system that lets them know what is going on and where progress is less than anticipated. Such a system allows them to play "catch-up ball" when necessary. Many firms have missed the boat but managed to correct their mistake. Consider McDonald's, the leading fast food franchiser. Initially it sold hamburgers and french fries, but over time the firm realized that customers wanted other fast foods, such as steak sandwiches and breakfast offerings. Eventually McDonald's added these items to its line. Examples such as this one suggest why it is important for a strategic plan to be reviewed and revised annually.

---

24. Donald C. Hambrick and Steven M. Schecter, "Turnaround Strategies for Mature Industrial-Product Business Units," *Academy of Management Journal*, June 1983, pp. 231–248.

25. For more on this subject see Alex R. Oliver and Joseph R. Garber, "Implementing Strategic Planning: Ten Sure-Fire Ways To Do It Wrong," *Business Horizons*, March–April 1983, pp. 49–51.

Table 5–2
The Ten Most Important Pitfalls in Strategic Planning

1. Top management assumes that it can delegate the planning function to a planner.

2. Top management becomes so engrossed in current problems that it spends insufficient time on long-range planning and the process becomes discredited among other managers and staff.

3. Failure to develop company goals that are suitable as a basis for formulating long-range plans.

4. Failure to assume the necessary involvement in the planning process of major line personnel.

5. Failure to use plans as standards for measuring managerial performance.

6. Failure to create a climate in the company which is congenial and not resistant to planning.

7. Assuming that corporate comprehensive planning is something separate from the entire management process.

8. Injecting so much formality into the system that it lacks flexibility, looseness, and simplicity, and restrains creativity.

9. Failure of top management to review with departmental and divisional heads the long-range plans which they have developed.

10. Top management's consistently rejecting the formal planning mechanism by making intuitive decisions which conflict with formal plans.

George Steiner, *Strategic Planning: What Every Manager* Must *Know* (New York: The Free Press, 1979), p. 294.

In this way, the company ensures that its plan is as current as possible and takes into account the latest changes in the environment. Updating the plan involves effective decision making, a topic that will be explored in the next chapter.

Summary

1. Two major characteristics differentiate strategic planning from planning in general. The first is the value system promoted by strategic planning. The second is the philosophy behind the process.

2. There are four elements in strategic planning: formulation of the basic mission, setting of strategic objectives, determination of strategy, and the use of portfolio planning.

3. Strategic planning is important for two reasons. First, it helps organizations cope with their external environment. Second, it assists them in redefining or reformulating their strategies or both.

4. Many organizations can profit from strategic planning. In particular, large businesses are finding this type of planning very helpful.

5. In determining the basic mission of the organization, top management must ask itself: What business are we in? What business should we be in? Will we need to change this mission over the next five years? Corporate culture is also important. It relates to values, such as defensiveness or aggressiveness, that set a pattern for a company's activities, opinions, and actions.

6. During the 1960s many firms used an investment planning approach as a substitute for strategic planning. Today this has changed. Organizations look for internal growth opportunities, and when they do buy other firms, they seek compatibility or a synergistic fit. Strategy is tailor-made to fit the situation.

7. Portfolio planning involves breaking the company into small business units (SBUs). Each SBU is a discrete, independent, product-market segment serviced by the firm. It is a business within a business. Those firms with a large number of SBUs have turned to the use of a portfolio matrix. This matrix measures long-term product-market attractiveness and competitive position. Based on the two measurements, an SBU can be judged to be a star, question mark, cash cow, or cash trap. There are recommended strategies for dealing with each.

8. Once the organization has finished its portfolio management analysis, it knows which SBUs to push via further investment and which to prune via harvesting or direct disinvestment. The organization can then put its strategic plan into operation.

Key Terms

Cash cow An SBU with low long-term product-market attractiveness and a high competitive position. The strategy to employ with strong cash cows is to hold them, preserve market position, and generate dollars; with weak cash cows it is to harvest the unit and start moving toward divestment.

Cash trap An SBU with low long-term product-market attractiveness and a low competitive position. The strategy to take with cash traps is to manage them so as to maximize short-term cash flow.

Competitive position A portfolio matrix indicator that refers to the firm's business strength. Some of the factors commonly considered in measuring competitive position include growth rate, profitability, and management.

Concentric diversification A combination of integration and diversification. It involves the development or acquisition of new products that have marketing and/or technological synergies with the company's current products but which are normally not intended for sale to its present markets.

Corporate culture Values that set a pattern for a company's activities, opinions, and actions.

Long-term product-market attractiveness indicator A portfolio matrix indicator that measures market potential. Some of the factors commonly considered in this measurement are segment growth rate, competitive diversity, and segment profitability.

Question mark An SBU with high long-term product-market attractiveness and a low competitive position. The strategy to employ with these SBUs is to put some money behind them and see what happens. If the SBU develops into a star, fine; if not, the company should divest itself of the unit.

Star An SBU with high long-term product-market attractiveness and a high competitive position. The strategy to employ with stars is one of building and investing.

Strategic business unit (SBU) A discrete, independent, product-market segment serviced by a firm.

Strategic objectives   Return on investment, growth, market share, and other objectives that help determine future opportunities and call for a flexible/entrepreneurial leadership style that is willing to accept moderate to high risk.

Questions for Analysis and Discussion

1. There are two major characteristics of strategic planning: the value system it promotes and the philosophy behind the process. What does this statement mean? Explain it in your own words.

2. In what way can strategic planning help an organization cope with the external environment? Be specific in your answer.

3. What does Table 5–1 illustrate about the external environment of business? What conclusions can be drawn from the findings it presents? Explain.

4. In general terms, what companies need strategic planning? Defend your answer.

5. How does an identification of the basic mission help an organization formulate a strategic plan? What role is played by corporate culture?

6. In what way has strategic planning changed between the 1960s and the 1980s? Be sure to include a discussion of investment planning in your answer.

7. How do modern firms go about building market share? Maintaining market share? Surviving in a hostile environment? In each case, give examples.

8. What is meant by portfolio planning? What is an SBU? Bring both ideas together and discuss how a portfolio matrix can help an organization manage its various business units. Be sure to include a discussion of stars, cash cows, question marks, and cash traps in your answer.

9. What are some of the most important pitfalls that must be dealt with in putting a strategic plan into operation? Identify and discuss five of them.

Case

A Case of Portfolio Management

When the Robinson Products Company first designed its small hair blow dryer, management thought it would capture a large share of the market. Robinson's dryer was much smaller than the one sold by the competition, and it could be folded in two by swinging the handle parallel to the main blower. Robinson Products had put more than $3 million into designing and developing the dryer, but it was certain that these costs would be recovered quickly. However, that is not what happened.

When the machine was first introduced, sales were quite good. Unfortunately, one of the largest competitors came out with a similar hair dryer a month later. As a result Robinson's first-year sales were only 24 percent of forecast. Additionally, the company discovered that the competition had developed a much better advertising campaign.

Over the last three years Robinson's share of the market has fallen from 14 percent to just over 4 percent. Top management is now looking either to sell the product or simply to phase it out. The company knows that a strong advertising campaign would undoubtedly return a small profit but, as one of the top managers put it, "Why push a marginal product line? We have a lot of stars that warrant our investment." At the company's evaluation of product lines last week, the blow dryer was rated as having a low competitive position in a market segment with long-term product-market attractiveness. Now management has to decide what to do with the product.

1. Based on the portfolio matrix in Figure 5–3, how should this product be labeled: star, cash cow, question mark, or cash trap?

2. Given your answer to the above question, what approach should the company use in handling this product line? Explain your answer.

3. If the product line had a high competitive position but had been judged to have low long-term product-market attractiveness, how would your answer to the above question be different? Explain.

You Be the Consultant

A Need for Planning

When Anna and Jack Robinson first started their business, they had no idea how well they were going to do. The two had just received Ph.D.'s from a large state university and had gone to work in the engineering department of another university. Seven years ago they developed an energy-saving apparatus that can be of value in most homes in the United States. This apparatus, which sells for just over $75, can be attached to the water heater. It controls the water temperature and, with the roof hookup to which it is connected, uses solar energy to heat the water. After testing the product in a few hundred homes, Anna and Jack started their own company. They brought in a production expert who set up the manufacturing facilities and got their banker to help them with the financing. Before long they had a business that was grossing almost $2.5 million annually. That was four years ago.

Since then they have developed 16 more energy-saving devices that can be used around the house. Some of these are very similar to those sold by other firms. An example is a small digital clock that is connected to the electric meter but placed in the kitchen. This clock tells the home occupants how many kilowatts of energy they are using per hour. People who have these electric clocks report that they are far more energy-conscious when the number of kilowatts per hour is being flashed in front of them than when they simply try to conserve energy by turning off lights around the house and keeping the doors and windows closed so as to keep the heat in during the winter and the cool in during the summer.

These new energy-saving developments have had a dramatic effect on the company's gross income. Last week the Robinsons' accountant said that the company would gross between $8 and 9 million. On the one hand, they are ecstatic about the news. On the other hand, they realize that they have become a much larger enterprise than they ever expected to be. With this growth they need to plan for operations. This is something they have not done much about. They have been so involved in developing and testing new energy products that they have not bothered to study the competition, examine the market, or plan for the long term. Their banker has been urging them to develop a two-year financial plan that will provide them with some idea of the type of capital they will need to maintain operations. He has also urged them to make some plans regarding what to do with the profits.

The biggest problem facing the Robinsons is that they really do not know much about planning. They have a basic idea of planning fundamentals. However, they do not understand much about strategic planning, how to analyze the competition, how to evaluate their product lines, or how to put strategic objectives into operation. They realize that they will have to turn to outside help to assist them in these matters and are interested in bringing in a consultant.

Your Consultation

Assume that you have been brought in by the Robinsons to help them with their planning. Tell them what is meant by a strategic plan and why such a plan can be of value to them. Then set forth some of the basic elements of a strategic plan and explain what each means. Finally, develop a plan of action for the Robinsons, using your previous analysis to help you, and set forth some recommendations that will take the company through the next three years.

Decision Making in Action

Objectives

Planning and decision making are related in that plans are brought to fruition through decisions. In this chapter we will examine how decision making is carried out. Particular attention will be given to studying both rational and bounded rationality decision-making models. Consideration will also be given to the conditions under which decisions are made and to ways in which decision-making effectiveness can be improved. By the time you have finished studying all of the material in this chapter, you will be able to

1. define the term decision making and explain how the manager should go about reviewing decision-making situations;

2. compare and contrast programmed and nonprogrammed decisions;

3. describe the three conditions under which decisions are made and explain how these decisions are implemented;

4. set forth some of the steps a manager can follow in improving decision-making effectiveness;

5. compare and contrast the rational decision-making process with the bounded rationality process;

6. explain how each of the following affects decision making: satisficing behavior, simplification, subjective rationality, and rationalization; and

7. explain how the following can be of value in improving decision-making effectiveness: use of management science tools and techniques, creativity, and the matching of decision-making situations with leadership styles.

The Nature of Decision Making

As we saw in Chapter 2, *decision making* is the process of choosing from among alternatives. Sometimes this process is a simple one. In making the final choice the manager can rely on simple guidelines and techniques such as rules, policies, procedures, or basic quantitative analysis. At other times the process is a complex one. In these cases the manager must draw on intuition, judgment, gut feeling, and highly mathematical tools and techniques. Table 6–1 illustrates these ideas.

In deciding how to approach each particular situation, the manager needs an understanding of the basic nature of decision making. Specifically, this requirement involves (1) knowing how to review the situation properly, (2) understanding the types of decisions that will be involved, (3) determining the conditions under which the decision will be made, and (4) having a fundamental grasp of the techniques involved in making effective decisions. The following section examines each of these kinds of knowledge.

Reviewing the Situation

The first thing a manager facing a decision needs to do is review the situation. He or she must answer three key questions. The first two are designed to help the manager sidestep personal action. The third is designed to help the manager formulate a response.

Will the problem resolve itself?

The first question is: Will the problem resolve itself? If nothing is done, will the matter go away? If the answer is yes, the manager can ignore the problem. A classic example is found in the case of managers who receive reports, memos, and other written communiqués that are labeled "for your attention and action." In most cases the manager does not have to read this material or do anything with it. The material is simply informational. It can be glanced at and then filed.

Is a personal decision required?

The second question is: Does the issue require a personal decision? Many times the matter can be delegated to a subordinate. It is not important enough to warrant personal consideration.

How should the problem be handled?

If the issue does require a personal decision, the third question is: How should the problem be handled? Having determined that the issue cannot be sidestepped, the manager must develop a plan of action. Managers who review decision-making situations by asking these three questions in the order in which we have presented them find they can greatly reduce the amount of time and effort expended in choosing from among alternatives.

Types of Decisions

The manager needs to have a fundamental grasp of the various types of decisions. Table 6–2 provides one framework for categorizing them. Notice

Table 6–1
Decision-Making Continuum

Simple Problems	Complex Problems
Rules, policies, procedures, basic quantitative analysis	Intuition, judgment, gut feeling, highly mathematical tools and techniques

Table 6–2   Traditional and Modern Techniques of Decision Making

Types of Decisions	Decision-Making Technique	
	Traditional	**Modern**

Programmed:
Routine, repetitive decisions
Organization develops specific
processes for handling them
	1. Habit
	2. Clerical routine:
	   Standard operating
	   procedures
	3. Organizational structure:
	   Common expectations
	   A system of subgoals
	   Well-defined informa-
	   tional channels
		1. Operations research:
		   Mathematical analysis
		   Models
		   Computer simulation
		2. Electronic data processing

Nonprogrammed:
One-shot, ill-structured, novel
policy decisions
Handled by general problem-
solving processes
	1. Judgment, intuition, and
	   creativity
	2. Rules of thumb
	3. Selection and training of
	   executives
		Heuristic problem-solving
		technique applied to:
		a. Training human decision
		   makers
		b. Constructing heuristic
		   computer programs

Source: Herbert A. Simon, *The New Science of Management Decision,* Revised Edition, © 1977, p. 48. Reprinted by permission of Prentice-Hall, Englewood Cliffs, N.J.

from the table that there are two basic types of decisions: programmed and nonprogrammed.

Programmed decisions are those that are traditionally made using standard operating procedures or other well-defined methods. Some standard modern techniques include the use of operations research, mathematical analysis, and computer simulation. Programmed decisions are the easiest for managers to make because they can rely on pre-established patterns or programs to provide an answer.

Programmed decisions use well-defined methods.

Nonprogrammed decisions are unique or out of the ordinary. They are often ill-structured, one-shot decisions. Traditionally they have been handled by techniques such as judgment, intuition, and creativity. More recently decision makers have turned to heuristic problem-solving approaches in which logic, common sense, and trial and error are used to deal with problems that are too large or too complex to be solved through quantitative or computerized approaches. In this area of nonprogrammed decision making managers have the opportunity to prove themselves. In fact, many management training programs on decision making are designed to help managers think through problems using a logical, nonprogrammed approach. In this way they learn how to deal with extraordinary, unexpected, and unique problems.

Nonprogrammed decisions are ill-structured.

Decision-Making Conditions

Decisions are made under one of three possible conditions: certainty, risk, and uncertainty. As seen in Figure 6–1, these conditions are based on the amount of knowledge the decision maker has regarding the final outcome of the decision.

Figure 6–1
Decision-Making Conditions

The amount of knowledge the decision maker has regarding the outcome of the decision determines the decision-making condition.

Certainty

Sometimes the outcome of a decision is known with certainty.

Under conditions of **certainty** the manager has enough information to know the outcome of the decision before it is made. For example, a company president has just put aside a fund of $50,000 to cover the renovation of all executive offices. This money is in a savings account at a local savings and loan (S&L) association which pays 5.25 percent. Half will be drawn out next month and the rest when the job is completed in 90 days. Can the president determine today how much interest will be earned on the money over the next 90 days? Given the fact that the president knows how much is being invested, the length of investment time, and the interest rate, the answer is yes. Investing the funds in an S&L is a decision made under conditions of certainty. The ultimate outcome in terms of interest is known today.

Another example of decision making under certainty is found in the case of an organization with a warehouse full of machine parts. Assume that these parts can be used to produce any one of three machine models: A, B, or C. Each model requires a different combination of parts and has a different profit level. For example, model A is the simplest, uses the fewest parts, and has the lowest profit. Model C is the most complex, uses the greatest number of parts, and returns the highest profit. Given the fact that the parts are all on hand, the company can make any model or combination of models it wants. If we assume the firm wants to maximize profit, the only question that needs to be answered is: Which model or models should be assembled in order to reach this objective? This question may be difficult to answer through visual analysis of the inventory report, but it can be answered by using mathematical decision-making tools. The company can determine with certainty the outcome of its decision.

Risk

At other times the outcome is only partially known.

Most managerial decisions are made under conditions of risk.[1] **Risk** exists when the individual has some information regarding the outcome of the decision but does not know everything. When making decisions under conditions of risk, the manager may find it helpful to use probabilities. To the degree that probability assignment is accurate, he or she can make a good decision.

Consider the case of a company that has four contract proposals it is

---

1. David B. Hertz and Howard Thomas, "Decision and Risk Analysis in a New Product and Facilities Planning Problem," *Sloan Management Review,* Winter 1983, pp. 17–31.

Table 6–3
Computation of Expected
Values

Contract Proposal	Profit	Probability of Getting the Contract	Expected Value
1	$100,000	.6	$ 60,000
2	200,000	.5	100,000
3	300,000	.4	120,000
4	400,000	.2	80,000

interested in bidding on. If the firm obtains any one of these contracts, it will make a profit on the undertaking. However, because only a limited number of personnel can devote their time to putting bids together, the firm has decided to bid on one proposal only—the one that offers the best combination of profit and probability that the bid will be successful. This combination is known as the *expected value*. The profit associated with each of these four contract proposals, as presented in Table 6–3, varies from $100,000 to $400,000. Notice that the contract offering $400,000 is the least likely to be awarded to the company. Conversely, the first contract is much more likely to be awarded to the company, but it offers the smallest profit of the four. On which of the proposals should the firm bid? As the table shows, the answer is number three. It offers the greatest expected value.

This example illustrates the importance of probability assignment when decisions are made under risk. If we reversed the probabilities so that Proposal #1 had a 20 percent success factor and Proposal #4 had a 60 percent success factor, the manager would opt for the latter proposal. The effective manager must investigate each alternative in order to be as accurate as possible in making probability assignments.

Uncertainty

At still other times the outcome is unknown.

Uncertainty exists when the probabilities of the various outcomes are not known. The manager feels unable to assign estimates to any of the alternatives. While the situation may seem hopeless, mathematical techniques have been developed to help decision makers deal with uncertainty. Some of these are heavily quantitative in nature and are outside the scope of our present consideration.[2] Some nonmathematical approaches have been developed to supplement these techniques, however, and they do warrant brief discussion. One is simply to avoid situations of uncertainty. A second is to assume that the future will be like the past and assign probabilities based on previous experiences. A third is to gather as much information as possible on each of the alternatives, assume that the decision making condition is one of risk, and assign probabilities accordingly.

Using these approaches actually requires sidestepping the uncertainty factor. It is assumed not to exist; and this can be a wise philosophy. After all, by definition, uncertainty throws a monkey wrench into decision making. The manager's best approach is to draw back from this condition either

2. Richard M. Hodgetts, *Management: Theory, Process, and Practice,* 3rd edition (Hinsdale, Illinois: Dryden Press, 1981), Chapter 8.

by gathering data on the alternatives or by making assumptions that allow the decision to be made under the condition of risk.

Making Effective Decisions

When a manager does have to make a decision, he or she should strive to be as effective as possible. One way of ensuring effectiveness is to follow the steps in the decision-making process. These will be discussed shortly. A second way is to use guidelines that help carry out this process. While many guidelines can be of help, the following seven, set forth by Irving Janis and Leo Mann, have been found to be of particular value:

1. Thoroughly canvas a wide range of alternative courses of action.

2. Survey the full range of objectives to be fulfilled and the values that are implied in the choice.

Effective decision-making guidelines

3. Carefully weigh whatever is known about the costs and risks of negative consequences as well as the positive consequences that can flow from each alternative.

4. Intensively search for new information relevant to the further evaluation of the alternatives.

5. Correctly assimilate and take into account any new information or expert judgment to which one is exposed, even when the information or judgment does not support the course of action initially preferred.

6. Reexamine the positive and negative consequences of all known alternatives, including those originally regarded as unacceptable, before making a final choice.

7. Make detailed provisions for implementing or executing the chosen course of action, with special attention to contingency plans that might be required if various known risks were to materialize.[3]

These guidelines are somewhat utopian. The manager does not always have either the time or the resources for carrying out all of them. They do serve, however, as a basis for rational decision making.

Rational Decision-Making Process

The **rational decision-making process** describes how decisions are made in the ideal.[4] As we shall see shortly, most decisions are not made in quite this way. Some of the steps are either shortcircuited or bypassed entirely. Nevertheless, when the problem or issue is a simple one that is addressed in logical fashion, the steps as outlined in Figure 6–2 do describe how decisions are made.

3. Irving Janis and Leo Mann, *Decision Making* (New York: Free Press, 1977), p. 11.
4. Noreen M. Klein, "Utility and Decision Strategies: A Second Look At The Rational Decision Maker," *Organizational Behavior and Human Performance*, February 1983, pp. 1–25.

Figure 6–2   Steps Involved in the Rational Decision-Making Process

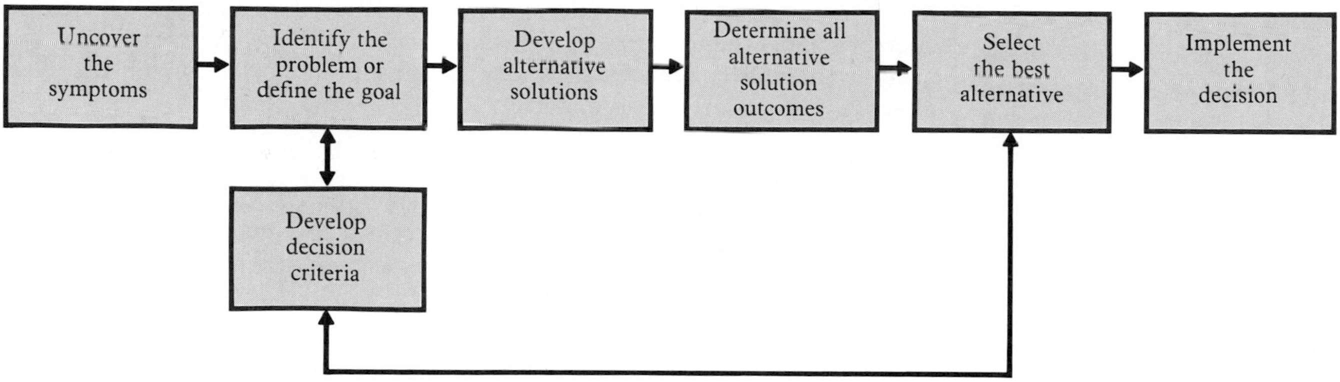

```
┌──────────┐   ┌──────────┐   ┌──────────┐   ┌──────────┐   ┌──────────┐   ┌──────────┐
│ Uncover  │   │Identify the│ │ Develop  │   │Determine all│ │  Select  │   │Implement │
│   the    │──▶│problem or │──▶│alternative│──▶│alternative │─▶│ the best │──▶│   the    │
│ symptoms │   │define the goal│ │solutions│   │  solution  │ │alternative│   │ decision │
└──────────┘   └──────────┘   └──────────┘   │  outcomes  │ └──────────┘   └──────────┘
                    ▲▼                        └──────────┘        ▲
               ┌──────────┐                                       │
               │ Develop  │                                       │
               │ decision │                                       │
               │ criteria │                                       │
               └──────────┘                                       │
                    ▲                                             │
                    └─────────────────────────────────────────────┘
```

Uncover the Symptoms

The first step in rational decision making is to uncover the symptoms of the problem. The company that produces an outmoded product will find its market share slipping away. The manager who fails to obtain average raises for personnel will find an increase in absenteeism and tardiness among the workers. In each case the problem presents itself through its symptoms.

Identify the Problem or Define the Goal

Having uncovered the symptom, the manager must identify the problem or the desired goal. In other words, he or she must answer the question: Why did the symptom arise? More specifically, the question might be: Why is the company's product outmoded, or why are worker absenteeism and tardiness increasing?

Develop Decision Criteria

The next step is to develop criteria for evaluating the alternative courses of action. In the case of the outmoded product, the objective might be to recapture the old market share. The manager who failed to get average raises for the personnel might compare the cost of these raises with the expenses associated with the lost work output.

Develop Alternative Solutions

At this point the decision maker lists all of the possible solutions to the problem. Some may be very unlikely; others may border on the absurd. In rational decision making all are listed. Not all of the solutions are explained in detail, however. The decision maker focuses on the ones that seem most likely to solve the problem.

Determine All Alternative Solution Outcomes

All of the alternative solutions are then examined in terms of outcome. What will happen if each is implemented? Whenever possible the manager attempts to quantify the answer.

Select the Best Alternative

After determining the probable outcomes of alternative solutions, the manager evaluates them using the decision criteria. Which one best meets the criteria that have been established? At this point, selection of the best alternative is a fairly simple matter.

Implement the Decision

The final step in decision making is to carry out the decision. The solution is put into effect. If the decision has been well thought out and there are no problems in communicating what is to be done, this step should be fairly easy.

Bounded Rationality Considerations

The rational decision-making process is an ideal approach. Unfortunately, in practice decision making is not often carried out this way. The manager's knowledge may be limited or bounded in a number of ways. The following discussion examines four of the most important kinds of limitations and then describes the bounded rationality process.

Satisficing Behavior

To most managers many choices are merely "good enough."

Rational decision making assumes that the manager will choose the alternative that offers the greatest return or benefit. This kind of manager, often referred to as **economic man,** always strives for the maximum payoff. In contrast, **administrative man** exhibits **satisficing behavior,** choosing a course of action that is merely satisfactory. Most managers are happy most of the time with a satisfactory return. They are "satisficers" rather than maximizers. Herbert Simon has distinguished between the two in this way:

> Whereas economic man maximizes—selects the best alternative from among all those available to him—his cousin, administrative man, satisfices—looks for a course of action that is satisfactory or "good enough." Examples of satisficing criteria, familiar enough to businessmen if unfamiliar to most economists, are "share of the market," "adequate profit," "fair price."[5]

The decision maker, in many cases, is content with a satisfactory solution. This statement is particularly true when such a solution is easy to implement. Why spend 100 hours of work to get a 20 percent return on a project investment when for 10 hours of work an 18 percent return can be obtained?

Simplification

Simplified models of reality are often employed.

A great deal of empirical evidence shows that many decision makers employ a simplified model of reality. If the manager has made a successful decision concerning a similar problem in the past, he or she quickly opts for the

---

5. Herbert A. Simon, *Administrative Behavior,* 3rd edition (New York: Free Press, 1976), p. xxix.

same type of decision again. The manager molds the problem to the solution instead of molding the solution to the problem.

If the situation is new, the manager may gather information about the problem. He or she is likely, however, to try to formulate an answer quickly. As a result, the first pieces of data uncovered are used as a foundation for the solution even when the information they present is inconclusive or incomplete. Managers may become overly concerned with making these data fit into a total composite solution. Unfortunately, such attempts at an early and simple answer often result in the screening out of all new incoming information, especially when this information challenges some of the initial input or indicates that the early solution may be wrong. Realizing that any acceptance of new information will require a reformulation of the entire answer, the manager ignores this input. The result is a simple, but erroneous, solution.[6]

Subjective Rationality

In determining the possible outcomes of alternative solutions, the manager is sometimes forced to assign probabilities subjectively. In this process, known as **subjective rationality,** probabilities are assigned based on personal judgment. Research shows that most people are ineffective when making such subjective assignments. They simply do not know how to determine the likelihood of a particular outcome, so they guess—and they do so incorrectly.[7] Moreover, as the complexity of the decision-making situation increases, most people become more and more conservative. As a result they become increasingly inaccurate in assigning probabilities. Others stop trying to obtain additional information, even when it can be secured easily and inexpensively, and start relying more heavily on personal judgment. Still others fall prey to one of the biggest problems of subjective probability assignment: they overestimate the likelihood of rare events and underestimate the likelihood of common events.

Sometimes managers make subjective probability assignments.

What accounts for such behavior? Numerous personality traits can be cited, including aggression, autonomy, intelligence, and fear of failure. Whatever the reason, subjective rationality leads to erroneous decision making.

Rationalization

Many decision makers rationalize their choice.

Empirical evidence also shows that many decision makers are rationalizers.[8] They go further than just choosing satisficing solutions: they choose those they can justify.

If time is short, the first feasible solution often is implemented. The decision maker rationalizes this choice by noting that there was no time for considering other possible solutions.

6. For more on this see: Richard M. Hodgetts and Steven Altman, *Organizational Behavior* (Philadelphia: W. B. Saunders, 1979), p. 287.

7. Cameron L. Peterson and Lee Roy Beach, "Man as an Intuitive Statistician," *Psychological Bulletin*, July 1967, pp. 29–46.

8. Roger Hagafors and Berndt Brehmer, "Does Having to Justify One's Judgments Change the Nature of the Judgment Process?" *Organizational Behavior and Human Performance*, April 1983, pp. 223–232.

Figure 6–3 Bounded Rationality Model

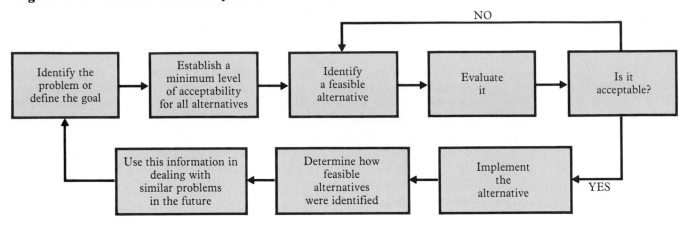

Even when a great deal of time is available, decision makers often make a final choice before examining all alternatives. As soon as this choice is made, all other alternatives are found to have some problem or shortcoming. As a result, the early choice becomes the final alternative. The decision maker defends or rationalizes this choice against all others. In the process the objectivity of rational decision making is replaced by the subjectivity of **bounded rationality.**

Bounded Rationality Process

As seen in Figure 6–3, eight steps are involved in bounded rationality. Notice that after the problem is identified or the goal is defined, a minimum level of acceptability is established. This is the satisficing factor at work. After a decision is implemented, it serves as a basis for dealing with similar problems in the future.

A close analysis of Figure 6–3 reveals that the bounded rationality model can save the manager a lot of time. It is also a more behaviorally acceptable approach for dealing with difficult or complex problems. So instead of comparing it with the rational decision making model to determine which is better, let us simply say that the bounded rationality model shows more accurately how decision making is actually carried out.

Improving Decision-Making Effectiveness

The major concern of American industry today is increasing productivity (output/input). This concern is being addressed through improved decision-making effectiveness. Whether a manager follows the rational decision making model or the bounded rationality model, he or she can improve decision-making effectiveness in several ways. Depending on the particular situation, these include (1) the use of management science tools and techniques, (2) creativity, and (3) the matching of decision-making situations and leadership styles. The following discussion examines these three approaches to decision-making effectiveness.

Use of Management Science Tools and Techniques

In some cases more effective decisions can be made through the use of management science tools or techniques.[9] Commonly referred to as *operations research* (OR), management science tools have four basic features: (1) they emphasize gathering and using information that helps the manager make a useful decision; (2) they try to determine the highest profit/lowest cost decision commensurate with the end results; (3) they employ mathematical models; and (4) they rely on the computer to perform the necessary mathematical calculations.

Quite often an organization will develop a specific OR tool or technique to help it solve a particular problem. In other cases there is already a prepackaged program for dealing with the problem. In either event, OR techniques have been used frequently to solve many different types of problems. Five of the most common techniques are described in the following discussion. In all but the last case, only a qualitative description of the technique is provided. There are two reasons for treating the subject in this way. First, our objective is to show how management science techniques can be of value in decision making, not how to perform quantitative analysis. Second, modern managers need to know what these tools can do, but they themselves do not need to know the specific mathematical mechanics except in the case of such "hands on" tools as decision trees, the last technique to be examined.

Inventory Problems

No firm wants to have too much inventory on hand. The greater the amount of inventory, the higher the cost of storage and insurance as well as the possibility that the goods will become obsolete or that demand for them will decline. On the other hand, if there is too little inventory on hand the organization will be continually running out of stock, the costs of ordering inventory will rise, and customers may soon turn to more reliable suppliers.

How can inventory be balanced so that these problems do not occur? The answer is found in an OR program known as the **economic order quantity (EOQ) formula.** By taking the costs associated with carrying inventory and balancing them against annual demand for the product, an organization can determine an ideal inventory level. The formula tells how much to reorder each time.

The formula is

$$\sqrt{\frac{2(D)(F)}{(P)(C)}}$$

where

D = expected annual demand

F = fixed cost associated with placing and receiving a single order

P = price per unit

C = carrying costs associated with storage, insurance, taxes, spoilage, etc., as a percentage of inventory value

"I don't know whether to have prune danish or a jelly doughnut, Miss Edwards. Will you run it through the computer for me?"

Balancing demand and carrying costs

---

9. Jacob W. Ulvila and Rex V. Brown, "Decision Analysis Comes of Age," *Harvard Business Review,* September–October 1982, pp. 130–141.

To see how this formula works, assume that a manager has a product line with an expected annual demand of 500,000 units, a reorder cost of $10, a price of $100, and a carrying cost of 10 percent. Putting these values into the formula results in the following:

$$\sqrt{\frac{2(500,000)(\$10)}{(\$100)(.10)}} = \sqrt{\frac{10,000,000}{10}}$$
$$= \sqrt{1,000,000}$$
$$= 1,000$$

The manager should reorder 1,000 units every time. Ordering more units a lesser number of times drives up the carrying costs; ordering fewer units a greater number of times drives up the reordering costs. The EOQ formula helps the manager balance these two costs.

Of course, the manager does not actually compute the formula and place the order. Firms using the EOQ have their decision making computerized, so the computer tells the purchasing manager what to reorder and how many items to request. This determination is based on the current depletion of inventory, the EOQ, and the amount of time between when an order is placed and when it is filled. For example, if the current depletion of inventory is 10 units a day, the EOQ is 100 units, and delivery takes three days, the 100 units must be ordered at least three days before they are needed. Otherwise there will be a shortage of this good. The EOQ formula helps the organization manage its inventory problems.

Allocation Problems

Many times an organization finds that it has a large number of parts or materials to use for producing its products. If the organization has two or more product lines, however, it has to decide whether to put all the resources into one product line or to produce some of each. This is an allocation problem because the manager needs to determine how to allocate or assign the parts for production.

One way of solving the problem is to produce as many units as possible of the most profitable product and allocate the remaining parts to the next most successful lines in the order of profitability. The most profitable product may take three times as many parts as the next most profitable line, however, thereby severely limiting the number that can be produced. So this is not always the best strategy for maximizing profit. In fact, sometimes the answer is to make a combination of product lines such as 500 units of Product A, 350 units of Product B, and 200 units of Product C. The answer is determined by finding the ideal mix or the combination of products that will yield the highest profit. When the number of parts and product lines is more than a handful, this answer can be difficult to work out in one's head. In this case, OR can help. Linear programming formulas can quickly and easily determine the best mix. What is a difficult problem to work out mentally can be resolved via a mathematical approach.

Ideal allocation of resources

Queuing Problems

Queuing problems are waiting-line problems. These arise any time there is a need to balance service with waiting time. Numerous examples can

Balancing customer waiting time and service

be cited, from the time it takes to be served at the local supermarket to the time it takes to load a truck at the warehouse and send it on its way. The longer the waiting time, the greater the loss of business. Since many purchasers will not return to the store if they have to wait one hour in a supermarket line, the store needs to look into opening more checkout lines. In the case of the warehouse, the firm needs to examine the payoff from increasing the number of people loading the trucks as well as the cost of building more loading stations.

Of course, there is a limit to the amount of service the organization should provide. If service is too great, customers may be very happy and trucks may be loaded quickly but the business will lose money because the cost of the service more than outweighs any benefits. The cost curve associated with service is illustrated in Figure 6–4.

Using an OR approach known as the *queuing theory,* the organization can balance waiting lines and service. In this way waiting is reduced to an acceptable level while profit is maximized.

Replacement Problems

Over time every organization has to replace obsolete or worn-out machinery and equipment. If kept too long these assets become inefficient and increasingly expensive to operate. The question for the manager is: When should replacement take place?

There are OR programs that can answer this question, depending on its exact nature. For example, consider a large factory floor where there are thousands of overhead lights. When should each be replaced? There are basically two answers: as each goes out or all at once. An OR program for dealing with this problem can help compare the cost of replacing each

Figure 6–4
Cost and Service

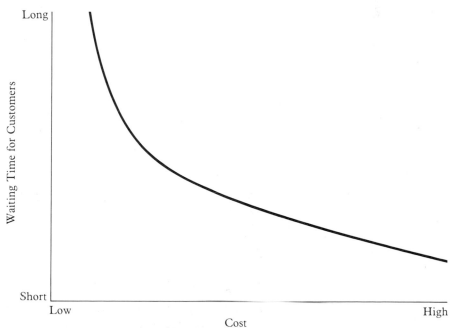

An economical replacement decision

light as it goes out with the cost of changing all of them at the same time. In most cases the company will replace all of the lights at a predetermined time because that is more cost effective.

Another typical replacement problem is determining when to fix worn or used machinery. By keeping a log on machine breakdown, the company can forecast the number of hours before the next breakdown will occur. Then it can decide whether to do preventive maintenance first or to go ahead with the next job. By simulating machine breakdown, OR can help the manager decide the best time for conducting preventive maintenance. Once again, an OR approach can produce an efficient answer.

Decision Trees

A decision tree depicts a decision graphically.

A **decision tree** is a graphic illustration of a management decision in which those aspects of a decision that are often implicit are made explicit. In constructing such a tree the manager begins by setting forth all of the alternative approaches to the problem, the payoffs associated with each, and the probability of success for each. From this information an expected value is then computed and the path with the greatest expected value is chosen for implementation. Figure 6–5 shows a decision tree for plant expansion.

In this decision tree, the manager is confronted with three alternatives

Figure 6–5 Decision Tree for Plant Expansion

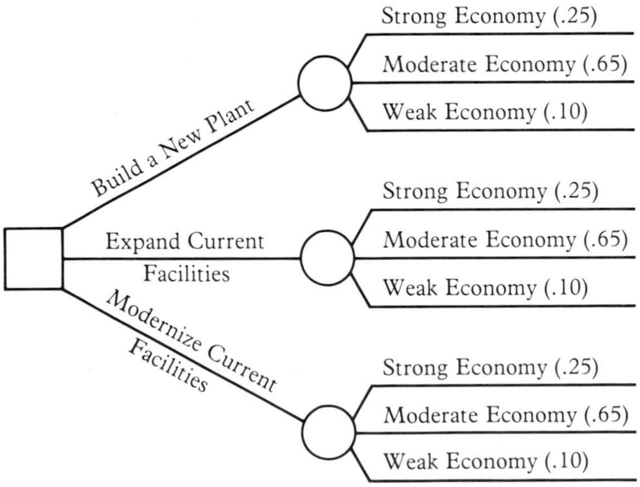

	Conditional Value for Each Outcome	Probability of Each Outcome	Expected Value of Each Outcome	Expected Value of Each Decision Alternative
Build a New Plant				
Strong Economy (.25)	$3,000,000	.25	$750,000	
Moderate Economy (.65)	1,000,000	.65	650,000	
Weak Economy (.10)	400,000	.10	40,000	$1,440,000
Expand Current Facilities				
Strong Economy (.25)	2,000,000	.25	500,000	
Moderate Economy (.65)	1,500,000	.65	975,000	
Weak Economy (.10)	100,000	.10	10,000	1,485,000*
Modernize Current Facilities				
Strong Economy (.25)	1,000,000	.25	250,000	
Moderate Economy (.65)	500,000	.65	325,000	
Weak Economy (.10)	300,000	.10	30,000	605,000

*Alternative to implement.

for dealing with current production facilities: building a new plant, expanding the current one, or modernizing present facilities. The decision maker has determined that one of these alternatives must be implemented. The decision tree can help the manager make the choice. To see how it can help, let us first examine the tree in greater depth.

Note that the tree is constructed from left to right. The decision maker first identifies the alternatives under consideration. Next he or she determines the conditional value of each outcome. This is the value or benefit the firm will obtain under each of three possible economic states. For example, if the firm builds a new plant and the economy is strong, the company will make $3 million. If the economy is weak, the company will make only $400,000. Third, the decision maker determines the probability of each of these economic states. Notice that the likelihood of a strong economy is 0.25 while the likelihood of a moderate economy is 0.65 and the likelihood of a weak economy is 0.10. Fourth, he or she computes the expected value of each outcome by multiplying the conditional value by the probability of its occurrence. Finally, the decision maker computes the expected values of each decision alternative by adding up the expected values for each of its outcomes. In Figure 6–5 the highest expected value is associated with expanding current facilities, so that is the alternative the manager should implement.

The expected value for each decision alternative is determined.

Decision trees are very useful in helping managers deal with nonrecurring events. They help decision makers see clearly the alternatives and the likely outcomes of each. Two points of clarification are in order, however. First, once the manager has constructed the decision tree, assigned the probabilities, and computed the expected values of each alternative, he or she must choose the one with the highest expected value. The manager cannot go back and say, "Oh, I've always wanted to build a new plant so let's do that." If this is what the manager wanted all along, why did he or she waste time with decision-tree analysis? Decision trees help the manager analyze alternatives objectively, and the answer they point to should be implemented, not altered. Second, in interpreting decision trees, the manager must remember that the expected values are only relative measures of values used to compare one alternative with another. For example, if the firm expands current facilities and the economy is strong, the company will make $2 million. It will not earn the expected value of $1,485,000. Depending on the state of the economy, the firm will earn $2 million, $1.5 million, or $100,000.[10]

Decision trees are useful for nonrecurring events.

Creativity and Group Decision Making

In some cases decision making can be improved through the use of creativity or group decision analysis or both. This is particularly true when the problem requires an innovative or unique approach.

---

10. For more on decision-tree analysis, see Efrain Turban and Jack R. Meredith, *Fundamentals of Management Science,* revised edition (Dallas, Texas: Business Publications, Inc., 1981), Chapter 4.

Creative Thinking Process

Creative thinking and decision making actually go hand in hand. In particular, creative thinking can help generate alternative solutions to the problem under review.[11] The **creative thinking process** involves four steps: preparation, incubation, illumination, and verification.

Preparation is the stage in which the decision maker gets ready mentally. During this period he or she gathers all of the available information on the problem. This stage involves problem definition and analysis. At this time the decision maker becomes saturated with data.

After gathering data the decision maker sits back and lets his or her subconscious mind work on the problem. This is the *incubation* period. During this time the brain analyzes and rearranges information, often presenting it in a new or innovative way. At this stage the decision maker also develops alternative solutions to problems. Of course, if no solution is forthcoming after a period of time, such as 10 days, the decision maker is wise to go back to the preparation stage and review the data again.

In the *illumination* stage the decision maker realizes the answer to the problem. The answer usually does not come like a bolt out of the blue. More commonly it comes in bits and pieces, revealing itself slowly. This characteristic of illumination is particularly true in the case of complex problems. As the decision maker works out parts of the problem, he or she writes them down until the entire solution has been determined.

Verification is the last stage of creative thinking and involves testing the answer. In most cases there is a need to refine or rethink some part of it. For example, an inventor usually has to do some trial-and-error work to eliminate minor bugs. Modification and improvement smooths the way for implementing the solution.

Brainstorming

Sometimes creative thinking is an individual process but groups can use it as well. In fact, groups are often superior to individuals when it comes to generating creative ideas. One of the most popular approaches to group creative thinking is brainstorming.

Brainstorming was developed by Alex F. Osborn as a method of encouraging creative thinking in an advertising agency. Since then the technique has been applied in many situations where the objective is to obtain a large number of ideas for solving a problem. A brainstorming session begins with the group leader telling the members the problem under analysis and encouraging them to be as imaginative and creative as possible in their recommended solutions. During the session criticism is forbidden, and group members can say what they want. Emphasis is placed on quantity, and as one group member calls out ideas, other group members are allowed to combine some of them or improve them in any way they see fit.

These sessions usually last from 40 to 60 minutes and involve six to nine participants. The members sit around a table, so that they are able

First comes mental readiness . . .

then subconscious analysis . . .

followed by an answer . . .

which is then refined and used.

Brainstorming encourages imaginative, creative solutions.

---

11. Charles E. Wilson, "Managerial Mind Sets and the Structural Side of Managing," *Business Horizons*, November–December 1983, pp. 21–27.

to communicate quickly and easily. As ideas are called out, a secretary or recording machine keeps track of what is said. In some cases ideas are written down on a blackboard so that group members can expand or piggyback on them more easily.

Of course, many of the ideas thrown out may be of little value. Some are superficial, others too imaginative to be workable. To the extent that brainstorming helps generate plausible solutions that could not be obtained in routine ways, however, it is a valuable decision-making technique.

Gordon Technique

The Gordon technique addresses technical problems.

Another group participation, problem-solving technique has been developed by William J. Gordon. It is used for handling technical problems.[12] Commonly referred to as the **Gordon technique,** it is similar to brainstorming in that it employs free association. When this approach is used, however, only the group leader knows the problem under consideration. He or she gives a hint or a stimulus to the other group members, and the discussion begins.

> For example, if the group leader wanted the participants to come up with ideas on auto engine designs that might lead to better mileage, the key phrase might be "better mileage." From here the members would toss out all sorts of ideas. Some ideas might be valuable in redesigning current engines, while others might be more useful on some other project in the future. In any event, the Gordon technique is an excellent method for obtaining creative ideas for solving technical problems.[13]

In most cases the group sessions last from two to three hours. The members often come from diverse backgrounds, although all are capable of understanding and responding to the technical problem. As with brainstorming, in most cases group size is six to nine people. With this technique a blackboard is always used so that ideas can be written down and seen by all.

When creative solutions for technical problems are needed, the Gordon technique can be very useful. In particular it provides an approach for generating innovative solutions to what is often a mechanistic, engineering-oriented challenge. The result can be a solution superior to that obtained by typical individual or group decision-making processes.

Matching Decision-Making Situations and Leadership Styles

Some researchers have noted that decision-making effectiveness can also be improved by matching leadership styles and problem situations. In illus-

---

12. Charles S. Whiting, "Operational Techniques of Creative Thinking," *Advanced Management Journal,* October 1955, p. 28.

13. Richard M. Hodgetts, *Introduction to Business,* 3rd edition (Reading, Mass.: Addison-Wesley Publishing, 1984), p. 471.

trating how this can be done, let us first identify five types of management decision styles:

1. The manager can solve the problem or make the decision personally by using the information that is available at that point in time.

2. The manager can obtain the necessary information from the subordinates, and then decide on the solution to the problem. In obtaining the information the manager may or may not tell the subordinates what the problem is. Their role in making the decision is confined solely to providing the necessary information rather than generating or evaluating alternative solutions.

There are five types of management decision styles.

3. The manager can share the problem with relevant subordinates on an individual basis, obtaining their ideas and suggestions without bringing them together as a group. Then a decision, which may or may not represent the views of the subordinates, can be made.

4. The manager can share the problem with the subordinates as a group, collectively obtain their ideas and suggestions, and then make a decision that may or may not reflect the subordinates' influence.

5. The manager can share the problem with the subordinates as a group. Together all can generate and evaluate alternatives and try to reach a consensus on a solution. The manager's role here is one of a chairperson. The manager does not try to influence the group to adopt his or her solution, and he or she is willing to accept and implement any solution that has the support of the entire group.[14]

In deciding which of these decision styles to use, the manager asks a series of diagnostic questions. The answers to these questions help the individual decide what to do. These seven questions are presented in Figure 6–6. A close examination of the figure reveals that the questions at the top (A through G) help dictate which of the five decision styles to use. For example, if the manager feels that there is a quality requirement such that one solution is likely to be more rational than another (Question A) and acceptance of the decision by subordinates is not critical to implementation (Question D), then management decision style #1 should be used. The manager can solve the problem or make the decision personally by using the information that is available at that point in time. The same logic can be used in going through all of the other paths in the flow chart.

Using diagnostic questions to choose decision styles

This framework for analyzing decision making is very useful. It helps the manager identify the various approaches that can be employed in making decisions. At the same time it offers flexibility. For example, if the manager has a group problem, he or she can share it with subordinates on an individual basis (management decision style #3) or in a group (management decision style #5). There is no one set way of handling everything. As Victor Vroom, one of the individuals who helped develop Figure 6–6, has noted, however, when several management styles are possible, the manager should select the one that will cost the least in terms of time or resources. Thus some

---

14. Victor H. Vroom, "A New Look at Managerial Decision Making," *Organizational Dynamics*, January 1973, p. 67.

Figure 6–6 A Decision Process Flow Chart

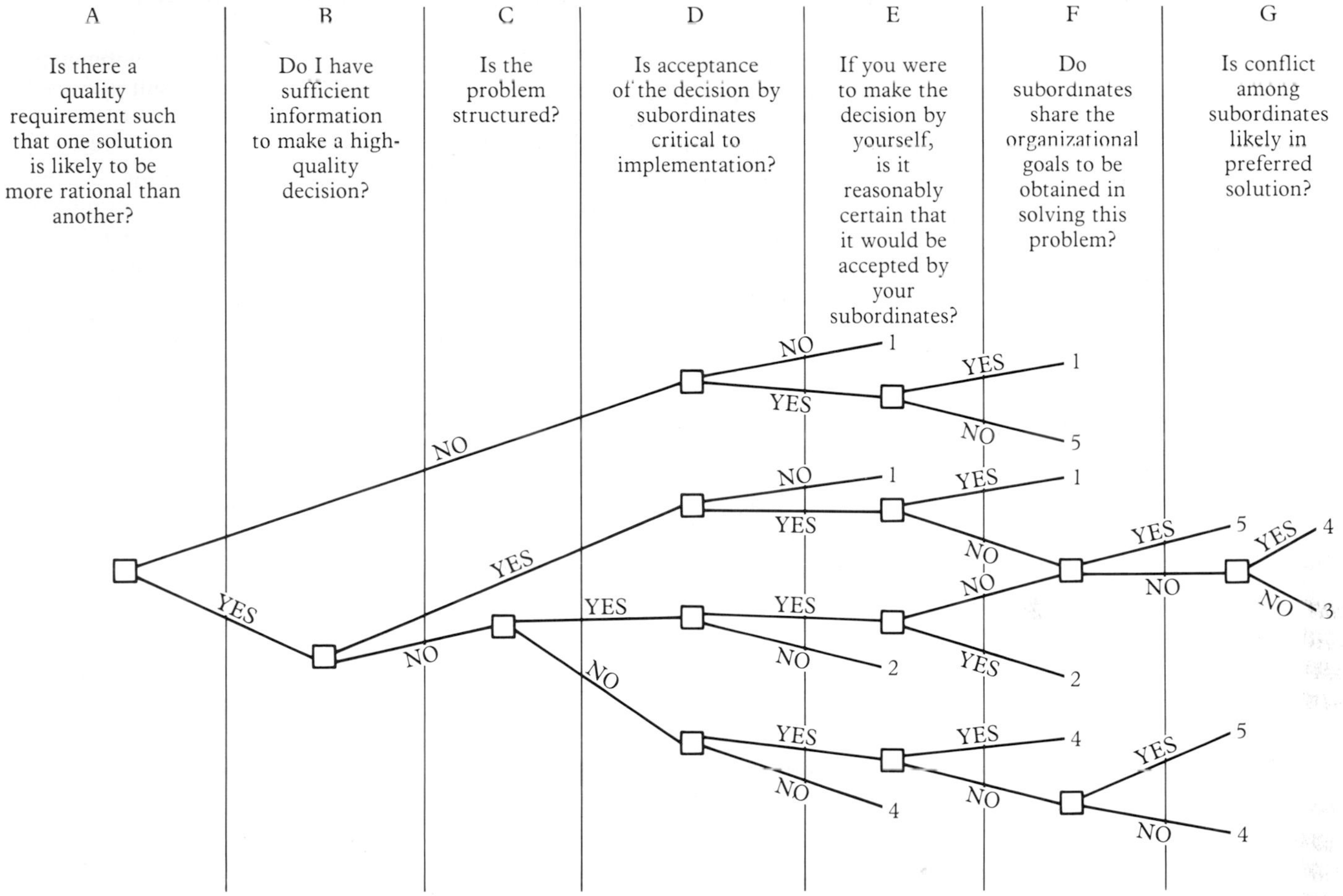
A
Is there a quality requirement such that one solution is likely to be more rational than another?
B
Do I have sufficient information to make a high-quality decision?
C
Is the problem structured?
D
Is acceptance of the decision by subordinates critical to implementation?
E
If you were to make the decision by yourself, is it reasonably certain that it would be accepted by your subordinates?
F
Do subordinates share the organizational goals to be obtained in solving this problem?
G
Is conflict among subordinates likely in preferred solution?

Reprinted, by permission of the publisher, from "A New Look At Managerial Decision Making," Victor H. Vroom, *Organizational Dynamics*, Spring 1973 © 1973 by AMACOM, a division of American Management Associations. Page 70. All rights reserved.

judgment on the manager's part is involved in the process. The decision process flow chart is only a recommended guideline for improving decision making; it is not a mechanistic approach for solving all problems.

Summary

1. Decision making is the process of choosing from among alternatives. Sometimes this process is a simple one and rules, policies, procedures, or basic quantitative analysis can be used in making the decision. At other times the process is a complex one and requires the manager to draw on intuition, judgment, gut feeling, and highly mathematical tools and techniques.
2. In understanding the basic nature of decision making, the manager needs to know four things. The first is how to review the situation properly. In doing so, there are three questions the manager must answer: Will the problem resolve itself? Does the issue require a personal decision? How should the problem be handled? The second thing the manager should know is the difference between programmed and nonprogrammed decisions. The third is the

conditions under which decision making is carried out: certainty, risk, and uncertainty. The fourth is the guidelines for making effective decisions.

3. When making decisions under risk conditions, the manager needs to make probability assignments. These allow him or her to determine what combination of profit and probability of success each alternative offers. The result is known as the expected value. By comparing the expected values of all alternatives, the manager can opt for the alternative with the greatest expected value.

4. When making decisions under conditions of uncertainty, the manager feels unable to assign probability estimates to any of the alternatives. As a result, he or she may use the mathematical techniques that have been developed to help deal with this problem. Other suggestions include simply avoiding situations of uncertainty, assuming that the future will be like the past and assigning probabilities based on previous experiences, and gathering as much information as possible about each alternative while assuming that the decision is being made under a condition of risk and assigning probabilities accordingly.

5. Rational decision making consists of seven basic steps: (1) uncovering the symptoms, (2) identifying the problem or defining the goal, (3) developing decision criteria, (4) developing alternative solutions, (5) determining all alternative solution outcomes, (6) selecting the best alternative, and (7) implementing the decision.

6. Bounded rationality considerations refine the rational decision-making model. These considerations include satisficing behavior, simplification, subjective rationality, and rationalization. The result is a bounded rationality model consisting of the following steps: (1) identifying the problem or defining the goals, (2) establishing a minimum level of acceptability for all alternatives, (3) identifying a feasible alternative, (4) evaluating it, (5) determining whether it is acceptable, (6) if it is not, going back to step three; if it is, implementing the alternative, (7) determining how feasible alternatives were discovered, and (8) using this information in dealing with similar problems in the future.

7. Decision making can be improved in a number of different ways. One is by using management science tools and techniques. Some of the most helpful include those that solve inventory, allocation, and replacement problems. Another important tool is the decision tree. By determining the alternatives, the conditional values for each outcome, the probability of each outcome, and the expected value of each outcome, the decision maker can determine the expected value of each decision alternative. The decision alternative with the largest expected value is then chosen for implementation.

8. Creative thinking involves four steps: preparation, incubation, illumination, and verification. During the preparation stage the decision maker gets ready mentally. During incubation he or she sits back and lets the subconscious mind work on the problem. During the illumination period the solution comes to the decision maker. During the verification period the answer is tested, and modified if necessary, to smooth the way for implementation.

9. Brainstorming is a group approach to creative thinking. The group leader tells the group members the problem under analysis and encourages them to be as imaginative and creative as possible. Criticism is forbidden; freewheeling is encouraged; and individuals are allowed to combine ideas or piggyback on them in an effort to improve them. The Gordon Technique is another group creative thinking approach. However, it is used only to deal with technical problems. The group leader does not spell out the problem but rather gives the participants only a hint or stimulus before the discussion begins.

10. Some researchers have noted that decision-making effectiveness can also be improved by matching styles and problem situations. The five styles described

in the latter part of the chapter are combined with the problem situations presented in Figure 6–6 to illustrate this idea. Managers who want to improve their decision making can use this type of approach to help them make more effective decisions.

Key Terms

Administrative man   An individual who looks for a course of action that is satisfactory or good enough.

Bounded rationality   A model of decision making that illustrates how most managers make decisions by requiring minimum levels of acceptability and using "satisficing" criteria.

Brainstorming   A group creative-thinking technique. It involves telling the group members what the problem is and then encouraging them to be as imaginative as possible, allowing each to expand and piggyback on the ideas of others in the group in an effort to improve earlier suggestions.

Certainty   A decision-making condition under which the manager has enough information to know the outcome of the decision before it is made.

Creative thinking process   A process used for generating innovative or unique approaches to problem solving. It consists of four steps: preparation, incubation, illumination, and verification.

Decision tree   A graphic illustration of a management decision that shows the various alternatives, the conditional values of each outcome, the probabilities of each outcome, the expected value of each outcome, and the expected value of each decision alternative.

Economic man   An individual who always strives to implement the decision that will provide the maximum payoff.

Economic order quantity (EOQ) formula   An inventory control formula. The purpose of the EOQ is to balance demand for a product against the costs associated with carrying the inventory.

Gordon technique   A group participation, group-problem-solving technique that is commonly used for handling technical problems. The group leader gives the group members a hint or stimulus about the problem and encourages them to be as creative as possible in arriving at suggested solutions.

Nonprogrammed decisions   Decisions that are unique or out of the ordinary. They are often ill structured and are handled by judgment, intuition, and creativity.

Programmed decisions   Decisions that rely upon habit, routine, standard operating procedures, or some other well-defined method.

Rational decision-making process   A process that describes how decisions are made in the ideal. It involves the following steps: (1) uncovering the symptoms, (2) identifying the problem or defining the goal, (3) developing decision criteria, (4) developing alternative solutions, (5) determining all alternative solution outcomes, (6) selecting the best alternative, and (7) implementing the decision.

Risk   A decision-making condition under which the manager has some information regarding the outcome of the decision but does not know everything.

Satisficing behavior   Decision-making behavior in which the individual chooses a course of action that is merely satisfactory or good enough.

Subjective rationality   The assignment of probabilities based on personal judgment.

Uncertainty   A decision-making condition under which the manager feels incapable of assigning probabilities to the various outcomes.

Questions for Analysis and Discussion

1. In handling simple problems, a decision maker often relies on rules, policies, procedures, and basic quantitative analysis. In handling complex problems, a decision maker employs intuition, judgment, gut feeling, and highly mathematical tools and techniques. Are these two statements accurate? Explain.

2. What are the three questions a manager should ask in reviewing a decision-making situation? Briefly discuss each.

3. How do programmed decisions differ from nonprogrammed decisions? Compare and contrast the two.

4. Decisions are made under one of three possible conditions: certainty, risk, and uncertainty. What does this statement mean? Be complete in your answer.

5. Are there any guidelines that can help a manager improve his or her effectiveness? State and explain at least five.

6. How does the rational decision-making process work? Describe each of the steps. Then compare it with the bounded rationality model. How are the two similar? How do they differ?

7. What is meant by the term "satisficing behavior"? How does it help describe decision-making behavior?

8. In what way do the following characteristics describe decision making in action: simplification, subjective rationality, and rationalization? Explain.

9. How can management science tools and techniques be of value in dealing with problems in these areas: inventory, allocation, and replacement? Explain each.

10. In your own words, what is a decision tree? How can a decision tree help the manager make effective decisions? Be complete in your answer.

11. How can leadership styles be tied together with decision-making situations? Explain, being sure to include the steps in Figure 6–6 in your answer.

Case

One, Two, or Three?

For the last six months Chuck Beatty, a product development manager, has been engaged in the design and market testing of three new electronic games. Chuck's company has five product development managers. Each is responsible for working with the design, engineering, and manufacturing departments to produce one electronic game every six months. Each is also responsible for working with three marketing people to market-test the product. Since the company puts such an emphasis on turning out a winner each time, it is typical for each product development manager to start with three to five games and, for either technical or marketing reasons, to reduce the final choice to one. Over the last two years Chuck has had the best-selling game each time. The other product development managers admit Chuck is the best. He would like to keep it this way.

The next new electronic game is to be presented by the product development managers to the manufacturing and marketing executives in six days. Right now Chuck is in the throes of making a final decision. He has taken

Exhibit 1
Decision Tree

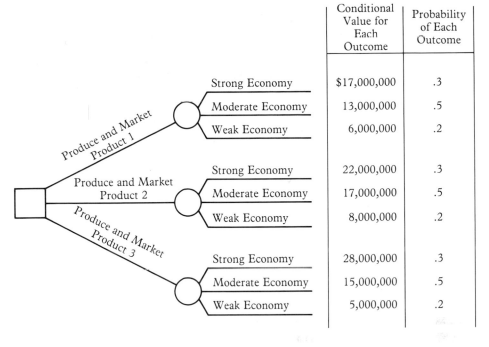

	Conditional Value for Each Outcome	Probability of Each Outcome
Produce and Market Product 1		
Strong Economy	$17,000,000	.3
Moderate Economy	13,000,000	.5
Weak Economy	6,000,000	.2
Produce and Market Product 2		
Strong Economy	22,000,000	.3
Moderate Economy	17,000,000	.5
Weak Economy	8,000,000	.2
Produce and Market Product 3		
Strong Economy	28,000,000	.3
Moderate Economy	15,000,000	.5
Weak Economy	5,000,000	.2

all of the manufacturing data he has available and constructed the decision tree in Exhibit 1.

To the best of his knowledge, this tree is accurate. The marketing people on the project have told him, however, that a new survey they conducted last week shows that forecasted profits for Product 1 may be 35 to 50 percent higher than initial estimates suggested. Chuck is unsure whether to include this information or go with what he has currently. Time is short, and he must make a final decision soon.

1. Describe Chuck's decision-making process. Is it closer to the rational or bounded rationality process? Explain in detail.

2. Is Chuck making a decision under conditions of certainty, risk, or uncertainty? Defend your answer.

3. Drawing upon the information in the decision tree, decide which product Chuck should opt for. Would your answer change if the conditional profits for Product 1 were increased by 40 percent? Explain.

You Be the Consultant

The $10 Million Project

Memorial Hospital has been in existence for more than 80 years. Built just after the turn of the century, Memorial has expanded its facilities three times. Today the hospital has 575 beds and offers a wide range of health services. In fact, a large portion of the institution's budget is spent for medical equipment and research.

A recent survey conducted in the local community reveals that Memorial Hospital is considered to be the best health care facility in the city. In an effort to keep this reputation, Mary McKenna, the hospital administrator, is planning a $10 million capital expenditure proposal designed to increase the number of beds, the overall facilities, and the health care services. At the present time she has a report put together by an outside consulting group that shows that the local population will grow by 44 percent during the next 10 years. A large percentage of this growth will be among the elderly (60 years and older), which is not surprising since Memorial is located in a major southeastern city famous for its mild winters.

Based on an analysis of this consulting report, Mary's initial conclusion is that the hospital will need to increase the number of beds by 75 and expand its emergency room and outpatient services to approximately double their present size. By coupling these demands with the other changes needed to modernize the facilities, Mary has arrived at an initial estimate of $10 million. Before taking this proposal to the board of trustees, however, she wants to work up the report in depth so that every part of it is clear and can be justified.

Mary believes that the best way to do this is to call together her immediate subordinates and discuss the proposal with them. In analyzing the decision process, she has concluded that (1) there is not a quality requirement such that one solution is likely to be more rational than another; (2) acceptance of the decision by the subordinates is critical to implementation; and (3) the subordinates do indeed share the organizational goals to be obtained in solving this problem. Mary also believes that a creative approach to writing and presenting the report might be helpful. It would help pull together all of the data in a unique way and might go a long way toward selling the trustees on the proposal.

Over the last five years, under Mary's direction, Memorial has made money each year. Prior to her arrival, however, the hospital head managed finances poorly, and Mary knows that many of the board members are fiscally conservative. She is going to have to do a good selling job to get them to go along with her proposal. Among other things, she will have to show the board how the expenditure will result in increased revenue and maintenance of the hospital's current reputation. Some of the board's biggest arguments are going to be: "Why do we need to spend all of this money? What are we going to get for this? Is this really a wise decision? Can't we accomplish almost the same thing for a lot less?"

Mary has decided to use the next six months getting everything in order. Then she will give the board members a copy of her report, ask them to read it over and note their questions, and schedule a day for intensive discussion. Mary is convinced that this selling job will take almost six months, but she can do it if she lays the proper groundwork now.

Your Consultation

Assume that you are Mary's personal consultant. Help her better understand how to put this report together and present it. First, explain the decision-making process she should use. Second, help her match this decision-making situation with her leadership style in dealing with subordinates. (Use Figure 6–6 to assist you.) Third, describe to her how creativity in decision making can be promoted and tell whether such an approach would have any value. Fourth, drawing upon your study of the material in this chapter, tell her anything else you believe would be helpful to her. Be as complete as possible in your recommendations.

Comprehensive Cases

The MDP Corporation

History

The MDP Corporation is engaged principally in manufacturing, engineering, construction, and worldwide marketing of steel-based products and services predominantly for heavy industrial applications. While the company's statutory head office remains in Tennessee, worldwide operations are handled by a corporate executive group in Chicago, Illinois.

Commitment to Growth

Founded in 1882 as a builder of steel bridges, MDP has—particularly during the last decade—achieved a high degree of product, service, and geographical diversity through a program of acquisitions. The key to this development has been its commitment to its own expertise and its highly selective approach in acquiring other companies. The characteristics MDP looks for in evaluating a potential acquisition include

1. strong management at the operating level,

2. a reputation for well-known, engineered proprietary products that are marketable worldwide,

3. the expertise and experience to make possible a healthy interchange of ideas and skills with other businesses within MDP, and

4. a demonstrated record of profitability, growth, and return on investment.

Through selective acquisition of companies meeting these criteria, as well as internal growth, the company has been able to provide an increasing degree of leadership in the markets it participates in.

Product Lines

Before the 1970s, MDP's primary business was fabricating and erecting steel bridges, buildings, and building products. Its skills in fabrication and erection of steel structures, honed over the past century, earned the firm a reputation as the builder of nearly every major bridge and landmark building in America.

Over the years MDP has become recognized worldwide for contributions to the art of welding and joining steel. This firm's technical knowledge is a result of its research and development in Tennessee, which is almost wholly devoted to the study of welding techniques and materials. The company is also known for rolled steel produced at Midwest Rolling Mills (MRM). MRM products are sold directly to customers and distributed through a coast-to-coast network of company-owned and operated steel service centers.

Additionally, the firm fabricates and installs (a) structures for electric utility industry powerhouses, specialty bridges, cranes, and transmission towers, (b) specialized structures for nuclear power installations such as heavy water process columns, cooling towers, pressure vessels, reactor cores, and airlocks, and (c) a diversity of hydraulic gates, penstocks, spiral cases, and hydraulic turbines for the hydroelectric power industry. MDP also builds grain- and coal-handling facilities, specialty weighing scales, crude oil pumping units, chemical processing plants, heavy industrial cranes, and materials-handling systems and equipment.

From the 1970s to Date

During the 1970s, the company embarked on a period of diversification and growth through acquisition. By the close of the decade, MDP was a major North American enterprise with business interests throughout the world. During this period, the company adhered to its philosophy of acquiring businesses that shared its own expertise of steel-based products and services marketed worldwide, primarily to industrial accounts. Overall corporate management was handled by the corporate executive group working in close collaboration with the various units. As a result of its acquisitions and management approach, the firm became well known for its structural steel, plate steel fabrication, and steel erection services. The product line expanded to include (1) engineered fasteners, (2) precision-machined helicopter parts, (3) preengineered buildings, (4) cranes and hoists, (5) chain saws, (6) tugboats, (7) offshore marine terminals for moving liquid and slurry cargoes, (8) design and construction of petroleum refineries and chemical processing plants, (9) alloy metals forging for high-technology applications, (10) design, construction, and management of dry bulk materials-handling facilities, (11) foam seating and carpet underpadding for the automotive industry, and (12) processing and packaging machinery for the food, pharmaceutical, and beverage industries.

Most recently, MDP acquired the Blackwell Corporation, thereby expanding its products and services to include the design, production, and marketing of excavators, cranes, and compaction and concrete finishing equipment for the construction industry, hydraulic equipment, bearings, and service mechanisms for specialty industrial applications, and woodlands production and harvesting equipment.

Today the company and its subsidiaries have more than 60 operating plants in six countries and employ more than 16,000 employees. It markets products and services in more than 100 countries while also providing significant financial and licensing services worldwide. In addition, the group operates a substantial number of engineering and sales offices in the United States, Canada, Europe, the United Kingdom, the Middle East, and the Far East.

As the company entered the 1970s, annual sales were $168 million. During that decade, MDP achieved a 28 percent compounded annual growth rate in earnings per share—better than 95 percent of the Fortune 500. Over the course of the 10-year period that concluded December 31, 1980, the firm multiplied sales fivefold, increased operating income sevenfold, and increased dividends per share eightfold.

With the acquisition of Blackwell in 1981, the company's annual volume increased about $500 million to the $1.5 billion level. While growth, diversification, and overall progress had been notable up to that point, however, management did not intend to rest on its laurels. As the firm moved into the 1980s, it did so with a well-planned road map in hand which, if properly executed, could produce another attractive decade for the company's shareholders.

Financially, MDP was targeted for sales of $5 billion and an operating income of $270 million by the end of the 1980s. Good progress toward this goal was achieved with the acquisition of Blackwell Corporation. Continuing execution of the company's plans should make it a source for an even wider range of industrial, steel-based products and quality services for a widening spectrum of customers and prospects.

Targeted Areas for Management Strategies

Products from many of the company's operating units are used the world over for both light and heavy construction projects. They range from manual tools to large, heavy-duty equipment for lifting, digging, drilling, and compacting. Also included in MDP's line are complete preengineered buildings as well as custom-designed steel structures and building components. The diversity of construction products manufactured by the company is significant. Cranes, excavators, and compaction equipment are produced under other familiar names. The following directory lists the overall operations of the firm and the divisions into which they can be organized:

Divisional Name	Products Manufactured
Elray Company	Hydraulic excavators for light duty carry the Elray name. These versatile machines are used for trenching and rough grading. Elray also manufactures hydraulic rough terrain and truck cranes in smaller sizes. Elray excavators and cranes are self-propelled, carrier- or crawler-mounted.
Gamco Company	Gamco compaction equipment ranges from walk-behind plate and double-drum vibratory compactors to large segmented-wheel earth compactors, soil stabilizers, landfill refuse compactors and road rollers produced in single- or double-drum vibratory or static configuration. Gamco manufacturing and/or distribution locations are also found in Great Britain, France, Austria, Japan, and South Africa.
Bisset Manufacturing	Bisset manufactures revolving cranes and specialized equipment for lifting and pulling extremely heavy loads. These cranes are used in shipyards

Divisional Name	Products Manufactured
	for construction, repair of vessels, maintenance, and loading. The petroleum industry uses these cranes aboard barges, ships, and drilling platforms for functions essential to exploration and production processes. These cranes also have stevedoring and heavy construction uses.
Blackwell Group Offices	Administrative and selected marketing functions are conducted at Blackwell's group offices.
Blackwell Excavation Corp.	Heavy-duty hydraulic excavators and cable cranes carry the Blackwell Corp.'s name. Excavators are used for strip mining, harbor dredging, trenching, and rough grading. Excavators and cranes are crawler-mounted.
Blackwell Construction Equipment	Blackwell Construction Equipment manufactures and markets a variety of equipment under Blackwell and other trade names. Included are concrete trowels, vibrators and engine alternators, and construction forklifts.
Tennessee-Blackwell Co.	Tennessee manufactures hydraulic boom, lattice boom, and tower boom cranes that are self-propelled, carrier- or crawler-mounted in a full range of sizes.
Stepco-Blackwell Co.	Stepco manufactures drilling equipment for water wells, shallow oil and gas wells, oil and mineral exploration. Rotary and cable tool rigs are used throughout the world. Stepco also produces crawler-mounted trenchers.
Riverside-Blackwell	Riverside Division manufactures pulpwood harvesting and paper mill machinery, including hydraulic log loaders and feller, forwarder, and de-limber machines.

The Problem

In developing management strategy, the corporate executives are pondering the creation of these divisions as working entities. The major concern appears to be in the area of strategic planning. Will these divisions function as a cohesive whole? Will corporate management be able to coordinate the efforts of each division toward overall corporate goals?

The setting of financial goals must be accompanied by careful planning in the management of all the company's divisions. MDP's acquisitions have led to tremendous financial growth, yet an overall strategic plan seems to be in danger.

The divisional breakdown of the corporate acquisitions is an initial step important for organization. The next steps, however, are the keys to maintaining certain management controls and guidance throughout the 1980s.

Various plans must be implemented to develop the divisional managers knowledge of and commitment to corporate strategic goals. Actually, corporate education must take place before the divisions grow beyond the controls of central management. Otherwise, the diversifications and acquisitions of

MDP will lead to its eventual destruction. Destruction can only be prevented if top management begins researching alternative courses of action for planned development and managerial education.

Alternative Course of Action No. 1   To hold major management update meeting in Tennessee, Alabama, or other location convenient for the various divisions.

Advantages
1. All divisional managers would be together in one location to hear the same story at one time.

2. Each manager would have the opportunity to meet key management personnel from all corporate divisions.

3. Managers would have the opportunity to share concerns.

Disadvantages
1. All the divisional managers might not be available at the same time for a meeting.

Alternative Course of Action No. 2   To jointly contact divisional dealer network with sales and service personnel.

Advantages
1. Factory personnel and distributors would have the opportunity to meet selling outlets face to face.

2. Managers would learn firsthand how the selling outlet relates to product offerings.

Disadvantages
1. The distribution network might not have enough personnel to accomplish this marketing approach within a given time frame.

2. Joint contacts with distribution and factory personnel might result in some personnel not "hearing" what should be related as concerns. Managers sometimes will not relate what their concerns are among various divisions.

Alternative Courses of Action No. 3   To release new literature depicting divisional product offerings and send special press releases to trade magazines.

Advantages
1. Literature with divisional names on them could be utilized by sales outlets and be included in quotation presentations.

2. The literature would be good for at least five years or more.

3. Magazines would be kept in offices for a great length of time— i.e., a trade story is in print for a number of months.

4. Press releases would show machines and point out which divisions develop the product.

Disadvantages
1. Cost factor—One brochure, one press release or releases may not be suitable to selling geographical area.

Alternative Course of Action No. 4   To offer incentives to divisional salesmen and issue a monthly newsletter. Follow up with a phone call by central corporate executives.

Advantages
1.   Salesmen like gifts as incentives.

2.   A monthly newsletter could show photographs of salesmen with customers.

3.   The use of executive personnel to call salesmen and ask questions would be very positive.

Disadvantages
1.   Salesmen might not want others knowing to whom they were selling.

Alternative Course of Action No. 5   To visit contractors' sites and construction areas in an effort to understand, first hand, the various products and their utilization.

Advantages
1.   Managers would have an opportunity for first-hand experience.

2.   The company would be able to develop a current mailing list.

3.   Top management would be in a position to evaluate the environmental condition of each operational site.

Disadvantages
1.   Seasonal conditions might prevent visiting.

2.   Safety regulations might prohibit visits.

1.   As a central corporate manager, which course of action do you consider the best available?

2.   What are the reasons for your choice? Explain in detail.

3.   How would you implement your plan? Discuss the specific steps you would employ.

4.   What are the problems associated with large acquisitions and diversifications in relation to central strategic planning?

5.   Would you offer any other possible courses of action for management? Explain.

Northwest Machines

History

The Northwest Corporation was founded in 1942 as a typewriter machine company. Its initial focus was on the development of technically advanced typewriters. With a sales force of 31, the company began to market manual and electric typewriters during the World War II period. Its efforts proved fruitful. The United States government purchased 3,000 of its machines for stateside use and another 1,000 for use in overseas military installations.

After the war, profits and sales continued to grow, allowing Northwest to maintain its research and development efforts designed to produce more efficient office products. By 1952, the company had 8,000 employees and six years later, total employment stood at 15,000.

During the late 1950s, developments in the area of tabulating (adding) machines allowed the firm to branch out into the area of data processing. This expansion and diversification marked a period of tremendous growth. During the 1960s, data processing became more and more important for effective operations of large and medium-sized firms. Northwest rode the crest of this wave and by 1975 it had a nationwide network of 10 regional headquarters and a labor force of 80,000 employees.

The advent of electronics brought substantial changes in data processing machines and typewriters. Equally important, however, was the development of data processing as a technique for advanced management and operational control.

With continuing improvements in computer programming techniques, data processing machines were able to help managers make decisions in areas such as product scheduling, inventory management, and capital investment, and to handle "what if" questions. For example, by using computers to simulate a plant's performance, managers were able to turn hindsight into foresight. The computer thus became an important aid to decision making at the highest level.

Northwest considered the cornerstones of its success in this industry to be

1. *Respect for the Individual*
   Caring about the dignity and rights of each person in the organization

2. *Customer Service*
   Giving the best service of any company in the world

3. *Excellence*
   Believing that all jobs and projects should be performed and produced in a superior way.

Building its business on these three cornerstores, Northwest established a reputation as a corporation that maintained the highest standards of performance.

In 1980, Northwest had a nationwide work force of 100,000 employees. Rapid expansion had required broad organizational changes, resulting in a structure composed of 12 divisions and a number of subsidiaries. The Corporate Office, consisting of the chairman of the board, the president, and the senior vice presidents, manages the overall affairs of the enterprise.

Organizational Structure

One of the firm's divisions is the Data Processing Division (DPD), which has marketing responsibility within the United States and its territories for Northwest's information-handling systems, equipment, computer programming, systems engineering, education programs, and other related services to customers who need larger systems. (See Exhibit 2.)

Exhibit 2

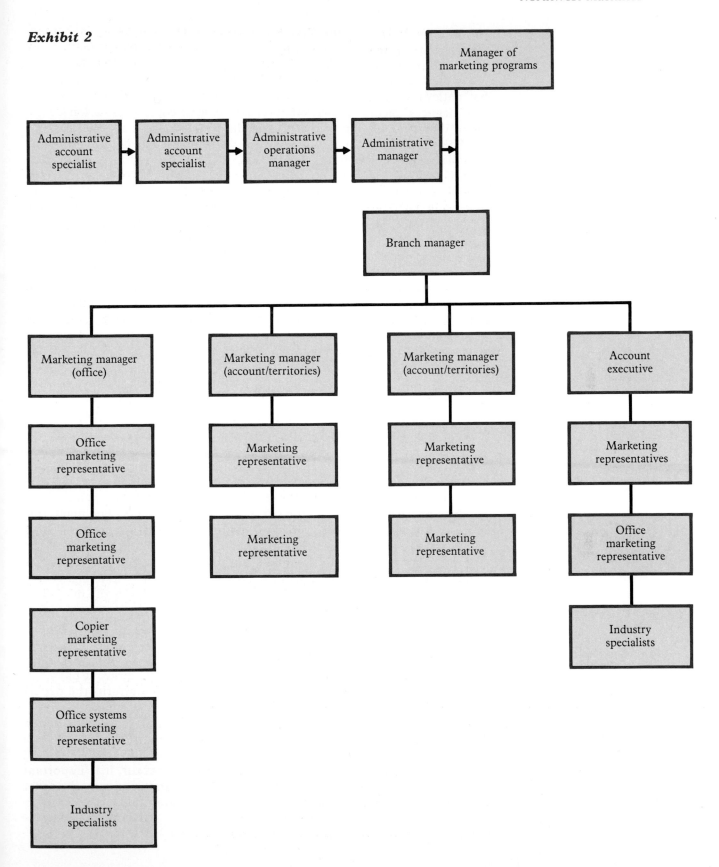

Another division is the Systems Division (SD), which has nationwide market requirements responsibility and service responsibility for low- to moderate-price information-handling systems and related programming.

A third division is the Office Machines Division (OMD). This division has nationwide market requirements responsibility for electronic, electric, and magnetic media typewriters, text processors, copiers, dictation equipment, direct impression composing products, and related supplies.

The particular branch office discussed in this case deals primarily with the three preceding divisions—DPD, SD, and OMD. Within the last year, the office has undergone a major reorganization of divisions, phasing in new divisions and phasing out old ones. Currently, more emphasis is being placed on DPD and less on SD as the latter is slowly being moved out of this particular branch. Reporting directly to the branch manager in this branch office are the marketing managers, who coordinate and supervise all marketing operations within a specified territory, and the account executive, who is responsible for servicing major customers. The branch structure also includes the position of office marketing manager. This individual leads a team of marketing reps, with each specializing in a particular product area, office products including copiers, and office systems. (See Exhibit 2.)

On the administrative side, reporting directly to the branch manager is the administration manager. The administrative operations manager (AOM), in turn, reports to the administration manager, who has the choice of involving the branch manager or not. Reporting to the administrative operations manager are the administrative account specialists (AAS). There is a very close working relationship between the administration manager, the AOM, and the AAAs.

There is also a great deal of interaction between the administrative side of the house and the marketing side. The marketing representative goes out of the office to sell the product to the customer, spending the majority of his or her time in the offices of these customers. The marketing representative is also responsible for completing the proper paperwork, which includes the legal documents stating terms of the purchase, lease, or rental of equipment, and obtaining customer signatures. The terms include guidelines on payment, delivery, and installation. The AAS is involved in this work too. Each AAS is assigned specific accounts (as is the marketing rep), and the AAS and rep on the same account have to work together. After the rep goes out and makes a sale, he or she is responsible for coming into the office to let the appropriate AAS know about the needs and desires of the customer. The AAS accesses the proper paperwork, based on the given information, completes the areas concerning price, terms of payment, etc., and then feeds the information into the system and returns the paperwork to the marketing rep for proper signatures, often including administrative and marketing management signatures as well as that of the customer. (Thus, management on both sides is involved.) Then, it is the AAS's job to follow up on all of the details of the sale, such as delivery, installation, and renewal of agreements. If special circumstances occur, it is important for the marketing rep to keep the AAS informed and vice versa in order to ensure high-quality customer service.

The Problem

Three weeks ago, a problem developed in the organization. For the last year, Andy Subvoda had been working hard to land a major contract with one of the large banks in town. On five different occasions, he had been to see the bank president and visit with the top personnel. After an extended series of meetings, the bank decided that it would buy a new computerized information system from Northwest. This contract is the largest one that has been secured by any Northwest marketing rep this year.

The AAS who is supposed to coordinate his efforts with Andy is Jack Strasser. Three months ago, while Andy was working hard on landing the contract, he told Jack what he was doing. Jack said that he understood and was ready to jump in and help out at any time.

The minute Andy learned that the bank was going to be placing a large order with him, he contacted his marketing manager and told her the good news. She was overjoyed, but encouraged him to "get with your AAS immediately and make sure that he is on top of what is going on. Let's not lose this order due to some paperwork foulup." Andy assured her that everything would be all right and immediately went to see Jack. Part of their conversation went as follows:

> "Jack, remember that bank account sale I've been pushing? Well, I got it. They called me this morning and told me that they were agreeable to buying from us. All we have to do now is take care of the paperwork and we're set."

> "Andy, that's great news. However, I've got quite a lot of work here on my desk. I don't think I can get to the paperwork associated with your deal for at least 10 days."

> "You must be kidding. This is the biggest contract we've landed in almost 18 months! We have to get this deal closed as quickly as possible."

> "Look, I'll give it a try. But I've got plenty of work here. Call me in two days and let's see where I stand then."

Andy could hardly believe his ears. Nevertheless, he waited two days before getting back with Jack. The latter told him that things were still pretty hectic and, "I just don't know when I'll be able to get around to your project." Andy found himself screaming at Jack before he hung up the phone. He then immediately called his boss and asked for an emergency meeting.

During the meeting Andy could hardly control himself. He felt that at any second he was going to fly into a rage. His boss understood how he felt, and she worked to keep him calm. "Let's see what we can do about the situation. Let me call the administration manager and see if we can get some action on this matter," she told him. "I don't intend to see this order lost just because some AAS is sitting on his can."

Unfortunately, the conversation with the administration manager did not go according to expectations. The latter indicated that his people were pretty tied up with other jobs and it was only fair that all work be handled on a "first come, first served" basis. By the time she had hung up, Andy's boss felt the same way Andy did. "I don't know who organized this structure," she said, "but it is a total mess. It seems that you can't get anything done around here unless you stand in line. Well, I'm not going to put up with that." She then picked up the phone and dialed the number of the branch manager.

1. In your own words, what type of organizational structure does Northwest employ?

2. What type of relationship exists between the marketing people and the administrative people? Describe it.

3. What is the major problem presented in the case? What has caused this problem?

4. Is Andy's boss taking the right approach to solve this problem? How can the branch manager help her out? If the latter does help, will this lead to any future problems? Identify and describe two.

5. How would you recommend that this problem be resolved? Be sure to protect the integrity of the organizational structure while simultaneously resolving the issue. Balance a concern for the organizational relationships with one for efficiency and effectiveness.

THREE

Organizing and Staffing the Structure

This part of the book studies the ways in which managers design their organizational structures and staff the positions within the enterprise. Some of the specific questions that will be answered in this section include: How does strategy influence structure? What are some of the most typical organizational designs? What factors help determine how many subordinates should report to one manager? How is authority used to coordinate both the personnel and the work? What are some of the basic advantages and disadvantages associated with the use of committees? What are some of the most common costs and benefits associated with job design? How does an organization go about determining its human resource needs? Who is responsible for recruiting? What are some of the most popular forms of training and development used in today's organizations?

Chapter 7 addresses the topic of overall design. What does the enterprise's organizational chart look like? Why? In this chapter, you will learn the three internal and three external factors that most influence organizational design. You will also study the most popular forms of departmentalization, including functional, product, territorial, and matrix. The role of job analysis, job descriptions, and job specifications in the organizing process will also be presented.

Chapter 8 is a natural follow-up to the previous chapter. Now that you know how the structure is designed, you are ready to examine the people in that structure. In this chapter, you will learn the most common types of coordination found in modern organizations and how authority is used to bring coordination about. The subject of decentralization will also be broached, and key factors that influence the degree of decentralization will be identified and studied. Attention will also be focused on such key coordination topics as delegation, the role of committees, and job design.

Chapter 9 is concerned with recruiting and selecting the workforce. At this point, you will learn about human resource planning and the link between strategic planning and employment needs. You will also find out how organizations forecast employment needs and use the recruiting and selection process to obtain the necessary personnel. The subject of orientation, so valuable in retaining personnel and ensuring that their work performance is as high as possible, is also covered.

Chapter 10 examines the training and development of organizational personnel. At this point, you will learn about human information processing and its value to organizational training. Attention will be focused on both employee training and management development programs, with consideration given both to the types of programs modern enterprises use and how they measure results to evaluate the overall effectiveness of these programs.

When you have finished studying all of the material in these four chapters, you will have a sound understanding of the way managers organize and staff their structures. You will also be aware of the many pitfalls and problems that confront them as they attempt to implement these efficiency measures.

Designing the Overall Structure

Objectives

This chapter examines the ways in which modern enterprises organize their overall structures. This examination covers both the internal and external forces that influence organizational design, as well as the specific forms of departmentalization used in organizations. Consideration is also given to the influence of span of control on structural design and the role played by job definitions. By the time you have finished reading and studying the material in this chapter, you should be able to

1. define the term organizing;

2. identify and describe the three internal and three external factors that most influence organizational design;

3. compare and contrast mechanistic and organic structures;

4. explain how the following major forms of departmentalization work—functional, product, territorial, matrix;

5. discuss the effect of span of control on organizational design and discuss how managers can determine ideal spans for their own particular departments or units; and

6. discuss the role of job analysis, job descriptions, and job specifications in the organizing process.

The Nature of Organizational Design

Organizing defined

As we saw in an earlier chapter, organizing is the process of assigning duties and coordinating the efforts of personnel in their pursuit of the enterprise's objectives. This process has two specific facets: structure and coordination. Having identified objectives and strategy during the planning

177

Figure 7–1   Designing the Overall Structure

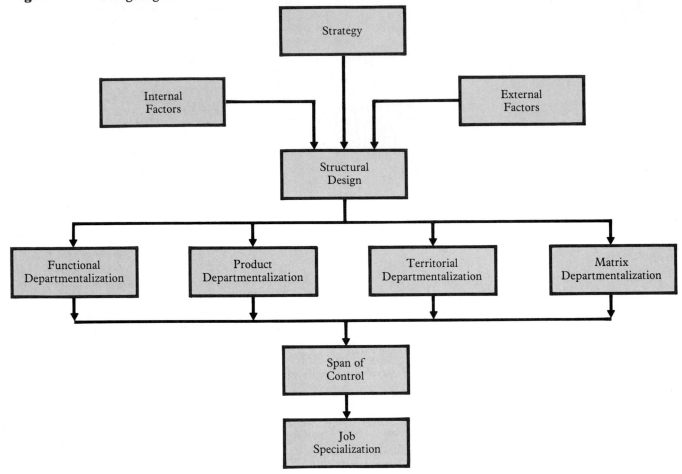

phase, the organization has to determine who will do what and how intra- and interdepartmental coordination will be attained.[1] Figure 7–1 shows how structural considerations are addressed.

Structural Considerations

Strategy influences structure. Strategy influences structure. If the organization intends to sell its goods or services in the local area, the structure used will be different from that employed by an enterprise operating in a 10-state area or by one with branches in overseas locations. Moreover, as organizations change their strategies, they also modify their structures. For example, a firm selling a single product or service in a stable environment usually opts for a functional organizational structure in which personnel are organized according to the activities they perform. As the company increases its offerings to several products, it may change to a product form of organization. If the firm becomes a multiline manufacturer it will typically change again, opting

1. Richard S. Blackburn, "Dimensions of Structure: A Review and Reappraisal," *Academy of Management Review*, January 1982, pp. 59–66.

for a territorial or matrix structure. These four forms of organizational design will be explained later in the chapter.

Internal and external factors also help dictate the most effective structure. One internal force, for example, is the characteristics of the employees. The way the employees want to be managed influences the type of structure used. One external force is the dynamism of the external environment. Firms in a competitive environment are organized differently from those in a stable environment.

An organization's structure usually takes the form of one or more of the following four kinds of departmentalization: functional, product, geographic, or matrix (again see Figure 7–1). In creating an overall structure the organization also has to determine the specific design of each department. How many levels should each contain? What are the effects of having just a few as opposed to many? Which is most efficient and why? How can the manager determine what is best for each specific department? What are the major factors to be examined? These questions are all answered in the section of the chapter that addresses the span of control concept.

Finally, each department contains personnel who carry out the necessary duties and tasks. Job descriptions are used to acquaint them with their assignments and tell them to whom they report and who reports to them.

In this chapter, the four major parts of Figure 7–1 will be studied in detail. The first area of consideration is the internal and external factors affecting structure.

Internal and External Factors

Three internal and three external factors influence organizational structure. These factors help dictate whether the structure is basically bureaucratic or highly innovative. They also influence the form of departmentalization.

Internal Factors

The three internal variables that have the greatest effect on organizational structure are (1) the size of the organization, (2) the diversity of its operations, and (3) the characteristics of the personnel.

Organization Size

As an organization increases in size, control and coordination requirements are likely to increase. When an organization has 25 people, business can be carried out on a very informal basis. As the number increases to 250, however, it becomes more difficult to use such procedures, and a more formal organizational arrangement is required. These findings have been supported with empirical data, some of it collected by John Child, who conducted research involving 82 British firms selected from a series of different industries, including advertising, insurance, electronics manufacturing, newspaper publishing, confectionary manufacturing, and pharmaceuticals. He reports that organizations that increased their degree of formalization to parallel their growth in size tended to achieve higher levels of performance than those that did not.

Large organizations are usually more bureaucratic than small organizations.

Much as critics may decry bureaucracy, we found that in each industry the more profitable and faster-growing companies were those that had developed this type of organization in fuller measure with their growth in size above the 2,000-or-so employee mark. At the other end of the scale, among small firms of about 100 employees, the better performers generally managed with very little formal organization. The larger the company, the higher the correlation between more bureaucracy and superior performance.[2]

These findings do not mean, however, that all large organizations turn into huge bureaucracies. When personnel are spread out among a number of different locations, formalization at each locale is likely to be less than it would be if all personnel were located under a single roof. For this reason, we are likely to find greater bureaucracy in a large manufacturing plant than in a retail chain with stores spread over a five-state region.

Size is a causal factor in many cases.

Moreover, while many research studies have investigated the effect of size on structure, the relationship between the two is not totally clear.[3] Some studies have found a strong relationship and argue that it is causal, while others have either found no such relationship or argue that size is a consequence rather than a cause. Yet it is safe to say that while size alone does not dictate organizational structure, it does play a role, in combination with the other internal and external factors discussed here.

Diversity of Operations

Diverse organizations have complex structures.

An organization that offers a wide range of products or services is organized differently from one that offers only a few. It is likely to have a series of product groups, each headed by a manager who supervises the particular line. It is also likely to have more salespeople, each specializing in certain product areas.

An organization with a narrow range of products and services can usually get by with a much less sophisticated structure. It has fewer lines to push, and its support services are much more restricted. Even if the company's volume of sales is as great as that of a large, diversified organization, a simple organizational design is sufficient. Decision making, communication, and control can be carried out without a sophisticated structure.

Characteristics of the Personnel

Not everyone responds the same way to organizational rules, policies, procedures, and control methods. One reason is that young workers who have been raised in more affluent conditions than their parents usually are less willing to be subjected to bureaucratic rules. For these people, more flexible designs are needed. Conversely, older employees tend to accept restrictions more willingly.

Second, the training, education, and experience of personnel help dictate the best design. Engineers, accountants, marketing specialists, and other

---

2. John Child, "What Determines Organization Performance? The Universals vs. the It-All-Depends," *Organizational Dynamics,* Summer 1974, p. 13.

3. For more information see Jeffrey D. Ford and John W. Slocum, Jr., "Size, Technology, Environment, and the Structure of Organizations," *Academy of Management Review,* October 1977, pp. 564–566.

highly educated employees tend to work more effectively under democratic rule. They want a say in what goes on; they want to feel that they are contributing; they want the opportunity to use their training and expertise. Those with less education and training often feel comfortable in a more bureaucratic setting. In fact, many of them like the direction and guidance provided by organizational rules and policies. If placed in an environment where there is too much latitude and discretion, they often feel uncomfortable because they want more structure.

Some people like rules and regulations; others do not.

To accommodate the characteristics of the personnel, many organizations find they have to alter the degree of control/autonomy accorded to a particular department or work unit. Only by blending the organization's needs with those of the employees are they able to obtain the desired efficiency.

External Factors

The three external factors that have the greatest effect on an organization's structure are (1) environmental stability, (2) technology, and (3) a variety of external pressures.

Environmental Stability

The nature of the external environment helps shape organizational structure. If the environment is a stable, placid one, the company generally has a formal organizational chart, well-defined jobs, and a set way of doing things. If the environment is dynamic and changing, the company tends to ignore such formalities as the personnel rely heavily on teamwork and informal relationships to meet the ever-present challenges.

Mechanistic designs are highly structured; organic designs are not.

Today, in the study of organizational structure, well-defined formal structures are referred to as **mechanistic** and their informal, minimally structured counterparts are called **organic.** This mechanistic-organic framework is the result of research by Tom Burns and G. M. Stalker.[4] After investigating 20 industrial firms for the purpose of studying how the technological and market environment affected the management processes, they discovered that organizations operating in a stable environment had a much different structure from that used by companies operating in an unpredictable setting. Table 7–1 presents the essence of their findings.

The Burns and Stalker research examined the effect of the environment on overall organizational design. The external environment can also affect specific departments, however. For example, a research and development (R&D) department is likely to be interested in developments in the external environment. Has there been a new breakthrough by the competition? What new patents have been applied for at the U.S. Patent Office? Do any of them offer potential for current or future product development?

Because of its interest in the external environment and the changes taking place there, an R&D department is likely to have an organic structure. In this characteristic it differs from a manufacturing department, where the focus is usually internal and the objective is to produce the goods as

4. Tom Burns and G. M. Stalker, *The Management of Innovation* (London: Tavistock Publications, 1961).

Table 7-1   Organizational Structure in Different Types of Environments as Reported by Burns and Stalker

Stable Environment				Dynamic Environment
Rayon Mill	**Electrical Engineering**	**Radio & TV Manufacturing**	**Other Electronics Firms**	**Electronics Development Manufacturer**
• Highly structured • Carefully defined roles • Carefully defined tasks	• Somewhat flexible structures • Roles somewhat defined • Tasks somewhat defined	• Relatively flexible structure • No organization chart • No great degree of role or task definitions	• Flexible structure • No organization charts • Reliance on informal cooperation and teamwork	• Very flexible structure • No organization charts • Emphasis on teamwork and interpersonal interaction to ensure goal attainment

efficiently as possible. The manufacturing department is likely to have a mechanistic design. So the mechanistic-organic framework developed by Burns and Stalker applies to specific departments as well as overall organizational structures.

Of course, the intraorganizational mix can produce headaches for top management. Each department may develop a different kind of structure, have very different objectives, vary in terms of whether it is most concerned with short-range, medium-range, or long-range goals, and have different managerial styles. These characteristics—structure, objectives, time orientation, and management style—are often used to measure **differentiation,** the degree to which each department is developing its own specific posture with regard to its external environment. Research shows, however, that effective top managers know how to obtain the right degree of **integration,** which can be defined as the amount of collaboration that has to exist between departments in order to achieve unity of effort.[5]

Regardless of specific departmental arrangements, successful organizations have the following characteristics: (1) the individual departments effectively address their specific external environments and (2) personnel exhibit the right degree of cooperation and teamwork to ensure overall organizational effectiveness. In every industry the degree of differentiation and integration varies from firm to firm. Those enterprises having the combination that best meets the demands of their environment are the most successful.

Effective organizations address the demands of their external environments.

Technology

Technology consists of the equipment, computers, and other machinery that help an organization attain its objectives. Technology is employed

---

5. Paul R. Lawrence and Joy W. Lorsch, *Organization and Environment* (Homewood, Illinois: Richard D. Irwin, Inc., 1967).

Table 7–2

Comparison of Organizational
Characteristics Among the
Firms in Woodward's Study

Organizational Characteristics	Unit and Small-Batch Production	Large-Batch and Mass Production	Process Production
Number of employees controlled by first-line supervisors	Small	Large	Small
Relationship between work groups and supervisor	Informal	Formal	Informal
Basic type of workers employed	Skilled	Semiskilled & unskilled	Skilled
Definition of duties	Often vague	Clear-cut	Often vague
Degree of delegation of authority	High	Low	High
Use of participative management	High	Low	High
Type of organization structure	Flexible	Rigid	Flexible

internally, but its use is dictated by the external environment. If every other company in an industry is using computers for inventory control, the one that does not will find its profits and efficiency suffering.

Technology is one causal variable in organizational design.

Research shows that technology does indeed influence structure. For example, Joan Woodward surveyed 100 firms and identified differences between them in terms of structure, management operating processes, and profitability. She then grouped the firms according to the kinds of technology they used. The firms fell into three basic groups: (1) those using unit or small-batch production technology for making one-of-a-kind items or a small number of units produced to customer specifications, (2) those using assembly-line technology for large-batch and mass production, and (3) those using process production technology to produce liquids, gases, and crystalline substances. After examining the most successful firms in each category, Woodward discovered that the unit and small-batch firms used organic structures. So did the process production firms. The mass production firms, meanwhile, employed mechanistic designs. Table 7–2 provides a further comparison of the organizational characteristics that Woodward found among the successful firms in each category.[6]

Numerous external forces affect organizational design.

Since Woodward's research was conducted, numerous other studies have been launched in an effort to discover exactly how much of an impact technology has on organizational design. A number of these studies support Woodward's findings that technology is one causal variable in organizational structure. It should also be realized, however, that technology is not equally influential in shaping the structure and style of all organizations or parts of them. It appears to have the greatest influence in small, production-oriented units and the least influence at the upper levels of organizations

---

6. Joan Woodward, *Industrial Organization: Theory and Practice* (London: Oxford University Press, 1965).

and in nonproduction units such as staff service.[7] While technology is important, it is only one of a handful of key variables influencing organizational structure.

External Pressures

Every successful organization attempts to accommodate external pressures that it cannot sidestep. A typical example is government regulation, as in the case of a utility. Realizing that its rate structure, plans for expansion or replacement of current facilities, and customer service all come under the critical eye of regulatory boards, a utility typically has a department or unit addressing each of these areas. In some cases, for example to deal with rate increase requests, a committee consisting of personnel from the finance, operations, and legal areas may be organized to write the proposal. The utility's structure is designed to meet the regulatory pressures the organization is certain to face.

Another major source of external pressure is the organization's resource suppliers. Large business firms that are unionized typically have industrial relations departments that handle contract negotiations and assist the management in resolving union grievances. The structure of the company enables it to meet the pressure of union demands. The same is true in the case of resource suppliers such as major stockholders. In organizations where one or a handful of people hold a large percentage of ownership, such as Edwin Land at Polaroid or Hugh Hefner at Playboy Enterprises, the organization is set up to accommodate their wishes.

A third major source of external pressure is generated by clients and customers who provide a sizable portion of a company's business. Aerospace contractors who obtain 70 percent of their business from federal contracts are organized in a way that obliges the government. They have at least a representative, if not an office, in Washington and are set up to respond to this very important client. A firm that sells 40 percent of its output to a national retail firm is organized to address the particular needs and wishes of this customer. It may have a local office in the same city as the retail firm's headquarters, and the manufacturing personnel are in close touch with the retail company's people regarding any changes in product line or new items to be manufactured.

A fourth major source of external pressure is competitors. If an organization is in a very competitive environment, it has to respond quickly to changes in the industry. A price cut has to be met at once; a new product line has to be matched as soon as possible. In recent years government deregulation of business has brought about an increase in the competitive nature of many industries. The airlines are one example. So is the trucking business. In fact, of all six internal and external fctors examined in this section, more firms are concerned with competition than with any of the others.

---

7. For an excellent review of the literature on this subject see Ford and Slocum, *op. cit.,* pp. 562–564; David F. Gillespie and Dennis S. Mileti, "Technology and the Study of Organizations: An Overview and Appraisal," *Academy of Management Review,* January 1977, pp. 7–16; Mariann Jelinek, "Technology, Organizations, and Contingency," *Academy of Management Review,* January 1977, pp. 17–26; and Donald Gerwin, "The Comparative Analysis of Structure and Technology: A Critical Appraisal," *Academy of Management Review,* October 1979, pp. 41–51.

Specific Influence of the Factors

If an organization is affected by only one or two of these structural factors, the effect is easy to measure. A small business that operates in a stable environment offering a service for which there is little competition may need to be concerned only with the impact of government regulation (licensing, health and safety laws, and minimum wages, for example). A large public utility has to consider at least two of these factors: government regulation and technology.

For some companies, only one factor is important.

If an organization is affected by three or more factors, the effect is not as easy to measure. For example, a multinational enterprise such as IBM is affected by all six. How should these enterprises be organized? The answer depends on the specific influence of each factor. In each company, some have a minor effect while others have a major impact. In the case of IBM, technology, market stability, and size are the most crucial factors. The firm needs to offer the most efficient equipment possible (technology), keep abreast of the competition (market strategy), and have an overall organizational design for coordinating its far-flung operations (size). The next most important factors are external pressure (the specific needs of the customers) and diversity of operations (how to organize systematically and monitor the various product offerings). The least important one is the characteristics of the people in the organization, because in addressing the other factors IBM creates an organizational environment in which creative and high-achieving people can work well.

For others, all six are important.

Each organization must examine its own environment to determine which variables are most important for it individually. After conducting a thorough review of research in this area, William Glueck concluded that the three most important variables for organizations in general are size, environmental stability, and diversity of operations. The second group consists solely of technology. The last group is made up of external pressures and the characteristics of the personnel.[8]

The overall effect of the variables must be weighed.

In any event, if most of these six variables point toward a particular type of organizational structure, that is the one the enterprise should choose. If the variables point toward different structures, the firm must decide which variables are most important to it and select a structure that accommodates them. Finally, if the most important factors do not point to any one particular type of design (such as mechanistic or organic), management should seek a compromise or blend between the two.

The important factors are reflected in the specific organizational design, which can take a number of different forms. These forms are referred to as types of departmentalization.

Departmentalization

Departmentalization defined

Departmentalization is the orderly arrangement of activities and functions that must be performed by organizational personnel. The specific form of departmentalization depends on the needs of the organization. In broad terms, however, there are four major forms of departmentalization: functional, product, territorial, and matrix.

---

8. William F. Glueck, *Management*, 2nd edition (Hinsdale, Illinois: Dryden Press, 1980), p. 406.

Functional Departmentalization

Functional departmentalization is very popular.

Functional departmentalization is the arrangement of the enterprise around the key functions or activities that it must perform. In the case of a manufacturing firm, such major departments as production, marketing, finance, and engineering usually report directly to the chief executive officer (CEO). Figure 7–2 illustrates such a structure. In the case of a hospital (see Figure 7–3), it is common to find financial, nursing, support service, ancillary, and medical staff departments under the direct control of the administrator or CEO. In the case of a department store, typical functions include merchandising, publicity, and finance; in the case of a meat packer, typical departments are dairy and poultry, beef, lamb and veal, by-products, and agricultural research.

A functional departmentalization arrangement is the most popular of all because it is easy to understand and employ. Personnel are organized based on what they do, and if new lines or functions are added they can be accommodated easily. As certain areas increase in size, *derivative departments* can be created. For example, if the marketing department becomes too large for one individual to manage, it can be broken down into two derivative departments: selling and advertising. The functional arrangement

Figure 7–2 Typical Functional Structure for a Manufacturing Firm

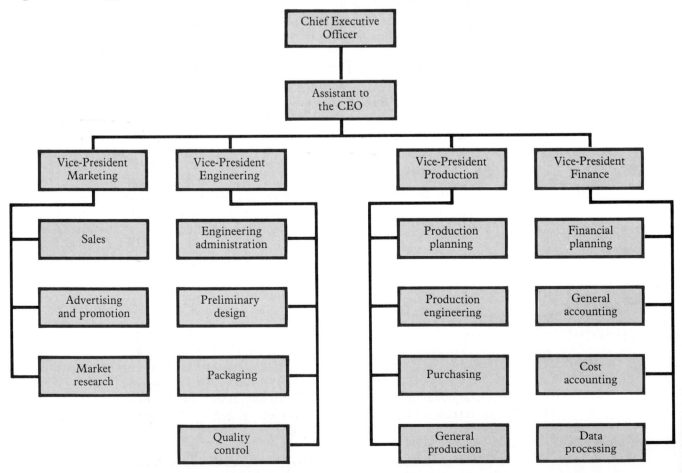

Figure 7–3 Typical Hospital Organizational Chart

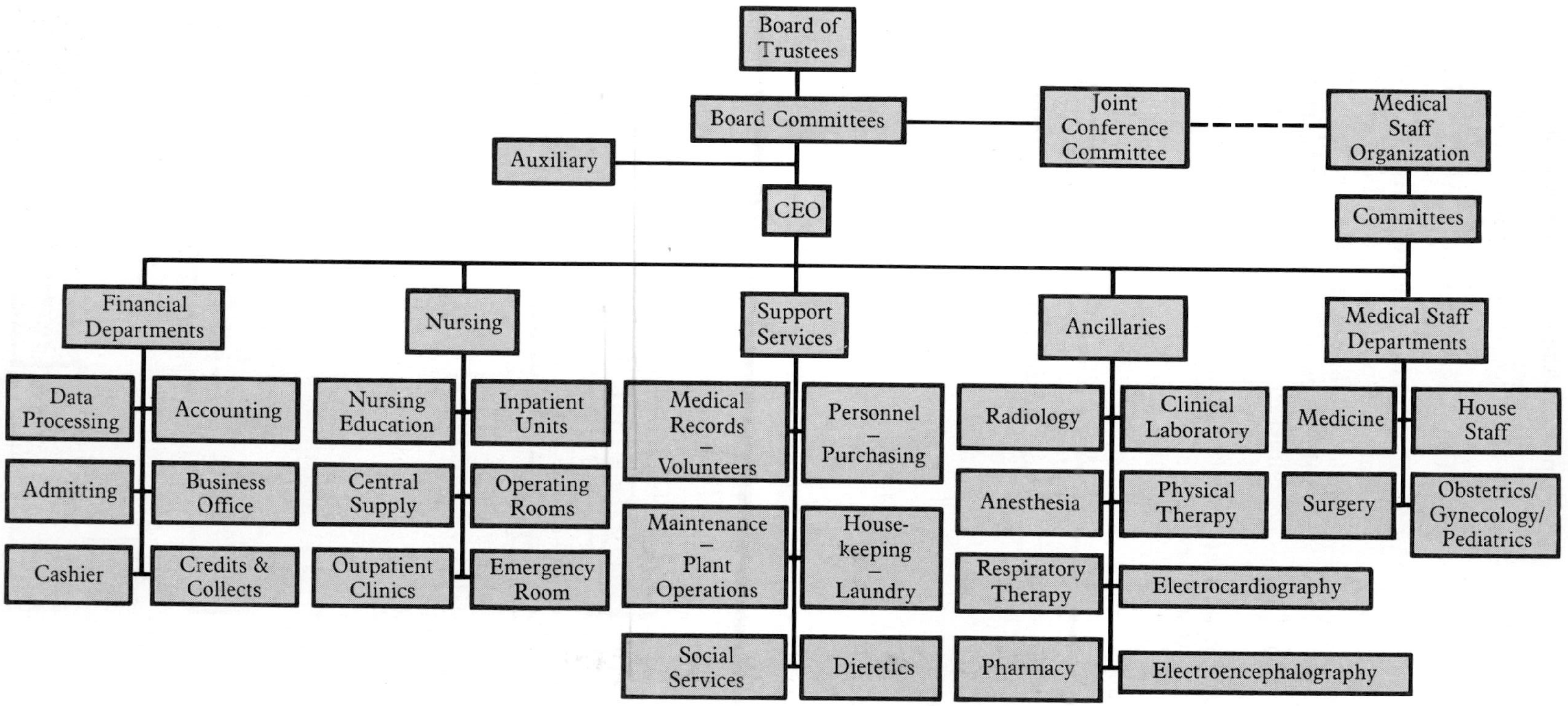

permits the organization to break large departments into smaller and more manageable subfunctional areas.

Product Departmentalization

Product departmentalization occurs when an enterprise organizes itself around product lines. Many firms, as they increase their number of product lines, find a functional structure too unwieldy. In an effort to concentrate the necessary attention on each offering, they organize around product lines. Figure 7–4 shows a typical product departmentalization structure for a manufacturing firm.

Product departmentalization helps create profit centers.

Notice how product departmentalization helps the enterprise create *profit centers*. Each product area is a semi-autonomous business that has what is needed to manufacture and sell the product. Note too how the basic functions of a manufacturing firm—production, marketing, and finance—are incorporated into the product arrangement. Many large multiline corporations (General Motors, Ford, Du Pont, General Electric) employ this organizational form. The arrangement also helps the firm develop general managers who, when they eventually move into top positions, have had the requisite training needed for strategic planning.

Figure 7–4   Product Departmentalization Arrangement for a Manufacturing Firm

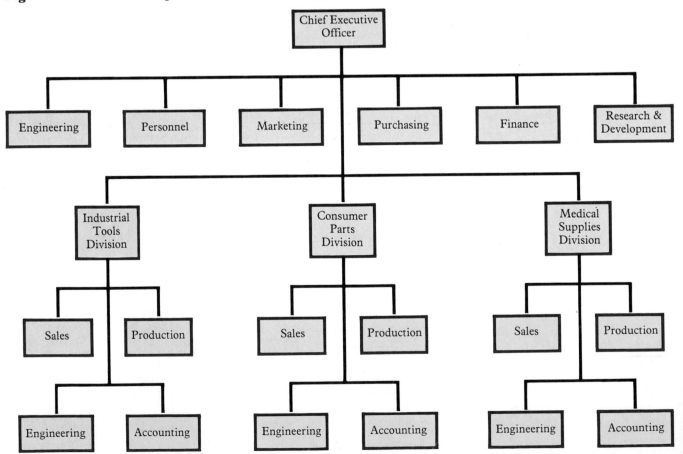

Territorial Departmentalization

Territorial departmentalization is used for servicing physically dispersed customers.

Territorial departmentalization is employed by many organizations trying to serve customers who are physically dispersed. Retail stores are a classic example. As a retail chain begins to grow, more and more stores are opened in different locales. There may be a store downtown, one in the eastern suburbs, and another in the western suburbs. Then the organization may expand to other cities and towns so that over time there are 50 to 60 stores located throughout a five-state region. In the case of the giant retailers like Sears, J. C. Penney, and K-Mart, there are literally thousands of outlets.

Another common example is found in the case of firms that expand into foreign markets. These firms have national and international departments.

Figure 7–5 presents the organizational chart for a retail store that has expanded internationally. This chart bears some resemblance to the structure in Figure 7–2 in that there are functional departments reporting to the CEO. These departments are responsible only for supporting store operations, however. As in the case of product departmentalization, most operating decisions are made at the store level. It is also important to note that within each store there is a series of departments organized according to both function (accounting, personnel, payroll) and product (home appliances, toys, electronic products, books). The result is a mix of all

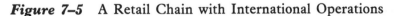

Figure 7–5   A Retail Chain with International Operations

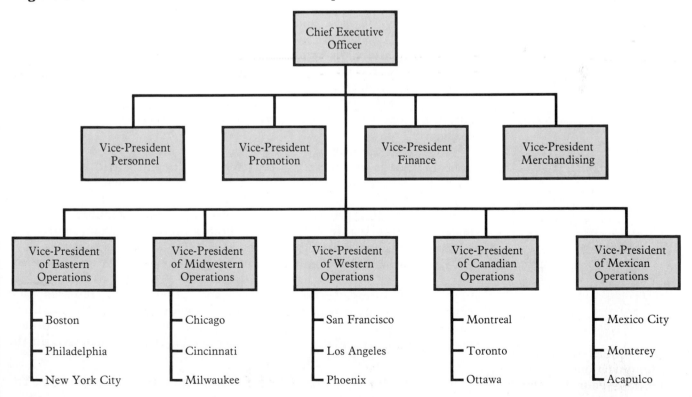

three types of departmentalization: functional, product, and territorial. This mixture of different organizational arrangements is even clearer in the case of the matrix organization.

Matrix organization

A **matrix organization** is a *blend* of functional and product (and in some cases territorial) departmentalization in which there is a dual command system that emphasizes both inputs and outputs. Allen Janger has described some of the most typical arrangements this way:

Typical matrix organization arrangements

> *The product-function matrix,* which overlays a functional "resource" organization with a number of product managers who are charged with achieving "business results" and whose responsibilities cut across the functional organization.
>
> *The product-region matrix,* which overlays a regionally divisionalized structure with a number of product managers who are charged with achieving "business results" for their product lines and whose responsibilities cut across regional lines.
>
> *The multidimensional matrix,* whose regional divisions are organized into product-functional matrixes and which are, in turn, part of a product-region matrix.[9]

The emphasis is on both inputs and outputs.

A matrix structure uses a *dual* command system in which personnel have two types of bosses: *resource managers* and *business managers.* Resource managers provide the personnel. In a business matrix structure these managers come from such functional areas as manufacturing, engineering, R&D, and marketing. Business managers receive the personnel from the resource managers and are charged with coordinating the employees' efforts in such a way as to ensure the profitability of the particular business or product line. The resource managers are concerned with the *inputs;* the business managers are concerned with the *outputs.* The matrix structure helps the organization balance these two concerns, something that can often be difficult when one of the other typical departmentalization arrangements is employed.

Sometimes the matrix is used to accomplish a particular objective such as to build a spacecraft or a piece of hardware, and when the project is finished, the matrix is disbanded. At other times the matrix is used for ongoing operations such as managing product lines. When the structure is used for handling geographically dispersed operations, a multidimensional matrix emerges. Figure 7–6 illustrates both a product-function matrix and a multidimensional matrix as used by Dow Corning.

The first matrix in Figure 7–6, the product-function matrix, was introduced by Dow Corning to handle its domestic U.S. operations. The marketing, manufacturing, technical service and development, research, and economic evaluation/controller managers provide resources for the firm's various businesses. They also provide people to serve on the business boards, which give advice and assistance to the business manager. In the

"No wonder we have a communications problem—your box isn't connected to anyone."

---

9. Allen R. Janger, *Matrix Organization of Complex Businesses* (New York: The Conference Board, Inc., 1979), p. vii.

Figure 7-6 Dow Corning's Product-Function Matrix and Multidimensional Matrix

Dow Corning's Product-Function Matrix

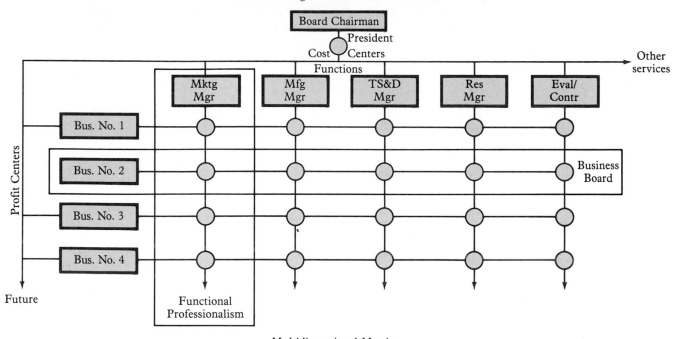

Multidimensional Matrix

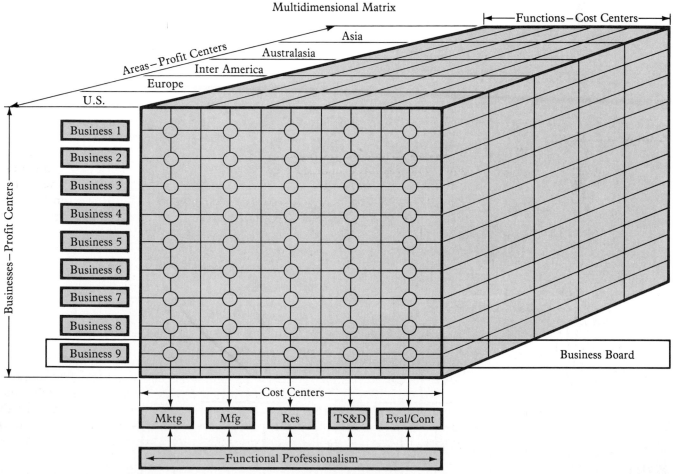

Source: Allan R. Janger, *Matrix Organization of Complex Business* (New York: The Conference Board, 1979), p. 31. Reprinted with permission.

international areas the firm eventually replicated this product-function matrix, giving the design a 3-D effect (functional-product-territorial). Each area—the United States, Europe, Inter-America, Australasia, Asia—is a regional profit center set up along matrix lines. In coordinating the business activities of these areas on a companywide basis, Dow Corning introduced a product region matrix by assigning an additional worldwide product-line "business results" role to each of the U.S. business managers. At the same time, the functional managers have responsibility for worldwide development of their functions.

The matrix design can become quite complex, creating as many problems as it solves. This is why the structure is never a first choice. It evolves gradually as the organization realizes that the other structural designs are not getting the job done. Some firms such as Skandia, the Swedish insurance company, have moved to a matrix structure and then gone back to a more classical organizational arrangement. So the matrix is not the ultimate in organization design. In some cases it proves to be only a temporary structure as the enterprise searches for some hybrid form of departmentalization that will help it operate more efficiently.

Matrix is not the ultimate in organizational design.

Span of Control

Span of control defined

Another important structural consideration is **span of control,** which refers to the number of people who report directly to a manager. This span affects organizational design. A **narrow span of control,** in which two or three

Figure 7–7 A Tall Structure (A Span of Control of Two)

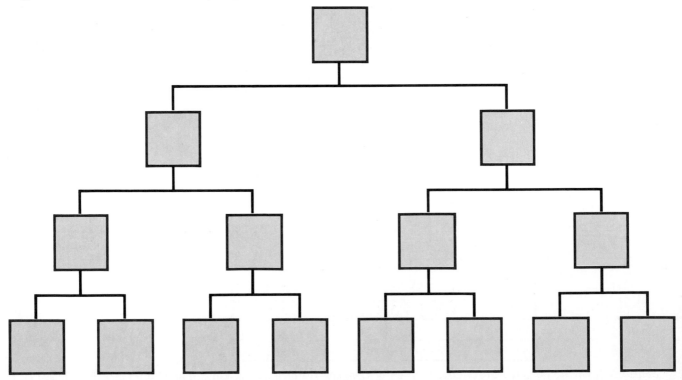

Figure 7–8   A Flat Structure (A Span of Control of Ten)

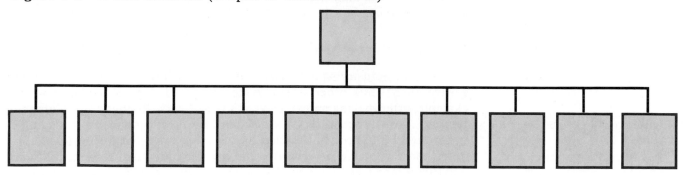

people report to a superior, results in a **tall organizational structure.** Conversely, a **wide span of control,** in which as many as 10 or 15 people may report to the same person, results in a **flat organizational structure.** These two different types of structure are illustrated in Figures 7–7 and 7–8, respectively.

The Matter of Effectiveness

For many years management theorists and practitioners argued over the "ideal" span. Some people felt it should be narrow; others said it should be wide. In recent years, however, the focus of consideration has shifted from defining ideal spans to identifying factors that make one span more effective than another. This idea is illustrated in Figure 7–9, which shows that effectiveness of supervision can be influenced by the number of people managed.

   If the number of subordinates is small, the manager may spend too much time trying to control them. He or she has a great deal of available time and may use it to keep an eye on what everyone is doing. On the other hand, if the number of subordinates is too large, the manager is unable to keep track of what everyone is doing. If someone needs assistance

Figure 7–9
The "Optimum
Span" Concept

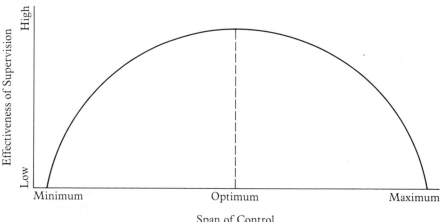

on a project, the manager may not be able to provide it because too many people are vying for his or her time.

Research in the Area

Some studies argue for wide spans.

Research in industry shows that some organizations are very effective with a wide span while others seem to do quite well with a narrow one. For example, after making an extensive study of Sears, Roebuck and Company, James C. Worthy found that a wide span of control produced a less complex structure for the firm and tended "to create a potential for improved attitudes, more effective supervision, and greater individual responsibility and initiative among employees."[10] In more recent years management writers such as Peter Drucker have echoed support for wider spans, noting that "a basic rule of organization is to build the *least* possible number of management levels and forge the shortest possible chain of command."[11]

Others support narrow spans.

On the other hand, there is also research support for narrow spans. Rocco Carzo and John Yanouzas tested the relative efficiency of the two types of structures under controlled conditions and found that, once the groups learned their tasks, those operating under a tall structure had both higher profits and higher rates of return. This finding led them to conclude that "the tall structure, with a great number of levels, allowed group members to evaluate decisions more frequently, and . . . the narrow span of supervision provided for a more orderly decision process."[12]

Still other researchers have found that the size of the firm can have an important effect on whether a flat or a tall structure is better. For example, Lyman Porter and Edward Lawler surveyed more than 1,500 managers and found that in firms with less than 5,000 people, managerial satisfaction was higher in flat structures, while among those with more than 5,000 people, managerial satisfaction was higher if the company had a tall structure.[13]

Current Views

At the present time the focus of attention is less on studying spans of control that exist in various organizations and more on identifying the factors that actually influence the ideal span of control.[14] One of the earliest studies was reported by Harold Stieglitz, who described how the Lockheed Corporation assigned point values to span of control factors.[15]

---

10. James C. Worthy, "Organizational Structure and Employee Morale," *American Sociological Review*, April 1950, p. 179.

11. Peter F. Drucker, *Management: Tasks, Responsibilities, Practices* (New York: Harper & Row, 1974), p. 546.

12. Rocco Carzo, Jr. and John N. Yanouzas, "Effects of Flat and Tall Organization Structure," *Administrative Science Quarterly*, June 1969, p. 191.

13. Lyman W. Porter and Edward E. Lawler, III, "The Effects of 'Tall' Versus 'Flat' Organization Structures on Managerial Job Satisfaction," *Personnel Psychology*, Summer 1964, pp. 135–148.

14. David D. Van Fleet, "Span of Management Research and Issues," *Academy of Management Journal*, September 1983, pp. 546–552.

15. Harold Stieglitz, "Optimizing Span of Control," *Management Record*, September 1962, pp. 25–29.

In the case of job functions, for example, Lockheed assigned a rating of "1" to the job if all of the functions were identical, a "2" if the functions were essentially similar, and so on, up to a "5" if the functions were fundamentally distinct. The same approach was used in handling other span of control factors such as complexity of functions, coordination, and planning time required. The higher the number of points, the lower the span of control recommended.

Although this is the best known attempt to develop a quantified approach for dealing with span of control, there is still a great deal of interest in studying the factors that influence the ideal span of a particular job. David Van Fleet and Arthur Bedeian have pointed out that the important thing is not the specific number of subordinates supervised by a particular superior but the effect of the span on overall performance. Figure 7–10 illustrates their approach to the topic.

The most important thing is how the span affects performance.

Notice that the factors on the left side of the figure influence the span of control number. This number, in turn, influences a series of other variables. By the end of the process, these variables have been reduced to three: administrative costs, productivity, and job satisfaction, which, in turn, influence the overall effectiveness of the span. Figure 7–10 does not offer any solution to the question: What is the ideal span of control? But it does highlight the important factors that must be taken into consideration when examining span of control relationships. After conducting an exhaustive review of the literature on this subject, Van Fleet and Bedeian concluded that

> . . . there is a limit to the number of subordinates a superior can effectively supervise, manage, or control. Clearly this limit will vary depending upon the individual superior, members of his or her group, and the situation. Further, an optimum . . . may exist which is . . . different from that limit.

Figure 7–10 Organizational View of Span Relationships

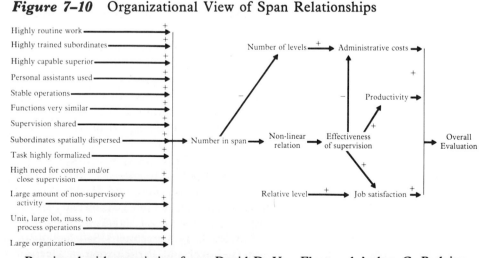

Reprinted with permission from: David D. Van Fleet and Arthur G. Bedeian, "A History of Span of Management," *Academy of Management Review,* July 1977, p. 364.

> More precise definitions need to be used in future research regarding the span of (control) concept. Future research must clearly identify not only the "factors" which may affect the span, but also the criteria upon which any value judgments of "too large" or "too small" are to be based.[16]

Job Specialization

The final aspect of organization design that warrants consideration is job specialization. This concept was at the heart of Frederick Taylor's task concept, described in Chapter 2. In accordance with this concept, the work of every worker was spelled out in advance so that the individual knew exactly what was expected of him or her. This basic form of specialization is still in existence today. In fact, it forms the basis for division of labor and is crucial to departmentalization. Job specialization is promoted through the use of job descriptions.

Job Descriptions

A **job description** is a written statement that sets forth the duties and responsibilities associated with a particular job. The basic purpose of any job definition is to clarify the functions to be performed by the employees, or to provide them with *role clarity*. The greater the clarity, the more likely it is that employees will perform their work in a satisfactory manner. In fact, numerous studies have found that role clarity has both a significant and a positive impact on such key organizational variables as job satisfaction, absenteeism, turnover, and effectiveness.[17]

Unfortunately, not every organization has well-developed job descriptions. The result is *role ambiguity,* a situation in which different people, all doing the same basic job, have different understandings of their roles and responsibilities. Some see themselves as having a great deal more authority and responsibility than others do. Obviously this form of role ambiguity affects the way they do their jobs. Additionally, if their superiors all have different expectations regarding their performance, this too has an impact on the situation.

The surest way of dealing with role ambiguity problems is to determine exactly what each individual should be doing. Then a comprehensive and clear job description can be developed. The employee and the superior can discuss job expectations, and performance evaluation can be tied to them. This entire process begins with what is called job analysis. While it is easier to apply such an analysis to lower-level jobs than to upper-level ones, an organization should use it for every position in the hierarchy, if only to generate a general description of that particular job.

---

16. David D. Van Fleet and Arthur G. Bedeian, "A History of Span of Management," *Academy of Management Review,* July 1977, p. 364.

17. Robert H. Miles and M. M. Petty, "Relationships Between Role Clarity, Need for Clarity, and Job Tension and Satisfaction for Supervisory and Nonsupervisory Roles," *Academy of Management Journal,* December 1975, pp. 877–883; Randall S. Schuler, "Role Perceptions, Satisfaction and Performance Moderated by Organizational Level and Participation in Decision Making," *Academy of Management Journal,* March 1977, pp. 159–165.

Job Analysis

Job analysis

Job analysis is the process of observing, studying, and reporting pertinent information related to the nature of a specific job. This information is of three types: (1) an identification of the job, (2) a complete and accurate description of the tasks involved in the job, and (3) a specification of the requirements the job makes on the employee.

There are many ways of analyzing a job. Some of the most common methods include (1) examining previous job analyses or job descriptions of the position, (2) observing both the job and the job occupant, (3) interviewing the job occupant, (4) having the job occupant or the supervisor or both complete a questionnaire about the job, (5) having the job occupant keep a log or a diary of work activities, (6) recording job activities via film or audio techniques, and (7) analyzing equipment design information from blueprints and design data. Of these methods, numbers 1, 4, and 7 are the fastest but may also provide the least reliable data. Methods 2, 3, 5, and 6 are more accurate but also more costly.

Developing Job Descriptions

Job description

When the job analysis is complete, the job description can be prepared. One of the best sources for use in writing job descriptions is the *Dictionary of Occupational Titles.* In fact, some organizations that need job descriptions for new positions simply go to this dictionary and either directly copy the descriptions they require or modify them slightly to fit the specific job. Table 7-3 provides an example of a job description prepared using the latter procedure.

Notice in the table that there is a general description of the job. It is followed by a list of the most important job duties to be carried out by the person occupying the position.

Developing Job Specifications

Job specification

From the job description, job specifications are prepared. A **job specification** is a written statement that describes the specific qualifications a person must have in order to carry out the job effectively. For the job of the project manager in Table 7–3, the specifications would include the type of education, experience, training, knowledge, skills, and abilities required to perform the job properly. In many situations, especially for lower- and middle-level jobs, the job specifications spell out the minimum amount of experience required (such as two years or three years) as well as the education needed (engineering degree, master of business administration, for example). Perhaps the biggest problem that modern organizations face in the use of job descriptions and job specifications is that the description is too vague and the specifications do not tie closely to the job. If a person were to pick up the job description and read it, he or she would not know exactly what the job required. The individual would have a general idea but that is all. Another problem is that the specifications often seem to have little direct relationship to the work. Why does this job require a college degree in engineering? Why does this job require 10 years of actual managerial experience?

Table 7–3

Job Description for a Project Director

General Description of the Job

Plans, directs, and coordinates the activities of the designated project to ensure that the aims, goals, and/or objectives that are specified for the project are accomplished within the prescribed priorities, time limitations, and funding constraints.

Job Duties:

Reviews project proposals or plans to determine the time frame and funding limitations.

Determines the methods and procedures for accomplishing the project, staffing requirements, and allotment of funds to the various phases of the project.

Develops the staffing plan, and establishes the work plan and schedules for each phase of the project in accord with time limitations and funding.

Recruits personnel according to the staffing plan.

Confers with the staff to outline project plans, designates personnel who will have responsibilities for phases of the project, and establishes the scope of authority.

Directs and coordinates the activities of the project through delegated subordinates and establishes budgetary systems for controlling expenditures.

Reviews the project reports on the status of each phase and modifies schedules, as required.

Confers with project personnel to provide technical advice and to assist in solving problems.

Table 7–4

Ambiguous and Behaviorally Defined Objectives in a Job Description

Ambiguous job objectives	Terminal job objectives
1. To demonstrate satisfactory ability on the job and perform at required standards.	1. To operate the press such that a minimum of 120 pieces are produced correctly each hour, with no more than one incorrect (defective) piece produced in any hour.
2. To develop a positive attitude toward the work; to be dependable.	2. To give evidence of willingness to perform the job by not being absent from work except for those reasons and on those days specified by the union agreement; and by being at the proper work place when the shift bell sounds.
3. To be able to communicate effectively with subordinates.	3. To notify each division head of all changes in the budget by written memo to each no later than one day after notification of such change reaches your desk.

Source: Craig Eric Schneier, "Content Validity: The Necessity of a Behavioral Job Description," *Personnel Administrator,* February 1976, p. 42. Reprinted from the February 1976 issue of *Personnel Administrator,* 30 Park Drive, Berea, Ohio 44017, $26 per year.

Behaviorally defined objectives

In recent years more and more attention has been called to the fact that job descriptions and job specifications are too general and too ambiguous. Researchers such as Craig Schneier have suggested tying everything to behaviorally defined objectives.[18] In this way, when people read the job description they know exactly what the job calls for and the type of education and training that is required to perform it well. Table 7–4 provides an example of ambiguous and terminal behavior in job objectives. Notice that the descriptions that are spelled out in detail are more complete and easier to understand than their less descriptive counterparts.

Well-written job descriptions and job specifications are extremely important in overcoming role ambiguity and promoting organizational efficiency. They are also important in helping ensure that the organization is not found guilty of employment discrimination because it establishes job qualifications that are not job-related or because it screens out women or minorities who apply for the position.

Summary

1. Organizing is the process of assigning duties and coordinating the efforts of personnel in their pursuit of the enterprise's objectives.

2. Strategy influences structure. A single-product organization that is determined to penetrate the local market has a much different structure from a multiline company that wants to expand overseas.

3. The three internal factors that have the greatest influence on organizational structure are the size of the organization, the diversity of its operations, and the characteristics of the personnel. As an organization gets larger it usually becomes more formalized. As the enterprise increases the scope of its operations its structure changes to accommodate the new demands placed on the organization. If personnel want a less bureaucratic design, management is more likely to adopt it than if the employees want a more bureaucratic structure.

4. Three external factors have a great effect on organizational structure: environmental stability, technology, and various external pressures. Organizations operating in stable environments tend to use a mechanistic structure while those in dynamic environments are more likely to opt for an organic design. This principle holds true for both the organization at large and departments in particular. Technology also influences structure, especially that of small, production-oriented units. Also, organizations subject to such external pressures as government regulation, resource suppliers, clients, customers, and competitors organize to accommodate the demands of these forces.

5. In examining the overall effect of all six variables, an organization must first decide which of these has the greatest impact on operations. Then, working in descending order, it must determine the degree of importance of each variable and how each can be accommodated.

6. There are four major forms of departmentalization. One is functional departmentalization, which involves the arrangement of the enterprise around the key functions or activities that it must perform. A second is product departmentalization, which occurs when an enterprise organizes itself around its major product lines. A third is territorial departmentalization, which is employed by organizations trying to serve customers who are physically dispersed. The last is the

18. Craig Eric Schneier, "Content Validity: The Necessity of a Behavioral Job Description," *Personnel Administration*, February 1976, pp. 38–44.

matrix organization, in which there is a dual command system and management attempts to balance a concern for inputs with a concern for outputs.

7. Span of control refers to the number of people who report directly to a manager. If the span is narrow, the organization has a tall structure; if the span is wide, the organization has a flat structure. The ideal span depends on a number of factors. In evaluating these factors the organization should keep in mind the impact of each factor on overall effectiveness.

8. Job specialization is promoted through the use of job descriptions. A job analysis helps to ensure that these descriptions are both complete and clear. From this analysis, a job description can be written. Then job specifications can be prepared. In recent years researchers have been encouraging organizations to tie their job descriptions to behaviorally defined objectives.

Key Terms

Departmentalization   The orderly arrangement of activities and functions that must be performed by the organizational personnel.

Differentiation   The degree to which each department in an organization goes about developing its own specific posture in regard to its external environment.

Flat organizational structure   An organizational structure characterized by a small number of hierarchical levels and a wide span of control.

Functional departmentalization   The organizational arrangement of the enterprise around the key functions or activities that it must perform.

Integration   The amount of collaboration that exists between the organization's departments and other units in achieving unity of effort.

Job analysis   The process of observing, studying, and reporting pertinent information related to the nature of a specific job.

Job description   A written statement that sets forth the duties and responsibilities of a job.

Job specifications   A written statement that describes the specific qualifications that a person must have in order to carry out a job effectively.

Matrix structure   A hybrid combination or blend of functional, product, and/or territorial departmentalization in which there is a dual command system that puts emphasis on both inputs and outputs.

Mechanistic structure   An organizational structure that is often effective in a stable environment. It is characterized by rules, policies, procedures, organizational charts, and other forms of structure.

Narrow span of control   A span of control in which only a small number of people, usually from two to six, report to a superior.

Organic structure   An organizational design that is often effective in a dynamic environment. It is characterized by a lack of rules, policies, procedures, organizational charts, and other forms of structure.

Product departmentalization   The organizational arrangement of an enterprise around its major product lines.

Span of control   The number of people who report to a superior.

Tall organizational structure   An organizational structure characterized by a large number of hierarchical levels and a narrow span of control.

Technology   The equipment, computers, and other machinery that help an organization attain its objectives.

Territorial departmentalization   The organizational arrangement of an enterprise along geographic lines.

Wide span of control   A span of control in which a large number of people, often between eight and fifteen, report to a superior.

Questions for Analysis and Discussion

1. What is meant by the term organizing? State the definition in your own words.
2. How does strategy influence structure? Give an example.
3. Does an organization's size have any effect on its structure? Explain your answer.
4. In what way do diversity of operations and the characteristics of the personnel have an effect on organizational structure? Explain the impact of both factors by using examples.
5. Would a successful firm operating in a stable environment have a different type of organizational structure from one operating in a dynamic environment? Why or why not? Defend your answer.
6. Would all of the departments in a mechanistic structure be highly bureaucratized? Would all of the departments in an organic structure be highly non-bureaucratized? Explain your answer.
7. How much of an impact does technology have on organizational structure? Explain.
8. What are some of the major types of external pressures that influence an organization's structure? Identify and describe at least three.
9. How can an organization go about deciding how to address the internal and external factors that influence organizational structure? Which ones should get the most attention? Should any be ignored?
10. How does functional departmentalization work? What are some of its benefits?
11. Why have some firms opted for a product departmentalization arrangement? What benefits does it offer?
12. When is territorial departmentalization likely to be used by organizations? What kinds of firms are most likely to use it?
13. A matrix organization is a blend of functional and product (and in some cases territorial) departmentalization arrangements. What is meant by this statement?
14. In what way does span of control help determine whether an organization has a flat or a tall structure? Illustrate by using an example.
15. Using research as the basis for your answer, tell which type of span is superior: narrow or wide? Defend your choice.
16. What types of factors influence the ideal span of control? In answering this question, incorporate Figure 7–10 into your answer.
17. In what way can well-written job descriptions help an organization deal with role clarity and role ambiguity?
18. What role do job analyses and job specifications play in the organizing process? Explain.

Case   # The Newly Proposed Structure

The Philby Corporation has been in operation for six years. During this time the company has increased its product lines from one to six, and sales have climbed from just under $100,000 in the first year to more than $16 million last year. Because of this rapid sales growth, Philby has focused most of its attention on manufacturing problems. The corporation has a rule that it will not allow backlog orders to extend more than 90 days. If they do, the firm employs subcontractors to help out.

This year promises to be another big one for Philby. Management is not as concerned as usual with manufacturing problems, however. The large plant that was constructed last year went into full operation three weeks ago, and it now appears that Philby will not have to rely on subcontractors in the future. In fact, if the plant is as efficient as it seems to be, the company should be able to meet all orders within 40 days after they are received.

Having resolved this problem, management is now turning its attention to the company's organizational structure. Currently the firm is organized along functional lines. Reporting directly to the president are the vice-presidents of marketing, finance, and production. The latter, of course, has been of greatest importance to the firm in past years, and any organizing concerns the firm had in the past were related to improving production operations. Now, however, the president believes a total reorganization is in order. He feels that the company has done a good job of handling product production but should focus more attention on the marketing side of operations. His idea is to redesign the structure and convert it from a functional to a product arrangement. Each product line will be given its own manager, who is to be responsible for handling the advertising, selling, and order placing for that particular line. Each manager will also be given some financial control over the operations of the product line, although there will continue to be a centralized finance department reporting directly to the president. Finally, the production department will be reorganized, with specific managers appointed to oversee the manufacture of each of the product lines. While no new production facilities will be built, the company's internal structure will be organized to help manufacturing support and respond to the various product line managers.

If this new structure works well and the firm continues to grow, the president is talking about going to territorial departmentalization. This change will not take place for at least three more years, however.

1. What does the current organizational structure look like? Draw it.

2. What will the newly proposed product organizational structure look like? Draw your version of it.

3. If the company does adopt a territorial departmentalization arrangement, how will this be integrated into the product departmentalization structure? Be sure to draw the territorial structure in a way that makes clear how the new arrangement will work.

You Be the Consultant

Organizing for Dynamic Growth

A large multiline manufacturer is located in the Midwest. The company has eight product lines. Four are consumer goods; the other four are industrial products. Figure 7–11 provides a partial illustration of the company's organizational chart.

The company had only three product lines five years ago. Because of an aggressive acquisitions program, however, it was able to buy three more. The last two were developed in-house. This rapid expansion has resulted in an average sales increase of 38 percent annually. The board of directors would like to continue this rate of growth but realizes that there are risks associated with expanding too fast. The primary problem the board is concerned about is control. The members are convinced that when an organization grows too quickly, things start to go haywire and costs escalate dramati-

Figure 7–11   Partial Organizational Structure

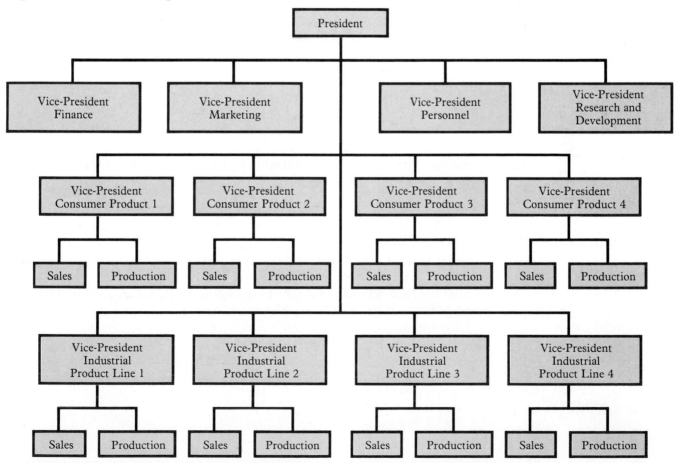

cally. On the other hand, both the board and top management are committed to vigorous expansion.

In line with this strategy, the company has decided to expand into foreign markets. The ventures planned will be in Europe (England, France, and Germany initially), South America (Brazil, Argentina, and Chile at first, others later), and the Far East (Japan at first, China in a few years). In the European theater the concentration will be on selling all of the company's current product lines. In South America and the Far East only the industrial products will be marketed.

Management believes that a demand exists overseas for its products. Initial marketing research conducted by local research firms in all three international areas has supported this conviction. The main reason for the demand is that the company's strong research and development program has allowed it to produce industrial machinery that is superior to anything being offered by the competition.

On the negative side, while management believes that it can make a great deal of money overseas, it is concerned about the link that will exist between the American-based home office and the international offices. While the firm is expanding overseas it will also be looking for additional acquisitions in the states. Coupled with the company's vigorous marketing of current product lines is the president's desire to plan for "stable growth." He believes this can be done if the company has the "right" structure. After giving the matter a great deal of thought, he and his top management advisory staff have concluded that a matrix design would be most effective. This arrangement would allow the organization to emphasize both inputs and outputs. Of course, it is also a very sophisticated type of design and could result in "overorganization" if things are not done properly. This is why he is going to use outside consultants to help out.

Your Consultation

Assume that you have been called in by the president to serve as the consultant in designing the desired matrix structure. After carefully studying the material in this case, draw the matrix design you would propose. Then explain how it would work. Be sure to explain how your structure would increase efficiency and pull together all of the various departments and units into a working team. Also, tell the president how the structure would be of value if more product lines were added (or why the structure would be ineffective if more product lines were added, in which case tell him how the firm will then have to be reorganized to accommodate this latest growth).

Coordinating the People and the Work

Objectives

This chapter studies the ways in which modern organizations coordinate their personnel and the work they do. In the previous chapter consideration was given to the "building blocks" of organizational design. This chapter examines the way in which the people and the work are brought together within this design. In essence, the enterprise needs to coordinate the efforts of its employees in such a way as to attain objectives efficiently. The ways in which this coordinative effort are carried out are the focus of attention here. By the time you have finished studying the material in this chapter, you will be able to

1. define the term coordination and explain some of the most common types of coordination that exist in modern organizations;

2. describe the four most common types of authority and explain the value of each in coordinating the personnel and the work;

3. explain how decentralization can be measured and describe four of the key factors that influence the degree of decentralization in an organization;

4. define the term delegation, explain how this process works, and explain the ways in which managers can go about dealing with delegation-related problems;

5. describe the three most common types of committees found in organizations, how they function, some of the basic advantages and disadvantages associated with using them, and how they can be used most effectively;

6. discuss the most common approaches to job design and illustrate how each can be of value in coordinating the work and the employees; and

7. list some of the most common costs and benefits associated with job design.

Coordination

Coordination is the synchronization of human effort.

Coordination is the synchronization of the efforts of individuals and groups for the purpose of attaining organizational efficiency. The structural components that were described in the previous chapter—departmentalization, span of control, and job specialization—are useful in organizing personnel, but organization is not enough. The enterprise must also coordinate personnel's efforts. Coordination is particularly important when the work is of an interdependent nature.[1]

Interdependency

Few individuals in modern organizations work in isolation. Most must coordinate their efforts with the efforts of others. In doing so, they exhibit one or more of the following types of interdependency: pooled, sequential, and reciprocal.[2]

Pooled interdependence

The simplest form of interdependence is **pooled interdependence.** It occurs when units, departments, or divisions all pool their efforts to help the organization attain its objectives, but coordination between them is minimal. Retail chain stores are an example; for the most part they operate independently of each other.

Sequential interdependence

Sequential interdependence occurs when work units rely on other work units to get the job done. Figure 8–1 illustrates this kind of interdependence. Each group is dependent on the one behind it. A bottleneck in any link of the chain affects overall organizational performance. A bottleneck may occur in an assembly line, for example.

Reciprocal interdependence

Reciprocal interdependence occurs when the inputs of one unit become the outputs of another. Figure 8–2 illustrates this kind of interdependence. A car rental agency, for example, has its own auto maintenance facilities. As the fleet of cars is rented, the wear and tear caused by use results in the need for maintenance. So the better the personnel who rent these cars do their jobs, the more business they create for the maintenance people. The output from the maintenance department, in turn, provides an input for the rental fleet personnel.

Figure 8–1
Sequential Interdependency

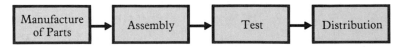

Manufacture of Parts → Assembly → Test → Distribution

1. Joseph L. C. Cheng, "Interdependence and Coordination in Organizations: A Role-System Analysis," *Academy of Management Journal*, March 1983, pp. 156–162.

2. James D. Thompson, *Organizations in Action* (New York: McGraw-Hill, 1967), Chapter 5.

Figure 8–2
Reciprocal Interdependency

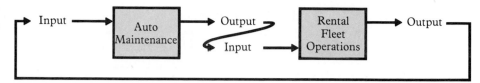

In every modern organization at least one of these three forms of interdependency exists. In large organizations with diversified operations, all three can be found.

Achieving Effective Coordination

There are three ways to achieve effective coordination. Two are formal in nature and one is both formal and informal.

Delegation of authority

The first way is through the use of delegated authority. By giving managers the right to order employees to carry out certain functions or the right to combine their efforts with the efforts of other managers, formal coordination can be achieved.

Use of committees

The second way is through the use of committees. Sometimes tasks or assignments require cooperation or synchronization of effort by individuals or groups from different units or departments. In achieving this coordination, committees are formed that draw members from all of the groups involved. In the case of sequential and reciprocal interdependencies, coordination through the use of committees is quite common.

Restructuring the work

The third way is through the use of job design in which work is restructured so as to blend personnel needs and organizational requirements. If done properly, job design can foster higher motivation and increased work quality and quantity.

In the rest of this chapter, these three ways of achieving coordination are examined in detail. The initial focus of attention is on authority.

Authority

Authority is the right to command.

As we saw earlier, **authority** is the right to command. Through the proper use of authority, formal coordination can be achieved.

There are a number of different types of authority. Four of the most important, used in the departmentalization arrangements discussed in Chapter 7, are line, staff, functional, and project authority.

Line Authority

Line authority is direct authority.

Line authority is direct authority. It is used by superiors in giving orders to their subordinates and helps establish the chain of command in an organization. Figure 8–3 illustrates line authority in action. The CEO gives orders to the vice-presidents who, in turn, have authority over their respective subordinates.

Figure 8–3   Line, Staff, and Functional Authority

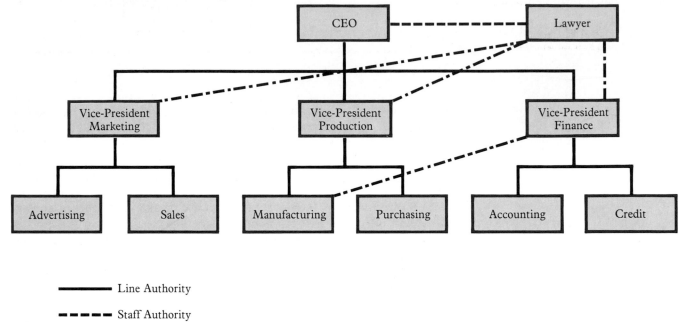

Line Authority

Staff Authority

Functional Authority

Staff Authority

Staff authority is auxiliary authority.

Staff authority is auxiliary authority. Those with staff authority assist, advise, recommend, and facilitate organizational activities. One of the most common examples of staff authority is the lawyer who advises the CEO. (See Figure 8–3.)

Functional Authority

Functional authority is authority in a department other than one's own.

Functional authority is authority in a department other than one's own. This authority is delegated to an individual or department in regard to a particular practice or process being carried out by individuals in other units. For example, the lawyer may have functional authority to demand that all public speeches by the vice-presidents first be cleared by the legal department. The vice-president of finance may have the right to require the head of the manufacturing department to provide cost production data on a weekly basis. (See Figure 8–3.) In a manner of speaking, functional authority is a slice of line authority that can be exercised in another unit.

Line-Staff and Functional Authority Problems

When an organization is small, all coordination may be handled through the use of line authority. When staff authority is added, line-staff conflicts sometimes result. Line people may resent having staff people suggest solutions to their problems. Staff people may feel that the line personnel refuse to implement their good advice. In order to prevent such problems from undermining coordination and cooperation, four basic rules should be enforced by the organization: (1) the line people must keep the staff people

Resolving line-staff problems

aware of the kinds of problems that staff can help out with; (2) staff personnel must provide their advice and assistance in such a way as to reduce the amount of time and effort needed by line people in understanding these recommendations; (3) staff people must be prepared to sell their ideas to line people as opposed to demanding action or implementation; and (4) line people must be willing to listen to staff advice and use it in the best interests of the organization.

The use of functional authority also presents problems. The major one is that it can undermine the integrity of managerial positions. After all, if the vice-president of finance can give an order directly to the head of manufacturing, does he or she not undercut somewhat the authority of the production vice-president? To reduce these kinds of problems, three guidelines should be followed: (1) before anyone is given functional authority, managers whose personnel will be affected should be made aware of the situation; (2) the nature and scope of the functional authority held by any manager should be spelled out precisely; and (3) whenever possible, functional authority should *not* extend more than one hierarchical level below that of the manager holding this authority.

Handling functional authority problems

Project Authority

Project authority is the authority a matrix manager has over the individuals assigned to the project. These personnel are only loaned to the matrix manager, who is more of a coordinator than anything else. He or she lacks the authority to fire, demote, promote, or raise the salary of any of these personnel. Such authority is the domain of the functional manager. Figure 8–4 provides an example. Notice how the line authority of the functional managers runs down the structure while the project authority of the matrix (project) manager runs across the structure.

The project manager is a coordinator.

When the line authority of the functional manager is contrasted with the "coordinative" authority of the matrix manager, it becomes obvious that the latter has much less formal authority than the former. In fact, the matrix manager has an "authority gap." To close this gap, four techniques have been found to be of value. First, the matrix manager must be *competent* so that all the personnel involved realize that the individual knows what he or she is doing. Second, the matrix manager must be *persuasive,* able to generate the necessary support from both the functional managers and the personnel. Third, he or she must be willing to *engage in reciprocity* by trading favors with the functional managers. ("Help me out now and I'll return the favor at a later date.") Fourth, the matrix manager must be *able to live with uncertainty* as he or she tries to coordinate project efforts and get everything done within the assigned time, cost, and quality parameters.

Dealing with "authority gap" problems

The use of line, staff, functional, and project authority can be found in all large organizations. The degree of each, however, is affected by the amount of decentralization that exists in the structure.

Decentralization

Decentralization is a philosophy of management regarding which decisions to send down the line and which to keep near the top for purposes of

Decentralization defined

Figure 8–4   Matrix Organization

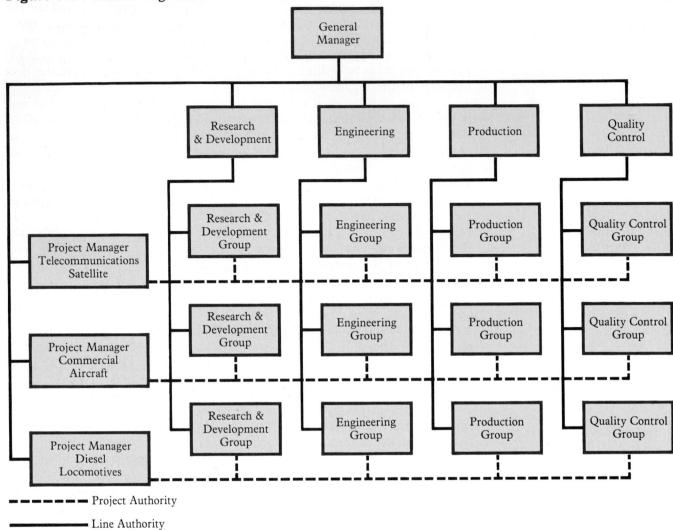

organizational control. In every organization, except those owned and operated by one person, there is always some degree of decentralization and some degree of centralization. To determine whether an organization is basically decentralized or centralized, one must examine the nature and scope of its decision making. Who makes which decisions? How important are these decisions? At which level of the hierarchy is this person located? The answers to these questions help determine the degree of decentralization. In broad terms, four criteria can be employed in measuring the degree of decentralization.

Measuring Decentralization

The first way to measure decentralization is to find out the number of decisions made at the lower levels of the management hierarchy. While

Quantity of decisions

Quality of decisions

Impact of decisions

Amount of control

Cost encourages centralization.

Size encourages decentralization.

Desire for independence encourages decentralization.

So does the availability of managers.

this number can be quite large, even in a centralized structure, quantity is one useful initial gauge.

The second way is to find out where the important decisions are made. One of the best ways to measure importance is through cost. At what level do managers have the authority to approve expenditures of $1,000? $5,000? $10,000? The higher the amounts that managers at the middle and lower ranks have the authority to approve, the greater the degree of decentralization.

The third way is to examine the impact of decisions at lower levels in the hierarchy. Managers who make decisions that affect functional areas other than their own have more impact than those whose decisions are confined exclusively to their own functional area.

The fourth way is to measure the amount of control managers have over their areas of operation. An individual who can make decisions without informing his or her superior has more decentralized authority than someone who must keep the boss informed. A manager who has to consult with the superior before making a decision has even less decentralized authority. The fewer people a manager has to consult and the lower in the hierarchy the manager is located, the greater the degree of decentralized authority.

Factors Influencing Decentralization

Is decentralization superior to centralization? The answer is no. Whether an organization should be highly decentralized or basically centralized depends on its own particular environment, both internal and external. Five of the most influential factors in this area are cost, size, the employee's desire for independence, the availability of managers, and the nature of the enterprise.

Cost   In general terms the greater the cost involved, the more likely it is that the decision will be centralized. Many organizations ensure this practice by setting financial limits that indicate when the decision must be referred to a higher authority.

Size   As an organization increases in size, it usually becomes more decentralized. Top management is unable to control personally as much as it did before. More hierarchical levels are created, and units are given increased authority over their own operations.

Desire for Independence   If the middle and lower-level managers want more authority over their areas, they are likely to get it. If they want little authority, centralization is likely to exist. The motivational effect of giving the managers what they desire is too important to be ignored. Of course, there are limits to the amount of decentralization the organization will approve, but the basic desire for independence will often, to the degree possible, be accommodated.

Availability of Managers   The more managers an organization has, the greater the possible extent of decentralization because managers are individuals to whom authority can be delegated. Conversely, a shortage of managerial talent means that the top managers may have to make most of the important decisions themselves. This factor illustrates the importance of managerial recruiting, selecting, and training.

Dynamic environments also lead to decentralization.

Nature of the Enterprise   Organizations operating in a dynamic environment are often more decentralized than those functioning in a stable environment. The reason is quite simple. In a dynamic setting the top managers are being confronted continually with new problems and challenges. Realizing that they cannot handle everything themselves, they delegate much responsibility to their subordinates, thereby freeing themselves to handle the most important problems. In a stable environment the opposite often occurs. The top staff is capable of handling most things themselves.

Which is Better?

Neither centralization nor decentralization is necessarily the better choice.

Is decentralization preferable to centralization? Sometimes it is; sometimes it is not. Each situation must be considered separately. Certainly decentralization seems to fit well with the American desire to democratize things. In a stable environment, however, where the middle and lower-level managers prefer a centralized structure, the benefits of decentralization may well be limited. Table 8–1 sets forth some of the primary benefits of and drawbacks to centralization and decentralization. After carefully weighing these features, the organization can decide what degree of decentralization will provide it the most benefit.

Table 8–1   Benefits and Drawbacks to Decentralization and Centralization

	Decentralization	Centralization
Benefits	Reduces the total responsibility to more manageable units.	Assures uniformity of standards and policies among all organization units.
	Encourages more involvement of the personnel in the decision-making process.	Allows the use of outstanding talent in managers by the whole organization rather than a single unit.
	Shortens lines of communication.	Ensures uniform decisions.
	Brings decision making closer to those affected by the decision.	Helps eliminate duplication of effort and activity.
	Disperses power and authority among many people.	
Drawbacks	Allows a lack of uniformity of standards and policies among organizational units.	Makes great demands on a few managers instead of spreading responsibility.
	Necessitates making of decisions without capable managers, who may be unavailable or unwilling to participate.	Forces top managers to possess a broad view, which may be beyond their ability.
	Can create coordination problems among the various organizational units.	Gives vast amounts of authority and power to a few people.
	Can lead to interunit rivalry, which can interfere with the organization's overall effectiveness.	Reduces a sense of participation for all but a few.
	Requires training programs which can be time-consuming and costly.	

Delegation

Delegation defined

Delegation of authority is the process of assigning duties to subordinates, giving them the authority to carry out these tasks, and creating an obligation on their part to complete the assignments in a satisfactory manner. It is the means the superior uses to ensure that all of the department or unit work is divided up among the personnel. Everyone is given something to do.

Boss-Related Problems

Reasons for managerial reluctance to delegate authority

Many managers are somewhat reluctant to delegate a great deal of authority to their people. Why? Perhaps the major reason is that they think they can do the job better. Other typical reasons include (1) a lack of confidence in subordinates, (2) an inability to train the subordinate to do the task properly, (3) an unwillingness to let go of authority, and (4) a refusal to let others make mistakes.

Subordinate-Related Problems

Reasons for subordinate reluctance to accept the delegation of authority

On the other side of the coin are subordinate-related problems. Some individuals do not want to have authority delegated to them. Some of the most common reasons are that they (1) lack self-confidence, (2) are afraid of harsh criticism, (3) perceive that inadequate rewards are associated with the increased responsibility, and (4) realize that the boss would rather not delegate authority in the first place.

Dealing with These Problems

How can a manager go about overcoming typical boss-related problems in the delegation of authority? How can he or she work with subordinates in surmounting their resistance to its delegation? Five of the most useful recommendations are the following:

1. Spell out all assignments in terms of the expected results. Let people know exactly what they are to accomplish.

2. Match the person with the job. Determine which subordinates are most qualified and from this pool choose the one who has the best combination of training and experience.

Action-oriented steps

3. Keep all lines of communication open. In this way if there is a problem, both superior and subordinate can communicate easily with each other.

4. Set up a control procedure for seeing that the job is being done properly and provide assistance as needed. Be careful, however, not to interfere with work progress or to give the impression of being too close-control oriented.

5. Use job performance as a basis for rewards. Those who are willing to assume responsibility and get the job done right should be placed at the head of the list when raises and promotions are given out.

Committees

Like authority, committees are important in coordinating activities. Of course, this is not all they do, but it is one of their most vital roles. In fact, the larger the number of employees, the more likely it is that an organization has formal committees.

Types of Committees

In an organizational setting, there are three common types of committees: ad hoc, standing, and plural executive.

Ad Hoc Committees

Ad hoc committees are those formed for a particular purpose. The words "ad hoc" in Latin mean "for this," and so it is with the committee that is formed to meet a particular objective. As soon as the objective has been accomplished, the committee is disbanded.

Ad hoc committees, often referred to as task forces or project teams, are typically formed for handling complex problems that cut across departmental or divisional lines. For example, an organization planning to install a new computer system for control purposes may form an ad hoc committee to study how the plan should be implemented. In such cases, to work through a committee is usually wiser than to order the implementation of the plan through a directive from top management. By having representatives from all of the major departments that will be affected by the installation, the organization accomplishes three objectives. First, it ensures that representatives of each unit have the opportunity to find out how the system will work and what its benefits or disadvantages will be. Second, it allows the committee to put together recommendations that will take advantage of these benefits while sidestepping or avoiding many of the drawbacks. Third, having been involved in the decision, the members of the committee can then serve as representatives to their own unit to explain why the implementation is taking place. By allowing personnel to participate in the actual decision, management gets them behind the project.

Not all ad hoc committees are interdepartmental in nature, however. Some are put together by senior executives to whom the individual members report all along. In these cases the members of the committee are usually asked to make an analysis of a particular problem or project and report their recommendations directly to the superior.

In any event, when the project group completes its recommendations, its task is over and the committee is dissolved. Ad hoc committees have no authority to order their recommendations implemented, unless such authority is expressly given to them. They are purely advisory. Of course, if they do their job well the manager who is ultimately responsible for making the decision may well implement their recommendations. This is the manager's decision, however, and not the committee's.

Standing Committees

Standing committees are permanent in nature. They are not disbanded. In large organizations they often take the form of finance committees and

Ad hoc committees are temporary.

Standing committees are permanent.

personnel committees, and there is always enough work to justify their existence. In the case of a personnel committee, for example, there are sufficient questions related to such issues as discrimination, pay, and promotion procedures to keep the group meeting on a weekly basis for an indefinite period.

Membership on these committees is usually rotated. For example, the personnel committee may consist of 10 members, each of whom is elected for five years. The terms will be staggered so that every year two members are going off and two new ones are coming on. In this way there is always a large percentage of the membership that is familiar with both the issues and the procedures.

Some standing committees spend much of their time addressing problems. Most, however, examine situations and forward their recommendations to a higher authority.

Plural Executive Committees

Plural executive committees can order implementation of recommendations.

The term **plural executive** refers to a committee that has the authority to order the implementation of its own recommendations. The most common plural executive committee is the board of directors, although other standing committees can also be plural executives. In the latter cases these committees typically report directly to the CEO or the board of directors.

The biggest problem with the plural executive concept, except in the case of the board of directors, is that it is often a mistake for a committee to be given authority to make specific decisions. A well-known American Management Association study of committees in organizations reported that in some cases committees do not do a good job. Individuals are more effective. Table 8–2 presents the findings of this study. Notice from the

Table 8–2   The Effectiveness of Individual and Committee Action in Carrying Out Management Functions (In Percentages)

Management Function	Can be effectively exercised by a committee	Can be effectively exercised by a committee but more effectively by an individual	Individual initiative is essential but it can be supplemented by a committee	Individual action is essential and a committee is ineffective
Planning	20	20	25	35
Control	25	20	25	30
Formulating Objectives	35	35	10	20
Organization	5	25	20	50
Jurisdictional Questions	90	10		
Leadership			10	90
Administration	20	25	25	30
Execution	10	15	10	65
Innovation	30	20	20	30
Communication	20	15	35	30
Advice	15	25	35	25
Decision Making	10	30	10	50

results that only in the case of **jurisdictional question** issues—those arising between two or more departments or units regarding who has authority in a given matter—were committees considered more effective than individual managers. The study points out the great danger of overusing committees to get things done. They should be used for promoting coordination and cooperation but seldom for actual decision making. They complement the role of the executive but should not serve as a substitute for it.

Advantages of Committees

A number of important advantages are associated with the use of committees. Most of these involve either the coordination of effort through group problem solving or the promotion of cooperation and understanding among organizational members. Four key advantages are that committees promote group judgment, representation, coordination, and motivation.

Group Judgment

Committees have wide experience.

Some problems and issues are best resolved by committees. The old adage that "two heads are better than one" certainly applies here. A group of qualified people is much better able to focus its wide range of experience on an issue than is a single individual. The committee's ability to stimulate ideas and suggestions can often bring about extremely good results.

Representation

Interested parties are represented on committees.

Many problems or issues facing an organization affect two or more departments or units. Committees that contain representation of such interested parties can often deal effectively with these matters. For example, the design and implementation of a new cost control report may affect both the marketing and production departments. So each may be given two representatives on the committee. If the finance department is the one that wants the new report, it is also given two representatives. At the same time, five other individuals from various departments may be assigned to round out the membership. Note that the production and marketing people may object to some of the suggestions from finance but that they do not have enough votes to force their opinion on the committee. Meanwhile finance is put in the position of having to explain the format and logic of the report; it does not have enough votes to force its recommended report on the other two departments. The disinterested members play the crucial role of deciding what will eventually be done. While the interested groups are represented on the committee, no one group dominates it.

Coordination of Plans and Activities

Committees help coordinate organizational activities.

Committees help coordinate activities between organizational units. This function is particularly important given the dynamics of modern structures, with their multilevel departments and far-reaching operations. Sometimes managers cannot pull everything together by themselves. A committee is needed:

. . . in one study 90 percent of the respondents agreed with the statement that "committees promote coordination among departments." There was similar agreement on this point among various levels, although lower-middle management agreed slightly less (a little over 80 percent) than upper-middle and top management (about 90 percent) agreed with the statement.[3]

Motivation

Participation on committees can be motivational.

Committees can also be motivational in that they provide their members an opportunity to participate and play a role. Quite often when people have a hand in fashioning a particular decision, they get behind it and work for its implementation.

Disadvantages of Committees

Committees also have their shortcomings, however. Some of these relate to coordination per se, while others relate to inefficiency and high cost.

Indecision or Compromise

Committees often make mediocre decisions.

Sometimes, rather than helping get things done, committees prove to be a source of indecision or compromise. Regardless of the number of meetings, nothing is accomplished. Either the discussions wander off to peripheral issues or the group simply "agrees that it cannot agree." In the latter case a decision is reached, but it is so watered down that the result is meaningless. This situation often occurs when one group on the committee feels that a particular line of action should be taken (develop Product A), a second group supports a different line of action (develop Product B), and the eventual decision is to do more marketing research on the benefits of both products. While the organization is doing this research, the competition produces a brand new product and sweeps the market.

Time and Money

Time is money.

Committees can prove to be a great waste of time and money. Whether they are or not depends on their results. The important thing to keep in mind is that time is money. To determine if a committee is giving the organization its money's worth, the organization must weigh their costs and benefits. Suppose that a particular committee consisting of seven senior managers meets once a week for four weeks, three hours each time, before reaching a final decision. This decision results in an overall profit of $50,000 and 5 percent of this amount is attributed to the quality of the committee's decision. Was the committee effective from a time and cost standpoint? The following table answers this question.

Executive	Hourly Salary	×	Number of Hours	Cost
1	$50		12	$ 600
2	48		12	576
3	46		12	552
4	45		12	540
5	42		12	504
6	42		12	504
7	42		12	504
				$3,780

---

3. Harold Koontz, Cyril O'Donnell and Heinz Weihrich, *Management,* 7th edition (New York: McGraw-Hill, 1980), p. 456.

The committee has not been effective. The cost was $3,780 but the benefit of the committee was only $2,500 ($50,000 × 0.05). The reason for committee ineffectiveness is often found in the high cost per hour. In our example, the cost of the seven executives was $315 an hour. For the organization to benefit from such a committee, the payoffs must be extremely high. Otherwise it is best to have the decisions made by a smaller committee or a single manager.

Lack of Responsibility

No one is personally responsible.

When working in a group, many people make decisions that are different from those they would make if they were personally charged with the same responsibility. One reason is that in a group they feel sheltered from personal responsibility. If a decision proves to be wrong, the individual can always point out that he or she did not agree with the majority or, if the individual did agree, he or she can argue that "I'm only one of many who participated in the decision, so don't pin the blame on me." In either event, no one is personally responsible. Even if the organization wants to follow up and find out who caused the mistake, it cannot.

Making Committees Effective

Since committees are vital to the operation of most medium-sized and large modern organizations, it is important that they be used effectively. For this objective to be accomplished, attention must be focused on three areas.

Determine objectives and structure.

First, the objectives, authority, and organization of the committee should be spelled out clearly. What is the committee to do? Does it have the authority to implement its recommendations, or are these merely forwarded to higher authority? How should the committee organize itself? Who is to do what? How often will meetings be held? When and where will the group meet?

Get good leadership. . .

Second, the committee must be led skillfully by its chairperson. This individual plays a key role in determining both the focus and the pace of committee discussions. In addition to drawing up the agenda, the chairperson must stimulate participation and encourage teamwork.

and competent members.

Third, the committee members must cooperate in pursuing the group's objectives. This means that they must read the agenda, come to the meeting prepared to work, participate actively in the discussion, team up with the other members to resolve differences and deal with problems, decide what needs to be done before the next meeting, and carry out their assignments within the established time period.[4]

---

4. For some additional ideas on using committees effectively see: Cyril O'Donnell, "Ground Rules For Using Committees," *Management Review,* October 1961, pp. 63–67 and George M. Prince, "How To Be A Better Committee Chairman," *Harvard Business Review,* January–February 1971, pp. 98–108.

Job Design

A third major way of coordinating the people and the work effectively is to use job design. Over the last 10 years a great deal of attention has been directed toward the need for less job specialization. A change is being accomplished through what is called job design (or, in the case of ongoing jobs, job redesign). **Job design** is the process of introducing work changes for the purpose of increasing the quality or the quantity of work or both. A close analysis of the most common approaches to modern job design reveals that there are six very popular methods: job engineering, job rotation, job enlargement, the sociotechnical approach, goal setting, and job enrichment. The following discussion examines each of these approaches, giving particular attention to the last four.

Job Engineering

Time and motion analysis is used.

Job engineering uses time and motion analysis to achieve the most efficient interface between the worker and the machine. This approach was discussed in Chapter 2 when the scientific management movement was analyzed. Job engineering can be very important, especially in manufacturing firms, although its use is certainly not restricted to these industries. The biggest problem with job engineering is that the emphasis on the work may be allowed to overshadow consideration of the worker. Instead of blending the worker and the work, this approach forces the worker to adapt to the machine.

Job Rotation

Boredom can be reduced.

Job rotation involves moving a worker from one job to another. The basic purpose of the approach is to reduce the boredom of the task. The technique has been used in many different types of work, particularly in assembly-line jobs, where each person does one (or a few) things. By rotating the individual worker from one job to another, as shown in Figure 8–5, management attempts to increase job interest.

Figure 8–5
Job Rotation in Action

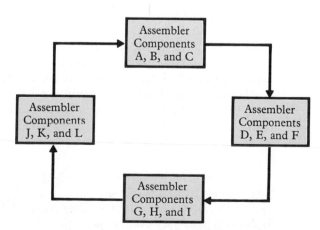

Job Enlargement

Job enlargement is a design technique that involves giving the worker more to do. When applied to the job rotation example, it would mean giving an assembler more than three components to assemble. In fact, the worker might be given all 12 so that he or she would put together the entire product. In job design terminology, job enlargement makes use of **horizontal loading:** the worker is given *more of the same things* to do. From a physical standpoint, job enlargement can bring about greater output because it reduces the amount of time spent in passing partially completed components to the next assembler. From a psychological standpoint, job enlargement can bring about greater output because it can lead to greater job satisfaction and a feeling of accomplishment on the part of the worker.

Horizontal loading provides the worker with more of the same things to do.

Sociotechnical Approach

The **sociotechnical approach** is one in which a group or team of workers is made responsible for getting the job done. This approach balances the social and technical aspects of the job. In contrast to the three previously discussed approaches, this one relies less on job design techniques and more on improving the quality of work life (QWL) and the overall work climate on the job. The sociotechnical or QWL approach is "a process of joint decision making, collaboration and building mutual respect between management and employees."[5] In recent years a number of important projects using QWL have been reported. One of the best known is that at Volvo, the Swedish auto maker. Commenting on his firm's approach to job design, the company president has noted:

A group approach

> The design for Kalmar incorporated pleasant, quiet surroundings, arranged for group working, with each group having its own individual rest and meeting areas. The work itself is organized so that each group is responsible for a particular, identifiable portion of the car—electrical systems, interiors, doors, and so on. Individual cars are built up on self-propelling "carriers" that run around the factory following a movable conductive tape on the floor. Computers normally direct the carriers, but manual controls can override the taped route. If someone notices a scratch in the paint on a car, he or she can immediately turn the carrier back to the painting station. Under computer control again, the car will return later to the production process wherever it left off.[6]

Other organizations have also reported success with a sociotechnical approach to job design. Some of the most widely reported examples include those at General Foods, Weyerhaeuser, Heinz, and Nabisco.

Many of the design programs used by these firms rely heavily upon worker input regarding changes that should be made. The idea has been gaining acceptance in the United States, and many people attribute this development to the success the approach has had in countries like Japan,

---

5. Deborah Shaw Cohen, "The Quality Of Work Life Movement," *Training HRD,* January 1979, p. 24.

6. Pehr G. Gyllenhammar, "How Volvo Adapts Work To People," *Harvard Business Review,* July–August 1977, p. 107.

where the **quality control circle** (or quality circle for short) has been employed profitably for years.

In Japan a quality circle typically consists of from five to ten employees. All of the employees are assigned permanently to their circle, and their work is related in some way to that of the others. The task of each circle, headed by a foreman, is to study any problems of production or service that fall within the scope of its work. Each group meets for one to two hours each week to discuss changes and projects it wants to undertake.

> A typical project may involve a problem in quality which one or more circle members have identified. . . . The group may then begin a systematic study of the problem, collecting statistics on the type and nature, perhaps even counting the number of defects per part at each of the stages in the production process covered by members of the circle. At the end of the study period . . . members meet again to analyze the data, drawing charts and graphs to determine the problem's source: Is it a defective design being supplied by engineering, a mis-designed part coming from suppliers, a machine improperly set up, or a lack of coordination among members of the circle? Once the problem is identified, circle members suggest steps that should be taken to correct it.[7]

Of course, the quality circle concept is not a panacea for organizations facing sociotechnical problems. If used properly, however, it can be extremely useful in helping to meet these challenges. Some of the most important behavioral ideas that must be kept in mind when this approach is used include the following:

1. Quality control circles are a method of employee development as well as a means for improving organizational output and efficiency. If employee development is ignored, efficiency will suffer.

2. Membership in a quality circle should be voluntary. No one ought to be forced to join a quality circle; being forced to join may negatively affect the person's contribution to the group.

3. Participants should all be fully trained. Their training should not only be technical but should also provide them with insights regarding conference techniques and group dynamics so they will know how to work more effectively in groups.

4. Quality circles are group efforts, not individual efforts. This means that showboating and competition must be minimized and that cooperation and interdependent behavior must be encouraged.

5. The quality circle's project should be related to the members' actual job responsibilities. In this way the members are working to improve the quality of their own jobs, something in which they ought to have a high interest.

Quality circle guidelines

6. The quality circle program should help employees see the relationship between their work and the quality of the product or service being

---

7. William G. Ouchi, *Theory Z: How American Business Can Meet the Japanese Challenge* (Reading, Mass.: Addison-Wesley, 1981), p. 263.

generated by their efforts. This quality and improvement awareness development should be used to commit the members further to quality.

7. If there is a quality control department in the organization, the relationship between the department and the quality control circle should be clarified before the circle begins its job. Clarification of responsibilities prevents intergroup fights and squabbling. The best way to handle the situation usually is for the circle to complement the quality control department.

8. If the organization is just starting to use the quality control concept, a pilot study is in order. Then, if the circle produces results and wins the acceptance of managers and employees alike, its use can be expanded.

9. Management should make use of the suggestions set forth by the quality control circle. If none of the recommendations are adopted, the circle will lose its effectiveness and both membership and morale in the circle will drop off.

10. Management must be willing to grant recognition for all ideas that are set forth by the circle. If this is not done, the program is likely to backfire.[8]

Goal Setting

Goal setting is a job design approach that emphasizes building goals, feedback, and incentives into the structure of the job. The logic behind the process is really quite simple. The better people understand their goals and the more challenging and interesting they are, the greater the likelihood that they will prove to be motivational. Figure 8–6 presents an integrated model of job design. Notice on the left side of the figure that task goals and enrichment are *interactive*. Goals help enrich jobs and enriched jobs have goal clarity and challenge. Because the interactive effect of goal setting and job enrichment is so strong, organizations that use a goal-setting approach are also interested in job enrichment, although the reverse is not necessarily true.

Challenging goals are motivational.

Job Enrichment

Job enrichment is an extension of job rotation and job enlargement techniques. In essence, job enrichment is a process that attempts to build psychological motivators into the work. In particular, it often involves giving the worker more authority both in planning the work and in controlling its pace and procedures.

Psychological motivators are built into the job.

8. The ideas in this section can be found in: Ed Yager, "Examining the Quality Control Circle," *Personnel Journal,* October 1979, pp. 682–684; Andrew J. DuBrin, *Contemporary Applied Management* (Plano, Tex.: Business Publications, Inc., 1982), pp. 120–122; and Jeremiah J. Sullivan, "A Critique of Theory Z," *Academy of Management Review,* January 1983, pp. 132–142. For more on quality circles see Richard M. Hodgetts and Wendell V. Fountain, "The Defense Department Evaluates a Quality Circle Program," *Training and Development Journal,* November 1983, pp. 98–100.

Figure 8–6   An Integrated Model of Job Design

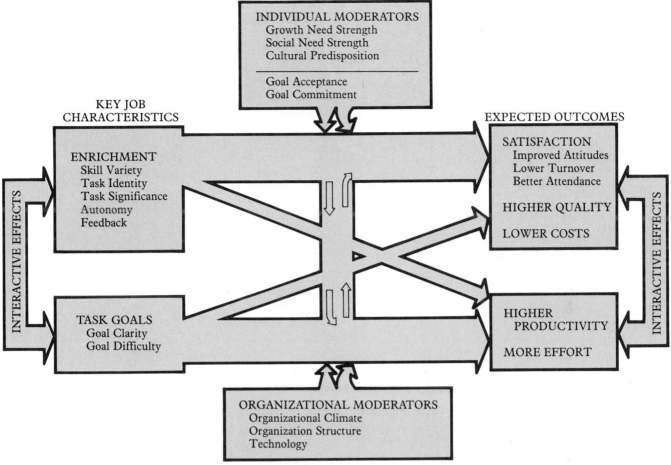

Dennis D. Umstot, Terence R. Mitchell, and Cecil H. Ball, Jr., "Goal Setting and Job Enrichment: An Integrated Approach to Job Design," *Academy of Management Review,* October 1978, p. 877. Reprinted with permission.

There are many forms of job enrichment in organizations. Some of these include (1) giving the worker the opportunity to build an entire unit rather than just one part of that unit, (2) allowing the worker to decide when to make preventive maintenance on a machine and how to do so, and (3) letting the employee check his or her own work rather than having a supervisor or quality control person perform this function. To obtain a more complete grasp of job enrichment, we need to see how the complete process works. To do so, we will analyze the job characteristics model.

Job Characteristics Model

Perhaps the most comprehensive conceptual framework for examining the effects of job enrichment on work attitudes and behavior is the **job characteristics model.**[9] This model, presented in Figure 8–7, explains

_____

9. J. Richard Hackman, Greg Oldham, Robert Janson, and Kenneth Purdy, "A New Strategy For Job Enrichment," *California Management Review,* Summer 1975, pp. 57–71.

Figure 8–7 Job Characteristics Model

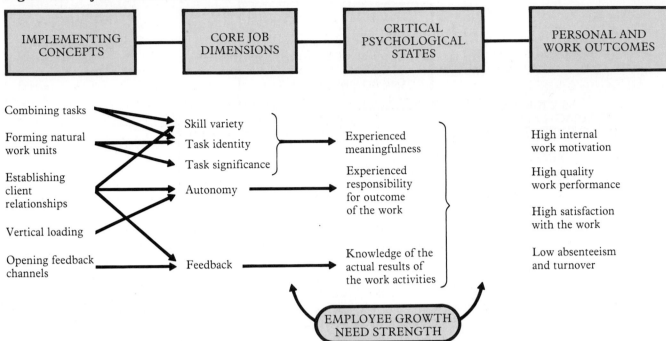

R. Richard Hackman, Greg Oldham, Robert Janson, and Kenneth Purdy, "A New Strategy for Job Enrichment," *California Management Review,* Summer 1975, p. 62. Reprinted with permission.

the psychological impact of various job characteristics and predicts the effects that specific psychological states have on both work attitudes and performance. The most effective way to examine the model is to work backwards from work outcomes to job design concepts.

Personal and Work Outcomes Personal and work outcomes are the results that are attained from a job enrichment program. These outcomes may be high work quantity, high work quality, high job satisfaction, and low absenteeism and turnover. Other more "psychological" behaviors include showing initiative, cooperating with fellow workers, making creative suggestions, and pursuing self-development and training.

Critical Psychological States Desired work outcomes are a result of **critical psychological states.** If these states can be created, positive work outcomes may result. If the organization cannot create these states, the desired personal and work outcomes will not materialize. As seen in Figure 8–7 there are three such states: (1) *experienced meaningfulness of the work,* or the state in which the worker feels that the work is important, worthwhile, and valuable; (2) *experienced responsibility for work outcomes,* or the state in which the worker feels personally responsible or accountable for the results of the work; and (3) *knowledge of results of work activities,* or the state in which the employee understands, at all times, how well he or she is performing the job.

These motivators create positive work outcomes.

Core Job Dimensions **Core job dimensions** are the causal factors that bring about these psychological states. There are five dimensions in all, and their effect is illustrated in Figure 8–7. The first is *variety of skill,* or the degree to which the job requires the person to do different things

Causal factors

and use a number of different skills, abilities, and talents. The second is the *identity of the task,* or the degree to which the job allows for completion of a whole and identifiable piece of work. The third is the *significance of the task,* or the degree to which the job has an impact on the lives of other people, both internal and external to the organization. These three characteristics affect the experienced meaningfulness of the work.

The fourth dimension is *autonomy,* which refers to the amount of freedom, independence, and discretion that the worker has in functions such as scheduling work, making decisions, and determining how to do the job. This characteristic directly affects the worker's sense of experienced responsibility for work outcomes.

The last dimension is *feedback,* or the degree to which the job provides the worker with clear and direct information about job outcomes and performance. This dimension directly affects the worker's knowledge of the results of work activities.

Implementing Concepts   Core job dimensions are built into the work through the application of job design concepts. While many such concepts can be applied, five of the most useful have been incorporated into Figure 8–7. They include (1) *combining tasks* so as to increase both skill variety and task identity, thereby allowing the individual to feel that he or she is doing more meaningful work; (2) *forming natural work units* by identifying basic work items and grouping them into natural categories; (3) *establishing client relationships* by allowing employees the most direct contact possible with those for whom the work is being done and setting up criteria by which the client can judge the quality of the product being received; (4) establishing **vertical loading** by giving the worker more control over both the planning and the control of work activities; and (5) *opening feedback channels* so that either the client or the employee, personally, can monitor work performance.

Employee Growth Need Strength   Before ending the discussion of the job characteristics model, we need to consider the concept of employee growth need strength (see the bottom of Figure 8–7). While the model does pull together much of what is known about job enrichment and puts it into understandable form, it does not predict that all workers will have positive personal and work outcomes if their jobs are designed according to job enrichment principles. The person must *want* the psychological rewards that come with the design. The need for growth must be strong. Otherwise, the employee will be just as happy if no change is made in the work.

Cost and Benefits

Over the last two decades, considerable attention has been focused on how to design enriched jobs and autonomous work groups. Only recently, however, has there been an attempt to assess the economic costs and benefits associated with job design.[10] The results of one survey, covering both business and governmental agencies, is reported in Table 8–3. The data reveal

Job enrichment techniques

People must want psychological rewards.

---

10. J. Richard Hackman, "The Design of Work in the 1980's," *Organizational Dynamics,* Summer 1978, p. 15.

Table 8–3
Impact on Performance
Caused by Job Enrichment
Changes

	Number of Projects		
Item	Unfavorable Change	No Change	Favorable Change
Quality			
Number of items produced that were rejected for failure to meet quality standards	1	5	28
Amount of work that had to be recycled	2	3	22
Resource Utilization			
Labor force idle time	2	9	18
Production output	1	9	40
Operating Benefits			
Accident rate	1	10	4
Order expediting	1	7	8
Grievance rates	1	11	12
Absenteeism	1	11	26
Turnover	4	15	28

Source: Antone F. Alber, "The Real Cost Of Job Enrichment," *Business Horizons,* February 1979, p. 67. Reprinted with permission.

that, in general, job enrichment changes had a favorable effect on the organizations involved. This study, however, should not be allowed to overshadow a consideration of the specific costs involved.

Specific Costs

A number of specific costs are associated with the implementation of job enrichment programs. Many of these are design related and include wage/salary increases, facility change costs, inventory costs, charges for implementing the new work design, and expenses incurred in training employees to carry out the newly expanded jobs.

Design-related costs

While not every job redesign results in higher wages or salaries, many do. The employees take on more work and responsibility, and many organizations feel it is only fair to give them more money. Of course, management hopes to make up these salary increases through greater efficiency and output.

In many cases job enrichment also involves changes in work procedures and work flow, particularly in assembly line or manufacturing jobs. In these cases the organization often has to expand the amount of floor space needed for the work and to purchase more tools and equipment. The result is an increase in facility costs.

An accompanying cost is that of inventory. Especially in manufacturing-related work, sequentially arranged work stations are abandoned in favor of semi-independent functioning work areas. Each person becomes more autonomous. This change requires each worker to have his or her own stockpile of inventory.

A fourth cost is that for implementation. Some organizations hire consultants to help with implementation. Others use in-house personnel. These expenses must be considered when the organization examines the costs or designs the work.

When job enrichment results in a more complex job, training of the personnel is often required. The most common forms are on-the-job, although in a small percentage of cases the training is sophisticated enough to require the personnel to be trained off the job. Surprising as it may seem, researchers such as Antone Alber report that most organizations assign a very low priority to training in the overall design effort.[11] Additionally, some managers actually misread the value of job enrichment because they allow the initial increase in costs or decrease in productivity to affect their evaluation. The managers fail to realize that there is a time period during which employees are still mastering the new jobs and that efficiency is lower during this phase.

Specific Benefits

Performance-related benefits

The benefits associated with job enrichment are performance related in nature. Some of the most common include increased work quantity and quality, better use of resources, increased operating benefits, and lower absenteeism and turnover.

Many organizations that have had success with their job enrichment programs have achieved work output increases. Drawing on his own research in the field, Alber reports that

> . . . a manager in a large manufacturing company and another manager in a service-related activity of a bank both stated that a "significant improvement in supervisor/employee relations" occurs. The job utilization analyst of another bank reported better use of management time: "The supervisor's desk has been moved out of the mainstream of production and she now spends her time supervising, counseling, computing, graphing individual productivity, and approving loans."

> Another manager reported that organizational changes resulting from the enrichment project have eliminated unnecessary work: "The team of low-level supervisors stopped doing what they didn't have to do. For example, they reduced the amount of paperwork by one-third, and it turned out that what they eliminated wasn't being used anyway."[12]

Another benefit is higher work quality. Many times when the nature and scope of the work are increased, the job becomes more meaningful, the employees better understand the importance of the job, and the number

---

11. Antone F. Alber, "The Real Cost Of Job Enrichment," *Business Horizons,* February 1979, p. 66.

12. *Ibid.,* pp. 66–67.

of errors declines. Notice in Table 8–3 that the number of firms reporting improved quality was almost 30 times greater than the number reporting reduced quality!

One of the most commonly reported benefits of job enrichment changes is increased resource use. For example, the amount of labor force idle time goes down and machine use time goes up. Of course, these developments do not always occur immediately. In fact, numerous researchers have reported that output declines initially, if only because the employees lack training or are unsure of what the management is up to with its job enrichment efforts. ("Why are they redesigning this work? Why are they interested in making this job more interesting or enjoyable?")

Another payoff is the operating benefits, including improved safety features, better scheduling of work, improved labor relations, and increased levels of job satisfaction. It should be noted, however, that not everyone wants to have his or her work redesigned. Many employees admit that they like things as they are.

Still another benefit of job enrichment programs is reduced absenteeism and turnover. Sometimes, of course, these things will worsen. In most cases, however, researchers report an improvement.

Making Job Enrichment Pay Off

To make job enrichment pay off, an organization must reduce the design and performance-related costs and keep the benefits high. It can accomplish these objectives, in many cases, through the implementation of management practices such as the following:

Practical management practices

1. Find out what employee attitudes are toward job design and work to get the support of the personnel for these changes.

2. Do not underestimate the amount of time that will have to be spent on training the workers to handle these newly designed jobs.

3. Redesign the work intelligently so that there is a blend between the needs of the workers and those of the organization.

4. Emphasize the nonmonetary return to the employees by showing them how the jobs are now much more interesting and challenging than before.

5. Analyze the overall effect of the change on the organization itself. If possible use a pilot project to see how things go.

6. When one job design project proves itself, use this as a model for others; do not attempt to reinvent the wheel each time.

7. If the job enrichment program goes well, stick with it; if the program does not appear to be doing well, work to straighten out any problems that exist and wait a reasonable amount of time before throwing in the towel. Maybe the project will not work, but give it a chance.[13]

---

13. *Ibid.,* p. 72.

Summary

1. Coordination is the synchronization of the human efforts of individuals and groups to attain organizational efficiency. Coordination is particularly important in the case of interdependent work. Interdependency can take one of three forms: pooled, sequential, and reciprocal.

2. Authority is the right to command. There are four common types of authority. Line authority is direct authority such as that which a superior has over a subordinate. Staff authority is auxiliary, as in the case of a lawyer who provides advice to a top manager. Functional authority is authority in a department other than one's own, as in the case of the finance vice president who has the authority to order the head of manufacturing to provide cost production data. Project authority is the authority a matrix manager has over the individuals assigned to the project.

3. Decentralization is a philosophy of management regarding which decisions to send down the line and which to keep near the top for purposes of organizational control. Every organization, except those owned and operated by one person, is decentralized to at least some degree. There are a number of ways of measuring decentralization, including studying the quantity of decisions made at different levels, the quality of these decisions, the impact of the decisions on lower levels, and the control the individual has in his or her own area of operation. Some of the major factors influencing decentralization include cost, size, desire for independence, availability of managers, and the nature of the enterprise.

4. Delegation of authority is the process of assigning duties to subordinates, giving them the authority to carry out tasks, and creating an obligation on their part to complete the assignments in a satisfactory manner. In the delegation of authority there are a number of boss-related and subordinate-related problems. The effective manager works to overcome these.

5. Committees are extremely valuable in coordinating activities. Basically, there are three types of committees: ad hoc, standing, and plural executive. Some of the major advantages of committees are that they make group judgment possible, provide for the representation of interested parties, help to coordinate plans and activities, and provide motivation. Some of the major disadvantages include their tendency toward indecision or compromise, their costs in terms of time and money, and their tendency to promote lack of responsibility. In using committees effectively, organizations must focus their attention on the objectives, authority, and organization of the committee, the leadership of the committee, and the support of the membership.

6. A third major way of effectively coordinating the people and the work is through the use of job design. Job design is the process of introducing work changes to increase work quality and quantity. Some of the most common approaches to job design include job engineering, job rotation, job enlargement, the socio-technical approach, goal setting, and job enrichment. An examination of the job characteristics model helps us to understand the effects of job enrichment on work attitudes and behavior. This model considers personal and work outcomes, critical psychological states, core job dimensions, and implementing concepts.

7. In recent years attention has been focused on assessing the economic costs and benefits associated with job design. Some of the specific costs include wage and salary increases, facility change costs, inventory costs, charges for implementing the new work design, and expenses incurred in training employees to

carry out the newly expanded jobs. Some of the benefits include increased work quality, better use of resources, increased operating benefits, and lower absenteeism and turnover.

Key Terms

Ad hoc committee   A committee that is formed for a particular purpose and that is disbanded upon completion of the objective.

Authority   The right to command.

Coordination   The synchronization of the human efforts of individuals and groups for the purpose of attaining organizational efficiency.

Core job dimensions   Causal factors that can bring about critical psychological states that are vital to positive work outcomes.

Critical psychological states   Psychological states that, if created, can result in positive work outcomes such as increased quality and quantity of work and reduced absenteeism and turnover.

Decentralization   A philosophy of management regarding which decisions to send down the line and which to keep near the top for purposes of organizational control.

Delegation of authority   The process of assigning duties to subordinates, giving them the authority to carry out these tasks, and creating an obligation on their part to complete the assignments in a satisfactory manner.

Functional authority   Authority in a department other than one's own.

Goal setting   A job design approach that emphasizes building goals, feedback, and incentives into the structure of the work.

Horizontal loading   Increasing the number of tasks or activities that a worker is doing by giving him or her more of the same to do.

Job characteristics model   A comprehensive conceptual framework for examining the effects of job enrichment on work attitudes and behavior through a consideration of personal and work outcomes, critical psychological states, core job dimensions, and concepts for implementing job design.

Job design   The process of introducing work changes to increase the quality or quantity of work or both.

Job engineering   The use of time and motion analysis to achieve the most efficient interface between the worker and the machine.

Job enlargement   A job design technique that involves giving the worker more to do through the use of horizontal loading.

Job enrichment   An extension of job rotation and job enlargement that attempts to build psychological motivators into the work.

Job rotation   Moving a worker from one job to another to reduce boredom.

Jurisdictional questions   Questions or issues that arise between two or more departments or units regarding who has authority in a given matter.

Line authority   Direct authority such as that possessed by a superior over a subordinate.

Plural executive committee   A committee that has the authority to order the implementation of its recommendations.

Pooled interdependence   A form of interdependence in which all units or departments are contributing to similar objectives but the actual coordination between them is minimal.

Project authority   The authority a matrix manager has over the individuals assigned to the project.

Quality control circle   An approach to job design in which work groups meet to discuss and recommend changes in the way the jobs are being done.

Reciprocal interdependence A form of interdependence in which the inputs of one unit become the outputs of another.

Sequential interdependence A form of interdependence in which work units are linked together in the form of a chain and each depends on the one in front of it for inputs.

Sociotechnical approach An approach to job design in which a group or team of workers is made responsible for getting the job done.

Staff authority Auxiliary authority held by individuals who advise, assist, recommend, or facilitate organizational activities.

Standing committee A committee that is permanent in nature, as in the case of the finance or personnel committees that exist in many organizations.

Vertical loading A concept used in job design which involves giving the worker more control over both the planning and control of work activities.

Questions for Analysis and Discussion

1. In your own words, what is meant by the term coordination? How do the following types of coordination work: pooled, sequential, reciprocal? Explain, giving an example of each.

2. What is meant by the term authority? In your answer use examples of line, staff, functional, and project authority.

3. Numerous line-staff problems and dilemmas result from the improper use of functional authority. How can a modern organization go about dealing with typical line-staff problems? Offer at least three suggestions. How can the enterprise minimize problems in the use of functional authority? Again offer three suggestions.

4. How can a project manager deal most effectively with the "authority gap" problem? What techniques are useful? Describe at least three.

5. In your own words, what is meant by the term decentralization? How can decentralization be measured? Cite and explain three ways.

6. What are some of the factors that influence the degree of decentralization in an organization? Identify and describe three.

7. Is decentralization superior to centralization? Or is centralization superior to decentralization? Defend your answer.

8. What is meant by the term delegation of authority? What are some of the most common boss-related problems related to delegation of authority? What are some of the most common subordinate-related problems? How can these problems be resolved? Explain.

9. What is meant by each of the following types of committees: ad hoc, standing, plural executive? When are committees most effective? When do they tend to be of limited value?

10. Overall, what are two of the most important advantages of committees? What are two of the most important disadvantages? Explain.

11. What can be done to improve the overall effectiveness of committees? Give at least three suggestions.

12. Some of the most popular approaches to job design include job engineering, job rotation, and job enlargement. How does each work? Be complete in your answer.

13. How does a sociotechnical approach to job design work? In what way is a quality circle an example of a sociotechnical approach?

14. How does goal setting in job design work? In what way is it related to job enrichment?

15. In your own words, what is job enrichment? How does it differ from job enlargement?

16. In what way does the job characteristics model help explain job enrichment? In your answer be sure to explain all of the major parts of the model.

17. From a cost and benefit standpoint, what are some of the typical costs associated with the implementation of job enrichment programs? What are some of the specific benefits to be derived? Overall, do you think that job enrichment has proven to be a useful tool for modern managers or is the idea basically ineffective? Defend your answer.

Case   # Ted's Idea

Last week Ted Kantor returned from a management seminar. The seminar had covered a host of different management-related topics, including job design. Ted was intrigued by some of the ideas of the trainer and is now thinking of trying to apply some of them in his own work environment.

Ted is the manager of a small (30 people) assembly-line department. The personnel assemble one product only, a small portable electric kitchen appliance. The parts are produced at another location and sent to Ted's area. His people then assemble, test, and package each unit. The process consists of the following five distinct steps:

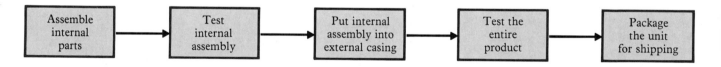

Some parts of the process take longer than others. For example, the assembly of the internal parts requires 20 minutes, while the testing of the internal assembly takes only 5 minutes. Putting the internal assembly into its casing requires 15 minutes (the assembler has to ensure a proper fit and then place three screws into the casing), while testing the entire product takes only 10 minutes (this involves a visual examination of the product as well as a test to determine whether the unit works properly). Packaging of the product requires another 10 minutes. There are three work groups in the department: one does internal assembly; one does the internal testing and placing of the parts into the casing; the last tests the overall product and then packages it.

Ted believes that the current assembly method is good but that there is room for improvement. In particular he feels that some form of job enlargement, a sociotechnical approach (maybe some version of the quality circle), or job enrichment would be a good idea. His first step is going to be to talk to the assemblers themselves to see what ideas, if any, they might have for redesigning the work. If the response is positive, then he intends to work with them in deciding what to do.

1. If Ted does opt for job enlargement, how would this redesign work? How would each person's job change?

2. If a sociotechnical approach were used, what would it involve? Include in your answer a discussion of the quality circle.

3. Drawing upon your understanding of the job characteristics model, explain how job enrichment can be used in redesigning this work. How would it be carried out?

You Be the Consultant

Losing It In-House

Aldag, Inc. is a well-known national manufacturer of medical supplies and equipment. The firm sells to both hospitals and clinics as well as to doctors' offices.

At the present time Aldag estimates that its share of the medical supplies market is 12.3 percent and its share of the medical equipment market is 10.6 percent. Return on investment has declined over each of the last five years, however. This year it will be even lower: the vice-president of finance has estimated a return on investment of 5.3 percent.

The chairman of the board, Ted Heckman, is not pleased with this declining ROI. He reasons that with gross sales increasing at an annual rate of 15 percent and the firm holding a large market share, returns should be much higher. His own personal evaluation is that there are too many internal inefficiencies. Specifically, organizational bottlenecks and a distinct lack of coordination are costing the firm money. "We do just fine in the external market," Ted told a few board members, "but we do not do well in-house. What's the use of beating the competition if we simply throw away our profits with inefficient organizational procedures?"

One of the things that Ted is specifically referring to is an internal report drawn up by a special organizational evaluation committee appointed by the board. The committee members were charged with making an internal analysis of company operations. When they finished their 90-day investigation, they sent their report to the board. The following is a brief summary of four of their major findings:

1. There is an overuse of functional authority (see Figure 8–8). In particular, the legal and finance departments currently have the right to give orders in a number of other departments and this is leading to both coordination and control problems.

2. There is insufficient delegation of authority in the finance and production departments. The managers refuse to delegate authority as widely as they should. This is as true at the top levels of these departments as it is at the middle levels.

3. The R&D and personnel departments have each established committees with interdepartmental membership. The purpose of the R&D committee is to generate and discuss new product ideas. This committee was meeting weekly. Now it meets monthly and attendance is poor. The same basic situation exists for the personnel committee, which was established to review the training needs of all departments. This committee is not living up to its responsibility.

4. The manufacturing department has a series of 23 assembly line processes used for putting together medical equipment products. In most cases semifinished parts are passed from one individual to another. This is both time-consuming and, in the minds of many of the assemblers, dull work. A new approach to job design is needed.

Figure 8–8   Aldag, Inc. Organizational Chart

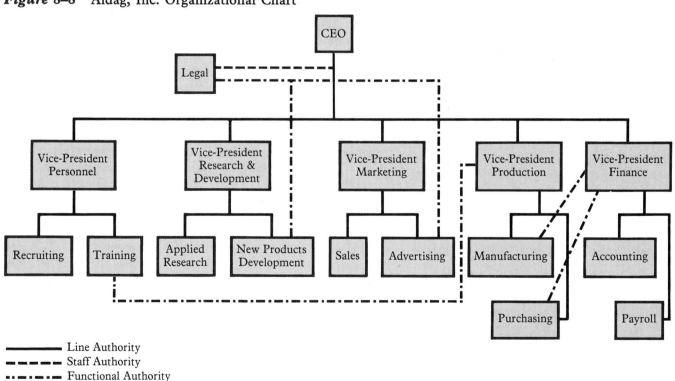

Your Consultation

Assume that the president has provided you a copy of this in-house report and asked you to be the outside consultant. Read the case again, carefully noting the organizational problems the firm currently faces. Then give your recommendations. In those instances where you feel that a particular problem requires more information indicate (a) the type of information you would seek to gather, (b) the likely outcomes you would find, and (c) most important of all, how you would resolve the problems. Be as specific as possible in your recommendations.

Recruiting and Selecting the Workforce

Objectives

Every ongoing organization must be concerned with recruiting and selecting a workforce. Some enterprises want to expand their current operations; others want to move into totally new areas. At the same time these organizations face personnel retirements, resignations, and terminations. As a result of such developments, the typical workforce is in a state of flux. For this reason recruiting and selecting are very important to modern organizations. Unless human resource talent can be acquired and retained, the enterprise's chances of reaching its objectives are severely limited. This chapter examines the way in which the recruiting process actually works, studies the ways in which recruits are selected for positions in the workforce, and reviews the role of orientation for new employees. When you have finished studying all of the material in this chapter, you should be able to

1. define the term "strategic human resources planning";

2. describe the linkage between strategic planning and employment needs;

3. tell how modern organizations go about forecasting their employment needs;

4. explain how the recruiting process works, including both sources and methods of recruiting practices;

5. describe the selection process, including selection criteria, specific steps that are followed in the process, and the use of assessment centers; and

6. discuss the values and benefits of orientation.

236

Strategic Human Resources Planning

Strategic human resources defined

Strategic human resources planning is the process of identifying the numbers, skills, and occupational categories of personnel the organization will need in the future to ensure the attainment of its strategic objectives. At the heart of this process is the question: "What are the potential internal and external threats, opportunities, and trends taking place in human resources that may have an impact on the strategic success of the organization?"[1] Human resources planning is closely linked to the strategic planning process, which was discussed in Chapter 5. Many of the same questions that govern the establishment of strategic objectives also influence the recruiting and selecting of personnel.

Strategic and employment planning are closely linked.

Human resources planning begins with the same question that strategic planning begins with: What business are we in? The remaining steps in the two kinds of planning are also parallel, as both go on to evaluate the plan and set new objectives. Human resources planning and strategic planning go hand in hand. Table 9–1 illustrates this idea.

The strategic plan sets the direction in which the organization will go. The human resources plan ensures that the enterprise has the necessary people to follow the strategic plan. Sometimes it calls for hiring additional personnel with particular talents. At other times it requires the organization to train and develop the current personnel. In this chapter, consideration will be focused on the first of these demands—recruiting and selecting additional personnel. This specific process is outlined in Figure 9–1. Notice that three key external forces affect this process: government regulation, economic factors, and demographic and social trends.

Table 9–1
The Strategic Plan—Human
Resources Plan Linkage

Strategic Plan	Human Resources Plan
What business are we in?	What specific human skills are needed in this business?
What external market forces (technological, economic, social, etc.) will we have to address?	What human skills and capabilities will the personnel need in coping with these external forces?
What are the current internal resources with which we can fashion a viable strategy?	How qualified are our current personnel in helping us meet our basic mission?
In what specific markets should we concentrate our resources and what objectives should we pursue?	Are our present personnel sufficient or do we need to recruit and hire more people?
What resources do we still need to acquire in order to attain these objectives?	What kinds of additional people should we hire? What recruiting and selecting process do we need?
After the plan has been put into effect, what changes are in order?	Do we need to let anyone go? Hire more people? Train and develop any present personnel?

---

1. Stella M. Nkomo, "Stage Three in Personnel Administration: Strategic Human Resources Management," *Personnel,* July–August 1980, p. 75.

Key External Forces

Each of the three key external forces in Figure 9–1 is important, although, depending on the specific situation, one may prove to be more important than the others. For many organizations, government regulation is at the top of the list.

Government Regulation

Many laws and executive orders prohibit discrimination in employment. The most encompassing is the *Civil Rights Act of 1964*. Title VII of this act specifically forbids employment discrimination on the basis of race, color, religion, sex, or national origin.

Numerous laws regulate employment practices.

Another major piece of legislation is the *Equal Pay Act of 1963,* which requires equal pay for individuals doing jobs that require substantially equal skill, responsibility, and effort while working under similar working conditions. This act was amended in 1972 to include administrative, executive, and professional employees.

Figure 9–1
Strategic Human Resources
Planning Process

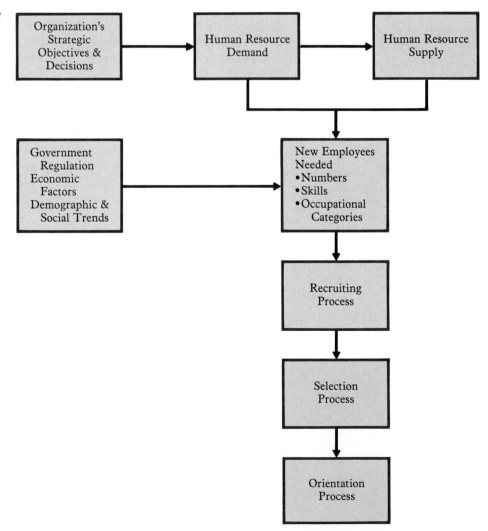

A third major act is the *Age Discrimination in Employment Act of 1967,* which prohibits discrimination against people between the ages of 40 and 65. This act governs all employers with 20 or more workers.

A fourth act is the *Rehabilitation Act of 1973,* which requires organizations to take affirmative action for the employment of individuals with physical or mental handicaps. Specific regulations have been developed and issued by the federal government regarding the kinds of actions that are required and the organizations that are covered.

In addition to these acts, a number of executive orders have been issued by various presidents. *Executive Order 11246,* issued by President Lyndon B. Johnson, prohibits the same actions as does Title VII of the Civil Rights Act but carries the additional requirement that contractors develop a written plan of affirmative action and establish numerical integration goals and timetables for achieving this equal opportunity objective. *Executive Order 11478,* issued by President Richard M. Nixon, forbids discrimination by the federal government on the basis of race, color, religion, sex, national origin, political affiliation, marital status, or physical handicap.

These acts and legislative orders are important to the human resources plan because they define the limits within which an organization can act. As each year goes by, they are supplemented by still other regulations. One of the more recent deals with mandatory retirement and allows people who wish to continue working until age 70 to do so. This new retirement age is in marked contrast to the previous mandatory retirement age of 65 in most organizations. In an effort to deal with changing regulations, many businesses are finding that equal employment opportunity (EEO) guidelines must be developed and followed. Table 9–2 illustrates a partial framework that can serve as a guide in developing an overall affirmative action compliance strategy. Working within a framework such as this one, the organization can carry out its hiring and promotion efforts. In large enterprises, a Personnel Department is charged with staying abreast of the latest government regulations and ensuring that the firm is operating within regulatory boundaries. In small organizations the top managers assume this responsibility.

Economic Factors

During the 1970s, productivity in the United States continued its slow decline. What accounts for this problem? One answer is rising labor costs. Another is that personnel are not working as efficiently or as effectively as they should be. Since labor costs, for all practical purposes, cannot be reduced very much (if at all), the best thing an organization can do is to ensure that the personnel are well trained and capable of doing their jobs. Additionally, the enterprise should know which employees can be moved up in the case of a vacancy, which employees need further training, and which are questionable in terms of continued employment.

Some companies keep an employee replacement chart.

Some companies deal with these questions by keeping an **employee replacement chart.** This chart, illustrated in Figure 9–2, shows which personnel are performing extremely well, which are satisfactory, and which need to improve their performance. The chart also describes the promotion potential of each person.

In dealing with economic forces, however, an organization also needs to be able to conduct employment forecasting. It must be able to project

Table 9–2   Partial Framework for an Affirmative Action Compliance Strategy

Areas for Action	Overall Objectives of Affirmative Action	Possible Tactics and Specifics
Increasing minority/female applicant flow	To insure that minorities and females are not systemically excluded from the communication of employment opportunities available in the facility; and to encourage those individuals to apply.	1. Include minority colleges and universities in campus recruitment programs. 2. Personal and regular contacts with employment referral agencies, such as Job Corps or Urban League. 3. Participate in job fair or career day programs at area high schools and vocational schools. 4. Place employment advertising in minority-oriented print and broadcast media. 5. Encourage current minority/female employees to refer other minority/female individuals to the organization (for example, memo, "finder's fee"). 6. Retain applications of unhired minority/female applicants to be reviewed as vacancies occur.
Demonstrating top-management support for EEO policy	To indicate to all employees that top management considers affirmative action and equal employment opportunity to be legitimate and important activities for the organization.	1. Prepare written reports evaluating progress toward affirmative action goals as other management control reports are prepared. 2. Involve the line supervisors in the establishment of the affirmative action hiring goals. 3. Appoint an EEO coordinator who is both highly visible within the facility and from a department other than personnel. 4. Participation by the top executive in the EEO training and orientation of line supervisors. 5. Route progress reports and related material on affirmative action through senior executives' offices. 6. Include affirmative action issues and progress on the agenda of departmental meetings.
Keeping employees informed	To communicate to employees the specifics of the affirmative action programs, including their rights, benefits, and opportunities as organization members.	1. Discuss EEO matters, such as program success and new program efforts in internal publications (house organ, newsletter). 2. Display EEO policy statement in work areas. 3. Provide and publicize the availability of career development counseling.

Areas for Action	Overall Objectives of Affirmative Action	Possible Tactics and Specifics
		4. Make the affirmative action plan available for employee review.
		5. Post promotion opportunities within the work areas.
		6. Explain the EEO policy, job posting, complaint procedures, tuition refund programs, and so on, during the new employee orientation procedure.

Source: Reprinted, by permission of the publisher, from "Conducting an Internal Compliance Review of Affirmative Action," Kenneth E. Marino, *Personnel,* March–April 1980, pp. 30–32. © 1980 by AMACOM, a division of American Management Associations. All rights reserved.

Four common employment forecasting techniques

job vacancies or new positions. Basically, four methods are used in modern organizations to forecast employment needs.

The least sophisticated approach is often called the **expert-estimate technique.** It calls for knowledgeable executives to decide how many people will need to be hired during the next 6 to 12 months.

A second approach is the **trend-projection technique.** This method relies heavily on past events and tries to tie employment needs to one or more causal factors. For example, the company might say: "In the past for every increase of $100,000 in sales we have had to hire four new people. Since we project an increase in sales this year of $1 million, we will have to hire another 40 workers."

The third forecasting method is the **unit demand forecast.** In this method a "bottom up" approach is used. Each unit manager analyzes his or her unit, job by job, to determine employment needs. This information is then passed on to the superior, who carries out the same process. The data are thus passed up the line, from one level to the next, until they arrive at the top. Headquarters, in turn, sums up the estimates, and the result becomes the organization's overall employment forecast.

A fourth approach is a version of **modeling and multiple-predictive techniques** in which the organization uses mathematical models that take into account a series of employment-related data such as sales, gross national product, and discretionary income. Based on the results of the sophisticated analysis, a conclusion is reached regarding hiring needs. This approach is not very common and tends to be restricted to large, multiline corporations.

Of these four techniques, the ones most commonly used in small organizations are the expert-estimate or trend projection techniques. These are simple and do not take much time. In larger organizations the unit demand forecast is often employed.

Demographic and Social Trends

A number of important demographic and social trends have contributed to the composition of today's workforce. These trends are having a serious

Figure 9–2   Employee Replacement Chart

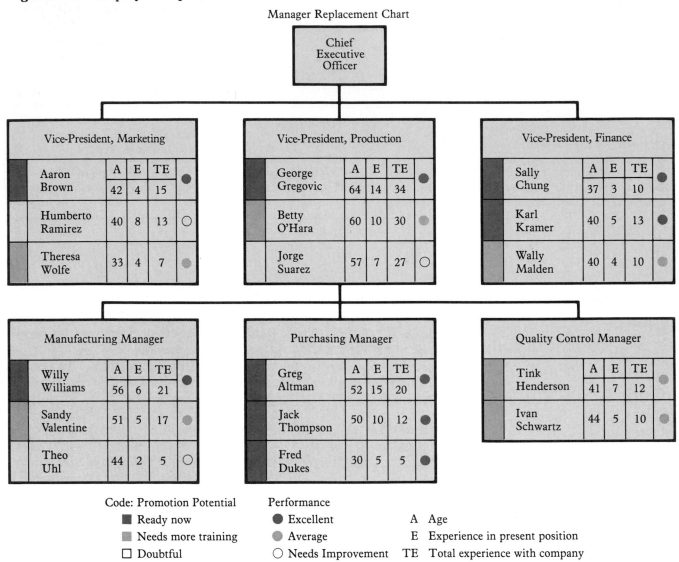

Manager Replacement Chart

Code: Promotion Potential	Performance	
■ Ready now	● Excellent	A Age
▨ Needs more training	◐ Average	E Experience in present position
□ Doubtful	○ Needs Improvement	TE Total experience with company

The composition of the workforce is changing.

impact on the way organizations staff their operations. One of the most significant is the post-World War II baby boom. People born in the 1945–1955 decade began entering management positions in 1975 and will continue to move into these positions until 1990, assuming that the average person gets into middle management when he or she is between 30 and 35 years old. These people are having to fight for the limited number of management positions available. Because this trend is coupled with the extension of the mandatory retirement age from 65 to 70 and the influx of women and minorities into the labor force, human resource plans must be thought out very carefully.

In recruiting and selecting personnel, an organization also has to address the specific work demands of the personnel. These demands are being influenced by changing values. Employees are demanding, and getting, not only more enriched jobs but, in many cases, flexible work schedules as well.

More hours in fewer days

Flexible work schedules can take a number of different forms. One is the **compressed work week,** which involves fitting the normal work week (35 to 40 hours) into fewer days. For example, instead of working eight hours a day five days a week, an individual may work 10 hours a day four days a week. In some cases the individual may have a 36-hour week, working 12 hours daily three days a week.

Choosing one's hours

Another variation of flexible work schedules is flexible hours, or **flextime** for short. Under this arrangement employees are permitted to choose their own work hours. For example, the person who likes to come to work early and leave early may be given a schedule of 7 A.M. to 3 P.M. Another who likes to come in later in the morning may be given a schedule of 10 A.M. to 6 P.M. There are certain periods of the day, however, when everyone is at work. These periods are called **core hours.** Some of the benefits associated with flextime include increased job satisfaction, increased productivity, reduced commuter time, and more personal time for leisure and family activities.[2] In addressing social trends, modern organizations are finding it necessary to use techniques such as these.

The Recruiting Process

Recruiting defined

Recruiting is carried out within the guidelines created by the key external forces discussed earlier in this chapter. **Recruiting** is the process of attracting job candidates who have the abilities and attitudes necessary to help the organization achieve its objectives. Recruiting is a natural follow-up to human resource planning. As soon as the enterprise knows the number and types of individuals it needs, it can focus attention on recruiting these people.

The value and importance of the recruiting process is perhaps best illustrated through an examination of the costs associated with recruiting various specialists and managers. One researcher[3] has estimated that recruiting costs the following percentage of the first-year salary of these managers:

Senior engineer	68%
Accountant	61
Secretary	51
Supervisor	40
Middle manager	33
Top manager	35

2. Warren Magoon and Larry Schnicker, "Flexible Hours at the State Street Bank of Boston, *Personnel Administrator,* October 1976, pp. 34–37.

3. Robert Sibson, "The High Cost of Hiring," *Nation's Business,* February 1975, p. 85.

Who Recruits?

Recruiting responsibility is delegated differently in different organizations.

The responsibility for recruiting personnel is delegated differently in different organizations. In small companies managers with personnel vacancies often become actively involved in the recruiting process. Larger organizations usually form recruiting committees. The members of these committees recruit and interview applicants.

In large organizations the Personnel Department is often charged with doing the recruiting. This department places recruiting advertisements with the media and conducts initial interviews with applicants. Keep in mind, however, that while various committees or departments may play an active role in recruiting, the manager for whom the individual will be working usually makes the final decision regarding hiring.

Where to Recruit

To find job applicants, the organization must know where to recruit. Many sources are available, depending on the specific needs of the enterprise. Table 9–3 shows some of the major sources of job applicants for blue-collar, white-collar, and managerial positions.

Current personnel are tapped first.

The most readily available source of job applicants is the company's current personnel. One way of tapping this source is through a job-posting system in which the organization notifies its people of openings through company publications and bulletin boards. Many firms post all permanent

Table 9–3
Sources for Recruiting Personnel

Sources	Blue-Collar	White-Collar	Managerial, Technical, Professional
Internal			
Job posting and bidding	X	X	
Friends of current workers	X	X	
Skills inventories	X	X	X
External			
Walk-ins	X	X	
Agencies			
Temporary help		X	
Private employment agencies		X	
Public employment agencies	X	X	
Executive search firm			X
Educational distributions			
High school	X	X	
Vocational/technical	X	X	
Colleges and universities			X
Other			
Unions	X		
Professional associations			X
Military services	X	X	X
Former employees	X	X	X

and transfer opportunities, giving in-house people at least one week to apply before turning to outside sources.

Many firms also encourage present employees to tell their friends and relatives about job openings. Of course, certain equal opportunity programs prohibit organizations from giving jobs to people solely on the basis of employee friendship. It is a good way to generate a pool of applicants, however.

Skills inventories help in identifying qualified candidates.

Some organizations also turn to the use of **skills inventories,** employee records that contain information on each person's training and experience. Sometimes these inventories are quite simple and contain only the individual's job experience, i.e., five years as a welder or four years as an advertising manager. At other times they are much more detailed and include education, training, strengths, weaknesses, present performance, and potential for promotion (ability and the possible position). By examining these skills inventories, the organization can determine the likelihood of filling current vacancies with in-house personnel. Of course, small organizations are not likely to have such records. The time and expense associated with gathering the initial information and keeping everyone's record up to date limits the use of skills inventories to larger organizations.

Table 9–3 lists almost all of the external sources of recruits that an organization ever needs. Notice that there are employment agencies that a business can call upon for assistance. In the case of executive recruiting or temporary help, these agencies can be very effective. They do charge a fee, however. If an enterprise does a lot of hiring, it often sidesteps this expense by using its own recruiting force. The following discussion examines four of the most popular methods of recruiting.

Methods of Recruiting

The specific method of recruiting depends on the needs of the company. Some forms, such as advertising, can be used to draw personnel for all levels, while an executive recruiting agency provides assistance only in filling upper-level positions.

Media Advertisements

Media advertising is the most common form of job advertising.

The most common form of advertising is the daily newspaper help wanted ad. These ads can be found in any local paper. National papers such as the *Wall Street Journal* and *New York Times* also carry ads, but they list jobs offered in all areas of the country in a wide array of organizations. People looking for employment can match their needs with those of potential employers, by looking at ads in the appropriate kind of paper, local or national.

Executive Recruiting Firms

Executive recruiting firms are used by organizations looking for top managers. The purpose of these recruiting firms is to find the "right match" between a company and a job candidate. Large recruiting firms operate nationwide with offices on both coasts and a few in between. These recruiters are always on the lookout for successful executives willing to move to another firm. Executives may also go to them looking for placement with another company. For this reason the recruiting firm's initial client is not always a company. The company hiring the executive pays the fee, however, and it can run as high as one year's salary.

College Recruiting

College recruiting is also widely used.

Many companies that are looking for personnel, especially management trainees or college-educated people, turn to college recruiting. In this process the organization assigns one or more of its people to serve as interviewers who travel the college circuit, calling on schools in the nearby area (in the case of a local firm) or throughout the country (in the case of a national firm).

Interviewing is an expensive process. First, people have to be trained in the techniques of effective interviewing. This training may include trial interviews in which recruiters are videotaped and allowed to see themselves in action, and instruction in the way to ask and answer questions and size up prospective employees. Unless the students are sufficiently impressed by the recruiter, they are not likely to be attracted to the company. In the opinion of students, four of the most common flaws in interviewers include (1) a lack of interest in the applicant, (2) a lack of enthusiasm, (3) a tendency to ask questions that are either too personal or create stress in the interviewee, and (4) failure to allow the applicant time to talk or ask questions.[4]

Summer Internships

Some firms offer summer internships.

Another approach, also geared at recruiting college students, is the summer internship. This is a hiring arrangement in which a student works for a summer and then returns to school. An internship gives the organization a chance to look the student over before offering full-time employment. It also provides the organization with an "ambassador" on campus who can tell other students how good the company is.

In recent years a number of businesses have offered summer internships, including Kaiser Aluminum, Chase Manhattan Bank, Standard Oil of Ohio, and First National City Bank. Government agencies, hospitals, and other nonprofit organizations have also made them available. In many cases organizations use these internship programs to attract women, blacks, or other minorities. Their use has been mostly restricted to large firms, however, because of the high costs involved. Interns typically require a great deal of supervision and before they really start to produce the summer is over and they are back at school. Nevertheless, for firms that have the interest, desire, and money to spend, the internship arrangement can be a very rewarding one.

---

4. William F. Glueck, *Personnel: A Diagnostic Approach*, revised edition (Dallas, Tex.: Business Publications, Inc., 1978), p. 173.

The Selection Process

Selection defined

After the firm has recruited potential personnel, it must decide which ones to hire. At this time, the selection process begins.[5] **Selection** is the process by which an enterprise chooses the applicants who best meet the criteria for the available positions.

Selection Criteria

In order to ensure that the best available candidates are selected, an organization must compare the applicants against the criteria established for the job. These criteria can be grouped into five basic categories: education, experience, physical characteristics, personal characteristics, and personality types. Before examining these categories, however, we must note that any criterion used for selection must be *job related*. The criterion must assist in predicting which applicants are most likely to do the best job. To make this prediction, an organization must use selection instruments that are both valid and reliable.

Validity and Reliability

Validity is vital.

Validity means that a selection instrument measures what the organization wants it to measure. If the company wants to hire a typist, the test that is administered must measure typing skills and expertise. If the firm wants to hire a supervisor, the test must help in distinguishing between those with supervisory skills and those without them.

So is reliability.

Reliability means that a selection instrument provides a consistent measure of something. If a typist gets a 97 on the test today, he or she should get approximately 97 tomorrow. If a supervisory applicant scores high on the test today, he or she should also do well tomorrow. The higher the reliability of the instrument, the more confidence management can place in it.

Of validity and reliability, validity is more important. For an instrument to be valid, it must also be reliable. The reverse is not necessarily true, however. In computing the validity of a selection instrument, a company may use either of two basic approaches. One is to look at current employees, find one (or more) job-related factors common to their performance, designate it as a potential predictor, and then determine if it is actually related to job performance. This approach is called *concurrent validity*. A second possibility is to use a screening test in the hiring process, see how well the hired applicants do, and correlate the test scores with their respective performances. This approach is called *predictive validity*. When attempting to screen job applicants, effective organizations all seek to develop valid predictors. Of the four criteria generally employed in the selection process, some tend to be valid while others are not.

"Looks like young Lanks has a good business head on his shoulders."

5. Ann Coil, "Job Matching Brings Out the Best in Employees," *Personnel Journal*, January 1984, pp. 54–60.

Education

Education can be a valid screening criterion.

For some jobs, education is a valid screening criterion. Practicing physicians must have medical degrees. Universities can require the doctorate as a prerequisite for a tenure-earning position. For many other jobs, however, education may help but there is no direct proof that a person with education will be more effective than one without it. Selling is an example. Will a salesperson with an undergraduate degree in marketing be more effective than a person without such a degree? Unless the firm can prove that the individual will be, the criterion of a college degree should be dropped. And there are many examples to support the limitations of education as a selection criterion. One study found that nonschool experience is an important factor in prediction of success.[6] A second discovered that grades and quality of school were insignificant as predictors of future earnings.[7] Education is not always a very useful criterion to use in selecting candidates.

Experience

So can job experience.

A second popular criterion for selection is experience. Employers usually want more experience as opposed to less and feel that someone who has done the particular job before (or one similar to it) should be hired before someone to whom the job is completely new. Experience is equated with ability. To some degree, this logic is justified. If the employer can find out how well the applicant has done in the past, this information can also be used as a gauge in evaluating the likelihood that the person will do well in the current job.

Physical Characteristics

While it may sound silly, some employers (consciously or unconsciously) use physical characteristics as a selection criterion. This screening approach can take many forms. For example, when a bank has only one female teller and wants more, the next woman who applies for a teller's job is going to have the inside track over a man. The same situation might involve other minorities if an organization was trying to increase the number of minorities in the work force.

Physical characteristics are not.

Physical characteristics also enter the screening selection process when the manager asks: Does this applicant *look* like a supervisor (or whatever level manager is being hired)? Is he or she tall enough? Big enough to command respect? Strong enough to carry out the job? Except in the case of stamina, where the company can require a physical exam to ensure that the person has the physical strength to do the job, the use of physical characteristics in the selection process is, at best, arbitrary and is likely to get the organization in trouble eventually.

---

6. Leonard Nadler, "Recognition of Non-Collegiate Learning Experiences," *Training and Development Journal,* July 1975, pp. 8–11.

7. Charles R. Link, "Graduate Education, School Quality, Experience, Student Ability, and Earnings," *Journal of Business,* October 1975, pp. 477–491.

Personal Characteristics and Personality Types

Nor are personal characteristics . . .

The last two criteria relate to personal characteristics and personality types. Personal characteristics include such things as marital status, children, and age. Some organizations are reluctant to hire someone who has been divorced. (Is this person very stable?) Others look unfavorably on single people. (Why is he or she not married? What is wrong with this person?) A second personal characteristic is the number of children. (If this person has five children, will he or she give the organization as much time as is needed to get the job done? Or will this person be spending too much time at home with the family to the detriment of the job?) Finally, there is the criterion of age. Some people are considered too young for a job; others are considered too old. In the case of young people, the question tends to be: Does he or she really have the experience and knowledge to get this job done? In the case of old people the question is: Can he or she get the work done without being overwhelmed? In any case the decision is often not to hire the individual. The young person is passed over with the comment, "Let's wait and let him or her get more experience." In the case of the older applicant the response is, "He or she is over the hill; we need a younger person."

or personality types.

In considering personality types, an organization considers whether the applicant is basically an introvert or an extrovert. Does the applicant seem to have the outgoing style needed for successful salesmanship? Does the applicant seem to have the restraint and quiet judgment needed in an effective top manager? Almost every position in the organization has its "right personality traits" that are used in determining whom to hire. This approach to selection is, at best, arguable. It assumes that the people making the selection will be able to identify successful personality traits and determine whether the applicant has them. Besides the fact that personality tests are being used less and less because of the difficulty of establishing a link between test scores and desired job behavior, many organizations today realize that there are more accurate ways of selecting candidates.[8]

Steps in the Selection Process

The selection process consists of six basic steps, although some organizations sidestep a few to reduce time and expense. In describing this process we will use the above-noted criteria, where applicable and valid. Otherwise they will be ignored. The following discussion examines the selection process in sequential order beginning with the preliminary screening interview.

Preliminary Screening Interview

In some cases applicants apply for a job in person. They simply walk into the employment office or job location and announce that they would like to be considered for a particular position. Many times these people lack either the experience or the training to do the job effectively. This fact can be determined in just a few minutes of general interview screening.

---

8. Ellen J. Wallach, "Individuals and Organizations: The Cultural Match," *Training and Development Journal,* February 1983, pp. 22–26.

In these cases, the preliminary screening interview serves to reduce the number of applicants to be considered and the amount of organizational time expended in filling job vacancies.

Completion of Application Blank

Most firms use application blanks.

If the applicant does pass the preliminary screening interview, or if the organization does not have such a process, the next step is the completion of an application blank. Almost all organizations use an application blank of some sort, although the amount of information requested varies. The application blank can help screen candidates in that the information requested may indicate clearly that they lack necessary training or experience.[9] The information also may help a company predict success on the job by allowing it to see, for instance, whether those with no background in sales do better or more poorly than those with one or two years' experience. Decisions based on application form data should also be supported by empirical evidence, however. Merely to assume that an applicant without selling experience will not do as well as one with it is insufficient justification for screening the applicant out. The company should have data on employee performance in the past to support its decision. Otherwise, a charge of discrimination can be raised.

Many organizations have also found that some of the biographical data they requested in the past have no relevance to the person's ability to do the job. As a result, they have revised the application form to omit such information. Of those parts that remain, some organizations weigh the data so that some information is considered more important than other information.

In recent years biographical data has increased in importance because many organizations have discovered that some of the tests and other selection techniques they were using are invalid. Until better techniques are developed, biodata will probably continue to be used as an important selection input.

The Employment Interview

The third step in the selection process is the employment interview. This is one of the most widely used tools in selection. In general terms, there are three types of interviews: structured, semistructured, and unstructured.[10]

Three types of interviews

In the **structured interview,** the interviewer uses a prepared list of questions and does not deviate from them. In a **semistructured interview** only the major questions to be asked have been prepared in advance and the interviewer may either expand on them or ask other questions that open new areas of discussion. The **unstructured interview** is one in which the interviewer asks whatever seems appropriate and adapts the discussion

9. Richard S. Lowell and Jay A. DeLoach, "Equal Employment Opportunity: Are You Overlooking the Application Form," *Personnel,* July–August 1982, pp. 49–55.

10. John W. Cogger, "Are You a Skilled Interviewer," *Personnel Journal,* November 1982, pp. 840–843.

to the responses, choosing areas in which further questions appear warranted and ignoring those in which additional discussion seems fruitless.

The most commonly used type of interview combines structured and unstructured approaches. It provides the interviewer general guidance while still allowing him or her to pursue subjects that warrant greater discussion.

The biggest problem with interviews is their validity and reliability. Exactly what is the purpose of the interview? Many candidates find that when they are interviewing for a job each person with whom they visit asks them basically the same questions. So the interviewers really do not learn a great deal about the candidate. Also, there is the very great danger that the interviewers will be overinfluenced by the applicant's appearance or the answers he or she gives to questions. Other commonly cited deficiencies include the following:

1. The interviewer does too much talking and never lets the candidate develop his or her responses.

2. The questions are inconsistent in that different interviewers ask different questions. Between them they have a lot of information, but not enough to make comparisons regarding the responses.

3. Some interviewers rate almost all applicants as average; particularly strong or weak applicants get the same rating as everyone else.

Interviewer deficiencies

4. Some interviewers allow one or two responses to affect their overall view (good or bad) of the candidate.

5. If the interviewers talk to three or four poor candidates in a row, the next individual (regardless of how mediocre he or she is) ends up getting an undeservedly high rating.

6. The interviewer has a stereotype of the ideal applicant and allows this profile to influence the rating.

7. Many interviewers have their own favorite questions designed to throw the applicant off balance enough to inadvertently reveal his or her real nature. They then try to interpret the results by playing "junior psychologist."

8. Some interviewers ask questions related to an applicant's race, sex, religion, age, or some other generally inappropriate factor.[11]

The best way to overcome problems like these is to provide training for the interviewers. From this training, they should learn how to (1) listen to what and how the applicant communicates, (2) be aware of the nonverbal cues the applicant is sending, (3) remain aware of the job requirements and how well the candidate will fill the bill, (4) maintain a balance between structured and unstructured questions so as to learn as much relevant information as possible, and (5) avoid making a decision on the individual before talking with other interviewers to learn how they feel.

11. Terry W. Mullings and Ronald H. Davis, "A Strategy for Managing the Selection Interview Process," *Personnel Administrator*, March 1981, pp. 66–67.

Employment Tests

Performance tests are many and varied.

Some organizations use selection employment tests. These tests are many and varied. One of the most common is the *performance test,* in which the applicant is asked to perform a job-related task. For example, the applicant may be asked to operate a piece of machinery or make a decision regarding how to handle a disciplinary problem. Performance tests tend to have high validity and reliability because they systematically measure behavior directly related to the job.

A second type of test falls under the heading of *performance simulation.* This type of test is designed to measure a person's space visualization (as in the case of a draftsman), psychomotor ability such as finger dexterity (as in the case of an assembler of components) or clerical abilities (such as the ability of a secretary to check numbers and names).

A third type of test is the *paper-and-pencil variety.* These tests often measure mental ability. Two of the most common are the Otis Quick Scoring Mental Ability Test and the Wechsler Adult Intelligence Scale. While these types of tests are still popular today, their validity and reliability are not as high as those of performance-related tests.

The least reliable employment tests are those used to measure *personality or temperament.* Such tests have low validity because it is too difficult to relate their findings to job-related behavior. Consequently many organizations have dropped them.

Reference Checks and Recommendation Letters

If the applicant successfully completes the steps to this point, the organization usually checks the person's references. Of greatest interest to the employer is the applicant's performance in previous jobs.[12] If the individual is applying for his or her first job, the organization relies heavily on the comments in the letters of reference regarding the applicant's overall ability, effort, initiative, and integrity. These letters are not always very reliable because the writer may be providing an evaluation based on limited input (the applicant may have been a student in one of the writer's classes, or the person writing the letter may know the applicant's family and believe that the applicant will be a good worker). Nevertheless, if the applicant seems to be qualified and the reference letters provide no information to the contrary, the firm is likely to view the applicant positively.

Physical Examination

A physical exam is often required.

The last step in the selection process, before the actual hiring decision, is the physical exam. Merely because the person seems qualified to do the job does not mean he or she can do the work. Is the applicant in good health? This is an especially important question for someone who will be doing manual labor or holding a top-management position. For this reason, many firms require a physical exam.

---

12. James D. Bell, James Castagnera, and Jane Patterson Young, "Employment References: Do You Know the Law?" *Personnel Journal,* February 1984, pp. 32–36.

Of course, the person may pass the physical and still develop medical problems later on. Passing the exam is no guarantee that the person will not have a heart attack within the next five years. Organizations require it, however, if only to cover themselves from liability in case the applicant's family files suit claiming that the individual had a bad heart and never should have been hired for strenuous labor. By having a physical exam report in its possession, the company is in a position to challenge the family and point out that, to the best of its knowledge, the worker was in excellent health when hired.

Assessment Centers

In selecting managers, many organizations use an assessment center. The purpose of an **assessment center** is to identify the management applicants with the greatest potential. The ultimate purpose of the center is to answer the question: Of all those who are likely to do well, which are most likely to succeed in the job?

The assessment center concept was used by German military psychologists during World War II, but the first use of the approach by industry was that by AT&T in 1956.[13] That study examined the characteristics that affected the career progress of young employees from the time they took their first job in the Bell System until they moved into middle- and upper-management levels. The results were impressive. Of the 422 people in the study, 42 percent of those who were judged to have middle-management potential achieved that level, while only 4 percent remained at their original level in the hierarchy. At the same time, of those predicted not to rise, 42 percent did not move up, while only 7 percent achieved middle-management positions.[14]

Since this original study, other firms have employed assessment centers in selecting managers. Some of the best known include IBM, Ford Motor, General Electric, J. C. Penney, Merrill Lynch, and General Telephone, as well as the FBI, the Civil Service Commission, and the Social Security Administration.

How They Work

Assessment centers are designed to predict performance success more accurately than educational background, interviews, paper-and-pencil tests, and performance appraisals can. In an assessment center, a number of assessors evaluate the way the applicants perform. After watching the applicants in action for one to five days, depending on the position for which they are applying, the assessors gather, discuss the data, and agree on the evaluation of the applicants. While assessment centers may differ from organization to organization, the following six elements are considered essential to each:

13. Wayne F. Cascio, *Applied Psychology in Personnel Management,* 2nd edition (Reston, Va.: Reston Publishing Company, Inc., 1982), p. 243.

14. Ron Zemke, "Using Assessment Centers to Measure Management Potential," *Training/HRD,* March 1980, p. 26.

1. A series of assessment techniques must be used. At least one of these must be a simulation or exercise in which the applicants are required to use behaviors related to dimensions of performance on the job. This simulation may be a group exercise, fact-finding exercise, interview simulation, etc. (See Table 9–4 for an example.)

2. A number of assessors must be used. These people must have had thorough training so they know exactly what to look for in the applicants.

Elements of assessment centers

3. The final decision regarding what to do (hire, promote, etc.) must be a result of a group decision by the assessors.

4. The simulation exercises that are used must have been developed to tap a variety of predetermined behaviors, and have been pretested prior to use to ensure that they provide reliable, objective, and relevant behavioral information.

Table 9–4 A Typical Two-Day Assessment Center

Day 1 Orientation meeting

Management game—"Conglomerate." Forming different types of conglomerates is the goal, with four-person teams of participants bartering companies to achieve their planned result. Teams set their own acquisition objectives and must plan and organize to meet them.

Background interview—A one-and-a-half-hour interview conducted by an assessor.

Group discussion—"Management Problems." Four short cases calling for various forms of management judgment are presented to groups of four participants. In one hour the group, acting as consultants, must resolve the cases and submit its recommendation in writing.

Individual fact-finding and decision-making exercise—"The Research Budget." Participants are told that they have just taken over as division manager. Each is given a brief description of an incident in which the predecessor has recently turned down a request for funds to continue a research project. The research director is appealing for a reversal of the decision. The participant is given fifteen minutes to ask questions to dig out the facts in the case. Following this fact-finding period, he or she must present a decision orally with supporting reasoning and defend it under challenge.

Day 2

In-basket exercise—"Section Manager's In-Basket." The contents of a section manager's in-basket are simulated. Participants are instructed to go through the contents, solving problems, answering questions, delegating, organizing, scheduling and planning, just as they might do if they were promoted suddenly to the position. An assessor reviews the contents of the completed in-basket and conducts a one-hour interview with each participant to gain further information.

Assigned role leaderless group discussion—"Compensation Committee." The Compensation Committee is meeting to allocate $8000 in discretionary salary increases among six supervisory and managerial employees. Members of the committee (participants) represent departments of the company and are instructed to "do the best you can" for the employee from their department.

Analysis, presentation, and group discussion—"The Pretzel Factory." This financial analysis problem has the participant role-play a consultant called in to advise Carl Flowers of the C. F. Pretzel Company on two problems: what to do about a division of the company that has continually lost money, and whether the corporation should expand. Participants are given data on the company and are asked to recommend appropriate courses of action. They make their recommendation in a seven-minute presentation, after which they are formed into a group to come up with a single set of recommendations.

5. The techniques used in the assessment center must be designed to provide information that can be used in evaluating the dimensions, attributes, or qualities previously determined.

6. The assessment by the evaluators must be made after the exercises are completed, not during the exercises.[15]

Overall Value

On the positive side, a number of organizations have reported great success with their assessment centers. For example, at IBM, 1,086 nonmanagement employees were classified as having either potential for successful assignment beyond the first-level management or having no potential beyond this level. Of those assessed as having such potential, 30 percent achieved second-level positions. Conversely, only 10 percent of those rated first-level were promoted beyond this level. Additionally, 20 percent of those promoted against the prediction were eventually demoted, in contrast to only 9 percent of those who were promoted in accordance with the prediction.[16]

On the other hand, there is some concern about the fact that most of the validation studies to date have been restricted to large business organizations. A second concern is that unless the organization knows how to run an assessment center, the evaluators may not really know what they are doing or why they are doing it. A third area of concern is whether these assessment centers can be defended in a court of law. In one recent case an assessment center was used to select the deputy police chief of a large midwestern city. While the judge upheld the validity of the process, he questioned some of the methods used.

On an overall basis, however, assessment centers certainly do seem to be an important step toward the effective selection of managers. Commenting on this idea, Fred Luthans, a well-known behavioral scientist, has written:

> There is little question that the assessment center is a much more comprehensive and valid approach to selection than are tests and interviews. By use of the simulated exercises, the approach is much more directly related to job performance than is a question on a personality test asking whether the employee likes to sleep with a light on or off. The big companies have given a great deal of effort and financial support for relating actual job dimensions to the exercises used in their assessment centers. At this stage of the development of assessment centers, the procedures and actual conduct of the sessions in medium-sized and smaller business firms and the potential of the approach for use outside the selection process must be given further attention. Overall, the future looks bright for the use of assessment centers in the selection . . . processes of organizations.[17]

15. "When Is an Assessment Center Really an Assessment Center?" *Training HRD,* March 1980, p. 24.

16. Zemke, *op. cit.,* p. 30.

17. Fred Luthans, *Organizational Behavior,* 3rd edition (New York: McGraw-Hill, 1981), p. 595.

Orientation

Orientation defined

Orientation is an important follow-up to selection. **Orientation** is the process of introducing new employees to the organization and to their superiors, their work groups, and their tasks. If this process is carried out properly, a number of advantages can be obtained. If it is done poorly, the enterprise will often find the new employees unsure of what they are doing or inefficient in getting it done or both.

Basic Advantages

Sufficient research in industry has been conducted to prove that some specific benefits are associated with proper orientation. One of these is a reduction in the start-up costs for new employees. Better oriented workers reach standard performance faster than their counterparts who are not well oriented.

A second advantage is the reduction in anxiety concerning job failure. When an individual knows what is expected and how long it will take to become proficient at the job, the nervousness that accompanies the new work is often greatly reduced. Proper orientation also makes the individual aware of some of the hazing techniques often employed by more experienced workers who enjoy ribbing new employees. This knowledge reduces tension by helping the new worker "catch on" earlier.

A third benefit is reduction in employee turnover. When workers feel they are ineffective or unneeded, the tendency to quit increases. Effective orientation helps reduce this costly practice.

A fourth advantage is the time saved by supervisors and co-workers. The better the individual's orientation, the less likely it is that he or she will need to seek help from others.

Finally, a well-designed orientation program helps the worker develop positive attitudes toward the employer and job satisfaction. The individual is more likely to identify with the enterprise and the work.

Numerous research studies have indicated that these advantages do exist. The most extensive study was conducted at Texas Instruments (TI) which found that anxiety and tension among new workers had a negative effect on their output and led to dissatisfaction and turnover. TI decided to investigate whether an orientation program could reduce anxiety and increase competence and satisfaction. As a result, two groups of new recruits were formed. One group was given the traditional orientation program, which consisted of a two-hour briefing by the Personnel Department on the first day of work, including a short description of the work the new employees were to be doing and the company's rules and regulations. These recruits were then taken off to be introduced to their supervisor, who gave them a short job introduction.

The other group was given the same two-hour orientation and then another six hours of social orientation. During this latter period four basic things were done: (1) the employees were told that their opportunity to succeed with the firm was good; (2) they were encouraged to disregard typical hazing procedures often inflicted on new workers by more experienced ones; (3) they were encouraged to ask their supervisor for any needed help; and (4) they were told to get to know their supervisor.

Research supports proper orientation.

The results were dramatic. The experimental group had 50 percent less tardiness and absenteeism, training time was cut 50 percent, and waste was reduced by 80 percent. Effective job orientation does indeed pay off.

Orientation in Action

Orientation programs vary widely. In small firms they tend to be very informal, while in large organizations each new employee is put through a prepared schedule. In addition to the typical tour of the facilities, other common items on the orientation agenda include (1) a brief discussion of the company's history and general policies, (2) a description of its services and products, (3) an explanation of its organizational structure, (4) a brief rundown of its personnel policies, benefits, and employee services, (5) a recitation of the overall rules and regulations to which all employees are asked to adhere, and (6) an introduction to the work group with which the employee will be working.

Some programs are formal; others, informal.

In small organizations much of the orientation is handled verbally. In large ones the employee usually is given a booklet or brochure that explains and elaborates on many of the rules, policies, and procedures that were discussed verbally. Some companies even follow up on the orientation process by asking their new people to fill out a form similar to that in Figure 9–3. This follow-up form helps the superior judge how well the new subordinate understands the job, and it pinpoints areas in which the person may be confused about his or her duties.

In the case of management trainees, orientation often goes one step further. Many of these individuals are new college graduates starting their first full-time job. Because the company realizes that first impressions are very important to the trainee's career and employee development, supervisors are often trained to serve effectively as role models for this group. The supervisors are taught how to praise, encourage, and develop the trainees. Such techniques are very valuable in ensuring their commitment to the organization. Daniel Kanouse and Philomena Warihay, consultants in the area of human resources administration, have put the idea this way:

> . . . what workers want most is a feeling of self-worth and what organizations want most is profitable self-perpetuation. Employee desires for self-esteem are being expressed throughout America. "Industrial concerns are subject to increasing pressures seeking improvement in the work force and in the environment. . . . There are signs of crisis in almost every major institution. Many of these are centered around people—the desire of individuals for a richer quality of life in their everyday lives and on the job." Organizations determined to meet both their own and their employees' goals need a method for systematically addressing the way they deal with their human resources. Concerned members of management can initiate a change in their utilization of human resources as a point where it will make the greatest impact—at the beginning—with effective employee orientation.[18]

---

18. Daniel N. Kanouse and Philomena I. Warihay, "A New Look at Employee Orientation," *Training and Development Journal*, July 1980, p. 38.

Figure 9–3   Orientation Follow-Up Form

JOB INFORMATION

1. The job of my department is to _____

   My assigned area is _____

   The most important part of my job is _____
   _____

2. My department head's name is _____
   His/her office is located _____
3. I receive my time card from _____
   Time cards must be turned in on day _____
   to (person) _____. Pay day for our
   department is _____
   If I am out of the hospital on pay day, I can get my
   pay from _____ The cashier's
   office is where _____
4. If I feel ill while at work, I should _____
   _____

   If I become ill while at home, I should notify my
   supervisor by calling (hosp. phone no.) _____
   dept. ext. _____ at least one hour before I am
   expected at work
5. My locker or checkroom is located _____
6. The hours I am scheduled to work are assigned by _____

   Any change in my work schedule (days off, etc.) is
   arranged in advance by _____
   My lunch hour and relief are assigned by _____
7. Work assignments are given to me by _____
   I can get help on the job from _____
8. Some of the things I do on my job are:
   A. _____
   B. _____
   C. _____
   D. _____
   E. _____
9. In doing my work I handle the following (check the boxes)

   PAPER [ ]   EQUIPMENT [ ]

   SUPPLIES [ ]   FOOD [ ]

   PRODUCTS [ ]   PATIENTS [ ]

10. If I work with papers:
    Papers I handle   They come   When I finish
    daily include   from   they are used by

    _____
    _____
    _____
    _____

11. If I use equipment, I use _____
    _____
    _____

To keep the equipment in good working order I must
_____
_____
_____

12. If I work with supplies, products or food—the way
    I handle them is important because _____
    _____
    _____

13. My work helps Lenox Hill Hospital give better patient care by
    _____
    _____
    _____

14. When I need supplies, I get them from
    (person) _____ (place) _____
    (time) _____ (day) _____
15. To keep things running smoothly, I should bring to my
    supervisor's attention such things as _____
    _____
    _____

16. How well I do my work can be measured by _____
    _____

17. 2 Safety rules that apply in my job are:
    1. _____
    _____
    2. _____
    _____

18. I have had the most difficulty with _____
    _____
    _____
    _____

19. Things I'd like to know more about are _____
    _____
    _____

20. Things I like best about my job are _____
    _____
    _____
    _____

SUGGESTIONS I HAVE _____
_____
_____
_____

Source: Joan E. Holland and Theodore P. Curtis, "Orientation of New Employees," as found in Joseph E. Famularo, *Handbook of Modern Personnel Administration* (New York: McGraw-Hill Book Company, 1972), Chapter 23, pp. 23–10 through 23–13. Reprinted with permission.

Summary

1. Strategic human resources planning is the process of identifying the numbers, skills, and occupational categories of personnel the organization will need in the future to ensure the attainment of its strategic objectives. This process is closely linked to strategic planning.

2. Three key external forces affect human resources planning. One is government regulation, as reflected in such legislation as the Equal Pay Act of 1963, Civil Rights Act of 1964, Age Discrimination in Employment Act of 1967, and the Rehabilitation Act of 1973. A second is economic factors, which modern organizations address through such means as employee replacement charts and employment forecasts. The third is demographic and social trends, which are resulting in such developments as flexible work schedules.

3. Recruiting is the process of attracting job candidates who have the abilities and aptitudes necessary to help the organization achieve its objectives. The responsibility for recruiting personnel is delegated differently in different organizations. In small firms recruiting is done by the managers for whom the individual will be working. In large organizations a recruiting committee or a Personnel Department handles the task.

4. Some of the most common ways of generating job candidates internally include job posting, the contacting of friends of current workers, and the use of skills inventories. The most common sources of external candidates include agencies and educational institutions. When external sources are used, some of the most frequent methods of recruiting include media advertising, the use of executive recruiting firms, college recruiting, and the use of summer internships.

5. Selection is the process by which an enterprise chooses those applicants who meet the criteria for the available positions. The most important characteristic of selection is that the selection techniques be both valid and reliable. Validity means that the selection instrument measures what the organization wants it to measure. Reliability means that the selection instrument provides a consistent measure of something. Some of the criteria often used in screening candidates include education, experience, physical characteristics, personal characteristics, and personality types.

6. There are six basic steps in the selection process: (1) the preliminary screening interview, (2) the completion of an application blank, (3) the employment interview, (4) employment tests, (5) reference checks and recommendation letters, and (6) the physical exam. For screening managers, another popular approach is the assessment center.

7. Orientation is the process of introducing new employees to the organization and to their superiors, their work groups, and their tasks. If this process is carried out properly, a number of important advantages can be obtained.

Key Terms

Assessment center A method of selecting managers that involves predicting performance of candidates through the use of simulation exercises and other tools and techniques for evaluating job-related behavior.

Compressed work week Scheduling the normal weekly hours into fewer days so that, for example, individuals work four 10-hour days rather than five eight-hour days.

Core hours The time periods during the day when, regardless of the flexible work schedules of the various employees, everyone is at work.

Employee replacement chart   A chart that shows which personnel are performing extremely well, which are satisfactory, and which need to improve their performance, as well as the promotion potential of each person.

Expert-estimate techniques   A method of forecasting employment needs in which a knowledgeable executive, or committee, decides how many people will be needed over the next six to 12 months.

Flextime   A flexible work schedule in which employees are permitted to choose their own work hours.

Modeling and multiple-predictive techniques   A method of forecasting employment needs that involves the use of mathematical models that take into account a series of employment-related data such as sales, gross national product, and discretionary income.

Orientation   The process of introducing new employees to the organization and to their superiors, their work groups, and their tasks.

Recruiting   The process of attracting job candidates who have the abilities and attitudes necessary to help the organization achieve its objectives.

Reliability   The degree to which a selection instrument provides a consistent measure of something.

Selection   The process by which an enterprise chooses the applicants who best meet the criteria for the available positions.

Semistructured interview   An interview in which the major questions to be asked are prepared in advance and the interviewer may expand them and ask others.

Skills inventories   Employee records that describe each person's training and experience as well as, in some cases, the person's strengths, weaknesses, present performance, and potential for promotion.

Strategic human resources planning   The process of identifying the numbers, skills, and occupational categories of personnel the organization will need in the future to ensure the attainment of its strategic objectives.

Structured interview   An interview in which the interviewer uses a prepared list of questions and does not deviate from them.

Trend-projection technique   A method of forecasting employment needs that involves trying to tie employment needs to one or more causal factors.

Unit demand forecast   A method of forecasting employment needs that involves a bottom-up approach in which each unit manager analyzes the needs of his or her unit and passes the information up the line to the superior.

Unstructured interview   An interview in which the interviewer asks whatever seems appropriate and adapts the discussion to the responses, choosing those areas where further questions appear warranted and ignoring those where additional discussion seems fruitless.

Validity   The degree to which a selection instrument measures what the organization wants it to measure.

Questions for Analysis and Discussion

1. In your own words, what is meant by the term strategic human resources planning? What is the link between strategic planning and human resources planning?

2. How does government regulation affect employment planning? In your answer be sure to discuss the following: Civil Rights Act of 1964, Equal Pay Act of 1963, Age Discrimination in Employment Act of 1967, and the Rehabilitation Act of 1973.

3. Of what value is an employee replacement chart? How can it be used in human resources planning?

4. How do each of the following employment forecasting techniques work: expert-estimate, trend-projection, unit demand, and modeling and multiple-predictive? Explain your answer.

5. What is meant by a compressed work week? Flextime? Core hours? How do modern organizations use these concepts?

6. In your own words, what is meant by recruiting?

7. Using Table 9–3 as your guide, tell when the following would be of value in recruiting: skills inventories, executive search firms, college recruiting? Explain.

8. What is meant by the term selection? What role should validity and reliability play in the selection process? Put the answer in your own words.

9. How useful are each of the following in terms of selection: education, experience, physical characteristics, personal characteristics, personality types? Explain your answer.

10. In your own words, what are the six basic steps in the selection process? Briefly describe each.

11. What are some of the problems associated with using interviews in the selection process? Identify and discuss two.

12. How does the assessment center concept work? It is of any value? When should it be used?

13. Is orientation of any value? Explain, being sure to include in your answer some of its basic advantages.

| Case | # Now for the People |

The Baumbeck Corporation is a speciality design and manufacturing firm located on the West Coast. Over the last five years, the company has expanded its market from a five-state region to the entire nation. The corporation's CEO feels that if the firm continues this blanket approach to the market, it can achieve an annual sales increase of 20 percent for at least the next decade.

Two months ago Baumbeck bid on a large government contract and yesterday learned it had won the bidding. The contract calls for the design, manufacture, test, and delivery of specialized telecommunications equipment. This equipment is very sophisticated, and while the firm had the expertise for the initial proposal, it is not capable of designing the final specifications. Nor is it currently able to provide the appropriate tests to ensure that the various subsystems of the equipment all work as they should. This problem does not upset the CEO, however. He feels that the most important objective—securing the contract—has been attained. Now the focus of attention can swing to obtaining the needed personnel.

The company knows what it has to do. Fifteen new engineers must be hired within the next six months. The initial hirings must be among those who have had experience in the design of telecommunication systems. Baumbeck realizes that there is a shortage of these people but also knows that the firms against which it competed for the contract have such people. There are others located in the large aerospace firms.

The company would also like to hire one or two professors of engineering for a two-year stint. These professors, it feels, will provide both theoretical insights and a fresh approach to the design of the subsystems. The president and head of engineering both believe that some of the most creative thinkers in systems design can be found in universities. "If nothing else," the engineering vice-president has commented, "they will give us a new look at things and, I believe, help us better understand how to design these subsystems most efficiently."

The remainder of the new workforce to be hired will have to be obtained from competitive firms. The company's initial plan is to try to identify some of these individuals and contact them privately. If this approach does not work, a broader approach will be used.

1. How should the firm go about recruiting the experienced telecommunication engineers? The college professors? The other engineers?

2. If the firm were to obtain a pool of applicants in each of the three groups, how could it select the best ones? Explain.

3. Would orientation be of any value? For which groups? Defend your answer.

You Be the Consultant

A Matter of Fine Tuning

As demand for their industrial machinery has increased, Calhill & Turner have begun setting up operations in different locales around the country. The company's first plant was in Massachusetts, the second in California, the third in Texas. Six days ago, the board of directors decided that the firm would move into Ohio.

The company is currently in the process of determining how many people will be needed for the Ohio plant. Initial estimates range from 225 to 250. Of these, approximately 20 percent are to be management personnel and the rest will be skilled or semiskilled workers.

If Calhill & Turner follow past practices, they will draw as many of the needed managers as they can from their current plants. The remainder will be hired locally. Skilled and semiskilled workers, meanwhile, will all be hired from the Ohio area or from adjacent states.

The firm expects that the new plant will do $15 million of business in its first year of operation. During each of the next four years the annual projected increase is $5 million annually. Initially, new business orders will be handled by the original workforce. Additional orders will be taken care of by new personnel who will be hired beginning 18 months after the plant opens.

In deciding who will be sent in as head of the plant, the company is going to select one of five top managers who have indicated an interest in the job. They will be screened using an assessment center program that was developed and installed two years ago by an outside consulting firm. Calhill & Turner are quite pleased with the results of this assessment center concept so far: not one manager who was promoted after being selected through an assessment center has failed to do the job well.

The managers who will go to Ohio to work in the new plant are those who have been rated as "promotable now" by their respective superiors and who have indicated a desire to move. The ratings are listed on manager replacement charts that are developed and kept up-to-date on a biannual basis by all managers who have three or more subordinates.

The skilled and semiskilled workers will be hired based on past experience and a series of job-related tests that the firm has developed to help identify those who are most adept at the work. First preference in selecting will be given to skilled workers, after which attention will be focused on hiring semiskilled workers.

In selecting the latter personnel, the company intends to use a very detailed job application form that will provide both important background data and references that can be used to determine previous work performance. The firm is also having its Personnel Department examine Ohio's hiring laws to ensure that all EEO guidelines are followed. "We've hired people for three locations now," said the president, "and each time we have found ourselves confronting new problems. We have a general recruiting and selecting plan worked out, but in every case it needs fine tuning."

Your Consultation

Assume you are a consultant to the president of this company. Review the preliminary plan sketched out in this case and note the additional steps the firm should take in recruiting and selecting personnel for its Ohio plant. Then offer the president your detailed plan for staffing these facilities. Be as complete as possible in your plan.

10

Training and Developing the Organization's Personnel

Objectives

The previous chapter addressed the ways in which modern organizations recruit and select personnel. This chapter examines the ways in which these organizations train and develop their people. The objectives of this chapter are to examine the nature of training and to study how organizations actually train their employees and develop their managerial personnel. When you have finished reading all of the material in this chapter, you should be able to

1. define the term training and discuss the role that learning plays in the training process;

2. explain how human information processing works and why it is important to organizational training;

3. discuss the role of top management in the training process;

4. describe how organizations analyze their specific training needs;

5. identify and describe specific types of employee training and management development programs; and

6. list specific steps that can be used in evaluating a training program.

The Nature of Training

Training and learning defined   **Training** is the process of altering employee behavior and attitudes in a way that increases the probability of goal attainment. When training is properly conducted, learning occurs. **Learning** is the acquisition of skills, knowledge, and abilities that result in a relatively permanent change in behavior.

264

Learning and Job Training

All people are capable of learning, although there are certainly differences in the way they learn. Some learn fastest if they are shown how to do something; others do best if they are told how to do it; still others learn fastest when they are actually allowed to carry out the task. For this reason, training methods vary, as does the locale in which the training occurs. Usually, the organization does the training using company facilities. Sometimes, however, an off-the-job location is used because it is more conducive to learning, or because the program is sponsored by a training or educational organization, such as a university, and is open to everyone on a first-come, first-served basis.

In order to ensure conditions conducive to learning, the facilities should be laid out in a way that encourages attention and ease of participation. Learning is also more likely to occur if the trainer can keep the participants alert. For this reason organizations typically use a variety of learning methods, including lectures, discussions, projects, and simulation exercises.

The company must establish a link between the training and its value to the trainee by showing the trainee the usefulness of the program. It can establish this link in two ways: by having the trainer explain and illustrate the practicality of the training and by having the superior reinforce the training by praising the subordinate for using the newly acquired methods or ideas back on the job.

Depending on the nature of the material, the training sometimes can be done in a matter of hours and the trainee can master the subject quickly. At other times a longer training period is necessary. In a situation where the trainee is being taught to carry out a simple task, such as operating machinery, learning usually occurs quickly; for more complex undertakings, such as analyzing financial statements, learning may be much slower at first and may then pick up dramatically.

People learn in different ways.

Figure 10–1 shows some typical learning curves. In the **negatively accelerated learning curve,** learning occurs very quickly but as the individual masters the material the rate of learning slows up. This curve describes the learning pattern of trainees who have high initial motivation and are studying easy-to-learn material. In the **positively accelerated learning curve,** the opposite occurs: learning starts slowly but increases very rapidly as the new material is absorbed. This curve describes the learning pattern of individuals who have low initial motivation or who have had insufficient past preparation in the subject under study. Finally, the **skills acquisition pattern learning curve** shows a situation in which learning seems to stop for a time. After the person learns some material initially, the learning rate levels off before he or she learns the rest. This leveling off, or plateau, can occur for several reasons: (1) loss of motivation, (2) the need for synthesis of the early material, and (3) the need to eliminate any incorrect learning that has occurred. The skills acquisition learning curve is one of the most common learning curves because many people need time to digest their initial learning before moving on.[1]

---

1. Richard M. Hodgetts and Steven Altman, *Organizational Behavior* (Philadelphia, Pennsylvania: W. B. Saunders, 1979), p. 71.

Figure 10–1   Three Typical Learning Curves

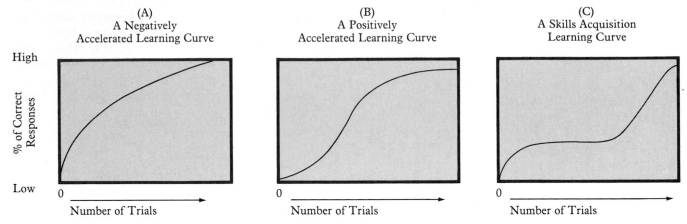

Human Information Processing

In recent years a great deal of attention has been focused on studying how people gather and use information. This subject is often referred to as **human information processing,** or HIP. The reason for studying HIP is that not all people process information in the same way.[2] Some are logical and take a fact-gathering approach; others are intuitive and perceptive. Differing approaches should be used in training these two kinds of people. This area of HIP is popularly referred to as "right-brain, left-brain" thinking. People who are "right-brained" tend to be more subjective and inductive, while those who are left-brained tend to be more objective and deductive. Researchers such as Henry Mintzberg have observed that *good planners* exhibit the strengths of the left hemisphere processor, while *good managers* exhibit the strengths of the right.[3]

Left-brained people focus on facts.

Right-brained people focus on possibilities.

Other researchers have gone even further and have sought to tie left-brain, right-brain thinking to management training. William Taggart and Daniel Robey, for example, offer the decision styles presented in Figure 10–2. Notice from the figure that individuals who are left-brained focus on facts and tend to develop a practical approach to things. At the other extreme are the right-brained people, who focus on possibilities and tend to develop an enthusiastic and insightful approach to things. In the middle are the combinations of intuition and thinking (NT) and sensation and feeling (SF). Each of the four managers described in the figure approaches situations differently. For example, the following table tells how each of them might handle a subordinate whose performance has been rated marginal:

2. Weston H. Agor, "Brain Skills Development in Management Training," *Training,* April 1983, pp. 78–83.

3. Henry Mintzberg, "Planning on the Left Side and Managing on the Right," *Harvard Business Review,* July–August 1976, pp. 49–58.

Type of Manager	Response
ST	"Improve your performance or you're fired!" (factual, impersonal, practical)
NT	"If your performance does not improve, you will be transferred to another position." (focused on possibilities, impersonal, ingenious)
SF	"You need to change. What can we do to help you?" (factual, personal, sympathetic)
NF	"You can improve your performance. Let me suggest an approach." (focused on possibilities, personal, insightful)[4]

Sometimes the effective manager needs to be highly factual and impersonal. At other times he or she needs to be insightful and personal. There are also occasions when the manager should adopt a style between these two extremes (the NT or SF manager). Since left-hemisphere-dominant

Figure 10–2   The Range of Decision Styles in Human Information Processing

	ST Sensation/Thinking	NT Intuition/Thinking	SF Sensation/Feeling	NF Intuition/Feeling
Focus of Attention	Facts	Possibilities	Facts	Possibilities
Method of Handling Things	Impersonal analysis	Impersonal analysis	Personal warmth	Personal warmth
Tendency to Become	Practical and matter of fact	Logical and ingenious	Sympathetic and friendly	Enthusiastic and insightful
Expression of Abilities	Technical skills with facts and objects	Theoretical and technical developments	Practical help and services for people	Understanding and communicating with people
Representative Occupation	Technician	Planner	Teacher	Artist

LEFT HEMISPHERE ←——— DECISION STYLE ———→ RIGHT HEMISPHERE

Manager ←———————————→

Source: William Taggart and Daniel Robey, "Minds and Managers: On the Dual Nature of Human Information Processing and Management," *Academy of Management Review,* April 1981, p. 190. Reprinted with permission.

---

4. William Taggart and Daniel Robey, "Minds and Managers: On the Dual Nature of Human Information Processing and Management," *Academy of Management Review,* April 1981, p. 191.

trainers turn out left-hemisphere-dominant trainees,[5] attention is now being directed toward stressing not only the traditional, left-hemisphere analytic style but also the right-hemisphere creative style. The challenge has been described by Professors Taggart and Robey in this way:

> It is neither trite nor exaggerated to say that management is both an art and a science. But accepting this statement as valid presses us to consider how we can develop manager/artists by providing learning experiences to improve right-hemisphere decision skills. At the same time, we must continue to educate managers for success as manager/scientists. This means retaining the left-hemisphere curriculum that we are familiar and comfortable with. Balancing the curriculum to encompass the complete range of processing styles and strategies that our framework suggests is a major challenge for management in the 1980s.[6]

The Role of Top Management

Some organizations have very successful training programs while others do not. One of the primary reasons is that in some organizations management supports training while in others it does not. Unless there is a positive attitude toward training beginning at the very top, the overall impact of training is limited. Moreover, in some cases verbal support is not enough; active participation is required. Management must be prepared to (1) make it clear that training has a high priority, (2) reward those who train their people, and (3) where needed, actively participate in training programs to keep abreast of the latest developments in their own areas of expertise.

A proactive approach to training.

This philosophy results in a *proactive* approach to training. Instead of waiting for training deficiencies to become apparent, the organization anticipates and plans for the types of training that will keep the workforce up-to-date. Organizations use numerous strategies to attain this objective. Eight of the most helpful are for organizations to

1. Include human resources management and development in the strategic planning process.

2. Project important trends that will affect what management expects of the employees, including technological, social/psychological, economic, political, and intellectual trends.

3. Resist the lure of using training just to handle immediate, short-run problems.

Proactive strategies

4. Hold managers accountable for seeing that the individuals in their units and departments are properly trained.

5. Set a regular, criterion-based planning and review process that can be used to build a pool of potentially promotable individuals.

6. Encourage input from those who will be trained, in designing and implementing training programs.

7. Conduct human resource audits to measure the organizational climate.

5. *Ibid.,* p. 194.
6. *Ibid.*

8. Review management practices and job satisfaction to measure how well things are going in the organization and to pick up early-warning signals that indicate the need for additional training and development.[7]

What specific types of training do employees need? The answer depends on the person's job. At the lower levels of the hierarchy, training is often quite simple and learning involves memorizing procedures or operating equipment. At the upper levels training is more complex and learning involves improving interpersonal relations or developing an understanding of the way to carry out strategic planning. Before deciding on the specific type of training that is required, however, the organization must analyze its training needs.

Analyzing Training Needs

Some organizations, especially large ones, try to keep up-to-date records on employee training needs. Most, however, either rely on periodic assessments for discovering who needs training (and of what type) or simply depend on the individual superior to give subordinates the most effective on-the-job training possible.

Needs analysis surveys

Fortunately, there seems to be a trend, especially among the more successful enterprises, toward conducting *needs analysis surveys*. A sample questionnaire used for this purpose is provided in Figure 10–3.

Needs and Objectives

Determining training objectives

By using needs analysis questionnaires or procedures, an organization does more than simply pinpoint the types of training that are needed.[8] It also provides a basis for determining training objectives. What is the purpose of training? How can the organization know when this objective has been accomplished? To answer these questions, the organization must spell out objectives clearly and establish criteria for determining goal attainment.

While these tasks are easier to do for lower-level jobs than upper-level ones, they should be attempted for all. The following table provides some examples:

Objective	Criterion to Use in Determining When an Objective Is Met
To operate a word processor (lower-level employee)	When the trainee is able to enter a five-page report into the memory, make all typing and editorial changes, and obtain a complete and correct printout.

7. Patricia McLagan, "How Top Executives Can Develop Training's Proactive Potential," *Training/HRD*, October 1980, pp. 43–46.

8. Edward H. Wolfe, "Supervisory Development: The Need for an Integrated Strategy," *Training and Development*, March 1983, pp. 28–31.

Figure 10–3 Needs Analysis Survey Form

Employee _____ Department _____

Check One   Prototype _____ Operational _____

Form Completed By _____ Title _____ Date _____

INSTRUCTIONS

This form was designed to enable you to list skills and evaluate the degree of relevancy of these skills to positions in our own department. In addition you will be asked to assess the degree of proficiency in designated skill areas distinguished by the employees occupying these positions. To accomplish this task, you are asked to follow the steps outlined below.

A) **Prototype Form**

1) Rank the **General Job Skills** in order of your perception of their importance to successfully performing the subject job.

2) Review the **Specific Job Skills** section; this is the preliminary listing prepared by the survey coordinator based on existing job descriptions, and add or delete skills as you feel appropriate.

3) Rank the **Specific Job Skills** in order of your perception of their importance to successfully performing the subject job and divide into five groups as the coordinator has done for the General Skills listing (this is the skill group level).

B) **Operational Form**

After the Prototype Form has been finalized (through rater consensus) with respect to both the type and degree of relevance of skill areas, you will be asked to evaluate each employee's degree of proficiency in each skill area. Please use the scale below.

NO PROFICIENCY   1   2   3   4   5   HIGH LEVEL OF PROFICIENCY

General Skills	General Skills in Ranked Order		Group	Place "x" on Employee Evaluation					
				1	2	3	4	5	*
Planning		1							
Controlling		2	V						
Writing Ability		3							
Oral Communications		4							
Company Credibility		5	IV						
Decision Making		6							
Creativity		7							
Initiative		8	III						
Adaptability		9							
Problem Solving		10							
People Sensitivity		11	II						
Self Evaluation		12							
Relationship to Supervisor		13							
Work Attitude		14	I						
Organizing Ability		15							

Specific Skills	Specific Skills in Ranked Order	Group	Place "x" on Employee Evaluation					
			1	2	3	4	5	*

* Check when there's a discrepancy of more than two points (employee vs. group) or when the employee is rated below 3 in Groups III and below.

| To discipline an employee effectively (middle-manager) | When the trainee can go through a role-playing session, using all of the steps presented in the earlier training, and explain why and how to discipline the employee while still maintaining his or her respect and trust. |
| To present a financial report effectively to the board of directors (upper-level manager) | When the individual is able to read, synthesize, and summarize financial data; have it worked up in the form of graphs, charts, tables, and other visual aids; present it to a group of top line managers; and be able to field questions from them. |

Notice that in the first case the objective can be measured objectively. The second, and more important, the third, require subjective evaluation by other people. Nevertheless, these approaches are the best that an organization can use and, if the people who are evaluating the training know what to look for, they are good enough.

Employee Training

After the organization has examined the training needs of its personnel and has established training objectives, implementation of the training can begin. The four principal types of employee training are apprentice training, vestibule training, on-the-job training, and off-the-job training.

Apprentice Training

Apprentice training is for new employees.

Apprentice training is given to people who are new to the job. Typically, this training is done both on the job and off the job. It is designed to give employees an understanding of the rules and procedures they must follow in carrying out the work as well as a chance to apply these ideas in an actual job setting. The length of the apprentice training period varies. For example, in the case of engravers, foundrymen, and barbers, it can be as short as one to two years. In other cases, such as for tool and die makers, plumbers, and electricians, the time period can run as long as five years.

Vestibule Training

Vestibule training simulates the work environment.

Vestibule training takes place in an environment that simulates the actual workplace. For example, the trainee may run a lathe under the close supervision of a trainer until he or she can operate the machine properly. At this time the individual is sent to the shop floor. Manufacturing organizations and other businesses where technical skills are vital to the job usually train their people in such an off-the-job setting. This approach ensures that the trainees know how to do the job properly before they are allowed to become full-fledged members of the workforce. It also allows the company to use the training facility over and over again once the necessary equipment and machinery are set up. The result is a very economical training method.

On-the-Job Training

On-the-job training is typical. The most widely used type of training occurs on the job. Sometimes it is formal in nature; frequently it is informal. Typically the trainee is shown how to do the work by either the supervisor or an experienced employee. On-the-job training is a particularly helpful approach, especially in jobs where there are a number of "tricks of the trade" that cannot be picked up except through experience. By becoming familiar with these techniques at the very start, the trainee is able to do a better job in much less time than the worker who has to learn everything through trial and error. Another major benefit of on-the-job training is that it is relatively simple and usually not very costly. After all, how much time and effort does it take for an experienced worker to show a new employee how to feed a machine or process a form more effectively? The only real problem occurs when the person doing the training does not know how to do it. In this case the trainee may become more confused than ever. For this reason, some organizations do not allow supervisors or anyone else to train a new worker until they have learned training techniques. Table 10–1 presents the four major steps involved in training.

Off-the-Job Training

Off-the-job training is done away from the actual workplace. Many companies have their own classroom facilities for this purpose. Those that do not often hold their training sessions at a conference room in a nearby hotel. Usually the training is done by company personnel, but in some **Sometimes outside sources are used.** cases companies rely upon professional training organizations such as the American Management Association, the American Society for Training and Development, or local university professors who are skilled in particular areas. Companies with large training programs often use off-the-job training. The methods employed in off-the-job training are discussed in the next section.

Training Methods

Many different training methods can be employed, depending on the training objectives. Learning how to run machinery, for instance, requires the trainee to play a much more active role than learning about new government guidelines regarding equal opportunity. In the first example the trainee is shown how to do the job and is then asked to do it. In the second example the trainee remains seated and listens to a lecture presented by someone who is thoroughly familiar with both the content and the implications of the new guidelines.

The more actively involved trainees are, the greater the cost of the training. For example, if 10 individuals must learn how to run a particular machine, the trainer must watch and correct each in turn. If a great deal of training is involved, the organization may have to assign more than one trainer to the program. Conversely, if the material can be presented in lecture form, the cost per trainee is lower. After all, it matters little to **Lectures are cost-effective.** the speaker if there are 6 people in the session or 26. When possible, organizations prefer to use lectures or a combination of lectures and discussions in training.

Table 10–1
The Proper Way To Train

> **Step 1   Preparation**
> 1.   Put the learner at ease.
> 2.   Find out what the person already knows about the job.
> 3.   Get the individual interested in learning the job.
>
> **Step 2   Presentation**
> 1.   Tell, show, illustrate, and question in order to put across the new knowledge and operations.
> 2.   Instruct slowly, clearly, completely, and patiently, one point at a time.
> 3.   Check, question, and repeat.
> 4.   Make sure the learner really knows.
>
> **Step 3   Performance Try-Out**
> 1.   Test the learner by having him or her perform the job.
> 2.   Ask questions beginning with why, how, when, or where.
> 3.   Observe performance, correct errors, and repeat the instructions if necessary.
> 4.   Continue until you know the trainee knows.
>
> **Step 4   Follow-Up**
> 1.   Put the individual "on his or her own."
> 2.   Check frequently to be sure the person is following instructions.
> 3.   Taper off extra supervision and close follow-up until the trainee is qualified to work with normal supervision.
>
> **Remember**   If the learner hasn't learned, the teacher hasn't taught.

Programmed instruction requires no trainer.

In contrast to lectures, **programmed instruction** is a technique that does not require the presence or intervention of a trainer. Under this popular but expensive training method, the learner can work at his or her own pace, and the subject matter is usually set up so that the individual learns in small amounts. After mastering one small portion of the text material, the trainee moves on to the next. Sometimes the learner's responses are written; at other times the person is asked to do something, like turning on a machine or feeding in a piece of sheet metal. As the trainee performs the task, he or she receives immediate feedback on how well things are going. For example, if a written response is involved, the trainee is told the right answer immediately upon completion of the work. If the trainee has given the correct answer, he or she is allowed to proceed. If not, he or she is told to go back and reread or restudy some of the earlier material. A typical direction would be: "If you answered 'nine' to the above question, go on to page 23. If you did not give the answer 'nine,' go back to page 20 and reread the material in this section one more time."

Coaching and counseling provides individual help.

Unlike programmed instruction, **coaching and counseling** requires personal contact between the trainee and the trainer. The superior talks to the subordinate to find out how well the individual is doing, what kinds of problems he or she is having, and how they can be dealt with. Some managers set aside time every week to talk to new subordinates and review their progress. This personal contact tells subordinates that the boss is concerned for their welfare and encourages them to ask questions, raise issues, and discuss problem areas. This type of training is so important that it is used to develop managers as well as lower-level employees.

Job rotation helps build a pool of talent.

After becoming adept at one job, the employee may be ready for **job rotation,** a training method in which the individual is moved from one job to another. Rotation is often motivational because the person is continually doing something different. It also gives the worker a chance to use a variety of skills and abilities. Many organizations also find that job rotation allows them to develop a pool of talent that can do a series of different jobs. If there is a high degree of absenteeism in one area, individuals from other areas can be transferred there temporarily since they too understand and know how to do that work.

Management Development

Management development defined

Management development is the process by which managers obtain the necessary skills, experiences, and attitudes that they need to become or remain successful leaders in their respective organizations. There are a number of specific reasons for using management development, many of which parallel the reasons for employee training. Four of the most important include (1) reducing or preventing managerial obsolescence by keeping the individual up-to-date in the field, (2) increasing the manager's overall effectiveness, (3) increasing the manager's overall satisfaction with the job, and (4) satisfying some of the requirements of equal employment opportunity by, for example, developing women and other minorities for managerial positions.

The Obsolescence Issue

Modern organizations are particularly sensitive to the problem of managerial obsolescence. There are three major causes of obsolescence. One is the manager's inability to keep up with technological changes in the field. A second is the promotion of individuals to positions for which they are unqualified—i.e., the Peter Principle, which holds that people rise to their level of incompetence. A third is the fact that, as managers get older, they find it difficult to keep up with the latest developments in their field.

Causes of managerial obsolescence

Of course, obsolescence hits some organizations harder than others. It is most prevalent in companies in high-technology industries and those in which a large percentage of the managers are near retirement. Some researchers have reported that managerial obsolescence is highest in the over-55 age group and among engineering personnel where technical knowledge is vital. On the other hand, it has been found that those with higher levels of education and strong work ethic motivation are least likely to become obsolete.[9]

9. Frederick Haas, *Executive Obsolescence,* AMA Research Study 90 (New York: American Management Association, 1968); Lawrence Baughler and John Lee, "Personal Obsolescence: The Employee's Perspective," *Southern Journal of Business,* November 1971, pp. 52–61; Richard Shearer and Joseph Steger, "Manpower Obsolescence," *Academy of Management Journal,* June 1975, pp. 263–275; Frank O.

After making an extensive review of the literature on obsolescence among professional and technical employees, Herbert Kaufman reported that the major factors causing obsolescence are limited intellectual and cognitive abilities, low motivation, low self-esteem, and personal rigidity.[10] How can this problem be addressed effectively? The alternatives are to fire the person, to move the person to another job, or to provide the person with management development programs that address the particular deficiencies. The latter is the preferable alternative. The following discussion examines how it can be implemented.

Development Methods

Smaller organizations seldom have formal development techniques; most are informal. Large enterprises, however, tend to have elaborate and formal programs which often combine on-the-job and off-the-job development. Table 10–2 illustrates the effect that organizational size can have on the specific type of program used. Some of the techniques employed in management development are the same basic ones used in employee training. The major difference is the emphasis given to certain tools and techniques.

Table 10–3 presents some of the most common types of development programs, as reported in the recent literature. It is evident from the tables that the types of training given supervisory managers is not the same as that provided at the middle and upper levels of the hierarchy. Notice that supervisory training tends to involve more in-house workshops, coaching plus on-the-job experience, and self-study courses. At the opposite extreme, executive development consists of more external conferences and seminars, participation in university programs, association and professional conferences and workshops, and consultant programs. Middle management development is in between these two extremes, although it tends to be closer to the executive type than the supervisory type.

Training often varies by hierarchical level.

Development Techniques

A number of different techniques are employed in management development. The purpose of these techniques is to help develop managerial abilities by simulating on-the-job conditions and forcing the participants to deal with them. Four of the most common development techniques are role playing, the case method, management games, and the in-basket technique.

Role Playing

Role playing involves the acting out of a particular situation to show the players and the onlookers how to deal with the matter. The purpose of role playing is to familiarize the participants with various kinds of on-the-job behavior they will face on a day-to-day basis and to discuss the best way to handle such situations.

Hoffman, "Is Management Development Doing the Job?" *Training and Development Journal,* January 1983, pp. 34–39.

10. Herbert Kaufman, *Obsolescence and Professional Career Development* (New York: Amacon, 1974).

Table 10–2 Program Type and Level Versus Organization Size

Program Level	Medium to Large: Less than 2,000 Managers	Organization Size Very Large: 2,000–8,000 Managers	Giant: over 8,000 Managers
Executive	Programs largely individualized. Primarily out-company, some internal on contract, some completely ad hoc. Oriented toward conceptual skills and strategy.	Programs divided between in-house and out-company. Oriented toward conceptual skills, strategy, and environmental understanding.	Programs largely in-house and centralized, supplemental lectures, some out-company exposure. Oriented toward interface of internal and external environment.
Middle	Programs mixed between in-house (supplemented by lecturers) and out-company. Oriented toward human and conceptual skills and analytical abilities.	Programs largely in-house, with little out-company. Conducted on centralized corporate basis. Oriented toward human and decision-making skills, geared to company policy.	Programs predominantly in-house, either corporate or division centralized. Orientation is on human, decision-making, and conceptual skills.
Supervisory	Programs on-site in division. Orientation is on basic technical and human skills, geared to company procedures.	Program on-site in division. Orientation is on basic technical and human skills, including company procedures.	Programs on-site in division. Orientation is on basic technical and human skills, including company procedures and policy. Program instructors are centrally trained.

Table 10–3
Type of Development
Received

Type of Development	Percent Receiving		
	Executive	Middle	Supervisory
External conference/seminars	27.7%	26.1%	17.3%
In-house workshops	22.9	21.6	34.7
Coaching plus on-the-job experience	13.3	29.5	33.4
Participation in university programs	10.8	10.2	4.0
Association/professional conferences and workshops	16.8	4.5	0
Consultant programs	7.2	5.7	5.3
Self-study courses	1.2	2.3	5.3

A particular situation is acted out.

In role-playing sessions the trainer usually asks a few of the participants to assume specific roles. One might be asked to play a senior executive who has to tell a subordinate that he or she is being terminated. The other plays the role of the subordinate who is being let go. The players may be told what has led to the current situation, or they may simply be given their roles and allowed to act them out as they see fit.

Using the information at hand, the participants proceed to act out their roles. The most important one is that of the top executive. The trainer will be interested in seeing that the person playing this role employs the proper style, tactics, and persuasive skills in telling the subordinate the bad news and getting the person to accept it.

After the scene has been acted out, the trainer analyzes the actions of the players, pointing out what the "senior executive" did right and how the person could improve through a better choice of words or approach. ("Don't say, 'you're fired!' That is too threatening. Say, 'We are going to have to let you go.' Don't just say, 'your work has been poor and you know it.' Cite statistics backing the statement up. Don't be defensive over having to let someone go when they don't measure up.") During this process, the role players begin to get a better understanding of how it feels to have to let someone go or be the person being let go. The rest of the training group may also be asked to play roles, in which case they too will get some actual experience. Or they may simply be observers and empathize with the plight of the two role players. In any event, they receive useful training.

Sometimes, in an effort to improve the ability of the participants to deal with certain situations, the role playing is videotaped and then played back so the players, trainer, and other participants can analyze what happened. As the tape is reviewed the trainer will discuss what took place, ask questions, make comments, and provide substantive input regarding how to deal with similar situations in the future.

Case Method

A specific problem is analyzed.

The **case method** employs a written description of a decision-making situation. The trainees are asked to read the case, identify the problems, analyze them, and offer recommendations for action. Sometimes the case is quite short and presents only one problem. It may, for example, be a two- to three-page case in which a manager is confronted with the issue of which one of four product lines to promote through increased advertising expenditures. The narrative provides background and data on each line as well as information related to the effect of advertising on each. The trainee's job is to analyze the data and determine which line will profit the most from advertising. The person is then asked to make a recommendation and explain the reasons behind it.

The case may also be an extensive one covering overall operations, particularly when top managers are involved. After providing a general history of the firm and an overview of product lines and services, the narrative discusses current strategies and tactics. The reader is then left with the challenge of identifying the problems and presenting recommendations along with the reasons for them.

The case method approach requires the trainees to be able to analyze data and present their findings. When they are finished, the trainer often provides input regarding the "right" answer and then tells the participants what actually happened and why. The respondents can then see how closely their recommendations paralleled those of the executives who initially faced the same situation.

Management Games

Operating conditions are simulated.

Management games are simulation exercises designed to replicate the operations of functional areas or overall enterprises. In the former case, they are referred to as *functional games* and require the participant to manage a particular area or department: sales, advertising, production, purchasing. In the latter case, they are called *general management simulations* and require the participant to make overall operating decisions in areas such as selling price, production scheduling, purchasing, hiring, firing, and financing of overall operations.

Some of the biggest benefits of management games include the emphasis they put on decision making, the provision for feedback of results, and the requirement that all decisions be made with inadequate data—a condition that simulates reality. On the other hand it can be costly to operate and administer these games and, in some cases, the participants complain that the simulation model is unrealistic.

In-Basket Technique

Day-to-day decisions are made.

The **in-basket technique** is used for both management development and as part of assessment center packages. The technique involves giving each of the trainees a box of material containing typical items from a specific manager's mail and a telephone list. Included in this material are both important and pressing matters that should be handled immediately and routine issues that can wait. The trainee is evaluated on the number of decisions made during the allotted time, the quality of these decisions, and the priorities used in making them. While the technique is expensive, trainees like it and organizations have found it useful in predicting effectiveness.

A method related to in-basket management development is the Kepner-Tregoe rational manager concept.[11] This technique centers around a fictional Apex Company that has 400 employees. The exercise uses the in-basket technique, role playing, and many other methods. Each trainee is assigned to one of four roles in the company: production manager, sales manager, purchasing and shipping manager, or division general manager. The people playing these roles have their own offices, talk to one another on the phone, and meet to solve problems. After 90 minutes, they switch and take on another role. After playing all four roles, they are evaluated on how well they performed. This exercise is a very comprehensive one. Some of the benefits of its use include greater awareness of the decision process, improved problem-solving ability, and a deeper understanding of how the management team functions.

---

11. Charles Kepner and Benjamin Tregoe, *The Rational Manager,* (New York: McGraw-Hill, 1965).

Development Needs and Management Level

The development needs of managers vary by hierarchical level. Lester Digman conducted a survey of the supervisory, management, and executive development practices and needs of both public and private organizations in the Midwest. The areas represented by these 84 organizations included manufacturing, wholesale/distribution, retail, finance, health care, transportation, utilities, construction, insurance, social services, schools, and federal, state, county, and city governments.[12] He found that most organizations prefer to develop their own managers from within. The better-managed enterprises had more advanced developmental practices and had to go outside to hire much less often than did the typical organization (71% versus 92%, respectively). In developing managers, these companies preferred on-the-job experience, aided by coaching and counseling, and in-house training. When in-house training was unavailable, the organization turned to outside sources. Professor Digman also found that well-managed firms trained their supervisors more frequently than did the average firm. The result was that their people were better prepared for higher-level positions earlier in their management careers.

What kinds of development do managers need? The answer is somewhat influenced by the manager's level in the hierarchy (see Table 10–4). For example, Digman reported that at the upper levels there was a decided

Table 10–4   Most Frequent Development Needs at Each Level of Management

Executive Level	Middle Level	Supervisory Level
1. { Managing time / Team building	1. Evaluating and appraising employees	1. Motivating others
3. { Organizing and planning / Evaluating and appraising employees	2. Motivating others	2. Evaluating and appraising others
	3. Setting objectives and priorities	3. Leadership
5. { Coping with stress / Understanding human behavior	4. Oral communication	4. Oral communication
	5. Organizing and planning	5. Understanding human behavior
7. { Self-analysis / Motivating others	6. Understanding human behavior	6. Developing and training subordinates
9. { Financial management / Budgeting	7. { Written communication / Managing time	7. { Role of the manager / Setting objectives and priorities / Written communication
11. { Setting objectives and priorities / Holding effective meetings	9. Team building	10. Discipline
13. Oral communication	10. { Leadership / Decision making / Holding effective meetings / Delegation / Developing and training subordinates	11. { Organizing and planning / Managing time / Counseling and coaching
14. Labor/management relations		14. Selecting employees
15. Decision making / Developing strategies and policies	15. Selecting employees	15. Decision making

12. Lester A. Digman, "Management Development: Needs and Practices," *Personnel*, July–August 1980, pp. 45–57.

Development needs vary by hierarchical levels.

shift toward general business areas (planning, organizing, evaluating, and appraising employees) and personal skills (time management and understanding human behavior). At the middle and lower levels the emphasis tended to be more behavioral in orientation, with evaluation, motivation, communication, and leadership holding high priorities.

Evaluating Training Programs

Are training and development worth the cost? Surprisingly, many firms are unable to answer this question objectively because they do not conduct any form of evaluation. They simply assume that if the training program covers areas of known deficiencies, the benefits are worth the expenses. Given the fact that many organizations are spending thousands of dollars in this area annually, a more formal evaluation process is needed. The following 10 steps can be used in evaluating training.[13]

One: Compute the Cost of Each Training Component

Direct and indirect costs are included.

There are many costs involved in training and development, including trainer costs, facilities and equipment costs, materials and supplies expenses, and the salaries of the trainees. (Remember that when the trainees are not at work, output is being lost. So the salaries these people earn while being trained are part of the overall cost.)

Two: Rank Each Program Based on its Perceived Value

Programs are evaluated on the basis of importance.

By drawing upon knowledgeable personnel within the enterprise, the organization must rank the relative value of each training program, from the most important to the least important. For example, the most effective training might be entry-level technical training, while the executive development program might rank second, and the orientation program last. The purpose of this type of ranking is to provide a basis for computing potential savings.

Three: Compute Potential Savings

A "PS" rating is determined.

Next to the relative value rankings of the various programs, a computation of the relative cost of each program should be made. An example is provided in Table 10–5. Notice that the organization now has two ratings for each program: value and cost. The total of these two is the potential for savings, or the "PS" rank. The lower the PS number, the higher the potential savings. For example, in Table 10–5 entry-level technical training has a higher potential savings than does EEO training, and the latter has a higher potential savings than does communication skills training.

---

13. The data in this section can be found in Basil S. Deming, "A System for Evaluating Training Programs," *Personnel*, November–December 1979, pp. 35–41.

Table 10–5   Program Evaluation Worksheet

Training Component	(1) Relative Cost	+ (2) Relative Value	= (3) Potential for Savings (PS Rank)	(4) Effect of Training	(5) Priority for Evaluation
Executive development program	2	3	5 (2)	Unclear	2
Upward mobility program	3	2	5 (2)	Ineffective	1
Secretarial training	7	4	11 (4)	Effective	10
EEO training	8	6	14 (6)	Unclear	4
Supervisory training	4	8	12 (5)	Ineffective	3
Communication skills training	11	9	20 (11)	Unclear	7
Basic adult education	5	11	16 (8)	Unclear	6
Technical training					
—entry-level	1	1	2 (1)	Effective	9
—to improve performance	6	10	16 (8)	Effective	11
—for program change	10	7	17 (10)	Effective	12
Orientation training	12	12	24 (12)	Unclear	8
Management intern program	9	5	14 (6)	Unclear	5

Four: Evaluate the Effect of the Training

Training objectives are reviewed.

The next step is to find out whether the programs are achieving their objectives. It involves (1) reviewing the training objectives and (2) asking the trainees and their superiors if the training was helpful back on the job. An overall rating of the respective programs can be done on a forced-choice basis: training appears effective, training appears unclear, training is ineffective. An example is provided in column 4 of Table 10–5, where the effect of the programs has been reported.

Five: Determine Which Programs Should Be Evaluated First

Programs with the lowest "PS" factors are reviewed first.

The organization now must check the PS factors of programs judged to be unclear or ineffective in regard to job performance. Those with the lowest factors are candidates for immediate evaluation. After all, they are the most expensive and most valuable; if they are also judged to have poor or uncertain effects on job performance, they should be the first to undergo the initial evaluations. In Table 10–5 the upward mobility program is most eligible for evaluation. The executive development program is second in line. Notice that while the entry-level technical training program has the highest potential for savings, it was judged to be effective, so the priority for evaluation is much lower.

Six: Establish Evaluation Objectives

Now managers and evaluators have to explore a number of basic questions: Are the training objectives clear? Are they acceptable to management? Can a cause-and-effect relationship be established between learning and performance? Is cost effectiveness a critical element? Should the training process be analyzed to improve instruction? Working together, managers and evaluators must determine specific objectives that can be used for evaluating the respective program.

Specific objectives are determined.

Seven: Estimate the Cost of Evaluation

Once the basic objectives and the evaluation design are determined, an estimate of the cost of evaluating the program must be made. In many cases this is not a very difficult undertaking. The evaluator can often make an estimate or provide a reasonable cost range. The two most important things the evaluator must do are (1) to include all of the costs, both direct and indirect, that are associated with the program, and (2) to allocate the costs over the life of the program. For example, if a new executive development program is going to require 3 trainers and involve 7 executives, the salaries of these 10 people should be allocated to the program. The total cost of the equipment should not be allocated, however, because this machinery will be used over again. A small fee of perhaps $50 can be allocated for the use of the slide projector, overhead viewgraph, film projector, and other equipment.

Evaluation costs are considered.

Finally, the cost of evaluating the program must be considered. A typical rule of thumb is that evaluation costs should be no more than 10 percent of the total program cost. If the program is being run for the first time, however, and no evaluation procedures have been worked up, this 10 percent rule can be violated. As the program is run again and again, the evaluation procedures will have already been established and the costs will then be much lower than 10 percent.

Eight: Monitor the Evaluation Process

Monitoring is the maintenance activity. Unless the organization follows up and ensures that the program continues to achieve its objectives and be worth the cost, the process may break down. The evaluator may meet resistance from the supervisors from whom the employee performance data is being collected. Or after the program, some of the evaluation forms may not be filled out in their entirety, providing only piecemeal information regarding the overall value of the program.

Maintenance functions are performed.

Nine: Study and Diagnose the Evaluation Reports

The evaluation reports should be read carefully. Do they provide the kind of information that will permit the program to be judged effectively? Or are they too general or skewed toward determining whether certain ideas or concepts were presented while ignoring the value of the program to the participants? Does the evaluation need to be revised? Remember that this evaluation should relate to the original objectives so that it indicates whether these goals were or were not attained.

Evaluation reports are examined.

Ten: Make Decisions Based on the Findings

Sometimes nothing is done.

The last phase of program evaluation is to decide what to do in light of the results. Sometimes nothing is done because the results are unclear or are based on faulty data collection. At other times nothing is done because the people who are empowered to make the decision are afraid of the effect change might have on the organization. At yet other times, although change appears to be warranted, nothing is done because the cost would be too great. Too much time and energy would have to be expended in redoing or revising the program.

The first rule to follow in determining what to do is to emphasize changing those programs for which the smallest investment will produce the greatest benefits. The second rule is to evaluate the magnitude of the proposed changes and balance the savings with the efforts necessary to make them and the problems that will result from implementation. The organization should begin making changes by opting for the program that provides the best cost/benefit ratio. Then it is a matter of the organization's own judgment regarding how far to go in making changes in the various programs.

Table 10–6   Change Decision Sheet

Recommendation	Type of Change Required	Constraints	Probable Payoff	Priority of Selection	Implementation Decision
Have executive development program participants assigned to senior executives who guide them and monitor their activities.	Evaluation of participants shifts from trainers to executives; thorough orientation needed by executives who would participate; evaluation subsystem would have to be designed.	Executive might not be objective because of close working relationships developed with participants.	Regardless of some subjectivity in evaluator-participant relationship, it has strong growth potential for the participant.	1	Implement
Extend executive development program from two years to three.	Administrative	Participants are anxious to get back into regular assignments by the end of their second year; salary costs to organization is more than $140,000 per year.	The value of developmental experiences may diminish over time. Probable payoff is likely to be smaller than that of first two years.	2	Do not implement now; survey executives who served as mentors to get their opinions.

Reprinted, by permission of the publisher, from "A System for Evaluating Training Programs," Basil S. Deming, *Personnel,* November–December 1979, © 1979 by AMACOM, a division of American Management Associations, p. 40. All rights reserved.

Table 10–6 provides an example of how two proposed changes in the executive development program identified in Table 10–5 were handled. Notice that one recommendation was implemented and another was put on hold.

Usefulness of Specific Training Methods

The preceding discussion described how training programs can be evaluated and when it is appropriate to make changes based on the cost/benefit ratio. On a more general level, trainers and researchers have long been interested in the specific benefits associated with various types of training techniques, both on the job and off the job. Table 10–7 presents some of their findings.

Notice from the table that there are five different bases on which programs can be evaluated: whether or not the participant is actively involved; whether the method allows for feedback of results; whether the materials are organized in a meaningful way; whether the individual has an opportunity for practice and repetition of the learning; and whether the training

Table 10–7   Evaluation of Usefulness of Training Methods

	Motivation: Active participation of learner	Reinforcement: Feedback of knowledge of results	Stimulus: Meaningful organization of materials	Responses: Practice and repetition	Stimulus-response conditions most favorable for transfer
On-the-job techniques					
Job-instruction training	Yes	Sometimes	Yes	Yes	Yes
Apprentice training	Yes	Sometimes	?	Sometimes	Yes
Internships and assistantships	Yes	Sometimes	?	Sometimes	Yes
Job rotation	Yes	No	?	Sometimes	Yes
Junior board	Yes	Sometimes	Sometimes	Sometimes	Yes
Coaching	Yes	Yes	Sometimes	Sometimes	Yes
Off-the-job techniques					
Vestibule	Yes	Sometimes	Yes	Yes	Sometimes
Lecture	No	No	Yes	No	No
Special study	Yes	No	Yes	?	No
Films	No	No	Yes	No	No
Television	No	No	Yes	No	No
Conference or discussion	Yes	Sometimes	Sometimes	Sometimes	No
Case study	Yes	Sometimes	Sometimes	Sometimes	Sometimes
Role playing	Yes	Sometimes	No	Sometimes	Sometimes
Simulation	Yes	Sometimes	Sometimes	Sometimes	Sometimes
Programmed instruction	Yes	Yes	Yes	Yes	No
Laboratory training	Yes	Yes	No	Yes	Sometimes
Programmed group exercises	Yes	Yes	Yes	Sometimes	Sometimes

From *Training in Industry: The Management of Learning,* by B. M. Bass and J. A. Vaughan. Copyright © 1966 by Wadsworth Publishing Co. Reprinted by permission of the publisher, Brooks/Cole Publishing Co., Monterey, Calif. 93940.

No one type of training is always superior.

can be transferred with the worker when the individual moves to a different job.

Table 10–7 shows that no one training method is better than any of the others. The method selected depends on the needs of the organization and what it can afford to offer. For example, as noted earlier, the lecture approach can be a very cost-effective one, but it is not suitable for an organization that wants to use highly motivational training methods. Or, as Table 10–7 indicates, if the trainer feels that the trainee must have reinforcement through feedback of the results, job rotation is a poor choice but programmed instruction is not. While cost is certainly one criterion that can be used in deciding the type of training method to use, other more subjective goals are often more important. In the final analysis, the "best" training method is the one that meets the needs of the organization and its personnel.[14]

Summary

1. Training is the process of altering employee behavior and attitudes in a way that increases the probability of goal attainment. Learning is the acquisition of skills, knowledge, and abilities that result in a relatively permanent change in behavior.

2. People learn in different ways, as illustrated by the negatively accelerated learning curve, the positively accelerated learning curve, and the skills acquisition pattern learning curve. Today a great deal of attention is being focused on studying how people gather and use information. This subject is often referred to as human information processing and is concerned with such topics as right-brain and left-brain thinking.

3. To ensure effective training of personnel, the support of top management is critical. Unless top management gets behind the training effort, it can prove worthless.

4. Many organizations attempt to determine training needs by carrying out what is called a needs analysis survey. This survey pinpoints areas in which training is needed. Then the training must be tied to specific, and if possible, measurable, objectives.

5. There are four principal types of employee training: apprentice training, vestibule training, on-the-job training, and off-the-job training. In conducting these types of training, companies may use a number of different methods. Some of them include lectures/discussions, programmed instruction, coaching and counseling, and job rotation.

6. Management development is the process by which managers obtain the necessary skills, experiences, and attitudes that they need to become or remain successful leaders in their respective organizations. One of the most critical problems addressed by this training is managerial obsolescence.

7. A number of different types of management development methods are used by modern organizations. These were presented in Table 10–3. The specific choice of method tends to depend on the manager's hierarchical level.

---

14. Frank O. Hoffman, "A Responsive Training Department Cuts Costs," *Personnel Journal*, February 1984, pp. 48–51.

8. In management development, a number of different techniques are employed. Some of the most common include role playing, the case method, management games, and the in-basket technique.

9. In the final analysis, an organization can only determine if the training and development are worth the cost if some form of evaluation is carried out. Ten steps can be used for evaluating training. The usefulness of each program is determined not only by its cost but by its value in helping meet the objectives of the program.

Key Terms

Apprentice training   Training that is given to people who are new to the job. It is done both on the job and off the job and is designed to give the participants an understanding of the rules and procedures that must be followed in carrying out the work.

Case method   A training technique that employs a written description of a decision-making situation. The participants are required to read the narrative, identify the problems, analyze them, and offer recommendations for action.

Coaching and counseling   A training method in which the superior talks to the subordinate to find out how well he or she is doing, what kinds of problems he or she is having, and how they can be dealt with.

Human information processing   The study of how people gather and use information.

In-basket technique   A training technique used in management development. It involves giving each of the trainees a box of materials containing typical items from a specific manager's mail and a telephone list and requiring them to deal with as many of these items as possible in the allotted time.

Job rotation   A training method in which the individual is moved from one job to another.

Learning   The acquisition of skills, knowledge, and abilities that result in a relatively permanent change in behavior.

Management development   The process by which managers attain the necessary skills, experiences, and attitudes that they need to become or remain successful leaders in their respective organizations.

Management games   Simulation exercises used in management programs. They are designed to replicate the operations of functional areas or overall enterprises to give trainees an opportunity to make "real-life" decisions, get feedback, and make other decisions in light of the results.

Negatively accelerated learning curve   A learning curve in which learning occurs very quickly at first and then begins to taper off.

Positively accelerated learning curve   A learning curve in which learning starts slowly and then picks up dramatically.

Programmed instruction   A training technique that allows the learner to read and master small amounts of text material while working at a comfortable pace.

Role playing   A training technique that involves the acting out of a particular situation to show the players and the onlookers how to deal with the matter.

Skills acquisition pattern learning curve   A learning curve in which learning starts off quickly, levels off, and then picks up again.

Training   The process of altering employee behavior and attitudes in a way that increases the probability of goal attainment.

Vestibule training   Training that takes place in an environment that simulates the actual workplace, as in the case of a manufacturing firm that trains lathe operators in an area away from the factory floor.

Questions for Analysis and Discussion

1. In your own words, what is meant by the term training? What role does learning play in the training process? Be sure to include in your answer a discussion of typical learning curves.

2. Why would a person interested in training want to learn about human information processing? Why would a study of this subject be of value?

3. How important is the role top management plays in the organization's training effort? Explain your answer.

4. What is a needs analysis survey all about? When would an enterprise want to carry one out? Of what value would the survey be?

5. How can criteria for training objectives be determined? Cite some examples.

6. What are the four principal types of employee training? Identify and describe each.

7. In your own words, what is meant by the term management development? Be complete in your answer.

8. How common is managerial obsolescence? What causes it? How can modern organizations deal with this problem?

9. What are some of the most common development techniques used in management development? Identify and describe three of them.

10. How do management development needs differ by hierarchical level? Explain, incorporating the data in Table 10–4 into your answer.

11. How can an organization go about evaluating its training programs? Offer specific suggestions.

| Case |

Wechsler's Training Offerings

While most of its competitors are having a difficult year, Wechsler, Inc., a midwestern manufacturing firm, is doing better than ever. Last week it received $1.2 million in new orders and it now has four-and-a-half months of backlog.

In order to fill these new orders, the company has just hired 10 new machinists. These new employees all need training in how to run the specialized machinery used in the production process. The firm has also hired three new supervisors and promoted one more from within. These four people are all scheduled for supervisory training.

Last week the organization sent around a list of the latest training courses being offered under the auspices of the Personnel Department. Six seminars are scheduled for the new three-month period: Effective Communication, Time Management, Motivation Techniques, Effective Leadership, Job Planning, and Performance Evaluation. Each of the six is fully described in a one-paragraph outline that details the specific topics to be covered and discusses what the participant will learn.

The list of courses is being circulated throughout every department in the organization. Each manager is being asked whether he or she would like to attend any of them and which subordinates, if any, would profit from attendance.

After the list has made the rounds, the head of the Personnel Department will draw up a final roster showing who will be attending each of the seminars. Inevitably, some seminars will attract 20 people while others will have more than double that number. Since the department has found the ideal number of participants per session to be between 15 and 20, management people are assigned to one session, where possible, while workers go to another. Additionally, if the number of managers is large enough to form two groups, they are divided up so that no one attends a session with his or her direct superior.

In the past Wechsler, Inc. has found that its approach to training works quite well. Most of the feedback has been positive. The only real complaints have been that the number of programs offered is not large enough (some people believe the firm should offer two or three every month) and that they do not last long enough (usually a program lasts from a half day to a full day and sometimes participants argue that at least twice as much time should be allotted to the topic).

The head of the Personnel Department received back the latest list of training requests yesterday. He is now in the process of deciding how to accommodate all of them.

1.   What type of training should be given to the new machinists? The new supervisors? Be complete in your answer. Also, of the six programs being offered by the firm, which ones would be of most value to the managerial people? The nonmanagerial people?

2.   What types of training methods and techniques would you expect to be used in the following seminars: Effective Communication, Time Management, and Effective Leadership? Explain your answer.

3.   In addition to the six programs listed in the case, what other ones would be of value to the personnel? Identify and describe three.

You Be the Consultant

Helping Out the University

Every year a large southern corporation conducts a needs analysis survey of its managerial personnel. This survey seeks to answer two questions: (1) What types of training do your subordinates need? (2) What types of training would you, personally, like to receive? This approach, management reports, has been very helpful in assisting people at all hierarchical levels to overcome the problem of managerial obsolescence.

Management attributes the organization's success in dealing with obsolescence to two things. First, every manager is required to analyze the specific needs of his or her own department. The result is what the enterprise calls a "defined" need; in other words, the manager defines the training needs of the subordinate. Second, each individual is asked to explain his or her own training requirements, producing what the enterprise calls a "described" need. By addressing both defined and described needs, the organization is able to handle all training need deficiencies and ensure that no managerial obsolescence occurs.

The latest needs analysis survey among the middle managers shows that the following development needs were most frequently mentioned:

1. Motivation of others

2. Appraisal of subordinates

3. Verbal communication

4. Setting of objectives and priorities

5. Written communication

6. Leadership

The first was mentioned by 74 percent of all middle managers; the sixth was on 46 percent of all lists. Since the seventh training need was on only 25 percent of the lists, management feels that this training can wait and that the first six should be addressed immediately.

The survey results from top management were different. Based on 102 questionnaire responses, the most frequently cited needs were the following:

1. Time management

2. Stress management

3. Strategic planning

4. Financial management

5. Organizational design

6. Performance evaluation

The first was mentioned by 85 percent of all top managers, the sixth by 50 percent. The seventh mentioned training need was on only 21 percent of all lists.

The seminars and other training sessions designed to meet these needs are put together by outside organizations. The head of the Personnel Department has convinced the president that, in the long run, it is cheaper to use outside sources than to hire trainers and build a full-time Training and Development Department.

Each year the Personnel Department conducts the needs analysis survey and puts together the final list of programs. Each program on the list is described in detail. For example, the time management seminar has been described this way.

> *Time Management*   One-day seminar. Each participant will review the way he or she spends time during an average week, survey current time needs, identify typical time management problems, learn some of the most useful principles of time management, and put together an action plan for incorporating and using time management principles on the job.

These program descriptions are sent to six professional training and development groups, including one university in the nearby area. These groups work up a proposal package for each program that includes the training techniques and methods that will be used as well as the specific content and the total price. The head of the Personnel Department and the vice-president of finance make the final decisions regarding who does what training.

Your Consultation

Assume that you have been hired by the university to prepare the proposal. Acting as the consultant, describe the basic training techniques and methods you would use for the middle and top management programs identified in the case. Use Table 10–7, when appropriate, to help you. Also provide one specific objective for each program that could serve as a guide in measuring whether the program was effective.

Comprehensive Cases

The First National Bank of America

Background

The First National Bank of America (FNBA) is a large bank located in a metropolitan city. FNBA is situated in the center of the financial district, offering easy access to commercial clients and convenient service to individual customers who work in the surrounding area. The bank operates on a philosophy that gives commercial clients a higher priority than individual customers. This policy has proven profitable, and by all indications it will continue. Mr. Ell, president of the bank, believes profits can also be attributed to the very conservative policy exhibited in all aspects of the bank's business. The bank has a reputation for being ultraconservative.

There are 2,600 employees at FNBA, of whom 10 percent are managers. Most of the upper management group (officers within the bank) received their undergraduate and graduate degrees from well-known universities. Almost all have master's degrees in business administration (MBAs). Every one of them has completed the American Institute of Banking (AIB) program, which is sponsored by the American Bankers Association (ABA) and trains bank personnel in the theory and practice of banking. This background (MBA degrees from prestigious universities and AIB attendance) is considered by the president of the bank to be all that is necessary for training managers. He believes it will sustain the personnel throughout their careers at the bank.

An in-house training and development program was recently established for the lower-level managers who do not have college degrees. The president and executive vice-president believe that this training will totally supplement the formal education of these managers.

In a recent discussion between Mr. Ell and Mr. Mack, the executive vice-president, Mr. Ell expressed grave concern over problems with manager promotion and morale. Mr. Ell stated, "When it's time to fill a management position, it's difficult to find a manager to promote who has had experience in other areas of the bank." Reflecting his conservatism, Mr. Ell is hesitant to approve promotions for managers who have had no experience in a different operational area. He also feels that many of the managers who have been with the bank for seven or more years are becoming obsolete in their positions and ineffective and unhappy in their jobs. Mr. Mack suggested to Mr. Ell that the entire management team should undergo a training program. Mr. Ell is basically agreeable to the idea, but feels that if it is carried out, a cost-benefit analysis of the training should be conducted.

Facilities

The building in which the bank is located is a new, modern structure. The normal teller, new accounts, and consumer loan services are contained on the main floor. There are three basements which house safe deposit boxes and bank vaults for currency storage. The upper levels contain the computer department (which comprises two floors), commercial lending, the accounting department, and all other departments and support systems. The third floor provides a cafeteria for employees which offers a free lunch as part of the employee compensation package. The top floor of the building contains very plush executive offices and the executive dining room.

The Personnel Department's training and development facilities are located on the third floor. Modern audiovisual and duplicating equipment is available for use in both the classroom and meeting room environment. Books, publications, and videotapes are furnished to the Training Department freely by the manager of the facility, a vice-president who carries the title director of human resources.

Domestic Operations

The domestic operations of the bank account for 90 percent of all personnel (the other 10 percent is devoted to foreign operations). There are two divisions within domestic operations: commercial and individual consumer. These divisions are subdivided as follows:

Commercial	Consumer
Demand Deposit	Demand Deposit
Lending (including an audit group)	Savings
Trust	Lending
	Trust

This division of activities allows the bank to customize service, depending upon the category to which the customer belongs. The commercial customer transacts a larger dollar volume (per customer) and requires more employee time than does the individual customer.

Foreign Operations

Although the foreign, or international banking, sector of operations accounts for only 10 percent of the bank's overall personnel, it is an extremely important function of the bank. International banking responsibilities include exchanging foreign currencies for customers, lending funds to foreign clients, and engaging in the Euro-Dollar market by means of the bank's foreign branches. To gain a better perspective on the relationship of the various departments of the bank, and of the domestic and foreign operations, see Exhibit 1: Organization of Departments.

Personnel

Following the pattern of most other large banks, the FNBA divides its employees into two categories: officers and nonofficers. The officers are

Exhibit 1   First National Bank of America: Organization of Departments

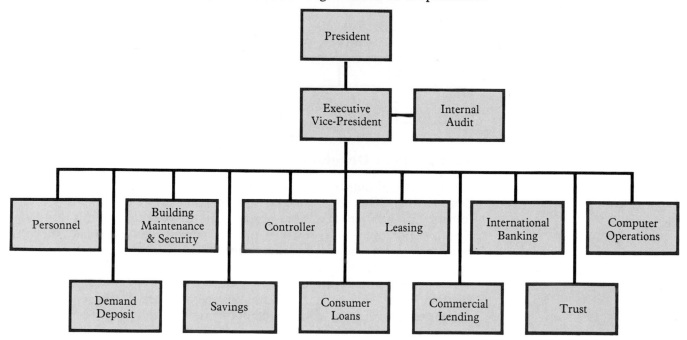

those in management positions with college degrees and usually MBAs. Immediately upon being promoted to officer, the person receives a substantial salary increase and is eligible for a one-month vacation per year, as well as other compensatory benefits and privileges. The levels within the rank of officer are (from top to bottom): president, executive vice-president, vice-president, cashier and assistant-cashier (initial level for an officer). Each vice-president is responsible for a department (see Exhibit 1). Within each department are numerous lower-level managerial positions. For example, in the Demand Deposit Department there are five subdepartments (see Exhibit 2).

There are many management opportunities within the bank for nonofficers. The highest management positions are filled by officers of the bank, however. Most of the current training and development of employees is directed toward the managers who are not officers.

Training Methods

All employee training is done in the training and development center in the bank; none is conducted at remote locations. Despite the number of current training programs, the president is still concerned that managers are not being groomed properly for their next position in managerial succession.

The director of human resources believes that one of the primary reasons that managerial positions are not being well filled is that employee needs are not being assessed. He also believes that a systematic, periodic evaluation of all managers and potential managers would help alleviate the problem.

Exhibit 2

First National Bank of
America: Organization of
Demand Deposit Department

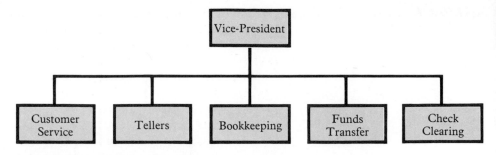

Management Development

The director of human resources recently received a memo from the president stating: "Our top managers are becoming obsolete, ineffective, and unhappy in their jobs. Let's put our facilities to work to cure this problem." The director must now devise a plan to correct this problem. The plan must take into account the various departments within the bank, the levels of managers and the special problem of honing the skills of the officers. One of the methods the director is considering is job rotation. For job rotation to be successful, long training periods are necessary before an employee can manage another department, and this requirement causes personnel shortages in the department from which the manager was transferred. In spite of this drawback, rotation remains a viable solution that must be enacted immediately. The director is also thinking about job enrichment programs that can be instituted at each level of operations.

1. What are the advantages of hiring people with MBAs and expecting them to be fully qualified for their duties for many years to come? What are the disadvantages?

2. Should the AIB courses be considered part of training and development? Explain.

3. What are the dangers of the president's policy of not promoting managers to "new" departments until they have had some experience in the "new" department?

4. What are the differences, if any, between training upcoming managers who will work with commercial customers and those who will work with individual customers?

5. Consider yourself the director of human resources at the bank. How would you design a comprehensive plan of training and development for management, recognizing interdepartmental differences and domestic and foreign operations? Be complete in your answer.

G.K. Norman & Company, CPAs

Structure of the Firm

The primary function of a certified public accounting firm is to perform audits of the financial statements of clients. Tax, accounting, and management advisory services are also provided as needed. Each client is entrusted to a partner in the firm. That partner is wholly responsible for the work performed for that client. Since clients are the primary source of revenue to the firm, it is vital that the services performed by the firm's professional staff be totally satisfactory to the client.

The partners are also the owners of the firm. There are also other employees who consist of the professional staff and the office staff. The professional staff at G.K. Norman & Co. is made up of accountants with a wide range of experience. The office staff is composed of a receptionist, typists (clerical and statistical), three secretaries, and an office manager. Overall, the firm has 14 partners, 41 professional staff members, and nine office staff members.

The professional staff is divided into three classifications: bookkeepers, junior accountants, and senior accountants. The bookkeepers (sometimes referred to as paraprofessionals) are unlikely to advance upward in the firm because they usually do not have college degrees. They have taken courses in accounting and have had bookkeeping experience. Bookkeepers prepare worksheets and are assigned bookkeeping duties that would be inappropriate (from a cost standpoint) for a junior or senior accountant to perform. Junior accountants are new graduates or accountants with less than three years of experience. Senior accountants have more than three years of experience. One new partner is chosen every three years from the ranks of the senior accountants.

The distribution of partners and professional staff at G.K. Norman is as follows:

Function	Number of Partners	Number of Professional Staff
Managing Partner	1	0
Financial Statement Review	1	0
Tax Department	2	1 Senior
		2 Juniors
Audit & Personnel	1	0
Audit Department	9	10 Seniors
		25 Juniors
		3 Bookkeepers
Total	14	41

Work Environment

The professional staff spends an average of two-thirds of its time at client locations and one-third at the office. Time spent with clients is usually devoted to performing financial statement audits. These audits can take anywhere from a few days to three or four weeks to complete. The average is two weeks. Because most of the work is performed at the client's location, the environment may vary from a clean, modern office to a dirty, noisy factory. Travel time spent going to and from the client is dependent on the distance from the staff member's home to the client and on road and traffic conditions.

The main office of G.K. Norman is located in the business district of a large city, in a very old building that has not been modernized. The air-conditioning system does not work well. The space the firm occupies is at a premium. Senior accountants are located two to an office. Junior accountants and bookkeepers share two large offices that each contain five to 10 people. Four telephones are allotted to each of the two offices containing the junior accountants.

The income tax season begins January 15th and ends on April 15th of each year. During this three-month period, the staff is expected to work late three nights per week, as well as eight hours every Saturday and Sunday. The extra hours are required to handle the heavy workload caused by the April 15th deadline for individual income tax returns.

Work assignments are given to staff members by the various partners. Staff members are not accountable to a specific partner but may receive assignments from many different partners. During the "normal" work season this method of receiving work assignments is confusing and burdensome to staff members. But when the tax season arrives the situation becomes extremely overpowering because the staff member must complete current assignments from one partner and also finish revisions of previous work done for other partners. Each partner demands top priority.

Professional Staff Requirements

G.K. Norman looks for specific requirements when hiring new employees. It looks at the applicant's grade point average in accounting, comparing it to the overall grade point average of college students. Since the staff member will be in constant contact with clients, an outgoing personality and a neat appearance are also deemed essential by the firm. An applicant is always regarded as an eventual partner. As such, the individual must exhibit the leadership qualities representative of the firm.

Once hired as a staff accountant, the individual is expected to act professionally. Staff members are expected to display the teamwork and comraderie necessary to conduct an audit with other employees of the firm. Finally, as a sign of competence, the staff member is expected to pass the CPA exam within three years of joining the firm.

Planning

The client list at G.K. Norman has been growing continually since the firm's inception. Each year brings more clients and progressively more work. The average turnover among the professional staff has been one senior accountant and five juniors per year. Last year only one junior accountant was hired. The firm is currently shorthanded because of resignations and terminations. In addition, the workload is increasing as the client list lengthens.

The partner responsible for personnel recently read an article entitled "Strategic Human Resources Planning" and brought before a meeting of the partners his concerns regarding the firm's difficulty in forecasting employment needs. He suggested that before hiring occurs, the firm should first determine the following: How many people are needed? At what levels? From what schools should they be sought?

The needs of the firm, as outlined during the meeting, were structured around the Audit Department. It was deemed necessary to recruit two experienced seniors from either another CPA firm, the Internal Revenue

Service, or industry (a controller or internal auditor). Uncertainty existed about exactly how many juniors should be hired, but the partners agreed that they should be recent graduates or students who will graduate shortly.

Recruiting Methods

The firm has been recruiting externally through the use of blind newspaper ads. This technique has had limited results because potential employees want to know the name of the company to which they are applying. As an alternative to blind newspaper ads, the partner in charge of personnel has considered recruiting directly from schools, using employment agencies, or starting an internship program. Although he is still committed to external recruitment and would like to try another method, the partner is not sure which new method would be most effective.

Salaries offered by the firm are not competitive with those paid by comparable firms. The firm offers no profit sharing, pension benefits, or tuition reimbursement plan. Other firms extend to their employees all or some of these benefits. The partners are at a loss to explain why they are unable to attract highly qualified employees. The firm believes that it is enough to advertise the growth of the firm as a lure to prospective professional employees.

Selection Methods

The personnel partner initiates the selection process by analyzing responses to the blind ads, measuring them by predetermined criteria. The partner screens the applications (resumes) sent in response to the blind ad, looking for job-related qualifications and non-job-related social qualifications.

Job-related characteristics include education, reliable transportation (other than public), and leadership qualities. If the applicant has had no related work experience (which is usually the case for juniors), the partner relies heavily on knowledge of the school attended, accounting courses taken, and grades achieved. A senior-level applicant will have had a minimum of three years' job experience which will be taken into consideration in the selection process.

Reliable transportation essentially means that the professional staff member must have a car. Staff members travel constantly from one client to the next. Many clients are not accessible by means of public transportation, and some are located outside of the city. In many instances a staff member must leave one client and travel across town to the next client.

Leadership qualities are equally important in both the junior and senior applicant. The partner examines the record of school association memberships, extracurricular activities, and other accomplishments of the recent graduate. A senior applicant needs to show a record of promotions and must have held positions of leadership and responsibility.

The non-job-related characteristics the partner looks for in an applicant are personal and physical attributes. A well-dressed single person under the age of 30 is the most desirable applicant. Working long hours does not seem to have the adverse effect on a single person that it does on someone who is married. A staff member is a reflection of the firm and, as such, the partner would prefer an individual who is medium to tall in height, not overweight, and who has a pleasant appearance. Such characteristics are not absolutely essential, however, merely desirable.

Once past the resume scrutiny, the applicant undergoes a preliminary interview with the partner in charge of personnel. After this screening, he or she is interviewed by other select partners of the firm. Finally, the applicant has lunch with other staff members. The luncheon enables the candidate to ask questions of his or her peers and gives staff members the opportunity to have input regarding the candidate.

Orientation

The firm does not have a formal orientation procedure. The partners believe that if the new staff member is a "go-getter," he or she will get the introductory tasks accomplished on an individual basis. They also feel that much valuable time is lost in "handholding" the new employee. The personnel partner is aware that studies have shown that a good orientation process reduces the anxiety levels of new employees, but has concluded that this function is totally unimportant.

Management Decisions

A more aggressive recruiting and selection policy is being developed in an effort to add more junior and senior staff members to the firm. The partners are convinced that change is necessary to supplement the turnover caused by resignations and terminations and to fill the gaps generated by the growth of the firm.

Newspaper ads will continue as the only means of recruitment. The ads will now be open ads, however, stating the firm's name, address, and telephone number. Benefits will be increased with the addition of tuition reimbursement for professional staff members. Finally, the firm will substantially increase the number of candidates being interviewed, expecting this practice to result in a larger number of people being hired.

1. Explain the effect that each of the following has on recruitment efforts: (a) lack of benefits, (b) below-average pay scale, and (c) undesirable office environment.

2. What, if any, legal problems may arise because of the selection criteria used by the personnel partner?

3. List the job-related requirements necessary to obtain a professional staff position with G.K. Norman & Company, CPAs.

4. Could the partners improve their planning procedure in regard to forecasting staffing requirements?

5. What other sources and methods of recruiting can the firm use in addition to those they currently employ?

6. How would an orientation program for new employees benefit the firm? Explain.

FOUR

Leading and Influencing the Personnel

This part of the book presents some major concepts of individual and organizational behavior. It also describes some of the tools and techniques that modern managers use to influence both kinds of behavior. The chapters in this part of the book follow a natural sequence of subjects, starting with the study of human behavior in action, progressing to a consideration of motivation and management, group behavior at work, and managerial leadership, and culminating with an examination of interpersonal and organizational communication.

Chapter 11 addresses the subject of human behavior in action. Why do people act as they do? In this chapter, you will learn about some of the major models of human behavior. You will also study the perception process, learning how perception is affected by attribution, stereotyping, and the halo effect. Attention will also be focused on three alternative models of management: traditional, human relations, and human resources, as well as on some of the primary principles of learning. The last part of the chapter examines forces that are vital in shaping personality, including biology, culture, the family, and work organizations.

The focus in Chapter 12 is on motivation at work. In this chapter, you will find out how motivation works and become familiar with some of the most important content and process theories of motivation. These theories are extremely useful in explaining why people act as they do. Attention will also be directed to the effect of money and values on employee motivation.

Chapter 13 examines group behavior in organizations. It describes formal, informal, and combination groups and explains why people join groups. Consideration is also given to identifying and describing the most meaningful characteristics of groups, comparing and contrasting the most common types of power within groups, and discussing group dynamics in action.

Managerial leadership is discussed in Chapter 14. After discussing some of the common traits typically found in effective leaders, the chapter focuses on identifying and describing leadership styles and explaining some of the latest research in the field. Particular attention is given to the contingency

and path-goal theories of leadership, the practical value of the leader-follower continuum, and the situational theory of leadership.

The last chapter in this section examines managerial communication.
Communication is vital to the leading and influencing process because unless
people understand what is being communicated, they are unlikely to act
in the desired manner. In this chapter, interpersonal and organizational
communication processes are described in depth. Barriers to both types
of communication are then identified and described and ways of dealing
with these barriers are presented.

When you have finished studying the material in this part of the book,
you will have a sound understanding of the way managers lead and influence
their people. You will also be familiar with some of the latest tools and
techniques that can be used to handle people's problems and ensure a
smooth flow of operations.

11

Human Behavior in Action

Objectives

To understand human behavior in organizations, we must first examine human behavior in general. Why do people act as they do? This is a difficult question to answer in just one chapter, so this chapter will concentrate on the primary factors that influence human behavior: perception, learning, and personality. When you have finished studying the material in this chapter, you whould be able to

1. describe some of the major models of human behavior;

2. describe the perception process and tell how it is affected by attribution, stereotyping, and the halo effect;

3. compare and contrast the assumptions and managerial implications of Theory X and Theory Y;

4. discuss the three alternative models of management: traditional, human relations, and human resources;

5. describe some of the primary principles of learning and explain the role played by positive and negative reinforcement; and

6. define the term personality and describe the role played by each of the following in shaping personality: biology, culture, the family, and work organizations.

The Nature of Human Behavior

Human behavior is a complex subject. In an effort to understand it, many individuals and researchers alike have sought to simplify things either by seeking answers to questions such as "Who am I?" or by constructing overall models of human behavior.

Who Am I?

Many people, in an effort to understand themselves, ask: "Who am I?" They believe that under the many roles they play in life there is one true self whose identity still eludes them. Some psychologists, however, believe this "search for unity" is fruitless.

> This is because [the] self consists of numerous identities—perhaps as many as a person has interests or associates. And although the alter egos are quite distinct, they may coexist happily and never challenge each other in an identity crisis.[1]

In an effort to provide some answers to the question "Who am I?" a number of short psychological tests have been developed. Figure 11–1 presents one that is designed to identify high self-monitoring people.

Figure 11–1

"Self-Monitoring"—A Quick Test

The following 10 statements are an abbreviated test from the self-monitoring scale described in the accompanying article. Answer True to each statement you feel describes you, False to each one that does not. To score yourself, see instructions at end of test.

TRUE	FALSE	
☐	☐	1. My behavior is usually an expression of my true inner feelings, attitudes and beliefs.
☐	☐	2. I can make impromptu speeches, even on topics about which I have almost no information.
☐	☐	3. When I am uncertain how to act in a social situation, I look at the behavior of others for cues.
☐	☐	4. I rarely seek the advice of my friends to choose movies, books or music.
☐	☐	5. I am not particularly good at making other people like me.
☐	☐	6. Even if I'm not enjoying myself, I often pretend to be having a good time.
☐	☐	7. I would not change my opinions (or the way I do things) in order to please someone else or win their favor.
☐	☐	8. I have trouble changing my behavior to suit different people and different situations.
☐	☐	9. I feel a bit awkward in company and do not show up quite so well as I should.
☐	☐	10. I can look anyone in the eye and tell a lie with a straight face (if for a right end).

To obtain your score, count one point for each False response to statements 1, 4, 5, 7, 8, and 9. Count one point for each True response to statements 2, 3, 6 and 10. High self-monitoring people earn scores of at least 7; lows get no more than 3 points.

Source: © 1981 by the New York Times Company. Reprinted by permission.

---

1. Dava Sobel, "For Some People, Studies Find, 'One True Self' Isn't Enough," *New York Times*, November 24, 1981, p. 19.

Self-monitors are people who constantly assess the opinion climate around them and change their behavior appropriately. This characteristic is neither good nor bad in itself; it simply represents a type of lifestyle. If you had a high score on the test in Figure 11–1, you are a self-monitor. Such people are pragmatic and engage in specific activities with specific people. They may talk politics with one person, discuss art and music with another, and trade baseball stories with a third. They play different roles depending on the other person. Also interesting is the fact that they never give a party for all of their friends at the same time. This behavior enables them to continue their independent relationships with different people.

Self-monitors are pragmatic.

Models of Human Behavior

The preceding discussion provides a psychologically based and only partially complete view of human behavior. Other approaches, which attempt to present an overall model of human behavior, have also been developed. The following discussion examines three of the most popular combination models.

Rational and Emotional Models

One model presents people in terms of their ability to reason . . .

The **rational model** of human behavior presents individuals in terms of their ability to reason. Theorists using this model see the individual as a highly rational person. When faced with a particular decision or situation, the individual gathers all of the available data, analyzes it, evaluates each course of action, computes (if only mentally) a cost/benefit ratio for each, and then chooses the course of action that offers the greatest benefit. According to this model the individual is a serious, computational, analytical person.

another in terms of their emotions.

At the other extreme is the **emotional model** of behavior, which views the individual as being heavily controlled by emotions, many of which are unconscious responses to the surrounding environment. This model is quite popular with scholars of Freudian persuasion, who believe that individuals are in a constant state of inner turmoil brought about by conflicts between the three major subsystems of the personality: the id, the ego, and the superego. The **id** is the core of the unconscious. It consists of raw, instinctual drive and continually struggles for gratification and pleasure. The **ego** is the conscious and logical part of Freudian man. It uses intellect and reasoning to interpret reality. The **superego,** often depicted as the conscience, is part of the unconscious. The Freudian view is that these three personality subsystems conflict, causing people to be controlled by their emotions.

Behavioristic and Humanistic Models

Some theorists focus on observable behavior.

Some theorists subscribe to the **behavioristic model.** They believe the individual can be described solely in terms of observable behavior. They are unconcerned with thoughts and feelings. This group believes that all behavior is environmentally determined. At the extreme, perhaps, are behavioristic model proponents such as John B. Watson, who wrote:

> Give me a dozen healthy infants, well formed, and my own specified world to bring them up in, and I'll guarantee to take any one at random and train him to become any type of specialist I might select—doctor, lawyer, artist, merchant-chief and yes, even beggarman and thief—regardless of his talents, tendencies, abilities, vocations and the race of his ancestors.[2]

Others use a more philosophical approach.

The **humanistic model** is regarded as more of a philosophy than a scientifically based theory. In essence, this model views the individual as being able to surmount irrational behavior through conscious reasoning. People control their own destinies, this model holds. Rather than being shaped by the external environment, as the behaviorists argue, each person fashions this environment through careful, conscious reasoning. Thus, human potential is viewed as unlimited.

Economic and Self-Actualizing Models

The economic model emphasizes self-interest.

The **economic model** pictures people as being totally self-interested. Each person uses his or her abilities to calculate the greatest personal payoff from any action. This calculation includes determining how to get the greatest satisfaction or the smallest discomfort from the least amount of effort. The individual is characterized by the term *economic man,* which describes a person who always tries to maximize personal benefits. The economic model also views people as competitive and, above all, concerned with their own survival.

The self-actualizing model emphases growth and maturity.

At the other extreme is the **self-actualizing model.** This model views people as being motivated by the opportunity to grow, mature, handle challenge, accept responsibility, and become all they are capable of becoming. Proponents of this model argue that people desire self-fulfillment; they want to self-actualize in the sense of using their total potential.

These models are all partially accurate and partially inaccurate in describing the nature of human behavior. Certainly they are useful as points of departure in understanding how and why people act as they do. The overall picture is incomplete, however, without a consideration of the roles played by perception, learning, and personality.

Perception

Perception is an individual's view of reality. Since no two people have ever had all of the same experiences in life, no two ever perceive all things in the same way. The following examples illustrate the perceptual differences that can exist in modern organizations:

Examples of perceptual differences

- The purchasing agent buys a part that she thinks is best, not the part that the engineer says is the best.

- A subordinate's answer to a question is based on what he "heard" the boss say, not on what the boss actually said.

---

2. J. B. Watson, *Behaviorism* (Chicago: University of Chicago Press, 1930), p. 104.

- The same worker may be viewed by one supervisor as a very good worker and by another supervisor as a very poor worker.

- The same widget may be viewed by the inspector to be of high quality and by a customer to be of low quality.

- The male chief executive officer of a large firm feels that women have an equal opportunity for advancement into top management, but the female assistant personnel manager feels there is no way she can break into top management's "good old boy" network.

- The head engineer who tours the factory floor once a week in a electric cart feels this is a pleasant place to work, but a punch press operator thinks this place ranks right next to the state prison.[3]

The Nature of Perception

The key to understanding perception is recognizing that each situation is interpreted by the individuals who are witnesses to it. What one person "sees" may be totally different from what another sees. One group of writers put the idea this way:

> The cognitive map of the individual is not, then, a photographic representation of the physical world; it is, rather, a partial, personal construction in which certain objects, selected out by the individual for a major role, are perceived in an individual manner. Every perceiver is, as it were, to some degree a nonrepresentational artist, painting a picture of the world that expresses his individual view of reality.[4]

The perception process can be broken down into a series of subprocesses. Figure 11–2 illustrates this idea.

First there is the external environment in which the person exists. This environment can be described in terms of the physical environment (objects and things) and the sociocultural environment (individuals and groups). The physical environment is made up of the geographic locale and area in which the person lives. The sociocultural environment is made up of the norms, values, attitudes, and other behavioral characteristics of those who are in the physical environment.

In this physical setting, the perceiver confronts a specific "stimulus" or situation. He or she learns about a new work rule, is asked to fill out a new control report, or is told to attend a meeting. Whatever the stimulus is, it brings together the environment and the person.

The result is a registration of the stimulus. The person realizes that an order has been given or a request has been made. This realization is followed by an interpretation of that order or request. The person asks himself or herself: What have I been asked to do? What response am I supposed to make?

3. Fred Luthans, *Organizational Behavior,* 3rd edition (New York: McGraw-Hill, 1981), pp. 84–85.

4. David Krech, Richard S. Crutchfield, and Egerton L. Ballachey, *Individual in Society* (New York: McGraw-Hill, 1968), p. 20.

Figure 11–2   The Perception Process in Action: From Start to Finish

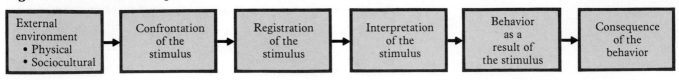

The next step is the actual response or behavior. It can take a number of forms. The simplest occurs when the individual complies with the order and does what has been asked. A second response, often unseen, is a change in the person's attitude brought about because he or she either approves or disapproves of the request. When people make value judgments, their personal attitudes usually change and become either more positive (I like this manager and the way he or she treats me) or negative (I do not like this manager and the way he or she treats me).

The last step in perception is the consequence or outcome. It takes place after the behavior is complete and serves either to reinforce the behavior (as in the case of a reward such as a salary raise) or to encourage the individual not to act this way in the future (as in the case of a penalty such as a demotion).

Perception in a Social Context

In studying human behavior in organizations, we must examine perception in a social context. *Social perception* is concerned with how a person perceives others. In a formal organizational setting, social perception goes on continually; and in an effort to understand it, psychologists have been particularly interested in the characteristics of both the perceiver and the perceived. Some of the things they have learned about the perceiver include the following:

Characteristics of perceivers

1. Knowing oneself makes it easier to perceive others accurately.

2. One's own characteristics affect the characteristics one is likely to see in others.

3. People who accept themselves are more likely to see the favorable side of others.

4. Accuracy in perceiving others is not a single skill; it requires a combination of skills.[5]

Researchers have also learned a great deal about the characteristics of the perceived. Some of their findings include the following:

1. The status of the person who is being perceived has a great influence on the way others perceive him or her.

---

5. Sheldon S. Zalkind and Timothy W. Costello, "Perception: Some Recent Research and Implications for Administration," *Administrative Science Quarterly*, September 1962, pp. 227–229.

Characteristics of the perceived

2. The person being perceived is usually placed into categories in order to simplify the perceiver's perceptual activities. The two most typical categories are status (how the person ranks in regard to others in the organization) and role (what the person does in the organization).

3. The visible traits of the person being perceived greatly influence the perception others have of him or her.[6]

These findings indicate that an individual's personal characteristics and those of the people being perceived all influence the way the individual sees other people. Perception is a two-way street. This idea becomes even clearer when we consider perceptual factors such as attribution, stereotyping, and the halo effect.

Attribution

Attribution defined

Attribution refers to the way in which an individual explains or interprets the personal behavior of others. For example, if a manager feels that a particular subordinate does better work than anyone else in the department because he or she stays late every evening, this perception is certainly going to affect the manager's evaluation of the individual. Likewise, if the manager believes that getting a master's degree in business administration will improve one's work performance, this perception will result in a much different career strategy from the one that would be adopted if the manager feels an advanced degree will be of virtually no value. Of course, sometimes people interpret behavior incorrectly. They misread or misunderstand the "real" situation. Nevertheless, attribution helps partially explain human behavior in organizations. So, too, does stereotyping.

Stereotyping

Stereotyping influences perception . . .

Stereotyping is the tendency to perceive another person as belonging to a single class or category. Based on this classification or categorization, the other person is imbued with certain traits that he or she may or may not possess. For example, in an organization where there is strong management-union dissent, a person who is labeled "a manager" by a union member is also being labeled untrustworthy, arbitrary, and capricious. On the other hand, when a manager in the same organization uses the term to describe a coworker, it means that the person is hard working, trustworthy, and reliable.

There are many examples of stereotyping both within and outside of organizations. People often change their occupational titles when the connotations of these titles become negative. For example, many insurance salespeople now refer to themselves as financial advisers. They do not want to be stereotyped as insurance sellers because of the negative image this title conjures up in people's minds. Similarly, within an organizational setting certain departments are often reputed to hold all the bright people while other departments are viewed as the dumping ground for deadwood. A

---

6. *Ibid.*, p. 230.

simple mention of the department someone comes from causes the listener to stereotype the individual as competent or incompetent.

Halo Effect

as does the halo effect.

The **halo effect** is similar to stereotyping. The major difference is that in stereotyping the person is perceived according to a single category while under the halo effect the person is perceived on the basis of one trait. The halo effect is common in performance evaluations when the person doing the rating allows one of the ratee's traits (intelligence, appearance, dependability, cooperativeness) to affect the overall rating. For example, if the manager who is rating a subordinate believes that no one can really master the job without a college degree and this person does not have a college degree, the manager rates him or her average or below average. On the other hand, anyone who does have a college degree receives a very favorable rating regardless of actual work performance.

Theory X and Theory Y

Perception of others also affects the way managers motivate and lead their personnel.[7] For example, if a manager believes that the subordinates are lazy and need to be prodded along, he or she is likely to use a leadership style quite different from the one that would be chosen if he or she regarded the subordinates as self-starters. This basic approach to examining leadership behavior was presented by Douglas McGregor in his now-famous Theory X and Theory Y.[8]

Theory X Assumptions

Theory X is a set of assumptions that many managers use in supervising and leading their personnel. These assumptions are based on the manager's perception of the way subordinates ought to be led. In McGregor's view, managers who subscribe to Theory X employ the following assumptions:

Theory X assumptions

1. The average person has an inherent dislike of work and, where possible, will avoid it.

2. People have little ambition, tend to shun responsibility, and prefer to be directed.

3. Above all else, people want security.

4. In order to get people to attain organizational objectives it is necessary to use coercion, control, and threats of punishment.[9]

---

7. See for example: Michael J. Gent, "Theory X in Antiquity, or the Bureaucratization of the Romans' Army," *Business Horizons,* January–February 1984, pp. 52–56.

8. Douglas McGregor, *The Human Side of Enterprise* (New York: McGraw-Hill, 1960).

9. *Ibid.,* pp. 33–34.

These assumptions, if accepted by the manager, lead to the use of a "carrot and stick" approach. In front of the worker are placed job security and other financial rewards—the carrot. If the worker does not move forward, the stick (loss of pay raises, demotions, outright firing) is used.

Theory Y Assumptions

The assumptions of **Theory Y** are quite different from those of Theory X. Theory Y employs a more optimistic, dynamic, and flexible philosophy. Managers who subscribe to this theory use entirely different methods. The assumptions of Theory Y are

Theory Y assumptions

1. Work is a natural phenomenon and, under the right conditions, people not only will accept responsibility but also will seek it.

Table 11–1
A Comparison of Theory X and Theory Y

Selected Management Functions	Theory X Managerial Behavior	Theory Y Managerial Behavior
Planning	Superior sets objectives for subordinates.	Superior and subordinates jointly set objectives.
Decision making	Superior makes decisions and announces them to subordinates.	Superior establishes broad guidelines and lets subordinates make decisions within these parameters.
Organizing	Superior determines what everyone will do and all authority is based on job position and title.	Superior and subordinates jointly determine job design. Authority is based on job knowledge and initiative as well as hierarchical position.
Communicating	All communication flows from superior to subordinates.	Communication flows in all directions: vertical, horizontal, lateral, and diagonal.
Motivating	Motivation is based on threats, fear, and the potential loss of job security.	Motivation is based on helping subordinates achieve a feeling of self-fulfillment for a job well done.
Leading	Leadership is autocratic; people do as they are told—or else.	Leadership is participative and teamwork is both encouraged and nurtured.
Controlling	Subordinates are evaluated based on past mistakes. Those who have erred are punished.	Subordinates are evaluated based on accomplishments. Mistakes are used as learning examples for preventing further occurrences.

2. If people are committed to organizational objectives, they will exercise self-direction and self-control in pursuing these aims.

3. Commitment to organizational objectives is a function of the rewards associated with goal attainment; the more the organization is willing to give to its people, the harder the latter will work in pursuing enterprise goals.

4. The capacity for ingenuity and creativity is widespread throughout the population but under conditions of modern industrial life, this potential is only partially tapped.[10]

Table 11–1 shows how a Theory X manager differs from a Theory Y manager in carrying out selected management functions.

Managerial Implications

Theory X and Theory Y are not prescriptions or suggestions for management behavior. They simply describe assumptions that reflect the manager's perception of the workforce. A Theory X manager is not always hard and tough; a Theory Y manager is not always flexible and easygoing. Every manager adjusts to the specific situation. The implications for management are related to the beliefs the manager has regarding how actually to get things done. Table 11–1 clearly illustrates this idea. Notice from a reading of the table that under Theory X everything seems to be influenced by three basic perceptions: people dislike work, must be forced to do things,

"They haven't much confidence in me."

10. *Ibid.*, pp. 47–48.

and do not willingly assume responsibility. Under Theory Y just the opposite is true: people like work, do best under self-direction, and are willing to assume responsibility.

Another significant managerial implication relates to the manager's role. Under Theory X the manager perceives the need to control everything. The attitude is: "If I am not around these guys will do nothing." Under Theory Y the manager perceives the need to get the subordinates involved and let them carry out most of the assignment. The attitude is: "If I turn work over to these people, I know they will get it done within the time, cost, and quality parameters I establish." Under Theory X the manager assumes that the workers need close control; under Theory Y the manager assumes they need general direction and guidance. The difference in philosophy is extremely important.

It is equally important, however, to note that not every worker wants increased responsibility and control; not all are self-directed and self-motivated. It is therefore unrealistic to believe that managers should subscribe to Theory Y assumptions in every situation. Sometimes Theory X assumptions are more realistic. Managers who have had experience in assembly-line plants often perceive their employees according to Theory X rather than Theory Y. On the other hand, managers in white-collar occupations often find their perceptions of employees better represented by the assumptions of Theory Y. In any event, it is important to realize that managerial perceptions influence the way superiors deal with subordinates.

Three Theories of Management

Another way in which perception affects human behavior in organizations has been noted by Raymond E. Miles, who points out that the managerial task is to integrate organizational variables (goals, structure, technology) with human variables (abilities, values, attitudes, personal needs). The result is an efficient sociotechnical system in which the needs of both the organization and the personnel are met.

Into this environment the manager brings his or her own personal concepts about how to deal with people. Miles's model goes past Theory X and Theory Y and incorporates both the policies of the manager and the expectations of management. Table 11–2 illustrates his three-theory model.

This table shows that there are three theories of management: traditional, human relations, and human resources. In practice managers subscribe not to one of these theories but to two. The first is the one they use to manage their own subordinates. The second is the way they believe they should be managed by their own superior.

The **traditional model** emphasizes controlling and directing. The underlying assumption in this model is that the members of the organization will comply if they are given specific tasks and procedures and if they are properly selected, trained, and paid for their efforts.

The **human relations model** is a modified version of the traditional model. The major difference is that the human relations model pays attention to personal needs such as social and egoistic needs. Social needs are addressed by allowing personnel to interact with other members of the workforce and feel part of a team. Egoistic needs are met by allowing people to feel that they are doing something important and meaningful.

Perception influences leadership style.

The emphasis is on controlling and direction.

Attention is paid to social and egoistic needs.

Table 11–2 Alternative Models of Management

Traditional Model	Human Relations Model	Human Resources Model
Assumptions		
1. Work is inherently distasteful to most people 2. What workers do is less important than what they earn for doing it 3. Few want or can handle work which requires creativity, self-direction, or self-control	1. People want to feel useful and important 2. People desire to belong and be recognized as individuals 3. These needs are more important than money in motivating people to work	1. Work is not inherently distasteful. People want to contribute to meaningful goals which they have helped establish 2. Most people can exercise far more creative, responsible self-direction and self-control than their present jobs demand
Policies		
1. The manager's basic task is to closely supervise and control his subordinates 2. He must break tasks down into simple, repetitive, easily learned operations 3. He must establish detailed work routines and procedures and enforce these firmly but fairly	1. The manager's basic task is to make each worker feel useful and important 2. He should keep his subordinates informed and listen to their objections to his plans 3. The manager should allow his subordinates to exercise some self-direction and self-control on routine matters	1. The manager's basic task is to make use of his "untapped" human resources 2. He must create an environment in which all members may contribute to the limits of their ability 3. He must encourage full participation on important matters, continually broadening subordinate self-direction and control
Expectations		
1. People can tolerate work if the pay is decent and the boss is fair 2. If tasks are simple enough and people are closely controlled, they will produce up to standard	1. Sharing information with subordinates and involving them in routine decisions will satisfy their basic needs to belong and to feel important 2. Satisfying these needs will improve morale and reduce resistance to formal authority—subordinates will "willingly cooperate"	1. Expanding subordinate influence, self-direction, and self-control will lead to direct improvements in operating efficiency 2. Work satisfaction may improve as a "by-product" of subordinates making full use of their resources

Source: From *Theories of Management: Implications for Organizational Behavior and Development* by R. E. Miles. Copyright 1975 by McGraw-Hill Book Company. Used with permission of McGraw-Hill Book Company.

The manager serves as a developer.

The **human resources model** presents the manager as a developer and facilitator who assists the subordinates in achieving goals. Under this model there is a great deal of participation in goal setting. Self-direction and self-control are not only encouraged but are rewarded. The employee is given the opportunity to become all he or she is capable of becoming.

These three theories are somewhat similar to McGregor's, with Theory X most represented by the traditional and (to some extent) the human relations model, and Theory Y most represented by the human resources model.

Miles has also found that many managers perceive themselves differently from the way they perceive their subordinates. They view the subordinates as having little drive or ambition and as best handled with a human relations approach. The managers see themselves as self-motivated and self-controlled and best managed with a human resources model.

Perception influences behavior in organizations at all levels of the hierarchy. It also helps explain both why people act as they do toward others and why they are satisfied or dissatisfied with the way others act toward them. Another important factor in understanding human behavior in action is learning.

Learning

Learning was examined in the last chapter in terms of its relationship to training. At that point it was noted that learning is a process involving a relatively permanent change in behavior. Learning remains with the individual until it is either displaced by some other behavior, such as a more efficient method of doing the same thing, or is no longer useful.

Acquisition of Learning: Some Principles

The discussion of learning curves in Chapter 10 focused on the differences in the ways that learning occurs. In more general terms, learning is a result of reinforcement. If individuals are praised or rewarded, they are more likely to remember what they have been taught than if they are either ignored or punished for their new behavior. This principle of learning is often referred to as **Thorndike's law of effect,** which can be stated this way: "Of several responses made to the same situation, those which are accompanied or closely followed by satisfaction (reinforcement) . . . will be more likely to recur; those which are accompanied or closely followed by discomfort (punishment) . . . will be less likely to occur."[11]

Reinforcement is important.

A second fundamental learning principle is: The more closely reinforcement follows the performance of an act, the greater the likelihood that the act will be repeated. This is because the individual is able to establish a causal link between the act and the reward.

Extinction described

A third fundamental learning principle is that failure to reinforce a particular behavior will result in **extinction.** When a reward is no longer forthcoming, the chances of the individual continuing to repeat the act diminish accordingly.

Spontaneous recovery explained

A fourth principle of learning is that of **spontaneous recovery,** which holds that if people experience a sequence of nonreinforced responses and then take a rest, immediately thereafter they will return to a higher level of performance than they exhibited before their rest. This principle indicates that not everyone has to be positively reinforced every time he or she does something. Additionally, it helps explain why some people come back from a vacation and do better work than they have in months.

---

11. Edward L. Thorndike, *Animal Intelligence* (New York: Macmillan, 1911), p. 244.

For purposes of studying human behavior at work, two basic types of learning warrant examination: classical conditioning and operant conditioning.

Classical and Operant Conditioning

Classical conditioning was discovered by the famous Russian physiologist Ivan Pavlov. While studying the automatic reflexes associated with digestion, he noticed that when a piece of meat was offered to his laboratory dog, the animal salivated. Pavlov called the food an unconditioned stimulus and the salivation an unconditioned response because the relationship between the two was unlearned. Whenever the dog saw the meat, it automatically salivated. On the other hand, when Pavlov rang a bell (a neutral stimulus), the dog did not salivate. It saw no relationship between the ringing of the bell and the presentation of the meat.

In an effort to determine whether he could condition the dog to salivate to a learned or conditioned stimulus like the bell, Pavlov began having the bell rung immediately before the food was placed in the dog's mouth. After several trials, he had the bell rung but no meat was placed in the dog's mouth. Nevertheless, the animal salivated. Pavlov had conditioned the dog to respond to a learned stimulus. He called this a conditioned stimulus (the bell) that brought about a conditioned response (salivation). The classical conditioning process is diagrammed in Figure 11–3.

Classical conditioning experiments have been very important in supporting stimulus-response (S-R) theories of learning. Although some behavior can be conditioned by this process, classical conditioning is of limited value in the study of human behavior in organizations. Of greater importance is the complex behavior of employees that is learned through conditioned reinforcers such as money, praise, and recognition. This type of learning is called operant conditioning.

Operant conditioning is learning that occurs as a consequence of behavior. In classical conditioning the response to be learned is already present in the animal and can be triggered by the presentation of the uncon-

Classical conditioning involves a stimulus and a response.

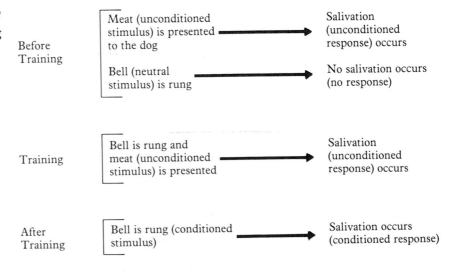

Figure 11–3
Classical Conditioning

Before Training

Meat (unconditioned stimulus) is presented to the dog ⟶ Salivation (unconditioned response) occurs

Bell (neutral stimulus) is rung ⟶ No salivation occurs (no response)

Training

Bell is rung and meat (unconditioned stimulus) is presented ⟶ Salivation (unconditioned response) occurs

After Training

Bell is rung (conditioned stimulus) ⟶ Salivation occurs (conditioned response)

ditioned stimulus (food). In operant conditioning, however, the desired responses may not be present in the subject. The individual may have to learn them. If the person does, he or she is rewarded. A second difference between the two kinds of conditioning is that in classical conditioning a stimulus is followed by an automatic response. For example, a person is stuck with a pin and flinches. In operant conditioning the individual first makes a response and then a stimulus follows. If the person makes the right response the stimulus is a reinforcer. Figure 11–4 provides some additional examples.

Learning is a result of behavior.

The important thing to remember about operant conditioning is that the individual has a choice of responses. The person can do what is expected or choose not to do what is expected. Unless the individual opts for the right choice, however, the reinforcer will not follow. Operant conditioning is of far more value in the study of human behavior in organizations than is classical conditioning. Individuals have to be trained and shown how to handle different situations and rewarded for doing them right. This principle forms the basis for social learning theory.

Social Learning Theory

There are two ways learning occurs in an organizational setting. One is through emulation of others; the other is through the use of positive and negative reinforcers. Emulation of others is commonly referred to as modeling.

Modeling

Modeling is a form of learning.

Modeling is a form of observational learning that involves imitating the behavior of others. Albert Bandura describes the approach this way:

Figure 11–4
Classical and Operant Conditioning: Some Specific Examples

Classical Conditioning

Stimulus ⟶ Response

The individual:

is surprised by a loud scream	jumps
is stuck by a needle	flinches
is tapped below the kneecap	flexes lower leg
is struck by a bright light	flinches

Operant Conditioning

Response ⟶ Stimulus

The individual:

works	is paid
talks to others	meets people
enters a restaurant	obtains food
gets work done on time	receives a salary increase

Although behavior can be shaped into new patterns to some extent by rewarding and punishing consequences, such learning would be exceedingly laborious and hazardous. If it proceeded solely on this basis . . . it is difficult to imagine a socialization process in which the language, mores, vocational activities, familial customs and educational, religious and political practices of a culture are taught to each new member by selective reinforcement of fortuitous behaviors, without benefit of models who exemplify the cultural patterns in their own behavior. Most of the behaviors that people display are learned either deliberately or inadvertently, through the influence of example.[12]

One of the most common examples of modeling occurs when people imitate their bosses, who serve as role models for subordinates. Through this process, subordinates learn what is "acceptable" organizational conduct and what is not. Additionally, they begin to develop rules and procedures for "fitting in" with the enterprise. Every organization has a culture or way of doing things. Successive managers are able to determine what this culture is and then adapt to its demands.

Modeling of this nature is important for two reasons. First, by imitating success people are more likely to be successful. Second, when managers are promoted, companies usually choose replacements who are similar in nature. Thus modeling improves a person's chances for promotion.

Of course, modeling can be dangerous if the person serving as the role model is suddenly fired or demoted. In such a case, everyone associated with that individual may suffer a stigma and be regarded as part of this manager's group. For this reason, it is important to differentiate between using someone as a role model and trying to clone oneself in a manager's image and likeness.

Positive and Negative Reinforcement

While modeling is used by individuals in shaping their own behavior, positive and negative reinforcement are processes employed by managers in shaping the behavior of subordinates. Modeling is internal in nature; positive and negative reinforcement are external in nature.

Positive reinforcement is a learning strategy in which a reward is given for the performance of some act, and the reward leads to the repetition of the act in the future. The important thing to remember about positive reinforcement is that any payoff given to the individual who performs the act must be viewed positively by the person receiving it. Otherwise it will not be a reward and will not serve to encourage repetition of the act. For example, if the person with the most sales during a particular month is given an all-expenses-paid vacation to Hawaii and the salesperson likes the reward, he or she is likely to strive for high sales during the next contest period. If the salesperson does not particularly want to go to Hawaii, however, and would prefer to have money instead, the reward is not much of a reinforcer. Merely the fact that someone is given a payoff does not

Positive reinforcement is a learning strategy.

12. Albert Bandura, "Social Learning Theory," in J. T. Spence, R. C. Carson, and J. W. Thibaut, *Behavioral Approaches to Therapy* (Morristown, N.J.: General Learning Press, 1976), p. 5.

mean that repetition is going to occur. Positive reinforcement only exists when the reward strengthens and increases the likelihood of repetition.

So is negative reinforcement.

Negative reinforcement is a learning strategy that strengthens and increases certain behavior through the termination or withdrawal of an undesirable consequence. The person who is being subjected to negative reinforcement begins to do what the boss wants and the boss, in turn, removes the undesirable consequence. For example, a worker may show up for work on time because he or she wants to avoid being bawled out by the boss. By showing up on time (the desired behavior) the worker eliminates the bawling-out (undesirable consequence). Both positive and negative reinforcement bring about the desired results. The former gives rewards, however, while the latter takes away undesirable consequences.

Positive and negative reinforcers can be used to shape behavior in organizations. Fred Luthans and Robert Kreitner, for example, have reported a number of cases in which, through the use of reinforcement schedules, managers have succeeded in increasing the productivity of their employees.[13] By initially giving rewards every time the person did something right and then gradually tapering off so that the rewards were given on a variable basis (such as every tenth time on average), managers shaped behavior in the desired way. The benefits of using reinforcement in the management of human resources have led Luthans to conclude that "understanding and then applying what is known about the administration of reinforcement can be of great assistance to modern human resource managers. In fact, one of the most important functions of all managers may well be the way they administer reinforcement to their people."[14]

Personality

Personality is a relatively stable set of characteristics and tendencies that determine the similarities and differences between people.[15] There are various elements in every personality, of course, but for purposes of simplification, we tend to think of people as a composite of all of their behavioral components. The result is that we often describe individuals by using such broad adjectives as aggressive, high achieving, calm, reserved, or generous. In a word or two, we try to sum up the individual. Naturally, this practice is misleading. Many factors make up an individual's personality. Nevertheless, there are some facts about personality that psychologists do accept, including:

1. Personality is an organized whole; otherwise the individual would have no meaning.

2. Personality appears to be organized into patterns. These are to some degree observable and measurable.

---

13. Fred Luthans and Robert Kreitner, *Organizational Behavior Modification* (Glenview, Ill.: Scott, Foresman and Company, 1975).

14. Luthans, *op. cit.,* pp. 259–260.

15. Richard M. Hodgetts, *Modern Human Relations At Work,* 2nd edition (Hinsdale, Ill.: Dryden Press, 1984), p. 80.

3. Although there is a biological basis to personality, the specific development is a product of social and cultural environments.

4. Personality has superficial aspects, such as attitudes toward a team leader, and a deeper core, such as sentiments about authority or the Protestant work ethic.

5. Personality involves both common and unique characteristics. Every person is different from every other person in some respects, while being similar in other respects.[16]

Personality Determinants

Four of the most important personality determinants used to examine individual behavior in organizations are biological, cultural, family, and external organizational forces.

Biological Contributions

Heredity plays a part.

Heredity is one of the most commonly cited biological contributors to personality. Genetic experts believe that some aspects of the human personality are affected, at least in part, by heredity. These aspects include such things as aggressiveness, sensitivity, verbal and math abilities, musical ability, and intelligence.

The role of the brain

A second biological approach concentrates on the role the brain plays in personality. One of the paths that this research has taken is to distinguish between left-brain and right-brain thinking. The basic ideas contained in this approach were discussed in the previous chapter. Table 11–3 presents additional information related to the characteristics and dimensions attri-

Table 11–3

Characteristics and Dimensions Attributed to the Left and Right Brain Hemispheres

Left Hemisphere (right side of body)	Right Hemisphere (left side of body)
Speech/verbal	Spatial/musical
Logical, mathematical	Holistic
Linear, detailed	Artistic, symbolic
Sequential	Simultaneous
Controlled	Emotional
Intellectual	Intuitive, creative
Dominant	Minor (quiet)
Worldly	Spiritual
Active	Receptive
Analytic	Synthetic, gestalt-oriented
Reading, writing, naming	Facial recognition
Sequential ordering	Simultaneous comprehension
Perception of significant order	Perception of abstract patterns
Complex motor sequences	Recognition of complex figures

16. James L. Gibson, John M. Ivancevich, and James H. Donnelly, Jr., *Organizations: Behavior, Structure, Processes,* rev. edition (Dallas: Business Publications, Inc., 1976), p. 98.

buted to the two brain hemispheres. At the present time there appear to be more questions about the role the brain plays in personality than there are answers. It does seem, however, that personality is, to some degree, determined by the brain.

Physical characteristics

A third biological factor is physical characteristics. The way a person looks affects the way he or she influences others. Appearance also influences the person's self-concept. People who are viewed positively by others are likely to feel good about themselves; people who are viewed negatively are likely not to feel good about themselves.

Cultural Contributions

Culture affects personality.

Culture consists of all the socially transmitted behavior patterns, such as the values, mores, and customs of a society. A society's culture dictates, to a large degree, why people act as they do. Culture affects personality in that it helps establish the environment in which the person grows up and matures.

Recently a great deal has been written about the cultural values and behavior of Japanese workers. Why are they able to turn out high-quality products at a lower cost than American workers? One reason, in the view of a Japanese management expert, William Ouchi, is that the Japanese operate under a different management style—one that is more conducive to their personality. Table 11–4 compares the management styles of American and Japanese managers. Notice the marked differences. Americans emphasize individual decision making and responsibility; the Japanese use group approaches. The Americans opt for rapid evaluation of personnel (every six to 12 months) and rapid promotion (every three to five years); the Japanese have much slower evaluation and promotion processes. In America there tend to be specialized career paths in which, for example, someone in accounting will go up the hierarchical ladder in this functional area; in Japan the career path is nonspecialized, so that a person may switch from bookkeeping to supervising the planning department. Finally, in America there is a limited concern on management's part with the individual's personal life; in Japan managers consider it part of their job to be fully informed of the personal circumstances of each subordinate.[17]

Table 11–4
Management Styles

American	Japanese
Short-term employment	Lifetime employment
Individual decision making	Group decision making
Individual responsibility	Collective responsibility
Rapid evaluation and promotion	Slow evaluation and promotion
Formalized control	Informal control
Specialized career path	Nonspecialized career path
Limited concern	Holistic concern

17. William G. Ouchi and Alfred M. Jaeger, "Type Z Organization: Stability in the Midst of Mobility," *Academy of Management Review*, April 1978, pp. 305–314.

Of course, in examining the true impact of culture on personality, one must look at the specific subculture from which the individual is emerging. Not every American worker performs best under the style described in Table 11–4; the same is true for the Japanese. The individual's economic and social status, age, and geographic region are additional considerations. The impact of culture cannot be overstated, however.[18]

Family Contributions

While culture helps determine the general environment in which a person learns about the world, the family initially selects and interprets this culture for the individual. The family also influences the way the person acts, both in the home and outside. For example, psychologist Paul Mussen notes:

> Warmth, support, and nurturance from the parents are critical antecedents of children's maturity, independence, self-reliance, competence and responsibility. . . . Other prerequisites are adequate communication between parents and children; the use of reason rather than punishment in achieving compliance; parental respect for the child's autonomy; encouragement of independence, individuality, and responsibility; and relatively firm control and high demands for mature behavior.[19]

Another family-related factor is *birth-order data.* Some people have suggested that an individual's birth-order rank helps fashion personality. For example, is the oldest brother of brothers likely to be a better worker than the youngest brother of brothers? Is the oldest sister of sisters a better worker than the youngest sister of sisters? Walter Toman has put together a series of profile sketches using birth-order data. The following are four of them:

Birth-order rank profiles

Oldest Brother of Brothers (OBB)   The OBB is considered to be a good worker when he wants to be. He can inspire and lead others competently, and often takes the greatest hardship upon himself. He can accept the authority of a male supervisor, however, only if he identifies with that authority. Ultimately the OBB wants the power for himself.

Youngest Brother of Brothers (YBB)   The YBB is seen as an irregular worker. Sometimes he is quite excellent in his achievements. Other times he is unproductive. The YBB is best at scientific or artistic endeavors. However, he tends to be careless with his money and often squanders it.

Oldest Sister of Sisters (OSS)   The OSS is the female counterpart of the OBB: assertive, dominant, and somewhat bossy. She is also competent, responsible, and efficient. She likes to have other women defer to her authority and will usually heed only the authority of older males.

---

18. Alan L. Wilkins and William G. Ouchi, "Efficient Cultures: Exploring the Relationship Between Culture and Organizational Performance," *Administrative Science Quarterly,* September 1983, pp. 468–481.

19. Paul Mussen, *The Psychological Development of the Child,* 3rd edition (Englewood Cliffs, N.J.: Prentice-Hall, 1979), p. 79.

Youngest Sister of Sisters (YSS)   The YSS can be any kind of worker from erratic to excellent. She is best at jobs requiring automatic skills and decision making. She may try to be creative but such efforts are usually too rushed or too chaotic to do much good. She is charming, pretentious, gullible, and emotional.[20]

Are such personality profiles really accurate? On the surface, they seem to make a lot of sense. Many people, upon reading the descriptions, agree with them. In terms of overall accuracy, however, the theory offers only general insights. More scientific research needs to be conducted before any definitive conclusions can be drawn.

Other External Forces

In addition to biological, cultural, and family influences on personality, there are external organizations with which individuals interact. These include groups and organizations at school, at play, and at work. In these settings, the individual begins to learn what is "proper behavior." For example, regardless of the group or organization, people soon begin to understand the basic goals of the organization, how these goals are supposed to be pursued, and the rules and standards they are to follow in their relationship to other members of the organization.

> Recent studies have indicated that socialization is important not only to new organization members but also in the superior-subordinate relationship, and when personnel switch jobs . . . or are promoted. Van Maanen also suggests specific socialization strategies such as formal or informal, individual or collective, sequential or nonsequential, or fixed or variable, which will lead to different outcomes for the individual and the organization. For example, a company may use a sequential socialization strategy to groom a person for a top management position by first rotating him or her through a series of relevant functional specialties. Another organization, say, a government agency, may take someone with political power from the rank and file and make him or her the head of the agency. This nonsequential strategy will result in different personal (i.e., the personality will be affected) and organizational strategies.[21]

Some organizations encourage dependency.

It is also important to realize that not all organizations encourage the full personality development of their personnel. In some cases the organization actually keeps its employees in a state of immaturity. For example, Figure 11–5 shows that, as a person matures, he or she goes through a series of changes resulting in the emergence of an individual who is active, independent, and capable of managing day-to-day affairs. This stage is quite different from the immature stage of the child. Not all organizations encourage this development, however. Many top managers like to keep their people dependent on the organization for direction and guidance. They give their subordinates only short-run information so that the

---

20. Walter Toman, "Birth Order Rules All," *Psychology Today,* December 1970, pp. 45–49.

21. Luthans, *op. cit.,* p. 128.

Figure 11–5

Development from
Immaturity to Maturity

Immaturity (Child)	Maturity (Adult)
Passivity	Activity
Dependence	Independence
Capable of behaving in a few ways	Capable of behaving in many ways
Casual, shallow interests	Deep, strong interests
Current time perspective	Past, present, and future time perspective
Subordinate position	Equal or superior position
Lack of awareness of "self"	Awareness and control of "self"

Source: Adapted from Chris Argyris, *Personality and Organization* (New York: Harper & Row, 1957), p. 50.

subordinates never really know for sure where the enterprise is heading. They also encourage subordinates to follow the lead of top management as opposed to acting independently and developing their own work styles. The result is easy to predict. Those who dislike control and guidance will leave the organization. Those who are content with this type of environment will stay. To some degree the organization helps form, or at least nurture, the personality of its members. This personality, in turn, helps dictate the type of motivation that is most effective in rewarding the personnel. The subject of motivation will be the topic of attention in the next chapter.

Summary

1. Human behavior is a complex subject. Some people have sought to study it by investigating questions such as "Who am I?" while others have opted for overall models of human behavior such as the rational/emotional models, the behavioristic/humanistic models, or the economic/self-actualizing models. While all of these approaches provide some information into the subject of human nature, the overall picture is incomplete without consideration of the roles played by perception, learning, and personality.

2. Perception is an individual's view of reality. The key to understanding perception is recognizing that each situation is interpreted by the individuals who are witnesses to it. No two may see exactly the same thing. Perception is a two-way street. This fact is illustrated by such perceptual factors as attribution, which refers to the way an individual explains or interprets the personal behavior of others; stereotyping, which is the tendency to perceive another person as belonging to a single class or category; and the halo effect, in which a person perceives another on the basis of a single trait.

3. Perception can also affect the way managers motivate and lead their personnel. Some managers accept Theory X assumptions, which, in the main, hold that the employee is lazy, works best when threatened or coerced and, above all, wants security. Other managers subscribe to Theory Y, which holds that people do not dislike work, do their best when under self-direction, and are willing to assume responsibility.

4. Another way to view the effect of perception on human behavior in organizations is to examine the three models of management: traditional, human relations, and human resources. Depending on the assumptions, policies, and expectations of the manager, any one of these three may be used. While many managers believe that their own people work best under the human relations model they believe they themselves should be managed via the human resources model.

5. The learning process involves a relatively permanent change in behavior. Research shows that learning is a result of reinforcement. If an individual is rewarded for doing something right, the chances of the person doing the same thing again are improved. In applying learning techniques to the job, organizations rely heavily on operant conditioning in their efforts to shape and mold desired behavior. Learning occurs in two ways in an organizational setting. First, managers become role models for their subordinates. Second, positive and negative reinforcement are used to reward and direct behavior.

6. Personality is a relatively stable set of characteristics and tendencies that determine similarities and differences between people. Some of the primary determinants of personality include biology, culture, the family, and external forces such as the groups and organizations with which the individual interacts. The average person both influences, and is influenced by, these forces in the external environment.

Key Terms

Attribution   The way in which an individual explains or interprets the personal behavior of others.

Behavioristic model   A model of human behavior that describes individuals in terms of observable behavior.

Classical conditioning   Unlearned behavior commonly associated with stimulus-response.

Culture   Socially transmitted behavior patterns such as values, mores, and customs.

Economic model   A model of human behavior that pictures people as being totally self-interested.

Ego   The conscious and logical part of Freudian man. It uses intellect and reasoning to interpret reality.

Emotional model   A model of human behavior that sees the individual as being heavily controlled by emotions.

Extinction   The result of a failure to reinforce a particular behavior.

Halo effect   Perceiving an individual on the basis of one particular trait such as intelligence, appearance, or dependability.

Humanistic model   A model of human behavior that views the individual as being able to surmount irrational behavior through conscious reasoning.

Human relations model   A model of management that describes the manager's job as one in which personal attention must be paid to both the job and the personal needs of the people.

Human resources model   A model of management that presents the manager as a developer and facilitator who encourages self-direction and self-control on the part of subordinates, allowing them to become all they are capable of becoming.

Id   The core of the unconscious. It consists of raw instinctual drive and continually struggles for gratification and pleasure.

Modeling   A form of observational behavior that involves imitating the behavior of others.

Negative reinforcement   A learning strategy that strengthens and increases certain behavior through the termination or withdrawal of an undesirable consequence.

Operant conditioning   Learning that occurs as a consequence of behavior.

Perception   An individual's view of reality.

Personality   A relatively stable set of characteristics that determine the similarities and differences between people.

Positive reinforcement   A learning strategy in which a reward is given for the performance of an act and the reward leads to a repetition of the act.

Rational model   A model of human behavior that views the individual as a highly rational person.

Self-actualizing model   A model of human behavior that views people as being motivated by the opportunity to grow, mature, handle challenge, and become all they are capable of becoming.

Self-monitors   Individuals who constantly assess the opinion climate around them and change their behavior appropriately.

Spontaneous recovery   A principle of learning that holds that if people experience a sequence of nonreinforced responses and then take a rest, immediately thereafter they will return to a higher level of performance than they exhibited prior to their rest.

Stereotyping   The tendency to perceive another person as belonging to a single class or category.

Superego   Often depicted as the conscience, it is part of the unconscious.

Theory X   A set of assumptions that hold that people (1) dislike work, (2) have little ambition, (3) want security above all, and (4) must be coerced, controlled, and threatened in order to attain organizational objectives.

Theory Y   A set of assumptions that hold that (1) if conditions are favorable, people will not only accept responsibility but will seek it; (2) if people are committed to organizational objectives, they will exercise self-direction and self-control; and (3) commitment is a function of the rewards associated with goal attainment.

Thorndike's law of effect   A law of learning that holds that actions that are reinforced are more likely to recur than are actions that are punished.

Traditional model   A model of management that describes the manager's job as one of controlling and directing people. It is based on the belief that people will comply only if their tasks are specified and they are properly trained and paid for their efforts.

Questions for Analysis and Discussion

1. How do the following models describe human behavior: rational and emotional models, behavioristic and humanistic models, economic and self-actualizing models?

2. In your own words, what is meant by the term perception? Describe the perception process in action.

3. What are some of the things psychologists know about perceivers? The person being perceived? List three of each.

4. How do the following affect perception: attribution, stereotyping, the halo effect?

5. What are the Theory X assumptions? Theory Y assumptions? Compare and contrast both sets of assumptions and discuss their managerial implications.

6. How does each of these models of management differ from the others: traditional, human relations, and human resources?

7. How do the following help explain the acquisition of learning: Thorndike's law of effect, extinction, and spontaneous recovery?

8. How does classical conditioning differ from operant conditioning? What role do modeling, positive reinforcement, and negative reinforcement play in learning?

9. In your own words, what is meant by the term personality? What facts about personality do psychologists accept?

10. What role do each of the following play in shaping personality: biology, culture, the family, work organizations? Be sure to discuss the effect of each.

| Case |

The Way They See It

Every year the Schalling Corporation conducts an overall analysis of its managerial staff. The company is particularly interested in identifying the most effective and least effective managers. This year, in middle management, the choice was not difficult at all. In one department turnover was less than 1 percent, work output was 14 percent above expectations, and four of the workers won an Outstanding Employee of the Month award. In another department turnover was 26 percent, work output was 39 percent below expectations, and none of the workers ever qualified for consideration as employee of the month.

As part of the year-end analysis report, each manager is required to make an evaluation of his or her personnel. The managers of the two departments mentioned here each made an analysis of their people and, in the process, explained their own managerial behavior. Part of their reports read as follows:

Manager 1: Most of the people in my department are hard working and conscientious. I find that if you take some time to explain how the work is to be done, and follow up later on by answering questions and helping out with problems, the people are pretty much self-motivated. Moreover, once a few of them get behind a project or undertaking, the rest follow in short order. There is terrific morale and it is infectious!

Manager 2: Most of the people in my department are basically lazy and have to be prodded continually. I have established a rule that anyone who is late more than two days in a month will be sent home for one day without pay. The rule has been in effect for three months now and tardiness is still quite high. However, I believe that we have turned the corner and it will start down. If not, I intend to add additional penalties. Also, I have noticed that when I am not around, the work quantity slows up dramatically. For this reason, I have begun increasing my visits around the department, thereby ensuring that everyone keeps working.

1. Which of the two is a Theory X manager? A Theory Y manager?

2. In your own words, what assumptions do the two managers use in directing their people? Be specific in your answer.

3. In what way might the managers' perceptions of their personnel be accounting for the results they are achieving with their respective work groups? Explain your answer.

Getting the Managers Ready

John Galworthy, president of a medium-sized insurance firm, has watched his company grow at an annual rate of 20 percent over each of the last five years. Realizing that the company will be six times larger than it is now if this growth rate is maintained for the next decade, John knows that the organization's management expertise will have to grow along with sales. Yesterday he had an hour-long conference with Dr. Henry O'Grady, one of his old business school professors. After explaining his goals to the professor, he asked Henry how the enterprise could ensure that its managers "really know how to manage." Here is Henry's response:

> What you are discussing is a tall order. There are a great number of things that your managers need to know. The technical side of their job, I imagine, they pretty much understand. I doubt whether there is a great deal they can be taught about insurance per se, although some training along the lines of salesmanship might be helpful.

> More to the point you are interested in, however, you will need to have your people trained in behavioral principles and guidelines. One of the first things is to find out what their current view of human behavior is. Why do they believe people work? What do they think motivates their personnel? The answer to this question will give us an idea of how they see their people and the way they feel these people should be managed.

> Then we need to familiarize them with the impact of perception on management style. Do they tend to stereotype workers? Are they guilty of using the halo effect? How do they see their workers—in Theory X terms or Theory Y terms? Do they subscribe to a human resources model of management?

> Next, they need to learn what positive reinforcement is all about, how to use it, and why it works. They also need to understand their own place as a role model for the subordinates.

> Finally, I would examine the subject of personality, find out what types of personalities the managers feel they are supervising, and what the best approach is to directing and leading these people. Also, what type of personality development does your company permit? Does it keep personnel in a general state of immaturity or does it allow them to grow and develop?

The president was impressed. He was also concerned, however, that this approach might be too theoretical to be of any practical value for his people. "Remember, Henry," he said, "I want to train these people as managers, not turn them into junior psychologists. Also, I want them to understand how this training transfers to the job setting."

Henry assured him that this was possible. "Remember, John," he said, "this is only the beginning of a management training program. First we need to sensitize your people to the world around them. We need to get and give information regarding how human beings function in modern organizations. Having done this we can then turn to the problems of motivation and leadership per se. You have to start an analysis of human behavior, however, by looking at the key factors involved: perception, learning, and personality. Then you can move on to more applied areas."

The president liked what he was hearing. "Okay," he said, "I want you to start as soon as you can. Bring your assistant with you and put together a set of mini-training programs that will help my managers to get a better understanding of human behavior in organizations. When you are finished with this phase of the project, we can talk about a follow-up program that will address more specific job-related issues."

Your Consultation

Assume you are the professor's assistant. Acting as a consultant to him, outline what you think should be covered in an early training program to help the management personnel understand human behavior in action. In your outline be sure to address the topics of perception, learning, and personality and explain how you would incorporate each of these topics in the training program.

12

Motivation at Work

Objectives

This chapter studies motivation at work. What drives people to work hard and do a good job? What role is played by money? Opportunity? Power? Prestige? The answers to these questions vary, depending on the individual. A large amount of research has been conducted on the subject of motivation, however, and in this chapter we will examine what is currently known about it.

Besides examining the nature of motivation, this chapter reviews some of the most important content and process theories of motivation, looks at the role played by money in the motivation process, and explores the impact of values. By the time you have finished reading the material in this chapter, you will be able to

1. define the term motivation and the three primary ingredients in the process;

2. describe how motivation works;

3. discuss in detail the four most important content theories of motivation: Maslow's need theory, Herzberg's two-factor theory, Alderfer's ERG theory, and McClelland's achievement motivation theory;

4. describe three of the most important process theories of motivation: Vroom's expectancy theory, Porter and Lawler's model, and Adams's equity theory;

5. explain the role of money in motivation; and

6. tell how values affect motivation in the modern organization.

The Nature of Motivation

Motivation defined

The word **motivation** comes from the Latin *movere,* which means to move. Today the term means stimulating people to action by means of incentives or inducements. This process is often generated through an *external* action such as offering someone more money to do more work. Whether or not this effort is successful is determined *internally,* however, because motivation is a psychological process. Furthermore, people are moved or motivated toward an objective only if they feel it is in their own best personal interest.[1] This fact was noted in Chapter 2 when Chester Barnard's acceptance theory of authority was discussed.

Primary Ingredients

There are three primary ingredients in motivation. These are best described in what can be called the *motivation formula:* motivation is a function of ability, effort, and desire.

Ability is the individual's capacity to do something. If a person has the ability to sell, he or she may be a terrific salesperson. But if the individual has little selling ability, he or she will never attain the same degree of success.

Effort is the time, drive, and energy the individual expends in the pursuit of an objective. Some goals cannot be attained by mere ability; they require the person to spend a considerable amount of effort as well. Many salespeople find, for example, that in order to close large sales, they have to make many calls on the customer before the latter is "sold" both on them and their product or service.

Desire is the wish, want, or urge for a particular objective. Unless someone truly desires to attain an objective, the chance of success is diminished and, even if the goal is attained, the degree of success is reduced. A salesperson who desires to make $1 million in sales during a given year has a much better chance of attaining this objective than does a colleague who hopes to sell $700,000 worth of merchandise.

Motion and Motivation

Motivation is more than movement.

Motion is often confused with motivation. Often people see someone working very hard and assume that the person is motivated. Motion or effort (in the form of energy) is only part of good work, however. People who are not in motion may also be motivated. Many times employees may sit down to read something or ponder the answer to a particular problem, and they are indeed motivated toward a particular objective. Motivation can exist without motion and vice versa. For this reason, an initial investigation of motivation is best approached from a needs standpoint. When this approach is taken, behavior can be reduced to three common aspects.

1. Chester I. Barnard, *The Functions of the Executive* (Cambridge, Mass.: Harvard University Press, 1938), p. 165.

Figure 12–1
One Model of Motivation

Common Aspects of Motivation

The three common aspects of motivation deal with (a) what energizes human behavior, (b) how this behavior is directed or channeled, and (c) how the behavior can be maintained using a "needs" approach. Figure 12–1 expresses this idea.

People engage in goal-directed behavior.

Referring to the figure, consider the case of a person who needs a new car (whether it be for transportation, status, ego, or whatever). This person is likely to engage in goal-directed behavior such as working overtime and saving money. The result is the purchase of the new car and the satisfaction of the need.

Obviously this example is quite simple. People have many needs and sometimes their needs conflict. A person may want to be at home with his or her family (affiliation need) and at the same time may want to earn the next promotion at the office (power, ego, status needs). The fact that we cannot see into someone's mind limits our ability to determine which need will win out and become the focus of goal-directed behavior.

Moreover, people do not always attain their needs. Sometimes they are unsuccessful in their efforts and may end up engaging in what appears to be irrational behavior (yelling, screaming, blaming others for their failure to succeed). Motivation is a very complex subject. Many researchers have studied this process, and one of the most popular approaches to explaining it is through the use of a "needs" approach. This is only one way of looking at the subject, of course, but it is an excellent starting point because a wealth of research has been collected about needs and their role in human motivation.[2] These approaches generally can be clustered under the heading of content theories.

Content Theories of Motivation

Content theories of motivation attempt to explain what motivates people. Whenever managers are asked what motivates their personnel and they begin making a list of factors, they are taking a content theory approach. The four major content theories of motivation, all of which use a needs approach, are those by Abraham Maslow, Frederick Herzberg, Clayton Alderfer, and David McClelland.

Maslow's Need Hierarchy

Perhaps the best-known "needs approach" to the study of motivation is that of Abraham Maslow.[3] Based principally on his clinical experience,

2. Terence R. Mitchell, "Motivation: New Directions for Theory, Research and Practice," *Academy of Management Review,* January 1982, pp. 80–88.

3. A. H. Maslow, "A Theory of Human Motivation," *Psychological Review,* July 1943, pp. 370–396.

Figure 12–2
Maslow's Need Hierarchy
(and the Way These Needs
Are Satisfied on the Job)

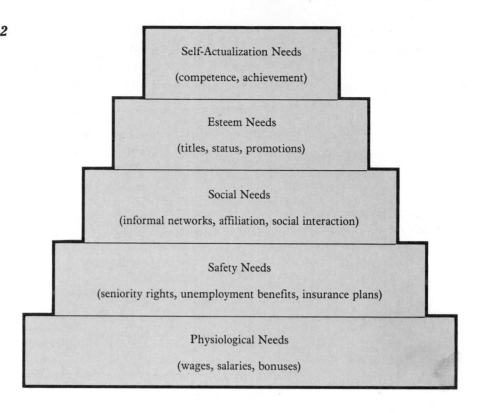

Self-Actualization Needs

(competence, achievement)

Esteem Needs

(titles, status, promotions)

Social Needs

(informal networks, affiliation, social interaction)

Safety Needs

(seniority rights, unemployment benefits, insurance plans)

Physiological Needs

(wages, salaries, bonuses)

Maslow, a psychologist, presented his theory in terms of a need hierarchy. This hierarchy is illustrated in Figure 12–2.

Unsatisfied needs are motivators.

Maslow's need theory holds that an individual strives for need satisfaction at a particular level. When needs at one level are basically satisfied, they no longer serve as motivators, and the individual moves on to the next level in the hierarchy. The upward movement continues until a lower-level need begins to manifest itself again. At this point the individual drops back to the lower level and attempts to satisfy this need.

The Five Levels

The five levels in the hierarchy represent basic need categories that can be described as follows:

1. **Physiological needs**   These are the most basic needs, often referred to as unlearned, primary needs. Typical examples include food, clothing, and shelter. Once these needs are basically satisfied, the next higher level of needs comes into play.

2. **Safety needs**   This level represents the individual's need for security or protection. It extends not only to physical safety but to emotional safety as well.

3. **Social needs**   This level represents the individual's need for affiliation, social interaction, and a sense of belonging. The person needs to give and receive friendship.

4. **Esteem needs**   This level represents the individual's need to "feel good" about himself or herself. Often referred to as ego needs, the needs at this level are satisfied through the acquisition of power and status. The individual needs to feel important or worthwhile, and power and status provide a basis for these feelings.

5. **Self-Actualization needs**   This level represents the apex of human needs. While it is the most difficult to describe, it is that level at which a person tries to become all he or she is capable of becoming. Many people pursue this need when they strive for competence or achievement in some area. They are trying to realize all of their potential.

Maslow never contended that everyone would be fully satisfied at a particular level before moving on to the next. He believed that people would seek the next level if they were "basically" satisfied at the current one. The higher they went, the lower the amount of basic satisfaction that would be realized, e.g., 85 percent at the physiological level, 50 percent at the social level, 10 percent at the self-actualization level.[4]

Application of the Theory

In Figure 12–2, Maslow's basic hierarchy has been converted into a content model of work motivation. When Maslow first presented his hierarchy, however, he did not intend it to be used for describing the motivation of organizational personnel. This use did not come about until more than 20 years later.[5] Much of what Maslow proposed has not been substantiated through research efforts. For example, one study of female clerks found his model fairly reliable as a way of measuring priority needs but open to question as an overall theory of work motivation.[6]

Another study, conducted among young managers at American Telephone & Telegraph over a five-year period, found that changes in managers' needs were attributable to their developing career concerns and not to the desire for the need gratification that Maslow described.[7] Mahmond Wahba and Lawrence Birdwell made a comprehensive review of the literature and found no support for Maslow's contention that satisfaction at one level led to activation of the next highest level. In addition, they discovered two primary clusters of needs, not five.[8]

---

4. *Ibid.,* pp. 388–389.

5. Abraham H. Maslow, *Eupsychian Management* (Homewood, Ill.: Dorsey Press, 1965).

6. Michael Beer, *Leadership, Employee Needs, and Motivation,* Ohio State University, College of Commerce and Administration, Bureau of Business Research, Monograph No. 129, Columbus, 1966, p. 68.

7. Douglas T. Hall and Khahl E. Nougaim, "An Examination of Maslow's Need Hierarchy in an Organizational Setting," *Organizational Behavior and Human Performance,* February 1968, pp. 12–35.

8. Mahmond A. Wahba and Lawrence G. Birdwell, "Maslow Reconsidered: A Review of Research on the Need Hierarchy Theory," *Proceedings of the Academy of Management,* 1973, pp. 514–520.

The theory's value is limited.

Research of this nature shows that while Maslow's theory may provide some insights into motivation, its value is limited. For example, the link between needs and motivation at work is not very well established. Nor is it clear exactly how many levels of needs each person has or whether everyone is actually motivated by all of these need levels. Maslow's ideas have been extended through the work of Frederick Herzberg.

Herzberg's Two-Factor Theory

Frederick Herzberg and his associates conducted motivation research among 200 accountants and engineers in the Pittsburgh area.[9] The researchers used the critical incident method to obtain their data, asking each person in the study to think of a time when he or she felt exceptionally good or bad about his or her job. Herzberg found the responses to be fairly consistent.

When reporting good feelings the participants in the study made comments related to their job experiences and to *job content.* When reporting bad feelings, they made comments associated with the environment or the *job context.* These two groups of factors—those related to job content and those related to job context—became the basis of Herzberg's **two-factor theory of motivation.** The job content factors (the satisfiers) were labeled motivators. The job context factors (the dissatisfiers) were called hygiene factors. Herzberg's theory is shown in Table 12–1.

Satisfiers and dissatisfiers were identified.

Motivators and Hygiene Factors

Herzberg called the job content factors **motivators** because they brought about satisfaction and resulted in motivation. The job context factors were labeled **hygiene factors** because, in Herzberg's view, they were like physical hygiene—they did not make things better but prevented them from getting worse.

Placing these two sets of factors, motivators and hygiene factors, in perspective, Herzberg concluded that hygiene prevented dissatisfaction, while motivators brought about satisfaction. Hygiene established a "zero level" of motivation; if management did not provide hygiene factors, dissatisfaction resulted. If hygiene factors were provided, then there was no dissatisfaction but there was no satisfaction either. Satisfaction resulted only from the presence of motivators.

Table 12–1
Herzberg's Two-Factor Theory

Hygiene Factors	Motivators
Salary	Achievement
Supervision, technical	Recognition
Working conditions	Responsibility
Interpersonal relations	Advancement
Company policies and administration	The work itself

9. Frederick Herzberg, Bernard Mausner, and Barbara Bloch Snyderman, *The Motivation to Work* (New York: John Wiley, 1959).

One of the most important aspects of Herzberg's theory is the attention it focuses on the need to provide hygiene at least. In the past many organizations have emphasized such factors as salary, working conditions, and interpersonal relations. Herzberg recommended providing these hygiene factors and "shutting up about them." The real emphasis, he said, should be placed on motivators like achievement, recognition, and the chance for advancement.

Herzberg's theory is similar to Maslow's. Herzberg's hygiene factors coincide with Maslow's lower-level (physiological, safety, and social) needs. His motivators coincide with Maslow's upper level (esteem and self-actualization) needs.

The basic two-factor theory is appealing if only because it seems to be intuitively correct. Many scholars and researchers have attacked the theory vigorously, however.

Criticisms of the Two-Factor Theory

One of the biggest arguments against the two-factor theory is that the conclusions drawn as a result of the research findings were not the only ones that could have been reached. Victor Vroom, a leading researcher in the area of motivation, put the argument this way:

> It is . . . possible that obtained differences between stated sources of satisfaction and dissatisfaction stem from defensive processes within the individual respondent. Persons may be more likely to attribute the causes of satisfaction to their own achievements and accomplishments on the job. On the other hand, they may be more likely to attribute dissatisfaction not to personal inadequacies or deficiencies, but to factors in the work environment, i.e., obstacles presented by company policies or supervision.[10]

The theory appears to be methodologically bound.

A second argument revolves around the fact that the theory appears to be "methodologically bound." This term means that the results are determined by the approach used in collecting the data. Other researchers have attempted to replicate Herzberg's theory using a data collection method other than the critical incident method and have not been able to get the same results.

Were the interviewers biased?

A third argument centers around the interpretations of the results by the interviewers. Since the respondents gave verbal answers, the interviewers may have misinterpreted some of the results and developed a theory that was at least partially fashioned by erroneous interpretations.

The dimensions are not independent . . .

Finally, critics of the theory argue that Herzberg set up an "either or" approach. According to his theory, something is either a hygiene factor or it is a motivator. Herzberg never proved, however, that something that is a hygiene factor for one person cannot also be a motivator for another. In fact, the two dimensions (motivators and hygiene factors) may not be undimensional or independent. Robert House and Lawrence Wigdor, after making a review of the literature on the subject, have concluded that:

---

10. Victor Vroom, *Work and Motivation* (New York: John Wiley, 1964), p. 129.

> Since the data do not support the satisfier-dissatisfier dichotomy, the
> . . . proposition of the Two-Factory theory, that satisfiers have more motiva-
> tional force than dissatisfiers, appears highly suspect. This is true for two
> reasons. First, any attempt to separate the two requires an arbitrary definition
> of the classifications satisfier and dissatisfier. Second, unless such an arbitrary
> separation is employed, the proposition is untenable.[11]

but the theory does have value.

On the positive side, it is important to realize that Herzberg made some important contributions to modern motivation theory. He provided a much better picture of job content factors and their relationship to motivation than anyone had before. Moreover, while his research findings may not hold true for every individual in every job, his basic theme—that more attention be paid to job content factors and less to job context factors— is an important one. For too long management has worried itself about the environment in which the work is carried out and given insufficient attention to the psychological side of motivation.

Alderfer's ERG Theory

More recently, Clayton Alderfer has provided an extension of the Maslow and Herzberg models.[12] Alderfer's model is more in line with existing research findings in that he uses only three basic need categories: existence, relatedness, and growth (**ERG** for short).

Existence needs are related to survival and safety. They correspond to Maslow's physiological needs and safety needs of a material type. They also coincide with some of Herzberg's hygiene factors, such as working conditions and salary.

Relatedness needs stress interpersonal and social relationships. They correspond to Maslow's safety needs of an interpersonal type, social needs, and esteem needs of an interpersonal type. They also coincide with Herzberg's hygiene factors, such as interpersonal relations and supervision, and motivators such as recognition and responsibility.

Growth needs are related to the individual's desire for personal development. In Maslow's need hierarchy they can be found at the top of the esteem level and at the self-actualization level. In Herzberg's theory they include advancement, achievement, and the work itself.

Movement along a continuum

Alderfer goes further than simply expanding the Maslow and Herzberg models, however. He suggests that needs be thought of as a continuum. Instead of moving from one hierarchical level to the next, as Maslow's theory suggests, or from one factor group to another, as Herzberg argues, people can skip along the continuum. Some may spend a great deal of time trying to fulfill one particular need and very little trying to satisfy another. For example, individuals from a middle-class background are highly likely to spend most of their time trying to fulfill relatedness and growth

---

11. Robert J. House and Lawrence A. Wigdor, "Herzberg's Dual-Factor Theory of Job Satisfaction and Motivation: A Review of the Evidence and a Criticism," *Personnel Psychology,* Winter 1967, pp. 385–386.

12. Clayton P. Alderfer, *Existence, Relatedness and Growth: Human Needs in Organization Settings* (New York: Free Press, 1972).

The theory is somewhat simplistic.

needs. In contrast people of low economic status may spend a great deal of time trying to satisfy existence needs.

While there has been no direct research on ERG theory, except for Alderfer's own work,[13] current motivation theorists have a great deal of respect for it. They feel it incorporates many of the strong parts of Maslow's and Herzberg's work while offering a less restrictive and limiting view of motivation. On the negative side, however, like Maslow and Herzberg, Alderfer does not really address the overall complexities of work motivation. This problem does not occur in all content theory research.[14] The work of David McClelland is an example.

Achievement Motivation Theory

David McClelland is most closely associated with **achievement motivation theory.** Over the last 35 years this theory has undergone considerable research and revision. The theory focuses on three specific needs: achievement, power, and affiliation. In contrast to the theories of Maslow and Herzberg, it is more limited in scope, tending to address only higher-level needs.

Those most interested in achievement motivation theory are concerned with the success and failure of organizational personnel. What do successful salespeople have in common? What characteristics do successful managers share? While achievement motivation parallels other content theories to some extent, it tends to go beyond the superficial treatment they afford. John Miner, a leading reseacher, states the difference this way:

> The two major motives of the theory, achievement and power, would seem to fall within Maslow's esteem category, although achievement motivation has some aspects in common with self-actualization. Affiliation motivation would clearly fall in the social category. However, despite these overlaps and the origins of both theories in clinical psychology and personality theory, need hierarchy theory and achievement motivation theory represent distinctly different concepts of the motivational process.[15]

Need for Achievement

Achievement need is the drive to attain objectives or accomplish things. Through research, McClelland identified the specific characteristics of individuals with a high need to achieve.[16] They are the following:

1. *Moderate risk taking* A high achiever is neither a high nor a low risk taker. High risks involve too much luck; low risks are not sufficiently

13. Clayton P. Alderfer, "An Empirical Text of a New Theory of Human Needs," *Organizational Behavior and Human Performance,* May 1969, pp. 142–1975.

14. Bronston T. Mayes, "Some Boundary Considerations in the Application of Motivation Models," *Academy of Management Review,* January 1978, pp. 51–52.

15. John B. Miner, *Theories of Organizational Behavior* (Hinsdale, Ill.: Dryden Press, 1980), p. 47.

16. David C. McClelland, *The Achieving Society* (Princeton, N.J.: Van Nostrand, 1961); David C. McClelland, "Business Drive and National Achievement," *Harvard Business Review,* July–August 1962, pp. 99–112.

challenging. High achievers like moderate risks where they have a chance of winning, with the results dependent on their abilities.

2. *Personal responsibility*   A high achiever wants to win or lose through personal effort. He or she wants to play a role in the successful attainment of an objective.

Characteristics of high achievers

3. *Feedback on results*   A high achiever likes to know the score in terms of how well he or she is doing. In this way, if the individual is doing well, he or she can continue; if he or she is doing poorly, appropriate corrective steps can be taken.

4. *Accomplishment*   A high achiever needs to accomplish things. The rewards themselves are not unimportant, but they are usually not the most important thing. For example, a successful salesperson may be happy making $125,000 annually, but the money is often nothing more than a counting device to let the individual know how well he or she is succeeding. Rewards are often secondary to the internal satisfaction that accompanies the goal attainment.

5. *Task preoccupation*   A high achiever tends to be preoccupied with a task until it is accomplished. The individual seldom leaves a job unfinished. For this reason, these people tend to be highly realistic and do not pursue objectives they cannot attain.

High achievers can be found in many occupations. One of the most typical is the area of sales, where it is possible to develop and nurture these five characteristics. It is also important to remember that high achievement, in and of itself, is not necessarily good, however. Many organizations have found that high achievers make excellent salespeople but extremely poor sales managers. These people are too interested in their own particular objectives to worry about others. If one is to become an effective manager, it is necessary to balance a concern for personal achievement with a desire to be helpful to subordinates.

Need for Power

During the mid-1970s McClelland expanded his initial interests and began studying the **need for power.** This need is manifested by a drive for control and influence. McClelland concluded that while achievement motivation is important in studying entrepreneurship, power is more important in an organizational setting. In fact, he determined that a good manager in a large company does not have a high need for achievement.[17]

According to McClelland, power motivation can be expressed in a number of different ways. The mode of expression, at least in part, is a function of the stage to which the power motive has developed in the individual. McClelland believes that there is a hierarchy of development and that people must experience one stage in order to reach the next. Some never

17. David C. McClelland and David H. Burnham, "Power is the Great Motivator, *Harvard Business Review,* January–February 1976, pp. 100–110.

Table 12–2
Power and Managerial
Performance

Maturity Stage	Power Motivational Pattern	Effect on Managerial Performance
I	The desire to influence others is low.	Usually this pattern does not provide sufficiently assertive behavior for effective managerial performance.
II	The power motivation drive has little to do with other people; it is basically concerned with doing things for oneself.	Unrelated to the management of people.
III (early)	High power motivation coupled with low affiliation and low self-control.	Not very effective. The manager tends to push his or her weight around too much and be rude to the personnel.
III (late)	High power motivation coupled with low affiliation and low self-control.	More effective. The manager uses power to help out subordinates while maintaining a visible presence. Subordinates identify more with the manager than with the organization itself.
IV	High power motivation of an altruistic type coupled with low affiliation and high self-control.	Very effective. Selfless leadership. The manager helps out subordinates and encourages identification with the organization. The individual takes a back seat to the organization itself.

rise above the first level, while others may be at any one of the four stages at a certain point in time. Table 12–2 illustrates these four stages.

McClelland also distinguished between personalized power and socialized power. *Personalized power* is characterized by win-lose situations and dominance-submission. A person exercising this type of power derives satisfaction from getting the better of others.[18] In contrast *socialized power* involves a mix of power motivation and pragmatism so that there is a "concern for group goals, for finding those goals that will move men, for helping the group to formulate them, for taking initiative in providing means of achieving them, and for giving group members the feeling of competence they need to work hard for them."[19] When used in this way, power is employed as a means of getting things done, as opposed to a basis for simply making a person feel good because he or she is able to boss others around.

Personalized versus socialized power

18. David C. McClelland, William N. Davis, Rudolf Kalin, and Eric Wanner, *The Drinking Man: Alcohol and Human Motivation* (New York: Free Press, 1972).
19. David C. McClelland, *Power: The Inner Experience* (New York: Irvington Press, 1975), p. 265.

Table 12–2 shows the relationships between the various types of power motivation and managerial performance. Individuals at lower developmental stages may function effectively in some managerial roles. The effective manager usually does not begin to emerge until late stage III, however.

This discussion illustrates that power motivation is extremely important to managerial performance. Power can manifest itself in many different ways, however. Some managers need power because it helps them dominate others (early stage III in Table 12–2); others need power because it helps them guide subordinates and develop a personal allegiance from them (late stage III); still others need power that allows them to be altruistic and develop subordinate talent that is well motivated and loyal to the organization (stage IV).

Power motivation is important for managers.

Need for Affiliation

The **need for affiliation** also plays a part in achievement motivation theory. Individuals with a high need for affiliation want to interact, socialize with others, and "belong." This need is best represented by the third level, social, on Maslow's hierarchy.

While achievement and power have been studied extensively, not much research has been done directly on affiliation.[20] In terms of managerial performance, however, there have been some interesting findings. One of them, reported by McClelland and Burnham, was the following:

> The general conclusion of these studies is that the top manager of a company must possess a high need for power, that is, a concern for influencing people. However, this need must be disciplined and controlled so that it is directed toward the benefit of the institution as a whole and not toward the manager's personal aggrandizement. Moreover, the top manager's need for power ought to be greater than his need for being liked by people.[21]

Affiliation need may subvert managerial performance.

If managers are too concerned about wanting to get along well with their people, their effectiveness will suffer. For this reason, affiliation plays a significant role in achievement motivation. Strong affiliation motivation interferes with and possibly even subverts, effective managerial performance. Of course, this is not to say that the effective manager has no need to affiliate with others. He or she must keep this need in perspective, however, and exercise self-control by maintaining proper social distance. Commenting on an example of managerial behavior in which the affiliation need was allowed to override all others, McClelland and Burnham offer the following case:

> When President Ford remarked in pardoning ex-President Nixon that he had "suffered enough," he was responding as an affiliative manager would, because he was emphathizing primarily with Nixon's needs and feelings. Sociological theory and our data both argue, however, that the person whose need for affiliation is high does not make a good manager. This kind of person creates poor morale because he or she does not understand that

---

20. Fred Luthans, *Organizational Behavior,* 3rd edition (New York: McGraw-Hill, 1981), p. 164.

21. McClelland and Burnham, *op. cit.,* p. 101.

Figure 12–3   A Summary of the Four Leading Content Theories

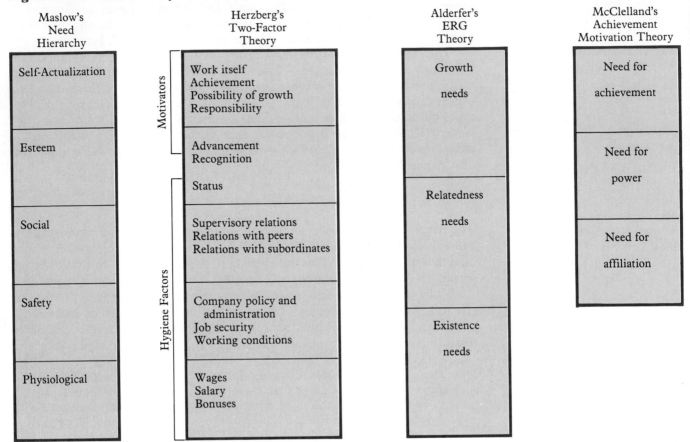

Conclusions regarding achievement motivation

When all three needs—achievement, power, and affiliation—are examined in terms of achievement motivation theory, three conclusions can be drawn. First, achievement drive is extremely important for entrepreneurs, salespeople, and others who depend exclusively upon their own abilities and drive for success. Power is most important for organizational managers, who must develop and nurture the talents of their personnel. Affiliation is most important for many of the nonmanagerial people but tends to have limited value for managers. These conclusions provide a general theory of motivation and help explain why some managers enjoy their roles while others do not seek managerial positions. Figure 12–3 provides a graphic summary of the four content theories described in this section.

Process Theories of Motivation

In contrast to content theories, **process theories** attempt to identify and explain how behavior is started, initiated, sustained, redirected, and termi-

---

22. *Ibid.,* p. 103.

Figure 12–4
Vroom's Expectancy Theory
Model

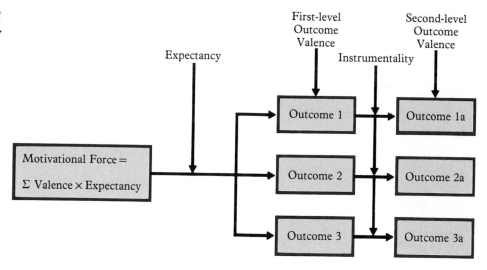

nated. The most important contributions to process theory have been made by Victor Vroom, Lyman Porter, Edward Lawler, and J. Stacy Adams.

Vroom's Expectancy Theory

In 1964 Victor Vroom proposed his **expectancy theory** of motivation[23] —a theory that derived from his belief that content models are inadequate in explaining the complex process of work motivation. Often referred to as "VIE" theory, the theory is built around three concepts: valence, instrumentality, and expectancy. Its basic assumption is that individuals are motivated to make choices among various alternative courses of action based on the results of these actions and how positively (or negatively) the individual views the payoffs.

Valence, instrumentality, and expectancy defined

By **valence,** Vroom means the strength of an individual's preference for a particular outcome. If a person has a positive valence, he or she prefers to attain the outcome as opposed to not attaining it. Valence can range from a +1 (very desirable) to a −1 (very undesirable). By **instrumentality** he means the perceived probability that a second-level outcome will follow from a first-level outcome, i.e., that if a person achieves the highest sales (first-level outcome) he or she will receive a bonus (second-level outcome). By **expectancy** he means the probability that effort will result in the attainment of a first-level outcome. Both instrumentality and expectancy can range from 0 (no chance) to +1 (certainty). Figure 12–4 illustrates Vroom's model.

Motivation is seen as a force.

As seen in the figure, Vroom refers to motivation as a *force.* This force is equal to the summation of valence times expectancy. Each outcome, whether first-level or second-level, has a valence and an expectancy (instrumentality is incorporated here). Overall motivation is a result of this valence and expectancy.

The theory addresses individual differences . . .

While theoretical in nature, Vroom's model is useful in explaining individual differences in work motivation. Each person has a unique combination of valences, expectancies, and instrumentalities. The model addresses these

---

23. Victor H. Vroom, *Work and Motivation* (New York: John Wiley, 1964).

differences. In addition, it helps clarify the relationship between individual and organizational objectives. J. G. Hunt and J. W. Hill commented on the statement this way:

> . . . instead of assuming (that) the satisfaction of a specific need is likely to influence organizational objectives in a certain way, we can find out how important to the employees are the various second-level work outcomes (worker goals), the instrumentality of various first-level outcomes (organizational objectives) for their attainment, and the expectancies that are held with respect to the employees' ability to influence the first-level outcome.[24]

but precludes direct application.

On the negative side, Vroom's proposition is not only theoretical but precludes direct application. After all, what manager is really going to try to determine worker motivation via a computation of expectancy and valence? On the positive side, research in the field supports Vroom's basic model, and the model has served as a springboard for additional investigation into the subject of motivation.[25] The Porter-Lawler model is an excellent example of such research.

The Porter-Lawler Model

Vroom's model is extended.

Lyman Porter and Edward Lawler have extended Vroom's model. In the process they have not only added more variables (expressed diagrammatically rather than mathematically, as in Vroom's case) but have also addressed the relationship between satisfaction and performance. Figure 12–5 is a diagram of their model.[26]

As the figure indicates, Porter and Lawler regard motivation as a force. This force is influenced by the value of the reward the individual is getting and the relationship the person sees between effort and the probability of attaining this reward. When effort is combined with abilities and traits (what the individual is capable of doing) and role perception (what the individual believes he or she should be doing), the outcome is performance (accomplishment). The result of performance is rewards. These rewards can be intrinsic (a feeling of having done a good job, self-satisfaction, personal enjoyment) or extrinsic (an increase in salary, a better office, a new title). The rewards, if perceived as equitable, result in satisfaction.

The performance-satisfaction link

Perhaps the most important part of the model is the righthand side, which addresses performance and satisfaction. The model presents satisfaction as the result of performance, i.e., if an individual performs well and receives an equitable reward, he or she will be satisfied. This "performance causes satisfaction" approach is in marked contrast to that of many behaviorists who, prior to this time, held that "satisfaction causes performance" or "a happy worker is a productive worker." Are Porter and Lawler right

---

24. J. G. Hunt and J. W. Hill, "The New Look in Motivation Theory for Organizational Research," *Human Organization,* Summer 1968, p. 105.

25. See for example: Alan C. Filley, Robert J. House, and Steven Kerr, *Managerial Process and Organizational Behavior,* 2nd edition (Glenview, Ill.: Scott, Foresman and Co., 1976), pp. 200–201.

26. Lyman W. Porter and Edward E. Lawler, III, *Managerial Attitudes and Performance* (Homewood, Ill.: Richard D. Irwin, Inc., 1968).

Figure 12–5   The Porter-Lawler Motivation Model

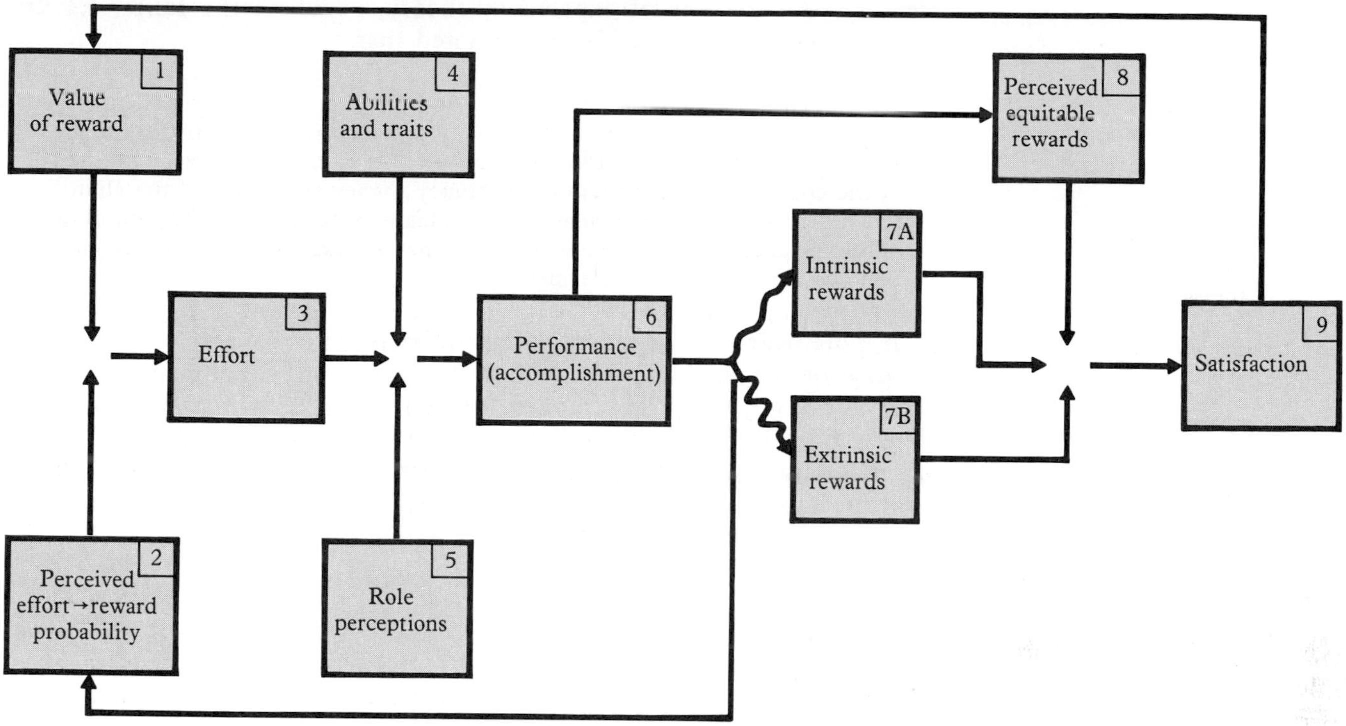

Source: Lyman W. Porter and Edward L. Lawler, III, *Managerial Attitudes and Performance* (Homewood, Ill.: Richard D. Irwin, Inc., 1968), p. 165. Reprinted with permission.

The theory has been refined . . .

in their contention that performance brings about satisfaction? Research studies do basically substantiate their conclusion.[27]

In more recent years, Lawler has proposed a number of refinements of the theory, suggesting that there are actually two types of expectancies. The first is the E → P, which is the probability that effort will lead to performance. The second is the P → O, which is the probability that performance will result in the desired outcome. In examining the E → P expectancy, he believes that the most important factors are the person's self-esteem, past experiences in similar situations, and communications from others. The P → O expectancy is influenced by many of the same basic factors, along with the attractiveness of the outcomes to the individual.

Overall, the Porter-Lawler model is an important contribution to the study of modern motivation. It identifies some of the most important

---

27. For example, see David G. Kuhn, John W. Slocum, Jr., and Richard B. Chase, "Does Job Performance Affect Employee Satisfaction?" *Personal Journal,* June 1971, pp. 455–459, 485; and Jay R. Schuster, Barbara Clark, and Miles Rogers, "Testing Portions of the Porter and Lawler Model Regarding the Motivational Role of Pay," *Journal of Applied Psychology,* June 1971, pp. 187–195; Rabi S. Bhagat, "Conditions Under Which Stronger Job Performance-Job Satisfaction Relationships May Be Observed: A Closer Look at Two Situational Contingencies," *Academy of Management Journal,* December 1982, pp. 772–789.

variables in motivation and proposes a relationship between them. Commenting on the value of expectancy theory, in which the Porter-Lawler model plays a large role, Miner has noted that:

> . . . expectancy theory has obtained considerable acceptance among students of organizational behavior. It is, however, primarily a theory for the scholar and the scientists rather than the practitioner. This fact is manifested in the continued outpouring of expectancy theory research and the almost total lack of applications that can be clearly traced to the theory. It is becoming increasingly evident, though, that applications are possible and that they might well prove fruitful.[28]

but it has its limitations.

A more negative assessment of the theory is that it is based on a hedonistic view of mankind. To the extent that a person is not hedonistic, the theory does not work. The model also suggests that human motivation is highly rational and conscious. Whenever unconscious motives cause people to behave unpredictably, expectancy theory misses its mark. Nevertheless, the expectancy theory approach is important in that it provides insights into human motivation at work.

Equity Theory

Exchange relationships

Equity theory, another process theory of motivation, is most closely associated with the work of J. Stacy Adams.[29] In essence, **equity theory** deals with exchange relationships among individuals and groups. The theory holds that, in deciding whether or not they are being treated equitably or fairly, people compare what they are giving to an organization to what they and others are getting from the organization. Table 12–3 lists some of the inputs and outcomes that are involved in this comparison process.

When a person concludes that, in comparison to others, what he or she is giving to the organization is equal to what is being received, equity exists. When one side of the equation (either the input or the outcome) is larger, an imbalance exists.[30] The person feels either anger (because of being underrewarded) or guilt (because of being overrewarded). This tension typically results in one or more of the following steps being taken:

Ways of dealing with inequity tension

1. The person alters the input by putting in more or less time (depending on whether there is an overreward or underreward).

2. The person attempts to alter the output by turning out more or less work (again depending on whether an overreward or underreward is perceived).

3. The person changes his or her perception of how much is being given or received, as in the case of the person who says, "Sure I make $500

---

28. Miner, *op. cit.,* pp. 160–161.

29. J. Stacy Adams, "Inequity in Social Exchange," in Leonard Berkowitz, ed., *Advances in Experimental Social Psychology,* Vol. 2 (New York: Academic Press, 1965), pp. 267–299.

30. Robert P. Vecchio, "Predicting Worker Performance in Inequitable Settings," *Academy of Management Review,* January 1982, pp. 103–110.

Table 12-3
Some of the Typical Inputs
and Outcomes Used by
Individuals in Measuring
Perceived Equity

Inputs	Outcomes
Education	Pay
Experience	Fringe benefits
Training	Job status
Skill	Seniority benefits
Job effort	Working conditions
Seniority	Job perquisites

a year less than anyone else in this department, but my job has a lot less tension and anxiety so I don't mind the difference."

4. The person simply stops comparing himself or herself with certain other people because there will always be a perceived inequity; instead the person chooses someone with whom a favorable comparison can be made.

5. The person acts against the individual or group with whom the comparison is being made by harrassing them or inducing them to do something (such as more work) and thereby improves the perceived input/output ratio.

If the inequity tension is sufficiently strong, the person usually employs more than one of these five approaches. The important thing to remember, however, is that until there is a perceived balance between inputs and outputs, tension will result and individuals will seek to adjust these inputs and outcomes appropriately. If people feel they are being treated inequitably, even if they are not, motivation is affected.[31]

Money as a Motivator

Before we conclude our discussion of modern motivation theory, some additional discussion of money as a motivator is in order. Earlier in the chapter it was noted that Herzberg felt that money was a hygiene factor— it does not bring about satisfaction but it does prevent dissatisfaction. Many people find this idea hard to accept. For them, money is indeed a motivator. As Table 12–4 indicates, this seems to be as true for athletes as it is for members of the general workforce. On the other hand, it is also true that money does not always motivate. For example, for someone in a very high income tax bracket, a raise of $500 has far less motivational potential than it would have for someone in a low income tax bracket. Moreover, the person's socioeconomic status must be taken into accout. Was the person raised to believe that having a lot of money was a good thing? Do the person's current friends and relatives place a high value on money? If the answer to these two questions is yes, money is far more likely to be a motivator than if the answer is no.

---

31. Richard A. Cosier and Dan R. Dalton, "Equity Theory and Time: A Reformulation," *Academy of Management Review*, April 1983, pp. 311–319.

Table 12–4

Baseball Salaries: Is Money a Motivator?

> Is money a motivator? Given the salary increases that baseball players have obtained over the last decade, it undoubtedly is. In 1971 the average major league baseball player was paid $31,543 a year. In 1976 this figure was up to $41,401. In 1981 the average was approximately $175,000. How well do the teams pay? According to the Major League Baseball Players' Association, this was the average annual player salary by team in 1980:

Team	Salary	Team	Salary
Yankees	$242,937	Giants	$148,265
Phillies	221,273	Braves	147,989
Pirates	119,185	Padres	138,978
Angels	191,094	Indians	127,505
Red Sox	184,686	Mets	126,488
Dodgers	183,124	Orioles	116,156
Astros	176,720	Royals	100,453
Cardinals	174,480	Tigers	86,998
Reds	162,655	Mariners	82,244
Cubs	160,209	Twins	80,538
Brewers	159,986	White Sox	72,415
Expos	158,196	Blue Jays	67,218
Rangers	148,792	A's	54,994

> Of course, some players have more lucrative contracts than others, as these examples illustrate:
>
> - Rich Gossage, pitcher (N.Y. Yankees). 1978–1983: $333,333 annually; $750,000 signing bonus plus $798,000 deferred; no-cut guarantee; five-year contract with Transmarine Management Corporation at $20,000 annually.
>
> - Craig Swan, pitcher (N.Y. Mets). 1980–1984: $425,000 in 1980 and 1981, $450,000 in 1982, $525,000 in 1983, and $625,000 in 1984. Also $675,000 signing bonus and guaranteed salary.
>
> - Dave Parker, outfielder (Pittsburgh Pirates). 1979–1983: $300,000 a year plus $625,000 signing bonus; up to $100,000 or more for MVP (most valuable player) balloting 6th through 1st place; $15,000 for Golden Glove award; bonus up to $150,000 for two million attendance; plus $5,625,000 deferred; salary is guaranteed and there is a no-trade clause.
>
> - Steven Stone, pitcher (Baltimore Orioles). 1979–1982. Annual salary of $175,000, of which $75,000 is deferred; a single room when on the road; $10,000 if starts 32 or more games, pitches 235 or more innings, or makes 50 or more appearances; $10,000 if Cy Young award winner; salary guaranteed.

The Manager and the Managed

Many managers believe that their employees are lazy because they will not work an extra hour for time-and-a-half, or because they will not produce an extra 10 percent despite the fact that the organization has an incentive plan that is tied directly to output. These managers fail to distinguish between their own personal values and those of their employees.

Managers assign significance to money . . .

Many managers are high achievers. They assign special significance to money rewards because doing so allows them to measure how well they are doing. Just because they use money as a counting device, however, does not mean their subordinates do also.

Furthermore, many managers regard money as a motivator because it is in their own best interest to do so. Why? Because money is a variable that is easy to manipulate. It can be given to those who obey the rules and denied to those who do not. It is a control device. If a manager can convince subordinates to accept money as a motivator, he or she can use money on a reward-penalty basis.

and often use it to manipulate.

Money and Need Satisfaction

Money can satisfy virtually all needs.

Money as a motivator is also difficult to understand because it means different things to different people. For the poor family that needs money for food, clothing, and shelter, for example, it is a means for satisfying the most basic needs. Without it the family would be in dire straits.

Money also helps attain safety needs. A person with a lot of money can purchase protection in the form of health and disability insurance and can also store up a sufficient amount of savings to handle other crises that may arise. In short, money can help protect a person from environmental dangers (unemployment, sickness, disability).

"Here's your severance pay, Wilson!"

Money helps people meet their social needs. A person with a lot of money can afford to throw parties, join a country club, and socialize with others. In fact, money often serves as a magnet that attracts others to the person who has it.

Money also provides an excellent basis for meeting ego needs. After all, someone who is making $250,000 a year can reason: "I must be good. Look at how much money I'm making." Money cannot guarantee that a person will feel good about himself or herself, of course, but it certainly can help.

Finally, money is important in meeting self-actualization needs in that the individual with money can focus on becoming a better person. Dozens of examples can be cited, from John Kennedy and Nelson Rockefeller, whose personal wealth allowed them to enter and excel in politics, to Ray Kroc, the founder of McDonald's, whose wealth allowed him to do such things as build the swimming pool for the 1984 U.S. Olympics and construct Ronald McDonald houses coast-to-coast.

It is an elusive motivator.

Naturally, money is not a prerequisite for all need satisfaction. The important thing to remember, however, is that some variables, such as money, allow an individual to fulfill more than one need. For this reason, money remains a rather elusive motivator. People use it in so many different ways, to fulfill so many varying desires, that it is impossible to say exactly what role it plays for people—except, of course, on an individual basis.

Of more importance to many of today's younger employees, however, is the chance to do things that are interesting, enjoyable, and meaningful. They believe that they will always be able to earn enough money to purchase what they need. The important thing is to earn this money in the most enjoyable or challenging way possible. In this way values enter the motivation process.

Values and Motivation

What do people want from their jobs? What are they willing to give to the organization in return for these rewards?

Not very long ago it would have been possible to answer these questions with the following list of values that most employees considered important:

- strong loyalty to the company

- strong desire for money and status

Traditional employee values

- strong desire for promotion up the management hierarchy

- critical concern about job security and stability

- strong employee identification with work roles rather then with personal roles[32]

Many of these values were shaped by environmental factors. People learned their skills at the organization's expense and planned their careers around

---

32. Lauren Hite Jackson and Mark G. Mindell, "Motivating the New Breed," *Personnel*, March–April 1980, p. 54.

that enterprise. Today a majority of employees acquire their skills and knowledge independently of the enterprise and are not as loyal as before. Additionally, it is no longer the norm for a person to enter an organization and work his or her way to the top. Employees today often find that the fastest route to the top is to change jobs and move to another organization at a higher level. Some of the values that characterize this contemporary employee have been identified as follows:

- low loyalty or commitment to the organization

- a need for rewards geared to accomplishments

- a need for organizational recognition of his or her contributions

- decreased concern for job security and stability

- a view of leisure as being more important than work

Contemporary employee values

- a need to perform work that is challenging and worthwhile

- a need to participate in decisions that ultimately affect him or her

- a stronger employee identification with his or her personal role rather than with his or her work role

- a need for communication from management regarding what is going on in the company

- a need to rise above the routine and approach tasks creatively

- a need for personal growth opportunities on the job[33]

Traditional and Contemporary Employees and Managers

In a recent study, Lauren Hite Jackson and Mark Mindell used two research instruments, the Employee Value Inventory and the Management Style Inventory, to measure employee and management values. Their results are reported in Figures 12–6, 12–7, and 12–8.

Figures 12–6 and 12–7 show that contemporary employees have profiles that are quite different from those of traditional workers. In fact, as explained in the figures, the values of today's employee are almost the reverse of the values of his or her counterpart in the past.

Figure 12–8 provides the profiles of contemporary and traditional managers. The five values reported in this figure are

- locus of control—a manager with a high locus of control believes that there is a strong relationship between managerial effort and organizational success. This manager also feels that advancement depends on achievement and that he or she has a great deal of control over subordinates' behavior.

Contemporary managerial values

- self-esteem—a high score here indicates that the manager considers his or her ideas to be creative, understood, and accepted. Managers with high self-esteem place high priority on employee feedback.

---

33. *Ibid.,* p. 55.

Figure 12–6   Value Profile of a "Contemporary" Employee

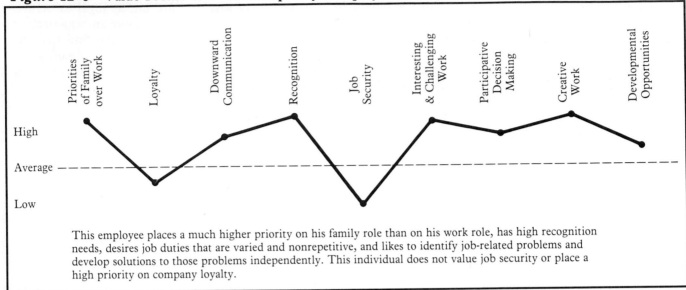

This employee places a much higher priority on his family role than on his work role, has high recognition needs, desires job duties that are varied and nonrepetitive, and likes to identify job-related problems and develop solutions to those problems independently. This individual does not value job security or place a high priority on company loyalty.

Reprinted, by permission of the publisher, from "Motivating the New Breed," Lauren Hite Jackson and Mark G. Mindell, *Personnel*, March–April 1980, p. 57. © 1980 by AMACOM, a division of American Management Associations. All rights reserved.

- tolerance of ambiguity—this value measures the degree to which managers are capable of functioning in an ambiguous or unstructured setting.

- social judgment—a high score on this scale characterizes managers with social perceptiveness, sensitivity, and a belief in the importance of good interpersonal relationships.

- risk taking—a person who scores high here tends to seek excitement rather than change and change rather than the status quo.

Taken together, the profiles of contemporary employees and managers, as reported by Jackson and Mindell, provide a clear, consistent picture. Today's employees do not intend to allow the organization to come before their family priorities. Meanwhile, on the job they are interested in what Herzberg referred to as motivators. These comments should not be taken as an endorsement of the two-factor theory, however. Rather they point to the fact that many employees simply want more control over their work and the chance to feel that what they are doing is meaningful and useful. Instead of supporting the two-factor theory, the results seem to point more to the desire for enriched jobs.

Managers have similar desires. They are less interested in being in direct control of subordinates and more interested in helping them get things done. They are also willing to operate in an unstructured environment, take risks, and work to develop good interpersonal relationships with their subordinates.

When motivation is placed in proper perspective, it becomes obvious that the manager and the employee must blend their interests. The values

Figure 12–7   Value Profile of a "Traditional" Employee

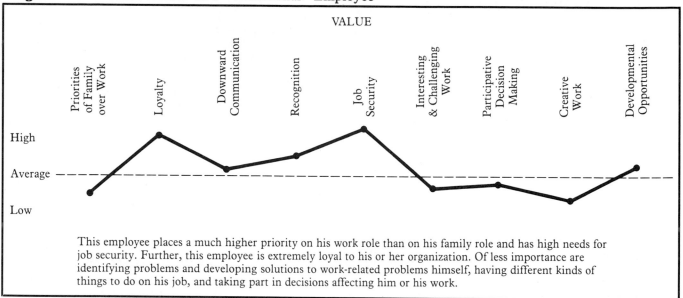

This employee places a much higher priority on his work role than on his family role and has high needs for job security. Further, this employee is extremely loyal to his or her organization. Of less importance are identifying problems and developing solutions to work-related problems himself, having different kinds of things to do on his job, and taking part in decisions affecting him or his work.

Reprinted, by permission of the publisher, from "Motivating the New Breed," Lauren Hite Jackson and Mark G. Mindell, *Personnel,* March–April 1980, p. 57. © 1980 by AMACOM, a division of American Management Associations. All rights reserved.

Figure 12–8
Profiles of "Contemporary"
and "Traditional" Managers

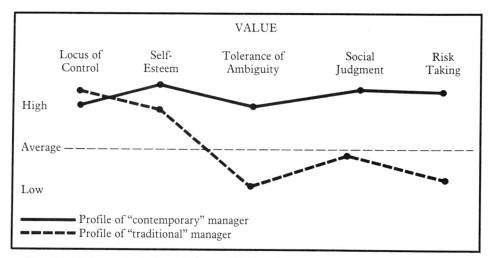

Reprinted, by permission of the publisher, from "Motivating the New Breed," Lauren Hite Jackson and Mark G. Mindell, *Personnel,* March–April 1980, p. 58. © 1980 by AMACOM, a division of American Management Associations. All rights reserved.

of the two groups cannot be at loggerheads.[34] If we think in terms of content theories, modern employees and managers both express a strong interest in higher-level need satisfaction. To the extent that an organization allows for the fulfillment of these desires, motivation can exist.

34. Jeffrey H. Greenhaus and Claudene Seidel, "The Impact of Expectations and Values on Job Attitudes," *Organizational Behavior and Human Performance,* June 1983, pp. 394–417.

Summary

1. Motivation means stimulating people to action through incentives or inducements. This process is often generated through external action but is determined internally since motivation is a psychological process.

2. There are three primary ingredients in motivation: ability, effort, and desire. There are also three common aspects of motivation. They deal with: (a) what energizes human behavior, (b) how this behavior is directed or channeled, and (c) how the behavior can be maintained.

3. Perhaps the best-known "needs approach" to the study of motivation is that presented by Maslow. Basically, his theory is that only unsatisfied needs serve as motivators, and that as lower-level needs are satisfied, upper-level needs manifest themselves. In his hierarchy, there are five levels: physiological, safety, social, esteem, and self-actualization.

4. Herzberg has extended Maslow's model and applied it to the workplace with his two-factor theory of motivation. According to this theory, something is either a hygiene factor, like money or working conditions, or it is a motivator, like increased responsibility and the opportunity for advancement.

5. Alderfer's ERG theory is built around three needs: existence needs such as survival and safety, relatedness needs such as social relationships and recognition, and growth needs such as advancement, achievement, and the chance for self-actualization.

6. McClelland's achievement motivation theory addresses three needs: the need for achievement, the need for power and the need for affiliation. McClelland holds that, of these three, the need for power is most important among managers.

7. Process theories attempt to identify and explain how behavior is started, initiated, sustained, redirected, and terminated. One of the most famous process theories is that of Vroom, who contends that motivation is the summation of valence times expectancy. While theoretical in nature, the model is useful in explaining individual differences in work motivation.

8. Porter and Lawler have extended Vroom's model by adding more variables and addressing the relationship between performance and satisfaction. In more recent years Lawler has proposed a number of refinements of the theory, especially by discussing the relationship of effort to performance and the relationship of performance to the desired outcome.

9. Equity theory deals with exchange relationships among individuals and groups. The theory holds that people compare what they are giving to an organization with what they are getting from it in deciding whether or not they are being treated equitably or fairly.

10. Money as a motivator is often misunderstood by managers because they assume that their subordinates attach the same importance to it as they themselves do. Money is also an elusive motivator because it can satisfy needs at any level of the need hierarchy and allow a person to fulfill more than one need at a time.

11. Values also influence motivation. The things that were important to employees 20 years ago are not necessarily those that are important to employees today. This means that if managers are going to be truly effective in motivating their people, they must understand what their employees regard as important and then help them attain these objectives.

Key Terms

Ability   An individual's capacity to do something.

Achievement motivation theory   A motivation theory that seeks to explain high achievement drive in people.

Achievement need   The need to attain objectives or accomplish things.

Affiliation need   The need to interact, socialize with others, and belong.

Content theories of motivation   Theories of motivation that attempt to explain what motivates people.

Desire   The wish, want, or urge for a particular objective.

Effort   Time, drive, and energy expended in the pursuit of an objective.

Equity theory   A process theory dealing with exchange relationships among individuals and groups in which employees compare what they are giving to an organization with what they are getting.

ERG theory   An extension of the Maslow and Herzberg models, this theory examines three basic needs: existence, relatedness, and growth.

Esteem needs   Needs related to feeling good about oneself.

Existence needs   Needs related to survival and safety. They coincide with Maslow's physiological needs, safety of a material nature, and Herzberg's hygiene factors such as working conditions and salary.

Expectancy   The probability that a specific action will yield a particular first-level outcome.

Expectancy theory   A theory of motivation that states that motivation is equal to the summation of valence times expectancy.

Growth needs   Needs related to an individual's desire for personal development.

Hygiene factors   Factors identified by Frederick Herzberg (in his two-factor theory of motivation) that will not motivate people by their presence but will lead to dissatisfaction by their absence. Examples include money, good working conditions, and technical supervision.

Instrumentality   The probability that a second-level outcome will follow from a first-level outcome.

Maslow's need theory   A theory of human needs postulated by the psychologist Abraham Maslow which holds that unsatisfied needs are motivators and that as lower-level needs are satisfied one moves further up the hierarchy from physiological to, ultimately, self-actualization needs.

Motivation   Stimulating people to action by means of incentives or inducements.

Motivators   Factors identified by Frederick Herzberg (in his two-factor theory of motivation) that bring about satisfaction and result in motivation. Examples include recognition, advancement, and the work itself.

Physiological needs   Basic human needs such as food, clothing, and shelter.

Power need   The need for control or influence over a situation.

Process theories   Theories of motivation that attempt to identify and explain how behavior is started, initiated, sustained, redirected, and terminated.

Relatedness needs   Needs that stress interpersonal and social relationships as well as safety needs and ego needs of an interpersonal type.

Safety needs   Needs for physical and emotional security or protection.

Self-actualization needs   The need to become all one is capable of becoming by realizing one's total potential.

Social needs   Needs for affiliation, interaction with others, and belongingness.

Two-factor theory   A theory of motivation formulated by Frederick Herzberg in which all job-related factors are divided into two groups: hygiene factors and motivators.

Valence   The strength of an individual's preference for a particular outcome.

Questions for Analysis and Discussion

1. In your own words, what is meant by the term motivation? How does Chester Barnard's acceptance theory of authority help explain how motivation works?

2. What are the three primary ingredients in motivation? Identify and explain each.

3. There are three common aspects of motivation. What does this statement mean? Explain your answer.

4. How do content theories of motivation differ from process theories of motivation? Compare and contrast the two.

5. In your own words, what is Maslow's need hierarchy all about? Be sure to discuss all five levels in the hierarchy.

6. In what way is Maslow's need theory helpful in understanding motivation?

7. What is Herzberg's two-factor theory all about? In your answer be sure to identify and define the two types of factors.

8. How useful is Herzberg's theory in explaining motivation in the workplace? In your answer be sure to discuss both the strengths and the weaknesses of the theory.

9. In what way does Alderfer's theory extend the Maslow and Herzberg models? How useful is Alderfer's theory?

10. What is achievement drive? What are the basic characteristics of high achievers?

11. How important is a need for power among successful managers? In your answer be sure to incorporate a discussion of the material in Table 12–2.

12. What is affiliation need? How important is it for success in a management position? Explain.

13. In what way are the Maslow, Herzberg, Alderfer, and McClelland motivation theories alike? Compare and contrast them.

14. What is Vroom's expectancy theory? In your answer be sure to discuss the terms valence, instrumentality, and expectancy.

15. How does the Porter-Lawler model expand Vroom's findings? What else does their model do to help us better understand motivation?

16. Of what value is equity theory to the study of motivation at work? Defend your answer.

17. What role does money play in motivation? Be as complete as possible in your answer.

18. How do personal values affect individual motivation? In your answer be sure to incorporate a discussion of Figures 12–6, 12–7, and 12–8.

Case | # Who Will It Be?

Every three months one of the country's largest drug manufacturers holds a sales contest. The individual who produces the most sales during this time is given a two-week, all-expense-paid vacation for two. If the person is not married, the difference is given in the form of a bonus payment.

The latest contest will end in four weeks. At present it appears that the winner will be one of three people: Helen Radwin, Karl Melcher, or

Roger O'Flaherty. The winner will be sent to London. The national marketing manager, Albert Chesser, is on the road quite a bit so he has had the opportunity to talk to all three of these salespeople. Here is his summary of how each feels about winning the contest.

Helen: Boy, am I excited! I have never won the sales contest before. Probably that's because it has taken me this long to hone my sales skills. Now I really feel as if I know both my product line and how to sell and it's all beginning to pay off. As far as London is concerned, I've never been there. It will be great to go. Every morning when I get up, I think about the trip. This starts me going and I can't wait to get out on the road and make my first call.

Karl: London must be beautiful this time of year. I sure would like to see it. My wife and I have never been to Europe. It would be a chance for both of us to take a vacation and relax. I'm not holding my breath about winning this contest, however. I've come close a couple of times before but I always get beaten out by someone. So if it happens this time, it happens. I'm just going to keep plugging along and do my best. I know that sooner or later I'm going to win one of these contests; so if I miss this one it's not going to be the end of the world for me.

Roger: I like sales contests, although I don't know if I particularly want to go to London. I won twice last year and three times the year before. In each case I was sent somewhere—Paris, Tokyo, Rio, Montreal. It's very nice. However, I didn't join the company to see the world. If I win this time, I think I'll ask the company to send me someplace locally for a week and then let me come home and put my feet up for the other week. Now, don't get me wrong. I love to win. However, I don't necessarily care for the rewards the company gives out. I suppose it's just getting to be "old hat" for me.

1. Which of the three individuals has the greatest valence for winning the contest? Which one has the strongest belief that he or she will win?

2. Which of the three salespeople is most motivated to win the contest? Defend your answer.

3. In addition to getting the free vacation, what other needs might be satisfied by winning the contest? Explain.

You Be the Consultant

The Survey Results

Sergio Campanella, administrator of a large hospital, just had a survey conducted among his managerial personnel. The focus of the survey was on what these individuals want from their jobs. In addition to a list of factors that were provided in the survey, the respondents were each given the opportunity to add additional factors. The top 15, based on the number of times they were ranked and where on the list they appeared (first, second, third), were the following:

1. A chance to do something that I feel is important.

2. The opportunity to use my skills and abilities.

3. The opportunity I get to help others.

4. The chance to learn new things.

5. The opportunity to excel at something I am good at.

6. The opportunities that are available for promotion.

7. The amount of freedom I have to do the job my way.

8. The amount of money I receive.

9. The respect I receive from those with whom I work.

10. The job security that is afforded to me.

11. The support I get from my boss.

12. The fringe benefits that are provided to me.

13. The praise I am given for doing a job well.

14. The information I receive regarding my specific job performance.

15. The chance to participate in decision making.

Sergio has had the responses classified both by department and by level in the organization. The classification reveals very little difference in the responses. The list basically represents the way all managerial personnel feel regarding motivational factors.

Sergio is a little unsure of what the results mean. He had believed that the first items on everyone's list would be money, job security, and fringe benefits.

Nevertheless, he is not discouraged. He still feels that he can use the results to develop a plan for motivating personnel over the next 12 months. It is all a matter of deciding how to take advantage of the survey information. At the same time, he will be conducting a similar survey at the workers' level. An initial effort along these lines was made last week when 35 people in one of the departments were surveyed. Although Sergio has not yet seen the results, the department head had them compiled and gave Sergio a brief verbal summary. From what Sergio can glean from the conversation, the results are very similar to those of the managerial survey.

On the negative side, Sergio is concerned that in both cases he was apparently unable to anticipate the responses of the personnel. On the positive side, if the results from both hierarchical groups are similar, it means that one overall motivational plan can be used for the entire organization. Right now Sergio feels his first priority should be to decide what action to take in light of the results.

Your Consultation

Assume you are Sergio's consultant. He has just called you in and shown you the results reported in the case. What is your conclusion regarding what the data show? Drawing upon the information in the chapter, can you cite any research findings that would support your conclusions? Finally, based on your findings, what specific actions would you recommend Sergio take? Be as complete as possible in your report to him.

13

Group Behavior in Organizations

Objectives

Every organization is made up of groups, formal and informal. Motivating and leading the members of these units requires a basic understanding of group behavior. This chapter studies the nature and characteristics of groups, the ways in which individuals within groups use power, and the way human interaction occurs both within and between groups. When you have finished studying all of the material in this chapter, you will be able to

1. define the term *groups;*

2. describe formal, informal, and combination groups;

3. explain why people join groups;

4. identify and describe the five most meaningful characteristics of groups;

5. describe the five most common types of power; and

6. discuss group dynamics in action.

The Nature of Groups

There is no universal definition of the word "group." Some researchers argue that two or more people constitute a group if they perceive themselves as a group. Others define the word in motivational terms, arguing that a group is a collection of individuals whose existence is beneficial to the members. Still others argue that if individuals *communicate and interact* with each other over time, they are a group.[1]

---

1. Richard M. Steers, *Introduction to Organizational Behavior* (Santa Monica, Calif.: Goodyear Publishing Co., 1981), p. 183.

Perhaps the best way to define the word is on the basis of common characteristics. Every **group** has three characteristics: (1) it is a social unit of two or more people, each of whom interacts with one or more of the others; (2) its members are dependent on each other in some way, if only to get their work done; and (3) its members receive satisfaction from their mutual association. These three characteristics—interaction, dependence, and satisfaction—are quite easy to understand. Unless individuals come in contact with each other, directly or indirectly, they cannot truly be members of a group. Nor would they come in contact if they were not dependent on one another for some reason. Finally, if any one of them did not derive satisfaction from this association he or she would attempt to leave the group. So in general terms, we can draw together these three characteristics and define a group as a social unit consisting of two or more interdependent, interactive individuals who are striving to attain common goals.

A group defined

Types of Groups

Every organization contains formal and informal groups as well as combination groups which combine the characteristics of the two.

Formal Groups

Groups can be formed by organizations or by the individuals themselves.

Formal groups are established by the organization and typically can be described as either functional or project groups. A **functional group** is made up of individuals performing the same basic tasks. For example, in a large organization one can expect to find all accountants in the accounting department, lathe operators in the production department, and salespeople in the marketing department. **Project groups,** as seen in Chapter 8, are multifunctional in composition and are formed to carry out a particular assignment. As soon as this objective is attained, the project group is disbanded.

Informal Groups

Informal groups are set up by the members themselves and often cross departmental lines and span hierarchical levels. There are various bases for their formation. Two of the most common are interests and friendship. People in an organization who have similar interests (both are in the R&D department working on the same invention) or personalities (they hit it off well together) are likely to be members of the same informal group.

Combination Groups

An individual can be a full-fledged member of more than one group. For example, someone can be in the accounting department (functional group), or a task force chosen to audit the operations of a subsidiary (project group), and in continual contact with two friends who work in the marketing department (informal group). Moreover, people do not always separate business from pleasure when interacting with other group members. For example, in most formal groups members spend time socializing as well

Many people are members of more than one group.

as "getting down to business." Conversely, while the informal group often serves as an outlet for social interaction, it is also commonly used for getting things done. For example, in auditing the operations of the subsidiary, the accountant may call and talk to one of his or her friends in marketing in order to get some inside information on the way salespeople write up their orders and the type of sales pattern that is typical for this subsidiary. The accountant uses the informal organization to supplement formal sources of information.

When the interactions of groups in a modern enterprise are depicted on an organization chart, there can be lines running all over the page. This point is illustrated in Figure 13–1, where special attention has been given to illustrating *only* the flow of informal communiqués. Four informal relationships are shown. Here is what has happened:

1. A worker has contacted the manager of Plant A to remind him that they are bowling for the league championship that evening.

2. One supervisor has contacted a fellow supervisor to ask some questions regarding how to properly fill out the new monthly control report.

Figure 13–1

Formal and Informal Relationships

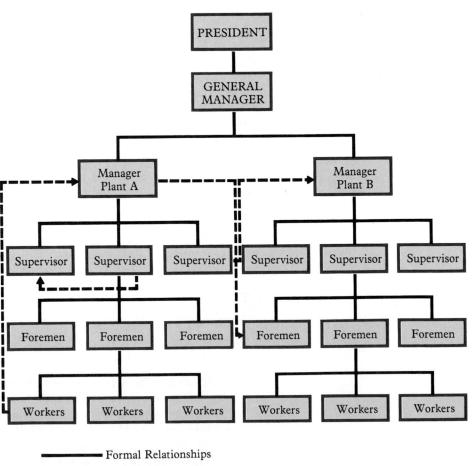

3. Another supervisor has contacted the manager of Plant B, a fellow college chum, and urged him to read an article in the business section of the local paper.

4. The manager of Plant A has contacted a foreman who lives down the block from him to ask if he can hitch a ride home this evening.

Notice from these explanations that some of the informal communiqués are business related and others are of a more personal nature. The manager is faced with the challenge of dealing with both formal and informal groups.

Why People Join Groups

Why do people join groups? A number of theories have been formulated to answer this question.

Theories of Group Formation

Closeness counts.

The most basic theory of group formation explains it in terms of "propinquity," which means nearness or close proximity. In other words, people affiliate with others because they are located near them. As applied to modern organizations, this theory holds that people who work in the same area are more likely to join the same group than are people who work a great distance apart.[2] Unfortunately, the theory is superficial, failing to address the real complexities of group formation.

So do activities, interactions, and sentiments.

A more comprehensive approach has been provided by George Homans.[3] His theory is based on three elements: activities, interactions, and sentiments. An *activity* is something that an individual or group does. An *interaction* is a communication, whether verbal or nonverbal, between people. A *sentiment* is an idea, a belief, or a feeling that an individual has about someone or something.

> The more activities persons share, the more numerous will be their interactions and the stronger will be their sentiments; the more interactions among persons, the more will be their shared activities and sentiments; and the more sentiments persons have for one another, the more will be their shared activities and interactions. The Homans theory lends a great deal to the understanding of group formation and process. The major element is interaction. Persons in a group interact with one another, not in just the physical propinquity sense, but also to solve problems, attain goals, facilitate coordination, reduce tension, and achieve a balance. Participants in an organization interacting in this manner tend to form into powerful groups.[4]

---

2. Leon Festinger, Stanley Schachter, and Kurt Back, *Social Pressures in Informal Groups: A Study of Human Factors in Housing* (Stanford, Calif.: Stanford University Press, 1963).

3. George Homans, *The Human Group* (New York: Harcourt Brace Jovanovich, 1950), pp. 43–44.

4. Fred Luthans, *Organizational Behavior,* 3rd edition (New York: McGraw-Hill, 1981), p. 319.

Similar attitudes are important.

Another theory explaining group formation is often referred to as **balance theory.** This theory contends that people are attracted to one another because of similar attitudes toward the same goals or objects. For example, they feel the same way about religion, politics, work, lifestyle, sports, or marriage. Perhaps the cliche "similarities attract" best describes the essence of balance theory, although it does tend to integrate two of the ideas that the other two theories focus on: propinquity and interaction.

So are reward-cost outcomes.

The theory that has received the greatest attention in recent years, however, is **exchange theory.** This theory is similar to equity theory, which was discussed in the previous chapter, in that it holds that a person's decision to join and remain with a group is based on the reward-cost outcome of the interaction. As long as what the person is getting from being a member of the group (friendship, support, satisfaction) exceeds the cost of being a member (time expended, favors given), he or she will remain a member. Propinquity, interaction, and common attitudes all play a role in this theory.

Economics of Group Formation

While these four theories certainly sum up many of the reasons why people join groups, it is not necessary to couch an answer in strictly theoretical terms. We can examine the question from the standpoint of economics or payoffs. And while balance theory and exchange theory certainly do pay some attention to this approach, we can go further. Many people join groups because it helps them satisfy one or more of their needs. This statement is particularly true when examined in terms of Maslow's need hierarchy. For example, in addition to feeling the obvious satisfaction of social needs

Groups help people satisfy needs . . .

. . . people in groups feel secure (safety), and such social interaction also helps them feel important (esteem). Additionally, members of a group may be of use to each other by demonstrating shortcuts for doing their jobs, thereby enabling the individuals to increase their pay and satisfy physiological needs in the process. Finally, group members often help each other in self-actualizing by encouraging the development of competence.[5]

and meet people with similar interests.

When presented in terms of balance theory, similar interests are also a very practical reason for joining a group. And we need not confine this similarity to one of viewpoint, i.e., two people see things the same way. It can be extended to include the need to cluster together to deal with problems or ward off danger. Workers and managers who are confronted with a situation that threatens the profitability of the firm or their continued employment are much more likely to band together and work as a team than are those who do not face such potential calamities.

Characteristics of Groups

Another way to examine groups is on the basis of their characteristics or distinguishing features. Five of the most meaningful are group size, norms, roles, status, and cohesiveness.

---

5. Richard M. Hodgetts, *Modern Human Relations At Work*, 2nd edition (Hinsdale, Ill.: Dryden Press, 1984), p. 102.

Group Size

Group size influences interaction . . .

Work groups can be found in various sizes; some are quite small (three to four people) while others are quite large (20 people or more). Research indicates that size may affect a number of behavioral variables. For example, as the size of the group increases, the way in which members interact with each other changes. Robert Bales and Edgar Borgatta found that as the group size went up, the time and attention given group harmony went down.[6] In small groups the members typically exhibited greater agreement and sought each other's opinions more frequently. In large groups data were communicated directly in the form of either suggestions or information. The need for group approval diminished, and, realizing that there was increased competition for attention, members were more direct and to the point with their communiqués.

as well as satisfaction.

On the other hand, research also shows that satisfaction tends to decline as group size increases. Porter and Lawler found that people working in smaller groups or work units reported higher levels of satisfaction than did those in larger units.[7]

Size also affects turnover . . .

Researchers have also found that as group size increases, so does turnover.[8] One of the primary reasons appears to be the difficulty of attaining upper-level need satisfaction. The work becomes highly specialized, group cohesion declines, and the average worker begins to find the job less appealing. The result is that the person quits.

and absenteeism.

A similar pattern exists in the case of absenteeism. In particular, absenteeism tends to be higher among blue-collar workers than among white-collar workers.[9] One explanation is that as group size increases, blue-collar workers are less able than white-collar workers to satisfy their upper-level needs because fewer avenues are available to them. For example, white-collar jobs tend to have more job autonomy and control than blue-collar jobs. The inability to satisfy upper-level needs may cause blue-collar workers to begin to stay away from work.

Richard Steers and Susan Rhodes made an investigation of both turnover and absenteeism in industry and found that two primary factors influence attendance: the individual's satisfaction with the job situation and pressures to attend. If a person is satisfied with a job, he or she wants to come to work. If there are pressures to attend, he or she is reluctant to stay away. Figure 13–2 shows Steers and Rhodes's model outlining the major influences affecting employee attendance.

Notice in the figure that one of the primary factors influencing job

6. Robert F. Bales and Edgar F. Borgatta, "Size of Group as a Factor in the Interaction Profile," in A. P. Hare, Edgar F. Borgatta, and Robert F. Bales (eds.) *Small Groups* (New York: Knopf, 1955), pp. 396–413.

7. Lyman Porter and Edward Lawler III, "Properties of Organization Structure in Relation to Job Attitudes and Job Behavior," *Psychological Bulletin*, July 1965, pp. 23–51.

8. Lyman W. Porter and Richard M. Steers, "Organizational, Work, and Personal Factors in Employee Turnover and Absenteeism," *Psychological Bulletin*, August 1973, pp. 151–176.

9. Richard M. Steers and Susan R. Rhodes, "Major Influences on Employee Attendance: A Process Model," *Journal of Applied Psychology*, August 1978, pp. 391–407.

Figure 13–2   Major Influences on Employee Attendance

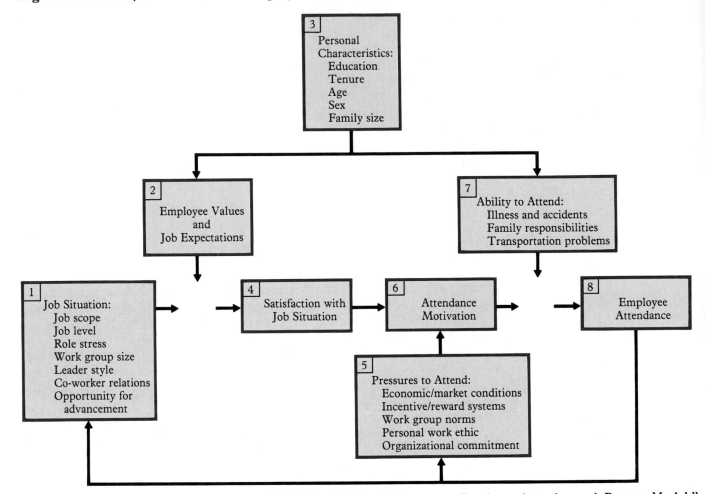

Source: Richard M. Steers and Susan R. Rhodes, "Major Influences on Employee Attendance: A Process Model," August 1978, p. 393. Copyright 1978 by the American Psychological Association. Reprinted by permission of the publisher and author.

attendance is the situation itself. If a person has a great deal of job scope (autonomy, responsibility, variety, feedback), a high job level, an acceptable amount of stress, opportunity for advancement, and so forth, he or she is favorably influenced to attend work. Another important set of criteria are the pressures to attend. If the person needs the job, is motivated by the reward system, is pressured by fellow workers to attend, or has a high organizational commitment, he or she is more likely to come to work. Some of the factors in Figure 13–2 are a result of group size. Others are a result of group norms, another important group characteristic.

Group Norms

Norms are behavioral rules of conduct.

Norms are behavioral rules of conduct that are adopted by group members. Norms tell how an individual ought to act. In essence, they serve five purposes: (1) to provide a frame of reference for viewing the environment, (2) to establish the attitudes and behaviors to be employed in this environment, (3) to help prescribe feelings about right and wrong attitudes and behavior, (4) to help determine tolerance (or lack of it) toward those who violate the norms, and (5) to help establish the positive and negative sanctions by which acceptable behavior is rewarded by group members and unacceptable behavior is punished.

Norms are important to group development for two reasons. First, they provide the members with an understanding of the way to act by telling them what is right behavior and what is wrong behavior. Second, they ensure that all of the members of the group act in unison. Without uniformity of action, the members might all be going in different directions. Thanks to these behavioral rules of conduct, however, all of the members act as one.

On the other hand, there are limits beyond which norms do not extend. The following list summarizes some of these limits:

1. Norms apply only to behavior; they do not carry over to private feelings or thoughts. Nor it is necessary to accept group norms privately, only publicly.

2. Norms are developed only for behavior that is viewed as important by most of the group members. They are commonly restricted to such areas as the amount of work people should be doing, the way in which they should interact with the manager, and the way they should behave with other members of the group. It is uncommon to find norms relating to one's personal life away from the group.

Limits beyond which norms do not extend

3. Norms usually develop over time. As the group increases its interaction and informal goals are developed, norms of conduct are formulated. This development of norms can be hastened, however, if some emergency arises. If new work rules are introduced, for example, the members need to know how to react.

4. Not all of the norms apply to all of the members. For example, younger members of the group may be required to show respect to the older members but the latter may be allowed to openly correct or criticize young people who have done things wrong. Such factors as seniority, age, and experience often dicate which norms apply and to what extent.

5. There are degrees of conformity. Not everyone has to toe the mark perfectly. For example, while a particular work group may have an informal output norm of 50 pieces an hour, a deviation of five pieces either way may be tolerated. Also, if someone in the group has a sick child and needs to earn additional income to meet the hospital bills, the output norm may not be applied to this person at all.

Individuals who want to be members of the group must adhere to these norms or be willing to suffer the consequences, which can take numerous forms. The most common is exclusion from social interaction with the other members. A second and somewhat related consequence is lack of assistance in job-related matters. A third is to be made the object of outright hostility or tension-building behavior such as name calling. The person may also be made to look foolish or ridiculous in front of the other members of the group or the supervisor, or, if things really get out of hand, he or she may be subjected to physical abuse of some sort such as being "accidentally" bumped by others or having work knocked on to the floor. The degree to which these negative consequences are carried is determined by the situation. If the group cannot afford to allow deviation from its ranks because the existence of the group is being threatened, the penalties are much more severe than if the person has a poor personality and is not popular with the group.

Role

A role is an expected behavior.

A **role** is an expected behavior. In many organizations job descriptions provide the basis for one's role. By carefully reading the description an individual can understand what he or she is supposed to be doing. The job description provides an initial basis for determining one's role. There is more to the topic of role, however, than a job description can explain.

Role-related problems

Sometimes a person does not fully understand what is expected of him or her because the description is either too general or too vague. When this occurs, **role ambiguity** can result. Most people deal with this problem by learning their responsibilities as they go along. Additionally, the further up the hierarchy people go, the more likely it is that they will face role ambiguity.

A second major role-related problem is **role conflict.** It occurs when an individual is forced to assume two roles but the performance of one precludes the performance of the other. For example, in order to be most effective, a supervisor believes that she needs to exercise a lenient leadership style. On the other hand, her boss has just told her that top management wants supervisors to crack down hard on output and that she will be evaluated heavily on her ability to make the workers toe the mark.

Finally, there are manager and employee **role perceptions.** The manager not only has a perception of his or her own role but also of each employees' role and of his or her own role as seen by the employees. The employees have the same set of three perceptions: their own role, the manager's role, and the manager's perception of their role. See Figure 13–3. These role perceptions influence both how people act and how they

Figure 13–3
Manager-Employee Role Perceptions

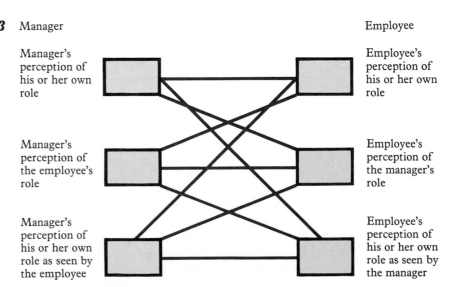

Manager   Employee

Manager's perception of his or her own role   Employee's perception of his or her own role

Manager's perception of the employee's role   Employee's perception of the manager's role

Manager's perception of his or her own role as seen by the employee   Employee's perception of his or her own role as seen by the manager

expect others to act. Knowing one's role and carrying it out is not enough for intragroup harmony. The other members of the group must feel that the individual is carrying out the "proper" role. For example, in many organizations managers are expected to maintain their distance from the other employees. Those who do not are regarded as acting improperly— not only by fellow managers but by employees as well!

Status

Status is the relative ranking of individuals.

Status is the relative ranking of individuals in organizations or groups. This ranking is typically based on criteria such as job position, job function, personality, and competence.

Determinants of Status

Hierarchical level helps determine status. . .

The employee's place in the organizational hierarchy helps dictate status. For example, a vice president has more status than a general manager; a supervisor has more status than a laborer.

as does one's job.

Another status determinant is the job the individual performs. For example, in manufacturing firms tool and die makers have more status than machinists; in sales organizations, the high-achieving salesperson has greater status than the office manager and the advertising manager has greater status than the purchasing manager.

Personality makes a difference. . .

Personality also affects status. An individual who gets along with others, is easy to work with, and is always ready to say a kind word is more likely to be given status by other members of the organization than an individual with whom no one can work easily because he or she is unpleasant.

as well as work competence.

Job competence also plays a role, because the better a person knows his or her job, the more likely it is that he or she will be accorded status by members of the peer group. Among workers with a high productivity objective, the greatest producer is likely to have high (if not the highest) status.

Status can be situationally determined.

Who will have the most status in the group, or in the enterprise at large, at any given moment? This question can be answered only by analyzing the specific situation. For example, if the group is confronted with a particular advertising problem, the person with the greatest expertise in this area undoubtedly will have the highest status. On the other hand, if the group is in the process of entertaining a potential client, the person with the most pleasing personality will move to the fore. If the group is having a weekly meeting, the chairperson will have the most status. If the group is meeting away from the job, the specifics of the situation must be analyzed again. Is it a business meeting? If so, the person with the highest rank (president, vice-president) may well have the greatest status. If it is a golf match, the person who is the best golfer has the greatest status. Figure 13–4 illustrates this idea.

The figure shows four people: an insurance company president, a company client, a professor of insurance, and an MBA student who is specializing in insurance. On the golf course, the insurance company client (who is the best golfer of all four) has the greatest status. In the company itself, the president has the most status. If the four go over to the university,

Figure 13–4
Status Varies with the Environment

	Golf Course	Insurance Company	University
Highest Status	Insurance company client	Insurance company president	Professor of insurance
	MBA student in insurance	Insurance company client	Insurance company president
	Professor of insurance	Professor of insurance	MBA student in insurance
Lowest Status	Insurance company president	MBA student in insurance	Insurance company client

they are in the bailiwick of the professor and he or she has the highest status.

Informal Organizational Status

Three basic groups

Status can also be examined from the standpoint of the informal organization. Within this kind of organization, there are three basic groups. First, people who are full-fledged members of the organization constitute what is called the **nucleus group.** Next people who are seeking admission to the informal organization and from whose numbers new members will be chosen constitute the **fringe group.** Finally, people who have been rejected for membership for reasons that include doing too little work, doing too much work, or having an unpleasant personality constitute the **outer group.**

Figure 13–5 shows arrows between the people who are members of the nucleus group, indicating that they interact and socialize with each other. The people in the fringe group have been placed in the inner portion of their circle, close to the nucleus group because this is the direction in which they want to move. Meanwhile, those in the outer group are placed toward the outer edge of their respective circle as far away from the nucleus group as possible, because they are not permitted admission.

Status Problems

Sometimes an individual's status is in doubt.

Although most members of groups, formal and informal, seek status, status-related problems must sometimes be addressed. The two most common are status incongruency and status discrepancy.

Status incongruency occurs when group members disagree regarding an individual's status. For example, if a vice-president has just been reassigned a parking spot in the supervisory area, the assignment is incongruent with his position. People immediately begin to ask: Is he about to be demoted? Or if a lower-level manager is suddenly given new carpeting in her office and a new desk, what does it mean? Is she about to be promoted? When status symbols are out of place, people have difficulty knowing how much respect or deference to accord to an individual. Things are not as they should be, and people begin trying to interpret the reasons. In the

Figure 13–5
Status Positions in Informal
Organizations

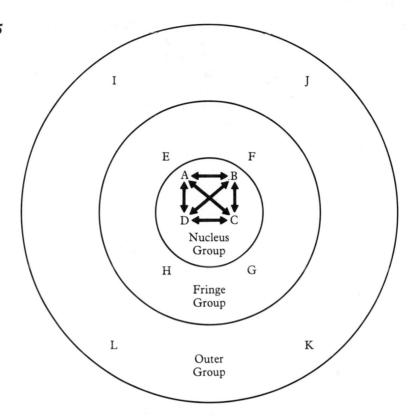

case of the vice-president, the truth may be that the company is putting
in a storm drain on his usual spot so he has to park elsewhere for a few
days until the job is done. In the case of the lower-level manager, the
company may be giving new carpeting and desks to all lower-level managers
and she has been chosen as the first one; no hidden meaning or intention
is involved.

Status imbalance may occur.

Status discrepancy occurs when people do things that simply do not
fit with their status in the group. There is an imbalance or discrepancy
between who they are and how they act. Top-level managers can create
such a discrepancy just as low-level managers can. For example, if a senior
vice-president begins to socialize with supervisors during lunch hour, his
actions may be regarded as "inappropriate" both by other top managers
and by lower-level managers. Analogously, a supervisor may attempt to
improve his or her status by trying to associate with upper-level managers,
only to be rebuffed by them and chastised by his or her peers. Status
discrepancy can occur any time people go outside of their own status level.

Cohesiveness

**Cohesiveness is important to
group membership.**

Cohesiveness is the extent to which individual members of a group are
motivated to remain in the group. The numerous determinants of group
cohesiveness have been covered in our earlier discussion of group formation
theories: (a) similarity of goals, (b) need for affiliation, (c) security, (d)
recognition, and (e) the belief that such an association will be useful in
achieving personal goals.

Of more importance are the consequences of group cohesiveness. What happens when a group is highly cohesive? The most probable result is that the group has considerable power over its members. Realizing that they have more to gain by remaining members of the group than by leaving, the group members agree to adhere to established norms and work for the continued survival of the group. Furthermore, with high cohesion there is more likely to be frequent communication among the members and more participation in group activities. Other results include less absenteeism and turnover and high levels of satisfaction.

High cohesion does not always lead to high output.

On the other hand, high cohesion does not automatically result in high productivity or performance. Numerous studies can be cited to illustrate that unless the group accepts management's goals as its own, productivity may be quite low. The group members may simply agree among themselves not to do a great deal of work. One of the most famous studies supporting this conclusion is that by Stanley Schachter in which he created four groups of participants and studied them under controlled conditions.[10]

All of the groups were to make checkerboard squares and then pass them through a window to other team members, whom they did not see, on the other side. Two of the groups were told that they would like their counterparts on the other side of the window; the other two groups were not told this. The effect was to create high cohesion among the first two groups and their "unseen" associates. Then, during the experiment one of the highly cohesive groups was encouraged by its unseen associates (actually the researchers themselves) to turn out more work and the other group was encouraged to turn out less work. The result was that the first of these two groups had the greatest output and the second had the smallest. Schachter showed that high cohesion alone does not guarantee high output. The goals of the group must be considered. If high cohesion is coupled with high output goals, productivity will be high. If high cohesion is coupled with low output goals, productivity will be low.

Other researchers have reported similar results. For example, a classic study of productivity among British coal miners was conducted by E. Trist and K. Bamforth.[11] They found that before the introduction of mechanization in the coal mines, coal was gathered by teams of six men who worked together as a cohesive unit. With mechanization, these small groups were broken up and each worker was given a specific task to perform. The old cohesive units ceased to exist. In many locales, however, the miners adapted the new procedures to suit themselves. The miners made the new technology work for them instead of working for the technology because they refused to work in noncohesive groups.

The adaptation of technology to social needs has also been incorporated at organizations like Saab-Scania, the Swedish auto manufacturer. In this case, however, the organization addressed itself to building highly cohesive work teams before making changes in the assembly line. Employees were

10. Stanley Schachter, Norris Ellertson, Dorothy McBride, and Doris Gregory, "An Experimental Study of Cohesiveness and Productivity," *Human Relations,* August 1951, pp. 229–239.

11. E. Trist and K. W. Bamforth, "Some Social and Psychological Consequences of the Longwell Method of Coal-Getting," *Human Relations,* February 1951, pp. 3–38.

brought into the decision-making process to help the organization deal with productivity and morale problems. The result of this step was impressive: unplanned work stoppages dropped from 6 percent to 2 percent of the total work time, extra work and adjustment needed to correct omissions and errors in the finished product declined by 33 percent, and turnover dropped from an average of 55 percent to 20 percent per year. Allowing the workers greater involvement in problem solving brought about increased cohesiveness among group members and greater commitment to group goals. In short, cohesiveness is vital to group survival and performance.

Power and Group Behavior

No discussion of group behavior in organizations would be complete without a consideration of power. As we saw in an earlier chapter, *power* is the ability to influence, persuade, or move another person to accept one's own point of view.[12] In modern organizations, power is used both by formal and by informal leaders.

Types of Power

There are five commonly cited types of power: reward, coercive, legitimate, referent, and expert.[13]

Reward Power

Positive payoffs

Reward power is held by individuals who have the ability and resources to reward people who do their jobs well. These rewards may take numerous forms, including pay increases, bonuses, promotions, praise, and increased responsibility. Both formal and informal leaders have reward power, and to ensure continued commitment to their organization's goals, they give or withhold rewards to their members. While the formal leader can make use of both intrinsic and extrinsic rewards, however, the informal leader must rely exclusively on intrinsic payoffs since the individual has no control over salaries, bonuses, or promotions.

Coercive Power

Negative consequences

Coercive power is held by people who have the ability to inflict punishment or other negative consequences on others, for example, by demoting them, docking their salary, or terminating their employment. This power also extends into the psychological arena, as when individuals are denied social need satisfaction by the person wielding coercive power. David Kipnis has summed up the range of this influence by noting that "individuals exercise coercive power through a reliance upon physical strength, verbal facility, or the ability to grant or withhold emotional support from others.

---

12. Hodgetts, *op. cit.* p. 132.
13. John R. P. French, Jr., and Bertram Raven, "The Bases of Social Power," in Dorwin Cartwright (ed.), *Studies in Social Power* (Ann Arbor, Mich.: Institute for Social Research, 1959), pp. 155–164.

These bases provide the individual with the means to physically harm, bully, humiliate, or deny love to others."[14]

Note that it is not necessary actually to use such sanctions; as long as the other party conforms because he or she wishes to avoid a negative outcome, the individual possesses coercive power. Because this power involves psychological as well as physical reward denial, it can be employed by both formal and informal leaders. Many behavioral scientists believe that "much of organizational behavior may be explained in terms of coercive power rather than reward power."[15]

Legitimate Power

Legitimate power is similar to authority.

Legitimate power arises from the values of the people who are being influenced. These people feel that the person influencing them has a legitimate right to do so, so they obey. Legitimate power is similar to authority because the person who has it also is in a position to reward and punish people who do not obey. Managers have legitimate power by virtue of their position in the firm. Additionally, a vice-president has greater legitimate power than a district manager, who has greater legitimate power than a supervisor. Legitimate power is often referred to as "delegated authority" since managers get it from their bosses and give some of it to their subordinates. This process helps fashion the scalar chain of authority, linking the top and bottom of the organization.

Referent Power

Referent power is based on identification with the leader.

Referent power is based on the follower's identification with the leader. This type of power is emotional in nature and can lead to enthuasiastic and unquestioning trust and loyalty. The followers obey because of *who* the leader is rather than *what* he or she asks them to do. A person can obtain referent power in various ways, such as by having a reputation for fairness, by possessing a "winning" personality, or by being able to empathize with others and bring them around to his or her own personal point of view.

Expert Power

Expert power depends on knowledge and ability.

Expert power derives from an individual's knowledge and expertise. Others listen to and follow the person with expert power because he or she is regarded as capable and knows how to do things right. Leaders who have demonstrated competence to implement, analyze, evaluate, and control group tasks are often seen as knowledgeable in their jobs. As a result, they acquire expert power and people rely on them for guidance and direction. Another characteristic of expert power is trust. Because this form of power is fairly impersonal and more concerned with task performance than with subordinates as people, it is important for the individual with expert power to wield it carefully. If the followers begin to learn that someone

14. David Kipnis, *The Powerholders* (Chicago: University of Chicago Press, 1976), pp. 77–78.
15. Luthans, *op. cit.,* p. 391.

is using expert power for personal gain or to their detriment, they will turn away from this person. The following excerpt about Henry Kissinger, former Secretary of State, tells how someone can lose expert power:

> . . . expert power is highly selective and besides credibility, the agent must also have trustworthiness and relevance. By trustworthiness is meant that the person seeking expert power must have the reputation of being honest and straightforward. In the case of Kissinger, events such as the scandal of Nixon's corrupt administration and Kissinger's role in getting the Shah of Iran into this country undoubtedly eroded his expert power in the eyes of the American public. He still has unquestionable knowledge about foreign affairs, but he has lost expert power because he may no longer be trustworthy.[16]

Of all the types of power, expert power is the one most difficult to retain because one's expertise may be surpassed by someone else's or the knowledge may become irrelevant. Nevertheless, because so many people in modern organizations rely upon knowledge as a source of power, including engineers, accountants, and other staff specialists, expert power continues to be nurtured and cultivated.

The Use of Power

Which of the five types of power is the "best" one to employ? Which should be one's last choice? While specific answers depend on the situation, research has been devoted to examining the use of each of the power categories. On the basis of organization studies conducted in a branch office, a college, an insurance agency, production work units, and a utility company work group, Jerald Bachman and his associates drew the following conclusions regarding each of the five bases of power:

Conclusions regarding power bases

1. Expert power is most strongly and consistently correlated with satisfaction and performance.

2. Legitimate power, along with expert power, is rated as the most important basis for complying with a supervisor's wishes but is an inconsistent factor in organizational effectiveness.

3. Referent power is of intermediate importance as a reason for complying and in most cases is positively correlated with organizational effectiveness.

4. Reward power is also given intermediate importance for complying but has inconsistent correlations with performance.

5. Coercive power is by far the least prominent reason for complying and is actually negatively related to organizational effectiveness.[17]

---

16. *Ibid.*, p. 394.

17. Jerald G. Bachman, David G. Bower, and Philip M. Marcus, "Bases of Supervisory Power: A Comparative Study in Five Organizational Settings," in Arnold S. Tannenbaum (ed.), *Control in Organizations* (New York: McGraw-Hill, 1968), p. 236.

These findings illustrate that informal bases of power can have a more favorable impact on organizational effectiveness than formal bases. Expert power, an informal basis, was more important than the other kinds of power in producing satisfaction and performance. Legitimate power, a formal basis, had an inconsistent effect on organizational effectiveness. And while referent power (an informal basis) was of intermediate importance, it ranked ahead of reward and coercive power (both formal in nature).

More recent work, such as that by Y. K. Shetty, supports these earlier findings. For example, in his review of both the empirical and theoretical literature related to the management of people at work, Shetty reported the following:

1. Expert power is closely related to a climate of trust and can result in internalized motivation on the part of the subordinates. This type of power can at least diminish, if not eliminate, the need for employee surveillance.

2. At least initially, legitimate power can be relied on. Continued dependence on it can create problems, however, such as the feeling of powerlessness and dissatisfaction, resistance, and frustration among the employees. If legitimate power does not coincide with expert power, an ineffective use of human resources can occur, resulting in lower productivity. Finally, the use of legitimate power may be inconsistent with some modern employees' work life values and may lead to minimum compliance and increased resistance.

Additional conclusions

3. Referent power can bring about internally motivated employees. The use of this type of power can also lead, however, to highly personal, selfish gains and manipulation of subordinates.

4. Reward power can directly influence employee behavior. Dependence on this type of power can produce problems, however, because in some organizations (a) there is very little money or few promotions that can be given out to those who comply with the manager's directives; (b) these rewards may have only a short-run impact; and (c) the use of such rewards may result in the subordinates' feeling manipulated and used.

5. Coercive power may bring about temporary compliance of subordinates or group members. It also produces numerous undesirable side effects, however, including fear, frustration, and alienation. The ultimate result is often poor performance, dissatisfaction, and turnover. When employing this type of power the manager must continually use surveillance of the employees to ensure that they are doing their work. Once out from under the watchful eye of the manager, many of them begin to slow up or stop working altogether.[18]

These conclusions echo those of Bachman and his associates. The informal bases of power—expert and referent—have a more favorable impact on organizational effectiveness than do the more formal power bases.

18. Y. K. Shetty, "Managerial Power and Organizational Effectiveness: A Contingency Analysis," *Journal of Management Studies,* May 1978, pp. 178–181.

Power and People

Some people are more easily influenced than others.

Some individuals are quite easily influenced. It does not take much effort to attain power over them. Conversely, some seem to be above all attempts at influence or domination. What accounts for these differences?[19] Why are some people easy targets of power while others are not? As researchers attempt to answer this question, it is becoming increasingly clear that the subject of power and people involves a *reciprocal* relationship. On the one hand is the individual who is wielding the power; on the other is the person or group toward whom it is being wielded—the power target. Six characteristics have been found to be especially important in determining how easily these targets can be influenced.[20]

One characteristic is the *dependency* of the individual or group on the person who is attempting to do the influencing. A manager often has subordinates in a difficult position. If they do not comply, reward or coercive power can be used against them. Of course, this is not always the case. If the manager needs the subordinates because they have certain skills that the department or unit cannot afford to lose, the shoe is on the other foot. Now the subordinates can use expert power either to reduce or overcome the manager's reward/coercive power options.

A second characteristic is the *degree of uncertainty* that others have regarding how to behave or go about attaining their desired objectives. The greater their uncertainty, the easier it is for someone to influence their behavior. In this case, expert power is one of the most influential means of doing so.

What makes people power targets

A third factor is the *personality* of the individual who is attempting to do the influencing. There are many reasons why personality can be influential. If the other members of the group are highly susceptible to influence, a person with a strong personality can dominate. If the group members have a high need for affiliation (one of the primary reasons for group membership), a person with a winning personality can often influence them. If they do not know how to achieve their objectives, the personable individual can persuade them to carry out a particular line of action.

Intelligence is a fourth factor, but in this case the relationship is inverse. The higher the intelligence of the members of the group, the lower their susceptibility to influence. For example, while highly intelligent people may be more willing to listen than the average person, they are also more likely to pick out flaws in someone's argument or statements. Additionally, highly intelligent people are accustomed to being held in high esteem, so attempts to influence them are usually less successful than the same attempts are with other people. Intelligent people are more resistant to influence.

Age is another important factor. Younger people tend to be more easily influenced than older people. Workers who have been around for a long time are more likely to resist attempts by management to influence them. Younger workers are more flexible and willing to go along with things, if

19. W. Graham Astley and Paramjit S. Sachdeva, "Structural Sources of Intra-organizational Power: A Theoretical Synthesis," *Academy of Management Review,* January 1984, pp. 104–113.

20. Stephen B. Robbins, *Organizational Behavior* (Englewood Cliffs, N.J.: Prentice-Hall, 1979), p. 276.

only to see how well they work. This is why the introduction of new work changes is often fought most strongly by older members of the work group.

Finally, *culture* influences the effectiveness of power. In western cultures such as the United States, individuality, dissent, and diversity are encouraged. People tend to fight attempts to be influenced; they try to protect their own identities. On the other hand, in oriental cultures there is an emphasis on agreement, uniformity, and cohesiveness. These cultural norms influence the way people respond to power sources.

Some of these factors are more important for some people than for others. Additionally, while three or four of them may be present at the same time, one is usually more important than the others. For example, even if the members of a group are highly intelligent, if they are uncertain how to handle a particular project, their uncertainty may overshadow everything else and the individual who offers a solution to their dilemma may emerge as the most powerful member of the group. On the other hand, regardless of an individual's personality, if the members of the group have no need to depend on him or her for anything, this person may be unable to influence the group.[21]

Group Dynamics

A group is more than the sum of its individual members. In the study of group behavior in the workplace, it is necessary to look at the way groups function both internally and with other groups. This is what **group dynamics** is all about.

Of course, there are many aspects of intra- and intergroup relations that can be examined. We will confine our attention, however, to two of the most important ones: how decisions are made within groups and how groups interact externally with other groups.[22]

Intragroup Behavior

Intragroup behavior consists of the interactions that occur between group members. The characteristics and dimensions of groups that were examined earlier in the chapter help explain some of this behavior. Group size, norms, roles, status, and cohesiveness all dictate acceptable behavior. Yet intragroup behavior depends on other conditions as well. These group factors are often supplemented by two others: the risky-shift phenomenon and groupthink. Both of these can seriously influence group decision-making.

---

21. For more on power see: David C. Calabria, "CEOs and the Paradox of Power," *Business Horizons,* January–February 1982, pp. 29–31.

22. Frederick C. Miner, Jr., "Group Versus Individual Decision Making: An Investigation of Performance Measures, Decision Strategies, and Process Losses/Gains," *Organizational Behavior and Human Performance,* February 1984, pp. 112–124.

Risky-Shift Phenomenon

The **risky-shift phenomenon** has long intrigued students of group behavior. The phenomenon can be explained quite simply: people tend to make riskier decisions when in a group than when acting independently.[23] Why is this so? Earl Cecil and his associates have provided five of the most common explanations:

Explanations for the risky-shift phenomenon

1. Making a decision in a group allows for diffusion of responsibility in the event the decision is wrong.

2. Risky people are more influential in group discussions than conservative people and so are more likely to bring others to their point of view.

3. Group discussion leads to deeper consideration of, and greater familiarization with, the possible pros and cons of a particular decision. In turn, greater familiarization and consideration lead to higher levels of risk taking.

4. Risk taking is socially desirable in our culture, and socially desirable qualities are more likely to be expressed in a group than alone.

5. According to a modification of the fourth explanation, a moderate risk is valued in our culture on certain kinds of issues, while on other kinds of issues moderate caution is valued. When the value of risk is engaged, people will choose a risk level which they believe is equal to or slightly greater than the risk the average person will take. When a decision-making group is formed, members discovering that they are more conservative than the average will become riskier. . . . Likewise . . . those discovering that they are more risky than the average will shift in a conservative direction.[24]

These explanations help tell why a group's actions may be different from the actions of any particular member of that group. Additionally, it should be noted that if there is group pressure toward accepting riskier courses of action, this pressure will often influence the superior to follow a similar course. Decision making within a group context is a two-way street: the subordinates influence the formal or informal leader and the leader influences the group. Of course, the people recommending the greatest risk are not followed automatically. Remember from explanation number five that the group decision often involves only a slightly greater risk than the average risk taken by the group members individually. Nevertheless, to repeat our earlier statement: The decision of a group is more than the

---

23. Dorwin Cartwright, "Risk Taking by Individuals and Groups: An Assessment of Research Employing Choice Dilemmas," *Journal of Personality and Social Psychology,* December 1971, pp. 361–378; Russell D. Clark, III, "Group-Induced Shift Toward Risk: A Critical Appraisal," *Psychological Bulletin,* October 1971, pp. 251–270.

24. Earl A. Cecil, Larry L. Cummings, and Jerome M. Chertkoff, "Group Composition and Choice Shift: Implications for Administration," *Academy of Management Journal,* September 1973, pp. 413–414.

sum of the individual decisions. The interaction of the members greatly influences the final course of action.

Groupthink

A second major phenomenon of intragroup behavior is groupthink. **Groupthink** is conformity to group ideas by members of the group.[25] Groupthink may have an especially adverse effect on highly cohesive groups because there is pressure by group members on those who are unwilling to go along with the majority. Irving Janis, who popularized the concept of groupthink, has noted that a number of historic fiascos by government policy-making groups can be accounted for by this phenomenon. Examples include the unpreparedness of the U.S. forces at Pearl Harbor, the invasion of Cuba at the Bay of Pigs, the escalation of the Vietnam War, and the Watergate scandal.[26]

Common symptoms of groupthink

In essence, groupthink has a number of common symptoms. One of these is the illusion, on the part of the group, that what it is doing is right. Second, any warnings the group has that its actions are wrong are either ignored or rationalized away. Third, if any member disagrees, pressure is placed on the person to "go along" with the group. Fourth, there is at least the illusion of unanimity among the members, especially when it comes to major areas of concern. Fifth, members of the group work to protect each other from adverse information that might shake the complacency they share. As a result, the group ends up isolating itself from the outside world.

Groupthink might seem farfetched until one remembers how the group feels about what it is doing. Typically the members believe their actions are humanitarian and are based on high-minded principles. ("Honest people everywhere would applaud us for our actions.") Second, in order to remain a member of the group, a person has to avoid criticizing it. ("Let's get behind the boss on this one.") Third, the high *esprit de corps* among the members results in their believing that people who criticize them are irrational and totally wrong. ("Those other guys are totally nuts.") Not only is the group isolated from the world around it, but it believes its actions are justified. Fortunately, not all groups fall victim to groupthink, and there are ways of avoiding any tendency toward this happening.

Groupthink illustrates the serious consequences of a work team's becoming victim of its own group norm. Fortunately, managers can combat this phenomenon by following a handful of simple rules. First, the manager must encourage the open airing of objections and doubts. Second, one or more outsiders should be invited into the group to challenge the views of the members. Third, one member of the original group should be appointed to function as a "lawyer" who is challenging the testimony of the other members. Finally, after reaching a preliminary decision, the group should hold a "second chance" meeting at which every member expresses, as vividly

---

25. Hodgetts, *op. cit.*, p. 415.

26. Irving L. Janis, *Victims of Groupthink* (Boston: Houghton Mifflin, 1972); Irving L. Janis, "Group Think," *Psychology Today,* November 1971, pp. 43–46; 74–76.

as possible, all his or her doubts and thinks through the entire issue again before making a final decision.[27]

Intergroup Behavior

Intergroup behavior consists of the interactions that occur between or among two or more groups. Sometimes these groups are in the same department; at other times they are not. In any event, they come into contact with each other. Two of the most common reasons are for coordination purposes or because a power struggle has arisen.

Coordination Purposes

Objectives, cooperation, and planning are needed.

The most typical reason for group coordination is goal achievement. When this is the purpose, the groups work to synchronize their efforts. Coordination requires an emphasis on three factors. First, each group must clearly establish what it is supposed to be doing. Second, there must be joint cooperation. Third, interfaces between the groups must be carefully planned, so that if one fails to meet certain targets or goals, the others can work to straighten out the situation. When groups are cooperating for the purpose of achieving high performance, planning and liaison work are vital. Unfortunately, not all intergroup behavior consists of harmonious cooperation. Sometimes power struggles develop in which one group attempts to dominate or influence the others.

Power Struggles

Groups secure power in many different ways.

Modern complex organizations tend to create a climate that promotes power seeking and political maneuvering. Groups carry out these power struggles in many ways. One of the simplest ways is by providing other groups with services they either cannot, or will not, provide for themselves. For example, the Industrial Relations Department in large organizations is responsible for negotiating union contracts and working out the finer points of management-union prerogatives. Whenever union-management problems arise, the people in Industrial Relations take on a great deal of power. They interpret how management is to act and how much leeway will be given to the union. Since most departments or units in the company are ill-equipped to interpret the terms of the contract, Industrial Relations holds sway over the others. The services it provides give it the necessary basis for this power.

A second basis of power is the degree of *integrative importance* the group holds. Figure 13–6 illustrates this concept. Since there is only one Quality Inspection Department, it constitutes a bottleneck. If this department approves of the manufactured, assembled, and painted units, they can be passed on to the Packing Department. If the quality inspection people do not approve, the units are sent back for the necessary reworking. If some people are absent from the manufacturing, assembling, painting, or packing groups, the flow of work is not necessarily slowed up. If one

---

27. Hodgetts, *op. cit.*, p. 123.

Figure 13–6 The Integrative Importance of Groups

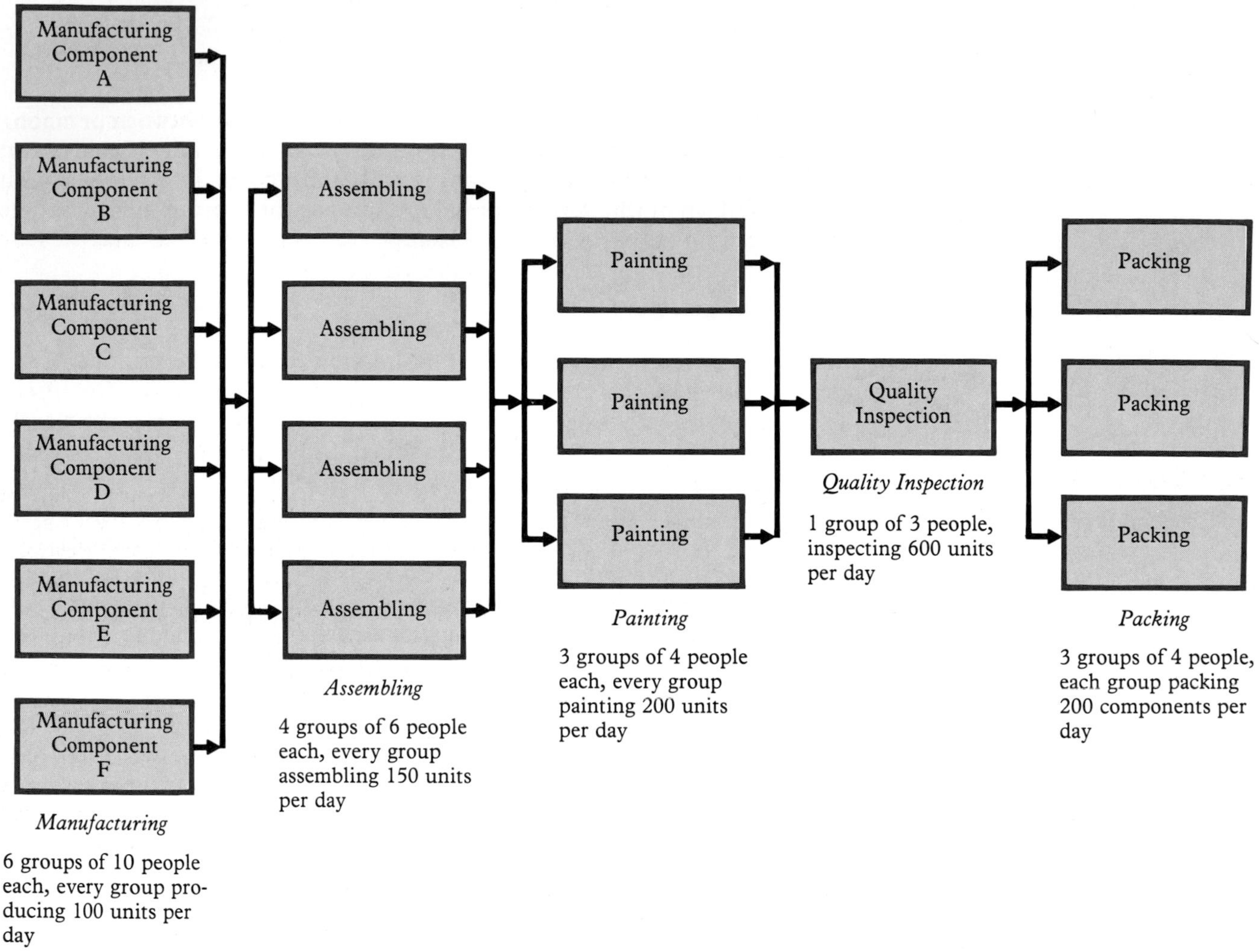
Manufacturing Component A
Manufacturing Component B
Manufacturing Component C
Manufacturing Component D
Manufacturing Component E
Manufacturing Component F
Manufacturing
6 groups of 10 people each, every group producing 100 units per day
Assembling
Assembling
Assembling
Assembling
Assembling
4 groups of 6 people each, every group assembling 150 units per day
Painting
Painting
Painting
Painting
3 groups of 4 people each, every group painting 200 units per day
Quality Inspection
Quality Inspection
1 group of 3 people, inspecting 600 units per day
Packing
Packing
Packing
Packing
3 groups of 4 people, each group packing 200 components per day

or two people are missing from the quality inspection group, however, the smallest one of all, overall output can be affected.

A third common intergroup power struggle is related to *budget allocation.* In virtually every organization there is a limited amount of money in the budget. Every dollar obtained by one department is lost to the others, so each department or unit tries hard to justify the need for more money. Quite obviously this is a win-lose situation. Not every department gets all of its budget requests.

Effective managers realize that power struggles are inevitable. They do not try to prevent these struggles, only to manage them properly. Proper management involves techniques of *conflict resolution.* The four most common forms of conflict resolution for dealing with intergroup power struggles are these: (1) confrontation—in which, because the groups have been unable to get along in the past, they are forced to face each other, discuss their common problems, and work to overcome them to the good of all; (2) collaboration—in which groups are shown how they can all achieve their aims if they simply cooperate; (3) compromise—in which each group gives up some of its demands, no group emerges as the clear winner, but the conflict is resolved; and (4) altering of the organizational structure—in which people are transferred to other departments or work assignments are changed in an effort to resolve the dispute.

Modern organizations generally use one or more of these approaches, depending on how serious the problems prove to be. Unfortunately, it is often easier to talk about how to deal with intergroup differences than it is to resolve them. A great deal of the success of such resolution is a result of the effectiveness of the group leadership, a topic that will be the focus of our attention in the next chapter.

Summary

1. A group is a social unit consisting of two or more interdependent, interactive individuals who are striving to attain common goals. In every organization there are two basic types of groups: formal and informal. Formal groups are established by the organization; informal groups are set up by the members themselves and often cross departmental lines and span hierarchical levels.

2. Formal groups fall into one of two categories: functional or project. A functional group is made up of individuals performing the same basic tasks. Project groups are multifunctional in composition and are formed for the purpose of carrying out a particular assignment. They are disbanded when the project is completed. In many cases individuals are members of more than one group.

3. People join groups for many different reasons. Some of the most common theories explaining group formation include: (a) propinquity theory—which holds that people affiliate with others because they are located near them; (b) Homans's theory—which holds that group formation is explained in terms of activity, interaction, and sentiment; (c) balance theory—which holds that people are attracted to one another because of similar attitudes toward the same goals or objects; and (d) exchange theory—which holds that a person's decision to join and remain with a group is based on the reward-cost outcome of the interaction.

4. Another way to examine groups is on the basis of their characteristics or distinguishing features. One of these is group size. Research shows that as size increases, satisfaction tends to decline, communication with other members of the group is more direct, the need for group approval diminishes, and absenteeism and turnover increase.

5. Norms are behavioral rules of conduct that are adopted by group members. They tell how an individual ought to act. While norms regulate group behavior, however, they do not apply off the job and they are limited in terms of who has to follow them and to what degree.

6. A role is an expected behavior. A role helps an individual understand how to behave in a group. Sometimes this understanding is hampered by such problems as role ambiguity, role conflict, and role perception.

7. Status is the relative ranking of individuals in organizations or groups. This ranking is determined by such things as a person's place in the hierarchy, the job he or she performs, personality, and job competence. The specific status of the person is often situationally determined, however. Status exists in both formal and informal organizations. In the latter, there are three basic groups: the nucleus group, which consists of full-fledged members of the

informal organization; the fringe group, whose members are seeking admission to the informal organization; and the outer group, whose members, for some particular reason, have been denied admission to the informal organization. Some common status-related problems that must sometimes be addressed are status incongruency and status discrepancy.

8. Cohesiveness is the extent to which individual members of a group are motivated to remain in the group. There are numerous determinations of group cohesiveness, including similarity of goals, need for affiliation, security, recognition, and the belief that such an association will be useful in achieving personal goals. It should be noted, however, that high cohesiveness does not guarantee high output. The group must also have a desire for high output.

9. Power is the ability to influence, persuade, or move another person to accept one's own point of view. There are five basic types of power: reward, coercive, legitimate, referent, and expert. Of these five, expert power is most strongly and consistently correlated with satisfaction and performance, while coercive power is the least prominent in attaining organizational effectiveness.

10. Power involves a reciprocal relationship. One person attempts to wield power and the other, known as the power target, is the individual toward whom it is wielded. Six characteristics have been found to be especially important in determining the influenceability of these targets: dependency, degree of uncertainty, personality, intelligence, age, and culture.

11. Researchers interested in group behavior in the workplace study group dynamics. Group dynamics involve both intragroup and intergroup behavior. In the case of intragroup behavior, two important factors merit attention. The first is the risky-shift phenomenon, or the likelihood that when in a group people will make riskier decisions than when they are acting alone. The second is groupthink, or the likelihood that an individual will conform with the ideas of the other members of the group because of an unwillingness to break with them.

12. Intergroup behavior consists of the interactions that occur between or among two or more groups. The most typical reason for such behavior is to promote coordination, which depends on three things: clearly established objectives, joint cooperation, and careful planning. Sometimes, however, power struggles develop between groups or one manages to obtain some degree of control over the others. When this happens, effective managers work to prevent things from getting out of control. Four of the most common forms of conflict resolution for intergroup power struggles are confrontation, collaboration, compromise, and an altering of the organizational structure.

Key Terms

Balance theory   A theory of group formation that holds that people are attracted to one another because of similar attitudes.

Coercive power   Power held by people who have the ability to inflict punishment or other negative consequences on others.

Cohesiveness   The extent to which individual members of a group are motivated to remain in the group.

Expert power   Power that derives from an individual's knowledge and expertise.

Exchange theory   A theory that holds that a person's decision to join groups and remain with them is based on the reward-cost outcome of the interaction.

Formal group   A group established by the organization, as in the case of a functional or project group.

Fringe group   Individuals seeking admission to an informal organization.

Functional group A group made up of individuals all performing the same basic tasks.

Group A social unit consisting of two or more interdependent, interactive individuals who are striving to attain common goals.

Group dynamics Intra- and intergroup behavior and functioning.

Groupthink Conformity to group ideas by members of the group.

Informal group A group set up by the organizational personnel themselves on the basis of such things as friendship or personal interest.

Legitimate power Power that arises from the values of the people being influenced, who feel that the person influencing them has a legitimate right to do so.

Norms Behavioral rules of conduct that are adopted by group members.

Nucleus group Full-fledged members of an informal organization.

Outer group Individuals who have been rejected for membership in an informal organization.

Project groups A group formed for the purpose of carrying out a particular objective and then disbanded.

Referent power Power based on the follower's identification with the leader.

Reward power Power held by people who have the ability and resources to provide rewards to those who do their jobs well.

Risky-shift phenomenon A development that occurs in groups when people make riskier decisions than they would when acting independently.

Role An expected behavior.

Role ambiguity A role-related problem that exists when a person is unsure of what he or she is expected to do.

Role conflict A role-related problem that occurs when an individual is forced to assume two roles but the performance of one precludes the performance of the other.

Role perceptions The way managers and subordinates perceive their own role, the others' role, and their perception of their own role as seen by the others.

Status The relative ranking of individuals in organizations or groups.

Status discrepancy A status-related problem that occurs when people do things that do not fit with their status ranking in the group.

Status incongruency A status-related problem that occurs when there is disagreement among group members regarding an individual's status.

Questions for Analysis and Discussion

1. In your own words, what is meant by the term group?

2. How do the following kinds of groups differ from each other: formal groups, informal groups, combination groups? Compare and contrast them.

3. Why do people join groups? In your answer include a discussion of such theories as propinquity theory, balance theory, exchange theory, and Homans's theory.

4. In what way does group size affect group behavior? Cite research findings to support your answers.

5. What are group norms? How do they affect group behavior? When do they not apply to group members?

6. What is a role? How do the following create role-related problems: role ambiguity, role conflict, role perception?

7. Of what significance is cohesiveness to group behavior? Does group cohesion have any effect on group output? Explain.

8. How is an individual's status within a group determined? What are some of the key variables that determine the person's status ranking?

9. In the informal group, who is a member of each of these subgroups: the nucleus group, the fringe group, the outer group?

10. How do status incongruency and status discrepancy affect one's group status? Use examples in your answer.

11. How would a manager use each of the following types of power: reward, coercive, legitimate, referent, and expert? Which would result in the highest satisfaction and performance among the group members? Which would bring about the lowest satisfaction and performance? Explain.

12. In what way is power a reciprocal relationship? What are some of the characteristics that have been found to be especially important in determining the influenceability of people as targets of power? Identify and describe four.

13. How does the risky-shift phenomenon work? What impact does it have on group dynamics?

14. How does groupthink work? What impact can it have on group behavior?

15. What are three of the most common ways in which groups attempt to gain power over other groups? How can effective managers work to resolve intergroup conflict resulting from these power struggles? Be complete in your answer.

| Case | # The Group Paper

Dick Biltmore is a junior at State University. For the term paper in his management class this semester, Dick decided to write on "Group Norms and Work Group Behavior." His father owns a locally based, medium-sized manufacturing firm, and Dick arranged with one of the supervisors to have himself assigned to a work group for five days. He took the second shift so it would not interfere with his class schedule. Initially, both his professor and his father believed he could obtain all the information he would need within this time period. Dick is not so sure he has been successful, however. Yesterday, he sat down with all of his notes and sketched out his findings. Here is summary of his observations:

1. There were 10 people in the group to which he was assigned.

2. Seven of these people seemed to get along quite well. Two of them were loners, however, and did not interact at all with the others and the last one was continually arguing with the other seven.

3. The amount of work that each did varied significantly. The two loners produced 115 widgets an hour, 15 more than the norm established by the company. The person who argued a great deal did 125 widgets an hour, but some (usually 10) of these were stolen by one or more of the seven people who got on well. Three of the seven people who get on well produced exactly 100 widgets an hour for their own account. This took about 50 minutes an hour. The other 10 minutes were spent helping out the other four people in their clique.

4. Of the four people being helped out, one was the group's main interface with the foreman. Whenever problems arose, this individual would work to straighten things out. He was identified by Dick as the informal group leader. A second person was 64 years old, had rheumatism, and was unable to keep up to company production standards. A third person produced 110 widgets for himself and was "given" 20 more by others. This individual's baby daughter was in intensive care, and he was working extra hard to meet the large medical bills that were accumulating. The fourth person was a part-time college student who was attending night school and paying his own tuition. The group admired his drive.

1. Was there an informal group in the room? Explain your answer.

2. What were the norms of this group? How were they enforced?

3. What would you advise Dick to include in his paper? Sketch out an outline for him.

You Be the Consultant

The Low Output Problem

Hand-held computer games have had exceptionally good reception by the consumer market. Hatwick Industries has a large contract with one of the nation's leading retail stores to provide such games. The firm is given the technical blueprints and 11 of the machines needed to produce the 10 computer games called for by its contract. The company's job is to manufacture the games according to specifications and then assemble, test, package, and send them to the respective retail outlets (see Figure 13–7). Output is a major consideration in that the firm must produce 1,000 of these games a day in order to stay on schedule.

Unfortunately, Hatwick's daily output has been slipping gradually. Six months ago, it was 1,037. Three months ago it was down to 988. Last

Figure 13–7
Hand-Held Computer
Production Process

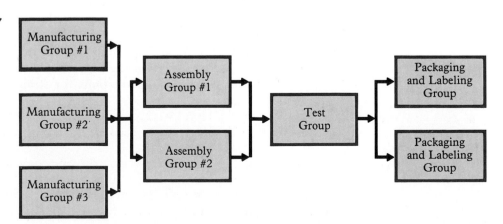

month it was 949. The most recent count shows that while output is higher on some days than others, current output is now averaging 934 units daily. In an effort to find out what is causing the problem, management has sent in a fact-finding group to analyze the situation. Here is what the team has discovered:

1. Among the three manufacturing groups, output varies significantly. Group 1 meets its output objectives each day. Group 2, which has extremely high morale, is producing 109 percent of its output objectives. Group 3, which also has extremely high morale, is producing only 35 percent of its output objectives.

2. Assembly Group #1 is doing fine. Group #2, however, continually falls behind, and the only way it has been able to keep up is by having the group manager pitch in and help out. This action has not gone unnoticed by the other groups, most of which feel the manager has no business doing this. They feel the manager should manage and leave the assembly work to the assemblers.

3. Both packaging and labeling groups are turning out only 94 percent of expected daily output. There is a great deal of concern in the two groups that the new packaging and labeling machines scheduled to be introduced next month will result in layoffs of some personnel.

4. The test group personnel are fighting with each other. The situation is so bad that the only solution appears to be to transfer some people out of the group to other jobs in the company.

5. In an effort to get the overall hand-held computer production process group back on target, the general manager has announced an incentive plan. All salary raises will be tied directly to group output. Those groups turning out less than they should can expect to receive salary raises in the 3 to 5 percent range; those doing more than their output quota can expect raises in the 10 to 14 percent range.

Your Consultation

Assume that you have just been called in by the president of this firm to act as a consultant regarding how to handle the situation. First, drawing upon your knowledge of norms, cohesion, status, group size, and other group-related characteristics, tell the president why some groups are not producing up to par. Then describe any other problems you have uncovered in the case and explain the reasons for these problems. Finally, offer the president your recommendations for straightening out the entire situation.

Managerial Leadership

Objectives

One of the most important functions of a manager is to be able to lead. In fact, effective leadership is often the key both to individual and to organizational success. This chapter explores the nature of leadership by examining leader traits, abilities, and behavior. It also describes two of the most popular contingency theories of leadership and reviews selective leadership theories on an applied level. When you have finished studying all of the material in this chapter, you will be able to

1. define the term leadership;

2. discuss some of the traits or characteristics commonly found in effective leaders;

3. compare and contrast autocratic, paternalistic, democratic/participative, and laissez-faire leadership styles;

4. describe the managerial grid;

5. explain the contingency and path-goal theories of leadership and discuss the value of each for practicing managers; and

6. discuss the leader-follower continuum and the situational theory of leadership and describe the practical value of each for modern managers.

The Nature of Leadership

The term leadership has been defined in many different ways. Bernard Bass, after making a systematic review of research on the topic, reports that "There are almost as many different definitions of leadership as there

Leadership defined

are persons who have attempted to define the concept."[1] It is generally accepted, however, that effective leadership consists of successful influence by the leader, resulting in goal attainment by the followers.[2] For our purposes, therefore, we shall define leadership as the process of influencing people to direct their efforts toward the attainment of some particular goal or goals.

The way in which this process of influencing is carried out varies from manager to manager.[3] Some spend a great deal of their time formulating objectives for subordinates, setting out detailed lists of what is to be done, and closely following up to ensure that everything goes according to schedule. Others prefer to set general objectives, allowing the subordinates to determine their own approach while maintaining an open-door policy for those who feel they require additional assistance. Still others provide the least amount of direction possible; if the subordinates run into any problems, they must work things out for themselves. The first of these kinds of managers delegates very little authority to subordinates; the second delegates a fair amount of work; the third delegates virtually everything. Which of these three styles is most effective? The answer is: All three may be equally effective. There is simply no such thing as one best leadership style. Perhaps this is why leadership is such an interesting topic and why it has led one well-known author to write, "Leadership has probably been written about, formally researched, and informally discussed more than any other single topic."[4] The result of all this research and interest has been the accumulation of a wealth of information about leadership behavior and leadership style. One of the primary areas of interest has been the traits and abilities that leaders have in common.

Traits and Abilities

A common approach to the subject of leadership is to try to isolate the traits and abilities that leaders possess and nonleaders do not. This approach has come to be known as the **trait theory.** From 1920–1950 a great deal of trait theory research was conducted in an effort to isolate the factors that contribute to leadership effectiveness. The biggest problem, unfortunately, was that investigators were unable to develop one universal list. Nevertheless, there are some general findings that many of them have reported. For example, after reviewing the literature of this period, Bass found uniformly positive evidence from 15 or more studies to support the following conclusions:

Some leadership traits

The average person who occupies a position of leadership exceeds the average member of his group in the following respects: (1) intelligence; (2)

1. Bernard M. Bass, *Stogdill's Handbook of Leadership* (New York: Free Press, 1982), p. 9.

2. *Ibid.,* p. 10.

3. Craig M. Watson, "Leadership, Management, and the Seven Keys," *Business Horizons,* March–April 1983, pp. 8–13.

4. Fred Luthans, *Organizational Behavior,* 3rd edition (New York: McGraw-Hill, 1981), p. 413.

scholarship; (3) dependability in exercising responsibilities; (4) activity and social participation; and (5) socioeconomic status.[5]

Additionally, he found 10 or more studies supporting the following findings:

a. The qualities, characteristics, and skills required in a leader are determined to a large extent by the demands of the situation in which he is to function as a leader.

b. The average person who occupies a position of leadership exceeds the average member of the group to some degree in each of the following aspects: (1) sociability, (2) initiative, (3) persistence, (4) knowing how to get things done, (5) self-confidence, (6) alertness to, and insight into, situations, (7) cooperativeness, (8) popularity, (9) adaptability, and (10) verbal facility.[6]

Because there is such intuitive appeal in discovering common leadership traits, this approach still remains popular in the literature today. For example, Harry Levinson, a well-known psychologist and frequent contributor to the *Harvard Business Review*, has offered the following 20 dimensions of leader personality as those that should be considered when choosing a top executive:

Dimensions of leader personality

1. The capacity to abstract, to conceptualize, to organize, and to integrate different data into a coherent frame of reference.

2. A tolerance for ambiguity.

3. Intelligence.

4. Good judgment.

5. The ability to take charge.

6. A capacity for attacking problems both vigorously and strategically.

7. An achievement orientedness.

8. A sensitivity to the feelings of others.

9. Participation as a member of the organization.

10. Maturity.

11. An ability to stand on his or her own while accepting information, criticism, and cooperation from others.

12. An ability to articulate.

13. High physical and mental stamina.

14. The ability to adapt and to manage stress.

15. A sense of humor.

---

5. Bass, *op. cit.*, p. 65.
6. *Ibid.*

16. Well-defined personal goals that are consistent with organizational needs.

17. High perseverance.

18. The ability to organize time well.

19. High integrity.

20. An appreciation for the need to assume social responsibility and leadership.[7]

Even in this discussion, however, Levinson admits that there is no statistical validation of these dimensions. Rather, he offers them merely as a way of calling attention to characteristics related to executive success. Nevertheless, such traits are important in understanding the nature of leadership. The specific relationship of each to leader effectiveness may not be clear, but when the traits are examined as a composite, they certainly provide a general picture of what is needed in a good leader.[8]

Behavior

Another important way to study leadership is to examine what leaders do. Many individuals believe that one can become a better leader by emulating successful leadership behavior. While this idea is debatable, there is currently a great deal of interest in leadership behavior. Many approaches have been used to describe how leaders conduct themselves. One describes leader-subordinate interactions.

Leader-Subordinate Interactions

As illustrated in Figure 14–1, leaders and subordinates can interact in four basic ways, depending on whether the manager's leadership style is autocratic, paternalistic, democratic/participative, or laissez-faire.

Autocratic Leadership   **Autocratic leadership** is practiced by managers who tend to be heavily work-centered, placing most of their emphasis on task accomplishment and little on the human element. These leaders fit the classical model of management, in which the workers are viewed as factors of production. It should not be assumed, however, that these leaders are ineffective: sometimes they are extremely successful. In crisis situations, for example, get-tough managers are often needed. Organizations having productivity, cost control, or high inefficiency problems often turn to autocratic leaders to straighten out the situation.

Autocratic leaders are characterized by an emphasis on close control and a willingness to delegate very little authority. They retain decision-making authority on all important matters, ensuring that they will have the final say. As represented in Figure 14–1, leader-subordinate interaction

Some leaders place little emphasis on people.

---

7. Harry Levinson, "Criteria for Choosing Chief Executives," *Harvard Business Review,* July–August 1981, pp. 114–118.

8. Morgan W. McCall, Jr. and Michael M. Lombardo, "What Makes a Top Executive," *Psychology Today,* February 1983, pp. 26–31.

Figure 14–1   Leader-Subordinate Interactions

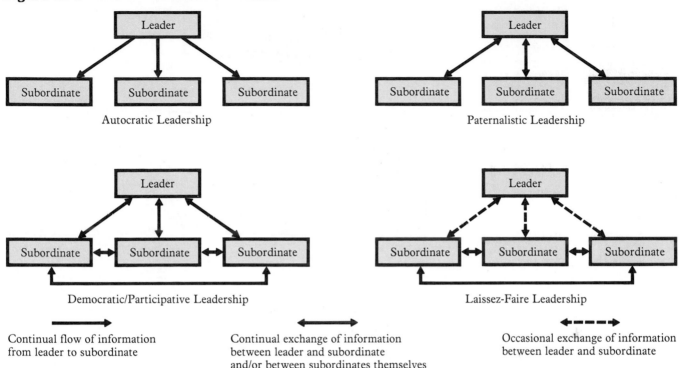

Autocratic Leadership

Paternalistic Leadership

Democratic/Participative Leadership

Laissez-Faire Leadership

Continual flow of information
from leader to subordinate

Continual exchange of information
between leader and subordinate
and/or between subordinates themselves

Occasional exchange of information
between leader and subordinate

is characterized by order giving on the leader's part. There is virtually no flow of information from the subordinates back to the leader. Communication is primarily downward and is used for conveying directives and orders related to the work itself. If there is any upward flow of information, it is commonly restricted to reports related to work progress and is used by the leader to monitor operations further.

Paternalistic Leadership   Paternalistic leadership is heavily work-centered but managers who adopt this leadership style also have some consideration for the personnel. In fact, they are sometimes confused with democratic/participative leaders because they seem to be as interested in the people as the work. One distinguishing characteristic, however, prevents them from being truly democratic: they believe in the philosophy "Do as I say and the organization will take care of you." These leaders tend to be very much like parents. They will look after their subordinates, but the subordinates have to behave themselves and stay in line. If there is any deviation, some form of punishment (demotion, poor performance evaluation, low salary increase) is likely to follow. When paternalistic leaders are described in terms of Theory X and Theory Y, they typically are identified as "soft" Theory X. Notice in Figure 14–1 that these managers have a continual exchange of information with their employees but that the employees do *not* interact with each other. In this way the leader still maintains final control. Everyone is managed directly by him or her, and intergroup teamwork never develops.

Many managers are paternalistic leaders because they believe their subordinates really want someone to look after them. Additionally, although

Others are parental in their approach.

"Now this one has a nice authoritative tone."

they do not believe that the workers are truly lazy (hard Theory X), they do feel that the workers have a tendency toward acting this way (soft Theory X philosophy). Paternalistic leaders tend to be most effective when dealing with subordinates who are insecure or who are just learning their jobs and welcome advice, assistance, and protection.

Democratic/Participative Leadership **Democratic/participative leadership** is characterized by a high concern for both people and work. As seen in Figure 14–1, democratic/participative leaders encourage a continual flow of information between themselves and their subordinates. They also support a continual exchange of information between the subordinates themselves. In bringing about this open flow of information in their unit or department, democratic leaders delegate a great deal of authority to their people and encourage them to play an active role in the operation of the enterprise.

Others have a high concern for people and work.

A number of advantages commonly result from this form of leadership behavior. Some of the most typical are that (1) decision making is improved because the leader is able to rely upon others for information and assistance before rendering a final judgment; (2) morale goes up because the followers like the openness and freedom of their work environment; (3) high achievement drive is nurtured and developed because the subordinates know what is expected of them and are given the necessary freedom to pursue these objectives; and (4) when changes have to be made, the personnel are less likely to oppose them because they will be playing a role in fashioning and implementing these new rules or regulations.

In the main, participative leadership is well thought of in the United States, perhaps because most Americans prefer to work in this type of environment. This approach does not work for every organization, however. Dale D. McConkey, a management researcher and writer, put the issue in perspective when he wrote: "Participative management . . . starts off by making clear to each manager that the primary reason he or she is employed is to help carry out the requirements of the organization. Then . . . each manager is asked how he or she can help carry out the organization's objectives and priorities. In responding to this question each manager is given the greatest possible (practical) latitude or participation in determining his or her own future within the organization which is *consistent with the requirements of the organization.*"[9] Some organizations do not function well in a highly participative environment; some subordinates do not respond well to this form of leadership behavior.

Participative management is not for everyone.

Three conditions are necessary for the effective use of participative leadership. First, this approach works best only when a manager is able to anticipate problems and plan ahead; if the problems turn into crises, the authoritarian style may be required. Second, both the subordinates and the manager must believe that this approach will be beneficial to them; if either feels it is inappropriate, it will not work. Third, the leader must remember that he or she has a responsibility to two groups: the subordinates and the enterprise. Democratic leadership does not mean turning over the management of the unit to the subordinates. It means developing group teamwork in the pursuit of the organization's goals.

Many organizations today express an interest in moving from their semi-authoritarian leadership approach to a more participative one. Such a change takes time to implement. Moreover, the organization has to be sure that it is ready to make such a transition. The readiness checklist in Table 14–1 is one of many that can be used for this purpose. The checklist can help an organization determine its overall readiness or current posture in regard to the major aspects of participative management. Many researchers recommend that at least three levels of management take part in completing these types of checklists so as to uncover any major problems that can accompany the decision to become a more participative enterprise.

Laissez-Faire Leadership   Laissez-faire leadership is employed by managers who are basically uninvolved in the operations of the unit. These managers tend to turn things over to the subordinates. If a leader does make an appearance, it is to check and see how things are going. There is no active involvement on the leader's part, however. As seen in Figure 14–1, there are only occasional exchanges of information between the leader and the subordinates.

Some leaders are basically uninvolved in operations.

Does laissez-faire leadership ever work well? The answer is that it can, but such situations are rare. The most commonly cited example of successful

---

9. Dale D. McConkey, "Participative Management: What It Really Means in Practice," *Business Horizons,* October 1980, p. 67.

Table 14–1   A Readiness Checklist for Participative Management

Factor	Major Thrust	Little if any 1 2 3	Exception rather than rule 1 2 3	Rule rather than exception 1 2 3	Extensive 1 2 3
Support and participation by top management	Active involvement vs. lip service				
Favorable environment for change	Willingness to change vs. protecting landed interests				
Open, nonthreatening environment	Trust and respect vs. fear				
Willingness of senior managers to share authority	Secure vs. insecure manager				
Quality of subordinate managers	Ability and willingness to accept responsibility				
Willingness of subordinates to accept objective measurement on the job	Results vs. effort or busyness				
Willingness to comply with disciplined approaches	Planning vs. seat-of-the-pants				
Environment predictable enough for planning	Stability vs. instability				
Participation in objective setting	Self-management vs. dictation from above				
Relationship between objectives of the organization and lower level objectives	Supportive vs. fragmented				
Verifiable objectives	Measurable vs. vague/nebulous				
Relationship between achievement of objectives and reward system	Results-oriented rewards vs. subjective ones				
Willingness to take risks	Innovative vs. playing it safe				
Free and open interdepartmental communications	Team building vs. empire building				
Degree of interdepartmental coordination among managers on matters of common concern	Freedom and willingness to consult with other involved managers				
Data/information in focus for decision making	Decentralization vs. centralized				
Job responsibilities clearly delineated	Agreement between superior and subordinate on job scope and content				
Priorities can be determined	Most important vs. less important				

Source: Dale D. McConkey, "Participative Management: What It Really Means in Practice," *Business Horizons,* October 1980, p. 72.

laissez-faire leadership is that of a manager in a research and development laboratory. The subordinates are usually all highly skilled, well-trained professionals. The manager's job is to provide them with the assistance and equipment they require to get their work done. The subordinates are typically highly motivated and do not need to be told what has to be done. By simply ensuring that they have what they need and staying out of their hair, the manager can achieve excellent results. This example is the exception to the rule, however. In most cases laissez-faire leaders are not effective because they fail to carry out the most important function of a leader—they do not attempt to influence their people to direct their efforts toward goal attainment.

The Managerial Grid

Another popular way of describing leadership behavior is through the use of the **managerial grid** developed by Robert Blake and Jane Mouton.[10] The managerial grid provides a detailed description of leadership behavior, in addition to serving as a training and development tool. At this point in the book, we will examine the grid only in terms of its descriptive value.
Basic Styles   The managerial grid, illustrated in Figure 14–2, is a two-dimensional leadership model. One axis is labeled "concern for production" and the other is labeled "concern for people." Each axis has nine degrees, ranging from low concern (1) to high concern (9). As a result, 81 leadership combinations are possible. Only five are considered to be major leadership styles, however. These are shown in the figure.

Basic management styles

    The 9,1 manager is most interested in production or work output and has a low concern for people. In direct contrast, the 1,9 manager is very interested in people but has a low concern for production. The 1,1 manager has a minimum concern for both work and people, exerting a minimum of effort in getting things done. The 5,5 manager is a middle-of-the-road type who balances an intermediate concern for production with a similar concern for people. Finally, the 9,9 manager has a high concern for both people and work.

    In contrast to a leader-subordinate interaction approach which describes how leader *can* act, the grid is designed to teach managers how they *ought* to act. Blake and Mouton, drawing on their research and experience, claim that the 9,9 style is the best one for all situations. In so doing they directly reject the contingency approach to leadership, which holds that the most effective style depends on the situation the leader faces at that particular time. Defending their position, Blake and Mouton argue that:

> Rejection of the "one best way" is equivalent to repudiating the proposition that effective behavior is based on scientific principles or laws. Yet the view that principles of behavior undergird specific events is consistent with all other areas of scientific inquiry. We know that principles of physics underlie a vast range of phenomena in inanimate nature. Principles of biology account for phenomena of life and make them predictable. By analogy,

---

10. Robert R. Blake and Jane Syrgley Mouton, *The Managerial Grid* (Houston, Tex.: Gulf Publishing Co., 1964).

Figure 14–2
The Managerial Grid

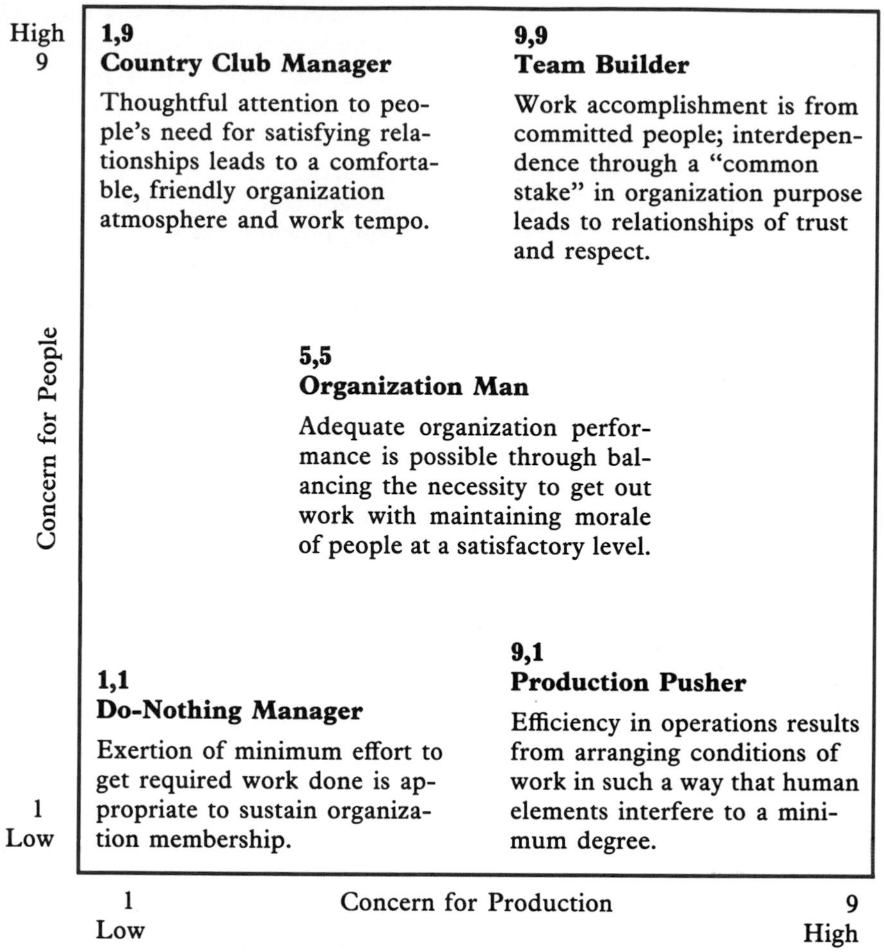

High
9

1,9
Country Club Manager

Thoughtful attention to people's need for satisfying relationships leads to a comfortable, friendly organization atmosphere and work tempo.

9,9
Team Builder

Work accomplishment is from committed people; interdependence through a "common stake" in organization purpose leads to relationships of trust and respect.

5,5
Organization Man

Adequate organization performance is possible through balancing the necessity to get out work with maintaining morale of people at a satisfactory level.

9,1
Production Pusher

Efficiency in operations results from arranging conditions of work in such a way that human elements interfere to a minimum degree.

1,1
Do-Nothing Manager

Exertion of minimum effort to get required work done is appropriate to sustain organization membership.

1
Low

Concern for People

1   Concern for Production   9
Low   High

behavioral science principles underlie human conduct, provide guidelines for soundness, and also make it predictable. . . .

Shifting from an "it all depends" to a "one best way" concept of leadership is what managerial effectiveness training is—or should be—all about.[11]

Contingency Theories of Leadership

At the present time the contingency approach to leadership is the most highly regarded. There are a number of contingency theories but they all have one thing in common: they tell how a leader should act in a particular situation. These theories make wide use of "if-then" propositions such as: if the leader is in a moderately favorable situation, he or she should use a people-oriented style; if the leader faces a crisis situation, he or she should be task oriented. These theories are also heavily research-based, in contrast to most other leadership theories, which are simply descriptive

---

11. Robert Blake and Jane Srygley Mouton, "Should You Teach There's Only *One* Best Way To Manage?" *Training HRD*, April 1978, pp. 25–29.

or are based on intuition or personal experience or both. The two that will be examined here are Fred Fiedler's contingency theory of leadership and Robert House's path-goal theory. These are currently the two most prominent contingency theories of leadership.

Fiedler's Contingency Theory

Fiedler's contingency theory has been well accepted because of its empirical nature. The development of this theory can be divided into two major stages. The first extended from the early 1950s to the early 1960s and was basically explorative. The second began with a statement of the theory, has been characterized by testing and modification to fit research findings, and continues to the present day.

Fiedler published his findings in 1964.[12] A few years later he published a comprehensive and detailed explanation of the theory.[13] In so doing he sought to explain the reasons why leaders are effective. At the heart of his contingency theory are a research instrument called the **least preferred coworker scale** (LPC) and a classification of three situational dimensions in which a leader functions.

The LPC and Situational Variables

The LPC (see Table 14–2) is a scale containing paired adjectives. The person filling out the instrument is asked to describe the coworker with whom he or she can work least well. This coworker does not have to be someone with whom the person is working currently; he or she can be a past colleague or subordinate. The interpretation of the LPC score was explained by Fiedler in this way:

The LPC score explained

> . . . we visualize the high-LPC individual (who perceives his least-preferred coworker in a relatively favorable manner) as a person who derives his major satisfaction from successful interpersonal relationships, while the low-LPC person (who describes his LPC in very unfavorable terms) derives his major satisfaction from task performance.[14]

Situational variables

Initially Fiedler hoped to find a relationship between the LPC score and the leader's performance. He eventually concluded, however, that more attention had to be given to situational variables. The three he found to be most important were (1) **leader-member relations**—the degree to which the group leader is accepted by the group members and is able to maintain their loyalty; (2) **task structure**—the degree to which rules, regulations, job descriptions, and policies are clearly specified; and (3) **position power**—the degree to which the leader is able to apply both positive (reward) and negative (punishment) sanctions. If the leader has good relations

---

12. Fred E. Fiedler, "A Contingency Model of Leadership Effectiveness," in Leonard Berkowitz, ed., *Advances in Experimental Social Psychology,* Volume 1 (New York: Academic Press, 1964), pp. 149–160.

13. Fred E. Fiedler, *A Theory of Leadership Effectiveness* (New York: McGraw-Hill, 1967).

14. *Ibid.,* p. 45.

Table 14–2
The Least Preferred Co-
worker (LPC) Scale

	8	7	6	5	4	3	2	1	
Pleasant	__ :	__ :	__ :	__ :	__ :	__ :	__ :	__	Unpleasant
	8	7	6	5	4	3	2	1	
Friendly	__ :	__ :	__ :	__ :	__ :	__ :	__ :	__	Unfriendly
	8	7	6	5	4	3	2	1	
Rejecting	__ :	__ :	__ :	__ :	__ :	__ :	__ :	__	Accepting
	1	2	3	4	5	6	7	8	
Helpful	__ :	__ :	__ :	__ :	__ :	__ :	__ :	__	Frustrating
	8	7	6	5	4	3	2	1	
Unenthusiastic	__ :	__ :	__ :	__ :	__ :	__ :	__ :	__	Enthusiastic
	1	2	3	4	5	6	7	8	
Tense	__ :	__ :	__ :	__ :	__ :	__ :	__ :	__	Relaxed
	1	2	3	4	5	6	7	8	
Distant	__ :	__ :	__ :	__ :	__ :	__ :	__ :	__	Close
	1	2	3	4	5	6	7	8	
Cold	__ :	__ :	__ :	__ :	__ :	__ :	__ :	__	Warm
	1	2	3	4	5	6	7	8	
Cooperative	__ :	__ :	__ :	__ :	__ :	__ :	__ :	__	Uncooperative
	8	7	6	5	4	3	2	1	
Supportive	__ :	__ :	__ :	__ :	__ :	__ :	__ :	__	Hostile
	8	7	6	5	4	3	2	1	
Boring	__ :	__ :	__ :	__ :	__ :	__ :	__ :	__	Interesting
	1	2	3	4	5	6	7	8	
Quarrelsome	__ :	__ :	__ :	__ :	__ :	__ :	__ :	__	Harmonious
	1	2	3	4	5	6	7	8	
Self-assured	__ :	__ :	__ :	__ :	__ :	__ :	__ :	__	Hesitant
	8	7	6	5	4	3	2	1	
Efficient	__ :	__ :	__ :	__ :	__ :	__ :	__ :	__	Inefficient
	8	7	6	5	4	3	2	1	
Gloomy	__ :	__ :	__ :	__ :	__ :	__ :	__ :	__	Cheerful
	1	2	3	4	5	6	7	8	
Open	__ :	__ :	__ :	__ :	__ :	__ :	__ :	__	Guarded
	8	7	6	5	4	3	2	1	

From *A Theory of Leadership Effectiveness* by Fred E. Fiedler. Copyright © 1967, McGraw-Hill Book Company. Used with the permission of the publisher.

with the group members, high task structure, and strong position power, the situation is favorable. If just the opposite is true, the situation is unfavorable.

Choosing the most effective leader

Fiedler then brought together the LPC scale, the situational variables, and his findings. The results are presented in Table 14–3 and Figure 14–3.[15] Notice that the "V" shaped curve can be used to determine what

15. For more on the LPC see: John K. Kennedy, Jr., "Middle LPC Leaders and the Contingency Model of Leadership Effectiveness," *Organizational Behavior and Human Performance,* August 1982, pp. 1–14.

Table 14–3
Fiedler's Findings on Leadership Style and Performance

	Major Situational Variables			
Condition	Leader-Member Relations	Task Structure	Position Power	Effective Leadership Style
I	Good	Structured	Strong	Task-Oriented
II	Good	Structured	Weak	Task-Oriented
III	Good	Unstructured	Strong	Task-Oriented
IV	Good	Unstructured	Weak	Human Relations
V	Moderately Poor	Structured	Strong	Human Relations
VI	Moderately Poor	Structured	Weak	No Data
VII	Moderately Poor	Unstructured	Strong	No Relationship
VIII	Moderately Poor	Unstructured	Weak	Task-Oriented

type of leader is most effective in a particular situation. In a very favorable situation ("A" in the figure), a task-oriented leader is best; in a moderately favorable situation ("B" in the figure), a human-relations-oriented leader is best; in a moderately unfavorable situation ("C" in the figure), a human-relations-oriented leader is best; in a very unfavorable situation ("D" in the figure), a task-oriented leader is best.

Leader Match   As well as identifying these relationships between leadership style and situation, Fiedler has also encouraged the use of a leader match concept. Since effective leadership is a function of *both* the individual leader and the situation, two alternatives are available to the leader who wants a better match between the two. The leader can either attempt to change his or her personality or work to change the situational variables and make them more favorable. Fiedler argues that it is too difficult to get leaders to change their personalities; it is more effective to change the situation. As a result, Fiedler and his associates have developed a self-

Matching the leader with the situation

Figure 14–3
Fiedler's Findings Regarding Leadership Effectiveness

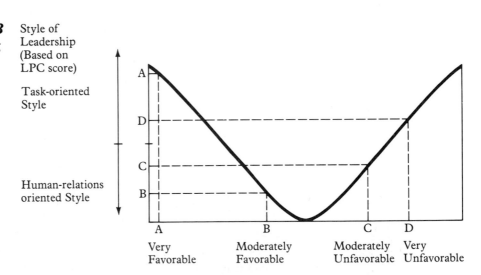

paced program instruction workbook for this purpose.[16] The booklet teaches leaders how to (1) assess their leadership style based on their LPC score, (2) assess the amount of situational favorableness that currently exists in their environment, and (3) change the situation so that it matches their style. The theory has been applied quite successfully.

Basic Value   How well has Fiedler's theory been accepted? At present it is well regarded. Much of what Fiedler has to say is grounded in empirical research, and he continues to address criticisms and conduct further testing. He himself described the situation best when he wrote:

> A number of the Contingency Model's critics have charged that ". . . the theory keeps changing to fit the data" and that it is becoming increasingly complex. Both of these observations are accurate. . . . The theory will, of course, continue to change as new data become available . . . We simply have to live with the fact that any attempt to predict pretzel-shaped relationships will require the development of pretzel-shaped hypotheses.[17]

The Path-Goal Theory of Leadership

The nature of the job affects the approach.

The **path-goal theory,** another contingency leadership theory, seeks to explain how the nature of the group's job affects whether a task orientation, human relations orientation, or some combination of the two will result in the greatest degree of group satisfaction and effectiveness. This theory has been popularized through the work of Martin Evans and Robert House.[18] It is actually derived from the expectancy theory of motivation in that it draws heavily on such concepts as valence and expectancy in explaining how a leader should act. In so doing, the path-goal theory blends the subjects of motivation and leadership.

In essence, the path-goal theory holds that the leader's job is to (a) clarify the tasks to be performed by subordinates (b) clear away any roadblocks that prevent goal attainment, and (c) increase the opportunity for subordinates to attain personal satisfaction. The major question, of course, is: What degree of task or human relations orientation will be best? As initially postulated, the theory suggested that in situations in which subordinates did not know what they were supposed to do or were unclear about the way to get the job done, a high task orientation was warranted. Conversely, when the subordinates knew what they were supposed to do and were capable of performing adequately, a human relations orientation was best.

What does this mean in practice? For one thing, it means that if subordinates are confused as to what to do next, then a lot of "initiating structure"

16. Fred E. Fiedler, Martin M. Chemers, and Linda Mahar, *Improving Leadership Effectiveness: The Leadership Match Concept* (New York: John Wiley, 1976).

17. Fred E. Fiedler, "Predicting the Effects of Leadership Training and Experience from the Contingency Model: A Clarification," *Journal of Applied Psychology,* April 1973, p. 113.

18. Martin G. Evans, "The Effect of Supervisory Behavior on the Path-Goal Relationship," *Organizational Behavior and Human Performance,* May 1970, pp. 277–298; Robert J. House, "Path-Goal Theory of Leadership Effectiveness," *Administrative Science Quarterly,* September 1971, pp. 321–338.

might be called for—you tell them what to do and how to do it. That way the leader gives them a clear path to follow. It also means that if subordinates' tasks are already very clear—as they might be on an assembly line—then the leader wants to "stay out of their hair." In this case, their "paths" are already clear enough. The path-goal theory also assumes that setting clear goals for subordinates and explaining to them why these goals are important are basic functions all leaders should perform.[19]

The theory can also be turned around to examine what will happen if the leader does not act properly. For example, if the leader fails to give adequate support to the subordinates performing the tasks, they will be dissatisfied and ineffective. Likewise, if the leader gives too much attention or direction to individuals who already know how to carry out their tasks, they will not like it and will be dissatisfied and not fully effective.

Research results are mixed . . .

How accurate has the path-goal theory proven to be? To date the results are mixed.[20] For example, some researchers have found that while increased task orientation on ambiguous jobs can lead to increased subordinate satisfaction, it does not necessarily lead to increased subordinate performance. Others have found that in an unstructured situation the subordinates welcomed attempts by the leader to be friendly and personable but did not want as much structure as had been predicted by the theory.

but the value of the path-goal theory cannot be disputed.

At the present time research on the theory is continuing. On an overall basis, the path-goal theory has value, especially as a supervisory theory of leadership. It not only suggests the type of leadership style that may be most effective in a given situation but also attempts to explain why that style is most effective, thereby serving as a basis for further research and refinement. Also, the linkage between the path-goal theory and the expectancy theory in work motivation may yet provide a basis for more effectively integrating the study of motivation and leadership.

Leadership Effectiveness

In recent years increased attention has been given to answering the question: How can leadership research be brought down to an *applied* level? Blake and Mouton attempt to answer this question with their grid training. Their critics decry the lack of flexibility provided by the approach, however— for example, its contention that the 9,9 style is *always* superior. Students and practitioners alike express an interest in a more contingency-based approach. The result has been the emergence of two different types of leadership effectiveness models. One is based heavily on management theory and attempts to integrate current knowledge into a logical framework for management action. The other is based more heavily on training and development in organizations and represents the experience and judgment of

---

19. Gary Dessler, *Management Fundamentals,* 3rd edition (Reston, Va.: Reston Publishing, 1982), p. 393.

20. For an excellent summary of research studies that have provided both supportive and mixed results on the theory, see Bass, *op. cit.,* pp. 445–447; Janet Fulk and Eric R. Wendler, "Dimensionality of Leader-Subordinate Interactions: A Path-Goal Investigation," *Organizational Behavior and Human Performance,* October 1982, pp. 241–264.

Figure 14–4
A Leadership Continuum

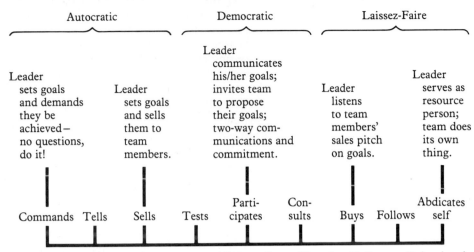

Figure 14–4
A Leadership Continuum

the particular researchers. Both approaches, however, are likely to rely heavily on Fiedler's leader match concept. The following discussion examines each of these two approaches.

Leader-Follower Continua

The approach that is perhaps the most popular for explaining how to achieve leadership effectiveness uses a synthesis of current information. One such comprehensive view has been offered by Robert W. Johnston, a management and organizational development specialist. He seeks "to develop a practical, conceptual model of leader-follower behavior designed for use as a tool for diagnosing, planning, and working through leader-follower issues for more productive relationships."[21]

Every leader can adopt a number of different styles. The three most commonly accepted are autocratic, democratic, and laissez-faire. These three are arrayed along a continuum and described in Figure 14–4.

A matching of the styles of the leader and the followers

In the same way, every follower also can adopt a number of different behavior patterns. In Johnston's terminology, these behavior patterns are dependent, interdependent, and independent; each of these is described in Figure 14–5.

When the leadership continuum in Figure 14–4 and the followership continuum in Figure 14–5 are brought together, the result is the leader-follower continuum depicted in Figure 14–6. Notice in this figure how the styles of the leader and the followers are matched. When the leader is autocratic and the follower is dependent, everything moves smoothly.

---

21. Robert W. Johnston, "Leader-Follower Behavior in 3-D, Part 1," *Personnel,* July–August 1981, p. 32.

Figure 14–5
A Followership Continuum

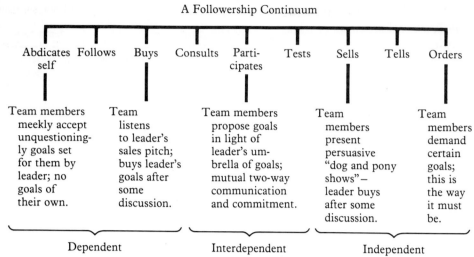

A Followership Continuum

| Abdicates self | Follows | Buys | Consults | Parti-cipates | Tests | Sells | Tells | Orders |

Team members meekly accept unquestioningly goals set for them by leader; no goals of their own.

Team listens to leader's sales pitch; buys leader's goals after some discussion.

Team members propose goals in light of leader's umbrella of goals; mutual two-way communication and commitment.

Team members present persuasive "dog and pony shows"— leader buys after some discussion.

Team members demand certain goals; this is the way it must be.

Dependent   Interdependent   Independent

The same is true when the leader is democratic and the follower is interdependent, or when the leader is laissez-faire and the follower is independent.

On a more specific level, Table 14–4 shows how the leader should act, given the followers' needs and the specifics of the situation. The Johnston model, of course, is much more complex than what is presented here. In essence, however, these figures and tables provide an accurate summary of Johnston's leader-follower behavior theory.

Why the theory has value

The theory is useful for four reasons: it encourages the leader to conduct self-analysis regarding his or her style; it focuses on the followers' styles, a topic that has not been given sufficient attention in the leadership literature; it helps explain how to achieve an effective leader-follower match; and it offers specific suggestions regarding the style to use given the needs of the followers and the specifics under which all are operating.[22]

The Situational Leadership Model

One of the most popular "applied" leadership theories to emerge in the last two decades is the **situational leadership model** developed by Paul Hersey and Kenneth Blanchard.[23] Originally known as the life cycle theory of leadership, the model has been gradually modified, retitled, and made more applicable. Figure 14–7 illustrates the latest model.

The four quadrants in Figure 14–7 are very similar to those of the

22. For more on this topic see: William Litzinger and Thomas Schaefer, "Leadership Through Followership," *Business Horizons,* September–October 1982, pp. 78–81.

23. Paul Hersey and Kenneth Blanchard, *Management of Organizational Behavior: Utilizing Human Resources,* 4th edition (Englewood Cliffs, N.J.: Prentice-Hall, 1982.)

Figure 14–6
The Leader-Follower
Continua

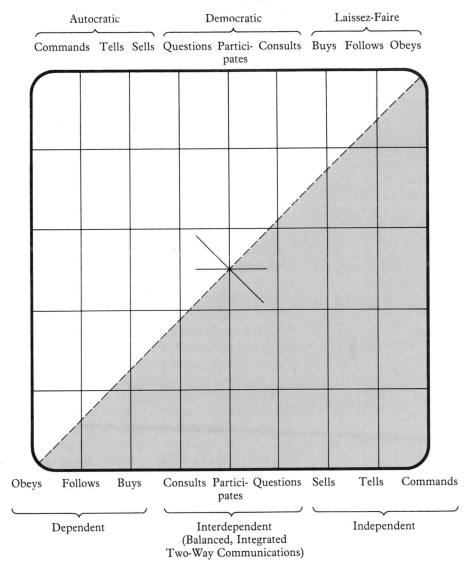

The Leader-Follower Continuums

Autocratic   Democratic   Laissez-Faire

Commands   Tells   Sells   Questions   Partici-   Consults   Buys   Follows   Obeys
                         pates

Obeys   Follows   Buys   Consults   Partici-   Questions   Sells   Tells   Commands
                             pates

Dependent   Interdependent   Independent
                         (Balanced, Integrated
                         Two-Way Communications)

☐ Leader's range of power, authority, and responsibility
☐ Follower's range of power, freedom, and responsibility

Reprinted, by permission of the publisher, from "Leader-Follower Behavior in 3-D, Part 2," *Personnel*, September–October 1981, by Robert W. Johnston, p. 56. Published by AMACOM, a division of American Management Associations. All rights reserved.

Matching leadership styles with maturity levels

managerial grid of Blake and Mouton. The general thrust is quite different, however. For example, unlike Blake and Mouton, Hersey and Blanchard argue that there is no one best leadership style. Instead, the most effective leadership style is determined by the task-relevant maturity level of the individual or group. As seen in Figure 14–7, there are four degrees of maturity, and each is related to a different leadership style. These styles

Table 14-4 A Synopsis of Three Choices of Leadership Behavior Considering Followers' Needs and Situations

Consider Being Autocratic When . . .	Consider Being Democratic When . . .	Consider Being Laissez-Faire When . . .
Leader/Manager:	**Leader/Manager:**	**Leader/Manager:**
Has complete power and no restraints on its use.	Has limited power and authority.	Has no power to compel action.
Has a way of saving matters in an emergency.	Has restraints on use.	Has no time pressures.
Has some unique knowledge.	Group might reject his/her authority and succeed at it.	Possesses tenure based on pleasure of the group.
Is firmly entrenched in his/her position.	Has *some* existing time pressures.	Has no sanctions to exert.
	Has *limited* sanctions he/she can exert.	Has no special knowledge.
Followers:	**Followers:**	**Followers:**
Are leader-dependent persons.	Expect to have some control over methods used.	Have more power than the leader.
Are rarely asked for an opinion.	Have predominantly middle-class values.	Dislike orders.
Have low educational background (not always).	Are physicians, scientists, engineers, managers, staff persons.	Will rebel successfully if they so choose.
Recognize emergencies.	Possess relatively scarce skills.	Choose own goals and methods.
Are members of a "labor surplus" group.	Like system, but not authority.	Are volunteers, loosely organized, or in short supply.
Are autocrats themselves.	Have high social needs.	Are physicians, scientists, or others with rare skills.
Have low independence drives.		
Work Situation:	**Work Situation:**	**Work Situation:**
Features tight discipline.	"Umbrella" organization objectives understood.	Has no clear purpose apparent except as the individual chooses.
Is characterized by strong controls.	Involves shared responsibility for controls.	Is unstructured.
Is marked by low profit margins or tight cost controls.	Has some time pressures.	Is one in which only self-imposed controls exist.
Includes physical dangers.	Consists of gradual changes or regularly spaced changes.	Has no time pressures.
Requires low skills from workers.	Involves actual or potential hazards occasionally.	Features few or only gradual changes.
Requires that frequent changes be made quickly.	Is one in which teamwork skills are called for.	Takes place in a safe, placid environment.
		Requires high individual skill or conceptual ability.
Effect of Autocratic Leadership if Carried to Extreme or Overused:	**Effect of Democratic Leadership if Carried to Extreme or Overused:**	**Effect of Laissez-Faire Leadership if Carried to Extreme or Overused:**
May result in poor communication, rigidity of operation, slow adaptation to changing conditions, and stunting of the growth of people.	May result in loss of ability to take individual initiative when necessary (in favor of group decisions); also may result in slow decision making in emergencies.	May result in organization fragmentation, member isolation, chaos, and anarchy.

Figure 14–7
Situational Leadership

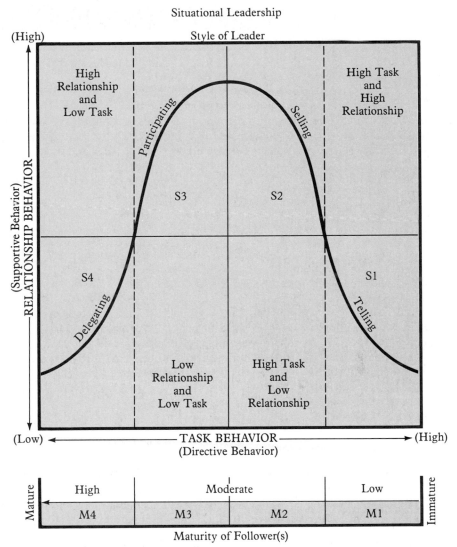

Situational Leadership

Paul Hersey/Kenneth H. Blanchard, Management of Organizational Behavior:
Utilizing Human Resources, 4th ed., p. 248. © 1982. Reprinted with permission of Prentice-Hall, Inc., Englewood Cliffs, N.J.

are referred to as telling, selling, participating, and delegating, and they represent different combinations of task and relationship behavior.

Task behavior relates to the extent to which a leader provides direction for subordinates, such as by telling them what to do, when, where, and how. *Relationship behavior* relates to the extent to which a leader engages in two-way or multi-way communication by providing assistance, advice, and socioemotional support. These two types of behavior, task and relationship, combine to provide four basic leadership styles: (1) high task and low relationship, (2) high task and high relationship, (3) high relationship and low task, (4) low relationship and low task. As seen in Figure 14–7, these four task-relationship combinations are labeled S1, S2, S3, and S4, respectively. Also, at the bottom of Figure 14–7 there are four degrees of follower maturity which match up with the four leadership styles. By deter-

mining the maturity level of the individual or group, a leader can identify the appropriate style (S1 through S4) along the prescriptive curve.

Choosing a Style

The style in the lower righthand corner of Figure 14–7 (S1) is considered most effective for individuals with low maturity. These people are both unable and unwilling to perform specific tasks. They need clear direction and close supervision. The leader should deal with these people by telling them what to do and by providing minimal supportive behavior to avoid being seen as tolerant of poor performance.

Individuals of low to moderate maturity should have a leader who can sell them on what needs to be done. These people are willing to do the work but are unable to take responsibility for a specific task or function. The leader needs to display directive behavior but must also be very supportive of the followers' willingness and enthusiasm. Through the use of two-way communication to explain decisions and gain subordinate support, the leader sells the followers on a course of action.

Subordinates with a moderate to high level of maturity are handled most effectively through the use of a participating leadership style. The followers at this level have the ability to perform specific tasks but they lack confidence or enthusiasm or both. By providing low task direction the leader allows them to use their own judgment and ability. At the same time the leader offers strong support and is continually available to listen and to praise. The leader's primary emphasis is to build up the personal confidence of the followers.

Individuals with a high level of maturity work best under a leader exercising both low task and low relationship behavior. The followers are self-directed and self-motivated. They can perform their jobs with a minimum amount of assistance from the leader, who therefore employs a delegating style.

How does the leader determine the maturity of the followers? Hersey and Blanchard recommend two simple steps:

1. Determine the goal or task to be accomplished by the followers.

2. Determine the maturity level of the follower or group that is relevant to the task by assessing:
   a. achievement motivation—the ability of the followers to set high but realistic goals.
   b. responsibility—the willingness and ability of the followers to assume responsibility.
   c. education/experience—the education and experience of the group related to the accomplishment of the task.

After determining the maturity level of the followers (M1, M2, M3, or M4) the leader simply draws a line from this level up to the leadership style curve in Figure 14–7. The point at which the line intersects with the leadership style (S1, S2, S3, or S4) indicates the most effective approach to employ.

The model can also be used to help followers develop in maturity by showing leaders how to move through the four styles on the prescriptive

Sometimes the leader must tell the subordinates what to do.

At other times a selling approach works best.

Leaders may participate . . .

or they may delegate.

Assessing the maturity of the followers

curve. The leader can adjust his or her style to move forward along the curve or to move backward, depending on the situation.

> The developmental cycle is accomplished through a series of two-step processes: first, the leader reduces directive behavior to encourage the follower to assume greater task-relevant responsibility; second, as soon as performance improvement is noted, the leader rewards the follower by increasing supportive behavior as positive reinforcement; and finally, as the follower reaches higher levels of maturity (M3 and M4), the leader responds by decreasing both task and relationship behavior, because very mature people tend to need autonomy more than socioemotional support.

The leader can help followers develop maturity.

> Conversely, the leader can arrest and reverse tendencies toward declining performance in followers by reassessing their maturity level and moving backwards through the prescriptive curve (the regressive cycle) to provide the necessary amounts of task and relationship behavior.[24]

Leadership Match and Effectiveness

At the heart of the situational leadership model is the issue of identifying the most effective style. Hersey and Blanchard have developed a diagnostic instrument that aids in this process. This instrument measures both job maturity and willingness to do the job. Of perhaps even greater value is a process they call "contracting for leadership style." After the leader and the follower agree on the goals the latter will pursue, they discuss the most appropriate leadership style to be used. In a manner of speaking, the two negotiate the style to be employed by the leader.

Negotiating a "contract" for leadership style

If the subordinate finds the choice to be unrealistic, he or she can then contact the leader and set up a meeting to negotiate a different style. For example, the subordinate may feel that the leader is not being sufficiently helpful and that a change from S3 back to S2 will improve work performance. Analogously, the leader may request a change in style because the subordinate is not producing the expected results. For example, the worker may have negotiated an S1 style but the leader may feel this choice is too time consuming because of the amount of attention that must be given to providing specific instructions and close supervision. An S3 style will give the subordinate more freedom, increased supportive behavior, and a chance to increase the amount of work output. This form of contracting results in a leadership match and tends to be superior to the typical situation in which the leader simply assumes the role that he or she believes will produce the best results without discussing this choice with the subordinates.

Degrees of leadership effectiveness

Of course, even with leader-subordinate discussion, the leader match may not be the best one. On the other hand, it may not be that far off. Given the fact that effectiveness is a dimension that ranges from most effective to least effective, if the leader match does not result in a choice of the best style it may produce a choice of the second best style. To assess the probability that the other styles will be successful, if the leader is unwilling or unable to use the ideal style, Hersey and Blanchard offer

---

24. Paul Hersey and Marshall Goldsmith, "A Situational Approach to Performance Planning," *Training and Development Journal,* November 1980, p. 39.

Table 14–5
Matching Maturity Level and
Leadership Style

Maturity Level	Most Effective Style	Second Most Effective Style	Third Most Effective Style	Least Effective Style
M1 Low	S1 Telling	S2 Selling	S3 Participating	S4 Delegating
M2 Low-Moderate	S2 Selling	S1 Telling or S3 Participating	—	S4 Delegating
M3 Moderate-High	S3 Participating	S2 Selling or S4 Delegating	—	S1 Telling
M4 High	S4 Delegating	S3 Participating	S2 Selling	S1 Telling

the leader match success probabilities presented in Table 14–5. Commenting on the table data, they note that:

> . . . the "desired" style always has a second "best" style choice, that is, a style that would probably be effective if the highest probability style could not be used. In attempting to influence people at the low to moderate (M2) and moderate to high (M3) maturity levels, you will notice that there are two second "best" style choices: which one should be used depends on whether the maturity of the individual is getting better, indicating that the leaders should be involved in a developmental cycle, or getting worse, revealing that a regressive cycle is occurring. If the situation is improving, "participating" and "delegating" would be the "best" second choices, but if things are deteriorating "telling" and "selling" would be the most appropriate backup choices.[25]

Why the model is useful

The situational leadership model approach is useful for four reasons. First, it encourages leader-subordinate matching, applying Fiedler's idea on a much more practical level. Second, it helps develop communication flows between leaders and subordinates through the "contracting for leadership style" process. Third, the model encourages managers to view leadership effectiveness as a continuum that ranges from most effective to least effective rather than as an "all or nothing" concept. Fourth, the developers of the theory set forth an easy-to-understand approach for matching maturity level and leadership style and offer success probabilities at each level (from M1 through M4) for each style (S1 through S4).[26]

---

25. Hersey and Blanchard, *op. cit.*, p. 236.
26. For more on this theory see: Claude L. Graeff, "The Situation Leadership Theory: A Critical View," *Academy of Management Review,* April 1983, pp. 285–291.

Summary

1. Leadership is the process of influencing people to direct their efforts toward the achievement of some particular goal or goals. Some of the common traits or characteristics found among successful leaders include intelligence, scholarship, dependability, social participation, and socioeconomic status.

2. Leader behavior can be described in many ways. One is through the use of leader-subordinate interactions as typified by autocratic, paternalistic, democratic/participative, and laissez-faire leadership styles.

3. Another popular way to describe leader behavior is through the use of the managerial grid. By examining the five basic styles on the grid—9,1 management, 1,9 management, 1,1 management, 5,5 management and 9,9 management—one can obtain an excellent understanding of the way leaders combine a concern for work with a concern for people in getting things done.

4. At the present time the contingency approach to leadership is the most highly regarded. One contingency theory has been proposed by Fred Fiedler. Combining the LPC score with situational variables, Fiedler reports that task-oriented managers do best in highly favorable or highly unfavorable situations while human-relations-oriented managers do best in moderately favorable or moderately unfavorable situations. Fiedler recommends matching the leader to the situation.

5. Another contingency leadership theory, path-goal, seeks to explain how the nature of the group's job affects whether a task orientation, human relations orientation, or some combination of the two will result in the greatest degree of group satisfaction and effectiveness. The theory holds that the leader's job is to clarify subordinate tasks, clear away roadblocks preventing goal attainment, and increase the opportunity for subordinates to attain personal satisfaction. While research continues, path-goal offers great promise as a supervisory theory of leadership.

6. Increased attention has been given in recent years to answering the question: How can leadership research be brought down to an applied level? Two different types of leadership models have emerged. One is based heavily on management theory; the other is grounded in training and development research.

7. Robert Johnston has offered one type of "applied" theory in developing his leader-follower continua. This approach is based on the idea that the leader must match his or her style with that of the followers. An autocratic leader will do best with dependent subordinates; a democratic leader will succeed with interdependent subordinates; a laissez-faire leader will excel with independent subordinates.

8. One of the most popular "applied" leadership theories is the situational leadership model developed by Hersey and Blanchard. This model is designed to help managers identify the maturity level of their subordinates and from this determine the leadership style that will be most effective. Along a continuum ranging from low to high maturity, the leader uses varying degrees of task and relationship behavior. Figure 14–7 illustrated this idea in detail. The model also recommends leader match preferences as explained in Table 14–5.

Key Terms

Autocratic leadership A leadership style characterized by a heavy emphasis on task accomplishment and very little on the human element.

Democratic/participative leadership A leadership style characterized by a high concern for both people and work.

Fiedler's contingency theory   A leadership theory that seeks to explain managerial effectiveness in terms of LPC score and situational variables.

Laissez-faire leadership   A leadership style characterized by the manager's general uninvolvement in the operations of the unit or department.

Leader–member relations   The degree to which a group leader is accepted by the group and is able to maintain the loyalty of the members.

Least preferred coworker scale   A scale containing paired adjectives that are used to describe the person with whom the respondent can work least well. It is used to classify the respondent as a task-oriented or human-relations-oriented manager.

Managerial grid   A two-dimensional leadership model used to measure a manager's concern for work and concern for people.

Paternalistic leadership   A leadership style characterized by the philosophy "Do as I say and the organization will take care of you."

Path–goal theory   A theory of leadership that seeks to explain how the nature of a group's job affects whether a task orientation, a human relations orientation, or some combination of the two will result in the greatest degree of group satisfaction and effectiveness.

Position power   The degree to which a leader is able to apply positive (reward) and negative (punishment) sanctions.

Situational leadership model   A leadership model that brings together task behavior, relationship behavior, and the maturity of the followers in identifying the most effective leadership style to employ.

Task structure   The degree to which rules, regulations, job descriptions, and policies are clearly specified.

Trait theory   An approach to the study of leadership characterized by attempts to identify the traits or abilities that are unique to effective leaders.

Questions for Analysis and Discussion

1. In your own words, what is meant by the term leadership?

2. Are there any traits or characteristics that seem to be of importance for effective leadership? Identify and describe five.

3. How do each of the following types of leaders act: autocratic, paternalistic, democratic/participative, laissez-faire? Describe each in terms of concern for work and concern for people.

4. One way of describing leadership behavior is through the use of the managerial grid. How can this be done? In your answer be sure to incorporate the five major styles described by Blake and Mouton.

5. Drawing upon your knowledge of Fiedler's contingency theory of leadership, explain what the LPC is all about. What were the three situational variables Fiedler found to be most important to effective leadership? How did he bring together the LPC and the situational variables in constructing his leadership model? In your answer be sure to incorporate a discussion of Table 14–3.

6. What did Fiedler conclude regarding leadership style and effectiveness? Who does best under what conditions? Be sure to include reference to Figure 14–3 in your answer.

7. According to the path-goal theory of leadership, what is the leader's job? How will the clarity or ambiguity of the subordinate's task affect the style of an effective leader?

8. Of what practical value to managers is the path-goal theory of leadership? Put the answer in your own words.

9. Drawing upon Johnston's leader-follower continuum, presented in Figure 14–6, describe the relationship between leadership style and follower behavior. Explain, incorporating a discussion of autocratic, democratic, and laissez-faire styles into your answer.

10. Drawing upon Johnston's findings, as presented in Table 14–4, when should a leader consider being autocratic? Democratic? Laissez-faire?

11. According to Hersey and Blanchard, how can one determine the maturity of subordinates? What type of leadership style is most effective when dealing with subordinates of low maturity? Low to moderate maturity? Moderate to high maturity? High maturity?

12. How does the Hersey and Blanchard model help explain leadership match? Use Table 14–5 in your answer.

| Case | # Ralph's Way |

Salespeople in the pharmaceutical firm where Ralph Holloway works have always made good money. In fact, those who do not are terminated. If they cannot sell, they are not kept around.

Over the last 15 years Ralph has become one of the company's outstanding salespeople. Two years ago he was number seven companywide; last year he was number six. Three months ago, however, he decided to make a career change, applying for a district sales manager's job and getting it. For the last 90 days Ralph has been supervising 12 salespeople.

Two of Ralph's people are new, having just finished their training at company headquarters. There they learned about the product lines, how the drugs work, what the competitive products are, and how to sell in the face of both doctor/hospital resistance and competition. Since the two new people are totally unfamiliar with their territory or how to call on doctors and hospitals, Ralph is spending a great deal of time working with them.

He is not confining himself to these two people, however. He is also spending time with the other 10 salespeople. During this time Ralph calls on medical personnel with the salesperson, helps with the presentation, and even pitches in to close the sale.

The new salespeople seem to like having Ralph along. They believe his advice and assistance are helping them improve their sales skills and overall performance. The other salespeople do not feel this way. They believe Ralph is too close-control in his approach. One of them put their feelings this way, "I know how to sell. Oh sure, it's nice to have Ralph along in terms of advice. He sure knows how to sell and can pick out little things I'm doing wrong or could do better. However, I don't need him to sell for me. He's supposed to be a manager now, not a salesperson. If anything, he tends to be too autocratic in his approach. He wants me to do things his way. I wish he'd just stay out of my hair and let me sell my way." Most of the other experienced salespeople feel the same way, although Ralph certainly does not. When talking to his boss last week, Ralph commented:

Sales are up 21 percent over this time last year and I think they are going to go even higher. One of the reasons is the two new people we have in the district. They are a lot better than the two they replaced. Also, my approach of working closely with the salespeople is helping a lot. It keeps them on their toes and assists them in developing their selling techniques. If more district sales managers would follow my leadership style, their sales forces would also improve.

1. Using the managerial grid as your guide, describe Ralph's leadership style. What style would the experienced salespeople like Ralph to use? Explain.

2. In terms of the path-goal theory of leadership, how should Ralph go about managing his people? Be complete in your answer.

3. What contingency-based recommendations would you offer to Ralph regarding how to lead his people? Draw upon Fiedler's and Hersey and Blanchard's ideas in constructing your recommendations. Provide Ralph with at least three useful leadership guidelines.

You Be the Consultant

Choosing the New CEO

Midwest General (disguised name) is a large private metropolitan hospital located in a north-central state. Five months ago the current chief executive officer (CEO) told the board of trustees that he was going to resign effective six months from that date. Since that time the board of trustees has been conducting an active search for a new CEO.

The present CEO has kept things on a very even keel. Since taking over the helm 10 years ago he has replaced the heads of all major departments. He has also managed to raise salaries to 107 percent of those in the local area and sponsored a fund drive that met its campaign goal of $50 million. Most of this money has gone into new equipment and facilities and has helped Midwest General increase its reputation in the local area. In fact, a regional survey conducted nine months ago found the hospital to be ranked number one by both doctors and the general public in terms of health care quality.

The current CEO is regarded by the hospital staff as hard driving, intelligent, honest, fair, and goal oriented. Many of his people have referred to him as "tough when he has to be tough." Overall, however, they think the world of him.

By early this month the board of trustees has reduced its list of potential candidates for the CEO's job to four. Each of these applicants has been invited in and interviewed by the board members and the staff, and a preliminary leadership profile has been put together on each. One of the elements of this profile is a rating of their leadership traits and abilities based on the interviews and discussions each had with the hospital personnel. Here is the composite profile that was constructed:

	Mr. A	Ms. B	Mr. C	Ms. D
Intelligence	H	MH	MH	MH
Self-Confidence	MH	H	H	H
Sociability	H	A	H	H
Initiative	H	H	H	A
Reliability	H	MH	H	H
Persistence	H	MH	MH	AA
Verbal Facility	H	AA	AA	H
Cooperativeness	AA	MH	H	H
Insight	A	H	A	A
Adaptability	L	A	H	AA

H = high   A = average
MH = moderately high   L = low
AA = above average

Each of the four applicants was also asked about his or her basic leadership style. Here is what each said:

Mr. A: The health care industry today is a very competitive one. The two biggest challenges are to provide the finest health care possible and to do so at the lowest possible price. The effective health care manager has to be on top of everything, every minute of the day. I'm a detail guy and that's the style I find works best today in health care.

Ms. B: I find you have to use the same style with health care people as they use with patients. Look after your people, treat them right, and encourage them to put their confidence in you. Do this and everything else will take care of itself.

Mr. C: Health care management requires a team approach. The CEO has to help set the goals and then delegate as much authority as possible to the subordinates. It's all a matter of showing people the way and letting them decide how to get there.

Ms. D: Health care professionals really do not need to be led. The effective CEO stays out of their way completely, devoting his or her time to public relations and fund raising. This is the key to effective administration in a health care setting.

Your Consultation

Assume that you are an outside consultant brought in to advise the board of trustees. Which of the four candidates would you recommend? Why? Be as complete as possible in explaining your reasoning to the board members.

15

Managerial Communication

Objectives

The success of every enterprise is influenced by the manner and effectiveness of organizational communication. Unless the personnel understand what they are supposed to do and the parameters within which goals are to be attained, overall efficiency and effectiveness suffer. This chapter examines the ways in which managerial communication works and the ways it can be improved. It explores intrapersonal, interpersonal, and organizational communication. When you have finished reading this chapter, you will be able to

1. define the term communication and describe how it works;

2. explain the intrapersonal communication process and the ways in which self, the self-concept, and intrapersonal variables influence this process;

3. identify and describe five of the major barriers to effective interpersonal communication;

4. discuss ways of overcoming these interpersonal organizational barriers;

5. identify and describe five of the major barriers to effective organizational communication; and

6. discuss ways of overcoming these organizational communication barriers.

The Basics of Communication

Communication involves the transfer of meanings.

Communication is the process of transferring meanings from sender to receiver. This process is used when there is something that the sender wants the receiver to know, understand, or act upon. Given this definition, there are three important aspects of communication: (1) the sender must

415

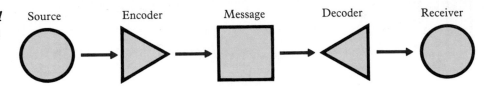

Figure 15-1
The Communication Process

communicate accurately and completely; (2) the receiver must understand the message; and (3) the receiver must be willing to act on it in an appropriate manner. In this chapter, all three of these aspects of communication will be examined. We will begin by explaining how meanings are actually transferred through what is known as the communication process.

The Communication Process

The communication process has three basic elements: a source, a message, and a receiver. The message is conveyed to and interpreted by the receiver through encoding and decoding. (See Figure 15–1.)

How it works

The source is the individual or party that wants to send a communiqué or message. For some particular reason, the source wants the receiver to understand something.

The source conveys the meaning to the receiver by using the **encoding process.** In other words, the source must put the message into a form that can be understood by the receiver.

The message is the sign or symbol used to carry the meaning. Typical examples include a written letter, a telephone, or a telegram.

The **decoding process** is carried out by the receiver, who interprets the message to determine what is being communicated. When the decoding process begins, the communication is out of the hands of the source and entirely in the hands of the receiver.

The receiver is the person or group to whom the message is communicated. If the receiver is on the same wave length as the sender, the decoding process will be accurate enough to convey the source's meaning. If not, the message will be misunderstood or not understood at all.

Communication in Action

When communication breaks down, it is usually because the receiver's understanding of the message is not the same as the sender's meaning. This problem is often overcome through the process of feedback, in which the receiver sends a message back to the sender. ("Is this what you meant?" "When do you need this done?" "Am I to start immediately or wait until I receive the materials you are sending?") The sender then clarifies the message through additional information. As a result, communication in action can be viewed as a series of messages flowing between the source and the receiver.[1]

When viewed in this way, communication in action can be illustrated as in Figure 15–2. Notice that the initial message sender (the encoder) is

1. John L. DiGaetani, "A Systems Solution to Communication Problems," *Business Horizons,* September–October 1983, pp. 57–61.

Figure 15–2
Communication in Action

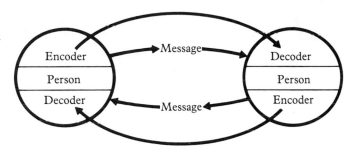

located on the left and the initial message receiver (the decoder) is located on the right. If the latter asks for further clarification of the message, these roles are reversed. The encoder becomes the decoder/interpreter and the decoder/interpreter becomes the encoder.

Feedback is essential.

Of course, it is not always the receiver who has to initiate the feedback. Sometimes the sender realizes that the message is not clear or that the receiver is having trouble following what is going on. In this case, the sender may well encourage feedback by asking pertinent questions ("Would you mind telling me what you heard me say?" "I can see by the look on your face that I am confusing you; exactly what seems to be unclear?" "How are you going to carry out the order I just gave you?") As a result, feedback is promoted and the communiqué has an improved chance of being effective.

Types of Communication

Managerial communication occurs in three forms. In **intrapersonal communication,** managers receive, process, and transmit information to themselves. This concept is important because unless we know how communication occurs within people, it is difficult to understand how it occurs between people. In **interpersonal communication,** meanings are transmitted directly between two or more people, on a person-to-person basis. Quite often, those involved can see each other, although, as in the case of telephone conversations, this is not always so. In **organizational communication,** finally, information is transferred formally throughout the organization, as memos, reports, and directives are sent up and down the hierarchical chain. This form of communication is the least personal, but in large enterprises it is a vital and efficient means of conveying information throughout the structure.

Intrapersonal Communication

In studying intrapersonal communication, we have to look at the manager's self and self-concept, the intrapersonal communication process itself, and intrapersonal variables that affect this process.

The Self

Everyone has many selves.

The study of intrapersonal communication begins with knowing oneself. Everyone has many selves. One is the *physical self,* which is the way the

Figure 15–3
The Johari Window

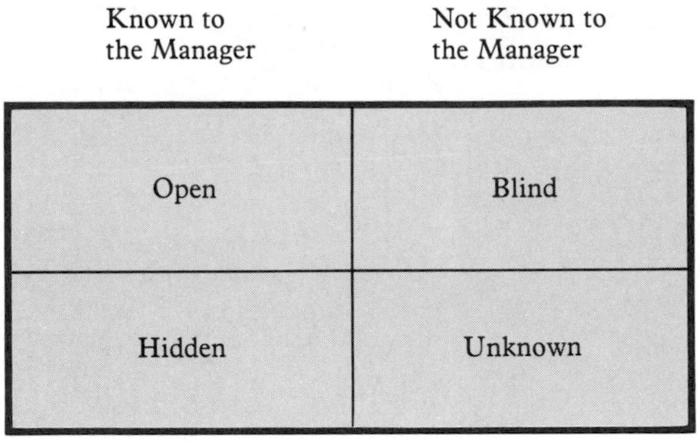

	Known to the Manager	Not Known to the Manager
	Open	Blind
	Hidden	Unknown

person looks (tall, short, fat, skinny). A second is the *emotional self*, which consists of conscious feelings (happiness, sadness, anger) and is accompanied by physiological changes (rapid heartbeat, tensed muscles, raised blood sugar level). A third self is characterized by *habits* and *repetitious behavior* of which the individual may be totally unaware (tapping one's fingers, scratching one's ear, biting one's lower lip). A fourth is the *public and private self*, which is illustrated in the Johari Window[2] shown in Figure 15–3.

This figure presents the public and private selves in terms of open and closed communication relationships. There are four sections to the window. The open section represents the things the manager knows about himself or herself and is willing to share with others. The hidden section represents what the individual is aware of but not willing to share. The blind section represents information of which the individual is unaware but which is known to others. The unknown section represents what is not known either to the manager or to others. Figure 15–3 presents four windows of equal size. In reality, however, these sizes require different proportions depending on the specific relationship under analysis. An open relationship with one's spouse would result in a very large open window and a quite small hidden window. Conversely, a business relationship with a subordinate whom one did not trust very much would result in a small open window and a large hidden one. Managers adjust their personal and private selves to fit the situation. Commenting on the value of the Johari Window, Larry Barker, a communications expert, has noted:

The Johari Window has practical value.

You can use the concept of the Johari Window to increase your self-awareness. This, in turn, should improve your communication with others. As you strive to shrink the blind and unknown segments, you may begin to discover a self you only partially knew before, a self that may or may not resemble the concept you've always had about that person you call "me." The more information you can bring into the open from the hidden, blind, and unknown areas, the better your interpersonal communication will be.[3]

---

2. Joseph Luft, *Of Human Interaction* (Palo Alto, Calif.: Natural Press Books, 1969).

3. Larry Barker, *Communication* (Englewood Cliffs, N.J.: Prentice-Hall, 1978), pp. 113–114.

The Self-Concept

The self-concept affects intrapersonal communication.

How managers feel about themselves, this feeling known as their **self-concept,** has a strong effect on their intrapersonal communication. A self-concept is developed through interactions with people and the environment. Positive past experiences encourage managers to act in certain ways; negative past experiences discourage them from acting in other ways. The result is a shaping or molding of the manager's concept of himself or herself.

Reference groups, with whom managers identify, also help establish their attitudes and values and affect the intrapersonal communication process. So, too, do the roles the manager plays in life. Some of these roles are ascribed in that the manager is expected to act in a given way. **Ascribed roles** are based heavily on sex, age, kinship, and general place in society. We see these roles reinforced when we hear people saying to others: "Act your age; you're too big to cry." "Older brothers are leaders, so take charge out there." "Women have a real chance to make something of themselves, so get on with it." **Achieved roles** are those earned through accomplishment. Depending on what a person does with life, he or she will end up with certain roles to play. An organization president, a chief financial officer, a district manager, and a union steward all have roles based on their achieved position. These roles are typically both business and social related.

The Process

Intrapersonal communication is the foundation on which interpersonal communication is based. This process is diagrammed in Figure 15–4. As the figure shows, every individual receives external stimuli that affect his or her thought and communication processes. These stimuli are of two types: overt and covert. *Overt stimuli* are received on the conscious level; *covert stimuli* are received on the subconscious level. When an individual is subjected to overt stimuli, he or she is aware of the messages being received. When subjected to covert stimuli, the individual may be unaware of the messages. A typical example occurs when one hears someone say something

Figure 15–4
Intrapersonal Communication Process

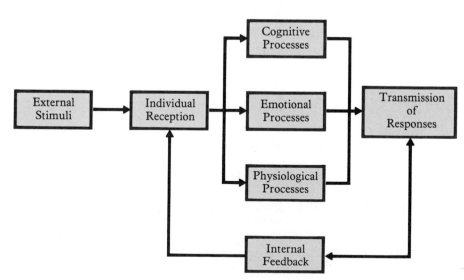

but it does not "register" until later on. The message was, at least originally, a covert one.

The process by which the body receives stimuli is called reception. Keep in mind, however, that the body does not accept all stimuli. A process called **selective perception** occurs in which only certain stimuli are accepted—the ones that are most important to the individual. For example, the manager who is concerned with budget data will pick up anything related to these data from a particular report and will ignore anything not so related, judging it to be extraneous.

Intrapersonal communication in action

After receiving the stimuli, the manager processes the data, using three types of processes: cognitive, emotional, and physiological. *Cognitive processes* include the storage, retrieval, sorting, and assimilating of information. This logical thinking stage process makes heavy use of memory, recognition, recall, and analysis. *Emotional processes* are nonlogical responses to stimuli. Some of the variables that play a key role in these processes include beliefs, values, opinions, attitudes, and prejudices. *Physiological processes* are physical in nature. Some of the major variables include brain activity, blood pressure, heart rate, and body temperature. These variables affect the way the individual feels and acts, thus helping dictate both the interpretation of stimuli and the response to them.

In intrapersonal communication, the transmission process takes place through nerve impulses in the brain as the individual sends messages to himself or herself. When the brain reacts to these nerve impulses, the transmission is complete.

The messages or stimuli are then sent back to the person in the form of self-feedback. This feedback can be both external and internal. External self-feedback is the part of the message in which one hears oneself and corrects any mistakes. For example, a manager may talk to himself in trying to straighten out a problem. As he does so, he corrects or adjusts recommended solutions until, in his mind, he says, "That's it. That's how we'll solve the problem." Internal self-feedback is picked up through nerve endings or muscular movement. When a manager is reading a memo and suddenly flinches because of something in the directive, she can feel the muscle tension in her face. She is getting internal self-feedback regarding how she feels about what she is reading.

Intrapersonal Variables

How a manager interprets communications is a function of intrapersonal variables. These variables fall into three general categories: personal orientation, personality traits, and defense mechanisms.

Personal Orientation

Where the manager is coming from

A manager's personal orientation is a reflection of his or her values, attitudes, beliefs, opinions, and prejudices. These characteristics affect the way the person sees the world and responds to it. If a manager believes that more women should be promoted to higher-level positions, this belief will influence his or her evaluation of female workers. If a manager places a high value on hard work, this will affect his or her perception of other employees.

A personal orientation dictates "where the manager is coming from" and influences the manager's approach to communication.

Personality Traits

What kind of person the manager is

Personality traits also help determine how a manager communicates. Although there are many such traits, five of the most important are manipulation, dogmatism, tolerance for ambiguity, self-esteem, and maturity. Manipulative managers try to dominate or control others through the skillful use of verbal and nonverbal communications. Dogmatic managers are closed-minded and are typically unwilling to accept new ideas or opinions regardless of fact or logic. Managers who have a low degree of tolerance for ambiguity find it difficult to communicate in general, abstract, or nebulous terms; everything has to be spelled out clearly. Self-esteem helps determine personal confidence and often influences the way in which a person communicates with others. Maturity affects the manager's desire for such things as independence, approval, and affection; it therefore influences the way the person both transmits and interprets communiqués.

Defense Mechanisms

How the manager deals with anxiety

When there is a conflict between one's inner psychological needs and the realities of the external world, anxiety results. If this anxiety is severe enough it can distort one's personal perception as well as one's view of the environment, bringing about a communication problem. To deal with this anxiety, people turn to the use of defense mechanisms. One of these is **rationalization,** which is an attempt to justify failures or inadequacies. Thus the person might say, "I would have gotten that promotion if they had judged the applicants on the basis of ability rather than past friendships." A second defense mechanism, **projection,** occurs when people ignore certain traits, motives, or behavior patterns in themselves and attribute them to others. The person says, "I can tell that Bob is still upset that I didn't get that promotion." A third is **reaction formation,** which involves dealing with "undesirable" behavior by taking just the opposite point of view. The manager who does not believe a college degree in business is very important but knows the company does, for example, may continually tell people, "We should never hire anyone who does not have a degree in business." Finally, **repression** is a defense mechanism that involves keeping down unpleasant or unacceptable feelings. The manager who really wants to tell off her boss but keeps these feelings well hidden is suffering from repression.

Interpersonal Communication

Interpersonal communication, the direct transmission of meanings between two or more persons, can be quite time consuming, especially if the manager eventually has to communicate the same message to a half dozen people. It is an extremely effective means of conveying information, however.

The interpersonal process can be diagrammed in the same basic way

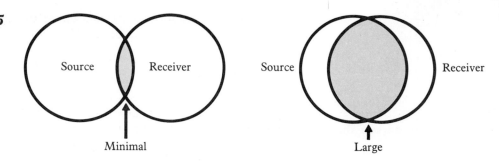

Figure 15–5
Degree of Message Understanding

as the communication process was in Figure 15–1. Additionally we need to realize that the source and the receiver must mutually understand one another. We can illustrate the idea by comparing two situations: one where the degree of understanding is minimal and the other where it is great. This comparison is made in Figure 15–5. Notice that the situation in the righthand diagram is more likely to produce effective results than is the situation in the lefthand diagram. Without considering the specifics of each situation, however, we cannot say how much message understanding is needed to produce the best results. We can only say a minimum amount is necessary in each situation. If it does not exist, communication breakdown will occur because of communication barriers.

Barriers to Interpersonal Communication

Barriers to interpersonal communication prevent the message from being understood in the way the sender intends. These barriers may be brought about by either the sender or the receiver, or they may be caused by environmental factors. Five of the major interpersonal communication barriers are perception, words, the source of the words, inconsistent behavior, and the environment.

Perception

People see things differently.

Perception is a person's view of reality. Personal values, education, and experience all influence individual perception. As a result, people often have different interpretations of the same situation. Consider the differences between the manager's perceptions and the subordinates in the following situation:

Situation 1

Manager said: "I need that report as soon as possible."

Manager meant: "I need that report as soon as you are done gathering those monthly sales figures."

Subordinate understood: "I'd better drop these monthly sales figures and get on that report right away."

Situation 2

Subordinate said: "If you need any help with that control plan, let me know."

Subordinate meant: "I'll be happy to look over a couple of sections of the plan and give you my input."

Manager understood: "If you need someone to rewrite or rework the plan, I'm available at any time."

Often, people see and hear what they want to. They interpret the communiqué based on what is in their own best interests, regardless of what was "actually" said.

Words

Not everyone has the same meaning for the same word. Sometimes a word has a technical meaning. For example, in the engineering world the word "burn" means to photocopy. Imagine an engineering manager's surprise if he tells a new secretary to burn the blueprints and finds out that the individual has literally done so.

Words can have different meanings.

Words also take on meanings based on how they are used locally. For example, if today is Tuesday, the statement "We have a meeting next Thursday" would be interpreted differently by Californians and New Yorkers. To most Californians, the statement would mean there is a meeting in two days. For many New Yorkers the word "next" means next week, so they would think the meeting was going to be held in nine days. To get New Yorkers to come to a meeting in two days, the communication would have to say "this" Thursday.

Then, too, words sometimes cause confusion because people do not know their meaning. For example, what is meant by the phrase "biweekly meetings"? How often is "biweekly"? Most people know it means either twice a week or every other week, but which is it?

Finally, consider interpretive statements such as, "Do you have a minute?"; "I'll be with you shortly"; and "We need to impress this new candidate." In each case, the speaker probably has a very good idea of what he or she is talking about. The listener may not, however, because meanings are not in words, they are in the individuals who use them.

The Source

Who says something can be important.

Sometimes what is said is not as important as who said it. This is particularly true when the receiver of the message has reason to believe that the sender is extremely knowledgeable, insightful, or trustworthy (or has the opposite characteristics). A typical example is provided by top managers who, when they are talking to other members of the management hierarchy, tend to be regarded as highly reliable. After all, they are part of the same team. On the other hand, when these top managers are discussing contract negotiations with the union, their statements may be regarded as inaccurate or misleading, especially if the negotiations are tough and the company feels it must hold the line on salary and benefits.

Analogous situations can be found throughout the organization. Individuals in departments or units where morale is high are more likely to believe communiqués from fellow workers merely because of their relationship to these employees. Conversely, when groups are fighting with each other it is common to hear each regarding the other's communiqués as self-serving, misleading, or just plain wrong.

Inconsistent Behavior

Inconsistency damages believability.

How a person says something often influences the way in which the message is received. When the speaker acts disinterested or unconcerned, the listener often attributes little importance to the message. If the speaker communicates something while going out the door and ends with the statement, "This is really important," the listener is not likely to believe it. Really important information is conveyed in a more quiet, calm, serious setting. When the message content is inconsistent with the message environment, the subordinate discounts its importance accordingly. Finally, when people say one thing but do another, their communiqués are eventually treated as noncredible. For example, the manager who tells his people that work begins at 8:30 A.M. sharp while he continues to show up at 9:10 A.M. is unlikely to reduce employee tardiness with his communiqué. The manager who tells her people that they all have to help hold down expenses while she gets approval to attend a meeting in Hawaii in December is unlikely to get much support for her cost-cutting efforts. There is simply too much inconsistency between what these managers are saying and what they are doing.

The Environment

The physical setting is also important.

Sometimes interpersonal communication fails because of noise or other environmental factors. If the listener cannot hear the speaker because too much activity is going on around them, communication breakdown is likely.

Environmental factors can also be more subtle, as when the setting is wrong. A manager who is talking to someone in the company cafeteria has to fight the never-ending interruptions by people who are dropping by to say hello or are waving from across the room. The same kinds of mental interruptions are also being encountered by the listener.

Finally, there is the environmental setting itself. The chairs in which the individuals are sitting, the colors in the room, and the location of the people (are they near each other or far apart?) all help convey nonverbal messages. These characteristics become part of the communication environment and can promote or hinder the reception of meanings.

Overcoming Interpersonal Communication Barriers

There are a number of ways to overcome interpersonal communication barriers. In large part, these methods are interdependent in that the use of one often involves the use of others. Nevertheless, for purposes of clarity we shall describe each individually. The following presents five of the most helpful approaches.[4]

---

4. See also Edward L. Levine, "Let's Talk: Tools for Spotting and Correcting Communication Problems," *Supervisory Management,* July 1980, pp. 25–37.

Accuracy and Empathy

Accuracy is vital . . .

Some communiqués fail because they are not conveyed accurately. Many examples of inaccuracy can be cited, some of which relate to written communication. When a manager is not confronting a subordinate on an interpersonal basis, the manager has to rely on message content to convey the desired meanings. To a large degree inaccuracy in written communications is related to perception. It can also be caused by other common written communication barriers, however, including poor sentence construction, improper grammar, lack of tact, and failure to plan the communiqué with the needs of the receiver in mind.[5]

One way to deal with problems like these is to use a written performance inventory like the one shown in Table 15–1. Notice that the problems involve qualities ranging from readability and correctness to appropriateness and thought. The inventory also emphasizes such behavioral factors as tact, diplomacy, motivational aspects, and persuasiveness.

as is empathy.

Empathy is the ability to see things from another person's point of view. When applied to communication, it means being able to look at a message from the receiver's standpoint and determine how this person will interpret the communiqué. To understand the receiver's standpoint, the manager must develop sensitivity. Perhaps the best way to develop empathy is by promoting two-way communication. As managers become more adept at this, their ability, figuratively speaking, to get into another person's shoes increases. Managers can also improve their ability to empathize by being able to read nonverbal communications.

Nonverbal Communication

Nonverbal communication incorporates a large range of factors, from body language to spatial relationships.[6] Body language relates to the way people sit, stand, and act in relation to others.[7] Spatial relationships relate to the surroundings in which the communiqué takes place. If managers understand the impact of this type of communication, they can use it effectively.

Body Language   In **body language,** body movements are used to communicate ideas, interests, opinions, and objectives on a nonverbal basis. When two people meet for the first time, the way they shake hands says something.

A handshake is important.

A soft handshake may be interpreted by the other person as a sign of weakness or an inability to take command. The same is true for the way people walk or stand. A fast, determined walk or an erect posture is often interpreted as a sign of a successful manager. Why? Because the individual seems to be saying, "I know where I'm going and I can see my way clear." He or she is coming across as believable and successful. Communiqués from such a manager are more likely to get the desired results.

So are the eyes . . .

Another important facet of body language is the eyes. Body language

---

5. John S. Fielden, "What Do You Mean You Don't Like My Style?" *Harvard Business Review,* May–June 1982, pp. 128–139.

6. Lynn Renee Cohen, "Nonverbal (Mis)Communication," *Business Horizons,* January–February 1983, pp. 13–17.

7. Julius Fast, *Body Language* (New York: Pocket Books, 1971).

Table 15–1

1. READABILITY

READER'S LEVEL
- ☐ Too specialized in approach
- ☐ Assumes too great a knowledge of subject
- ☐ So underestimates the reader that it belabors the obvious

SENTENCE CONSTRUCTION
- ☐ Unnecessarily long in difficult material
- ☐ Subject-verb-object word order too rarely used
- ☐ Choppy, overly simple style (in simple material)

PARAGRAPH CONSTRUCTION
- ☐ Lack of topic sentences
- ☐ Too many ideas in single paragraph
- ☐ Too long

FAMILIARITY OF WORDS
- ☐ Inappropriate jargon
- ☐ Pretentious language
- ☐ Unnecessarily abstract

READER DIRECTION
- ☐ Lack of "framing" (i.e., failure to tell the reader about purpose and direction of forthcoming discussion)
- ☐ Inadequate transitions between paragraphs
- ☐ Absence of subconclusions to summarize reader's progress at end of divisions in the discussion

FOCUS
- ☐ Unclear as to subject of communication
- ☐ Unclear as to purpose of message

2. CORRECTNESS

MECHANICS
- ☐ Shaky grammar
- ☐ Faulty punctuation

FORMAT
- ☐ Careless appearance of documents
- ☐ Failure to use accepted company form

COHERENCE
- ☐ Sentences seem awkward owing to illogical and ungrammatical yoking of unrelated ideas
- ☐ Failure to develop a logical progression of ideas through coherent, logically juxtaposed paragraphs

3. APPROPRIATENESS

A. UPWARD COMMUNICATIONS

TACT
- ☐ Failure to recognize differences in position between writer and receiver
- ☐ Impolitic tone—too brusk, argumentative, or insulting

SUPPORTING DETAIL
- ☐ Inadequate support for statements
- ☐ Too much undigested detail for busy superior

OPINION
- ☐ Adequate research but too great an intrusion of opinions
- ☐ Too few facts (and too little research) to entitle drawing of conclusions
- ☐ Presence of unasked for but clearly implied recommendations

ATTITUDE
- ☐ Too obvious a desire to please superior
- ☐ Too defensive in face of authority
- ☐ Too fearful of superior to be able to do best work

B. DOWNWARD COMMUNICATIONS

DIPLOMACY
- ☐ Overbearing attitude toward subordinates
- ☐ Insulting and/or personal references
- ☐ Unmindfulness that messages are representative of management group or even of company

CLARIFICATION OF DESIRES
- ☐ Confused, vague instructions
- ☐ Superior is not sure of what is wanted
- ☐ Withholding of information necessary to job at hand

MOTIVATIONAL ASPECTS
- ☐ Orders of superior seem arbitrary
- ☐ Superior's communications are manipulative and seemingly insincere

4. THOUGHT

PREPARATION
- ☐ Inadequate thought given to purpose of communication prior to its final completion
- ☐ Inadequate preparation or use of data known to be available

COMPETENCE
- ☐ Subject beyond intellectual capabilities of writer
- ☐ Subject beyond experience of writer

FIDELITY TO ASSIGNMENT
- ☐ Failure to stick to job assigned
- ☐ Too much made of routine assignment
- ☐ Too little made of assignment

ANALYSIS
- ☐ Superficial examination of data leading to unconscious overlooking of important pieces of evidence
- ☐ Failure to draw obvious conclusions from data presented
- ☐ Presentation of conclusions unjustified by evidence
- ☐ Failure to qualify tenuous assertions
- ☐ Failure to identify and justify assumptions used
- ☐ Bias, conscious or unconscious, which leads to distorted interpretation of data

PERSUASIVENESS
- ☐ Seems more convincing than facts warrant
- ☐ Seems less convincing than facts warrant
- ☐ Too obvious an attempt to sell ideas
- ☐ Lacks action-orientation and managerial viewpoint
- ☐ Too blunt an approach where subtlety and finesse called for

Source: John Feldon, "What Do You Mean I Can't Write?", *Harvard Business Review,* May–June 1964, p. 147. Reprinted with permission.

experts report that "our eyes (and face area around the eyes) are the most expressive and powerful parts of the body in terms of sending nonverbal messages."[8] Do not be fooled by the old adage that liars never look people in the eye. Actually, skilled liars have learned how to look right at their listener while telling their lies. On the other hand, changes in the eyes' pupil size may indicate whether a person is lying. Quite often when people lie they get emotional and this causes the size of their pupils to increase. Shifting of the eyes or blinking at a faster than normal rate also can indicate that a person is not being totally truthful. As the individual's stress level changes, the surface of the eyeball dries, causing increased eye movement. Still another thing to look for is "eye locks" between people during management meetings. Knowing who is looking at whom can help one understand the informal organization or the clique present in the meeting and figure out what different people are trying to do.

and touching . . .

Touching is another form of nonverbal communication. In addition to its use in shaking hands, touching is popularly used to convey orders and establish power relationships. Managers use it to let subordinates know who is in charge and to motivate them. For example, many managers put their hand on a subordinate's arm or shoulder when giving the person a directive. This touch creates a bond between them by which the manager says, "I'm counting on you to get this done right and I know you can do it. Now show me your stuff."

and physical attitude.

A physical attitude is another example of body language. It is a combination of gestures, postures, and face and hand signals. It is a composite of the way the individual acts when carrying out a task or completing an assignment. By studying this attitude, we get insights into the way the person goes about "selling" his or her ideas, objectives, and credibility. The manager uses body language as part of the strategy employed in swaying others to a given point of view. We need not confine our focus to managers exclusively, however. All organizational personnel use body language in communicating. Salespeople are an excellent example.

> . . . a good salesperson leans forward in an aggressive way when making a sales pitch; the prospect usually leans back. Also, a salesperson may use body language to spot certain facts about the prospective buyer. For example, sitting with arms folded is a traditional sign of resistance. When the prospect unlocks his arms and legs, he may be coming to the salesperson's side. Other traditional cues may be the prospect's uneasiness, displayed by juggling his foot or drumming his fingers, or doubt, displayed by holding his hands under his face.[9]

Space, Territory, and Status

Another nonverbal communication form is provided by space and territory. Where people stand in relation to others helps communicate a message. As seen in Figure 15–6, there are four principal zones of interaction in which interpersonal activities are conducted. The **intimate zone,** which

The four principal zones of interaction

8. Paul Preston, *Communication for Managers* (Englewood Cliffs, N.J.: Prentice-Hall, 1979), p. 159.

9. Richard K. Allen, *Organizational Management Through Communication* (New York: Harper & Row, 1977), p. 164.

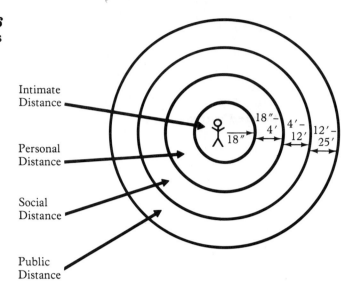

Figure 15–6
Personal Space Categories

Intimate Distance

Personal Distance

Social Distance

Public Distance

extends to approximately an arm's length from a person, is the area in which sensitive communications are carried out. This zone is typically reserved for close relationships. If strangers enter the area, they usually feel uncomfortable and start to move away. The **personal zone** extends from arm's length to approximately four feet from the body. This zone is for relatives and good friends. The **social zone** extends approximately four to eight feet from the body. This zone is the one in which we conduct most ordinary business and social activities. In offices, for example, most desks are wide enough to force people sitting on the opposite side to maintain this distance. The **public zone** extends approximately eight to 10 feet from the body and is the area over which individuals exert little personal control. Activity in this area can often be ignored. When individuals are engaged in conversation groups eight to 10 feet apart, they often can block out activities going on around them and concentrate on the affairs within the more comfortable social and personal zones.

How managers fill their own territory, such as their office, also helps them communicate with people. For example, an office's size and furnishings tell us something about the person. When a subordinate enters a manager's office and sits in front of the desk, he or she is typically in the manager's social zone. The subordinate and the manager are functioning in a typical superior-subordinate relationship. If the manager comes out from behind the desk and sits opposite the subordinate, this action is designed to put the subordinate at ease. The manager and the subordinate are communicating within the manager's personal zone.

Office size and furnishings convey status.

A related factor is such things as wall-to-wall carpeting, a wooden desk, plush furniture, and windows. All indicate executive status, which helps influence communication.

Positive Persuasion and Negotiation

Sometimes an interpersonal communiqué fails because the manager fails to use positive persuasion or negotiation or both. This is unfortunate because every time a manager communicates, he or she is actually attempting to persuade the receiver to accept a given point of view. Of course, sometimes the persuasive attempt is more obvious than other times. For example, consider the following dialogue:

Manager: Bob, I've been waiting for the right time to send you into the field. I think this is that time and I'd like you to take that new position we have open in Buffalo.

Subordinate: Why do I have to take a sales position in the field? Why can't I stay here at headquarters and continue working in marketing research?

Manager: The answer is simple. Every single person in this company who has succeeded in the marketing area has had field experience. It is a prerequisite for moving up.

Subordinate: You know, you're right. I never thought about that. Management does view this experience as important for promotion, doesn't it?

Positive persuasion is useful . . .

As you can see, the manager did more than just provide the subordinate with information. The manager presented it from the subordinate's point of view, showing this person why it was important to have field experience and using persuasion to get the message across. As we can see from the dialogue, the subordinate was positively influenced.

as is negotiation.

Sometimes the manager will find that negotiation is required, particularly when he or she is dealing with other managers or with subordinates who are key employees and work best when there is some give and take on both sides. When these conditions exist the manager has to be willing to concede some ground in order to gain an advantage. One of the simplest techniques is to concede something to the other party immediately. For example, the manager might say, "If you will give me some assistance on project A, I will reciprocate by helping you with project B." Or consider the case of the subordinate who wants to move to a new sales territory because he feels that his current one is too crowded (there are three other salespeople in the same area). In this case, the manager might negotiate by saying, "Okay, I'll give you the new territory you want, but you'll have to increase your sales there by 10 percent before you qualify for a bonus."

Sometimes the manager's freedom to give ground is limited and little equivocation on the part of the subordinates can be allowed. When this situation occurs, the manager must resort to more direct and assertive communication approaches. The manager has to say: "This is what I need you to do by next Thursday." "I've just talked to J.J. and we have to cut costs across the board by 10 percent. Let me have your plan for accomplishing this by the day after tomorrow." "I've asked you to drop by because I want you to look at these figures and provide me with a report by Friday regarding how we can cut fixed expenses by 7 percent." Notice in all of these examples that the manager is giving the subordinate a deadline. Instead of requesting assistance, he or she is demanding it. In each case, however, the manager is exercising tact and diplomacy. The subordinate is not being threatened; he or she is simply being informed of a business situation and told what is expected. If there is some reason why the subordinate cannot fulfill the manager's expectations, the subordinate has the opportunity to explain why. Some of the ways in which this feedback can be elicited are explained later in the chapter. For the moment, however, let us conclude our discussion of positive persuasion and negotiation by noting that the manager can adhere to a number of useful rules, including the following:

Some basic rules of persuasion and negotiation

1. Let the other person make the opening statement; you may learn the company's needs and be able to satisfy them on your terms.

2. Phrase questions for a positive answer. That gets the other side used to saying "yes," which is what you want said.

3. Make an early concession on a minor point; the other side may feel called upon to reciprocate.

4. Never promise unless you can deliver.

5. Never suggest a range of values; the other side will choose the end that suits it.

6. Defer key issues until the end, when you know most about the other side's stance.

7. Take a position of prominence. Stand up when talking, if necessary; don't let them stare down on you.

8. Pick the right time of day. Don't hit the boss when he or she is thinking of the next appointment.

9. Have the strong points of your case on the tip of your tongue, ready to be unleashed strategically.

10. Guard emotions. Never show anger unless you, know it will carry your point. Avoid gleeful expressions that could alienate.

11. Avoid snap decisions that you may regret. Better to insist on a delay to think the matter through.

12. Never underestimate the other side. It is already in a position of strength or you wouldn't be negotiating.

13. Remember that the boss is under pressure and faced with a decision that will reflect on him or her. Don't crowd.

14. Take along your sense of humor and be open and friendly.

15. Tell the truth. Exaggeration reduces your credibility.

16. Be yourself. Posturing is transparent.

17. End on a positive note regardless of the outcome, if only to express thanks and say that both sides have learned from the bargaining.

18. Adapt your messages to the receiver. Talk his or her language, and use examples and values that the receiver can appreciate.

19. Apply the "body messages" that strengthen your persuasive message.

20. Listen for the "relationship" messages when you negotiate or persuade. Don't simply rely on good content to bring about the persuasive goal you have in mind.[10]

---

10. Preston, *op. cit.*, pp. 190–191.

Listening

Listening involves four phases.

Another way to overcome interpersonal communication barriers is through effective listening. Research reveals that managers spend more of their time listening than they do reading, writing, or speaking.[11] Listening involves four distinct phases: hearing, attention, understanding, and remembering.

Hearing

Hearing takes place when the speaker's words are received by the listener. If the listener has poor hearing or there is noise in the local area, he or she may not hear what is being said.

Attention

Attention involves the selective perception of verbal messages. Usually a listener does not concentrate on each word but listens for the key ideas or phrases that he or she considers most important. The remainder of the message is either ignored or given minor consideration. The problem, of course, occurs when the listener daydreams or ignores some key facts or opinions. The best way to avoid this problem is by forcing oneself to focus on what is being said and fight attempts to daydream, interrupt, or throw off the speaker by acting bored, irritated, or disinterested.

Understanding

Understanding requires an accurate interpretation and evaluation of the message. What is the speaker *really* saying? One of the most effective ways to ensure understanding is to have the listener to recap the major points. If the manager is listening, when the subordinate is done the manager should say, "Okay, let me recap what I hear you saying." If the manager is speaking, a good recap question is, "Now before we close our discussion, I'd like you to give me your interpretation of what I want you to do." Remember that when trying to determine if understanding has occurred the manager must never ask *if* the other party understood the message but rather *what* the other party understood. The burden of understanding must be shifted to the listener. Then, if there is a problem the speaker can attempt to resolve it through additional clarification.

Remembering

The last stage of the listening process is remembering. The manager has to retain the essence of the message. Many managers retain information by taking notes and maintaining a file. In this way, they can consult their records when trying to recall what was said or agreed to. The human mind can remember and quickly recall only so much information. Note taking is an excellent supplement to the remembering stages of listening.

How can one improve one's listening ability? Some of the most useful guidelines include the following:

1. Ensure that the physical environment is conducive to listening by closing the door, shutting out noise, and sitting or standing close to the other person so as to create an atmosphere of trust and confidence.

2. Concentrate all of your physical and mental energies on listening to the other person.

3. Control your emotions by not getting upset at what the speaker says; otherwise, you will begin losing your concentration and the listening process will break down.

---

11. Ralph G. Nichols, "Listening: What Price Inefficiency?" *Office Executive*, April 1959, pp. 15–22.

Listening guidelines

4. Try to be objective by listening to the logic and consistency of the message rather than who is saying it.

5. Throughout the discussion demonstrate an interest and an alertness in what is being said; let the other person know you are listening.

6. Do not interrupt unless the speaker is confusing you by the order and logic of the presentation; and then do so only to get him or her back on track.

7. Encourage the speaker by nodding when you agree or understand a major point, and refrain from shaking your head "no" because this often throws the speaker off.

8. Listen closely for meanings and content but do not get hung up on specific words that are either used incorrectly or erroneously by the speaker.

9. As you listen, be sure you are fulfilling your basic responsibilities to the speaker by remembering (a) to concentrate on being appreciative, courteous, and kind (if this is an informal discussion); (b) to concentrate on fact, logic, and objectivity (if this is a formal discussion); and (c) to pinpoint important details, follow the logic as closely as possible, and be prepared to ask for additional clarity and explanation where needed (if this is a critical discussion).

10. Demonstrate patience with the speaker by acting calm and collected; give the speaker a chance to fully and completely explain what he or she has to say.[12]

Giving and Getting Effective Feedback

Both during and after listening, the manager must be able to give and get feedback. Feedback keeps the communication process going and ensures a continual flow of ideas back and forth.

Feedback is a circular process. After a message is transmitted to a receiver, a message is sent back to the sender. In the case of intrapersonal communication, the sender provides personal feedback. In the case of interpersonal communication, feedback comes from the receiver.

Feedback serves a number of important functions. First, it provides data from which to evaluate what is right or wrong about a particular communiqué. Second, it can serve to stimulate change by showing the receiver what needs to be communicated differently. Third, it reinforces the sender through rewards ("Keep it up, George, you're doing a fine job") or punishments ("Alex, you'll have to improve your performance or I'll have to let you go").

Getting feedback

The manager can employ a number of useful techniques to achieve effective feedback. Some of these relate to *getting* feedback. For example, the manager can make an opening statement like the following:

---

12. See also: John L. DiGaetani, "The Business of Listening," *Business Horizons,* October 1980, pp. 40–46.

- "Tell me more about this idea."
- "What makes you say that?"
- "How are you going to accomplish this?"

Notice that in each case the manager is encouraging the other party to offer feedback.

Giving feedback

Analogous statements can be used in *giving* feedback. For example, the manager might say:

- "Your ideas have merit, but before you continue let me share with you the latest thinking on this matter from top management."
- "I like your recommendations, but I think you should temper them in light of the latest financial report which I have just received."
- "Your progress has been much faster than I anticipated, so maybe now is the time for me to fill you in on the way in which your work is to dovetail with that of the people in advertising."

Again, feedback is promoted. The important thing to realize is that unless the manager can obtain and give feedback, communication remains basically a one-way process, and this is one of the major causes of communication breakdown.

Organizational Communication

Organizational communication involves the formal transfer of information throughout the hierarchy. In many cases, organizational communication is a series of interpersonal communiqués in which one person verbally conveys information to another and so on, until the last person in the chain or network is informed. At other times this communication pattern is of a written nature. Yet when the process is examined in an organizational context, as opposed to an interpersonal one, its dynamics are much greater because both formal and informal communication networks are involved.

Formal Communication Flows

There are four basic communication flows . . .

In an organizational setting, there are four basic communication flows: downward, upward, horizontal, and lateral. (See Figure 15–7.) **Downward communiqués** extend from superior to subordinate and are designed to convey such things as orders, directives, and guidelines for getting things done. **Upward communiqués** provide feedback on work assignments and are designed to keep the manager apprised of employee progress and problems. **Horizontal communiqués** occur between people on the same level of the hierarchy and are designed to ensure or improve coordination of work effort. **Lateral communiqués** take place between people on different levels of the hierarchy and are usually designed to provide information, coordination, or assistance to either or both parties.

These communiqués often are formal in nature, following the hierarchical chain of command, or they may be informal in nature and designed

Figure 15–7   Communication Flows

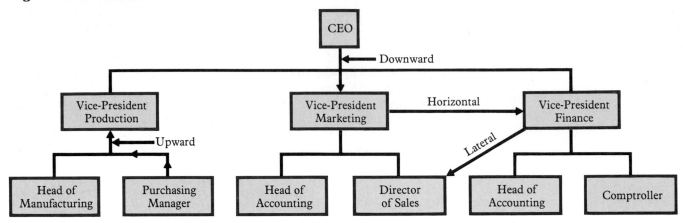

to cut through red tape and get things done as expediently as possible. When this approach is taken, the manager makes use of the informal organization.

Informal Communication Networks

Informal communication networks, often referred to as the **grapevine,** may take one of four forms: single strand, gossip, probability, or cluster chains. (See Figure 15–8.)

Figure 15–8   Informal Communication Networks

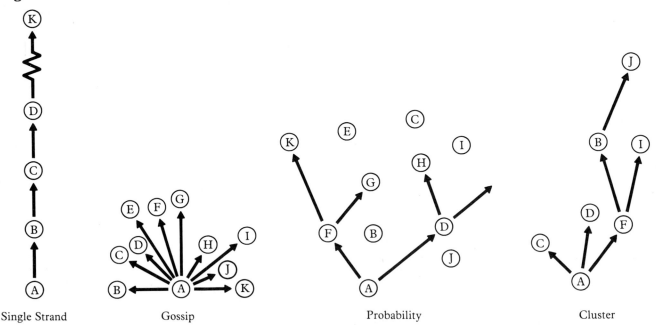

Source: Keith Davis, "Management Communication and the Grapevine," *Harvard Business Review,* September–October 1953, p. 45. Copyright © 1953 by the President and Fellows of Harvard College; all rights reserved. Reprinted with permission.

The **single-strand chain** is one in which each person passes the message to one other individual in the chain. The **gossip chain** is one in which the person with the information passes it to every other individual in the chain. The **probability chain** is one in which each person passes on information at random, without particular regard for who the receiver is, and the receivers use the same approach in their communication efforts. The **cluster chain** is one in which information is passed on selectively: the individual deliberately tells some people and does not tell others. Some of those getting the information pass it on to others while the remainder do not. The result is that a handful of people often account for all of the information that is passed along this informal chain.

Barriers to Organizational Communication

Whether messages are being transmitted along formal or informal lines, communication barriers can prevent understanding. Five of the major barriers to organizational communication are status, the number of links in the chain, expansion and contraction of messages, organizational politics, and economic threats.

Status

As noted earlier, in an organizational setting, who says something is often more important than what is said. This statement is particularly true when we examine communication in terms of hierarchical position. The president tends to have more status or credibility than the vice-president, who has more believability than the general manager, and so on down the line.

Status need not be confined to hierarchical position or title, however. Individuals with a reputation for getting things done, looking after their people, and knowing their job also have status in the organization. If a highly successful vice-president of sales says the new product line will produce revenues in excess of $5 million this year, the person's status may be enough to sway the president into agreeing to add $500,000 to the advertising budget despite arguments to the contrary by the vice-president of finance.

The problem with status, of course, is that the message itself is given secondary consideration. The source tends to be the most important factor.

Number of Links

When verbal communication is used, each person in the chain receives a message and then passes it on. Like the old parlor game, however, the message that goes in at the beginning is seldom the one that emerges at the end. Each person modifies it, adding or deleting some things in the process. Table 15–2 illustrates this phenomenon. Notice that each person not only changes the message slightly but also tends to drop out some negative information and embellish the positive picture.

Expansion and Contraction

Closely related to the barrier caused by the number of links is that of expansion and contraction of messages. As verbal messages come down

and four informal networks.

THE WALL STREET JOURNAL

"Send postcards to all our branch managers telling them of our economy drive."

Status is not confined to hierarchical level.

People modify verbal communiqués.

Table 15–2
The Number of Links Can Be a Communication Barrier

Unit Workers to Foreman	The new incentive payment plan doesn't look too bad. A couple of the guys are going to try it out. However, the salary offer is a good 2 percent too low and the fringe benefit package and new work rule proposals are lousy. We're telling the shop steward that if the company can't improve these, we should walk out.
Foreman to Supervisor	Some of the workers are going to support the new incentive payment plan, but the fringe benefit package and new work rules are going to be fought by the union. The proposed across-the-board salary increases are also a little low and we're going to get static on them, too.
Supervisor to Plant Manager	The workers seem fairly positive about our proposed incentive plan, but they don't like the fringe benefit package and they are somewhat opposed to the new work rules.
Plant Manager to Senior Vice-President	The workers really like the new incentive plan, but I don't think the union will agree to our fringe benefit package.
Senior Vice-President to Chief Executive Officer	The new incentive plan is being well received. We're getting a lot of positive feedback on it. I wouldn't be surprised if we had a new union contract signed by the end of next week.

the line, they tend to be expanded. Each person adds a little something. (See Table 15–3.) The reverse occurs with messages going up the line. In this case, they are contracted. One of the main reasons is that the higher one goes, the less time there is for long messages because time is money. A second reason for contraction is that managers typically hate to hear bad news. So the subordinate shortens the communiqué by reducing or **Messages are often altered.** omitting the negative parts. While this practice may be dangerous, no one wants to be penalized for being truthful, and some managers get the news and messenger confused. When it is time to evaluate the individual, all the manager remembers is the bad news the person always brings. This results in a less than accurate rating for the subordinate.

Organizational Politics

Throughout every organization there are managers who have built up little empires that they want to protect. There are also individuals with whom these managers work well and others with whom they do not. The result **Power plays may occur.** of all this is organizational politics, through which managers form alliances in an effort to achieve their objectives. Some people want to increase their power; others want money or autonomy over a given area of operations. Whatever the reason for the alliances, communication plays a key role in this process. People who know what is going on around the organization have the best chance to further their own aims. They are able to sift through the rumors and separate fact from fiction.

Organizational politics is a barrier to communication in three ways.

Table 15–3
Message Expansion

Chairman:	Bill, how many people would you estimate we have working in our claims division?
President:	Fred, how many people do we have employed in our claims division? Find out for me, would you?
Vice-President:	George, get me a list of everyone who works in our claims division. Include both part-time and full-time people at all levels as well as any new hires through last Friday. I think they want it because they are planning a cutback in personnel.
General Manager:	Kathy, I need a complete typewritten list of all employees in your division. Also, have their names, addresses, and telephone numbers included, as well as a copy of their latest performance evaluations. We're in the process of trimming back dramatically the number of personnel. We're going to get rid of a lot of deadwood.
Division Head:	Tim, I want a complete list of everyone working in this division as well as their addresses, phone numbers, latest performance evaluations, and job descriptions. Send a copy of all of this to the general manager. There's a cut-back coming and we'll have to decide who goes. Then block out all day tomorrow on my calendar so you and I can decide how we can cut 25 percent of the staff without losing too much efficiency.

First, in pursuing personal aims some managers keep people in the dark about what is really going on. Second, misinformation or rumor is typically started in an effort to camouflage what is happening. Third, managers or groups of managers begin making deals with each other in an effort to attain their objectives. When this occurs, communication is subverted for the sake of personal ambition, and the organization at large suffers.

Economic Threats

Whenever people's jobs and financial stability are threatened, they begin to communicate differently. An organization that introduces a new computer designed to help people with their paperwork must realize that these people may fear replacement by the machine. "If we cooperate," they reason, "we could end up out of work." As a result, they are not very open when explaining to the systems designer how the computer can be closely tied to their job. An analogous situation is found in the case of salespeople, who often do not tell the company about all of their sales leads for fear their sales quotas will be adjusted upward. "If you have that many potential customers," the sales manager will tell them "you'll have no trouble increasing your sales 30 percent above our previously agreed-upon quota."

People are threatened economically.

Economic threats are often psychological. The organization may have no intention of allowing anything negative to happen to the personnel, but the personnel are frightened and respond in a defensive manner. They reason that the less they communicate, the smaller the economic threat to them.

Overcoming Barriers to Organizational Communication

How can these barriers to organizational communication be overcome? Some of the most effective ways were discussed earlier when barriers to interpersonal effectiveness were examined. Five additional guides are extremely useful.

Know the Audience

Know who is getting the message.

Regardless of whether the manager is using written or verbal communication, and whether the formal or informal organization is involved, a knowledge of the audience is paramount. Who will receive this message? How are they likely to interpret it? What will the effect of this interpretation be? By answering questions like these, the manager follows the first rule of message communication: plan the communiqué.

Emphasize Value

Appeal to them.

One of the surest ways to get a person's attention and win him or her over is to communicate something of value or importance. Rather than saying, "We are putting in a new computer because it is faster and more efficient than doing this work by hand," the manager should say "This new computer we are going to be installing is designed to help you get your work done more efficiently and remove some of the time-consuming problems you are currently facing, allowing you more time for the rest of your job." Notice that the first statement presented the computer in terms of organizational value and could well be interpreted as an economic threat. The second presented the computer in terms of its value to the employee and was designed to win the latter's support of the work change. An emphasis on value can help overcome organizational communication barriers.[13]

Small Bites

Communicate simply.

Messages that are simple and to the point are more effective than those that are complex and indirect. Unfortunately, sometimes a message must be long and must contain a number of important ideas. It is important to break these messages into a number of small pieces. Then, presenting each piece, one at a time, the manager can gradually convey the entire message. The manager should begin with a simple point and then move on to the more complex parts. Unless the message is conveyed this way, the receiver will begin to lose attention or will become overwhelmed by its complexity.

Consult With Others

If the message is important, the manager should talk to someone about it or show it to someone. In this way if the message has a dual meaning or is likely to be misinterpreted by the receiver(s), the other person can notice

---

13. Edward L. Levins, "Let's Talk: Effectively Communicating Praise," *Supervisory Management,* September 1980, pp. 17–25.

Ask for advice.

the problems immediately. Remember that many of the messages we convey to others are crystal clear to us even though the receiver may have a great deal of difficulty with them. By allowing someone else to examine the communiqué, we reduce the chance of misinterpretation. Quite often others are able to pick up errors or interpretation problems that we ourselves (regardless of how many times we reviewed the message or read the memo), cannot see.

Encourage Trust and Openness

Encourage teamwork.

Another valuable guideline for improving organizational communication is that trust and openness among the personnel should be encouraged. This certainly is the best way to overcome the problems associated with organizational politics. As long as people succeed in their political maneuvers they will probably continue to engage in power plays. These kinds of activities must be discouraged through both words and deeds. Through words, the manager should make it clear that teamwork is a prerequisite for organizational success. Through deeds, the manager can give merit increases and promotions to members of the team who do not engage in dysfunctional organizational politics. Naturally, it is impossible to completely eliminate all efforts to use organizational communication channels to further one's own ends. These problems can be minimized, however, if the management sets its mind to this task.

In the final analysis, organizational communication effectiveness is determined by the willingness of the personnel to communicate with, trust, and work with others. If this organizational climate cannot be created, there is little chance that the enterprise can be either efficient or effective in the pursuit of its basic objectives.

Summary

1. Communication is the process of transferring meanings from sender to receiver. This process involves a source, encoding, a message, decoding, a receiver, and feedback. There are three basic forms of communication: intrapersonal, interpersonal, and organizational.

2. Intrapersonal communication involves the reception, processing, and transmission of information to oneself. This process was illustrated in Figure 15–4. A number of variables affect this process. Some of these include the self, the self-concept, personal orientation, personality traits, and defense mechanisms. Defense mechanisms include rationalization, projection, reaction formation, and repression.

3. Interpersonal communication involves the direct transmission of meanings between two or more persons. This process typically occurs on a face-to-face basis.

4. There are a number of barriers to interpersonal communication. Five of the major ones are perception, words, the source, inconsistent behavior, and the environment. Some of the best ways to overcome these barriers include accuracy, empathy, the effective use of nonverbal communication, positive persuasion and negotiation, listening, and giving and getting feedback.

5. Organizational communication involves the transfer of meanings up and down the hierarchy. Sometimes this occurs in the form of formal communication flows: downward, upward, horizontal, and lateral. At other times it takes place in the form of informal network communiqués as represented by the single strand, gossip, probability, or cluster chains.

6. Some of the most common barriers to organizational communication include status, the number of links, expansion and contraction, organizational politics, and economic threats. These barriers may be overcome by knowing the audience, emphasizing value, communicating in small bites, consulting with others, and encouraging trust and openness.

Key Terms

Achieved roles   Roles that are earned through accomplishment.

Ascribed roles   Roles based heavily on sex, age, kinship, and general place in society.

Body language   The use of body movements to communicate ideas, interests, opinions, and objectives on a nonverbal basis.

Cluster chain   An informal communication network in which individuals pass information on a selective basis.

Decoding process   The way in which a receiver interprets a message from a source.

Downward communication   Organizational communiqués that travel from superior to subordinate and are used to convey orders and directives.

Empathy   The ability to see things from another person's point of view.

Encoding process   The way in which a source conveys meaning to a receiver.

Gossip chain   An informal communication network in which the person with the information passes it to every other individual in the chain.

Grapevine   Informal communication networks used to convey information throughout the hierarchy.

Horizontal communication   Organizational communiqués that occur between people on the same level of the hierarchy and are designed to ensure coordination.

Interpersonal communication   The direct transmission of meanings between two or more persons.

Intimate zone   The zone of interaction that extends to approximately an arm's length from one's body.

Intrapersonal communication   The way in which individuals receive, process, and transmit information to themselves.

Lateral communication   Organizational communiqués that take place between people on different levels of the hierarchy and are usually designed to provide information, coordination, or assistance to either or both parties.

Organizational communication   The formal transfer of information throughout the hierarchy.

Personal zone   A zone of interaction that extends from an arm's length to approximately four feet from the body.

Probability chain   An informal communication network in which individuals pass information on a random basis.

Projection   The ignoring of certain traits, motives, or behavior in oneself and the attributing of them to others.

Public zone   A zone of interaction that extends approximately eight to 10 feet from the body.

Rationalization   An attempt to justify one's failures or inadequacies.

Reaction formation   Dealing with undesirable behavior by taking the opposite point of view.

Repression   Keeping down unpleasant or unaccepted feelings.

Selective perception   The acceptance from the external environment of only those stimuli that are of most importance or value to the receiver.

Self-concept   How people feel about themselves.

Single-strand chain   An informal communication network in which each person passes the message to one other individual in the chain.

Social zone   A zone of interaction that extends approximately four to eight feet from an individual.

Upward communication   Organizational communiqués that travel from subordinate to superior and are designed to provide feedback on progress and problems.

Questions for Analysis and Discussion

1. In your own words, what is meant by the term communication?

2. How does the communication process work? Be sure to include in your answer a discussion of the source, encoding process, message, decoding process, receiver, and feedback.

3. How does the self affect intrapersonal communication? How does the self-concept influence intrapersonal communication?

4. How does the intrapersonal communication process work? What role is played by intrapersonal variables such as personal orientation, personality traits, and defense mechanisms?

5. In what way are the following barriers to interpersonal communication: perception, words, the source, inconsistent behavior, and the environment? Be complete in your answer.

6. How can a manager improve the accuracy of his or her written communiqués? Include a discussion of Table 15–1 in your answer.

7. What is meant by the term empathy? What role does it play in effective communication?

8. What does a manager need to know about nonverbal communication? Offer four useful guidelines.

9. What rules should managers follow in using persuasion and negotiation? Offer six of the most beneficial guides.

10. How can a manager improve his or her listening skills? Be sure to include in your answer the four phases of listening as well as at least five useful guidelines.

11. How should a manager go about giving feedback? Getting feedback? Provide at least two opening statements for achieving each of these forms of feedback.

12. There are four basic communication flows. What does this statement mean? Be complete in your answer.

13. Informal communication networks take one of four forms. What are these four? Identify and describe each.

14. In what way are the following barriers to organizational communication: status, number of links, expansion and contraction, organizational politics, and economic threats?

15. How can managers overcome barriers to organizational communication? Identify and describe four ways.

Case	# Getting the Business

It seems that every Monday morning is a busy one for Karl Proctor, vice-president of the Commercial Loan Department. Monday of this week was particularly hectic because Karl had a very important meeting with a potential customer.

This individual had submitted his company's financial report to Karl a week ago. He told Karl, "I'd like to get a line of credit for $500,000. My construction business is expanding rapidly and my current bank is unable to provide me with the degree of financing I require. I need a bank I can grow with. I've looked around and gotten some excellent comments about your institution from other people in my line of work. I'd like to switch my business over to your bank if you can accommodate my credit needs. I want to make a decision within 10 days, however. If your bank turns me down, I'll need time to find someone else before my next fiscal year begins in 30 days."

Karl reviewed this applicant's financial records and did some in-depth checking. The man's business is doing quite well, but as a contractor, he is subject to economic ups and downs. A loan of $500,000 could be disastrous to the bank if the business went under. As a result, during his meeting with the businessman this Monday Karl tried to get him to agree to provide full collateral for all loans. Here is how part of the conversation went:

Karl: I've looked over your application and notice that at your previous bank you had a credit line of $200,000. Your business seems to get on fine with this line; you never have a real cash shortage. Why do you need a larger line now?

Applicant: I want to expand and bid on some new jobs across town. I know the economy is not in great shape, but these remodeling contracts I'm looking at promise to provide a return of 21 percent net.

Karl: I see. That sounds promising. However, I should point out that the assets on your business are only worth $210,000. If we were to give you a $500,000 line of credit you'd have to cosign as an individual and be willing to put up your personal assets as collateral.

Applicant: Oh, wow! I don't have to do that at my current bank. Why would I have to do it now?

Karl: Because your business assets have always had a greater value than your current line of credit. However, if you increase your loan line to $500,000 you'll have to increase your collateral coverage.

Applicant: Gee, I don't know. Maybe I should stay with my current bank.

Karl: You certainly can do that, but I can assure you that you'll also have to provide additional loan collateral coverage. Besides, for you $500,000 is probably only a temporary level. In two to three years you'll undoubtedly want to go higher. And since you are a fairly conservative risk taker, the chances of your having to sell personal assets to cover business loans is not very great. Additionally, our bank offers more business services than your current one. We're more equipped to help businesspeople meet their needs. Your bank gears itself toward individual accounts, not company business. Think about what I've said and call me later in the week. If you are interested in doing business with us, I'll bring your reports to our Wednesday weekly meeting and see what I can do.

The businessman thanked Karl, told him he would think about it, and left. The next day he called and told Karl he wanted the $500,000 line of credit and would agree to pledge his personal assets. This was approved at the Wednesday meeting. Early this morning the businessman's accountant was over at the bank opening up the necessary accounts and taking care of the requisite paperwork.

1. How did Karl manage to overcome the businessman's opposition to pledging his personal assets? What communication tools and techniques did he use?

2. In terms of effective negotiation, what principles or rules did Karl employ? Be complete in your answer.

3. How did Karl use the communication principle of "talk in terms of value to the other party"? How important was this in getting the businessman's account? Explain.

You Be the Consultant

Helping Sandra

Sandra Wentworth, administrator at a large metropolitan hospital, attends many meetings every week. One of the most recent was a meeting with the board of trustees. The board had received a report the previous month from a national health care accrediting association. The report criticized the hospital for not having more up-to-date equipment. It also strongly suggested that the hospital consider new construction to replace some of its antiquated facilities. The board took the report very seriously. "We have to revise our budget and address these new expenditures," the chairperson told the board. "And the sooner we do so, the better off we'll be. Can you imagine the problems we'll have if the local papers find out that some of our facilities are considered less than adequate by a national accrediting association?"

Sandra objected strenuously. "If you change the proposed budget and allocate additional funds for new equipment and new construction, you'll have to cut back on other important needs," she argued. "In particular, you'll be unable to give the employees anything more than a three percent raise, and the union won't take less than seven percent. We're negotiating with them right now, and our initial offer was three percent. We'll have to improve that percentage, and if the money isn't there, what will we do?" The board promised to rethink the matter, but Sandra has a feeling that they want to buy some new equipment and authorize some new building immediately. The rest might be funded over the next one or two years, but some steps have to be taken this year.

After the meeting Sandra decided to send a memo to the union representatives explaining the financial bind in which the hospital found itself and asking the union to "work with the management in meeting its primary obligation—the health and well-being of the patient; then we can turn our attention to the matter of personnel salaries." The memo was sent immediately, and within an hour union representatives were in Sandra's office accusing her of trying to undermine union efforts to get the best for their people. "You can hardly expect us to settle for a three percent raise when the cost of living is far in excess of this," one representative said. "Also, the new equipment and building should be totally funded out of a bond issue, not from general revenues. These funds are for day-to-day operations and should be used for salaries." Sandra promised to get back with the union representatives after she had again met with the board. This meeting will be held the day after tomorrow.

Later that morning Sandra had a call from Paul Reese, head of Public Relations. He feels that Sandra is not putting in enough time in the local community. He would like her to attend a breakfast or luncheon or give a talk at least twice a week. "You need the public visibility," he told her. "Community support is so important. Every time I can get your name in the paper or get you TV coverage, it helps the hospital." Sandra agrees with the man's basic philosophy. She doesn't see how she can afford this much time away from the institution, however. There are so many things to do that cannot be delegated to associate administrators. On the other hand, she knows she is going to have to get out at least once a week.

Sandra is concerned because when she was on a two-day-a-week outside speaking schedule, her assistants simply did not follow her orders. As a result, the work piled up and she was soon inundated with time-consuming, in-house tasks. This is when she stopped her outside schedule. "Sometimes," she told Paul, "if you want things done right you have to do it yourself. It seems that my biggest problem is communication. Everything I do is either misinterpreted or fouled up. I've been thinking about bringing in an expert on communication to help analyze the various communication barriers we have around here and how we can deal with them. I really think this would help us a lot. If you know of anyone, let me know."

Your Consultation

Assume that you have been called in to help Sandra with her communication problems. What kinds of interpersonal and organizational communication problems do you see in the case? What would you recommend that Sandra do in dealing with each? Be as complete as possible in your answer.

Comprehensive Cases

Gala Food Services, Inc.

Gala Food Services, Inc. provides food services to colleges, hospitals, and businesses. The firm was founded in 1948 by three students at a small college in Virginia. During their senior year, one of the students arranged to take over the operation of the cafeteria. Within a month, the three had the business operating profitably. During the year that followed, the new graduates incorporated the business and proceeded with their plans to become a specialized college food service company. Along the way, Gala diversified into a number of areas, including fast food restaurants. The focus of this case is on the operations they started and have maintained at the small Virginia college.

Operations

Under an arrangement with the management of the college, Gala, Inc. currently provides food for the entire student body. This service extends to live-in students who eat in their dormitory cafeteria, nonresident students who eat in the open cafeteria, and faculty who have their own dining room. Gala also caters special events on campus and operates all of the vending machines on the grounds. Additionally, the firm has a contract to provide meals to a monastery located across the street from the college. These meals are all prepared at the Gala kitchen located on campus. The resident students who make up the bulk of Gala's business receive excellent service. The students are consulted about their food preferences, and if someone needs a special type of meal, Gala is happy to accommodate the person. The company feels that its main objective should be to supply wholesome, palatable, and nutritious food in an efficient and courteous manner.

The physical location of the operations has never changed. Gala is located in the basement of the college's admissions building. This building is somewhat antiquated, so it has been necessary to spread out the overall operation. As a result, the food preparation and serving areas lie at opposite ends of the building from each other. The main office of the college is situated between the two. The food preparation area has its own bakery and salad preparation room, both located even farther in the back of the building, away from the rest of the operation. This layout has caused some problems for Gala's management. So has the operation at the monastery, because delivery of the food must be closely coordinated with the schedule of activities there. Unfortunately, until a new and more efficient building is erected on campus, Gala has no alternative but to work things out as best it can.

The firm has adopted five objectives and standards that it uses to guide operations. Its goals are to

1. maintain a high standard of quality in food, service, and sanitation;

2. establish a sound and stable organization;

3. provide good working conditions for the personnel;

4. develop a sense of responsibility within each employee; and

5. follow a sound, judicious philosophy in spending money and expanding operations.

Some of the people who work for Gala at its college facility are full-time employees. Most of these individuals are more than 30 years old. The rest are part-time college students, along with a few high school students. In all, 25 are full-timers and 75 are part-timers.

Gala likes to stress its "triangle approach" to the management of operations. This triangle consists of three factors: people, product, and service. In its handbook, entitled *The Gala Way*, the triangle or bond is represented this way:

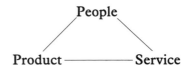

Gala believes that these three factors must be in harmony if the operation is to succeed. If one is out of step with the others, efficiency breaks down.

The Structure

Gala's food service organization at the college is presented in Exhibit 1. At the top of the structure is the district manager. This person's main function is to serve as the principal supervising officer for the operation. She indirectly supervises and directs all activities and monitors and implements quality standards in all areas of the operation by working closely with the food service director.

The food service director is Gala's principal representative at the college. In conjunction with the district manager, this person carries out the planning, budgeting, analysis, and reporting related to the operation. He also controls the account expenditures.

The food service director works closely with the two food service managers, who are responsible for assisting with the direction and supervision of the food service. One of the food service managers is responsible for the monastery operation and the vending machine operation on campus. The other is in charge of food service at the college itself. Both are responsible for ordering and purchasing the food as well as maintaining proper levels of inventory and working with the food service director. Although the director is more concerned with control of the overall operation and

Exhibit 1
The Gala Food Services
Hierarchy

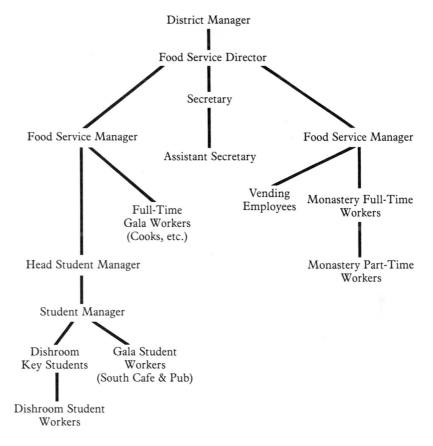

the managers are more concerned with seeing that operations are carried out efficiently, the director is charged with coordinating their efforts.

The director has a secretary and an assistant secretary. The secretary performs typing functions, keeps the district manager's calendar, and is responsible for ensuring a smooth flow of office work. The assistant secretary, hired only recently, is really more of a bookkeeper than anything else. Her duties include keeping the books for the vending operations, counting money taken in from the vending machines, preparing cash drawer banks for the snack area, checking student time cards, and handling other financially related tasks.

The head student manager is responsible for supervising the student manager, hiring and firing part-time personnel, and handling special food orders, catering requests, and banquets.

The student manager works closely with the head student manager and is assisted by dishroom area key students. Two of these students oversee the operation of the dishroom, ensuring that all workers are kept busy and that the area is well organized and clean.

Beneath the student managers in the hierarchy are the full-time and part-time workers, whose jobs extend from cooking and serving the food to cleaning up the dishes, pots and pans. These workers are located both at the college and in the monastery. Most of them work in the south café area.

Since the organization is small, virtually every person in the hierarchy has an influence on the operation's overall effectiveness and efficiency.

Communication flow can start anywhere in the hierarchy and move in any direction. Much of the decision making is carried out by the director, the food service director, and the food service managers. The student managers are also encouraged to share any ideas that they might have regarding more efficient operations. These opinions are listened to very closely. A diagram of the communication flows at Gala is presented in Exhibit 2.

Unfortunately, there do seem to be some communication problems at both the college and monastery operations. For example, in the college operation, there seem to be problems between the food service director and the food service manager. Some of the workers claim that they receive conflicting orders from the two. Others say that occasionally a manager will tell them the way to do something and an hour later tell them just the opposite. Furthermore, although the director is supposed to be in charge of the manager, the personnel feel that it sometimes works in reverse. On the other hand, the director sometimes jumps over the manager and gives orders directly to the head student manager. The same is true in the case of the head student manager and the student manager. Sometimes the employees wonder who is in charge. Still other problems, depicted in Exhibit 2, are that people communicate directly up the line, bypassing their boss in the process. As the district manager said the other day, "Some-

Exhibit 2
Gala Foods Communication
Flow

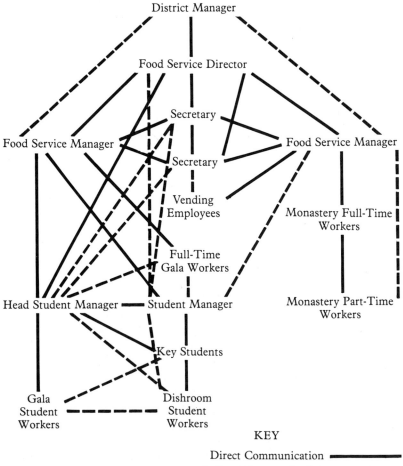

times I think we have no formal organization around here, only an informal one. And the informal one is just too darn informal."

1. Drawing on Exhibits 1 and 2, how would you describe the formal communication network in this organization? The informal communication network?

2. What specific communication problems exist in this organization? Use the data in the case and your interpretation of the two exhibits to arrive at your conclusions.

3. If you were advising the district manager regarding how to straighten things out, what would you recommend? Be complete in your answer.

4. Would your recommendations bring about any change in the organization's way of doing things? Would you make the structure more formal and less informal? How would your changes affect the future interpersonal relations of the personnel?

5. Are there any communication problems that the organization must learn to live with because it is too inefficient to change them? What are they? Describe each.

6. What managerial lessons can be drawn from this case that can help a manager become a more effective communicator? Identify and describe at least three.

Central Clothing, Inc.

Background

Central Clothing, Inc. (CCI) was founded in 1931 by Howard J. Girlax, Sr. When he opened his small shop on a side street of a downtown metropolitan district, Howard had no idea how large the operation eventually would become. In 1984, CCI had stores at five locations throughout the city, including the original building where it all began, and gross sales were in excess of $35 million.

Over the years, CCI has been well thought of in the community. Recently, however, there has been a distinct change in its product lines. Starting around 1976, the stores began extending their offerings to include more low-price and "trendy" clothing, and prices have dropped slightly compared with their earlier levels. A recent survey of store patrons reveals that CCI is seen as having changed from a traditional clothing retailer to one that offers more fad merchandise. The average age of the customers has declined, and research reveals that more and more of the clientele consists of out-of-towners who have moved to the metropolis within the last 18 months. The percentage of customers who have lived in the city for more than 5 years has dropped from 83 percent of all customers in 1978 to 44 percent in the survey taken last month.

The organization is still a family-run business. When Mr. Girlax, Sr. retired as president in 1971, he was replaced by his brother Samuel. Today, the presidency is held by Mr. Girlax's oldest son, Henry.

Organizational Structure

Henry Girlax sees his job as that of keeping control of all aspects of the business. "I have to maintain the image that my father helped create," he told the board of directors last month. Helping him keep control of the business are a number of staff personnel and store managers who are responsible for overseeing operations there. It is Henry who approves all long-range plans, however, and decides how operations will be carried out.

Reporting directly to him are four vice-presidents: finance, advertising, stores, and personnel. These people serve in a staff capacity, providing advice and assistance as well as coordinating their efforts with those of the respective store managers. (See Exhibit 3.)

The five store managers each operate in a semiautonomous fashion. Each manager is responsible for virtually everything that happens in the respective store. For the most part, the managers keep a tight rein on things. In order to maintain effective communication with the personnel throughout their unit and ensure that everything is going according to plan, all store managers hold weekly meetings. These meetings are conducted every Monday morning at 10 A.M. and last exactly one hour. At this time, problems are discussed, complaints are aired, compliments are

Exhibit 3   Organizational Chart: Central Clothing, Inc.

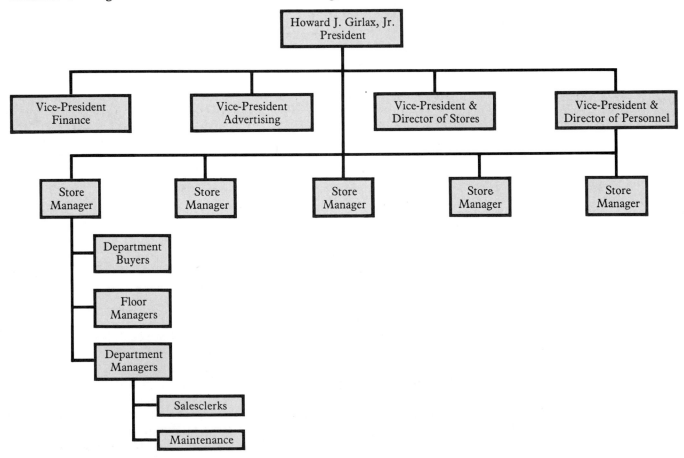

paid, product lines meriting advertising and sales promotion are identified and discussed, and other general business is transacted. During the week, in order to continue to keep a finger on the store's pulse, each store manager is expected to circulate through the store and actually lend a hand in selling to, or assisting, customers. Some of the store managers have drawn up a monthly itinerary for themselves, showing which department they intend to work in for an hour each day. The workers like this idea. They feel that the store manager is coming down to their level and getting involved in some of the nitty-gritty work.

Reporting directly to the store managers are the department buyers, who are responsible for choosing and purchasing the merchandise that will be sold in their particular department. Every three months top management formally recognizes the buyers who were most successful in selecting product lines or offerings that sold well. Every one of the buyers would like to win this recognition, although all admit that it is very difficult to determine exactly what will and will not sell. Buyers are continually scouring consumer magazines, looking at product lines and offerings advertised by the competition, and talking to their customers regarding what they like or dislike about new offerings. Buyers are also responsible for directing floor fixture arrangements and ensuring that the latter are tasteful and appealing.

Floor managers perform a variety of different tasks. Some of these include closing and opening all cash registers at the beginning and end of the day, handling returns and customer complaints and, when the department manager is unable to do so, making sure that department personnel are all performing their designated tasks.

Department managers report directly to the store manager. These individuals perform many of the same tasks as floor mangers. Additionally, these managers are responsible for handling markdowns and markups and ensuring that departmental personnel know what they are supposed to be doing. Department managers are also charged with training and developing their respective personnel.

Sales clerks report to their respective department managers. The jobs of these clerks vary according to the shift they work. Some are full-time and others are part-time and their status affects their job assignments. Full-time people assist the department managers in taking care of markdowns and markups. They also handle the cash register, assist customers, remove unwanted merchandise from the fitting rooms and return it to the proper place on the sales floor. Most of the part-time personnel also perform these tasks, but they are not allowed to approve checks and "okay" returns. This authority is held only by full-time salesclerks.

The maintenance people are responsible for all cleaning and repair work around the store. Most of these people are part-time personnel. They are divided up around the store and assigned to one specific department manager who supervises their work. Occasionally, the store manager will request that some of these people be assigned directly to a storewide project. In this case, the most senior member of the maintenance crew is charged with seeing that the work is done properly. The latter reports directly to the store manager on this particular project. For the most part, however, maintenance people work directly out of a particular department.

Personnel

The personnel can be grouped into two categories: workers and managers. Many of the workers are part-time only. All of the managers are full-time.

Store Workers

Most of the nonmanagerial staff are unskilled workers upon whom management relies to handle sales and maintenance-related functions. Many of the workers are recent high school graduates who will not remain with CCI very long. They view the company as a stepping stone to something better. Some of the workers are female college graduates who have returned to the workforce now that their children are old enough to go to school. In most cases, these women are trying to supplement the family income. They do not work for money alone, however. Many of them like the congenial atmosphere at CCI and feel it is a relaxing job that helps break the monotony of work around the house.

In the main, most of these workers are highly motivated by money. The average hourly wage is in the $3.50 to $4 range. No part-timer makes more than $5 an hour and both the workers and the management admit that a wage increase of 15 to 25 cents is a big incentive to the part-timers.

Most of these people work a minimum of 16 hours a week, a standard established by management more than 15 years ago. The logic behind the 16-hour rule is that it just does not pay either the company or the worker to have an employee come in for one or two hours at a time. Everyone works four-hour shifts and the typical pattern is to work two shifts during the week and one full day on the weekend. A year ago, management attempted to experiment with this "two shifts plus a weekend day" and allow everyone to choose their own work times. The decision was disastrous. Virtually no one was willing to work on weekends. Everyone wanted to work four weekdays or weeknight shifts. The new plan was abandoned two weeks after it was initiated.

The full-time unskilled workers represent only a small percentage of the worker force. These individuals are on a five-day schedule and rotate weekends so that once a month each of them works a Saturday-Sunday assignment. In this way, management ensures that there are always some full-time people around to provide continuity of operations. This is particularly important when one of the four-hour shifts is going off and the next one is coming on. Sometimes as much as 20 minutes may elapse during which sales and customer assistance drop off since the number of employees actively working declines dramatically. The full-time people try to take up the slack at this point in time.

Store Management

Most of the store managers are young women who are fresh out of college. Some are in the process of completing their degree, and a small number have worked their way up the line, having met the in-house management promotion requirements of five years of store experience before one can be considered for promotion.

Most of these managers are hard workers and they try very hard to do the best possible job. Basically their functions are to plan the activities of their respective areas and supervise the personnel who work there.

A recent meeting of store managers has revealed that there are a number of problems with these managers. The most important one is that they really do not know how to deal effectively with customers or employees. Several reasons have been cited for this problem. One is the level of maturity (or immaturity) of these young women. A second is their inexperience in the business. A third is that promotions at CCI are slow in coming, and many young managers feel that even if they do an outstanding job they will not be properly rewarded.

Another complaint raised about the store management personnel is that they are disorganized both in their work approach and the design and layout of their respective work areas. They also fail to manage their time well, often letting things slide until the last minute and then hurrying to get the job finished within the time period.

Finally, concerns have been raised about the fact that many of the store management personnel are as young as, or younger than, the employees they supervise. Because of this closeness in age, the manager and subordinates almost merge into one large clique. It is known that the two groups often socialize on a personal level both at work and outside. Top management feels that this impedes their ability to get things done effectively at the store.

The Consultant's Report

Three months ago, CCI had a consulting firm come in to analyze its operations. The consultants visited each store and talked to customers, workers, and managerial personnel. Here are some of their findings:

1. The sales quotas for each store are being met. In fact, return on investment this year is higher than it has been in the last five years.

2. Many customers are dissatisfied with the service they receive at the stores. The biggest complaint is that when they want to buy something it is difficult to find a salesperson willing to wait on them. A second major complaint is that the personnel discourage returns of merchandise, and customers who persist in their efforts for a refund often find themselves having to talk to a member of the upper management staff to get the return "okayed."

3. The departmental managers are concerned with the increase in tardiness, absenteeism, unkempt working display areas, and in general, the totally passive outlook of the personnel. The biggest complaints are made against the part-time people. One manager summed up her feelings with the cliche, "We just can't seem to hire good workers any more."

4. The part-time personnel feel that hourly wages are too low. The full-time personnel feel that salaries need to be raised. The managerial personnel believe that there is little chance for upward mobility and that to get ahead one has to stand in line for years.

The consulting firm wound up its report by telling management that the problem was one of motivation. The last part of the report said, "You have all of the help you need to run the stores. However, unless an effective motivational plan can be designed, you will continue to evidence high absenteeism and turnover." Mr. Girlax agrees with these comments and hopes to change things dramatically within the next few months.

1. What type of motivational system is CCI using at the present time? What is the philosophy of the top management regarding motivation? What does it feel really motivates the personnel?

2. How can the part-time personnel be motivated to do a better job? Offer some suggestions for action.

3. What should the company do about motivating the full-time nonmanagerial personnel? How would this motivation package differ from the one offered to the part-time personnel? Compare and contrast the two.

4. How can management motivate the managerial personnel? What needs to be done?

5. After reviewing your answers to the first four questions, review the case and list all of the problems you can find. Compare these problems with your recommended solutions. Are there any problems that are still unresolved? What would you recommend be done about them?

6. Of all the problems in this case, which one is the most crucial? Why? In what order should Mr. Girlax address the problems that currently exist? Offer him a priority approach.

7. Will Mr. Girlax be willing to carry out all of your recommendations or are there some changes he will not make? Explain, being sure to offer your interpretation of the implications that your answer has for future work performance at CCI.

The Kendall Food Corporation

Background

For five years, Ben Martin was the operating manager of a small Kendall Food store. Three months ago, he was promoted to resident manager of one of the firm's growing suburban units. During the first few months, Ben began an orientation process of getting to know the store, the managers, and the employees. He held weekly meetings with each department manager, with the operating manager, Allan Bartow, in attendance. (See Exhibit 4.) At these meetings he openly discussed problems, suggestions, and personnel, with emphasis on the future career paths of the people.

Having been recognized because of the outstanding job he had done at his previous store, Ben approached his new assignment in a similar way. He did so in close cooperation with Allan, who has been with the store for two years and knows all of the employees very well.

As the two men proceeded to plan the store's operations, Allan pointed

Exhibit 4   Kendall Food Corporation Organizational Structure

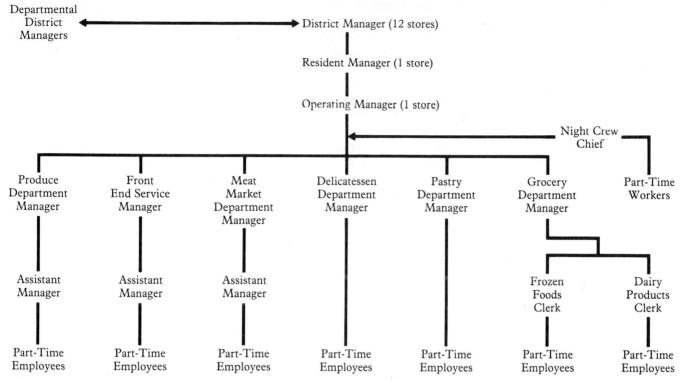

out a potential problem in the Grocery Department. The problem has been brewing for about a year. It involves Tom Cartwell and Randall Mocantee.

Tom Cartwell, the dairy products clerk, has been a participant in the management trainee program offered by the firm's home office. The procedure for a typical trainee is as follows:

- *Step #1*—Part-time employment (during college).

- *Step #2*—Assignment to a departmental opening for a 40-hour trainee.

- *Step #3*—Transfer every six months to a different department to learn operations there.

- *Step #4*—Assignment to night crew chief to learn the shelving and ordering procedures.

- *Step #5*—Assignment as frozen foods or diary products clerk.

- *Final*   —Eligible for promotion to grocery manager (the final step before being considered for operating manager). Tom is currently at step five.

Tom, according to Allan, is very upset with the grocery manager, Randall Mocantee. According to Allan, Tom complains continually about decisions by Randy that have made Tom look bad. Some of these have included the over-ordering and under-ordering of products, and the reassigning of key part-time help to other Grocery Department jobs. Tom's biggest concern is that he will not be able to do an effective job if Randy does not provide better assistance.

In relating this scenario to Ben, Allan reported that Randy had denied the allegations and said that Tom was an over-aggressive trainee. "He just doesn't understand how the overall department must operate. He thinks only of himself," Randy had told Allan.

In other departmental meetings, the managers all had expressed enthusiasm with Tom Cartwell, describing him as a steady, dedicated worker who showed great future promise. Some of the managers also had expressed concern that Randy was allowing himself to be unnecessarily riled by a young, aggressive trainee.

Ben realizes the potential seriousness of this problem. This type of situation could degenerate and spread through the store as a "hot topic" for gossip. In addition, Ben believes each man could actually be ruining his personal chances for promotion because of this problem.

After checking things out for himself, Ben has come to the conclusion that (1) Tom is an aspiring young trainee who has proven himself in other departments during his apprenticeship; and (2) Randy is next in line for the operating manager position, whether at this location or one of the other 12 in the district, and has proven himself over the years while gaining the respect of administrative personnel in the district office.

The course of action that Ben chooses will affect the store, the career paths of Tom and Randy, and, of course, his own stature as operating manager of the unit. The decision will require careful analysis and consideration of all factors.

Alternative Courses of Action

Ben can choose to transfer Tom Cartwell from the store, seeking to place him at another location. Or he may seek to get Randy assigned to another unit as operating manager.

Either of these alternatives requires consultation with the district office and an opening at another store. These uncontrollable factors make the alternatives somewhat inappropriate for the short term, although they are viable for the long-run career interests of both employees.

In approaching short-term solutions, Ben can convene an immediate meeting of Tom and Randy to discuss the problem and possibly negotiate a solution. With this approach, Ben would act as a facilitator in allowing his two employees a chance to communicate and formulate their own solutions. (Of course, this assumes they would actually come to some workable solutions during the course of the meeting.) Ben himself would have to demonstrate a willingness to allow the employees to solve their own problems.

Another short-run solution would be for Ben to conduct individual meetings with Tom and Randy to explain how he sees this problem developing. This possibility would also allow each employee his own input while letting Ben maintain his authority over the situation as he explained the outcome or future repercussions that could result if the matter were not resolved. Such a counseling session could provide insights for both employees and demonstrate Ben's immediate concern for his people. The negative side would be that each session could prove worthless, with each employee simply placing the blame on the other.

Finally, Ben could choose to do nothing at the present time. This alternative would leave the situation to be worked out by itself. Of course, while it would indicate that the conflict is only minor, this failure to act might foster a major problem (as indicated earlier in this case).

Ben sees himself as a new manager with a new store, facing an old management dilemma. The alternatives are there. The next move is up to him.

1. What course of action should Ben choose? Why?

2. Discuss the alternatives in relation to Ben's role as a manager.

3. Discuss the communications problems that are evident in this case and relate these to management.

4. What action should Tom and Randy take in regard to their careers?

5. Evaluate the importance of understanding effective communication in management.

6. Evaluate and discuss Ben's role as an effective communicator. Why is it such an important factor in management?

7. What if Ben chooses to do nothing? Discuss the possible outcome.

8. Compare and contrast each alternative in relation to the communication aspect of management.

Controlling Organizational Operations and Resources

This part of the book studies the ways in which modern organizations control their operations and their human resources. The control process has two important elements: physical resources and human beings. The tools and techniques used in controlling one are quite different from those used in controlling the other.

Chapter 16 focuses on the basics of operational control. It examines the control process in action; the way in which budgets work and the types of budgets commonly used by modern organizations; the nature of comprehensive budgeting and its value to overall control; financial statement analysis, break-even analysis, and program evaluation and review technique; the way overall performance control works; the ways in which management audits help an enterprise monitor its operations; and the role played by computerized information systems in helping managers control operations.

Chapter 17 examines the nature of operations management and its role in the controlling process. Particular attention is given to the major dimensions of operations management: product design, production planning, purchasing, inventory control, work flow layout, and quality control and to the way in which these dimensions are helping management improve productivity and meet the challenge from Japanese competition.

Chapter 18 examines the ways in which today's enterprises control personnel performance. In this chapter, attention is first focused on the performance appraisal process, how it works, some of the most common problems associated with it, and how these problems can be handled. The chapter then considers how conflict and change can be controlled. The last part of the chapter is devoted to an examination of some of the properties of organizational climate, the ways in which this climate can be measured, and the role that organizational development techniques can play in improving it. An answer is also provided to the question: Does organizational development really pay off?

When you have finished studying all of the material in this part of the book, you will have a working knowledge of the ways in which management controls its operations. You will also know some of the most popular tools and techniques used specifically in controlling organizational operations and personnel performance.

16

Controlling Organizational Performance

Objectives

At some point in time, every organization has to measure its progress and determine the adequacy of its performance. This control process can be applied at each level of the organization and can incorporate all enterprise activities. In carrying out the process, organizations employ many different control tools and techniques, from budgeting and financial statement analysis to break-even analysis, overall performance analysis, and management audits. Sometimes these tools are tied directly to the computer, which provides managers with the kind of information they need for carrying out timely and economical control.

This chapter examines the ways in which modern organizations control organizational performance. It analyzes the nature of the controlling process and reviews some of the primary ways to monitor organizational performance through the use of financial control. It also explores some of the major forms of operational control, as well as the overall performance control measures used by modern organizations. Attention is also focused on the role, scope, and purpose of management audits, and the role that computers and management information systems play in the control process. When you have finished studying the material in this chapter you will be able to

1. define the term controlling and describe the control process in action;

2. explain how budgets work and the types of budgets most commonly used by modern organizations;

3. describe how zero-base budgeting and comprehensive budgeting can improve budgeting effectiveness;

4. discuss financial statement analysis, break-even analysis, and program evaluation and review techniques and explain their value to the controlling function;

461

5. explain how overall performance control works and how management audits help an organization monitor its operations; and

6. describe the role played by computerized information systems in assisting managers to control organizational operations.

The Nature of Controlling

The controlling process defined

As we learned in a previous chapter, controlling is the process in which management evaluates performance using predetermined standards and, in light of the results, makes a decision regarding corrective action. Figure 16–1 illustrates the basic steps in this process.

The Control Process in Action

In studying how the control process works, we have to refer back to planning, for the two are closely linked. In fact, it is sometimes difficult to determine where one ends and the other begins.

Controlling and planning are closely linked.

Consider, for example, an organization that wants to capture 15 percent of its market. It currently holds 11 percent and has determined that strong advertising will help it close the gap. In January the firm begins a vigorous ad campaign, and when progress is measured in June, market share is up to 13 percent. What will the firm do now? Most likely it will keep up the ad campaign and may pump in even more money. The control process, which identified market share as 13 percent, has provided feedback for the next six-month plan. As this example indicates, the planning and control processes are irrevocably intertwined.

More specifically, the control process forces management to review the standards or objectives that were set in the planning process and decide the adequacy of progress toward them. Two areas of this process merit consideration.

Predetermined standards must exist.

First, there must be a predetermined basis for comparing performance and standards. Sometimes this basis will be heavily quantitative, as when the return on investment in one year is compared with that of the previous year. At other times the basis will be more qualitative, as when the public's view of the enterprise is examined and management attempts to answer the question: Is our image getting better or becoming worse?

Figure 16–1
The Control Process in Action

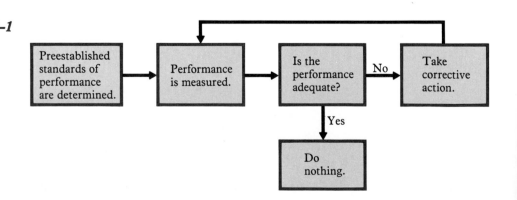

Not every deviation requires action.

Second, not every deviation from the plan requires corrective action. Sometimes the results can be considered good enough, as when there is a desired profit of $1 million and an actual profit of $988,000. Medium-sized and large firms often sidestep this problem by establishing a range of acceptable performance, such as a return on investment of between 14.8 and 15.2 percent. In this case action need be taken only if the return is outside this range. If it is less than 14.8 percent, such things as production efficiency, product quality, advertising, and sales programs might be analyzed to determine what is wrong. If the return on investment is higher than 15.2, the enterprise may simply want to set higher goals for itself in the future.

Characteristics of Effective Control Systems

Every control system should be accurate, timely, economical, and understandable. Accuracy is essential because if the information that is received is not correct, the resulting decisions are likely to make things worse rather

"Look, Henroid, getting ahead is knowing which string to pull."

than better. The information being fed back must be timely to allow management to obtain full benefit from the data, and it must be economical because it would be pointless, for example, for management to spend $1,000 on a reporting system that saved the company only $10 a month. The information also must be understandable, because unless the manager knows that it is all about, he or she may make unnecessary mistakes in interpreting and using it.

Effective control characteristics

In addition to having these four characteristics, a control system must help the manager focus on key control points, and it must be acceptable to managers. A manager does not have time to control every aspect of operations. As a result, the control system should single out specific areas that provide overall comprehensive control. Acceptability also is essential because if the data is impractical, calls for a great deal of extra analysis, or takes too long to implement, managers will find ways to work around the control system by developing their own feedback mechanisms that are easier and more efficient.

The material that follows illustrates key control tools and techniques used in modern organizations. In each case these six characteristics are incorporated into the specific control procedure or process.

Financial Control

One of the primary ways to monitor organizational performance is through the use of financial control. Some of the control techniques used in this process are quite simple while others are extremely sophisticated. Two major approaches to financial control used by both large and small organizations are budgets, the most popular method, and financial statement analysis, which is important in analyzing past performance, identifying problem areas, and determining a future course of action.

Budgets

Budgets defined

Budgets are plans that specify results in quantitative terms and serve as a control device for feedback evaluation and follow-up. There are many different types of budgets but all have three common characteristics: (1) they help establish goals and provide general direction to management by showing, in quantitative terms, what is to be done and how much it will cost; (2) they establish control points against which progress can be measured and performance can be evaluated; and (3) they provide a means for coordinating organizational activity on both an intra- and interdepartmental basis.

The way in which budgets are drawn up and approved varies by organization. Typically, the process begins at both the upper and lower levels of the hierarchy. At the upper levels top management examines overall forecasts related to expected annual revenue and determines how much it can afford to spend on operations. This number serves as the overall limit for all budget requests and is broken down by division or department for the organization at large. At the lower levels, each unit or department draws up its own budget and forwards the request to the respective superior. As these proposals make their way up the line, superiors compare the requests with the initial allocations they have received from higher-level management. In this way a paring of budgets takes place at all levels as management attempts to reconcile requests with available funds.

Few divisions or departments ask for less than what they think they can get. Most request more and hope to secure at least part of this additional amount. Still others have special problems or projects that do indeed require a greater amount of money than that initially allocated. Realizing this, management usually holds back part of the budgetary funds to cover emergencies or special cases.

Types of Budgets

A wide array of budgets are used in modern organizations. Most organizations make use of operating budgets and financial budgets. Some also employ various tools and techniques designed to tie these budgets as closely as possible to variations in the level of operational activity.

Operating budgets monitor expenses and revenues.

Operating budgets are used for monitoring expenses, revenues, and, in the case of business firms, profit. The *expense budget* is designed to control things like production, marketing, personnel, research, administration, and other expenses vital to the operations of the organization. The *revenue budget* is used to measure marketing and sales effectiveness or, in the case of public agencies, to keep track of fund allocations. In this way, both outflows and inflows are tied to a budget. A business firm may also use a supplemental budget known as the *profit budget*. It is particularly important to a division head or product manager who is charged with achieving a particular return on investment or profit.

Financial budgets integrate the financial and operational plans.

Financial budgets integrate the organization's financial plan with its operational plan. Will the firm have the money it needs to carry out its operations? To answer this question organizations commonly use four financial budgets: the *capital expenditure budget*, used for constructing or expanding buildings, property, equipment, and other physical assets; the *cash budget*, used to monitor the flow of funds and the pattern of receipts and cash disbursements; the *financing budget*, used to balance any shortages of capital whether they be short-, intermediate-, or long-range in nature; and the *balance sheet budget*, used for bringing together all of the other budgets and projecting how the balance sheet will look at the end of the period if actual results conform to budgets.

Budget Flexibility

One of the biggest problems with budgets is inflexibility. Managers often reveal this inflexibility when they say, "I'm sorry, but we can't buy that piece of equipment. It's not in the budget." In cases like this, the budget is being treated as a fixed entity instead of as a control tool that can be altered or changed to meet the needs of the organization. Perhaps the enterprise really should increase the budget to buy the piece of equipment.

Variable budgets are tied to volume of activity.

In an effort to avoid inflexibility, many organizations have turned to the use of **variable budgets.** These budgets are tied to volume of activity in that the more output the enterprise produces or the more sales it generates, the greater its expenditure budget. Conversely, if the organization finds it must contract operations, the budget is decreased. The costs affected by changes in activity are those directly related to production and sales.

Examples include materials, parts, maintenance, utilities, personnel salaries, advertising, and entertainment.

One of the major advantages of variable budgets is that they encourage the organization to examine its costs. In all, there are three types of costs: fixed, variable, and semivariable. A **fixed cost** is one that does not change, regardless of the amount of work being done. Property taxes, rent, and flood insurance are examples. **Variable costs** are expenses that vary directly with the quantity of work being performed. Raw materials, supplies, and scrap are all examples. **Semivariable costs** are those that vary with the quantity of work being performed but not in a directly proportional way. Examples include labor salaries, utilities, and machine maintenance. By systematically identifying and analyzing its costs, the organization is better able to control these expenses.

Advantages and Disadvantages

A number of important advantages are associated with budgeting, but managers also should be aware of some distinct drawbacks.

On the positive side, budgets help coordinate the work of units, departments and, if used on an overall organizational basis, the entire enterprise. They also provide feedback for correcting errors and, if properly installed, are able to generate this information on a timely and economical basis. Budgets help managers learn from their past mistakes and serve as a basis for the future allocation of resources. They help clarify planning efforts by communicating how progress will be evaluated and when this evaluation will take place. Finally, they help reduce anxiety and tension because they tell people what is expected of them.

On the negative side, however, budgets can create problems. One of the most common occurs when managers begin fighting with each other over budgetary allocations in an effort to maintain the size of their previous allocation or build onto it. A second problem is the failure of management to tell employees when they have deviated from their budget and give them an opportunity to correct the situation. Other problems arise when budgets are allowed to dictate what happens in the organization instead of being used as tools and techniques for controlling and monitoring operations, and when budgetary allocations are not tied directly to the job and therefore some departments have to cut back critical operations while others have plenty of fat.

Effective Budgeting

Many organizations seek ways to maintain the advantages of budgeting while sidestepping the disadvantages. One of the most effective approaches is to look at each department's or unit's budget solely in terms of objectives and resource requirements. If this approach is used, a department that received a large budget last year will not necessarily receive a large one this year. During the late 1970s this approach gained in popularity as **zero-base budgeting** (ZBB) was adopted by organizations throughout the private and public sector. In its essence, ZBB calls for the allocation of organizational funds on the basis of a cost-benefit analysis of major activities. This process is carried out via three major steps:

1. Each department justifies what it is going to be doing and how much it will cost. This constitutes the unit's "decision package."

The ZBB process

2. The unit then does a comparison of the costs and benefits of the activities in the decision package. Attention is also focused on alternative ways to perform these activities, such as hiring temporary help, and what the unit would do if it received additional money and could expand its activities.

3. Activities are then ranked in order of benefit to the organization. The budget proposal and the ranking are then passed up the line and the next manager in the hierarchy performs the same ZBB procedures.[1]

In recent years, the overall use of ZBB has declined. The amount of paperwork generated by the approach and the time and effort that were required for its implementation convinced many that there had to be a better way.[2] As a result, many organizations have developed their own simplified version of ZBB.

Comprehensive budgeting covers all phases of operations.

A second effective technique is **comprehensive budgeting,** in which all phases of operations are covered by budgets. Beginning at the bottom of the hierarchy and working up to the top, each unit develops a budget that fits in with that of the next highest level. In this way, management is able to integrate comprehensive planning (what each department will be doing) with comprehensive budgeting (how much money each department will need to accomplish these objectives).

Budgets should have some flexibility.

A third useful technique is that of not budgeting too strictly. If every penny is designated for particular activities and projects, the manager will have no flexibility in moving funds from one departmental program to another. This philosophy encourages waste. Since funds cannot be transferred to other projects, the department will simply spend them on the designated programs regardless of the cost/benefit ratio.

Communication is vital.

Finally, effective budgeting requires that everyone know what is going on. When personnel understand how much money they have to work with, the objectives that are to be accomplished, the time frame within which everything is to be done, and how performance will be evaluated, there is an excellent chance of developing high morale and teamwork. Budgets are more than just control tools. They are also important in effective planning, organizing, influencing, and leading. They are crucial to the overall management process.

Financial Statement Analysis

There are two major financial statements: the balance sheet (see Table 16–1) and the income statement (see Table 16–2).

Tools for measuring performance

The **balance sheet** is a financial statement that shows a firm's financial position at a specified point in time. It consists of three major parts: assets, liabilities, and owners' equity. Assets are the things the company owns.

---

1. Peter A. Pyhhr, "Zero-Base Budgeting," *Harvard Business Review,* November–December 1970, pp. 111–121.

2. Stanton C. Lindquist and K. Bryant Mills, "Whatever Happened to Zero-Base Budgeting?" *Managerial Planning,* January–February 1981, pp. 31–35.

Table 16-1 Jones Manufacturing, Inc. Consolidated Balance Sheet as of December 31, 1985

Assets			
Current assets			
Cash	$180,000		
Accounts receivable	160,000		
Notes receivable	55,000		
Inventory	330,000		
Total current assets			$ 725,000
Fixed assets			
Plant and equipment	$800,000		
Less: Accumulated depreciation	225,000	$575,000	
Building	$600,000		
Less: Accumulated depreciation	150,000	$450,000	
Land		250,000	
Total fixed assets			$1,275,000
Total assets			$2,000,000

Liabilities and Owners' Equity			
Current liabilities			
Accounts payable	$ 10,000		
Notes payable	30,000		
Income taxes payable	250,000		
Total current liabilities			$290,000
Long-term liabilities			
Mortgage payable	$180,000		
Notes payable	100,000		
Long-term bonds outstanding	200,000		
Total long-term liabilities			$480,000
Total liabilities			$770,000
Owners' equity			
Common stock	$500,000		
Preferred stock	200,000		
Retained earnings	500,000		
Total owners' equity			$1,230,000
Total liabilities and owners' equity			$2,000,000

Table 16–2
Jones Manufacturing Statement of Income for the Year Ended December 31, 1985

Revenue from Sales		
Gross sales	$4,000,000	
Less: Sales returns and allowances	250,000	
Net sales		$3,750,000
Cost of Goods Sold		
Beginning inventory	$ 330,000	
Purchases	1,870,000	
Total goods available for sale	2,200,000	
Less: Ending inventory	200,000	
Total cost of goods sold		$2,000,000
Gross profit		$1,750,000
Expenses		
Selling expenses	$ 700,000	
Administrative expenses	300,000	
General expenses	200,000	
Total expenses		$1,200,000
Net income before taxes		$ 550,000
Federal and state income taxes		250,000
Net income		$ 300,000

Liabilities are the firm's debts. Owners' equity is the difference between assets and liabilities and represents the net worth the owners have in the business.

The **income statement** summarizes a firm's financial performance over a given period of time, typically one year. The four major parts of an income statement are revenues, cost of goods sold, expenses, and net income.

Using these two financial statements, an organization can conduct analysis and determine where it is doing well and where it is doing poorly. The most common way in which this is done is through ratio analysis.

Ratio Analysis

A ratio is a relationship between two numbers.

A **ratio** is a relationship between two numbers. In regard to financial statements, it is possible to conduct balance sheet ratio analysis, income statement ratio analysis, and combination ratio analysis. The latter draws upon data from both the balance sheet and the income statement. The four most common types of ratio analyses relate to liquidity, debt, operations, and profit.

Liquidity ratios measure the ability to meet current debts.

Liquidity ratios are designed to measure how well the organization can meet its current debt obligations. Can it pay the monthly mortgage? Are there funds for meeting the payroll? Will the utility bill be paid on time? If an organization has the necessary cash, or can raise it quickly, it is said to be liquid. One of the most common ratios for measuring liquidity is the **current ratio,** which is computed by dividing current assets by current liabilities. For Jones Manufacturing in Table 16–1, this computation is $725,000/$290,000 = 2.5. The firm's current assets are two-and-a-half times its current liabilities. A standard rule of the road in manufacturing is 2.0 for the current ratio. So Jones Manufacturing, with a current ratio of 2.5, should have no trouble meeting its current debts. Liquidity is more than adequate.

Debt ratios measure the amount of financing by creditors.

Debt ratios measure the amount of financing being provided by creditors. One kind is the **debt/asset ratio,** which expresses the relationship between the firm's total debt and total assets. In the case of Jones Manufacturing $770,000/2,000,000 = 38.5$ percent. This means that 38.5 percent of all assets were purchased with debt. For a manufacturing firm, this ratio is acceptable. A second debt ratio is **debt/equity** which measures the amount of assets financed by debt compared to the amount financed by stock and profits that are retained in the firm. In the case of Jones Manufacturing this ratio is $770,000/1,230,000 = 0.642$ to 1. For every 64.2¢ of debt there is $1 of equity. Many banks prefer to keep this ratio below 1:1. In Jones Manufacturing's case, there is still some room for additional borrowing.

Operations ratios measure internal performance.

Operations ratios measure internal performance such as how fast inventory is turning over or how fast accounts receivable are being collected. Let us address just the first of these, the **inventory turnover ratio.** If a firm can turn its inventory over 12 times a year, it can get by with a much smaller inventory investment than a competitor with equal sales but an inventory turnover of only three. Inventory turnover is determined by taking the average inventory for the year (beginning inventory plus ending inventory divided by two) and dividing it into the cost of goods sold. Drawing upon data from both the balance sheet and the income statement, the calculations for Jones Manufacturing are

$$\text{Average inventory} = \frac{\$330,000 + 200,000}{2} = \$265,000$$

$$\text{Inventory turnover} = \frac{\$2,000,000}{265,000} = 7.55 \text{ turns}$$

The company is turning over its inventory 7.55 times per year. Although the manager would have to compare this turnover to that of the competition in determining its adequacy, for most manufacturing firms this is a very good turnover rate.

Profitability ratios measure performance vis-à-vis the competition.

Profitability ratios measure a company's effectiveness vis-à-vis its own performance and that of the competition. One of the most popular profitability ratios is **return on investment** (ROI), which is measured by comparing net income with total assets. In the case of Jones Manufacturing, this ratio is $300,000/2,000,000 = 15$ percent. This is quite good in light of the fact that we used net income after taxes in our calculations. If we opted for net income before taxes, the percentage would have risen to 27.5 percent. In its comprehensive form, ROI includes a large number of key factors. Figure 16–2 presents these and illustrates the relationship between them. By examining performance in each of these factors, an organization can identify problem areas and work to resolve them, increasing ROI in the process.

Figure 16–2 Return on Investment Computation

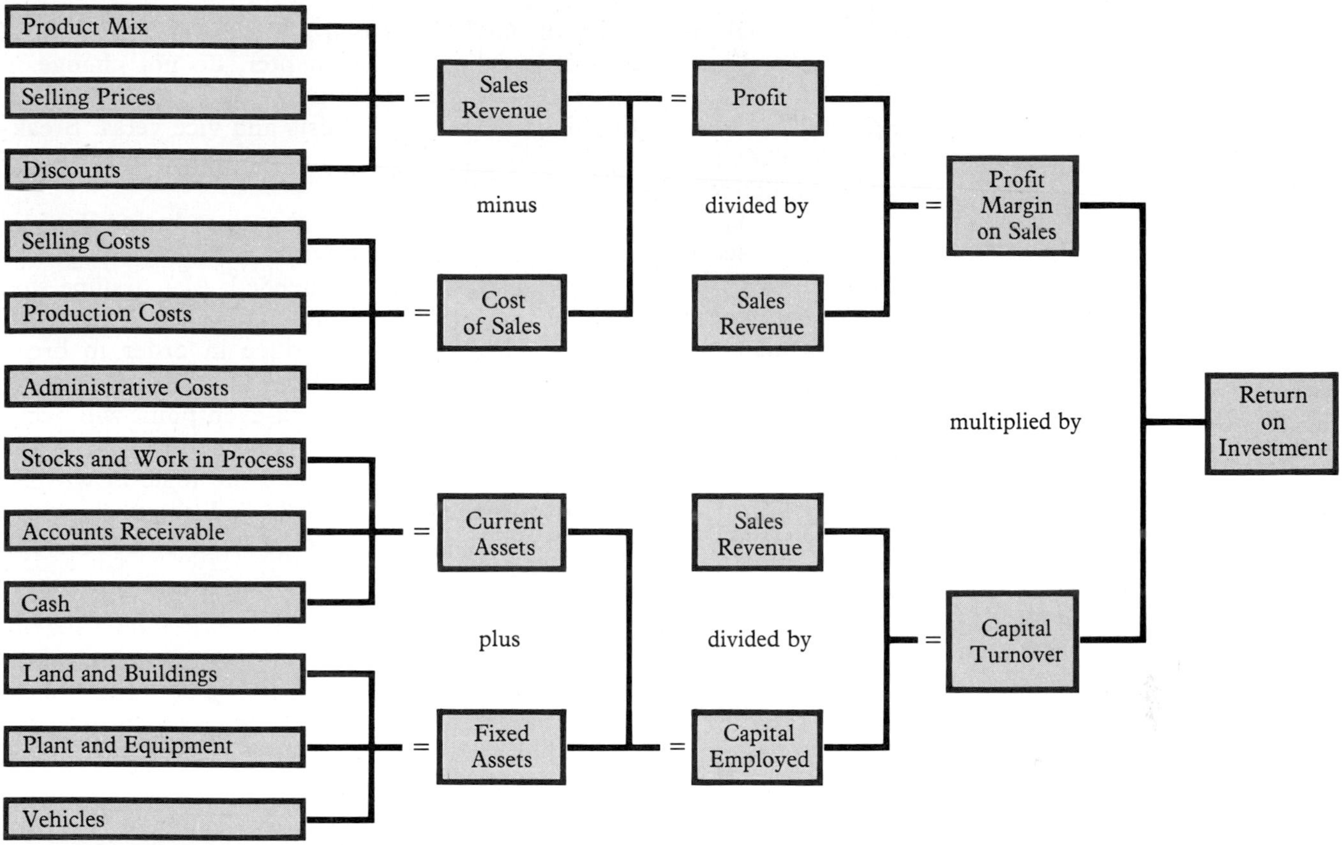

Operational Control

A second major form of control is operational control. The tools and techniques used in operational control are designed to help the organization monitor its operations or activities. One of the most popular tools, particularly among manufacturing firms, is break-even analysis. Another, used for controlling sophisticated or one-of-a-kind projects, is program evaluation and review technique.

Break-Even Analysis

The purpose of break-even analysis is to determine the point at which the firm covers all of the costs associated with producing a particular product. If the company cannot sell enough units to reach this point, it will lose money on the product. If the firm can sell more than this number of units, it will earn a profit. Before we explain how the break-even point is calculated, however, we should stress one point. A firm will not necessarily produce a product just because it can break even on it. In most cases, a return on investment objective is set, and if the firm cannot reach this target, which may mean selling 10,000 units above break-even, it will refuse to produce the good or will terminate current production.

Calculation and Advantages of Break-Even

Break-even occurs when costs are covered.

Break-even analysis requires an analysis of two types of costs: fixed and variable. Fixed costs, as noted earlier in the chapter, do not change in relation to output. Variable costs do change in relation to output, i.e., the greater the output, the higher the variable costs and vice versa. Break-even occurs when the organization can cover all of the fixed and variable costs associated with production of the product.

For example, suppose that Firm G is thinking about producing Product H. In order to set up all of the machinery and buy the necessary equipment to produce the product, a $50,000 investment is needed. Also assume that each unit will require $6 of labor, materials and parts and will sell for $10. How many units will the firm have to produce in order to break even? The formula for the break-even point (BEP) is fixed cost/selling price minus variable cost. In our example, the break-even point will occur at 12,500 units ($50,000/$10 − 6). This solution is graphed in Figure 16–3. Because of its simplicity, however, we can explain the logic in writing. On every unit sold, the company will clear $4 over and above the costs associated with building the unit. This $4 must be used to reduce the

Figure 16–3 Illustration of a Break-Even Point

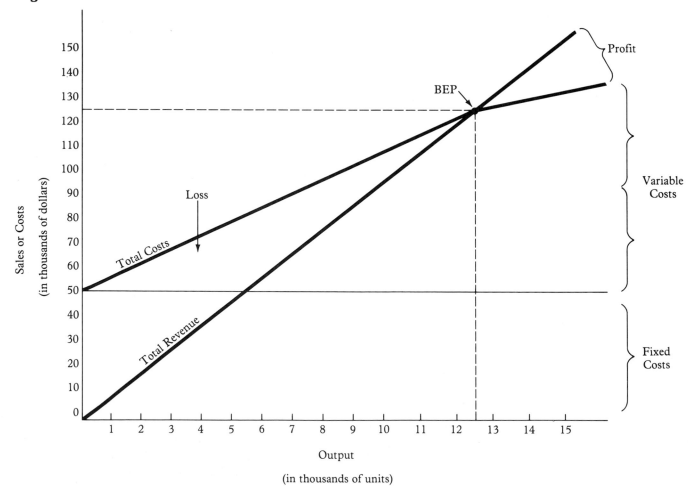

Output

(in thousands of units)

fixed cost associated with setting up the machinery and getting the production process in order. Since there was a $50,000 fixed cost, it will take 12,500 units, each contributing $4, to cover all fixed costs.

Once the firm has achieved break-even, assuming there is no change in selling price, fixed cost, or variable cost, it will make $4 on every unit produced and sold. The thing to keep in mind about break-even analysis is that it is usually not this simple. Quite often, the selling price, fixed cost, or variable cost will change, and this change will alter the BEP. For example, because of competition, the firm may find it necessary to lower the selling price from $10 to $9. When this happens, the BEP is raised. Conversely, if the variable cost per unit declines from $6 to $5.50, the BEP goes down. So the break-even point cannot be computed just once. The firm has to make these calculations on a periodic basis, and if costs are rising it can either raise prices in order to maintain profitability or begin to phase out production of the line.

Benefits of BEP analysis

One of the biggest benefits of break-even point analysis is that it forces the organization to analyze costs. It also helps the firm tie production to marketing demand, and it helps the manager integrate production with ROI objectives.

Program Evaluation and Review Technique

In some cases an organization needs to go beyond break-even point analysis in controlling operations. This is particularly true when the enterprise is engaged in a one-time, nonrepetitive project that is complex and requires the monitoring of many different activities. Typical examples include building sophisticated aerospace hardware, constructing high-technology telecommunication systems, and using state-of-the-art R&D to oxygenate polluted bodies of water. Given the fact that these projects typically are performed under a contract arrangement that penalizes late completion, management needs to monitor progress very closely. In so doing, management often uses a tool known as **Program Evaluation and Review Technique (PERT),** which is designed for one-time and complex projects. PERT was developed by the U.S. Navy and the consulting firm of Booz, Allen and Hamilton in connection with the Polaris missile. Since then, its use has been expanded to many other types of undertakings.

Stages of PERT

PERT has three stages: formulation, planning, and monitoring and control. In the formulation stage, the project is broken down into events and activities. An **event** in this context is defined as a milestone or specific accomplishment, such as completing the hiring of all necessary personnel for the project. An **activity** is defined as the effort, resources, and time associated with an event. Placing employment ads, interviewing candidates, and hiring qualified personnel may all be considered activities. These events and activities are then laid out in sequential order so that management knows what has to be done first, second, third, and so on. Then every event-activity is brought together in the form of a diagram or PERT network, and the time for each activity is indicated. An example of such a network, related to a lake restoration project, is presented in Figure 16–4. In this network,

First comes the formulation stage . . .

Figure 16–4
A PERT Network

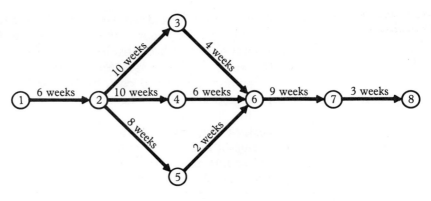

Event	Activity Associated with the Event
1	Lake restoration project begun
2	All necessary personnel hired
3	All materials purchased
4	All equipment assembled
5	Oxygenation plan finalized
6	All resources moved to lake project site
7	Oxygenation process carried out
8	Progress measured and evaluated

the activity associated with each event is indicated by an arrow, and the time for this activity is placed along the top of the arrow. For example, to complete Event 2 will require six weeks; to finish Event 5 will take eight weeks; to complete Event 8 will take three weeks.

followed by the planning stage . . .

In the planning stage, the **critical path** (the longest path) through the PERT network is computed. In Figure 16–4 there are three paths through the network. These paths, along with their respective times, are as follows:

Path	Time	Total
1–2–3–6–7–8	6 + 10 + 4 + 9 + 3	32
1–2–4–6–7–8	6 + 10 + 6 + 9 + 3	34
1–2–5–6–7–8	6 + 8 + 2 + 9 + 3	28

As can be seen, the second path is the critical one.

After this evaluation is made, the total of the critical path time is compared with the allotted time for the project. Assuming that this project has a completion date of 39 weeks, management will complete it in time if none of the activities take any longer than the estimates indicate. In fact, the critical path (1–2–4–6–7–8) can slip by as much as five weeks and the project still will be completed on time. If the contract time is 32 weeks, however, the critical path must be reduced by two weeks.

and, finally, the monitoring and controlling stage.

In the monitoring and controlling stage, steps are taken to ensure that the project does not run late. If the critical path must be reduced, management must decide how this should be done. For example the activities associated with Events 4 or 6 might be cut by a total of two weeks. The firm could take personnel off other activities where there was extra time and allocate them to activities on the critical path.

Advantages of PERT

PERT offers some very important advantages, including the following:

1. It helps management plan in detail, defining exactly what must be done in order to accomplish the project's objectives on time.

2. It forces management to make commitments regarding execution times and completion dates.

Why use PERT?

3. By identifying critical activities, it helps management monitor work progress more efficiently.

4. It assists management in identifying potential problem areas and formulating contingency plans.

5. The overall concept is easily understood because it provides a method for visualizing the entire project and explaining it to all who will be involved.[3]

Overall Performance Control

Financial and operational control are important at the lower and middle levels of the hierarchy. At the upper levels, however, managers are more interested in overall performance control. Typically, their attention is focused on five to seven key performance factors that provide the necessary control information for the organization at large. Identifying these key factors is the most important phase of overall performance control.

Identification of Key Factors

Some performance control factors are a result of strategic objectives.

The most common overall performance control factor is ROI. Other popular ones include market share, growth, profit, and customer relations. In deciding which factors are most important, the organization typically begins by reviewing its strategic objectives. Quite often, these objectives serve as both planning goals and key control points.

Others are tied to key success factors.

Additional key control factors are identified by answering the questions: Where do we need to do well in order to succeed? What are our key success factors? In every industry there are, at most, a handful of such factors. For example, in the computer industry, technology and customer service are two of the primary success factors. In laboratory animal breeding, research and development (R&D) is the most significant factor. In the

---

3. Efraim Turban and Jack R. Meredith, *Fundamentals of Management Science*, revised edition (Dallas, Tex.: Business Publications, Inc., 1981), p. 275.

automobile industry, production quality and customer service are of great importance. In the watch-making business, production efficiency and marketing effectiveness are two key success variables.

Some are highly quantifiable.

In some cases, these key factors are quantifiable. Every week, Detroit auto sales are reported. If General Motors wants to hold 60 percent of the market of autos produced domestically, the company can measure its progress on a weekly basis.

Others are partially quantifiable.

In other cases, the key factor is only partially quantifiable. An organization that wants to be a leader in R&D innovation cannot know its position on a weekly basis, so it must remain alert to environmental changes. Particular attention must be directed toward the competition's current product offerings and any news regarding new R&D developments in the industry. The organization does not know exactly what is happening in the environment, but it tries to assess these developments as objectively as possible.

Still others are qualitative.

In still other cases key factors are heavily qualitative in nature. Consider a company that wants to mesh long-, intermediate-, and short-range planning in an overall, comprehensive way. The state of progress is usually judged by an in-house management team, and the final decision regarding the company's progress is often based heavily on qualitative factors.

Tying Control to Performance

While key factor control allows the enterprise to focus on a limited number of performance variables, these variables often are tied closely to performance. For example, an organization may desire a 20 percent ROI, which can be attained only with a production of 500 units or more a day. In this case, the primary focus must be on production; ROI will be taken care of in the process. This is particularly true for businesses that can sell everything they can produce. During the early 1980s, many video game manufacturers fell into this category. The Rolls Royce auto division, of course, has been in it for years.

A second important fact in tying control to performance is that the required emphasis on specific key control variables may change. For example, in the early 1970s, a few firms introduced the digital wristwatch. In the initial version of this watch, the user pressed a button on the side of the watch and the time was displayed in red digital numbers. Depending on whether the casing was silver or gold, the watches retailed in the range of $250 to $400. The product was a novel one and in controlling overall performance, the manufacturers initially concentrated their attention on R&D. As sales began to increase and the market matured, however, attention shifted away from R&D to production and then to marketing. Figure 16–5 illustrates this pattern for a manufacturing industry similar to the one we are discussing.

Control is often tied to product/market evolution.

Notice in the figure that control emphasis must be tied directly to the product/market evolution. In product manufacturing, technology and R&D initially are more important than anything else. As the market matures, however, the emphasis moves to production and then on to marketing and finance. Unless R&D is used to develop a better product, its function is complete. At this stage the company's task is to produce the good as efficiently as possible and market it to the consumer. Since many firms are engaged in the production of goods or services, Figure 16–5 is an excellent

Figure 16–5   Product/Market Evolution and Key Area Control

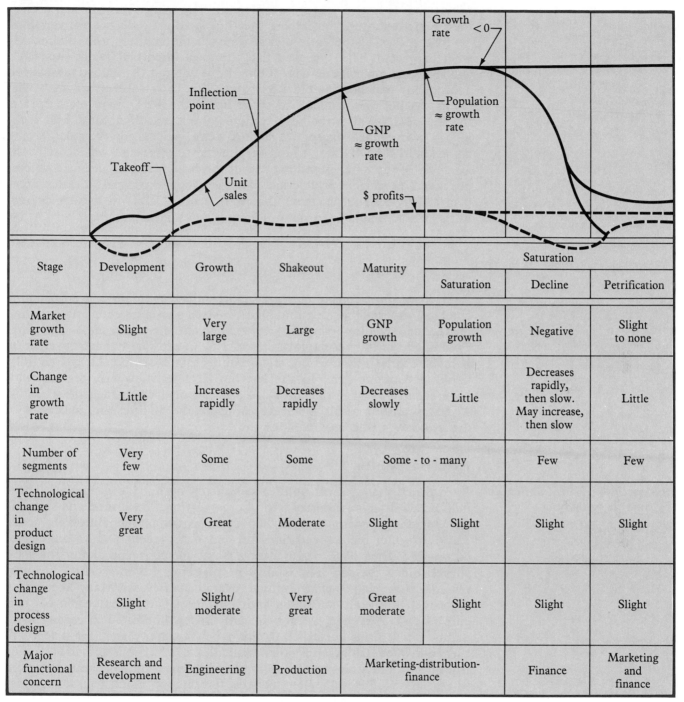

Stage	Development	Growth	Shakeout	Maturity	Saturation		
					Saturation	Decline	Petrification
Market growth rate	Slight	Very large	Large	GNP growth	Population growth	Negative	Slight to none
Change in growth rate	Little	Increases rapidly	Decreases rapidly	Decreases slowly	Little	Decreases rapidly, then slow. May increase, then slow	Little
Number of segments	Very few	Some	Some	Some - to - many		Few	Few
Technological change in product design	Very great	Great	Moderate	Slight	Slight	Slight	Slight
Technological change in process design	Slight	Slight/ moderate	Very great	Great moderate	Slight	Slight	Slight
Major functional concern	Research and development	Engineering	Production	Marketing-distribution- finance		Finance	Marketing and finance

Source: C. W. Hofer, "Conceptual Constructs for Formulating Corporate and Business Strategy" (Boston: Intercollegiate Case Clearing House, 9–378–754, 1977), p. 7. Reprinted with permission.

one with which to illustrate how key control factors are tied to specific operations. It is also useful in explaining why many firms do not achieve their desired strategic objectives: they fail to adjust their control variables.

In the case of the early digital watch manufacturers, this is precisely what happened. They believed that the most important factor was R&D and strove to maintain an edge. Other firms entered the industry, however, and quickly matched the old R&D capability. In retrospect, we know that (a) it was not very difficult to catch up to the R&D state of the art in this business; (b) after the basic technology was mastered, little more technology was needed except for adding extra gadgets like calculators and alarms, and this was easy to do; (c) the greatest expense was actually the assembly of the watches and the cost of the casing; and (d) ultimate success depended on efficient production and effective marketing. As a result, companies who designed controls that were strictly R&D in nature lost out to those who emphasized the production and marketing areas.

Management Audits

Regardless of the control measures an organization employs, it is becoming common, especially among intermediate-sized and large enterprises, to find management audits being used to supplement these measures. The term "auditing" typically is employed to refer to an external financial evaluation of an enterprise's transactions and accounts that is carried out by a certified public accounting firm. In the last few decades, however, organizations have begun to realize that they can also benefit from management audits. A **management audit** is an evaluation of the abilities and successes of the executives who are operating the enterprise.

External Audits

External audits are conducted by outside personnel.

An external management audit is conducted by outside personnel. These individuals examine industry trends, organizational resources, and strategic and operating performance to help management pinpoint problem areas. They also offer recommendations for action. In recent years a number of accounting firms have begun carrying out management audits for their clients. Since the company is already reviewing the enterprise's financial records, why not go on to evaluate overall operations? Many accounting firms feel that such consulting activities are a natural extension of their current task. Yet they are not the only group interested in management audits. Some firms specialize in this type of activity and, for a fee, will carry out an overall organizational evaluation of enterprise activities ranging from health of earnings, sales vigor, fiscal policies, and corporate structure to research and development policies, production efficiency, stockholder relations, and executive ability.[4]

External audits offer some important advantages. One is that the consultants can be objective without fear of reprisal by management. Also, in

---

4. Jackson Martindell, *The Scientific Appraisal of Management* (New York: Harper & Brothers, 1950), and *The Appraisal of Management* (New York: Harper & Brothers, 1962).

many cases they have seen similar performance in other firms and know what to look for and what to overlook during the management audit. And since the reputations of these firms are based on how well they help out their clients, they have everything to gain from doing a good job and nothing to lose.

Internal Audits

Internal audits are performed by in-house people.

An internal management audit is similar in nature to an external one. In making an evaluation, the audit team is generally directed by questions such as those presented in Table 16–3. Notice that these questions are directed toward analyzing key internal and external areas of management performance. Of course, depending on the firm, the questions also may address other areas, including research and development, production, personnel, financial performance, and customer relations.

Internal audits provide some important benefits to the enterprise. Because the inside people are more likely to know the inner workings of the organization, they should have less difficulty pinpointing both strengths and weaknesses than outside auditors would. In addition, the cost of using inside people is usually lower, and if there is a problem following through on some recommendations, the internal auditors can easily be called back for consultation.

In recent years, there has been a trend towards using internal auditors when possible. Of course, these people can be biased, and there is always the chance that they will be pressured to paint a rosier picture than actually exists. From a cost/benefit standpoint, however, many organizations are questioning whether external audits are worth the expense in terms of both company time and money. Some firms are compromising on the matter by using internal consultants whenever possible and bringing in outside consultants for special situations.

However management audits are done, they are an excellent way to supplement the overall control program. They provide a follow-up and appraisal of financial, operational, and key area control.

Computerized Information Systems

Over the last 25 years, computers have begun to play an increasingly important role in the control process. In particular, these machines are now being used to compile, analyze, and report information needed for control purposes.

The Computer Evolution

Computer power has increased.

Modern computer technology has evolved through a number of generations. The first generation of computers (1951–1958) used the vacuum tube as a basic element. These machines could do 1,000 five-digit decimal additions per second. The next generation of computers (1959–1964) replaced the vacuum tube with the transistor. Digital decimal additions rose to 10,000 per second. Third-generation computers (1965–1970) made use of small-scale integrated circuits, and additions per second increased to 25,000.

Table 16–3
Partial Outline for Evaluation
of a Firm

I. Product Lines and Basic Competitive Position

A. Past

What strengths and weakness in products (or services) have been dominant in this firm's history—design features, quality-reliability, prices, patents, proprietary position?

B. Present

What share of its market(s) does the firm now hold, and how firmly? Is this share diversified or concentrated as to number of customers? In what phases of their life cycles are the present chief products and what is happening to prices and margins? How do customers and potential customers regard this firm's products? Are the various product lines compatible marketing-wise, engineering-wise, manufacturing-wise? If not, is each product line substantial enough to stand on its own feet?

C. Future

Is the market(s) as a whole expanding or contracting, and at what rate? What is the trend in this firm's share of the market(s)? What competitive trends are developing in numbers of competitors, technology, marketing pricing? What is its vulnerability to business cycle (or defense spending) changes? Is management capable of effectively integrating market research, R&D, and market development programs for a new product or products?

II. Top Management

A. Identification of Top Management and Its Record

What person or group constitutes top management? Has present top management been responsible for profit-and-loss results of the past few years?

B. Top Management and the Future

What are top management's chief characteristics? How adequate or inadequate is this type of management for coping with the challenges of the future? Will the present type and quality of top management continue? Will it deteriorate, will it improve, or will it change its basic character?

C. Board of Directors

What influence and/or control does the Board of Directors exercise? What are the capabilities of its members? What are their motivations?

III. Summary and Evaluation Strategy

What other factors can assume major importance in this particular situation? (Use a checklist.) Of all the factors studied, which, if any, is overriding in this particular situation? Which factors are of major importance by virtue of the fact that they govern other factors? What are the basic facts of life about the economics and competition of this industry now and over the next decade? In view of this firm's particular strengths and weaknesses, what are levels of success in this industry? What are the prospects of its succeeding by diversifying out of its industry?

Source: Reprinted with permission from: Robert B. Buchele, "How to Evaluate a Firm," *California Management Review,* Fall 1962, pp. 6–7. © (1962) by the Regents of the University of California. Condensed from *California Management Review,* volume 5, no. 1, pp. 5–17 by permission of the Regents.

Clear-cut generations have not emerged beyond the third since the integrated circuit remains the primary technology. Changing technology is best represented by the increasing number of elements on a single chip. Medium-scale integration . . . in commercial use by 1970, packed from 10 to 100 elements per component . . . this was followed by large-scale integration . . . with 100 to 10,000 elements per chip. Very large-scale integration is expected to range up to 250,000. . . .[5]

Relative costs have declined.

More important for modern enterprises is the relationship between performance and price. As the power of computers has risen, the cost has declined. By 1980, one dollar of hardware expenditure could have purchased 100,000 times the computing power it would have in 1955!

As the range and power of the computer have risen, organizations have increased the ways in which they are using these machines. In the 1950s and 1960s computers performed a great number of paperwork functions such as payroll, accounting, and billing. Now their scope of operations is broadening with the development of computerized management information systems.

Management Information Systems

MIS defined

A **management information system (MIS)** is a formally designed data network used to provide managers with timely and useful information for effective planning and control. The system is specially designed so that managers get only the information they need, in the most useful form possible.

MIS Design

Every manager needs information. Specific demands vary, however, with the manager's function and hierarchical level. Using the latter as an example, we can compare the MIS needs of first-line managers and executives as in Table 16–4. If we added middle managers to the table, they would fall between the two, requiring less specific on-the-spot decision-making information than first-line managers but more than that needed by executives.

How can the organization ensure that its MIS design provides managers the data they need? There are four basic stages.[6]

Stages in MIS design

The first is a preliminary survey of what the MIS will entail. At this point, the informational, operational, and functional objectives of the organization are reviewed. The question the designers seek to answer at this stage is: What kinds of problems do the managers have to deal with and what kind of information can help them do so?

The second stage is that of conceptual design. What should the MIS look like? How can the purpose and nature of the system be communicated to the people who will be using it? At this point the designers work on

---

5. William M. Taggart, Jr., *Information Systems: An Introduction to Computers in Organizations* (Boston: Allyn and Bacon, Inc., 1980), p. 77.

6. Robert G. Murdick, "MIS Development Procedures," *Journal of Systems Management,* December 1970, pp. 22–26.

Table 16–4
Information Requirements
Based on Hierarchical Level

	First-Line Manager	Executive
This information will be gathered from:	internal environment	external environment
The nature of this information will be:	specific, narrow, well-defined	general, broad, ill-defined
The focus of the information will tend to be on:	technical issues	general issues
The accuracy of this information will be:	high	high-low, depending on its nature
The information will relate to:	the current situation	past, current and future situations
The information will be used for planning and controlling:	current operations	current and future operations
This information will be provided:	daily or weekly	monthly or quarterly

bringing together the system and the personnel so that the latter will know the value of the MIS and support it.

The third stage involves a detailed design of the information system. All of the specifics are worked out and, if the MIS is tied to the computer, the necessary program and other parts of the software package are completed at this point. Any personnel training related to the use of the system is also carried out during this stage.

The fourth stage is that of final implementation. At this point, the system is put into practice. If the designers have done their job right, management should find itself receiving both accurate and timely information.

MIS and Decision Making

In the last decade there has been a dramatic change in the way managers use information systems. In particular, reliance on written reports and similar forms of information is beginning to be replaced by what are called **decision support systems (DSS).** This is a collective term that refers to systems that are designed to provide the manager with information that is useful in making current decisions. Personal computer technology has gone a long way toward making these systems possible. Now, managers who know how to operate microcomputers and whose companies have the necessary computer software can request the current status of a project, make decisions regarding what needs to be done, and be assured that these commands are communicated to the people working on the project. The microcomputer is also allowing managers to make "what if" decisions for dealing with problems that occur on the line. As these machines become less expensive and managers become accustomed to operating them, we will probably see managers staying at home part of the day and making decisions from there and making decisions over the weekend on matters that will be carried out on Monday.

Microcomputers allow for on-line decisions.

By the early 1980s two impressive breakthroughs had made headlines in the computer field. IBM's personal computer, first introduced in 1981, soon began to dominate the industry. In 1983, when Apple introduced Lisa, it was touted as the most powerful and versatile personal computer available on the market.[7] The next year saw the introduction of IBM's PC jr. and Apple's Macintosh, offering still more computer power. Technological developments and the intense competition among computer manufacturers have created a climate in which new advances occur with regularity, making one day's technology obsolete the next.

Other important uses of computers in decision making are offered in the form of up-to-date printouts that provide managers with the current status of inventory, sales, receivables, and other similar information. Provided on a daily or weekly basis, these reports are useful when decisions do not have to be made on the spot. Managers unfamiliar with microcomputers (or computers in any form) usually encounter fewer problems with computerized printouts than they do with machines that allow them to ask for and receive information that they request. Until managers become more familiar with computers, we are likely to see some resistance to linking information systems, computers, and managers on an interactive basis.[8]

MIS and Human Behavior

Before completing our discussion of MIS implementation, we need to touch on the behavioral effects of this process.[9] As noted earlier in the chapter, MIS output must be acceptable to those who receive it.

Negative reactions may occur . . .

One of the biggest problems occurs when the users are not included in the design of the system. When this happens the information frequently is presented in the wrong form, requires too much time to decipher, or provides data of only marginal use. In any event, the managers make only minor use of the MIS output.

A second major problem is that many managers fear the information system because they are afraid of being subjected to excessively close control by upper management. These managers also view the MIS as a means of reducing the power they hold over their units. Many of them have come to run their departments like little empires and are reluctant to see this power base threatened.

---

7. Peter Nulty, "Apple's Bid to Stay in the Big Time," *Fortune,* February 7, 1983, pp. 36–41.

8. For more on the subject of computerized information systems, see: Robert J. Mockler and D. G. Dologite, "Put Data Processing Where the Action Is," *Business Horizons,* May–June 1981, pp. 25–31; Stephen R. Ruth, "Personnel and EDP in the 1980s," *MSU Business Topics,* Summer 1980, pp. 51–54; Peter G. W. Keen, "Decision Support Systems: Translating Analytic Techniques into Useful Tools," *Sloan Management Review,* Spring 1980, pp. 33–44; and Robert L. French, "Making Decisions Faster With Data Base Management Systems," *Business Horizons,* October 1980, pp. 33–36.

9. In addition to the discussion here, see Archie B. Carroll, "Behavioral Aspects of Developing Computer–Based Information Systems," *Business Horizons,* January–February 1982, pp. 42–51.

MIS systems also may trigger a feeling of insecurity. Some managers feel that MIS will uncover many of their shortcomings and, perhaps, will bring about their replacement. They reason that it will now be easier to identify managers who are not getting their jobs done efficiently, and no room for error will be tolerated.

Finally, there is the fact that MIS brings about change, and many people are wary of what will happen. They do not know what the ultimate effect of the MIS will be, and they start becoming defensive and fighting the system before they give it a chance.

but these problems can be dealt with.

How can management deal with these problems? The best way is to incorporate the user into the design of the system and show the individual how the MIS will assist in getting more work done. Doubts and worries should be seriously considered and action should be taken to show managers that they have nothing to fear from MIS. Then, after the system has been implemented, the organization should follow up and see that everything is going according to plan. If some managers are still concerned about the system, the superior should talk to them and help resolve their problems. There may, of course, be occasions when problems cannot be resolved completely, but if the organization approaches MIS implementation from the standpoint of both the user and the enterprise, behavioral problems can be minimized.

Summary

1. Controlling is the process in which management evaluates performance using predetermined standards and, in light of the results, makes a decision regarding corrective action. Controlling is closely linked to planning in that results serve as a basis for future decisions.

2. One of the most common control techniques is the budget. A budget is a plan that specifies results in quantitative terms and serves as a control device for feedback, evaluation, and followup. Two of the most common types of budgets are operating budgets and financial budgets. Operating budgets are used for monitoring expenses, revenues and, in the case of business firms, profit. Financial budgets integrate the financial plan of the enterprise with its operational plan.

3. Many organizations try to avoid budget inflexibility. One of the ways is by using variable budgets in which the volume of activity and the budget are tied together. Other useful approaches for increasing budget effectiveness include zero-base budgeting and comprehensive budgeting.

4. Financial statement analysis is an important financial control tool. Using data from the balance sheet or income statement, an organization can analyze financial performance. Four of the most common types of financial analysis are those related to liquidity, debt, operations, and profitability.

5. Another major form of control is that designed to monitor and evaluate operations. One of the most common tools used for this purpose, especially among manufacturing firms, is break-even analysis. Another, used for one-of-a-kind and computer projects, is PERT. By carefully spelling out all of the events and activities associated with the project and monitoring progress via the critical path, the organization can effect operational control.

6. In achieving overall performance control, an organization focuses attention on key control factors. Typical examples include ROI, market share, growth, and

profit. Others are identified as the enterprise analyzes how to tie performance and control together in a harmonious fashion.

7. Over the last 25 years, many organizations have begun using computers to help them ensure that managers have both accurate and timely information for decision purposes. The design of an effective management information system entails four basic steps: a preliminary survey, a conceptual design, a detailed design, and final implementation. The introduction of MIS can bring about dysfunctional behavior, but there are ways of dealing with these problems.

Key Terms

Activity   The efforts, resources, and time associated with completing a PERT event.

Balance sheet   A major financial statement that shows an enterprise's financial position at a specific point in time. It consists of three major parts: assets, liabilities, and owners' equity.

Comprehensive budgeting   A process by which all phases of operations are covered by budgets.

Critical path   The longest path in a PERT network.

Current ratio   A liquidity ratio computed by dividing current assets by current liabilities. Its purpose is to provide a measure of the enterprise's ability to meet current debt obligations.

Debt/asset ratio   A debt ratio used to express the relationship between a firm's total debt and total assets.

Debt/equity ratio   A debt ratio used to determine the amount of assets financed by debt and equity.

Decision support systems (DSS)   Systems that are designed to provide the manager with information that is useful in making decisions.

Debt ratios   Financial ratios used to measure the amount of financing provided by creditors.

Event   A milestone or specific accomplishment in a PERT network.

Financial budgets   Budgets that integrate the organization's financial plan with its operational plan.

Fixed costs   Costs that do not change in relation to output.

Income statement   A major financial statement that summarizes a firm's financial performance over a given period of time. It consists of four parts: revenues, cost of goods sold, expenses, and net income.

Inventory turnover ratio   An operating ratio computed by dividing average inventory into cost of goods sold. Its purpose is to provide a measure of how quickly the enterprise is turning over its inventory.

Liquidity ratios   Financial ratios designed to measure how well an enterprise can meet its current debt obligations.

Management audit   An evaluation of the abilities and successes of the executives operating an enterprise. It may be conducted either by external consultants or in-house specialists.

Management information systems (MIS)   A formally designed data network used to provide managers with timely and useful information for effective planning and control.

Operating budgets   Budgets used for monitoring expenses, revenues and, in the case of business firms, profit.

Operations ratios   Financial ratios used to measure internal performance.

Profitability ratios   Financial ratios used to measure a company's effectiveness vis-à-vis its own performance and that of the competition.

Program evaluation and review technique (PERT)   A planning and control tool used for handling one-time, nonrepetitive and complex projects.

Ratio   A relationship between two numbers.

Return on investment   A profitability ratio used to compare a company's performance with that of the competition. The calculation is: profit/assets.

Semivariable costs   Costs that vary with the quantity of work being performed, but not in a directly proportional way.

Variable budgets   Budgets that are tied to volume of activity so that the more output the enterprise produces, the greater the size of these budgets and vice versa.

Variable costs   Costs that change in relation to output.

Zero-base budgeting   A budgeting process in which funds are allocated on the basis of carefully developed decision packages and the use of cost/benefit analysis at each level of the hierarchy.

Questions for Analysis and Discussion

1. What is meant by the term controlling? Put the definition in your own words and then describe the control process in action, being sure to incorporate Figure 16–1 into your answer.

2. Every control system should have certain characteristics if it is to be effective. What does this statement mean? Be sure to include a discussion of at least five characteristics in your answer.

3. How is the budgeting process conducted in most modern organizations? Describe the process.

4. How do operating budgets differ from financial budgets? Of what value is each to the controlling process?

5. How can variable budgets help overcome a tendency toward budget inflexibility?

6. What are some of the most important advantages of budgeting? What are some of the major drawbacks? Identify and describe three of each.

7. How can ZBB help ensure an effective budgeting process? What other techniques can be used to improve effectiveness? Explain.

8. In what way does financial statement analysis help management control operations? Include in your answer a discussion of liquidity, debt, operations, and profitability ratios.

9. How does break-even analysis work? Explain with an example. Then discuss the benefits of this kind of analysis to the control process.

10. How is a PERT network constructed? Include in your answer a discussion of events, activities, and the critical path. What benefits does PERT offer? Discuss four of them.

11. What are some common key factors used in overall performance control? Identify and discuss three of them.

12. How do modern organizations tie control to performance? Include a discussion of Figure 16–5 in your answer.

13. How does a management audit work? What is the difference between external and internal management audits? Which is best? Explain.

14. Of what value is a management information system to a modern organization? What are the four basic stages in an MIS design? Describe each.

15. What behavioral problems are associated with the implementation of a new MIS? How can management try to resolve them? Explain.

Case | Ferdie's Expansion Plans

Ferdie Fernandez owns an optical manufacturing firm that specializes in the grinding of lenses for ophthalmologists and optometrists. The doctors' offices call in the prescriptions and the company makes the lenses and delivers them the next day. The company also wholesales eyeglass frames to small retail firms. The company is now thinking about expanding its operations.

At present, Ferdie is considering a contract with a local retailer to open an optical center in each of the latter's 10 outlets. Ferdie's firm would sell lenses, frames, and other accessories directly to retail clients. The fixed costs associated with setting up each store—including annual salaries, administrative overhead, inventory, and equipment for grinding the lenses—are $100,000. On average, each pair of glasses costs $25 and retails for $65. The contract that Ferdie is considering calls for the retailer to provide free space and utilities. Then, after break-even is reached, the manufacturer and retailer split all profits per pair of eyeglasses ($40) on a 50-50 basis. An initial estimate by both parties is that 5,000 sets of eyeglasses can be sold annually at each location.

In order to raise the necessary capital for opening the ten optical centers, Ferdie is going to have to seek bank financing. He will also have to develop a comprehensive budget so that expenses are closely controlled. In this regard, he is asking his accountant to help him devise an effective financial control system.

If all goes well, Ferdie has plans for the future. He currently pays $5 for each blank lens. If he could invest $700,000 in new machinery, he could make his own blanks. The annual variable cost associated with each blank is $3 for the first 200,000 blanks and $2 for every blank thereafter. Ferdie feels that if he can cut his own costs per lens and sell to other optical retailers, both local and national, he can increase his profits dramatically.

1. If Ferdie signs the contract with the retailer, how many pairs of eyeglasses will he have to sell per store in order to break even? If he sells 5,000 per store, how much profit will his firm make? What will be his ROI? If he sets a minimum ROI of 25 percent for his firm, how many pairs of glasses will he have to sell at each store?

2. What characteristics must Ferdie's control system have in order to be effective? Identify and describe five of these characteristics.

3. If Ferdie does get into the manufacture of blank lenses, what will be his annual break-even point? If he sets a minimum ROI of 20 percent, what is the minimum number he must sell? Could he sell this number by simply filling the demand he will have from his 10 retail outlets, or will he have to have outside customers as well? Show your calculations.

John's Proposed Expansion

When John Harrison started in business he had only $38 in his pocket. He bought 76 boxes of Christmas cards wholesale and began selling them door-to-door. Before that Christmas season was over, he had sold 1,600 boxes of cards at a profit of 50 cents each. John was 15 years old at the time.

During the 25 years since then, John has been quite successful in the retail business. Most of his success is a result of the three general merchandise drugstores he owns. When he opened his first store, John offered a typical line of merchandise: drugs (prescription and nonprescription), greeting cards, magazines, and candy. There was also a luncheon counter. Over time, however, he began to expand into other offerings: ice cream, paperback books, office and school supplies, and, most recently, appliances such as TVs, radios, heaters, and fans. John is also planning to put in a small store next to each of the current ones for the sale of beer, wine, liquor, mixers, and ice.

John believes that people will pay for convenience, and so far he has been right. His markup on paperback books and appliances, for example, is not extremely high. His return on investment on these lines, however, is in excess of 23 percent because of high inventory turnover. John believes he can also attain a high turnover on the new stores he is planning to open, ensuring him a continued high ROI.

Since location is so important to retail store success, John has also been looking into buying competitive stores. He has had his eye on one for more than six months and has made a tentative acquisition offer. The owner appears agreeable, and the two of them may be completing the deal shortly. In the interim, and before making a final determination on price, John has requested and obtained the right to look over the man's financial records. John is particularly interested in the store's ROI on its different lines. Also, this store is very conservative and has none of the latest offerings: paperback books, fast foods, appliances, or supplies. John believes that the addition of these lines could raise ROI by as much as 35 percent. If he can also put in a small store to handle beer, wine, and liquor, he believes he can boost ROI to 50 percent annually.

John foresees a few potential problems, however. One is that the initial offer to the owner calls for the latter to continue running the store for five years. This will allow the current owner to work to retirement, something he insists on doing. A second problem is the potential difficulty that might ensue when adding new lines, since the owner is not familiar with selling this type of merchandise. Third, John is not certain that the current clientele will welcome these changes. They are accustomed to a different product line. John may have to work on drawing in a new clientele. Finally, all of John's operations are controlled via computerized feedback. His store managers get computer printouts every Monday morning listing inventory on hand and on order. An ROI per product line is also provided, and once a month John meets with the store managers to evaluate progress and discuss changes in strategy.

Since he has never purchased a store before, John is concerned about whether he will be able to install his management system in an ongoing operation. He believes the best approach is to review the operations of the new business and determine its profitability. If things then look good, he will put in an assistant store manager to help ensure proper control of operations. From then on, it is going to be a matter of effective management.

Your Consultation

Assume that John has called you in as a consultant. After reviewing the facts in the case, outline the types of control procedures and techniques that should be used in controlling this new store. Be sure to discuss the roles of budgets, financial analysis, and key area control. Also, tell John how he can carry out a management audit of this new store. Be as complete as possible in your answer.

17

Operations Management and Control

Objectives

Many organizations produce goods and services that they sell to others. Manufacturing firms are an excellent example. These types of companies must be particularly concerned with operations management in the form of effective product design, production planning, purchasing, inventory control, work flow layout, and quality control. Additionally, many American firms are finding that they must increase their productivity if they hope to compete effectively. Operations management tools and techniques are very helpful to them in doing these things.

This chapter examines what operations management is all about and tells how it can help organizations control productivity and remain competitive. It examines the nature of operations management, giving particular emphasis to the production/operations process. Attention is also focused on the current productivity challenge and the role that operations management can play in meeting this challenge. The importance of product design, production planning, purchasing, inventory control, and work flow layout is explored as a way of describing the range and scope of operations management. Quality control is also addressed with particular attention given to the philosophical differences between American and Japanese firms. Finally, consideration is given to the importance of worker involvement and the role of monetary rewards in getting things done. When you have finished studying the material in this chapter, you will be able to

1. describe the production/operations process;

2. discuss the role of technology in operations management;

3. describe the current productivity challenge facing American firms and suggest how they can deal with it;

4. explain the product design process and the role played by value engineering and value analysis;

490

5. describe how the production planning process is carried out and the importance of master production schedules and product life cycles in this process;

6. state the role of purchasing and inventory control in effective operations management;

7. discuss the three major types of work flow layout and when each is used;

8. discuss the importance of quality control in operations management and tell how American firms can meet the Japanese challenge in this area; and

9. explain the importance of rewards when operations management is used for control purposes.

The Nature of Operations Management

Operations management is the process of designing, operating, and controlling a production system that transforms physical resources and human effort into goods and services. The field of operations management includes production management and is often referred to as "Ops Management" or "P/OM," which stands for production and operations management. In any event, over the last decade the field of operations management has received renewed interest. Not since the days of Frederick Taylor and his followers has management been as concerned with this subject. One reason is that, again and again, other countries, most notably Japan, are proving that they can produce lower cost and higher quality goods than the United States. In an effort to become competitive, management is again looking to the factory floor.

Operations management is receiving renewed interest.

Given these latest developments, students of management need at least a basic understanding of operations management. Other important reasons for a knowledge of the field include the following: (1) production, in one form or another, is a major area of concern for all organizations; (2) this function has extensive command over the total resources and assets of most organizations; (3) industrial societies depend heavily on the outputs of production organizations; and (4) the production function is directly related to many of society's most urgent problems including inflation, productivity, and resource scarcity.[1]

Production/Operations Process

The production/operations process has three basic phases: input, transformation process, and output. The **inputs** are the resources used in creating the goods and services. The transformation process uses machinery, tools,

1. Charles G. Andrew and George A. Johnson, "The Crucial Importance of Production and Operations Management," *Academy of Management Review,* January 1982, p. 145.

and techniques to convert the inputs into outputs. The outputs are the finished goods or services that will be sold to the customer or used to create still other goods or services.

Inputs

Inputs include materials and human talent.

The most common inputs are materials and human talents. In the production of an automobile, for example, materials include such things as aluminum, steel, glass, plastic, and rubber. The human talents include semiskilled and skilled laborers as well as management and the administrative staff. In the case of hospital health care, the inputs include ambulances, hospital rooms, beds, medicines, and equipment, while the human talents consist of the medical skills of the doctors and the nursing staff and the support services of the other personnel. As seen in Figure 17–1, the production/operations process relates to any conversion process used in producing goods and services.

Figure 17–1
Production/Operations Process in Action: Four Examples

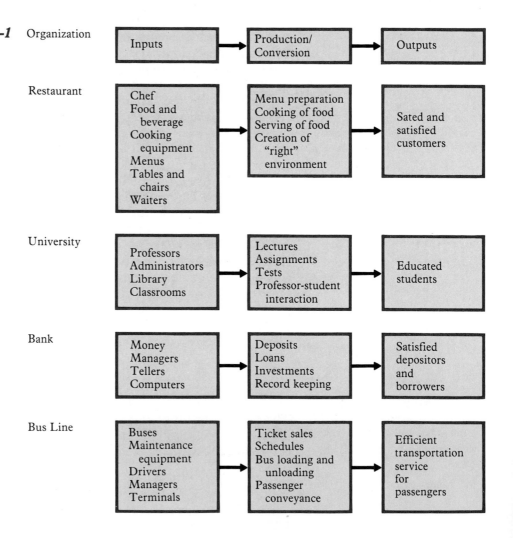

ducers will survive. Firms are finding that they can eliminate many staff managers without damage, but that it is not as easy to eliminate critical jobs in manufacturing or engineering. U.S. companies are now discovering that the operations aspect of their business has been neglected and given short shrift for too long. This brings us full-cycle. Consequently, once again, U.S. industry is beginning to see the need for POM [production/operations management]-trained individuals in order to beat the competition in producing quality products on time and at low cost.[6]

The current major challenge in the operations management area is to increase productivity. How can business turn out goods as cheaply, and with as much quality, as competitors such as the Japanese? In examining the link between operations management and productivity, we must look closely at productivity.

The Productivity Challenge

Productivity is measured by output/input.

Productivity is measured by using the equation: output/input. If a company produces 10 widgets with an input of $10, the cost per widget is $1. If through labor saving tools and techniques the firm can reduce its input to $9 and still turn out the 10 widgets, productivity has increased. Another way of improving productivity is to use the same input while increasing the output, for example by turning out 11 widgets with $10 of input. A third way is to increase output faster than input. For example, the firm might replace an old machine with a new, expensive one and find that the increase in output more than justifies the expense of the new machine because of the boost it gives to productivity. In the area of operations management and control, productivity is a key consideration.

By the mid-1970s it had become obvious that productivity was a major problem for many American firms. Statistics showed that the productivity levels of most industrialized countries were outrunning those of the United States. Of greatest concern, perhaps, was the fact that U.S. productivity was slowing up dramatically. From 1948 through 1965 the annual rate of productivity was 3.2 percent. During the 1970s it fell to an annual rate of less than 2 percent and from 1978 through 1982 it was virtually zero. Other industrialized nations were also slowing up, but not as fast. For the first time in decades, management began looking at operations management functions and trying to find out what could be done.

Productivity Truths

As management began to search for answers to the productivity problem, three basic truths came to the fore. Arnold Judson, a management consultant, has explained them this way:

Basic truths about productivity

1. Management effectiveness is by far the single greatest cause of declining productivity in the United States.

---

6. Vincent G. Reuter, "Trends in Production Management Education and Training," *Industrial Management*, May–June 1983, p. 3.

2. Most companies' efforts to improve productivity are misdirected and uncoordinated.

3. Tax disincentives, the decline of the work ethic, problems with government regulation, obsolete plant and equipment, insufficient R&D, and poor labor relations all have little to do with industry's faltering productivity.[7]

After conducting research among 236 top-level executives representing a cross section of 195 U.S. industrial firms, Judson found that there were a number of things American firms were doing wrong in their efforts to increase productivity. The major one was that their scope of productivity improvement was too narrow. They were focusing almost exclusively on cost savings in one or another part of the company. This piecemeal approach was providing short-run benefits only.

A second major problem was that many firms were focusing their efforts on the symptoms rather than on their causes. They addressed productivity problems as they appeared rather than trying to find out what was behind the problems in the first place.

Third, few companies had top management involved in their productivity efforts. In the main, the top staff were lukewarm in their support.

How must the productivity problem be addressed? Judson has recommended two important steps. First, management must view productivity as an overall organizational problem and not one that is confined to specific departments or units. Second, management must attack the problem on a long-term basis, developing and executing productivity plans that will solve today's problems and also address those that may arise in the future.[8]

Achieving Increased Productivity

Recent research reveals that firms seeking to increase their productivity have certain key elements in their programs. After talking to firms such as Beatrice Foods, Burger King, General Foods, Honeywell, Hughes Aircraft, and Kaiser Aluminum, Y. K. Shetty, a well-known researcher, reports that successful productivity improvement programs have six key elements.[9]

Top management support is needed.

First, as Judson also found, top management support is required. Unless an organization's managers and employees are convinced that a productivity improvement program has top management's support, they are unlikely to take the program seriously. This support can come in various ways. For example, at Beatrice Foods, the firm uses speeches, meetings, and a productivity philosophy booklet to illustrate its support for the program. At Honeywell a memo is used to announce the program, and then a meeting between top management and the general managers of the operating divisions lets the latter know that the program has executive support.

7. Arnold S. Judson, "The Awkward Truth About Productivity," *Harvard Business Review,* September–October 1982, p. 93.

8. For more on productivity and management see: Carlton P. McNamara, "Productivity Is Management's Problem," *Business Horizons,* March–April 1983, pp. 55–61.

9. Y. K. Shetty, "Key Elements of Productivity Improvement Programs," *Business Horizons,* March–April 1982, pp. 15–22.

Second, an organizational structure has to be established to support the productivity improvement objective. Quite often there is one person charged with this function, but he or she is given additional support in the form of a committee. For example, at Honeywell a corporate productivity administrator is responsible for assisting in the day-to-day implementation of productivity programs. A productivity steering committee, consisting of five top officials and the administrator, shares the responsibility for developing a program both to educate and to assist divisions and functional groups in measuring and improving productivity. Additionally, the firm uses productivity coordinators in its divisions, plants, and departments to chair group meetings with the workers in these units. At Beatrice Foods an operating service department is responsible for productivity efforts. It provides productivity improvement orientation and assistance to operating units and conducts productivity improvement projects. At Detroit Edison the top-level Productivity Committee is charged with surveying the firm's 65 departments, establishing productivity training programs for the managers and supervisors, and assisting the departments in establishing measurement systems and action programs.

A support structure is required.

Third, the company climate must be conducive to a productivity effort. Shetty reports that there are four major things that can be done to create the "right" company climate. The first is to make the employees aware that management is pushing for increased productivity. During this phase a company should announce its productivity objectives and describe the tools and techniques that are available to attain its goal. The second thing management must do is communicate with the employees to be sure that they understand these objectives. In the third phase the company must encourage employee involvement. This is typically done by putting the personnel on committees and involving them in discussions about ways to improve productivity. Finally, the company must recognize the contributions of the personnel through appropriate reward systems. Many companies give bonuses to individuals or groups that develop cost-saving techniques. Citations and employee- or manager-of-the-month awards are other common rewards used to recognize contributions.

A conducive corporate climate is important.

Fourth, the firm must design methods of measuring productivity progress and set realistic goals. Some of the most common measurements of progress include units per man hour, sales per payroll dollar, sales per employee, sales per asset dollar, and costs per unit. Given the wide range of possible measurements, each firm chooses those that are most useful for its own operations. In setting realistic goals, most firms seek attainable and quantifiable objectives on which they can secure data for measurement purposes. Then based on this information, the company can determine how well it is doing, where problems still exist, and how to correct them.

Productivity progress must be measured.

Fifth, the firm must be continually on the lookout for new techniques for productivity improvement. Some of the most common approaches include work simplification, value analysis, value engineering, automation, suggestions systems, time and motion studies, simulation models, and job enrichment. On an overall company basis, many companies are turning to product specialization, cutting away their excess plant and equipment, and turning out low cost, high quality, consumer demanded items.[10]

New productivity techniques must be sought.

---

10. See, for example: Agis Salpukas, "Plants to Be Smaller, More Effective," *New York Times*, February 2, 1984, p. D 1.

Implementation schedules must be formulated.

Sixth, there must be a schedule for implementing the productivity program and committing resources. As Shetty puts it, "productivity improvement . . . has to be planned and systematically pursued."[11] Recent research shows that many firms are indeed implementing productivity improvement programs. Since the early 1980s, business has been increasing the amount of money it has been pumping into R&D. The American work force is becoming more experienced at its jobs; more capital per worker is being invested; and productivity is beginning to rise. *Business Week* estimates that between 1980 and 1990 the output per hour of people working in the nonfarm business sector will rise by approximately 30 percent.[12]

Product Design

One of the major dimensions of operations management is **product design.** This phase of operations comes early in the process. During this phase management decides the specific physical dimensions of the goods or services to be produced. Quite often the process begins with research designed to generate new product or service ideas. After the research is complete, the company selects the ideas that are feasible, marketable, and compatible with the organization's strategy. Finally, it designs the product or service. During this final step the company addresses issues such as quality, cost, and reliability. Figure 17–2 provides an overall view of the product design process.

Figure 17–2
Product Design Process

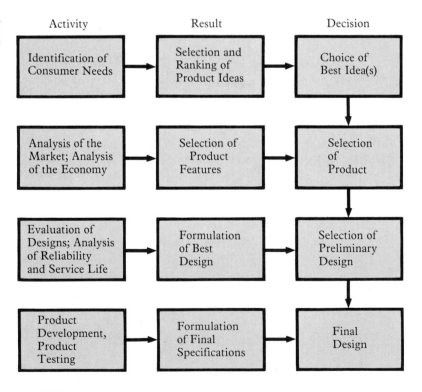

---

11. Shetty, *op. cit.,* p. 22.
12. "The Revival of Productivity," *Business Week,* February 13, 1984, p. 93.

In recent years management has come to realize that a well-formulated product or service can greatly increase profit. In fact, if the offering is well designed, the costs of making changes or correcting mistakes can be foregone and greater profit can be generated. Unfortunately, this seldom happens. Firms tend to be in too much of a hurry to get things produced. For example, a few years ago Ford Motor found that 2.7 million of its four- and six-cylinder engines had a design flaw. They were susceptible to wearing out in cold climates. In an effort to save money, two oil holes that would normally have been drilled into the piston connecting rods had been left out. The financial results were disastrous. The cost of correcting the flaw in the 56,000 recalls was $250 per car for a total of $14 million.[13] Such problems can often be minimized, if not avoided, if a firm uses effective value engineering and value analysis techniques.

Value Engineering/Value Analysis

Value engineering (VE) is the analysis of new products and the application of research and development concepts to these products for the purpose of designing the most efficient, lowest cost, highest quality output. **Value analysis** (VA) is the analysis of existing production products, specifications, and requirements demanded by production documents and purchase requests. Together VE/VA helps an organization attain its desired production objectives at the lowest cost and highest quality.[14]

If VE were properly applied in the design stage, VA could be eliminated. This usually does not happen, however. Typically something goes wrong and the company has to turn to value analysis to straighten it out. In doing so, many firms use a team approach. The team often consists of personnel from engineering, design, purchasing, production, marketing, quality, and cost departments. The group uses its collective judgment to improve both the design and the follow-up value analysis. The results can be impressive as seen by the following reported examples:

> A machinery contractor using regular carbide inserts doubled output by switching to coated carbide cutting tools without adding machines or increasing the size of the workforce.

Reported benefits of VA and VE

> A firm packaging bottles of shampoo for distributors in plain chipboard cartons changed to a 6-pack holder similar to that used in the beverage industry and saved over $100,000 in the first year.

> A large equipment manufacturer saved $18 for each dollar spent in VE/VA effort covering 2,000 projects and using a permanent four-man committee to head up the program.

> Honeywell, on defense contracts and within the company, found that the costs of VE/VA implementation were never more than one-tenth of the savings therefrom and that in a recent year they saved 18.1 dollars for every VE/VA dollar spent.[15]

---

13. "What Clouds Ford's Future," *Business Week,* July 31, 1978, p. 73.

14. Vincent G. Reuter, "Value Engineering/Value Analysis: Valuable Management Techniques," *Industrial Management,* November–December 1983, p. 2.

15. *Ibid.,* pp. 1–2.

Computer-Aided Design

Another product design development that is being used by many firms is CAD/CAM (computer-aided design/computer-aided manufacturing). In the case of CAD, for example, engineers can now produce blueprints without ever lifting a pencil. Using an input device, the engineer can draw directly on a cathode ray tube (CRT). The pen, which is connected to the CRT by a wire, feeds information to the computer system. Once the outline is placed on the CRT, the engineer can then rotate it, view the design from any angle, stretch it out, color or shade it, and change or add depth so as to produce a 3-D version of the drawing. The engineer can also call up reference drawings that have been preprogrammed into the computer's memory and incorporate them into the emerging design. If the engineer wants to redesign just a section of the drawing, he or she merely fits the redesigned piece into the sketch. The entire design does not have to be redrawn. As a result of such computer-aided techniques, the engineer can correct mistakes and make changes as he or she goes along. Then, when the design is finished, a hard-copy can be produced with just the touch of a button.[16]

CAM is also proving to be very useful. In particular, it allows manufacturers to produce different sizes of a particular part, as well as a number of different parts within a given size range, by simply changing the programmed instructions that guide the machine.

Applications of CAM

Caterpillar, the large tractor company, for example, uses CAM to make components for an engine drive assembly. About a dozen machines stand on both sides of a railroad-like track . . . along which a transfer device shuttles parts among the work stations, where some 30 to 40 separate machining operations are carried out. Operators at entry and exit points clamp the part on and off the transfer mechanism; the rest of the process is computer driven.

Another use of CAM is illustrated by a leading automobile manufacturer which uses the technology to weld gas tanks. In designing the tank, engineers chose a five-sided, irregular shape in which no two sides were parallel. Were the operation manual, someone would have to turn the tank at each stage; but with CAM, a complex welding system molds the individual sides precisely to the specifications—ensuring quality control even for such a nonstandard design.[17]

Production Planning

Production planning is the process whereby management meshes demand forecasts for goods and services with scheduled resource outputs. At this phase the firm's strategic sales forecast and production plan are brought

---

16. John McElroy, "CAD/CAM Comes of Age," *Automotive Industries*, July 1981, p. 36.

17. Bela Gold, "CAM Sets New Rules for Production," *Harvard Business Review*, November–December 1982, p. 90. For still more on this subject see: Yukimaro Kawatani, "Japan in the Computer Age," *Industrial Management*, January–February 1982, pp. 24–28.

together. After determining annual demand for each good and service, the firm breaks down these forecasts into short-term production plans with detailed schedules. The schedules describe manpower, equipment, and inventory requirements. During this process, management answers questions such as:

1. What product lines will be produced?

2. How much of each line will be produced?

3. How much material and other inputs will be needed to turn out each of these lines?

4. How many personnel will be required to produce these goods?

5. What types of technology and machinery will be needed to get all of this work done?

Master Production Schedules

If there are many different items being produced at the same time, coordination of production activities becomes extremely important. In meeting the challenge to coordinate activities, many firms use a master production schedule. This schedule takes into account all of the raw materials, subcomponents, components, machines, fabrication, and assembly operations that have to be carried out to produce the desired goods. If properly drawn up, the master schedule incorporates all of the production activities; and if properly implemented, it serves to ensure that everything is done efficiently and on time.

Unfortunately, bottlenecks occur frequently in production operations. Some crucial component does not arrive from the supplier, or a machine breakdown results in the need to delay the final assembly of a unit. When a bottleneck occurs, the master schedule can be consulted in order to find ways of working around the problem and to keep other jobs on time. In determining how to reschedule jobs, the master schedule is a vital document. It helps management keep track of the current status of all work and decide how to deal with problems. The schedule also provides a sound basis for decisions about staffing.

Product Life Cycles

Production planning and scheduling have to be tied to the product life cycle of the goods. Some products have very long life cycles (5 years or more) while others have very short ones. Working closely with the marketing department, the operations management people schedule production so that it coincides with the various phases of the products's life cycle.

In recent years many firms have found that the life cycle for their products is growing shorter. Competitors are flocking into the market place at a rapid rate, making older products obsolete more quickly. As a result, firms are turning to shorter production runs for their goods. When these runs are complete, the firm then tools up and begins production of another product. Quite often it is a more up-to-date version of the earlier offering.

Life cycles are tied to production schedules.

In this way the company reduces the problems associated with manufacturing goods for which there is little, if any, demand. The Japanese have been particularly skillful at tying production planning and scheduling to product life cycles. Casio, famous for its manufacture of watches and pocket calculators, is a good example. An engineering, marketing, and assembly company, with only a small investment in production facilities and marketing channels, Casio relies heavily on its production-marketing flexibility. It produces goods with very short product life cycles. As soon as Casio comes out with a product such as a calculator, it begins reducing the price to discourage competition. Then, within a few months, it introduces an improved version of the product, for example a calculator that plays musical notes when the numerical keys are touched.

> In Casio's case, the . . . strategy is to integrate design and development into marketing so that consumers' desires are analyzed by those closest to the market and quickly converted into engineering blueprints. Because Casio has this function so well developed, it can afford to make its new products obsolete quickly. Its competitors, all organized vertically on the assumption of a one- or two-year life cycle for this type of product, are at a severe disadvantage.[18]

Purchasing and Inventory Control

Two other major areas of operations management are purchasing and inventory control. The two are interrelated in that firms usually purchase materials and parts and store them until they are used. Not wanting to have too much on hand at any one time, however, they seek to balance the risk associated with stockouts against the costs of storing excess amounts.

Purchasing Practices and Organization

Almost every firm purchases some things from outside suppliers. Even large corporations rely on external vendors to provide them with some of the materials and parts needed in operations. As a result, it is important to have well-defined purchasing practices and an organizational structure that can efficiently handle purchase decisions.

Purchasing practices differ from firm to firm, but there are some general ones used by many. Some of the most common include the following:

1. A centralized purchasing department buys all of the major items that are supplied by outside vendors.

2. Minor purchases or one-of-a-kind items are bought directly by the departments that need them.

---

18. Kenichi Ohmae, *The Mind of the Strategist: The Art of Japanese Management* (New York: McGraw-Hill Book Company, 1982), pp. 117–118. For more on this topic see: Robert H. Hayes and Steven C. Wheelwright, "Link Manufacturing Process and Product Life Cycles," *Harvard Business Review*, January–February 1979, pp. 133–140.

Common purchasing practices

3. Buyers are required to have a solid understanding of the engineering specifications and requirements of all items being purchased from outside.

4. All purchases in excess of $10,000 are handled on the basis of low bid commensurate with the reputation of the supplier.

5. No special rebates or favors are accepted from any suppliers regardless of the conditions under which they are offered.

Guidelines of this nature are designed to ensure that the company is able to obtain the best quality merchandise at the fairest possible prices. In many cases these guidelines apply directly to the purchasing department since it is responsible for the purchase of expensive components and parts as well as for all large orders, regardless of the individual cost per item in the order. The centralization of large purchase orders is both logical and cost saving. From the standpoint of logic, as the purchasing people become increasingly familiar with how and where to buy, they begin to save the firm money. In shopping for vendors, they learn the questions to ask and the ways to size up the seller. Additionally, since they are doing this job on a full-time basis, they will eventually prove superior to the individual department personnel for whom purchasing is a side duty. By buying in large quantities, the purchasing department is also in a better position to negotiate the best possible price with the suppliers.

Inventory Control Practices

Earlier in the text the value of the economic order quantity formula was discussed. At that point it was noted that every firm attempts to balance product demand with the amount of product inventory on hand. Operations management is concerned with more than just computing an EOQ formula for each product line, however. Many firms are also using material requirements planning and just-in-time production methods.

Material Requirements Planning

MRP helps control materials and inventory.

Material requirements planning (MRP) is a systematic, comprehensive manufacturing and controlling technique used to increase the efficiency both of material handling and of inventory control. The master production schedule is the basis of an MRP system, and most MRP's are computerized because of the large amount of data processing that must be done. The formulation of an MRP begins with an annual sales forecast, which is used to get an initial idea of the demand for the company's products. Each of these products is "exploded" to determine the materials and parts that will be needed to produce it. The amount of inventory on hand is then subtracted from the total that will be needed, to arrive at the amount that has to be ordered. Then the time between the placement of an order and the expected delivery date is calculated along with lead time necessary to ensure that materials and parts are received in time for production. The forecast and the materials requirement plan often have to be revised on the basis of actual sales so that demand and supply can be kept in balance. When the system works properly, the firm can avoid costly ripple effects from either a sharp, unexpected drop in sales or delivery problems created by suppliers.

MRP is becoming increasingly popular because of the benefits it offers in controlling inventory and adjusting for changes in the economic environment. One national study of MRP found that the benefits of the system can be extremely high.

> Installation costs ranged from less than $100,000 for small companies to more than $1 million for large ones. But the average increase in annual inventory turnover was an astounding 50.3%. For the typical company with $65 million in annual sales, that made possible an inventory reduction of about $8 million, and a saving of $1.8 million per year in carrying costs calculated at recent interest rates. Some companies reported that MRP had enabled them to cut in half the amount of money tied up in inventories for each dollar of sales. The new system also improved service to customers: the average lead time for deliveries declined 18%.[19]

JIT Production

JIT production is hand-to-mouth.

Another development, related to inventory control, is just-in-time (JIT) inventory production. **JIT production** is the purchase or production or both of small quantities of products just in time for use. This hand-to-mouth approach leads to smaller inventories and reduces the need for storage space, inventory-related equipment such as forklifts and racks, and material support personnel. Most important, because of the absence of extra inventories, the organization is able to run an error-free operation.

In some ways, JIT production is not new. Large organizations have always sought to minimize inventories while maintaining full-scale production. For example, at the Anheuser-Busch brewery in St. Louis there is only a two-hour supply of unfilled cans on hand at any time. The firm brings in empty cans on a continuous basis to replace depleted inventory, allowing manufacturing to continue unimpeded. It is not necessary to produce a standard product, however, in order to use JIT production. It can also be employed in small operations and with multiple product lines.

The big problem with JIT production is that the company may run out of inventory from time to time, resulting in work stoppages. Yet this feature is not looked on negatively by operations management people. They see it as a way of pinpointing problem areas and working out solutions.

> . . . now the analysts and engineers pour out of their offices and mingle with foremen and workers trying to get production going again. Now the causes—bad raw materials, machine breakdown, poor training, tolerances that exceed process capabilities—get attention so that the problem may never recur.[20]

After these matters are resolved, inventories are often cut again, creating still more problems. These, too, are addressed as the operations management

---

19. Lewis Beman, "A Big Payoff From Inventory," *Fortune,* July 27, 1981, pp. 78–79.

20. Richard J. Schonberger, "A Revolutionary Way to Streamline the Factory," *Wall Street Journal,* November 15, 1982, p. 24.

people seek to improve efficiency still further. Is this really possible? Japanese firms have proven that it is, leading more American firms to follow suit.

Research shows that companies not using JIT production are now beginning to look seriously into adopting this technique. Richard Schonberger, an international expert on Japanese manufacturing techniques, has noted that the best way to adopt it is often "cold turkey." He recommends that firms get going and, "remove inventories from the shop floor, dismantle distance-spanning conveyors, move machines close together and permanently reallocate floor space that once held inventory." As a result, he predicts, "Spasms of work stoppage for lack of parts will soon get everyone involved in solving underlying problems."[21] For firms that want to employ a slower approach, incremental methods are available. One of the most common is to reduce machine setup costs. A second is to cut back inventory in an effort to implement JIT production. A third is to find local suppliers, thereby reducing delivery time.

> The only significant obstacles to JIT are those that stand in the way of any major change in management system: reorienting people's thinking. Much of that task has been done. Just-in-time programs have been established at General Electric, the big-three auto makers, Goodyear . . . and various other American industrial companies.

> Transforming our coughing, sputtering plants into streamlined just-in-time producers sounds like a 10- or 20-year project. It may not take that long because the innovating has been done for us. Taylor's innovation, scientific management, was readily exportable and implementable in Europe and Japan. . . . The Japanese innovation, just-in-time, is equally transportable.[22]

Work Flow Layout

Another critical area of operations management is **work flow layout,** the process of determining the physical arrangement of the production system. Work flow processes are important in converting inputs into outputs. If personnel and machines are scattered in a haphazard arrangement, productivity will suffer. If these machines can be arranged in an orderly, logical, cost-effective manner, productivity can be increased. In a well-designed work layout arrangement, some of the major benefits include (a) a minimization of investment, (b) more effective use of existing space, (c) a reduction in material handling costs and overall production time, (d) the maintenance of operational flexibility, and (e) the guarantee of employee safety and convenience.

Basic Layout Formats

Although there are many production layout configurations, there are three basic formats. These are the product layout, the process layout, and the fixed-position layout. All other layouts are simply variations of these three.

---

21. *Ibid.*
22. *Ibid.*

Product Layout

A product layout arranges resources in progressive steps.

In a **product layout,** machines, equipment, and personnel are arranged according to the progressive steps used in building the product. A good example is found in auto assembly plants. As the basic frame of the car moves down the line, parts are put on it until a finished auto emerges at the end of the line. (See Figure 17–3.) When large numbers of manufactured products are to be assembled, machines and personnel are often placed at fixed work-stations along the line with each making a contribution to the product as it moves past.

This type of layout has both advantages and disadvantages. On the positive side, the workers do not have to be very skilled. Most assembly lines are staffed with unskilled and semiskilled personnel. Additionally, one supervisor can usually oversee the work of many people. Some direct management costs tend to be low. On the negative side, the firm is locked into one type of layout. Changing to another major form is extremely costly. Second, the assembly line is no stronger than its weakest link. If a person cannot keep up or a machine goes down, it may be necessary to stop the line; if the firm runs out of an inventory item such as headlights for the cars, it will be impossible to continue assembly. Finally, in recent years more and more workers have begun to rebel against the monotony, boredom, and specialization of the line. They want more authority and control of their work environment.

Process Layout

A process layout groups components on the basis of function.

A **process layout** is one in which all components are grouped on the basis of the functions they perform. All lathe machines are placed in one area; all welding machines are placed together in another. In job shops

Figure 17–3
Basic Layout Formats

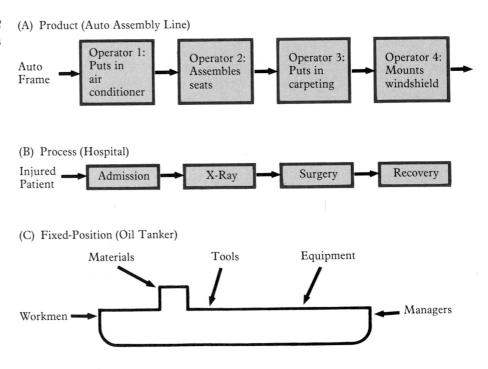

(A) Product (Auto Assembly Line)

Auto Frame → Operator 1: Puts in air conditioner → Operator 2: Assembles seats → Operator 3: Puts in carpeting → Operator 4: Mounts windshield →

(B) Process (Hospital)

Injured Patient → Admission → X-Ray → Surgery → Recovery

(C) Fixed-Position (Oil Tanker)

Materials   Tools   Equipment

Workmen →   ← Managers

where the product can be moved from one area to another, process layout works well. Yet the layout is not restricted to manufacturing. Hospitals (see Figure 17–3) also employ this layout. The patient is literally moved to some departments (X-ray, surgery) while others come to him or her (dietetics, pharmacy). In any event, the functional arrangement of a process layout is infinitely superior for hospitals to that of a product layout.

The process layout has both advantages and disadvantages. On the positive side, process layouts are more flexible than product layouts. They are also more suitable for the custom processing of diverse outputs because they can address themselves to the specific needs of such processing. On the negative side, work must be scheduled carefully. Otherwise some departments will be overscheduled while others sit idle.

Fixed-Position Layout

With fixed-position layout, the workers come to the work.

A **fixed-position layout** is one in which the workers come to the work. (See Figure 17–3.) Aircraft, diesel locomotives, and oil tankers are produced using this kind of layout. The product is too large or heavy to be moved so the workers and the equipment come to the product.

Like the other kinds of layouts, this one has both advantages and disadvantages. On the positive side, the resources are efficiently used because it is too costly to build the product any other way. Additionally, workers like this form of layout because it allows them to move about during their work day. On the negative side, this work design is expensive because it requires the firm to duplicate resources. For example, if there are three ships being built simultaneously, the company has to have three times as many crews and three times as much equipment and materials.

Quality Control

Quality control is the process of ensuring that goods and services are produced according to predetermined specifications. Earlier in the text, quality circles were discussed. These circles are certainly one way of improving output quality, but they are not the only way. Many other approaches currently are being used, as American managers begin to emphasize quality.

America's leadership in quality has been almost imperceptibly eroding for years. In the last few months, more and more U.S. executives have awakened to the fact that they are caught in a fateful struggle. They are turning their companies upside down to give quality specialists more clout. Vendors are being told to supply better parts or lose the business. In hundreds of factories, small groups of workers are sitting down periodically to search for ways of improving quality and productivity. Executive offices and factory floors ring with slogans. . . . at Ford Motor Co.: "If it's not right, we won't ship it, and we mean that." Intones a General Electric spokesman: "Quality is our No. 1 focus."[23]

23. Jeremy Main, "The Battle for Quality Begins," *Fortune,* December 29, 1980, p. 28.

Feedback and Feedforward

Feedforward control seeks to avoid problems.

In Chapter 16, the control process was examined. Using feedback, the process seeks to correct mistakes after they are made. Quality control also makes use of **feedforward control** to help *avoid* problems in the first place. This kind of control focuses on the quality of the production inputs and the work process. By ensuring that inputs and conversion/transformation processes are being handled properly, the organization reduces the likelihood of product recalls, consumer complaints, and lost business.

Operations management people work to balance the costs of feedback with the expenses associated with lack of quality. There is always a tradeoff between the two. For example, a company building an aircraft puts heavy emphasis on purchasing quality raw materials, subcomponents, components, and parts. As the work proceeds the firm also checks progress, ensuring that the craft is being built according to specifications. When the plane is completed, another series of quality checks is made. Finally, the machine is delivered to the customer. For the rest of its life, the plane's quality is judged on the basis of needed repairs and customer complaints.

Many of the control steps described in this example are feedforward in nature. Operations management people catch and correct quite a few errors. Some errors go undetected, however, and have to be picked up later. Still others are not sought because the cost of conducting the inspection is too high; it is more cost efficient to wait and get them later. In any event, the firm's goal is to produce a high quality good commensurate with market price. Unfortunately, in recent years many American firms have found themselves unable to keep up with Japanese competition.

Meeting the Japanese Challenge

Beginning in the late 1960s, the Japanese started to provide strong competition in a number of different fields including household electronics, optics, shipbuilding, and steel. Since then they have expanded their offerings to include air conditioners, automobiles, calculators, computers, musical instruments, textiles, and watches, to name but six. In each case they have been successful in no small measure because of product quality. This quality emphasis is based on two points ingrained at all levels of Japanese industry:

- Do it right the first time. It is a waste of time, material, men, and machines to separate good from bad production.

- Quality control is not a specialized production function. If there is a quality problem, it cannot be corrected by supervisors. Quality problems are due to problems in the production system and the system must be corrected.[24]

Japanese concepts of quality control are different from those followed by many western firms. (See Table 17–1.) Their ideas are put into practice by having the personnel assume a more involved role in responsibility for quality. Table 17–2 illustrates this contrast between American and Japanese

---

24. William A. Mahon and Richard E. Dyck, "Japanese Quality Systems From A Marketing Viewpoint," *Industrial Management,* September–October 1982, p. 10.

Table 17–1
Concepts Of Quality

Western	Japanese
Higher quality will bring about higher cost and lower productivity.	Higher quality will bring about lower costs and higher productivity.
Quality is the responsibility of the Quality Control Department people.	Everyone is responsible for quality control.
With large production runs, low costs per unit can be achieved.	With small production runs, low costs per unit can be achieved.
There is a tradeoff between cost, quality, and delivery.	There need never be a tradeoff between cost, quality, and delivery.
Poor quality should be kept at a minimum.	Poor quality should be totally eliminated.

Japanese firms encourage quality consciousness.

firms. At Matsushita, for example, the philosophy of quality control includes such key elements as encouraging quality consciousness in the personnel, involving them in quality control circles, removing the potential for human error through automation, designing quality into the process, securing good quality components, and randomly inspecting the product.

. . . design engineers meet twice a month with the component manager and quality reliability and related specifications. One to two product planning and cross-functional meetings take place each month for an exchange of ideas. Although the design engineer is responsible for design, he has frequent contact with customers. The first outline of the product plan includes careful calculation of quality, reliability, and cost. After this, drawings are made of the concept, and pilot production and testing begin. If the latter two processes are successful, a mass production sample is made, tested, and mass production begins. New or redesigned production systems are always

Table 17–2
Role of Personnel in Quality Control

American	Japanese
Management has a short-term view of operations.	Management has a long-term view of operations.
Employees are judged on productivity and their individual contribution.	Employees are judged on work contribution, quality, cleanliness, and assistance to others.
Employees perform specific tasks within well-defined job descriptions.	Employees perform their own jobs and others for which they have the ability and time.
Employees have low organizational commitment and are responsible for their jobs only.	Employees have high organizational commitment and share responsibility for accomplishment.
Scrap rates vary between 1 and 5 percent and there is a large amount of work in progress.	Scrap rates are usually less than one half of 1 percent and there is a minimum amount of work in progress.
Quality checks are performed by inspectors.	Quality checks are performed by each worker.
Unions have an adversary relationship with management. Strikes are accepted as legitimate bargaining tools.	There are company unions and no adversarial relationships. Most grievances are quickly settled; strikes are very rare.

considered in light of total quality control. Matsushita believes that each parameter of quality is new for each product, and design and production engineers determine the parameter jointly.[25]

In ensuring that the best quality components are received from the vendors, Japanese firms often have a personal financial investment in these suppliers. They also work closely with them, helping the vendors improve their quality and delivery time. The firms believe in "co-prosperity" with the suppliers. At Toshiba, for example, the Quality Assurance Systems Department develops instructions for component suppliers and makes an annual review of all vendors to determine which should be given additional business and which should be terminated.

Japanese firms also make heavy use of computerized operations. They have come to realize that a highly mechanized, technologically advanced production system is not only efficient but eliminates human error. This approach is complemented by random inspections made by quality control people. In the case of many products, the inspection is quite rigorous. For example, Matsushita carefully inspects one out of ten TV sets, switching the machine on for six hours and off for two, at a temperature of 40°C and 80 percent humidity to ensure that it will more than stand up to the demands of everyday use.

If there are quality problems, Japanese firms respond quickly. Quite often the design engineer who first drew the blueprints for the product becomes involved. If a redesign is needed, the engineer knows what has to be done.

The success of the Japanese is leading more and more American firms to study and emulate their methods. It has become obvious that this success is a result of both technology and more effective personnel practices. As the philosophy of American companies begins to change to accommodate the emphasis of production quality, we should see a closing of the quality gap between the two countries.

Operations Management and Rewards

Operations management is heavily concerned with product design, plant layout, and work quality. There is one area crucial to productivity and efficiency that warrants consideration, however, even though it is peripheral to the main concerns of operations management. That area is reward systems.

Reward Systems

Money is an important motivator.

When an organization implements an effective plant layout, it should achieve productivity increases. The overall success of the effort, however, is often a result of the reward systems that accompany the implementation. When motivation was discussed in Chapter 12, the value of intrinsic rewards was noted. Attention was also given to money as a motivator. To a large degree, the implementation of successful operations management concepts

---

25. *Ibid.*, p. 12.

depends more on monetary rewards than it does on the psychological satisfaction brought about by job enrichment. Mitchell Fein, a consultant and frequent contributor to the literature, reports that

> worker involvement programs which offer only job satisfaction as the prime reward for involvement will be supported by only a small proportion of the work force and tap a fraction of the potential for improvement in the organization.
>
> Worker involvement programs which offer financial rewards by sharing productivity improvement with employees through formal productivity sharing plans create high levels of involvement, produce results very quickly, and raise productivity to much higher levels than are attained by nonfinancial reward programs only.[26]

These findings point out the need to combine operations management decisions with personnel rewards. In this way greater control of productivity can be ensured.

Productivity plans tell how gains are to be shared with the workers.

Presently, there are a number of productivity plans designed to involve employees in productivity improvement and share the gains with the workers. According to the General Accounting Office, the most popular one is the **Scanlon plan.**[27] Under this plan the total payroll dollars are divided by the total dollar sales value of production in determining productivity gains. These are then shared with the workers. For example, consider a firm that has found from past performance that for $1 million in payroll it is able to produce goods worth $2 million in sales revenue. Under the Scanlon plan, if $2 million worth of goods can be produced for less than $1 million in payroll or more than $2 million worth of goods can be produced for $1 million in payroll, there is then a productivity gain. This gain is then shared between the workers and the management on a 75/25 basis.

Another popular productivity sharing arrangement is the **Rucker plan,** which is similar to Scanlon but more sophisticated in design. Under the Rucker plan, using past performance, the company establishes the relationship between the total earnings of the hourly rated employees and the production value created by the company. Productivity gains are then shared with the workers. David Belcher, a compensation expert, has explained the specifics of the Rucker plan this way:

> Assume that the company puts $.55 worth of materials, supplies, and power into production to obtain a product worth $1.00. Value added or production value is thus $.45 for each $1.00 of sales value. Assume also that analysis shows that 40 percent of production value is attributable to labor. The productivity ratio becomes 2.5, and for a payroll (plus benefits) of $100,000, standard production value is $250,000. If actual production value for the month is $300,000 a gain of $50,000 is available for bonus

26. Mitchell Fein, "Improved Productivity Through Worker Involvement," *Industrial Management,* May–June 1983, p. 4.

27. General Accounting Office, *Productivity Sharing Programs: Can They Contribute to Productivity Improvement?* U.S. GAO, Document Handling & Information Services Facility, PO Box 6015, Gaithersburg, MD 20760, AFMD-81, March 3, 1981, p. 22.

and is distributed 40 percent to labor and 60 percent to the company. Labor's bonus share for the month is $20,000.[28]

There are many other group productivity plans from the Kaiser Plan to Improshare, but they all have one thing in common: using some predetermined formula they reward employees for productivity increases. In some cases, these gains have proven to be dramatic. For example, using Improshare, a plan he developed, Fein reports that he was able to increase productivity in a highly mechanized brick plant by 30 percent in 3 weeks and raise productivity in a plywood plant by 24 percent in 4 weeks and 34 percent for the overall year.[29]

In all of these productivity sharing plans there are two major considerations. First, financial rewards must be given to the employees. Second, management must secure worker support. Without these two elements, operations management efforts are less than ideal. Job redesign coupled with improved work layout and technology is incomplete. There must be monetary rewards as well. Money is still a major motivator. In fact, in the view of many researchers it remains the most important one. Edwin Locke, a well-known behavioral scientist, and his associates have noted that, "For the last several decades ideological bias has led many [social scientists] to deny the efficacy of money as a motivator and to emphasize the potency of participation. The results of research to date indicate that the opposite point of view would have been more accurate."[30] Management must realize that in controlling operations it must tie its efforts to a reward system that encourages work participation. Only in this way will it be able to obtain the greatest benefits from the ideas set forth in this chapter.

Summary

1. Operations management is the process of designing, operating, and controlling a production system that transforms physical resources and human effort into goods and services. This is done through the production/operations process, which has three basic phases: input, transformation process, and output. The inputs are the materials and human talents used to produce the output. The transformation process consists of the production activities that take the inputs and combine them in some special way so as to produce the outputs. The outputs are the final results of the transformation process.

2. There have been many technological breakthroughs over the last decade. Some of these are being used to automate the work place. One of the most important is flexible manufacturing systems that allow companies to produce a small amount of output with the same efficiency previously reserved only for large production runs. Such advances are also helping American firms meet the productivity challenge.

3. Productivity is measured by using the equation: output/input. There are a number of reasons for the productivity lag in the United States. One is the failure of firms to develop an overall, long-range plan for dealing with the problem.

28. David W. Belcher, *Compensation Administration* (Englewood Cliffs, New Jersey: Prentice-Hall, Inc., 1975), p. 332.

29. Fein, *op. cit.,* p. 13.

30. Reported in *ibid.,* p. 6.

A second is a focus on productivity symptoms rather than on its causes. A third is the failure of top management to become active in the process. Some of the most effective ways of increasing productivity include getting top management involved, organizing to support the productivity objective, developing a climate conducive to this objective, designing methods of measuring progress and setting realistic goals, being continually on the lookout for new productivity improvement techniques, and developing a schedule for implementing the productivity program and committing the necessary resources.

4. One of the major dimensions of operations management is product design. This process usually begins with research designed to generate product or service ideas. Then the organization selects the ideas that are feasible, marketable, and compatible with its strategy. The last stage is the actual design of the product or service. In improving quality and reducing product problems, many firms use value engineering and value analysis. Value engineering is the analysis of new products and the application of research and development concepts to these products for the purpose of designing the most efficient, lowest cost, highest quality output. Value analysis is the analysis of existing production products, specifications, and requirements demanded by production documents and purchase requests. Other commonly used tools and techniques include computer-aided design and computer-aided manufacturing.

5. Production planning is the process whereby management meshes demand forecasts for goods and services with scheduled resource outputs. Production planning often involves the use of master production schedules and careful consideration of product life cycles.

6. Two other major areas of operations management are purchasing and inventory control. Purchasing practices and organizational arrangements are commonly drawn up to ensure the most efficient purchasing possible. Inventory control procedures often make wide use of material requirements planning and JIT production.

7. Another critical area of operations management is work flow layout. There are three basic layout formats. One is product layout in which the personnel are arranged according to the progressive steps used in building the product. A second is process layout in which all components are grouped on the basis of the functions they perform. The third is fixed-position layout in which the workers come to the work.

8. Quality control is the process of ensuring that goods and services are produced according to predetermined specifications. In this process, management typically makes use of both feedforward and feedback control. Many firms are also beginning to emulate Japanese approaches by encouraging personnel to do the job right the first time and by giving them authority and responsibility for quality control, as opposed to assigning this function to a special department.

9. The implementation of operations management concepts depends more on monetary rewards than it does on psychological satisfaction brought about by job enrichment. Today a growing number of firms are opting for productivity plans in which gains are shared by the employees and the management.

Key Terms

Feedforward control A control system that is used to help avoid problems rather than to deal with them after they have occurred.

Fixed-position layout A layout in which the workers come to the work.

Flexible manufacturing systems Computer-controlled systems that allow companies to produce desired outputs at low price and high quality.

Inputs   Materials and human inputs used in the production process.

JIT production   The purchase or production or both of small quantities just in time for use.

Material requirements planning   A systematic, comprehensive manufacturing and controlling technique used to increase the efficiency both of material handling and of inventory control.

Operations management   The process of designing, operating, and controlling a production system that transforms physical resources and human effort into goods and services.

Outputs   The final result of the transformation process, these goods or services are sold to customers or used in the creation of other goods or services.

Process layout   A layout in which all components are grouped on the basis of the functions they perform.

Product design   A phase of operations during which management decides the specific physical dimensions of the goods or services to be produced.

Production planning   The process whereby management meshes demand forecasts for goods and services with scheduled resource outputs.

Productivity   A performance measure determined by dividing output by input.

Product layout   The arrangement of machines, equipment, and personnel according to the progressive steps used in building the product.

Quality control   The process of ensuring that goods and services are produced according to predetermined specifications.

Rucker plan   A gain sharing productivity plan in which a company establishes the relationship between the total earnings of hourly rated employees and the production value created by the company in determining productivity gains to be shared by the employees and managers.

Scanlon plan   A gain sharing productivity plan that compares total payroll dollars to dollar sales value of production in determining productivity gains, which are then shared by the employees and managers on a 75/25 basis.

Transformation process   The production activities that take inputs and combine them in some special way so as to produce the desired outputs.

Value analysis   The analysis of existing products, specifications, and requirements demanded by production documents and purchase requests.

Value engineering   The analysis of new products and the application of research and development concepts to these products for the purpose of designing the most efficient, lowest cost, highest quality output.

Work flow layout   The process of determining the physical arrangement of the production system.

Questions for Analysis and Discussion

1. What is meant by the term operations management? Put the definition in your own words, being sure to include a discussion of the production/operations process in your answer.

2. Is the production/operations process confined to the manufacture of products or can it be used by nongoods-producing organizations as well? Explain your answer.

3. How has technology invaded the factory? Cite some examples and explain how this development is leading managers to redirect their attention to the factory floor.

4. What is meant by the term productivity? What do managers need to know regarding how they can achieve increased productivity in their operations? In your answer, cite at least four of the findings reported by Y. K. Shetty.

5. What is meant by the term product design? What importance do value engineering and value analysis have to product design/redesign? How can CAD and CAM be of value in product design?

6. What is production planning all about? In your answer be sure to discuss the importance of master production schedules and product life cycles.

7. Of what value are purchasing practices to effective operations management? What role does material requirements planning play in helping organizations control their inventory? What role does JIT production play? Be specific in your answers.

8. There are three basic work flow layouts and all others are simply variations of these three. What are these three basic work flow layouts and when would each be used? Use examples in your answer.

9. In your own words, what is meant by the term quality control? What roles are played by feedforward and feedback control in helping ensure the best quality?

10. You have just been asked to tell a group of business people how American firms can meet the Japanese challenge. What would you tell them? Identify and describe the three main points you would make to the group.

11. How important are reward systems to operations management? Explain your answer, being sure to incorporate a general discussion of productivity plans and their value for personnel motivation.

| Case | # Problems on the Line |

Shelling Products is a medium-sized manufacturing firm located on the West Coast. Founded by George Shelling, the company has always been run by family members. The firm specializes in the production of high tech components that are used in aircraft, computers, and sophisticated telecommunications satellites.

Last year the president of the firm, Margaret Shelling, was reviewing new product ideas with her top engineers. They pointed out to her that with the company's current experience, it could profitably produce modern technology consumer products. At the top of their list of suggestions was the portable telephone. Margaret had her marketing people check out the idea and found there were only a handful of firms that manufactured these portable phones, although the industry consensus was that by the end of the 1980s there would be many more competitors.

A month later Margaret contacted one of the nation's largest retail stores and asked them if they would be interested in a portable phone. Shelling Products would design, develop, and manufacture the unit, and the retailer would sell it. The idea sounded fine to the other company, especially since Shelling would be underwriting all design, development, and manufacturing costs.

It took Margaret's engineers two months to strip down competitive models, study them, design the Shelling offering, and get it into production. Then it was but six months until Shelling was ready to make its first shipment of the phones. The retailer mounted a vigorous advertising campaign to accompany the announcement that these phones could be purchased at any of its outlets around the country. Thanks to its high technology and efficient production system, Shelling's price was quite low and the retailer offered the phones for 25 percent less than the amount they could be purchased for from the competition. Best of all, the first phones arrived at the stores on December 1, just in time for Christmas. By the end of December, the retailer had sold most of the 25,000 units and placed an order for another 25,000 to be delivered by the end of January. Things could not have looked brighter for Shelling. Then the bottom fell out.

On January 15, Margaret received a call from the retailer's headquarters. The firm was being deluged with complaints from customers who were experiencing difficulty using the phone. The biggest problem was that the phone would suddenly cut off in the middle of a call. The second most common complaint was that the reception was extremely poor and people were unable to hear the other party. Based on the number of calls it has received, the retailer estimates that approximately 20 percent of all the phones have quality problems. It is urging customers to return the phones to the store in exchange for new ones. In turn the phones will be shipped back to Shelling for repairs. If the estimate of 20 percent defects is accurate, Shelling will just break even on the product. If any more than 20 percent are returned, the firm will lose money on the venture.

Margaret called a meeting of her engineers and design people earlier today to tell them the problem. "The first shipment of defective phones should be arriving later this week," she said. "We'll have to strip them down, find out what went wrong, and then repair them as soon as possible. I want this problem given first priority. Put all of your other work on hold." The head of engineering told her, "I'm going to personally head up this project. I'll get back to you with my findings within 72 hours of the time we receive the first shipment."

1. From your reading of the case, what went wrong? Why are so many of the phones defective?

2. Could this problem have been avoided or lessened through the use of better product design? Could value engineering and value analysis have helped? Explain.

3. What lessons should Shelling Products learn from this problem? Identify and discuss three.

You Be the Consultant

Cheaper, Smaller, and Better

Karl Vandenberg has long been an admirer of Japanese operations management techniques. In particular, he has marveled at the ability of the Japanese to produce goods that are cheaper, smaller, and of higher quality than those of the competition.

Karl believes that there is a very large consumer market for some Japanese goods currently being sold in the United States if they can be improved upon. The one that he has his eye on is the small portable TV. For his birthday this year, Karl received a TV/radio with a 2-inch TV screen. The unit works quite well, although there are some shortcomings. One is that the picture is not very clear. It is difficult to get extremely good reception without taking the portable outside away from all in-house interference. Last week Karl took the TV to a professional football game. His seat was under the second tier, and so while Karl was protected from the rain and snow, his reception was very poor. Additionally, throughout the game he found that he was unable to get any sound. He had to make do with a picture that was badly focused.

On his way back from the game Karl began thinking about what a good quality portable TV should look like. He believes that a much better picture is needed than the one provided by the current offering. He also feels that the unit should be able to bring in the sound regardless of where someone is sitting in a football stadium, a home, or a car. He is also convinced that while a black and white TV set is a good product, most people would prefer to have a color set. Finally, Karl is sure that a 2-inch TV screen is much too small. He believes that the manufacturer should change the workings of the set around. Most sets are approximately 3 inches high and 5 to 6 inches long and wide. The picture tube is located on one of the 3-inch sides. Karl would like to see the screen put on the top of the set, using the 30 or so square inches up there. As a result the back of the set would be very narrow but the tube itself could be as large as 8 inches. This change would bring about dramatic improvement in current models.

Karl does not think that most of these ideas are too farfetched. His manufacturing firm is one of the largest builders, assemblers, and packagers of TVs for the American market. The company does not design anything, however. The blueprints are provided to it by the firm whose name goes on the set. Karl's firm builds the product according to specifications and then assembles and delivers it to the marketer. Nevertheless, Karl feels that his expertise and knowledge of the field make him an ideal candidate to build a small, color portable TV. He has discussed this idea with the firm for whom he builds sets, and it is very interested in helping out. This company has suggested that they put their heads together and go into a joint venture partnership. In this regard, they have brought in a number of high tech scientists. One is a Nobel Prize winner from a large Ivy League university. Another is best known for the role she played in developing a popular portable computer for the business market. These experts have told Karl that there is no doubt that a small, color portable TV can be produced. They have suggested that the company piggyback on the Japanese by looking at the way the Japanese have built their sets and then see what changes will be necessary in order to produce a color version. As one of the experts put it, "It's just a matter of time before someone does it. Why not us?"

Based on these optimistic comments, Karl and the manufacturer have decided to proceed with their investment. A team of scientists and engineers will be assembled next week and given six months to develop a prototype of a small color portable. In the interim, Karl and his new partner will begin concerning themselves with ways to build these TVs as efficiently as possible. They realize that in order to beat back competitors who are likely to piggyback on their ideas they have to offer a good quality product at a reasonable price. They are convinced that this can be done if they pay close attention to operations management tools and techniques. This is why they are going to be bringing in a consultant to advise them on how the plant should be laid out and run so as to achieve the greatest possible efficiency.

Your Consultation

Assume that you have been called in as the consultant. After reviewing the facts of the case and drawing upon all you have learned in this chapter, outline a plan of action for Karl to follow. Be sure to include all of the operations management ideas that you believe will be of value to him. Present your ideas in chronological order beginning with the ones that will have to be implemented first and continuing on to those that affect the end of the production process. Be as complete and as helpful as possible.

18

Controlling Personnel Performance

Objectives

Effective managers need to control not only organizational performance but personnel performance as well. When people are not doing well, the manager needs to identify the problem and then work to correct it. This chapter studies the ways in which modern organizations evaluate personnel performance and change organizational behavior. It examines the performance appraisal process, highlighting common appraisal problems that must be overcome. It also explores organizational climate and shows how organizational development techniques help management control personnel performance. When you have finished reading all of the material in this chapter, you will be able to

1. explain how the performance appraisal process works and describe four of the most popular techniques for appraising performance;

2. identify and describe some of the most common problems associated with performance appraisal and tell how these problems can be dealt with;

3. discuss how conflict and change can be controlled by management;

4. identify and describe some of the properties of organizational climate and the ways in which this climate can be measured;

5. define the term organizational development and describe how some of the traditional approaches to organizational development work; and

6. answer the question: Does organizational development really pay off?

Performance Appraisal

Performance appraisal is one of the most common procedures used to control an organization's personnel. Analogous to the general control process, it consists of comparing desired and actual personnel performance.

Table 18–1
Primary Uses of Performance Appraisals

Use	Small Organizations Percent	Large Organizations Percent	All Percent
Compensation	80.6	62.2	71.3
Performance Improvement	49.7	60.6	55.2
Feedback	20.6	37.8	29.3
Promotion	29.1	21.1	25.1
Documentation	11.4	10.0	10.7
Training	8.0	9.4	8.7
Transfer	7.4	8.3	7.9
Manpower Planning	6.3	6.1	6.2
Discharge	2.3	2.2	2.3
Research	2.9	0.0	1.4
Layoff	0.6	0.0	0.3

Source: Alan H. Locher and Kenneth S. Teel, "Performance Appraisal—A Survey of Current Practices," *Personnel Journal,* May 1977, p. 246. Reprinted with permission.

Using the results, management can take corrective action and make decisions regarding future performance objectives.

Nature of the Appraisal System

Performance appraisal provides employee feedback.

The purpose of performance appraisal is to provide both managers and subordinates with feedback on how well the subordinates are doing. These appraisals, as seen in Table 18–1, are used to determine such things as merit pay increases, promotions, training, transfer, and discharge. In large measure, performance appraisal is the primary process used for evaluating and developing organizational personnel.

A well-designed appraisal system has five basic characteristics: (1) it is tied directly to the person's job and measures the individual's ability to successfully carry out the requirements of the position; (2) it is comprehensive, measuring all of the important aspects of the job rather than just one or two; (3) it is objective, measuring task performance rather than the interpersonal relationship of the rater and the ratee; (4) it is based on standards of desired performance that were explained to the personnel in advance; and (5) it is designed to pinpoint the strong points and shortcomings of the personnel and provide a basis for explaining why these shortcomings exist and what can be done about them.[1]

Characteristics of a well-designed system

There are many ways to design and implement a performance appraisal system so that it will have these characteristics. One of the most useful is to tie the appraisal closely to the objectives of the position. Figure

1. Beverly Kaye and Shelly Krantz, "Performance Appraisal: A Win/Win Approach," *Training and Development Journal,* March 1983, pp. 32–35.

Figure 18–1   A System of Managing and Appraising by Objectives

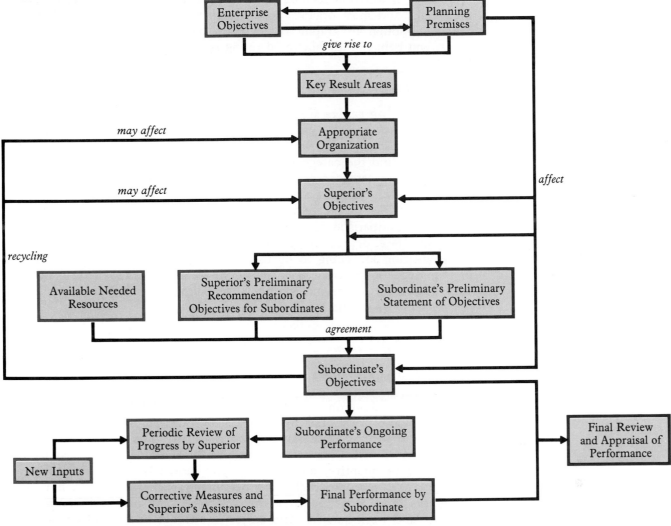

Source: Harold Koontz, "Making Managerial Appraisal Effective," *California Management Review,* Winter 1972, p. 49. Copyright © 1972 by the Regents of the University of California. Reprinted from *California Management Review,* volume 15, no. 2, pp. 46–55 by permission of the Regents.

18–1 illustrates one way of doing this. A close comparison of this figure with Figure 4–9 shows that this method is based on the management by objectives (MBO) approach. Not all performance appraisal systems are so closely tied to MBO, however. In fact, researchers such as Alan Locher and Kenneth Teel report that, on the average, only about 13 percent of all organizations use MBO for performance appraisals.[2] Nevertheless, the basic concept is useful in linking job performance and appraisal.

2. Alan H. Locher and Kenneth S. Teel, "Performance Appraisal—A Survey of Current Practices," *Personnel Journal,* May 1977, p. 247.

Techniques for Appraising Performance

A number of different techniques can be used in conducting performance appraisals, and most organizations design their own techniques. Four of the most popular are graphic rating scales, paired comparison, critical incidents, and behaviorally anchored rating scales.

Graphic Rating Scales

Graphic rating scales are the most widely used method of performance appraisal. They are also easy to fill out. Figure 18–2 illustrates one such scale. Regardless of the way these scales are constructed, however, it is common to find the category or factor listed on the left and the varying degrees of the category or factor listed along a continuum to the right. The form often contains a description of each category. Quality of work, for example, may be defined as "the caliber of work produced or accomplished in comparison to accepted quality standards." In some cases, as in Figure 18–2, degrees of the factor are also described. If the results of the evaluation are going to be used to compare people within the same unit or department, some sort of weight usually is given to each factor, such as a 1 for a marginal rating, 2 for below average, 3 for average, 4 for above average, and 5 for outstanding.

Graphic rating scales are easy to fill out.

Paired Comparison

Paired comparison is a ranking method in which each individual in a unit or department is compared with all of the others. Sometimes this comparison is done on an overall basis. For example, the manager ranks the five people in the unit from "best" to "poorest," mentally combining all of the important evaluation factors and using them to arrive at a final ranking. More often, the manager is given a series of job-related factors such as work quantity, work quality, job knowledge, dependability, and initiative and asked to rank each person on each factor. When ranked using this kind of paired comparison, Mr. A may be the best on work quantity and work quality, third on job knowledge and dependability, and last on cooperation and initiative. After all of the individual rankings are completed, the supervisor totals them up, averages them out, and determines who is the best worker.

In paired comparison a forced ranking choice is used so that only one person can be the "best." If a number of factors are used for evaluation purposes and two or more people come out with identical average scores, a further comparison is made. For example, if two people are tied for the best ranking in the unit, the manager goes back to the factor considered most important, such as work quantity. The worker who ranked highest on this factor gets the best rating in the unit. Remember that since no two people can get the same ranking on a particular factor, this comparison separates the best person in the unit from the second best worker.

Paired comparison uses forced rankings.

One of the things that many organizations like about the paired comparison is that it eliminates the possibility that a supervisor will give all the workers an excellent rating, something that is possible when the graphic rating scale is used. On the other hand, while it is often possible for the

Figure 18–2   Illustration of a Graphic Rating Scale

| Name | (Last) | (First) | (Initial) | Period Covered From | To |

| Pay Title | | Social Security Nr. | Status | | If Prob, Date Ends |

| Department | | Division | | Unit | |

CHECK ITEMS
⊞ Strong   ⊟ Weak
☑ Satisfactory Ⓞ Not applicable

INDICATE FACTOR RATING BY "X"

CHECK ITEMS	UNSATISFACTORY	NEEDS ATTENTION	SATISFACTORY	OUTSTANDING
1. QUANTITY OF WORK ☐ Amount of work performed ☐ Completion of work on schedule	Seldom produces enough work or meets deadlines.	Does not always complete an acceptable amount of work.	Consistently completes an acceptable amount of work.	Amount of work produced is consistently outstanding.
2. QUALITY OF WORK ☐ Accuracy ☐ Effectiveness ☐ Compliance with instructions ☐ Use of tools & equipment ☐ Neatness of work product ☐ Reports & correspondence ☐ Thoroughness	Too poor to retain in job without improvement.	Quality below acceptable standards.	Performs assigned duties in a satisfactory manner.	Performs all duties in an outstanding manner. Exceptional accuracy, skill or effectiveness.
3. WORK HABITS ☐ Attendance ☐ Observance of working hours ☐ Observance of rules ☐ Safety practices ☐ Personal Appearance	Too poor to retain in job without improvement.	Work habits need improvement.	Work habits satisfactory.	Exceptional work habits. Always observes rules and safe practices.
4. PERSONAL RELATIONS ☐ With fellow employees and supervisors ☐ With public	Too poor to retain in job without improvement.	Personal relations need improvement.	Maintains satisfactory work relations with others.	Exceptionally co-operative with public, co-workers and supervisors.
5. SUPERVISORY ABILITY ☐ Planning & assigning ☐ Training & instructing ☐ Disciplinary control ☐ Evaluating performance ☐ Delegating ☐ Making decisions ☐ Fairness & impartiality ☐ Unit morale	Poor supervisory ability. Work of unit frequently unsatisfactory.	Supervisory ability inadequate in some respects. Works results of unit below par at times.	Obtains good results from subordinates. Controls unit efficiently.	Outstanding ability to get maximum from unit and available resources.

(FOR SUPERVISORS ONLY)

RATER'S COMMENTS: *(attach additional sheets if needed)*

RATER'S RECOMMENDATION (for employees under consideration for a merit raise or permanent status)
This is to certify that the overall performance of the subject employee ☐ is ☐ is not   satisfactory.
The employee ☐ is ☐ is not   recommended for
☐ a merit raise   ☐ permanent status.

This report is based on my observation and knowledge. It represents my best judgment of the employee's performance.

RATER_____ Date_____

I have reviewed this report. It represents the facts to the best of my knowledge. I concur in the recommendation, if any, as to merit raise or permanent status.

REVIEWER_____ Date_____

In signing this report I do not necessarily agree with the conclusions of the rater. I understand that I may write my comments on the reverse side. I have received a copy of this report.
EMPLOYEE'S
SIGNATURE_____ Date_____

manager to distinguish easily between the best and poorest performers, it can be difficult to distinguish or rank those in the middle. So the paired comparison approach is not without its shortcomings.

Critical Incidents

Effective and ineffective behavior is recorded.

The **critical incidents** method requires the manager to record incidents in which the subordinate did something that was unusually effective or ineffective. For example, a sales supervisor may record: "When told by a customer that the piece of machinery was too inefficient for his company's needs, this salesperson immediately switched the customer to the top-of-the-line model and quickly closed the sale." Or a police sergeant may note: "This officer withheld his fire in a situation calling for the use of weapons because innocent bystanders might have been endangered in the process."

These critical incidents are recorded in a daily or weekly log. The book generally has predesignated categories such as planning, decision making, interpersonal relations, and controlling, so the entry can be made quickly. Commenting on the value of the critical incident, Wayne Cascio, a personnel psychologist and noted expert on performance evaluation, has written:

> These little anecdotes force attention on the situational determinants of job behavior and also on ways of doing the job successfully that may be unique to the person described . . . supervisors can focus on actual job behavior rather than on vaguely defined traits. Ratees receive meaningful feedback and they can see what changes in their job behavior will be necessary in order for them to improve. . . . In addition, when a large number of critical incidents are collected, abstracted, and categorized, they can provide a rich storehouse of information about job and organizational problems in general and are particularly well-suited for establishing objectives for training programs.[3]

Behaviorally Anchored Rating Scales

BARS are job related.

Behaviorally anchored rating scales, BARS for short, require a great deal of effort to construct. If the job is done properly, however, performance ratings are likely to be both accurate and reliable. The construction of the rating scales involves a number of distinct procedures. First, a group of employees or managers or both meets to identify and define the important dimensions of effective job performance. Next, another group takes each of these dimensions and develops critical incidents for each of them. These incidents are chosen to illustrate effective, average, and ineffective performance. Then a third group is given a list of the dimensions and the accompanying definitions and critical incidents used to illustrate them. This group is charged with eliminating the critical incidents that do not illustrate effective, average, or ineffective behavior in that dimension. A fourth group is then used to place a scale value on each incident associated with a dimension. Typically, a seven- to nine-point scale is used.

---

3. Wayne F. Cascio, *Applied Psychology in Personnel Management,* 2nd edition (Reston, Va.: Reston Publishing Co., 1982), p. 323.

Figure 18–3   A Behaviorally Anchored Rating Scale for Measuring the Organizational Ability of a Checkstand Worker

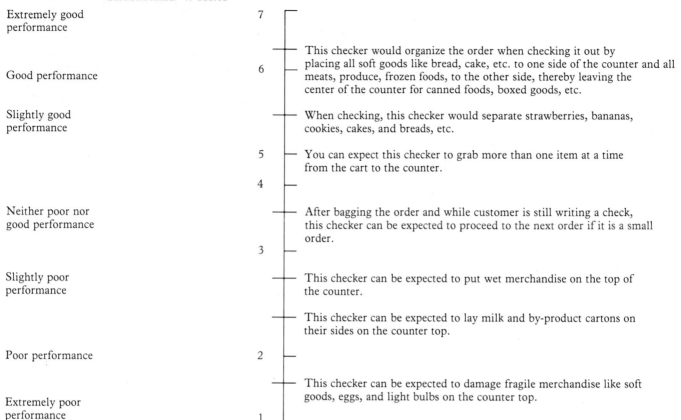

Source: Lawrence Fogli, Charles L. Hulin, and Milton R. Blood, "Development of First-Level Behavioral Job Criteria," *Journal of Applied Psychology,* February 1971, p. 7. Copyright 1971 by the American Psychological Association. Reprinted by permission of the publisher and author.

Figure 18–3 illustrates a BARS scale used to evaluate the organizational ability of checkstand workers in a supermarket. Using this scale, the supervisor can quickly and easily evaluate the grocery checker's organizational ability. Other scales would also be developed to address such dimensions as conscientiousness, knowledge and judgment, human relations skills, skill in operation of the register, and skill in bagging.[4] The scales are then pilot-tested.

A number of advantages are ascribed to BARS. One is that the appraisal instrument is job related, measuring the worker's ability to carry out or exhibit task performance behavior. Moreover, both workers and management participate in developing the instrument, and the steps involved in this process and in testing the instrument help ensure that it is both valid and reliable.

4. Lawrence Fogli, Charles L. Hulin, and Milton R. Blood, "Development of First-Level Behavioral Job Criteria," *Journal of Applied Psychology,* February 1971, p. 7.

Problems with Performance Appraisals

A number of problems can threaten the value of performance appraisal techniques. Most of these relate to the appraisal instrument's validity or reliability. **Validity** is the extent to which the instrument measures what it is supposed to measure. **Reliability** is the extent to which the instrument consistently yields the same results. In the case of an assembly-line worker, for example, a valid performance evaluation instrument is one that measures such performance-related dimensions as manual dexterity, speed, and ability to keep up with the line. If the instrument is reliable, assuming that the person's work performance does not change much, each time the individual is evaluated he or she should receive approximately the same rating. Unfortunately, in many instances performance appraisals lack validity or reliability. Specifically, some of the most common problems include central tendency, leniency or strictness errors, the halo effect, recency error, and personal biases.

Central Tendency

Some evaluators give everyone an average rating.

Central tendency occurs when the evaluator gives average ratings to just about everyone. No matter how good or bad their performance, the individuals are all given evaluations within a narrow range such as from low average to high average. Naturally, this tendency rewards the poorest workers and penalizes the best ones.

Leniency or Strictness Errors

Others are overly lenient or strict.

Leniency or **strictness errors** occur when the manager is either too easy or too hard on the employees. Leniency rewards the low and average producers by giving them more than they deserve. Strictness punishes the average and above-average producers by putting them in the same basic category as the low producers.

Halo Effect

Evaluators may be overly influenced by one or two factors . . .

As we learned in Chapter 11, the halo effect exists whenever a rater allows an individual's performance on one or two factors to influence how the person is rated on all factors. For example, a supervisor is supposed to rate an assembly-line worker on work quantity, work quality, attitude, perseverance, work habits, and interpersonal relations. The only factor that is measured quantitatively in the plant is work quantity, and on this factor the individual is high. Allowing this fact to influence the rating, the supervisor gives the worker the highest rating on all other factors as well. The supervisor has allowed performance in one area to influence the overall assessment.

Recency Error

overly influenced by the most recent performance . . .

Recency errors are related to employees' most recent behavior. Quite often, supervisors remember what an employee did last week but not what the individual did three months ago. As a result, the most recent behavior has a greater impact on the performance evaluation than does more remote behavior. When this error is present, an average worker who does excellent work in the month prior to the annual evaluation will get a better evaluation than an excellent worker who does poor work during this month.

Personal Biases

or influenced by personal bias.

Another common cause of evaluation error is personal bias on the part of the individual conducting the performance evaluation. One of these biases is called **similarity.** When this bias is present, a subordinate has the same values, attitudes, and habits as the supervisor is given a higher rating; conversely, a subordinate who does not seem to have these traits is given a lower rating. A second typical personal bias is a result of the amount of interaction that occurs between the manager and the employee. Some managers give a higher rating if they interact quite a bit with the individual; others give a lower rating in their effort not to be influenced by such interpersonal relationships.

Reducing Performance Appraisal Problems

A great deal has been written in recent years about the problems of performance appraisal systems and the ways to deal with them. One of the most common recommendations is to tie the appraisal directly to job-related behavior.[5] A second is always to use at least two appraisers, such as the direct supervisor and this person's boss.[6] This check is particularly important when a substandard evaluation is being given.[7] A third is to use objective factors in the appraisal whenever possible so that it is possible to pinpoint job performance more accurately and follow up later on by showing the employee where and how such performance can be improved.[8] Other suggestions include the following:

1. Ensure that each dimension or factor on a performance appraisal form represents a single job activity instead of a group of job activities.

2. Avoid terms like average, since different evaluators react differently to the term.

3. Ensure that raters observe subordinates on a regular basis throughout the evaluation period. It is even helpful if the rater takes notes for future reference.

---

5. William H. Holley and Hubert S. Field, "Will Your Performance Appraisal System Hold Up in Court?" *Personnel*, January–February 1982, pp. 59–64.

6. Ed Yager, "A Critique of Performance Appraisal Systems," *Personnel Journal*, February 1981, pp. 129–133; John D. McMillan and Hoyo W. Doyal, "Performance Appraisal: Match the Tool to the Task," *Personnel*, July–August 1978, pp. 12–20.

7. Patricia Linenberger and Timothy J. Keaveny, "Performance Appraisal Standards Used by the Courts," *Personnel Administrator*, May 1981, pp. 89–94.

8. Marvin G. Dertien, "The Accuracy of Job Evaluation Plans," *Personnel Journal*, July 1981, pp. 566–570.

Ways to reduce performance appraisal problems

4. Keep the number of persons evaluated by one rater to a reasonable number. When one person must evaluate many subordinates, it becomes difficult to discriminate; rating fatigue increases with the number of ratees.

5. Ensure that the dimensions used are clearly stated, meaningful, and relevant to effective job performance.

6. Train raters so they can recognize various sources of error and understand the rationale underlying the evaluation process.[9]

Controlling Conflict and Change

In addition to appraising performance, managers often find it necessary to control conflict and change. **Conflict** is opposition or antagonistic interaction between two or more parties.[10] **Change** is an altering of the status quo.[11] Conflict brings about change but the reverse is not always true. As a result, in the controlling of human resources, the manager may sometimes deal with one of these conditions and at other times with both.

Conflict Management

For a long time, management believed that all conflict was inherently bad. Today that view has changed as managers have come to realize that conflict can bring about necessary changes. As Stephen Robbins, a well-known writer on the subject, has noted:

> Conflict is the catalyst of change. If we do not adapt our products and services to the changing needs of our customers, actions of our competitors, and new technological developments, our organizations will become sick and eventually die. Is it not possible that more organizations fail because of too little conflict rather than too much?"[12]

Conflict can be caused by distrust, threats to status, or misperceptions.

On the other hand, conflict can be a result of distrust, fear, anxiety, tension, and other potentially dysfunctional causes. For example, when resources are being allocated it is not unusual to find individuals vying with each other for their share of the money or units competing for increased budget allocations. In such cases, given the fact that there are usually limited resources, when one party wins, others lose.

---

9. Richard M. Steers, *Introduction to Organizational Behavior* (Santa Monica, Calif.: Goodyear Publishing Co., Inc., 1981), p. 405. For ways in which suggestions such as these are likely to be implemented see: Ann M. Morrison and Mary Ellen Kranz, "The Shape of Performance Appraisal in the Coming Decade," *Personnel*, July–August 1981, pp. 12–21.

10. Stephen P. Robbins, " 'Conflict Management' and 'Conflict Resolution' Are Not Synonymous Terms," *California Management Review*, Winter 1978, p. 67.

11. Richard M. Hodgetts, *Modern Human Relations*, 2nd edition (Hinsdale, Ill.: Dryden Press, 1984), p. 392.

12. Robbins, *op. cit.*, p. 69.

Status is another common cause of conflict. The production people may resent having to accept product modifications initiated by the Engineering Department; the marketing research people may be angry over having to submit weekly budget expenditures to the Finance Department; the Personnel Department may not like having to comply with EEO guidelines developed by the Legal Department.

A third common cause of conflict is misperception. Individuals or groups misinterpret what others are doing or why they are doing it. This problem may be caused by differences in age, education, background, or values, or it may be a result of communication breakdown.

In any event, the manager must work to control the conflict by either guiding it along constructive lines or seeking to resolve it. How can this be done? Robbins, using a contingency approach, has presented some major resolution techniques along with the strengths and weaknesses of each. (See Table 18–2.) Depending on the specifics of the situation, the manager can choose the technique that offers the greatest chance of managing the conflict constructively.

Dealing with Change

Change is inevitable, particularly in modern organizations.[13] Work rules are revised, new equipment is introduced, product lines are dropped and added. As internal and external conditions change, the workforce has to adjust. Quite often it does this easily, but sometimes there is resistance to change. To deal with this situation, the manager must understand how the change process works.

The change process consists of three phases: unfreezing, introduction of the actual change, and refreezing. During the **unfreezing** phase the manager must analyze why the change is needed and the possible reasons for resistance to it. Many of the reasons for resistance can be traced directly to the manager. Typical ones include

Typical reasons for resisting change

1. failure to be specific about the change,

2. failure to show why the change is necessary,

3. failure to allow people affected by the change to have a say in planning it,

4. failure to consider the work group's habit patterns,

5. failure to keep employees informed about the change,

6. the creation of excessive work pressures during the change, and

7. failure to deal with employee anxiety regarding job security.[14]

Whatever the specific reasons for resistance, one of the most helpful ways to view the situation is in terms of **force field analysis.** On the

---

13. Nobel McKay and Serge Lashutka, "The Basics of Organization Change: An Eclectic Model," *Training and Development Journal,* April 1983, pp. 64–69.

14. Jack N. Wismer, "Organizational Change: How to Understand It and Deal with It," *Training/HRD,* May 1979, p. 31.

Table 18-2 Contingency Approaches for Dealing with Conflict

Technique	Brief Definition	Strengths	Weaknesses
Problem-solving (also known as confrontations or collaboration)	Seeks resolution through face-to-face confrontation of the conflicting parties. Parties seek mutual problem definition, assessment, and solution.	Effective with conflicts stemming from semantic misunderstandings. Brings doubts and misperceptions to surface.	Can be time consuming. Inappropriate for most noncommunicative conflicts, especially those based on different value systems.
Subordinate Goals	Common goals that two or more conflicting parties each desire and cannot be reached without cooperation of those involved. Goals must be highly valued, unattainable without the help of all parties involved in the conflict, and commonly sought.	When used cumulatively and reinforced, develops "peacemaking" potential, emphasizing interdependency and cooperation.	Difficult to devise.
Expansion of Resources	Make more of the scarce resource available.	Each conflicting party can be victorious.	Resources rarely exist in such quantities as to be easily expanded.
Avoidance	Includes withdrawal and suppression.	Easy to do. Natural reaction to conflict.	No effective resolution. Conflict not eliminated. Temporary.
Smoothing	Play down differences while emphasizing common interests.	All conflict situations have points of commonality within them. Cooperative efforts are reinforced.	Differences are not confronted and remain under the surface. Temporary.
Compromise	Each party is required to give up something of value. Includes external or third-party interventions, negotiation, and voting.	No clear loser. Consistent with democratic values.	No clear winner. Power-oriented—influenced heavily by relative strength of parties. Temporary.
Authoritative Command	Solution imposed from a superior holding formal positional authority.	Very effective in organizations since members recognize and accept authority of superiors.	Cause of conflict is not treated. Does not necessarily bring *agreement*. Temporary.
Altering the Human Variable	Changing the attitudes and behavior of one or more of the conflicting parties. Includes use of education, sensitivity and awareness training, and human relations training.	Results can be substantial and permanent. Has potential to alleviate the source of conflict.	Most difficult to achieve. Slow and costly.
Altering Structural Variables	Change structural variables. Includes transferring and exchanging group members, creating coordinating positions, developing an appeals system, and expanding the group or organization's boundaries.	Can be permanent. Usually within the authority of a manager.	Often expensive. Forces organization to be designed for specific individuals and thus requires continual adjustment as people join or leave the organization.

Source: Stephen P. Robbins, " 'Conflict Management' and 'Conflict Resolution' Are Not Synonymous Terms," *California Management Review,* Winter 1978, p. 73. Copyright © (1978) by the Regents of the University of California. Reprinted from *California Management Review,* volume 21, no. 2, pp. 67–75 by permission of the Regents.

one hand there are forces pushing for the change. On the other hand there are forces pushing against the change. The manager has to (a) increase the strength of the pressures pushing for the change, (b) decrease the strength of the forces resisting the change, (c) change a resisting force into one supporting the change, or (d) do a combination of these. Some of the ways in which this can be done include

Ways to reduce resistance

1. involving the employees in the planning of the change,

2. providing accurate and complete information regarding the change,

3. giving employees a chance to air their objections,

4. taking group norms and habits into account,

5. making only essential changes, and

6. learning to use proper problem-solving techniques.[15]

As the manager wins the battle to unfreeze the situation, attention can begin to switch to phase two: introducing the actual change. This phase may involve implementing new work procedures, switching over to new machinery, using a new MIS control system, or whatever the change calls

"The reason you're getting your own key to the washroom is because from now on, it's your office."

15. *Ibid.*

for. During this phase the manager must be most concerned with explaining how the new changes will work, seeing that the personnel understand how the changes will affect them, and trying to make the process part of their regular work routine.

The final phase of the change process is that of **refreezing.** At this point the manager reinforces the new behavior, rewards employees who are going along with the change, and encourages the other employees to do the same. If the refreezing phase is carried out properly, the workers will realize that there is little, if anything, to fear from the change, and they will go along with it. The following is an example of a situation in which this happened.

> The Accounting Department of a retail chain recently requested that all stores begin submitting some of their sales data on specially designed forms. These forms would help the Accounting Department tabulate the information more quickly and give feedback to the stores regarding cost and budget information. While the store managers were initially reluctant to ask their people to adopt the new forms, they did go along with the request. In turn, the head of the Accounting Department made it a special point to call each store manager to thank him or her for helping out and to explain how the newly submitted data would help the store get faster feedback for decision making. Made aware of the value of the new forms, the store managers began to urge their people to fill out the reports as completely as possible and get them in on time. The Accounting Department manager was thus able to sell the store managers on the change and keep them sold. In turn, the store managers did the same with their people.[16]

Organizational Climate

Performance appraisal, conflict, and change are personnel control issues that the manager faces on a periodic basis. If the organization is a good place in which to work, however, it is likely to have few problems related to conflict and change. On the other hand, if the environment is characterized by a great deal of distrust, anxiety, and fear, the organization probably will have many of these problems. That is why modern organizations are so interested in the topic of organizational climate.

Measuring the Climate

It is difficult to define the term organizational climate because there are so many properties in the work environment that serve to influence job behavior. Four of the most common include

- Decision-making practices—Are the personnel allowed to participate in the decision-making process, or are most important decisions made by the top managers?

Factors influencing overall climate

- Communication flows—Are the personnel informed about what is going on, or is the channel of communication basically one of orders flowing down from the top and progress reports flowing up from the bottom?

16. Hodgetts, *op. cit.*, pp. 413–414.

- Motivation—Do the people who work the hardest and do the best work get the greatest rewards, or is everyone treated the same regardless of contribution?

- Concern for the people—Does the organization try to improve working conditions and show that it is interested in the personnel, or is the enterprise most concerned with getting the work out regardless of human resource cost?

By designing questionnaires that provide answers to questions such as these, the organization can obtain feedback on its climate. Then it can develop programs to address the many problems that have been uncovered. Depending on what the management would like to know, all sorts of data feedback can be obtained. Figure 18–4 illustrates the results of a multilevel management survey conducted among units with the highest turnover. Both managers and nonmanagers in these units were asked to rate their superiors on a host of different organizational characteristics, from clarification of goals and objectives to feedback, delegation of authority, and the recognizing and reinforcing of good performance. The 50 percent line in the figure represents the average score received by all managers who were rated. Notice from the figure that in the units with the highest turnover a number of responses were significantly different from the norm (for example, goal clarification, goal pressure, delegation, and approachability). It is to these areas that management must direct its attention.

Feelings and attitudes must be measured.

One of the most important things to remember about measuring the organizational climate is that the information being collected provides insights into organizational behavior and feelings that are not readily available to management. In fact, many managers, upon finding how the workers in their unit feel about various conditions, remark, "I didn't know that. I thought things were a lot better than this." Without some form of instrument to measure organizational climate, management typically does not know how the personnel really feel about many things. This is as true at the worker level as at the management level. For this reason, Figure 18–4 could be used to collect information at all levels of the hierarchy.

Organizational climate is like an iceberg.

Another thing to remember about organizational climate is that it is very much like an iceberg. Part of an iceberg is visible (the ice above the water) and part of it is not (the ice below the water). An organization's climate is similar in that there are aspects that can be readily observed and others that are hidden. In the readily observed category are such things as the goals of the organization, its financial resources, its technological state and performance standards, and the skills and abilities of the personnel. In the hidden category are the attitudes, feelings, values, norms, supportiveness, and satisfaction of the personnel. When these hidden characteristics require attention, it can be provided through the use of organizational development techniques.

Organizational Development

When an organization uses a planned, systematic approach to effect change, it is said to be using **organizational development** (OD) efforts. Wendell

Figure 18–4 Multilevel Management Survey Results Concerning Managers in the Unit of an Organization with the Highest Turnover

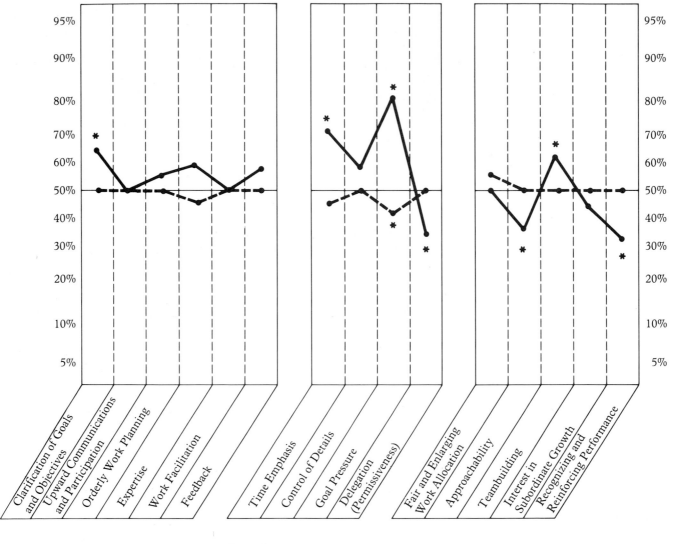

Legend:

———— 19 Managers Rating Their Superiors

■ ■ ■ ■ 65 Non-Managers Rating Their First-Line Superiors

＊   Significantly Different from Norm

Source: Clark W. Wilson, "Assessing Management and OD Needs," *Training and Development Journal,* April 1980, p. 73. Reprinted with permission.

L. French and Cecil H. Bell, two leading OD authorities, define the term this way:

OD defined

Organization [al] development is a long-range effort to improve an organization's problem-solving and renewal processes, particularly through a more effective and collaborative management of organization culture—with special emphasis on the culture of formal work teams—with the assistance of a change agent, or a catalyst, and the use of the theory and technology of applied behavioral science, including action research.[17]

OD not only emphasizes solving behavior problems, but also focuses on ensuring that they do not recur. It often requires changes in the attitudes, feelings, and perceptions of the people involved. For this reason, many OD efforts make use of an outside expert called a change agent, or catalyst. This person enters the organization, analyzes the situation, and then helps bring about a solution.[18]

Regardless of whether the organization uses an outside change agent or relies upon people within the hierarchy to play this role, OD efforts share some basic characteristics:

1. The emphasis is not on a one-shot solution to organizational problems but on an ongoing process in which organizational members learn how to interact successfully with others in solving these problems.

2. Intact work groups are used in the sense that everyone stays in his or her current work unit and remains in it throughout the OD change.

Basic characteristics of OD

3. The change agent uses applied behavioral science principles, not theoretical, abstract concepts.

4. The objective of the OD effort is to change the values and behavior of the employees so as to improve intra- and intergroup harmony.

5. The analysis and recommended changes are based on data collected within the organization rather than ideas or recommendations that have worked in other enterprises.

6. The efforts of the OD process are directed toward dealing with current problems and deciding how the personnel can solve them, working as a unit.

At the heart of the OD process are three basic components: diagnosis, action, and process maintenance. In the diagnostic component, information is gathered on characteristics of the organizational climate, including decision-making processes, communication patterns and styles, relationships between interfacing groups, the management of conflict, the setting of goals, and planning methods.[19]

The action stage is characterized by what are called OD interventions. This is a catchall term used to describe the structured activity in which individuals, groups, or units engage in accomplishing task goals that are related to organizational improvement. These interventions typically focus on problems central to the needs of the organization, rather than on hypothetical, abstract problems that may be peripheral to the members' needs.

17. Wendell L. French and Cecil H. Bell, Jr., *Organization Development* (Englewood Cliffs, N.J.: Prentice-Hall, 1978), p. 14.

18. Laurie Weiss, "Revisiting the Basics of Conflict Intervention," *Training and Development Journal,* November 1983, pp. 68–70.

19. Richard Beckhard, *Organization Development: Strategies and Models* (Reading, Mass.: Addison-Wesley, 1969), p. 26.

The dual aspect of OD interventions can be clarified with an illustration. Let us say that the top executives of an organization spend three days together in a workshop in which they do the following things: (1) explore the need for and desirability of a long-range strategy plan for the organization; (2) learn how to formulate such a strategy by analyzing other strategies, determining what the strategic variables are, being shown a sequence of steps for preparing a comprehensive plan, and so forth; and (3) actually make a three-year strategy plan for the organization. This intervention combines the dual features of learning and action: the executives engaged in activities in which they learned about strategy planning, and they then generated a strategy.[20]

After the action stage is complete, the OD practitioner monitors feedback and ensures that everything is going according to plan. Are the interventions proving to be timely and relevant? Are the activities producing the intended results? This phase is known as **process-maintenance.** During this phase the change agent ensures that there is continued involvement, commitment, and investment in the program by the members.

What specific type of OD intervention will the change agent use? It depends on the nature of the problem.[21] There are a number of traditional approaches, however, that can provide insights into the question. The following discussion examines some of these.

Traditional Approaches to OD

A number of traditional OD approaches are used in modern organizations. While there are far too many to address all of them here, three will be given consideration: sensitivity training, survey feedback, and grid training.

Sensitivity Training

The **sensitivity training** or T (training)-group approach has been used since 1946. The objectives of T-group sessions include one or more of the following:

1. to make participants increasingly aware of, and sensitive to, emotional reactions and expressions in themselves and others;

2. to increase the ability of participants to perceive, and to learn from, the consequences of their actions through attention to their own and others' feelings;

Objectives of T-groups

3. to stimulate the clarification and development of personal values and goals consonant with a democratic and scientific approach to problems of social and personal decision and action;

4. to develop concepts and theoretical insights that will serve as tools in linking personal values, goals, and intentions to actions consistent with these inner factors and with the requirements of the situation; and

---

20. French and Bell, *op. cit.*, p. 64.

21. Robert R. Blake and Jane S. Mouton, "Out of the Past: How to Use Your Organization's History to Shape a Better Future," *Training and Development Journal,* November 1983, pp. 58–65.

5. to foster the achievement of behavioral effectiveness in transactions with the participants' environments.[22]

There are two basic types of T-groups. In one the participants do not know each other; in the other they do. The latter type is more frequently used for in-house OD efforts than is the former. T-groups all function in about the same way, however. The participants are placed in an unstructured setting in which the leader of the group provides no direction. There are no agendas or rules. This often leads the participants to ask themselves questions such as: "What is going on here?" "Why isn't the leader providing direction?" "What are we supposed to be doing?" Gradually, however, they begin to focus attention on each other and on what is happening to them. Finally, the focus turns inward and the members begin to analyze each other.

Is T-group training of any real value? This approach has supporters as well as critics. For example, Jerry Porras and P. O. Berg found that positive results were reported by people who used it.[23] On the other hand, there is evidence that practitioners are not highly enthusiastic about sensitivity training, as seen by the fact that when personnel directors of large firms were surveyed, twice as many said they would not recommend its use as would recommend it.[24] What, then, is the current status of this OD technique? The answer is that its popularity is waning as other, newer approaches begin to replace it. Many people still think well of it, however. French and Bell, for instance, have written that

Benefits of T-groups

> The T-group is a powerful learning laboratory where individuals gain insights into the meaning and consequences of their own behaviors, the meaning and consequences of others' behaviors, and the dynamics and processes of group behavior. These insights are coupled with growth of skills in diagnosing and taking more effective interpersonal and group action. Thus the T-group can give to individuals the basic skills necessary for more competent action taking in the organization.[25]

Survey Feedback

Survey feedback is a comprehensive OD intervention in that it draws survey data from all levels of the hierarchy and then feeds this information back to the personnel who provided it. These personnel then analyze, interpret, and act upon this data. An employee attitude form similar to the one in Figure 18–5 typically is used in collecting this data.

---

22. Fred Luthans, *Organizational Behavior,* 3rd edition (New York: McGraw-Hill, 1981), pp. 614–615. See also: Leslie This and Gordon Lippitt, "Managerial Guidelines to Sensitivity Training," *Training and Development Journal,* June 1981, pp. 144–150.

23. Jerry I. Porras and P. O. Berg, "The Impact of Organization Development," *Academy of Management Review,* April 1978, pp. 259–260.

24. William J. Kearney and Desmond D. Martin, "Sensitivity Training: An Established Management Development Tool," *Academy of Management Journal,* December 1974, pp. 755–760.

25. French and Bell, *op. cit.,* p. 144.

Figure 18–5 Employee Attitude Survey

Describe working conditions in your unit by placing an "X" along each of the following continua.

Objectives are very vague.	1 2 3 4 5 6 7 8 9 10	Objectives are extremely clear.
Goal setting is done by a few who are often unaffected by the goals.	1 2 3 4 5 6 7 8 9 10	Goal setting is done by all persons who are affected by these goals.
Motivation is low.	1 2 3 4 5 6 7 8 9 10	Motivation is high.
Personal goals are suppressed for the "good of the organization."	1 2 3 4 5 6 7 8 9 10	Personal and organizational goals are integrated.
Communications are guarded.	1 2 3 4 5 6 7 8 9 10	Communications are open.
Relevant feelings are withheld.	1 2 3 4 5 6 7 8 9 10	Relevant feelings are shared.
Conflict is repressed or ignored.	1 2 3 4 5 6 7 8 9 10	Conflict is handled constructively.
Mutual support is low.	1 2 3 4 5 6 7 8 9 10	Mutual support is high.
Personal responsibility is low.	1 2 3 4 5 6 7 8 9 10	Personal responsibility is high.
The trust level is low.	1 2 3 4 5 6 7 8 9 10	The trust level is high.
Concern is mainly for work output.	1 2 3 4 5 6 7 8 9 10	Concern is mainly for people.
Procedures are inflexible.	1 2 3 4 5 6 7 8 9 10	Procedures are flexible.
Performance standards are low.	1 2 3 4 5 6 7 8 9 10	Performance standards are high.
Rewards are few.	1 2 3 4 5 6 7 8 9 10	Rewards are many.
Controls are imposed.	1 2 3 4 5 6 7 8 9 10	Controls are jointly determined.
Conformity is high.	1 2 3 4 5 6 7 8 9 10	Conformity is low.
The organizational climate is restrictive and tight.	1 2 3 4 5 6 7 8 9 10	The organizational climate is supportive and casual.
There is centralized leadership.	1 2 3 4 5 6 7 8 9 10	There is shared leadership.
There are many competitive relationships in the unit.	1 2 3 4 5 6 7 8 9 10	There are many collaborative relationships in the unit.
The superior's interpersonal skills are low.	1 2 3 4 5 6 7 8 9 10	The superior's interpersonal skills are high.

Research at the Institute for Social Research at the University of Michigan reveals that the following four steps are necessary if the survey feedback approach is to be optimally useful:

1. Organization members at the top of the hierarchy are involved in the preliminary planning.

2. Data are collected from all organization members.

3. Data are fed back to the top executive team and then down the hierarchy in functional teams.

Steps in survey feedback

4. Each superior presides at a meeting with his or her subordinates in which the data are discussed and in which: (a) subordinates are asked to help interpret the data, (b) plans are made for making constructive changes, and (c) plans are made for the introduction of the data at the next lower level.[26]

As the information is made available at each level, action plans are created for dealing with the necessary changes. In this process, the social, structural, goal, and task subsystems of the organization are changed. What makes this OD technique so valuable is that the personnel who are going to be affected by any changes help shape them. Also, the information being fed back to them is data they themselves helped generate. How successful has this technique been? French and Bell report that

> Survey feedback has been shown to be an effective change technique in OD. In a longitudinal study evaluating the effects of different change techniques in 23 different organizations, survey feedback was found to be the most effective change strategy. . . . Survey feedback is a cost-effective means of implementing a comprehensive program, thus making it a highly desirable change technique.[27]

Grid Training

Grid training is an outgrowth of the managerial grid approach to leadership, a topic that was introduced in Chapter 14. When used for OD purposes, grid training has a pre-phase and six major follow-up phases. In the pre-phase, selected key managers who will later be instructors in the program attend a seminar where they learn about the managerial grid. In this week-long seminar, they are taught about grid concepts, have a chance to assess their own leadership styles using the managerial grid questionnaire, develop team action skills, are taught problem-solving and critiquing skills, and learn how to analyze an organization at work. The participants are then put through the six major phases of the grid OD seminar. Here they learn what grid training is all about and how to conduct it in their own organization. With this knowledge the initial participants are in an ideal position to evaluate the program and determine whether or not it is a good idea for their own enterprise. If they decide to go ahead with grid training for everyone else in the organization, the first major phase can begin. The

---

26. *Ibid.,* p. 154.
27. *Ibid.,* p. 156.

six phases in this comprehensive OD effort, briefly described, are the following:

- *Phase 1: The Managerial Grid*   In this phase a grid seminar is conducted by the in-house managers who have already been trained in the grid approach. During this phase attention is focused on the leadership styles of the participating managers and on how they go about solving problems, critiquing, and communicating with subordinates. During this phase, the trainees also learn to become 9,9 managers.

- *Phase 2: Teamwork Development*   The objective of this phase is to perfect teamwork. This is done through an analysis of team traditions and culture and the development of planning, problem-solving, and objective-setting skills. The participants are given actual work problems to solve and are provided with feedback on how well they function in a team setting.

- *Phase 3: Intergroup Development*   The focus now moves to developing intergroup relations and getting work groups away from believing that they can attain their objectives and succeed only at the expense of other groups in the organization. The dynamics of intergroup cooperation and competition are explored.

Major phases in grid training

- *Phase 4: Developing an Ideal Strategic Corporate Model*   Now the focus switches to strategic planning, with the major goal being to learn the concepts and skills of corporate logic necessary to achieving excellence for the enterprise. The participants contribute to, and agree upon, important objectives for the organization. They are also encouraged to develop a sense of commitment to these objectives.

- *Phase 5: Implementing the Ideal Strategic Model*   The participants now work on implementing the corporate model that has been developed. Emphasis is given to organizing and developing planning teams whose job is to examine every phase of the enterprise's operations in seeing how the organization can be moved more in line with the ideal model.

- *Phase 6: Systematic Critique*   In this final phase, the results of the program are evaluated. Progress is determined, barriers and problems are pinpointed, and plans for future action are determined. This last phase serves to ensure that the organization does not slip back into its old way of doing things. The best of the present is saved, while efforts are made to improve the areas of performance that are below par.

Quite obviously grid OD is a comprehensive program. In fact, it takes from three to five years to fully implement grid training throughout an organization. Given the time and expense required to implement this program, an organization must be fully committed to the effort before embarking on phase one, or the end result is likely to be a waste of valuable resources. On the other hand, many organizations that have employed grid training have been quite pleased with the results. French and Bell, summarizing Blake and Mouton's OD approach, report:

> Grid organization development is an approach to organization improvements that is complete and systematic and difficult. Does it work? Blake,

Mouton, Barnes, and Greiner evaluated the results of a Grid OD program conducted in a large plant that was part of a very large multiplant company. The eight hundred managers and staff personnel of the four-thousand-person work force at the plant were all given training in the Managerial Grid and Grid OD concepts. Significant organizational improvements showed up on such "bottom-line" measures as greater profits, lower costs, and less waste. Managers, themselves, when asked about their own effectiveness and that of their corporation, likewise declared that changes for the better had resulted from the program.[28]

Does OD Really Pay Off?

Do OD programs really help organizations?[29] Research shows that they do. In particular, by developing teamwork, opening lines of communication, and creating bases for trust, enterprises often are able to reduce such undesirable behavior as absenteeism and turnover and the cost of replacing and training staff personnel.

One of the most interesting studies measuring the savings to an organization for eliminating human behavior problems was conducted by Philip Mirvis and Edward Lawler.[30] Using the branch system of a midwestern banking organization, they surveyed 160 tellers from 20 branches. These individuals were cashiers handling customer deposits, withdrawals, and other transactions. Mirvis and Lawler then calculated the loss to the bank caused by cashier absenteeism and turnover. Their results are presented in Table 18–3.

OD interventions can increase efficiency.

OD change agents quickly note that their behavioral interventions deal with problems such as absenteeism and turnover and can reduce the types of cost reported in Table 18–3. Mirvis and Lawler support these arguments. After measuring the intrinsic satisfaction (How satisfied are you with your job?), job involvement (How important to you is what happens in the bank?), and intrinsic motivation (Do you get a feeling of personal satisfaction from doing your job well?) of the tellers, they reported the data in Table 18–4. Notice from the data that as attitudinal measures increase, the costs associated with absenteeism, turnover, and teller shortages (errors caused by incorrect cash outlays) go down.

The results of studies such as these are important in evaluating OD efforts. In particular, they point out the dollar-and-cents benefits associated with maintaining a favorable organizational climate. This is why organizational development is so important and useful in helping management control personnel performance.[31]

---

28. *Ibid.*, p. 161.

29. Elizabeth S. Gorovitz, "Looking Beyond the OD Mystique," *Training and Development Journal*, April 1983, pp. 12–14.

30. Philip H. Mirvis and Edward E. Lawler, III, "Measuring the Financial Impact of Employee Attitudes," *Journal of Applied Psychology*, February 1977, pp. 1–8.

31. See for example: Barry A. Mace and Philip H. Mirvis, "A Methodology for Assessment of Quality of Work Life and Organizational Effectiveness In Behavioral-Economic Terms," *Administrative Science Quarterly*, June 1976, pp. 212–226.

Table 18-3
Cost Per Incident of Absenteeism and Turnover

Variable	Cost (in dollars)
Absenteeism	
Absent employee	
Salary	$ 23.04
Benefits	6.40
Replacement employee	
Training and Staff time	2.13
Unabsorbed burden	15.71
Lost profit contribution	19.17
Total variable cost	23.04
Total cost per employee	$66.45
Turnover	
Replacement acquisition	
Direct hiring costs	$ 293.95
Other hiring costs	185.55
Replacement training	
Preassignment	758.84
Learning curve	212.98
Unabsorbed burden	682.44
Lost profit contribution	388.27
Total variable cost	293.95
Total cost per employee	$2,522.03

Source: Phillip H. Mirvis and Edward E. Lawler, III, "Measuring the Financial Impact of Employee Attitudes," *Journal of Applied Psychology*, February 1977, p. 4.

Table 18-4   Dollars Saved Through Improved Job-Related Attitudes

Attitude	Change	Cost (in dollars) Per Teller Per Month			
		Absenteeism	Turnover	Shortage	Total
Intrinsic Satisfaction	Increase	2.40	10.17	25.98	38.55
	Remain the same	5.44	17.04	25.27	47.75
	Decrease	8.48	23.93	24.55	56.96
Job Involvement	Increase	5.74	7.08	23.62	36.44
	Remain the same	5.44	17.04	25.27	47.75
	Decrease	5.14	27.01	26.91	59.06
Intrinsic Motivation	Increase	4.45	11.55	24.41	40.41
	Remain the same	5.44	17.04	25.27	47.75
	Decrease	6.43	22.54	26.13	55.10

Source: Philip H. Mirvis and Edward E. Lawler, III, "Measuring the Financial Impact of Employee Attitudes," *Journal of Applied Psychology*, February 1977, p. 6.

Summary

1. Performance appraisal is an evaluation system that provides managers and subordinates with feedback on the subordinates' performance. A well-designed system has five basic characteristics: it is tied directly to the person's job; it is comprehensive; it is objective; it is based on standards of desired performance; and it is designed to provide the personnel with feedback on their strong points and shortcomings.

2. There are a number of popular techniques for appraising performance. One is the graphic rating scale, which allows the appraiser to easily evaluate a person by checking off his or her performance in a number of different categories. A second is the paired comparison, in which each individual in a unit or department is compared with all of the others. A third is the critical incidents method, in which effective or ineffective behavior is noted and used as a basis for evaluation. A fourth is the behaviorally anchored rating scale, in which employees and managers join together to identify and define dimensions of effective job performance and develop rating scales from their results.

3. A number of problems are associated with performance appraisals. Some of the most important include central tendency, leniency, strictness, the halo effect, the recency error, and personal biases. How can these problems be reduced? A number of suggestions were provided in the text, including the need to make performance evaluation as job related as possible.

4. In addition to appraising performance, managers often find it necessary to control conflict and change. Conflict is opposition or antagonistic interaction between two or more parties. Change is an altering of the status quo. Conflict management can be handled in many different ways. Some of the most effective were presented in Table 18–2. In dealing with change, the manager often must work to overcome resistance. This has to be done in a three-stage process: unfreezing old behaviors, introducing the desired change, and refreezing the new behaviors.

5. To control personnel performance, an organization should know what the organizational climate is like. There are many properties in this climate including decision-making practices, communication flows, motivation, and concern for people. These properties are often measured through such techniques as attitude surveys.

6. When an organization uses a planned, systematic approach to effect change, it is said to be using organizational development (OD). At the heart of the OD process are three basic components: diagnosis, action, and maintenance.

7. A number of traditional OD approaches are used in modern organizations. Three of the most common are sensitivity training, survey feedback, and grid training.

8. Does OD really pay off? Research shows that it does. By helping develop teamwork, open lines of communication, and create bases for trust, the enterprise often is able to reduce undesirable behavior such as absenteeism and turnover and increase bottom-line performance.

Key Terms

Behaviorally anchored rating scales   A performance appraisal system consisting of rating scales, designed by employees or managers or both, that are anchored to job related behaviors and are used to help managers distinguish between effective, average, and ineffective job performance.

Central tendency   A performance appraisal error in which an evaluator gives average ratings to almost everyone.

Change   An altering of the status quo.

Conflict   Opposition or antagonistic interaction between two or more parties.

Critical incidents   A performance appraisal method in which the manager records unusually effective or ineffective subordinate behavior and uses this information for evaluation purposes.

Force field analysis   The analysis of change through a consideration of the forces pushing for the change and of those pushing against it.

Graphic rating scales   Performance appraisal instruments that contain factors, and degrees of each, on which individuals are evaluated by their superior.

Grid training   A comprehensive OD intervention in which grid concepts are introduced, intra- and intergroup teamwork is developed, a strategic planning model is formulated and implemented, and a systematic critique is carried out.

Leniency   A performance appraisal error in which an evaluator gives very high ratings to almost everyone.

Organizational development (OD)   A long-range effort to improve an organization's problem-solving and renewal processes with the assistance of a change agent or catalyst.

Paired comparison   A performance appraisal method in which each individual in the unit or department is compared with all of the others.

Performance appraisal   An evaluation system that provides both managers and subordinates with feedback on the subordinates' performance.

Process-maintenance   The stage of an OD effort in which the change agent ensures that there is continued involvement, commitment, and investment in the program by the members.

Recency error   A performance appraisal error brought about when a rater allows an individual's most recent behavior to have a greater impact on the evaluation than the individual's overall behavior.

Refreezing   The final phase of the change process, in which the manager rewards workers who are going along with the change and encourages other employees to do the same.

Reliability   The extent to which an instrument consistently yields the same results.

Sensitivity training (T-group approach)   An OD technique designed to help participants become more aware of their own feelings and those of others.

Similarity   A performance appraisal error in which an evaluator gives higher ratings to subordinates who are viewed as having the same values, habits, and attitudes as the evaluator.

Strictness   A performance appraisal error in which an evaluator gives very low ratings to just about everyone.

Survey feedback   A comprehensive OD intervention that draws survey data from all levels of the hierarchy and then feeds the information back to the personnel who provided it.

Unfreezing   The first phase of the change process, in which the manager analyzes why change is needed and the possible reasons for resistance to it.

Validity   The extent to which an instrument measures what it is supposed to measure.

Questions for Analysis and Discussion

1. In your own words, how does the performance appraisal process work?
2. How are each of the following techniques used in the performance appraisal

process: graphic rating scales, paired comparison, critical incidents, behaviorally anchored rating scales? Be complete in your answer.

3. What are some of the most common problems associated with performance appraisal? How can these problems be dealt with? Explain.

4. What is meant by the term conflict? How can conflict be managed effectively?

5. In what way does force field analysis help explain the change process? Be complete in your answer.

6. The change process consists of three phases. What are these phases and what occurs in each?

7. Why do people resist change? How can such resistance be overcome? Be complete in your answer.

8. In your own words, what is meant by the term organizational climate? How can this climate be measured? What will the results tell management?

9. What is meant by the term organizational development (OD)? Be complete in your definition and description.

10. At the heart of the OD process are three basic components. What are they? Identify and describe each.

11. Of what value is sensitivity training? Does it have any drawbacks? Explain.

12. How does survey feedback work? Of what value is it to modern organizations?

13. When would an organization use grid training? How does this OD intervention work? What benefits does it offer? Be complete in your answer.

14. Does OD really pay off? Defend your answer.

| Case | # Getting a Fair Shake |

Clare Wickline is not happy. For the past seven weeks she has been the new supervisor of a work unit in a large West Coast enterprise. When Clare took over the unit, she was told that most of the workers were "okay" but she would have trouble with some of them. The departing manager, who was taking a job in an unrelated business, gave her the latest performance appraisals on all of the 23 employees. Four of them were rated excellent, four were rated good, 12 were rated average, and the last three were rated poor.

In this company the workers are briefly shown their performance evaluations. The boss then has a general discussion with each employee and tells the individual what he or she is doing well and what the person can do better. This short talk is used to measure and discuss progress and offer suggestions for future personnel development. When the salary raises come out, they are tied directly to the evaluation.

Initially, Clare used the most recent appraisals to help her in supervising the work group. She is now beginning to feel, however, that the ratings do not reflect the true potential and contribution of the individuals. For example, of the three who were rated poor, Clare has found that one of them is an excellent worker, two are good, and the other is average. On the other hand, of the four rated excellent, one of them is good and the others are either average or poor. The same pattern holds for most of the other workers. In each case the employee's attitude, performance, and contribution to the unit are not reflected by the performance appraisal.

The form used for the appraisal was a graphic rating scale that evaluated five factors: work quantity, work quality, appearance, attitude, and job knowledge. Clare is unsure about the way her predecessor arrived at his evaluations. She is beginning to get the impression, however, mostly from some of the workers, that he spent very little time finding out what everyone was doing. For the most part he relied on four informal group leaders to get things done. These were the employees who had the highest ratings. The three who were rated poor were those who had turned out the lowest work quantity during the one week in which a team of management consultants came by to review overall output in the unit.

Clare has talked to her boss and learned that the company has had very good success with its current graphic rating scale. She can use another form of appraisal technique if she prefers, however. The boss has told Clare that her predecessor was fired because he was highly ineffective in terms of his own work quantity, work quality, appearance, attitude, and job knowledge. "I wouldn't pay much attention to those performance evaluations he left behind," the boss told her. "They are probably highly biased and based strictly on non-job-related performance." Clare is currently putting together her quarterly review of each person's performance. She hopes to overcome many of the previous problems. "For once," she told her boss, "I'm going to see that these people get a fair shake."

1. If Clare did not choose to use a graphic rating scale in evaluating the performance of her people, what would you suggest she use? Defend your answer.

2. What particular problems were there with the way the previous supervisor evaluated the personnel?

3. How can Clare sidestep making these errors? What recommendations would you give her?

You Be the Consultant

Looking into the Grid

Carbrough Research and Development has just gone through some major changes, and it looks like there will be more in the near future. The company originally was a research and development (R&D) firm that specialized in making models and mockups for hard-to-build equipment. Jacques Carbrough, who founded the firm in 1939, gathered around him the best designers and research people he could find. As the firm's reputation began to spread, the company slowly but surely began to move into manufacturing. "Since we know so much about how to design complex equipment, why not manufacture the product as well?" was the way the founder's son, Jean, explained why the company moved into the production area.

During the 1950s and 1960s the company did extremely well. About this time the top management also began to notice that the firm was being divided into two distinct groups: the R&D-oriented people and the manufacturing people. The two worked independently of each other for the most part and there were no real problems. Given the fact that the top management consisted mostly of R&D types, however, some underlying feelings were beginning to cause friction.

During the 1970s the company began to expand its holdings. Taking a conglomerate approach, it started purchasing firms in diversified fields. The acquired companies included a plastics manufacturer, a chemical firm, a real estate development firm, a small but profitable insurance company, and a well-known, although modest, New England publisher.

Last week Jean Carbrough's son Paul was installed as the chief executive officer of the conglomerate. Since then he has been working hard to get a handle on things. Having come up the ranks through the R&D side of operations, he is somewhat at a loss regarding how to manage and control the enterprise's farflung acquisitions. In particular, Paul has noticed that while ROI and profit are up to expectations, something is lacking. When he was just starting out in the firm 20 years ago, there was greater esprit de corps. People seemed to trust each other more. There was an attitude of "Let's get together and do this as a team." That now seems to be gone. In its place is a rather stuffy bureaucracy in which people do what they are told to do and not much more. There seem to be distinct lines between "us" and "them" among the major divisions of the original company and between the company and its newly acquired subsidiaries.

Paul is convinced that this attitude and value system will affect operations negatively. It is only a matter of time. As a result, he has been thinking about what can be done to improve things. A few years ago he attended a training program designed to familiarize the participants with some basic OD interventions and their value to organizational efforts. Although he does not know a great deal about the managerial grid, he was impressed with what he heard and believes it might well be ideal in dealing with the problems he sees. In particular, Paul would like an OD technique that would bring all of the units together. He knows that other techniques can be used in dealing with more limited issues such as interpersonal conflict or team dissension. These, however, can be incorporated into the process along the way.

Paul's greatest concern is that the conglomerate is changing too quickly. The industries in which the company's diversified firms operate are extremely competitive, and they will have to hurry to keep up. Their basic nature may change and their relationship with the organization at large may become strained. In order to prevent this problem and maintain overall control of personnel performance, Paul would like to look seriously into employing the grid approach.

Your Consultation

Assume that you have just been called in by Paul to act as his consultant. First, describe to him how the grid OD approach works. Be as complete as possible in your answer. Then explain the benefits that this approach can have in terms of dealing with conflict and change, improving organizational climate, and improving bottom-line performance in the enterprise. Finally, discuss some of the responsibilities and problems that Paul's organization will encounter if it chooses the grid approach.

Comprehensive Cases

Inner-City Paint Corporation

History

Stanley Walsh is an entrepreneur in his mid-thirties who started his "dream come true," Inner-City Paint Corporation, in 1976. He began his career as a house painter and went on to become a painter for a large decorating company. Mr. Walsh primarily painted walls in large commercial buildings and hospitals. Eventually he came to believe that he could produce a paint that was less expensive and of higher quality than what was being used. His keen desire to start his own business resulted in the creation of Inner-City Paint Corporation.

Mr. Walsh built his firm on the basis of a high-quality product, personal and individualized service to the customer, and speedy delivery (usually within 24 hours). Because paint weighs so much (52½ pounds per five-gallon container), the cost of shipping the product can be prohibitive and Inner-City confines its business to the immediate Chicago area. Its main competitors are other small, local paint manufacturers. The primary market for the company's product is small to medium-sized decorating firms.

Facilities

Inner-City is located at its original site, a rundown warehouse on the fringe of Chicago's downtown business area. The majority of the space (16,400 square feet) is devoted to manufacturing and storage, with 850 square feet assigned as office space. The building is 45 years old and in disrepair. It is being leased at three-year intervals.

Product

Inner-City's chief product is flat white wall paint sold in five-gallon plastic cans and 55-gallon containers. Flat white is made with pigment (titanium dioxide and silicates), vehicle (resin), and water. The water makes up 72 percent of the product. The firm also produces paint in various colors on request. To produce a color, the necessary pigment used to create the color is tested in Inner-City's lab to ensure consistent quality.

The cost of materials to produce flat white paint is $2.40 per gallon. Colors are approximately 40 to 50 percent higher. Five-gallon, covered plastic pails cost Inner-City $1.72 each. Fifty-five gallon drums (with lids) are $8.35 each. Suppliers to Inner-City have recently required cash-on-delivery (C.O.D.) for raw materials.

To the average customer, flat white sells for $27.45 for five gallons and $182.75 for 55 gallons. Colors vary in selling price because of the variety in pigment cost and quantity ordered. Pricing was competitive and, until recently, Inner-City had shown steady sales growth. In the early 1980s, however, the slowdown in the housing market, combined with a slowdown in the overall economy, caused financial difficulties for Inner-City.

Management

Inner-City has been operating without management and financial controls. It grew from a small, two-person company with sales of $60,000 annually in 1976, to a company with sales of $1,800,000 and 38 employees last year. The president and majority stockholder is Stanley Walsh. He manages the corporation today in much the same way as he did when the business began. He personally opens all mail, approves all payments, and inspects all customer billings before they are mailed. He has been unable to detach himself from any detail of the operation and cannot delegate authority. As the company has grown, the time element alone has aggravated the situation. Frequently, these tasks are performed days after transactions occur and mail is received.

The office is managed by Mrs. Walsh, Mr. Walsh's mother. Two part-time clerks assist her, and all records are processed manually. Customers purchase on credit and usually pay their invoices in 30 to 60 days. In the case of nonpayment, the customer is telephoned after 60 days to inquire when payment will be made.

Inventory records are not kept. The warehouse manager keeps a mental count of what is in stock. He documents (on a lined yellow pad) what has been shipped for the day and to whom. That list is given to the billing clerk at the end of each day.

Employees

For the past eight months the plant has been managed by a man in his twenties whom Mr. Walsh hired from one of his customers. Mr. Walsh became acquainted with the man when he stopped at Inner-City to pick up paint for his previous employer. Before being employed by Mr. Walsh as plant manager, the man was a painter. He has no other work experience.

Thirty-five employees (many of whom are part-time) work in various phases of the manufacturing process. Most are nonunion, unskilled laborers. They take turns making paint and driving the delivery trucks.

Stanley Walsh does all of the sales and public relations work. He spends approximately half of every day making sales calls and answering complaints about defective paint. He is the only salesman. Other salesmen were employed in the past, but, Mr. Walsh felt they "could not be trusted."

Customer Perception

Customers view Inner-City as a company that provides fast service and negotiates on price and payment out of desperation. Mr. Walsh is seen as a disorganized person who may not be able to keep Inner-City afloat much longer. Rumors abound that Inner-City is in financial straits, that it is unable to pay suppliers, and that it owes a considerable sum for payment on back taxes. All of these notions contribute to a serious lack of confidence in the corporation on the part of customers. Therefore, paint contractors are reluctant to place large orders with Inner-City and come there only with short orders that must be filled quickly.

Financial Structure

The following are the most current financial statements of Inner-City Paint Corporation for the year ended six months ago. They were prepared by the company's accounting service. No audit has been performed, as Mr. Walsh did not want to incur the necessary expense.

Balance Sheet
June 30, 1984

Current Assets:

Cash	$ 1,535	
Accounts receivable (net of allowance for bad debts of $63,400)	242,320	
Inventory	18,660	
Total current assets		$ 262,515
Machinery & transportation equipment	47,550	
Less: Accumulated depreciation	15,500	
Net fixed assets		32,050
Total assets		$ 294,565

Current Liabilities:

Accounts payable	$217,820	
Salaries payable	22,480	
Notes payable	6,220	
Taxes payable	38,510	
Total current liabilities		$ 285,030
Long-term notes payable		15,000
Owners' equity:		
Common stock, no par, 1,824		
Shares outstanding		27,400
Deficit		(32,865)
Total liabilities & owners' equity		$ 294,565

Income Statement
for the Year Ended
June 30, 1984

Sales		$1,784,080
Cost of goods sold		1,428,730
Gross margin		$ 355,350
Selling expenses	$ 72,460	
Administrative expenses	67,280	
President's salary	132,000	
Office manager salary	66,000	
Total expenses		337,740
Net income		$ 17,610

Future

Stanley Walsh wants to improve the financial situation and reputation of Inner-City Paint Corporation. He is considering the purchase of a computer to organize the business and reduce needless paperwork. He has read about consultants who are able to spot problems in businesses quickly, but he will not spend more than $300 for such services.

The solution Mr. Walsh favors is one that requires him to borrow more money from the bank. He will then use the borrowed money to pay his current bills. He feels that as soon as business conditions improve, he will be able to pay back the loans. He believes that the problems Inner-City is experiencing are due to the poor economy and are only temporary.

1. What characteristics do you feel are necessary for effective control? Which of these characteristics, if any, has Stanley Walsh failed to use? How would these characteristics have been helpful as management tools at Inner-City Paint Corporation?

2. Did Stanley Walsh monitor the performance of the company using financial and operational controls? Explain.

3. How would a computer have aided Inner-City's control process?

4. What, in your opinion, do the financial statements of Inner-City Paint Corporation reflect?

5. If you took over Stanley Walsh's position, what would you do to improve Inner-City Paint Corporation's financial condition? Explain.

Case of the Missing Invoices

Background

The Price Corporation manufactures paper bags. Its sales are directed primarily at retail stores. The paper bag industry is very competitive. Since paper bags are a homogeneous product, sales depend on two key factors: low prices and fast service.

Kraft paper is a basic raw material in the production of paper bags. It is absolutely essential that Price Corporation have a ready supply of this paper. Any delay in receiving kraft paper causes the company to be unable to provide the fast service necessary to remain competitive. If Price cannot be relied upon, and a customer runs out of bags, the immediate result is the loss of that customer to a competitor.

Personnel

Mr. Produ is the production manager, office manager, and an owner-stockholder at Price, a closely held corporation with approximately $12,000,000 in annual sales. Ms. Booker and Ms. Keeper are accountants employed by Mr. Produ. The salesforce consists of four owner-stockholders and 12 salespeople. There are 63 employees in the plant.

Situation

Mr. Produ supervises the office on a daily basis. The other four owner-stockholders are responsible for sales and are rarely in the office. All mail is opened by Mr. Produ, and he distributes it to other employees at his convenience. Often, this may not be until the end of the day and sometimes not until the following day.

Customers pay Price Corporation within 30 to 60 days of date of invoice. Paying bills is the lowest priority for Mr. Produ, however. He insists on approving all Price Corporation payments on invoices but delays in opening mail that contains invoices to be paid. Frequently, mail received on Friday is not opened until Monday. Mail can accumulate on Mr. Produ's desk for three to four days.

All receiving reports (proof of delivery of raw materials and supplies) are given to Mr. Produ. These must be matched with incoming invoices. Receiving reports and invoices may never be matched, however, because they are lost among the stacks of paperwork on Mr. Produ's desk. Occasionally, receiving reports get lost in the jumble, and invoices remain unpaid. Even when this behavior leads to second and third requests for payment, letters and telephone calls from collection agencies and, finally, letters from attorneys, Mr. Produ ignores the bills completely.

Ms. Booker and Ms. Keeper, the accountants, are the people who must communicate with angry vendors regarding unpaid bills. They are also responsible for all phases of the accounting operations, as well as for preparing cash disbursements for vendor invoices. They have found it necessary to ask vendors to mail duplicate invoices and proofs of delivery (marked to their attention) in an effort to speed up processing of the accounts.

This method of processing accounts payable has proven costly to the Price Corporation. Time is wasted by personnel attempting to duplicate records already received, and late charges and attorney fees are being incurred. The reputation of the corporation has suffered, and the morale of all employees involved is now low. Mr. Produ likes his approach, however. He feels that his method controls manufacturing costs and gives him complete centralized management, which he needs.

1. Is there a timely payment procedure for processing documents that will still allow Mr. Produ to retain control of invoices being paid?

2. Good internal control in an accounting system requires the separation of duties. How could Mr. Produ accomplish this?

3. Why do you think Mr. Produ believes that for good control of the company, he must oversee things personally?

4. How will the relationships between Price Corporation and vendors change as invoices continue to be paid late, or not at all?

5. How would you improve Price Corporation's system of processing accounts payable? Be complete in your answer.

Mid-Con's Management Renewal

Background

Over the past decade, the Mid-Con Electrical Engineering Corporation has operated a profitable electrical engineering firm with a sound cash flow and an annual substantial growth in its market. During 1980 and 1981, declining numbers of new projects, as well as a depressed economy, led the company's management to respond with rapid and effective decisions. In an effort to remain "afloat," management found it necessary to reduce the workforce significantly. Although wages were tied to union standards, salary expenses were reduced for the remaining workers through a management-imposed three-day work week.

As viewed through the eyes of the company president, George Doyle, future business prospects look encouraging if his company can "weather this storm." In Mr. Doyle's view, "It's similar to a swimmer and a person in a boat in rough water. While it may appear more advantageous to be in a boat than to be swimming, the swimmer will gain advantage once the sea calms, for it is he who can direct his path and objective while the rider must go with the boat."

This optimistic and challenge-oriented president wants to continue to direct his company through the rough times rather than allow these rough times to direct the company. In order to survive, the company must establish new goals with the labor force in mind.

The Issue

George Doyle and his managers are seeking to establish new goals, objectives, and directions for the company. They need support and motivation from a decimated work force cut to three-day work weeks with no allowance for overtime. Everyone in top management realizes what a great obstacle they have to overcome. Exactly how can Mr. Doyle begin to motivate his workers to achieve company objectives?

In order to investigate the alternatives objectively, a special committee has been created to interview the workers, conduct meetings, gather data, and propose recommendations to the president. The committee consists of the executive assistant, the vice-president, the controller, the general manager, a foreman who holds seniority (11 years), and an outside consultant (a professor from a local university).

By conducting informal interviews at on-site locations, the committee has gathered data on worker attitudes. During these interviews, many workers felt reluctant to talk openly since job security was on their mind. Thanks to the attitude survey instrument (see Exhibit 1), the committee was able to evaluate the present attitude of workers toward the firm. Based on these

Exhibit 1
Employee Opinion Survey

Your answers to this survey will help us understand how our employees feel about the company and our effectiveness in working with people. It is completely anonymous. YOU DO NOT HAVE TO PUT YOUR NAME ON THIS QUESTIONNAIRE.

Directions: After reading each question, circle the letter (a), (b), (c), (d), or (e) next to the response you most closely agree with. Feel free to add any comments you wish.

1. How do you feel about the work you are doing?

    (a) Very pleased   (b) Somewhat pleased   (c) No feeling particularly one way or another   (d) Somewhat displeased   (e) Very displeased

    COMMENTS: _____
    _____

2. How would you rate the fairness of the way employee promotions are handled?

    (a) They are very fair   (b) They are fair enough   (c) They need to improve a great deal

    COMMENTS: _____
    _____

3. How do you feel about your manager's handling and discipline?

    (a) He/she does this very fairly   (b) He/she does this fairly
    (c) He/she is about average in this respect   (d) He/she does this poorly   (e) He/she does this very poorly

    COMMENTS: _____
    _____

4. How much trust and confidence do you have in your manager?

    (a) A great deal   (b) Quite a bit   (c) Some   (d) A little   (e) Very little or none

    COMMENTS: _____
    _____

5. Do you know what is expected of you in your job?

    (a) I know exactly what is expected   (b) I have a very good idea of what is expected   (c) I have a fairly good idea of what is expected
    (d) I have some idea of what is expected   (e) I don't know what is expected

    COMMENTS: _____
    _____

6. How do you feel about the cooperation between departments in the company?

    (a) Cooperation is excellent   (b) It could be improved   (c) There is no cooperation

    COMMENTS: _____
    _____

7. Compared to last year, how do you feel about your job?

   (a) Improved a lot   (b) Improved some   (c) About the same   (d) Not as good   (e) Much worse

   COMMENTS: _____

   _____

8. How free do you feel to tell your supervisor how you think?

   (a) Completely free   (b) Somewhat free   (c) Depends on the subject
   (d) Not free at all   (e) I'm afraid

   COMMENTS: _____

   _____

9. Compared to last year, how do you feel about the company?

   (a) I am proud to work here   (b) This is a pretty good place to work
   (c) I am not sure   (d) It is not as good   (e) I wish I didn't work here

   COMMENTS: _____

   _____

10. How well do you understand the various fringe benefits provided by the company?

    (a) Very well   (b) Fairly well   (c) Somewhat   (d) Not very well
    (e) Not at all

    COMMENTS: _____

    _____

11. Please complete this sentence:

    I think the company's effectiveness in working with people could be improved if:

    _____

    _____

12. Any additional comments:

    _____

    _____

    _____

simple measures, the committee has identified three problem areas or perceptions of problem areas:

1. lack of communication between management and labor;

2. lack of development of foremen and middle management; and

3. lack of goal setting and advancement within the firm.

The Alternatives

The special committee unanimously has agreed that a "management and organizational development program" should be designed and implemented at Mid-Con. Some major areas of concern that will have to be addressed are communication, time management, motivation, job enrichment, managerial performance standards, and management development. The committee feels, however, that Mr. Doyle's optimistic objectives will prove fruitful only with a motivated workforce. Thus, the following alternatives are being considered:

Alternative 1   Hire an outside consulting firm to develop the program for the company.

Notes   This would require time for the consulting firm to interview, analyze, and identify specific needs for Mid-Con. In addition, the costs could be extremely high.

Alternative 2   Hire a human resource manager.

Notes   This alternative would involve creating a specific job description, advertising the position, screening the applicants, selecting one, and, finally, orienting the person. In addition, a competitive, full-time salary would have to be provided.

Alternative 3   Use existing corporate talent. (People within the company develop the program.)

Notes   This approach would require the identification of qualified personnel already in the company who could be selected for either a special committee or an entirely new department for management and organizational development. In addition, their organizational positions would have to be reevaluated in order to be filled or phased out.

Evaluation

The advantages and disadvantages have been discussed with Mr. Doyle. The committee members like Alternative 1. They believe that a consulting firm could develop a professional program that would greatly benefit Mid-Con. In addition, the committee feels that the costs of the consulting firm compare favorably with the additional salaries that would be incurred with the other alternatives. Also, disruption of the company's work would be minimal since the consulting firm would be external to the organization.

Alternative 2 is considered a viable option, although the committee believes that the time and salary would be inadequate in solving the company's problems. It also fears that the workers might react negatively to having a "new management position" filled from the outside.

Alternative 3 offers the advantageous idea of using "in-house" people for the betterment of their own peers. The commiteee feels that these people might be more personally concerned than an outsider and more easily accepted by the other employees. Yet the committee also is aware that finding such talent might prove difficult and, even if it could be found, the company could have problems in filling the vacancies caused by the transfers.

In the committee's view, any of the three alternatives can be adopted if Mr. Doyle agrees. After pondering the input from the committee, Mr. Doyle has decided that the four most important aspects affecting his decision should be (1) the cost-benefit analysis (success vs. costs); (2) the probability of achieving objectives; (3) implementation time; and (4) the impact on the company's present operations.

Sitting quietly in his office, Mr. Doyle realizes that his decision may affect all of the company's future objectives. A decision must be made, however.

1. What decision should Mr. Doyle make? ·

2. What is the reason for your choice? Explain.

3. Would you have suggested any other plan?

4. What managerial issues are visible in this case? Explain.

Management and You

This last part of the book is designed to provide you with insights regarding the changes that are likely to take place in management during the next decade and the challenges and opportunities that await you should you choose a career in this field. The first chapter in this part describes the environment in which managers will be doing their work, while the second discusses some of the problems and opportunities that can be yours should you enter this field.

In addressing the subject of management in the future, Chapter 19 examines the codes of conduct and ethical practices in modern organizations and discusses the current and future status of women in top management positions. Attention is focused on attitudes, the quality of work life, and the way in which social values in the workplace are helping shape the world of management.

Chapter 20 focuses on management career planning and you. After providing a profile of currently successful executives and explaining the six career phases through which most managers go, it looks at the typical problems faced by managers both as they start out their careers and later on and suggests useful strategies in terms of career self-evaluation, career tactics, and career development planning. The latter part of the chapter focuses on the nature and effects of organizational stress, examining how and why some managers become highly susceptible to coronary heart disease and offering guidelines for managing stress to ensure a long, healthy career.

When you have finished reading the material in this part of the book, you will have a basic perspective on management. You will be better able to put everything you have learned in this book into an overall framework and see how it applies to you. Most importantly, you will have learned about some of the important challenges and opportunities that await you should you choose a career in the field of management.

19

Management in the Future

Objectives

During the next decade the world of management is going to change significantly. This chapter examines some of the major changes that will occur and presents a picture of the effect these changes will have on the way modern managers do their jobs. As you will see, many of these developments relate to changing values on the part of management, the employee, and society at large. The chapter examines the ways in which management values, attitudes, and interests will change during the next 10 years; it explores employee values, attitudes, and work life; and it analyzes the impact of social values in the workplace. When you have finished studying all of the material in this chapter, you will be able to

1. discuss codes of conduct and ethical practices in modern organizations;

2. explain the current status of women in top management positions and what their future looks like;

3. tell why there has been an increased interest in strategic planning among top managers;

4. discuss the values and attitudes that today's workers have regarding their company and their job;

5. explain how the quality of work life movement and modern technology will change the way workers do their jobs; and

6. identify and discuss how social values in the workplace are helping shape the world of management, giving particular attention in your discussion to employee assistance programs, the hiring of the handicapped, and the elimination of sexual harassment.

Management Values, Attitudes, and Interests

During the remainder of the 1980s and well into the next decade, we will be seeing changes in the way management conducts its business. Some of these developments will be a direct result of changing management values, attitudes, and interests. Because there are far too many changes for us to address all of them here, we will focus on three of the most important ones: (1) codes of conduct and ethical practices, (2) women in top management positions, and (3) strategic planning.

Codes of Conduct and Ethical Practices

Areas covered by codes of conduct

A **code of conduct** is a statement of ethical practices or guidelines to which an enterprise adheres. There are many such codes, some related to industry at large and others related directly to corporate conduct. These codes cover a multitude of subjects, ranging from misuse of corporate assets, conflict of interest, and use of inside information, to equal employment practices, falsification of books and records, and antitrust violations.

During the 1960s a number of codes of conduct were discussed in the business literature.[1] During the 1970s the revelations about the Watergate break-in and illegal or questionable payoffs at home and abroad resulted in a public outcry regarding codes of conduct and ethical practices.

How prevalent are codes of conduct today? Bernard J. White and B. Ruth Montgomery recently conducted a national survey and found that of the 673 chief executive officers who responded, more than 75 percent reported having such a code. (See Table 19–1.) White and Montgomery's findings are significantly different from the findings of S. Mathes and G. Thompson who conducted a similar survey during the 1960s. In the earlier survey only 60 percent of the respondents said that they had a code of conduct.[2]

What, specifically, do typical codes of conduct contain? Table 19–2 provides the general content of codes of 30 business firms randomly selected by White and Montgomery. Commenting on the overall nature of these codes, the authors noted:

> Most of the codes provide some "context," a general statement about the code of ethical issues in the company's management philosophy, and the role of the code in capturing and communicating rules and guidelines on such matters. Two-thirds include a blanket statement on the employee's responsibility for "compliance with all applicable laws and regulations." Beyond these general statements, the most frequently treated subject is conflict of interest. Nearly 65 percent of the codes made a statement about employees' responsibility to avoid conflict-of-interest situations. About half of all the codes detail the types of conflict of interest specifically prohibited: interests in competitors, suppliers, or customers, and conflicts created by relatives' or associates' interests.[3]

---

1. See, for example: Robert W. Austin, "Codes of Conduct for Executives," *Harvard Business Review*, September–October 1961, pp. 53–61.

2. S. Mathes and G. Thompson, "Ensuring Ethical Conduct in Business," *The Conference Board Record*, December 1964, pp. 17–27.

3. Bernard J. White and B. Ruth Montgomery, "Corporate Codes of Conduct," *California Management Review*, Winter 1980, p. 85.

Table 19–1 Percentage of Companies (Overall and by Size) Reporting Various Practices Related to Corporate Codes of Conduct

Question	Overall Response	Size categories*									
		1	2	3	4	5	6	7	8	9	10
Does your company have a code of conduct?	(N = 611)										
• yes	77%	40%	57%	74%	75%	72%	90%	85%	87%	92%	97%
Who receives a copy?	(N = 486)										
• officers/key employees	97%	83	97	94	98	100	100	98	96	100	100
• other employees	55%	46	60	35	54	58	42	60	46	70	68
Who signs it periodically?	(N = 481)										
• officers/key employees	85%	75	62	80	87	80	85	91	86	91	90
• other employees	(N = 451) 27%	23	27	12	17	30	25	23	31	47	39
Are procedures specified for handling violations of the code's provisions?	(N = 478)										
• yes	63%	41	46	38	54	58	55	66	75	85	83
Have procedures been enforced in the last several years?	(N = 463)										
• yes	62%	42	43	30	48	48	64	63	77	83	91

* The overall sample of 673 was broken into deciles by size. Category 1 is $0–60 million; category 2 is $60–132 million; category 3 is $132–201 million; category 4 is $201–300 million; category 5 is $300–467 million; category 6 is $467–717 million; category 7 is $717–1,150 million; category 8 is $1,150–1,900 million; category 9 is $1,900–4,000 million; category 10 is $4,000 million and above.

Source: Bernard J. White and B. Ruth Montgomery, "Corporate Codes of Conduct," *California Management Review,* Winter 1980, p. 82. Copyright © (1980) by the Regents of the University of California. Reprinted from *California Management Review,* volume 23, no. 2, pp. 80–87 by permission of the Regents.

Codes of conduct are becoming more prevalent.

Based on the results of such research, two important conclusions can be reached. First, codes of conduct are becoming more prevalent in industry. Management is not just giving lip service to ethics and moral behavior; it is putting its ideas into writing and distributing these guidelines for everyone in the organization to read and follow. Second, in contrast to earlier codes, the more recent ones are proving to be more meaningful in terms of external legal and social development, more comprehensive in terms of their coverage, and easier to implement in terms of the administrative procedures that are being used to enforce them.[4]

Of course, the most important question still remains to be answered: Will management really adhere to a high moral code? Many managers would respond to this question by answering "Yes." Why? The main reason is that it is good business. One top executive put the idea this way:

4. *Ibid.,* p. 86; for more on this topic see: Donald R. Cressey and Charles A. Moore, "Managerial Values and Corporate Codes of Conduct," *California Management Review,* Summer 1983, pp. 121–127.

Table 19–2
Codes of Conduct: Content
Analysis (n = 30)

Subject	Percentage in which Subject is Addressed
A. Date on code of conduct	77%
B. General statement of ethics and philosophy	80
C. Compliance with applicable laws	67
D. Observance of moral and ethical standards of society	20
E. Specific reference to Foreign Corrupt Practices Act	17
F. False entries in books and records	50
G. Misuse of corporate assets (general)	50
1. Political contributions	67
a. Acceptable under certain conditions if legal	37
b. All banned	30
2. Facilitating payments	20
3. Payments to government officials/political parties	63
4. Gifts, favors, entertainment	57
5. Secret payments	23
6. Undisclosed or unrecorded funds or assets	53
7. False, misleading support documents	37
H. Conflict of interest (general)	73
1. Interest in competition	50
2. Interest in suppliers	57
3. Interest in customer	50
4. Relatives or associates	50
5. Acceptance of gifts	77
6. Membership on boards of directors	30
I. Arrangements with dealers and agents	23
1. Foreign or third party payments	13
2. Responsibility for dealers' actions	43
3. Commission levels	33
J. Antitrust compliance	40
1. Relations with competitors	30
2. Relations with customers	30
3. Relations with suppliers	30
4. International transactions	13
K. International trade boycotts	10
L. Inside information	63
M. Relations with shareholders and security analysts	7
N. Confidential information	40
O. Equal employment opportunity	30
P. Partisan versus issue political activity	13
Q. Implementation/administrative procedures (for the code)	83

Source: Bernard J. White and B. Ruth Montgomery, "Corporate Codes of Conduct," *California Management Review,* Winter 1980, p. 84. Copyright © (1980) by the Regents of the University of California. Reprinted from California Management Review, volume 23, no. 2, pp. 80–87 by permission of the Regents.

Singly or in combination, [unethical] practices have a corrosive effect on free markets and free trade, which are fundamental to the survival of the free enterprise system. They subvert the laws of supply and demand, and they shortcircuit competition based on classical ideas of product quality, service, and price. Free markets are replaced by contrived markets. The need for constant improvement in products or services is removed.[5]

A second, related reason is that by improving the moral climate of the enterprise, the corporation can eventually win back the confidence of the public. This would mark a turnaround in that many people today question the moral and ethical integrity of companies and believe that business-people try to get away with everything they can. Only time will tell whether codes of conduct will serve to improve business practices. Current trends indicate, however, that the business community is working hard toward this objective.[6]

Women in Top Management Positions

Over the last decade the number of women in top management has increased.[7] Progress in this area has been slow, however. Nevertheless, the picture is going to be brighter over the next decade as management begins to realize more fully the importance of women in the executive suite. Commenting on the situation, *Newsweek* has written:

The day when women will routinely run big companies is still a long way off. But propelled by affirmative action laws, the feminist movement and the rising consciousness of corporations themselves, women executives have come a long way in the last decade. Women now occupy one-fourth of the managerial and administrative jobs in private industry. The number of women who are corporate officers of the 1,300 largest U.S. companies— judged too tiny to count just five years ago—stands at 477 . . . and the number of women directors of these companies now exceeds 300. And women are likely to move even more rapidly into the towers of corporate America in the future.[8]

At the present time only about 6 percent of all working women hold managerial positions. Additionally, most of these who have achieved executive status have done so in the areas traditionally open to women: public

---

5. Reported in Darrell J. Fashing, "A Case for Corporate and Management Ethics," *California Management Review,* Spring 1981, p. 84.

6. For more on this subject see: Kenneth E. Goodpaster and John B. Matthews, Jr., "Can a Corporation Have a Conscience?" *Harvard Business Review,* January– February 1982, pp. 132–141; Harold Johnson, "Ethics and the Executive," *Harvard Business Review,* May–June 1983, pp. 53–59; and Douglas S. Sherwin, "The Ethical Roots of the Business System," *Harvard Business Review,* November–December 1983, pp. 183–193.

7. J. Benjamin Forbes and James E. Piercy, "Rising to the Top: Executive Women in 1983 and Beyond," *Business Horizons,* September–October 1983, pp. 38–47.

8. Joseph M. Arena, "Women and The Executive Suite," *Newsweek,* September 14, 1981, p. 65.

Some men feel threatened by women in management positions.

relations, personnel, staff jobs, or the media and service industries. What is holding women back? One cause is male hostility. Some men feel threatened when they have to work for a woman. Researchers have also found that as the percentage of women in an organization increases, the number of insults and the degree of sexual harassment they suffer also increases.[9] Nevertheless, this barrier will begin to fall as men realize that they have to adjust.

Some women are not academically prepared for

A second reason for women's underrepresentation in the executive ranks is that in the past most women did not seek careers in management.[10] In college most majored in education or the liberal arts. That is now changing as women are flocking not only to undergraduate business schools but into MBA (Master of Business Administration) programs as well. Between 1971 and 1981 the number of women in MBA programs increased from 3.5 percent of total enrollments to more than 25 percent. (See Table 19–3.) This kind of education is bound to help their chances for breaking into the executive ranks.

careers in business.
Some women are taught not to be competitive.

A third reason for the small percentage of women in top management is cultural. Women have been taught not to be competitive, so when they get into the world of business they are unprepared for the politics and pressures that go with the job. In an effort to deal with these problems, business firms, as well as universities, are beginning to offer courses for women desiring management positions. In these courses the participants are provided with information and training designed to help them maneuver their way through the corporate jungle.

How does the future look? The answer is: good and getting better.

Table 19–3
Women and the MBA Degree

Class Year	Total	Women	Women as a Percent of the Total
1971	21,417	758	3.5%
1972	26,654	1,045	3.9
1973	30,511	1,533	5.0
1974	32,820	2,161	6.6
1975	36,450	3,080	8.4
1976	42,728	4,974	11.6
1977	46,650	6,681	14.3
1978	48,484	8,183	16.9
1979	50,506	9,675	19.2
1980	55,325	12,332	22.3
1981*	56,000	14,500	25.9

* Projections

Source: National Center for Educational Statistics, Association of MBA Executives, Inc. as reported in *Newsweek*, November 14, 1981, p. 66.

9. *Ibid.,* p. 66.

10. Lloyd D. Elgart, "Women on Fortune 500 Boards," *California Management Review,* Summer 1983, pp. 121–127.

But the future looks bright.

A few experts even say that the dream of the CEO's chair may not be as far away as many women think. Futurist Herman Kahn has predicted that 50 women may be CEOs of the 500 largest industrial companies by the year 2000. "I don't feel as if I'm on the express ride to the top," says Susan R. Weil, 34, manager of financial control systems at International Harvester Co., "but I also don't think it is any less likely that I will have the opportunity to be president of this group than any man at my level now."[11]

These comments are certainly supported by recent research data. For example, Alma Baron questioned approximately 8,000 male respondents, 85 percent of whom were middle or upper-middle managers, regarding their image of women in business. The purpose of the survey was (1) to find out how rapidly acceptance of women in management was occurring, and (2) to identify trends that could be useful for a company committed to moving women into the higher managment levels. Some of her major findings included the following:

1. Half of the respondents accepted women in managerial roles and less than 5 percent were negative toward women in these roles.

2. The higher the level of the executive's education, the more likely it was that he approved of women in managerial positions.

3. Men who work for women are more likely to accept them as managers, while men who do not work for women have a more negative opinion of them as managers.[12]

The survey confirms what we have been saying about women in management. The old stereotypes are fading. There is evidence that biases against women in business have lessened considerably in the last decade. This trend should continue in the foreseeable future.[13]

Continued Interest in Strategic Planning

During the next 10 years we will also see a change in the way management plans for the future. A true administrative science approach is emerging. This is due, in particular, to recent developments involving the collection and analysis of inter- and intra-industry business performance data on such key planning issues as strategy formulation, performance and its relationship to return on investment (ROI), the impact of product quality on ROI, the effect of modern technology on profit, and strategy implementation. Ten years ago, management scientists and behavioral scientists were chastising administrative scientists for their overreliance on intuition, gut feeling, hunch, and other less than scientific approaches. Progress since then shows

11. *Ibid.,* p. 68.

12. Alma S. Baron, "What Men Are Saying About Women in Business," *Business Horizons,* January–February 1982, p. 10–11.

13. For more on this see: Benson Rosen, Mary Ellen Templeton, and Karen Kichline, "The First Few Years on the Job: Women in Management," *Business Horizons,* November–December 1982, pp. 26–29.

that a more scientific approach is being taken, especially in the case of the strategic decision making used by top management.

Profit Impact of Marketing Strategy

The profit impact of marketing strategy (PIMS) is not the only example of the way administrative science is evolving in the 1980s, but it provides an excellent illustration of the way the process is occurring. PIMS originated as an internal project at General Electric, where it was used as a tool in both corporate and division-level planning. In the early 1970s the PIMS program was established as a developmental project at the Harvard Business School and was located at the Marketing Science Institute, a research organization affiliated with that business school. In the mid-1970s the program was organized as an autonomous institute known as the Strategic Planning Institute (SPI). Business firms that become members of the institute provide information describing the characteristics of their market environment, the state of their competition, the strategy being pursued by their various divisions, and the operating results obtained for each. This data is then analyzed for the purpose of determining answers to questions such as the following:

- What profit rate is "normal" for a given business, considering its particular market, competitive position, technology, cost structure and so forth?

- If the business continues on its current track, what will its future operating results be?

Important questions are being answered.

- What strategic changes in the business give promise of improving these results?

- Given a specific contemplated future strategy for the business, how will profitability or cash flow change, short-term and long-term?[14]

Results to Date

Information from the SPI has proven extremely useful to the member firms. In particular the institute has been able to generate a number of important findings regarding business strategy. One of the most interesting is that as business firms increase their levels of intensity per dollar of sales revenue (as in the case of airlines, bulk chemical-processing plants, and distributors of consumer goods requiring large inventories), their ROI declines. Why does this occur? The answer is that as firms invest more money in such things as capital equipment and plant, each becomes eager to produce at capacity. The results are frequent price wars, marketing wars, and other intensely competitive measures that collectively reduce revenue and increase costs. What should a firm do if the technology of its business clearly requires a high level of investment in plant, equipment and working capital? The SPI recommends that (a) the firm should not automatically assume that more is better in terms of investment intensity; (b) in evaluating a proposed investment that is clearly larger rather than

Findings regarding business strategy

---

14. *PIMS: The PIMS Program* (Cambridge, Mass.: The Strategic Planning Institute, 1980), p. 5.

merely proportional to an increase in capacity, the firm should consider the strategic effect as carefully as the cost effect of the project; and (c) it should adopt a market strategy that minimizes the profit-damaging effect of capital-intensive technology.

Another interesting finding reported by the SPI relates to product quality, market share, and ROI. The SPI puts the idea this way:

> The combined experience of the approximately 1,200 businesses now represented in the PIMS data pool indicates that *businesses selling high-quality products and services are generally more profitable than those with lower-quality offerings*. . . . Both return on investment and net profit as a percentage of sales rise as relative quality increases. Note, however, that the impact of differences in quality is greatest at the extremes of very low and high quality.[15]

Figure 19–1 illustrates PIMS research data related to product quality, market share, and ROI. Notice from the figure that higher product quality is positively related to ROI *independently* of market share. Firms with high product quality have greater returns than those with low product quality. If these companies also enjoy large market shares, so much the better in terms of ROI. Additionally, quality seems to be an important influence on profit in virtually all kinds of markets and competitive positions. This finding is illustrated in Table 19–4. Notice from the data that, on average, the higher the quality of the product, the greater the return on investment.

Overall Strategy Findings

Drawing upon its results to date, most of which have been from manufacturing firms, the SPI has begun reporting its findings on business strategy. Five of these are the following:

1. Business situations generally behave in a regular and predictable manner. In most cases, it is possible to measure the approximate results (within three to five points of after-tax ROI) of most businesses (almost 90 percent) over a moderately long period of time (three to five years) on the basis of observable characteristics of the market and the strategies

Figure 19–1
Product Quality, Market Share, and Return on Investment

	Market Share		
	Low	Medium	High
Product Quality — Low	11%	17%	23%
Product Quality — Medium	11%	17%	26%
Product Quality — High	20%	26%	35%

Returns on Investment

15. Robert D. Buzzell, *Product Quality: The PIMSLETTER on Business Strategy*, Number 4 (Cambridge, Mass.: The Strategic Planning Institute, 1978), p. 2.

Table 19–4
Quality and Return on Investment by Type of Business

Type of Business	Quality Level				
	Lowest	Below Average	Average	Above Average	Highest
	Average Return on Investment				
Consumer dura-bles	16%	18%	18%	26%	32%
Consumer non-durables	15	21	17	23	32
Capital goods	10	8	13	20	21
Raw materials	13	21	21	21	35
Components	12	20	20	22	36
Supplies	16	13	19	25	36

Source: Robert D. Buzzell, *Product Quality: The PIMSLETTER on Business Strategy,* Number 4 (Cambridge, Mass.: The Strategic Planning Institute, 1978), p. 5. Reprinted with permission.

being used by both the business itself and the competition. Since business situations can be understood by using an empirical scientific approach, the process of formulating strategy is now becoming an applied science.

Strategy-related conclusions

2. All business situations are basically alike in following the same "laws of the marketplace." Despite differences in product line, profitability, and company culture, all business firms seem to be governed by the laws of supply and demand.

3. The laws of the marketplace determine about 80 percent of the observed variance in operating results across different businesses. Simply put, this finding means that the characteristics of the served market, the business itself, and the competition make up about 80 percent of the reasons for success or failure. Operating skill or luck of the management constitutes the other 20 percent.

4. The expected impacts of strategic business characteristics tend to assert themselves over time. This finding has two major parts. First, if the fundamentals of a business change over time, for example when there is a decrease in the quality of the product line or the amount of vertical integration increases, profitability and net cash flow will move in the direction of the norm for the new position. Second, if a business's realized performance deviates from the expected norm, based on the laws of the marketplace, it will tend to move back toward that norm.

5. Business strategies are successful if their "fundamentals" are sound, unsuccessful if they are unsound. Simply put, if a business uses a strategy that is based on the empirical laws of the marketplace, it will tend to do better than a competitor that formulates strategy based solely on hunch, intuition, gut feeling, and personal opinion.

Quite obviously, findings such as these are very helpful to businesses that want to improve their strategy. These results also point out the value of systematic analysis of market conditions and reinforce many of the key ideas presented in Chapter 5.

During the next 10 years, we are going to be seeing even more attention focused on ways to analyze market conditions and formulate (and reformulate) strategic response. The approach that has been examined here is only one of a number that are beginning to gain popularity with business firms interested in learning how to become more effective in long-range planning and market strategy. It is, however, an important beginning.

Employee Values, Attitudes, and Work Life

Management's world will also change as a result of employee attitudes, values, and work life—all of which are in a state of transition.

Changing Values and Attitudes

The values and attitudes of workers have been in a state of flux for many years. Research data show that over the last quarter of a century there has been a major shift in these attitudes. This shift is occurring throughout industry and reflects employees' basic attitude changes toward both their companies and their jobs.

At the present time there is a marked difference in the satisfaction of employees at the upper levels of the organization and those at the other levels. This difference, commonly referred to as the **hierarchy gap,** exists in virtually every organization and in regard to just about every substantive issue, from pay and promotion to quality of work life. The following discussion, drawn from a major *Harvard Business Review* study, examines some of the most important developments that are occurring.

Views Toward the Company and the Job

Attitudes are less positive.

During the last 25 years there has been a continuing decline in the attitudes of employees toward the company as a place in which to work. Managers still rate their firm higher than do clerical or hourly employees, but there is far less positive attitude on the part of all the personnel than there was back in the 1950s. The same basic pattern appears when employees are asked to rate (1) their company as a place to work when compared with what it was when they started, (2) their department in terms of a "good" place in which to work, and (3) how much they like the type of work they are doing currently.[16] Commenting on the situation at large, Harvard University researchers have noted:

> It is the gap and the downward trend in hourly and clerical employees' satisfaction that we find so disturbing. Certainly, dissatisfaction is not new. To many, work may never be anything other than an unpleasant, inescapable fact of life; at best—a way to pay bills, associate with other people, and have scheduled things to do. Rapid advancement in technology and automation, the increasing impersonality of work and large organizations, and the

---

16. These findings can be found in M. R. Cooper, B. S. Morgan, P. M. Foley, and L. B. Kaplan, "Changing Employee Values: Deepening Discontent," *Harvard Business Review,* January–February 1979, pp. 117–125.

instability of time-honored values and traditions are certainly prime contributors to dissatisfaction. The impact of these forces on the working world is not yet as visible as was the dissent in colleges during the late 1960s, but discontent among hourly and clerical employees is every bit as pervasive and seems to be growing.[17]

When taken as a whole these findings, drawn from more than 75,000 workers in a wide array of industries ranging in size from less than 500 to more than 200,000 employees, present an ominous picture for the manager of the 1980s. There is decreasing satisfaction among both hourly and clerical employees. Additionally, while managers are more positive about the entire situation, they too agree with the hourly and clerical employees that their firms are not as good a place to work as they were once.

Extrinsic Motivators: Security and Pay

Security and pay are adequate . . .

If the personnel are dissatisfied with the organization, the initial conclusion is that security and pay are poor. Surprisingly, perhaps, this latest *Harvard Business Review* study found just the opposite. By the mid- to late-1970s employees were reporting that they were basically satisfied with these extrinsic motivators. (Of course, the recession of the early 1980s may have changed these attitudes somewhat.) While there has been a general decline in the satisfaction of the workforce, it cannot be traced solely to insecurity and low pay, the most commonly cited culprits.

Attitudes Toward Management and Supervision

as is supervision.

Also positive are the attitudes of the personnel toward management and supervision. In fact, researchers have found these attitudes improving. Apparently, efforts in recent years to upgrade management and supervision have been successful. On the other hand, these upgrading efforts, often accomplished through human relations training, have not been able to increase job satisfaction among many of the personnel.

Feeling Toward Esteem-Related Factors

But feelings of self-esteem are low.

In the domain of esteem-related factors, employees are particularly negative. These factors include opportunity for advancement, willingness of the organization to listen to problems and complaints, the respect with which one is treated, and company response to employee problems and complaints.

> These attitudes suggest that there are strong disincentives to perform well on a job, since some of the major rewards for good performance are missing, and employees perceive that management makes many decisions arbitrarily. It is here, in the area of providing opportunities for individual growth and challenge and of developing ways to recognize and respond equitably to the needs of the workforce, that efforts to change need to be focused. It appears clear that current changes in extrinsic areas such as pay and job security will be less likely to improve job satisfaction.[18]

17. *Ibid.,* p. 122.
18. *Ibid.,* p. 124.

"There's a good example of how long people stay with the company. That's our office boy—52 years with the firm."

Management Response

What should management do about these findings? The first thing is not to argue over their validity. There are many reasons to explain the current attitude trend. One is that today's newer workforce has different values from the workforce of a generation ago. A second is that the older segment of the workforce has changed what it believes. A third is that the workforce is just beginning to articulate what it has always valued. Whatever the reason, one thing is clear: the changes that have been reported here are representative of those in industry at large, and any change in them is unlikely in the foreseeable future. The goal of managment during the next 10 years must be to become aware of and prepare for employee needs via a pragmatic response. Many of the concepts discussed in Chapter 18 provide viable strategies for dealing with the changing attitudes of the workforce. In particular, the use of survey feedback and the development of two-way communication channels must become a reality in modern organizations.

Two-way communication must be promoted.

Although such findings may seem to paint a bleak picture of the outlook for effective employee relations, this is not necessarily the case. What is undeniably required, however, is that corporations recognize the new realities within which they must function. The crucial issues then become the degree to which management can successfully identify, anticipate, and address these changing values as they surface, or before they surface, in their own organizations. But, make no mistake about it, changing employee values are not myth. They will be the realities that companies must face in the 1980s.[19]

---

19. *Ibid.*, p. 125.

Table 19–5
Selected Examples of Flex-time in Industry

Banking

State Street Bank of Boston wanted to increase productivity, get better attendance, reduce overtime, and increase employee morale and job satisfaction.

Research design: Longitudinal attitude study, conducted one year after pilot study (1974–75).

Sample: 127 employees (mainly clerical) in corporate accounting, benefits, Bank Americard collection, and trust operations.

Research results:

1. Hard data:
   — Average sick-day leave went down in two departments and up in two.
   — Overtime costs declined from $38,258 to $21,115 over the study period.
   — Turnover dropped in three out of four departments. It also dropped faster than the bank's overall rate.
   — Efficiency dropped in two out of three departments.
2. Soft (attitude) data: Virtually all departments wanted to retain flexitime, but in two departments support for the program dropped slightly during the one-year study period.

Insurance

Metropolitan Life Insurance was aiming for a better coordination of work schedules and a way for employees to avoid rush-hour crowds and traffic.

Research design: A three-month pilot study.

Sample: 400 employees (jobs not specified, but presumed clerical).

Research results:

— Tardiness was eliminated.
— Employee morale improved.
— Need for personal time off declined.
— Employees tended to select the hours corresponding to those times when they were needed the most.

Manufacturing

Control Data Corporation had goals of maximizing employees' choice in establishing work hours, and ensuring that business needs as well as employee needs would be satisfied.

Research design: Pilot study, longitudinal over a three-year period, measuring attitudes. Also, hard data were monitored for such factors as absenteeism and sick leave.

Sample: 100 managers and 286 nonmanagerial personnel from the Aerospace and Microcircuit divisions.

Research results:

1. Hard data: Turnover, productivity, and sick leave showed slightly favorable trends.
2. Nonsupervisory personnel:
   — 85 percent felt morale improved under flexitime.
   — 73 percent felt that the pressure of getting to work on time had decreased.
   — 57 percent felt that driving time had decreased.
   — 66 percent felt that productivity had increased, while 11 percent felt it had decreased.
3. Managers: Felt that flexitime had a positive effect or, at worst, did not have a detrimental effect.

Source: Reprinted, by permission of the author, from "Flexitime in the United States: The Lessons of Experience," Donald J. Peterson, *Personnel,* January-February 1980 by AMACOM, a division of American Management Associations. Pages 24–26. All rights reserved.

Changing Work Life

Life *at* work is also going to be changing during the next 10 years as the quality of work life movement gains momentum and as modern technology alters the workplace.

Quality of Work Life Movement

The quality of work life (QWL) movement was initially discussed in Chapter 9, where concepts like flextime were introduced. As seen in Table 19–5, this QWL idea is being used by many different types of firms, and while not all companies have attained positive results, it remains a popular concept.[20]

Flextime and flexiweek are becoming popular.

Another work-related idea is that of flexiweek. **Flexiweek** is a working schedule in which employees have alternating four-day and six-day work weeks. As with flextime, the results are mixed: some firms have had very good success with the concept, others have not. Proponents of the idea point proudly to the various benefits flexiweek offers.

> Productivity could be affected by general adoption of flexiweek. The extra day of business operation could create many new job opportunities if markets could be developed. Part-time work potential is particularly strong. Given our present national concerns over unemployment, this fact alone makes flexiweek and its resurrection of the six-day work week worthy of serious consideration.[21]

Other commonly cited advantages include better distribution of auto traffic on urban expressways, longer weekends for employees, and increased psychological rewards for the workers.

Yet there is more to the QWL movement than flextime and flexiweek. Throughout this decade we are going to see an increase in union-management cooperation for the purpose of developing QWL approaches. Work design programs are now out of the theory stage and into the application stage.[22] This is an important development because of the tremendous increases taking place in technology in the workplace.

Modern Technology

Modern technology is going to continue to change life at work. Years ago, when working conditions were less than ideal, employees adjusted to the trials and tribulations of the workplace. Alvin Toffler, internationally known for his analysis of social change, recalled his own early experience in a factory this way:

20. Donald J. Petersen, "Flexitime in the United States: The Lessons of Experience," *Personnel,* January–February 1980, pp. 21–31.

21. Alan L. Porter and Frederick A. Rossini, "Flexiweek," *Business Horizons,* April 1978, p. 50.

22. "Quality of Work Life: Catching On," *Business Week,* September 21, 1981, pp. 72, 76, 80.

I swallowed the dust, the sweat and smoke of the foundry. My ears were split by the hiss of steam, the clank of chains, the roar of pug mills. I felt the heat as the white-hot steel poured. Acetylene sparks left burn marks on my legs. I turned out thousands of pieces a shift on a press, repeating identical movements until my mind and muscles shrieked. I watched the managers who kept the workers in their place, white-shirted men themselves endlessly pursued and harried by higher-ups. I helped lift a sixty-five-year-old woman out of the bloody machine that had just torn four fingers off her hand, and I still hear her cries—"Jesus and Mary, I won't be able to work again!"[23]

What the future holds

To a large degree, all of this is changing. The workers of the 1980s and 1990s will be operating under very different conditions. In particular, we are going to see the use of increased technology, with people learning new skills so that they can use these new developments. On the assembly line there will be more robots employed for welding and for ensuring quality control. In office work, computers will be used to provide and process information. These developments will not come at the expense of worker freedom or autonomy, however. Many of the latest developments in QWL will remain, and we will see even more, for two reasons. First, workers will not put up with a "back to the old days" movement because at that time they were mere adjuncts of the machine. Their values are far different from those of their fathers and grandfathers. Second, in order to make technology work, a new approach will be needed. A recent *Fortune* magazine study on life at work puts the idea this way:

Bosses will have to change the way they handle the workforce. The old "kick ass and take names" school of running a plant isn't effective with today's more educated workforce. Nor is reductionism, or Taylorism, which simplifies and narrows tasks down to the most elementary (and boring) functions. "Western civilization built itself by subdividing science and work, but reductionism has run its streak," says Paul Strassman, a Xerox vice-president for strategic planning. The principles of organizing laid out by Frederick Taylor, a turn-of-the-century mechanical engineer, become less applicable as technology evolves. Workers in the office and factory . . . need more knowledge and autonomy.[24]

As organizations begin to adapt to the needs of the employees, we will see dramatic changes in the way work is done. AT&T is an excellent example. When it was faced with becoming a competitor in a deregulated communications business, the firm changed the way some of its workers carried out their tasks. Today many telephone installers and repairmen (now known as systems technicians) no longer go to work in jeans carrying a sagging belt of loaded tools around their waist. They dress in slacks, shirt, and tie and have their tools stowed in a brief case. Instead of driving around in a van, they have a company sedan. The new appearance symbolizes a change in the status of these blue-collar technicians. The changes have been accompanied by increased training so that these people now can not

---

23. Alvin Toffler, *The Third Wave* (New York: William Morrow, 1980), p. 118.

24. Jeremy Main, "Work Won't Be the Same Again," *Fortune*, June 28, 1982, p. 59.

only solder a wire or bring a line into a building but, in many cases, can also reprogram a computer-controlled office switchboard. In this regard training is becoming a high-priority item for management.

Over the past couple of decades, major attention has been focused on training young and disadvantaged workers. "Now," notes Pat Choate, senior policy analyst for TRW, Inc. and a nationally known economist, "it is absolutely necessary to focus our attention on the whole workforce.[25]

Training will become important.

The overall effect of such training on American output will be positive. At Westinghouse Electric, for example, both secretaries and their bosses have been trained to use computer terminals on which they can write and send memos, edit letters, store and recall information, design charts, and perform various other communication functions. In short, technology is beginning to accommodate the desire of employees for meaningful jobs while simultaneously meeting the desire of organizations for increased productivity. The result will mean a better work life for employees at all levels of the hierarchy.

> As now, the unskilled or semi-skilled won't have the most interesting or best-paid jobs. But with the growth of the service economy, neither will they be scrapped in the jungle. For the others, the pluses seem to outnumber the minuses. Dehumanizing some of the new tasks may seem cruel, but how human was the work of clerks counting and sorting cancelled checks all day, of welders putting car parts together, of secretaries taking dictation and typing, of managers trying and failing all day long to get a colleague on the phone? These and many other deadening, irritating tasks are being taken over by robots and computers. People prepared for the new jobs will find their work freed of the curse of dull repetition, leaving them more time to be creative.[26]

Social Values in the Workplace

In addition to changing management and worker values and attitudes, social values will help shape the world of management during the upcoming decade. These values are a result of changes in both the external and internal environment. One change is the attention given to employees with personal problems such as alcoholism or drug addiction. At the present time employee assistance programs are beginning to spring up in larger organizations to deal with these problems. Before the decade is over this development will probably spread to medium-sized and smaller enterprises as well. Other major socially oriented developments will include the continued emphasis on hiring the handicapped and on developing policies and programs for eliminating sexual harassment in the workplace.

Employee Assistance Programs

In the past, employees who had alcoholism or drug addiction problems could expect to be fired by their employer. Individuals who suffered excessive degrees of stress found they either had to cope with the situation or

---

25. *Ibid.*, p. 60.
26. *Ibid.*, p. 65.

get out. Today, in many firms, this is no longer true. Thanks to the rise of **employee assistance programs (EAPs),** many companies are helping their people cope with a multitude of personal problems.[27] One of the major reasons why firms are developing such plans is economic. The cost of personal problems, in terms of absenteeism, poor workmanship, lost productivity, and related factors, is now running over $10 billion annually. Something has to be done.

An EAP is designed to help employees deal with many of the problems common to modern society: alcoholism, drug abuse, stress, mental exhaustion. At the present time there are approximately 2,000 EAPs nationwide. The pattern used in setting up these plans is typically the following:

Pattern for setting up an EAP

1. A policy statement is issued indicating that management is supportive of the program. The statement also points out that employees may sometimes need this type of personal assistance because of factors beyond their control, and the assistance will be available to them.

2. If there is a union in the organization, representation and support of the program are secured from this group.

3. Qualified counselors and other skilled personnel are retained and are used to help in diagnosis and referral to appropriate agencies where the individual can receive professional assistance.

4. A comprehensive insurance benefit package covering this assistance is provided to all employees.

5. A comprehensive approach for evaluating the effectiveness and impact of the EAP is developed.[28]

Procedure for handling problems

When does someone need the types of services provided by an EAP? This is not easy to say. Usually there are visible signs that something is wrong. For example, in the case of an alcoholic employee, attendance, general behavior, and job performance begin to decline, as illustrated in Figure 19–2. At this point the boss usually calls in the subordinate to discuss some of the job-related symptoms: poor work, exhausted appearance, and absenteeism. If the employee realizes that these symptoms are a result of alcohol, drugs, exhaustion, or some other personal problem and decides to straighten out immediately, the problem is on its way to being resolved. If things continue to deteriorate, however, the superior discusses the situation again, this time in the presence of a counselor. The superior then leaves the subordinate with the counselor so that they can discuss the situation privately. Quite often the subordinate admits to the counselor that there is a problem and agrees to join an employee assistance program. In other cases management has found that employees simply come in and ask for assistance without any prodding at all. Commenting on the way

---

27. Robert Witte and Marsha Cannon, "Employee Assistance Programs: Getting Top Management's Support," *Personnel Administrator,* June 1979, pp. 23–26, 44; and Thomas N. McGaffey, "New Horizons in Organizational Stress Prevention Approaches," *Personnel Administrator,* November 1978, pp. 26–32.

28. McGaffey, *Ibid.,* p. 28.

Figure 19–2   How an Alcoholic Employee Behaves

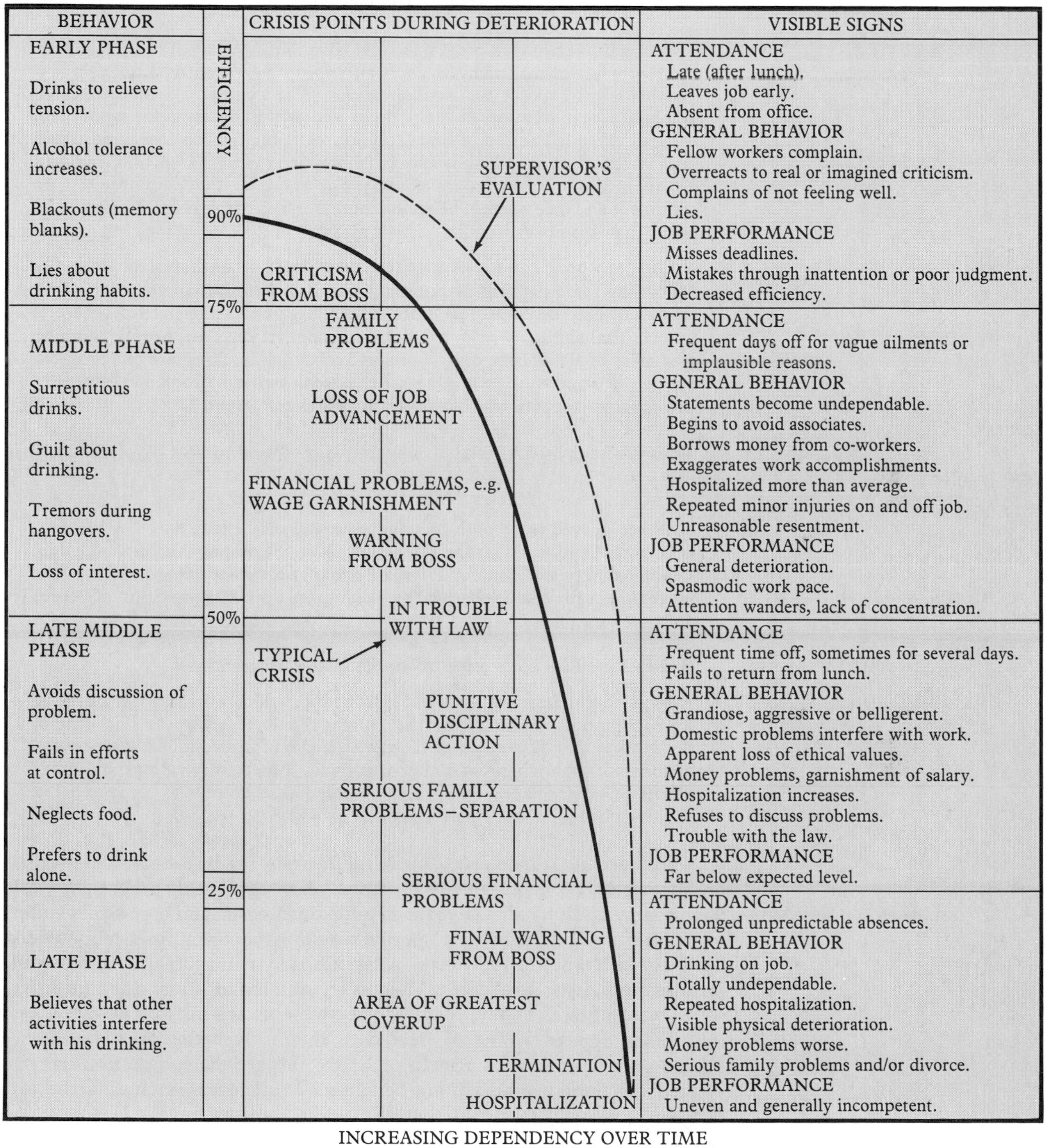

BEHAVIOR	EFFICIENCY	CRISIS POINTS DURING DETERIORATION	VISIBLE SIGNS
EARLY PHASE Drinks to relieve tension. Alcohol tolerance increases. Blackouts (memory blanks). Lies about drinking habits.	90% 75%	SUPERVISOR'S EVALUATION CRITICISM FROM BOSS	**ATTENDANCE** Late (after lunch). Leaves job early. Absent from office. **GENERAL BEHAVIOR** Fellow workers complain. Overreacts to real or imagined criticism. Complains of not feeling well. Lies. **JOB PERFORMANCE** Misses deadlines. Mistakes through inattention or poor judgment. Decreased efficiency.
MIDDLE PHASE Surreptitious drinks. Guilt about drinking. Tremors during hangovers. Loss of interest.	50%	FAMILY PROBLEMS LOSS OF JOB ADVANCEMENT FINANCIAL PROBLEMS, e.g. WAGE GARNISHMENT WARNING FROM BOSS	**ATTENDANCE** Frequent days off for vague ailments or implausible reasons. **GENERAL BEHAVIOR** Statements become undependable. Begins to avoid associates. Borrows money from co-workers. Exaggerates work accomplishments. Hospitalized more than average. Repeated minor injuries on and off job. Unreasonable resentment. **JOB PERFORMANCE** General deterioration. Spasmodic work pace. Attention wanders, lack of concentration.
LATE MIDDLE PHASE Avoids discussion of problem. Fails in efforts at control. Neglects food. Prefers to drink alone.	25%	IN TROUBLE WITH LAW TYPICAL CRISIS PUNITIVE DISCIPLINARY ACTION SERIOUS FAMILY PROBLEMS–SEPARATION SERIOUS FINANCIAL PROBLEMS	**ATTENDANCE** Frequent time off, sometimes for several days. Fails to return from lunch. **GENERAL BEHAVIOR** Grandiose, aggressive or belligerent. Domestic problems interfere with work. Apparent loss of ethical values. Money problems, garnishment of salary. Hospitalization increases. Refuses to discuss problems. Trouble with the law. **JOB PERFORMANCE** Far below expected level.
LATE PHASE Believes that other activities interfere with his drinking.		FINAL WARNING FROM BOSS AREA OF GREATEST COVERUP TERMINATION HOSPITALIZATION	**ATTENDANCE** Prolonged unpredictable absences. **GENERAL BEHAVIOR** Drinking on job. Totally undependable. Repeated hospitalization. Visible physical deterioration. Money problems worse. Serious family problems and/or divorce. **JOB PERFORMANCE** Uneven and generally incompetent.

INCREASING DEPENDENCY OVER TIME

Source: *The Miami Herald,* May 31, 1981, p. 1F. Reprinted with permission.

two of the most common problems, alcohol and drugs, are dealt with, Keith Davis, the noted human relationist, has written:

> Successful employer programs treat alcoholism as an illness, focus on the job behavior caused by alcoholism, and provide both medical help and psychological support for alcoholics. . . . The company demonstrates to alcoholics that it wants to help them and is willing to work with them over an extended period of time. A nonthreatening, no-job-loss atmosphere is provided: however, there is always the implied threat that alcohol-induced behavior cannot be treated indefinitely. For example, if an employee refuses treatment and incompetent behavior continues, the employer has little choice other than dismissal. . . .

> Company programs for treatment of drug abuse other than alcohol usually follow the same patterns as programs on alcoholism except that hard-drug treatment may be controlled more strictly because of the hard-drug user's greater probability of criminal behavior on the job. Most firms combine treatment of alcoholism, drug abuse, and related difficulties into one program for the treatment of people with behavioral-medical problems. Normally the program focuses on both prevention and treatment.[29]

How well have EAPs been working out? Psychologist Andrew DuBrin reports:

> EAP has proved to be both humanitarian and cost effective. . . . One successful application . . . is the Kennecott Copper Company facility in Ogden, Utah. Data are available for 150 male employees who averaged 12.7 months in treatment for conditions such as alcoholism. . . . A comparison of before and after treatment showed a 52 percent decrease in absenteeism, a 74.6 decrease in worker compensation payments, and a 55.3 percent decrease in direct medical costs after treatment in the program.

> More comprehensive research evidence is provided by a study of 11 major EAP programs conducted by the Human Ecology Institute. The general finding was that 57 percent of the cases referred for alcoholism were recovered or noticeably improved after treatment. Supervisory ratings and other means of performance assessment revealed that there was an associated positive change in work performance.[30]

Employee assistance programs help illustrate the impact of social values on the world of management. Twenty years ago these programs would have been viewed by management as unjustified costs, and employees suffering these types of problems simply would have been fired. Employees, for their part, would have viewed suggestions by management that counseling and other assistance were needed as an invasion of privacy or a meddling in private matters. Today, these social problems are out of the closet and both sides appear willing to deal with them. Over the next decade we should see the continued growth of EAPs. In particular, organizations can profit from their use in helping personnel at all levels, including the top, deal with personal problems that affect work performance.

---

29. Keith Davis, *Human Behavior at Work: Organizational Behavior,* 6th Edition (New York: McGraw-Hill, 1981), pp. 314, 315–316.

30. Andrew J. DuBrin, *Contemporary Applied Management* (Plano, Tex.: Business Publications, Inc., 1982), p. 218.

Hiring the Handicapped

Definition of handicapped

Another major social development will be an increased emphasis on hiring the handicapped. Efforts to encourage this trend have already been promoted through legislation such as the Rehabilitation Act of 1973 and the Vietnam era Veterans' Readjustment Assistance Act of 1974. The Rehabilitation Act has been particularly important because of its definition of a handicapped individual as anyone who (1) has a physical or mental impairment that substantially limits one or more major life activities, (2) has a record of such impairment, or (3) is regarded as having such an impairment. More specifically, the term **handicapped** has been used in referring to individuals who are visually or hearing impaired, partially paralyzed, missing a limb, or mentally retarded.

Research Findings

In the past, a number of employer beliefs have served to limit the chances of equal opportunities for the handicapped. Some of the most common of these beliefs are that (1) insurance and workers' compensation costs will rise because the handicapped will have a higher accident rate than the workforce in general; (2) these workers will have high absenteeism and tardiness; (3) the quality and quantity of their work output will be lower than that of the average worker; (4) the physical layout of the workplace will have to be modified at great expense to accommodate these workers; (5) co-workers will not accept them on an equal basis; and (6) the handicapped have to be treated differently from other workers. Research reveals that these beliefs are incorrect. For example, after conducting a systematic analysis of the literature on this subject, Sara Freedman and Robert Keller report:

Research findings regarding the handicapped

> Research on efforts to hire the handicapped has indicated positive consequences for both the individual and the company. DuPont . . . has released a study of 1,452 employees with a variety of disabilities that included orthopedic difficulties, blindness, visual impairment, heart disease, amputation, paralysis, epilepsy, hearing impairment and total deafness. The types of positions held included machine operators, craftsmen, professionals, and managers, to name just a few. A job performance survey rated 91 percent of the disabled employees as average or better than average to the regular workforce.[31]

The DuPont study also found that employee morale did not suffer. There were no significant morale differences between the handicapped workers and the rest of the workforce. Additionally, 96 percent of the handicapped had average or better than average safety records, and 79 percent were rated average or above on dependability.[32]

Findings at other firms support this general pattern. For example, Gopal Pati, a frequent contributor to the literature, conducted a study of 16 corporations employing approximately 800 handicapped workers. He found lower

31. Sara M. Freedman and Robert T. Keller, "The Handicapped In the Workforce," *Academy of Management Review*, July 1981, pp. 452–453.

32. Robert B. Nathanson, "The Disabled Employee: Separating Myth from Fact," *Harvard Business Review*, May–June 1977, pp. 6–8.

turnover and absenteeism and average or above-average performance among the handicapped. He also reported that insurance costs were not affected and that expenditures for accommodations were minor or nonexistent.[33] The California Governor's Committee also found support for hiring the handicapped.[34] Preliminary findings of a pilot study conducted at the Lockheed Missile and Space Company examined three cost indices: (1) days of sick leave, (2) dollar costs of claims under one insurance plan, and (3) number of medical care opportunities kept under a second insurance plan. The results indicated that handicapped persons had lower costs than the average employee. Numerous other studies also support the value of hiring the handicapped.[35]

Why have the handicapped performed so well? There are two basic reasons. First, as found by a number of research studies, many handicapped workers are more intelligent, more motivated, better qualified, and have higher educational levels than their nonhandicapped counterparts. Second, these results may also be a reflection of the fact that handicapped people have to be overqualified in order to get and hold a job. To the extent that the latter is true, handicapped people may well be kept in lower-level jobs long after similarly qualified, nonhandicapped personnel have been promoted.[36]

The Future of the Handicapped

During the next decade, we will see an increase in the employment opportunities provided for the handicapped. One reason is that, to a large degree, these individuals are an untapped source of personnel manpower for modern organizations. Second, we are likely to see more of them rise into the ranks of management as enterprises begin to realize that they have been approaching the hiring of the handicapped from the wrong point of view. As Robert B. Nathanson and Jeffrey Lambert, compliance planning specialists, have noted:

> No matter how well-trained, sensitive, well-meaning, or objective they may be, supervisory and managerial personnel, line workers, and other professional and nonprofessional staff are not immune to holding biases, beliefs or prejudices about persons who are disabled. These feelings and thoughts, deeply and often subconsciously rooted, are carried into daily interaction with disabled employees and can have a profound effect on their social and vocational integration into the business community.[37]

These attitudes take many different forms. Some of the most common include the following:

33. Gopal C. Pati, "Countdown on Hiring the Handicapped," *Personnel Journal,* March 1978, pp. 144–153.

34. Freedman and Keller, *op. cit.,* p. 453.

35. *Ibid.,* pp. 453–454.

36. *Ibid.,* p. 453.

37. Robert B. Nathanson and Jeffrey Lambert, "Integrating Disabled Employees into the Workplace," *Personnel Journal,* February 1981, p. 110.

Typical attitudes toward the handicapped

1. feeling sorry for the individual because he or she is disabled;

2. classifying all handicapped people on the basis of their deficiency, for example, thinking that all blind people have the same interests, abilities, and needs;

3. adopting an attitude of "Don't worry about anything; I'll protect you;"

4. feeling that handicapped people should not be hired because they will present too many problems for the organization to handle;

5. realizing that the individual has the capacity to do the job but hoping not to have to come into personal contact with the individual because of feelings such as "He gives me the creeps" or "Why does she have to be assigned to my area?"

6. expressing amazement at the individual's ambition and referring to the person as courageous, remarkable, or brave; and

7. encountering a feeling of anxiousness or tension in having to face those with physical disabilities.[38]

As organizations begin to gain experience regarding the values and attitudes of handicapped people and come to understand them better, attitudes like these will diminish. At the same time, management will begin to understand more clearly how to tap this labor source effectively. Attention will be focused on the individual characteristics of the handicapped and the best ways to train, place, and employ these people. In the process, both sides will find themselves making adjustments. For the present, management will find this area to be both a challenge and a problem requiring its time and resources; but the payoffs will prove worthwhile for both sides.

Dealing with Sexual Harassment

During the last decade, the issue of **sexual harassment** has become an important employer consideration. Particularly because of the legal obligations created under Title VII of the Civil Rights Act, management is finding itself having to pay closer attention to this type of behavior. While there is no uniform definition of the term sexual harassment, the following definitions are three attempts by official organizations to explain what it means.

What constitutes harassment?

[Sexual harassment includes a]ny repeated or unwarranted verbal or physical sexual advances (or) sexually explicit discriminatory remarks made by someone in the workplace which are offensive or objectionable to the recipient or which cause the recipient discomfort or humiliation or which interfere with the recipient's job performance. (*Continental Can Co. v. Minnesota*, 22 FEP cases 1808 [Minnesota, 1980])

Sexual harassment is any unwanted physical or emotional contact between workers or supervisors and workers which makes one uncomfortable and/or interferes with the recipient's job performance or carries with it either an implicit or explicit threat of adverse employment consequences. (Hearings before the House Committee on Post Office and Civil Services, 96th Congress, 1st Session [1979])

---

38. *Ibid.,* pp. 110–113.

Sexual harassment includes . . . continual or repeated verbal abuse of a sexual nature including, but not limited to, graphic commentaries on the victim's body, sexually suggestive objects or pictures in the workplace, sexually degrading words used to describe the victim, or propositions of a sexual nature. Sexual harassment also includes the threat of insinuation that lack of sexual submission will adversely affect the victim's employment, wages, advancement, assigned duties or shifts, academic standing, or other conditions that affect the victim's "livelihood." (Michigan Task Force on Sexual Harassment in the Workplace)[39]

When is management liable for sexual harassment in the workplace? Recent guidelines echo the sentiments of court decisions that hold that the employer has an affirmative duty to maintain a workplace that is free of sexual harassment and intimidation. More specifically, these guidelines hold that the organization is guilty if it knew or should have known of the harassment, or knowingly or constructively allowed the harassment to occur. On the other hand, if the enterprise moves to take immediate and corrective action to end the harassment, liability can be avoided.

Harassment and the Courts

When is the employer responsible?

A number of important questions about harassment and employer responsibility have been addressed in court decisions. Two of the most important of these are: Under what circumstances is the employer responsible for employee actions? Does the person filing the harassment charge have to demonstrate that the organization has a policy or practice of such harassment?

In reference to the first question, there is no uniformity of decision. Some court cases have held that an employer is not liable for acts unrelated to the performance of the supervisors' jobs, while others have held the employer strictly liable for supervisors' actions. After a thorough review of harassment cases, Patricia Linenberger and Timothy Keaveny report that the trend appears to be that an employer is indeed responsible for discriminatory practices by supervisory personnel. The reasoning is that if the organization wants to delegate its duties, it must remain responsible for the way in which these duties are carried out.[40]

In reference to the second question, again there have been mixed decisions by the courts. One of the most recent, by the Ninth Circuit Court of Appeals, held that an employer was liable under Title VII when the action complained of was committed by a superior, even though the superior's behavior was in clear violation of company policy. This court ruling represents the broadest interpretation of employer liability. It is unlikely that in the future the courts will hold employers to such broad liability. The ruling does show, however, how great the employer's responsibility can be. How can organizations work to protect themselves against such action? A number of important steps should be carried out.

---

39. Patricia Linenberger and Timothy J. Keaveny, "Sexual Harassment: The Employer's Legal Obligations," *Personnel,* November–December 1981, pp. 61–62.

40. *Ibid.,* pp. 64–65.

Taking Proper Action

Steps an employer should take to control sexual harassment

Most experts believe that the first step in controlling sexual harassment is a strong policy statement from top management condemning such behavior. This policy should contain a workable definition of the term sexual harassment. In particular, the definition should be as objective as possible. The policy statement should spell out possible sanctions against those who are guilty of such harassment and offer protection for those who make such charges. It should make it clear that retaliatory action against an employee who makes charges will not be tolerated. The employer also should establish an effective grievance procedure.

> The complement to a strong sexual harassment policy statement is an effective grievance procedure. The court cases highlight the need for such a mechanism by stating that employers *are* liable for the sexual harassment of employees or supervisors if management becomes aware of the problem and does nothing, or if management should have been aware of the harassment. Thus, it is clear that a procedure that provides the means by which employees can bring such complaints out into the open is necessary.[41]

The employer should also conduct a prompt and thorough investigation when made aware of a complaint. Finally, if someone is found guilty, disciplinary action must be taken.

Sexual harassment is not a new issue. As many organizations are learning, however, its consequences are. As a result, during the upcoming decade more of them will be thinking through the steps that must be taken to protect their female employees from harassment and themselves from legal action.[42]

Summary

1. A code of conduct is a statement of ethical practices or guidelines to which an enterprise adheres. Today these codes are becoming more prevalent. They are also proving to be more meaningful in terms of external legal and social development, more comprehensive in terms of their coverage, and easier to implement in terms of the administrative procedures that are being used to enforce them.

2. Over the last decade the number of women in top management has increased. At present, however, only about 6 percent of all working women hold managerial positions. Some of the reasons holding back their progress include male hostility, the failure of women to choose business careers, and cultural factors discouraging women from being competitive. Today this is beginning to change, and the future for women in the executive suite looks brighter than ever before.

---

41. *Ibid.,* p. 67.

42. Jeanne Bosson Driscoll, "Sexual Attraction and Harassment: Management's New Problems," *Personnel Journal,* January 1981, pp. 33–36, 56; Oliver L. Niehouse and Joanne Ross Doades, "Sexual Harassment: An Old Issue–A New Problem," *Supervisory Management,* April 1980, pp. 10–14; Patricia Linenberger and Timothy J. Keaveny, "Sexual Harassment in Employment," *Human Resource Management,* Spring 1981, pp. 11–17.

3. During the next 10 years there will be a major change in the way management plans for the future. A true administrative science approach is emerging thanks to progress by organizations like the Strategic Planning Institute. Through the analysis of business-related data, it is becoming possible to draw conclusions regarding how to formulate strategy and how to make strategic changes in the business plan when things go awry.

4. Management's world will also change as a result of employee attitudes, values, and work life. Today employees are not satisfied with their companies or their jobs. This dissatisfaction is not tied to security, pay, and supervision but to esteem-related factors such as the way employees are treated, their opportunity for advancement, the willingness of the organization to listen to their problems and complaints, and the respect with which they are treated.

5. Life at work is also changing. This is happening for two major reasons. The first is the quality of work life (QWL) movement. QWL concepts such as flextime and flexiweek are becoming more popular. At the same time organizations are finding that they have to adjust to modern technology by changing the way workers do their jobs. During the next 10 years we will see a change in management's philosophy of handling the workforce as well as an increased emphasis on training and retraining workers to ensure a harmonious blending of the workforce and modern technology.

6. Social values are also changing. These values are quite encompassing, and in the chapter, three illustrations were included, relating to employee assistance programs, hiring the handicapped, and sexual harassment. These developments are a result of changes both within and outside the organization. They reflect social changes, and during the next 10 years we will see increased attention focused on these kinds of programs.

Key Terms

Code of conduct   A statement of ethical practices or guidelines to which an enterprise adheres.

Flexiweek   A working schedule in which employees have alternating four-day and six-day work weeks.

Employee assistance programs   Programs designed to help employees deal with social problems such as alcoholism, drug addiction, and excessive stress.

Handicapped employees   Individuals who are visually or hearing impaired, partially paralyzed, missing a limb, or mentally retarded.

Hierarchy gap   The difference in perceived satisfaction between employees at the upper levels of the organization and those at the other levels.

Sexual harassment   Any unwanted physical or emotional contact between workers or between supervisors and workers which makes one uncomfortable or interferes with the recipient's job performance.

Questions for Analysis and Discussion

1. What is a code of conduct? What types of conduct does a code of conduct address? Be specific in your answer.

2. Why are modern businesses becoming more interested in improving their moral climates? Explain.

3. Why are there not more women in top management positions? What does women's future in the executive suite look like? Defend your answer.

4. Why is management becoming more interested in strategic planning? What new developments have occurred that are encouraging greater attention in this area? Explain.

5. How do workers feel about their company? Their job? Their pay? Supervision? Esteem-related factors? Discuss each separately and then draw overall conclusions about the values of modern workers.

6. In what way can we expect the quality of work life movement to affect the way work is done during the 1980s and 1990s? Will technology also play a role? Explain.

7. What is an employee assistance program? How does it work? Do you think we will see more of them during the next decade? Why or why not?

8. What have researchers learned about the abilities and performance of handicapped workers? In light of your answer, how likely is it that more attention will be devoted to hiring the handicapped? Support your answer with as many facts as you can muster.

9. What is meant by the term sexual harassment? Put the definition in your own words.

10. Is management liable for sexual harassment in the workplace? If management has an expressed policy forbidding such harassment, does this policy reduce or eliminate its liability for such actions?

11. How can management ensure that it is taking proper action to prevent or discourage sexual harassment? Be complete in your answer.

| Case |

A Point of Departure

Every year, a large southwestern-based corporation reviews its strategic plan in detail. At this time decisions are made regarding product line, promotion, pricing, and financing of operations for the next year. At the same time other related areas are discussed. This year the senior vice-president of planning raised the issue of a corporate code of conduct. He had made a survey of the firm's five largest competitors and found that all of them have corporate codes. Two of the companies have had one for more than five years; two drew them up within the last five years; and the other one came out with its code six months ago.

The basic idea sounds good to the top management team, but the president has some misgivings about spending time and money to draw up such a code. In particular, he has raised three key questions: What belongs in a corporate code of conduct? How difficult will it be to draw one up? Of what real value can the code be to the firm? Of these three questions, the last one concerns the president most. He particularly dislikes doing things just for window dressing. He has stated his position this way:

> Sure, it would be nice to have a formal corporate code of conduct. We could proudly display it in the main lobby of the building and we could have copies made for all of the employees. It would also make a nice addition to our annual report. But would it make us a better organization? Would people look at our code and believe that we are any more trustworthy, reliable, or honest than we were before the code existed?

The president's answer to these questions is no. As a result he is, at best, lukewarm to the idea. This does not mean that he opposes the vice-president who has proposed such a code, however. He simply wants to see such activity given a low priority. "If we are going to do something that will get us local or national attention and convince the public that we are indeed interested in playing an active role in the public arena," he has said, "it should be something like hiring more handicapped personnel or starting an active campaign to recruit and promote women into the upper ranks of the hierarchy."

The vice-president believes that these ideas are good ones. He does not regard a code of conduct as just window dressing, however. True, it will not be viewed as positively as hiring decisions involving the handicapped or women. Yet this does not make it unimportant. "Besides," the vice-president has told one of his colleagues, "we can use the development of a corporate code as the first step in a series of actions designed to make the company more responsive to the social environment. Then we can begin developing programs for helping the handicapped and women improve their positions in the firm. We have to start somewhere, however, and I think a code is the first place. It sets the pace for what is to come." As a result of this discussion, the vice-president has assigned one of his assistants the task of finding out what all of the other firms in the industry (there are 77) have done in terms of putting together a code of conduct. Using this information as a point of departure, the vice-president hopes to have a code drawn up and approved by the president within the next three months.

1. Exactly what does a code of conduct include? Give some specific examples of the things that would be found in one.

2. Of what value is such a code? Identify and discuss three advantages of having one.

3. What do you think of the president's point of view? Is his position a better one than that of the vice-president? Compare and contrast the two points of view, choose the one that makes the most sense to you, and then write a short paragraph defending your choice.

You Be the Consultant

Carl's Dilemma

Carl Bettenhouse is the CEO of a major consumer goods firm headquartered in New York City. Quite a bit of Carl's time is spent outside the office. Not all of his work is business, however. Because of the position he occupies, Carl is also very active in community activities. He serves on a number of boards of charitable organizations, is active in the theater league, and is currently involved in efforts to raise money for the restoration of historical buildings in the Washington, D.C., area.

Despite his involvement in nonbusiness activities, Carl makes it a point to know what is going on around the company. Every Monday morning two aides bring him up to date on everything that has happened during the week. He is given sales figures, cost data, and profit results. This information is useful in making organizational decisions; it also helps Carl answer questions asked by people he meets in social settings. Typical examples include: What business are you in? What products or services do you provide? Do you think your stock is a good investment? Carl likes questions like these because they give him a chance to break the ice and talk about a subject he knows quite well.

The other day, however, Carl found himself in a quandary. He was at a charity dinner designed to raise funds for an orphanage. Carl was enjoying himself, mixing with the guests, and discussing a variety of topics. In the process he happened upon a news reporter who was covering the dinner. The two began to talk and Carl learned that the reporter seldom covered such events. Usually she was assigned to business and industry stories. When she learned that Carl was a CEO her face lit up. For the next half hour the two talked about Carl's company. The news reporter was quite knowledgeable regarding business activity and some of the latest developments in Carl's industry. As the two talked, the topic eventually turned to social values and the way modern organizations are meeting their social obligations. Carl was well informed on what his company was doing in many different areas, including hiring the handicapped and setting up employee assistance programs. He expressed pride in the fact that his firm was the first one in its industry to have an EAP in place.

As the two continued talking about other things his company was doing, the conversation moved to women in top management. "How many female executives do you have in your organization?" the reporter asked Carl. Carl admitted that off the top of his head he did not know. This is when the reporter's attitude suddenly changed. "Well, Carl, it can't be very many," she said. "If there were you would have those statistics right at your fingertips. Every single thing I have asked you, you were able to answer with specific numbers and factual data. But when we get into the subject of women in the executive suite, you suddenly draw a blank. Apparently this is an area where your firm is not doing very much."

Carl was taken aback by this line of reasoning. He assured the reporter that she was quite mistaken. In fact, he invited her to come by his headquarters the next afternoon to meet with him and the vice-president of personnel and discuss the progress of women in top management at his firm. He offered her an exclusive story using his company as an example. "If we are not doing our job properly, tell your readers this. We have nothing to hide. The fact that I don't know as much about this area as I do about a lot of others should not be taken as an indication that our organization is lax in meeting its responsibilities to promote women into the upper ranks of management." The reporter told Carl she was delighted to hear this and agreed to meet with him at 3:00 P.M. the next day.

Later that evening, Carl placed a call to the vice-president of personnel and told him what had happened. "I want you in my office first thing in the morning," he told the vice-president. "Have with you all of the statistics you can gather regarding the total number of personnel employed by us, the number of women in this group, and the percentage of them who hold executive management positions. You and I had better review some of the questions she is likely to ask us and have data available to back up anything we say. This lady is very sharp and I don't want us to make any mistakes. If we do, we are likely to read about them in the newspaper later this week." The vice-president said he would have all of the information Carl needed and would be in his office at 10:00 A.M. sharp. He also told Carl that he was bringing along a new in-house consultant who knew quite a bit about the role and scope of women in the workforce in general and might be very helpful in providing information for answering some of the reporter's questions.

Your Consultation

Assume that you are the in-house consultant and have been asked to gather information about the current status of women in the executive suite. After a careful review of the material in this chapter, what would you tell Carl regarding the equal opportunities for women in top management? What is holding them back? What particular benefits do they offer to modern organizations? How many of them are there in the top ranks? Also, what information would you like to have about Carl's organization so that you could make the best possible case for the company's offering women opportunities equal to those of men? Be as complete as possible in your answer, using as many statistics and other facts as you can gather.

20

Management Career Planning and You

Objectives

Now that you have completed your study of what management is all about, it is time to turn to one last, crucial area: management career planning. This chapter looks at management as a career, examines a profile of successful managers, and suggests guidelines that can be useful to you in planning a management career of your own. When you have finished studying the material in this chapter, you will be able to

1. describe a profile of currently successful executives;

2. explain the six career phases that most managers go through;

3. discuss typical career problems faced by managers when they start out and later in their careers;

4. describe useful strategies in terms of career self-evaluation, career tactics, and career development planning;

5. describe the nature and effects of organizational stress;

6. tell how a Type A person works and why this person is highly susceptible to coronary heart disease; and

7. list specific steps that will help you manage stress, avoid burnout, and ensure a long, healthy career.

A Profile of Success

Before we begin a systematic analysis of how to manage a career effectively, let us examine a profile of some successful business leaders to find out who seems to succeed and why.

Functional Background

A few years ago, *Forbes,* the prestigious business journal, conducted an investigation of the backgrounds of the nation's top 801 chief executives.[1] The results of this study are shown in Table 20–1. Notice from the table that in the early 1980s more chief executives came from finance than from any other area. Does this mean that finance majors have the best chance of reaching the top? Not necessarily. David L. Kurtz and Louis E. Boone, who researched the subject of functional background, reported these conclusions:

> A study that used 20 years of data from each of 239 companies found that a new president had the same functional background as the previous chief executive in only 25 percent of the cases. The obvious lesson is that candidates for entry-level jobs should not select a functional area on the basis of the CEO's specialty. No particular functional background is essential for a chief executive in most industries today.[2]

No particular background is essential.

Compensation

How well are these executives compensated? In answering this question, we must note that many top managers receive the bulk of their annual compensation in bonuses, stock options, and other perquisites. Economic and competitive developments greatly influence this total package. In some years executives make very large amounts, while in other years, because of small bonuses or a depressed stock market, total compensation is much less. Nevertheless, speaking in very broad terms, executive compensation over the last decade has been quite good.

Compensation is quite good.

For example, a few years ago the New York Yankees gave Dave Winfield a multi-year contract that was reported to be worth $25 million. This was

Table 20–1
The Functional Backgrounds of Chief Executives

	Percent
Finance (142)	17.7
Administration (124)	15.5
Marketing, Sales, Retailing (101)	12.6
Legal (94)	11.7
Banking (93)	11.6
Production & Operations (89)	11.1
Technical (78)	9.7
Founder (44)	5.5
Other (36)	4.5

Source: Based on data reported in "It Ain't Hay, But Is It Clover?" *Forbes,* June 9, 1980, pp. 116–118, 120, 125–126, 129–130, 133–134, 136, 138, 141–142, 144, 146–147.

1. "It Ain't Hay, But Is It Clover?" *Forbes,* June 9, 1980, pp. 116–118, 120, 125–126, 129–130, 133–134, 136, 138, 141–142, 144, 146–147.
2. David L. Kurtz and Louis E. Boone, "A Profile of Business Leadership," *Business Horizons,* September–October 1981, p. 30.

a lot of money, but it did not match the compensation packages of Frank E. Rosenfelt of Metro-Goldwyn-Mayer and Steven J. Ross of Warner Communications, both of whom received more than $5 million in that year alone. In fact, as far back as 1979 *Forbes* reported that the average annual salary and bonus paid to CEOs, in the 801 firms it investigated, was $351,900. Top managers of the 1980s are well paid and, in many cases, their compensation packages are greater than those of well-known athletes and movie stars. Table 20–2 shows how compensation has changed in industries and in other fields between 1971 and 1981.

Birthplace

Birthplace makes no difference . . .

Does it make any difference where one is born? In the main, the answer is no. For example, in 1980, 33 of the top 801 executives studied by *Forbes* were born abroad in such countries as Canada, France, Italy, England, Japan, China, Germany, Austria, Israel, and Ireland, to name just 10. In recent years, foreign-born managers have headed such well-known firms as Colgate-Palmolive, Dow Chemical, General Electric, Gulf & Western, J. J. Heinz, Raytheon, Revlon, NCR, Time, and Coca Cola. The only pattern that does emerge when native-born CEOs are examined is that many of them come from industrialized states. For example, of the 801 CEOs in the *Forbes* study, almost half came from New York, Ohio, Pennsylvania, Texas, Illinois, California, or Massachusetts.

Job Tenure

but job tenure does.

One of the findings that does help distinguish successful managers is that they have "paid their dues." Chief executives get to their high positions on the basis of ability and performance. They also tend to be long-time employees of the firms they head. The *Forbes* study found that CEOs who were not the founders of their firms had worked for their companies for an average of more than 13 years before attaining chief executive status.

Overall Findings

The major success factor is competence.

Overall, the major factor in executive success is competence. You must know what you are doing. It also helps to have a specialty such as law, finance, accounting, or marketing, because you need a point of departure. You have to start out in a department and prove you are qualified to move up. From then on, drive and determination play key roles. You must want to succeed and be prepared to pay the price. One of the most effective ways to rise in the ranks is with a well-developed career plan. As this plan is implemented, you will find yourself going through what are called career phases.

Career Phases

In general terms, most people go through a series of career phases or stages. These phases do not last the same amount of time for everyone, and some people seem to have more difficulty at one (or two) phases than do most others. Nevertheless, six distinct career phases can be identified.

Table 20–2 Executive Compensation: 1971–1981

1971			1981		
Industry	**Largest Company**	**Chief Executive's Compensation**	**Largest Company**	**Chief Executive's Compensation**	**Increase (Decrease)**
WHAT'S HAPPENED TO EXECUTIVE COMPENSATION . . .					
Aerospace	Boeing	$ 80,000	Boeing	$ 957,551	1,096.9%
Food	Swift	$ 68,053	Dart & Kraft	$ 748,647	1,000.1%
Pharmaceuticals	American Home Products	$240,000	Johnson & Johnson	$ 968,542	303.6%
Publishing	Time Inc.	$203,025	Time Inc.	$ 633,367	212.0%
Metal Manufacturing	U.S. Steel	$300,000	U.S. Steel	$ 821,322	173.8%
Retailing	Sears Roebuck	$386,800	Sears Roebuck	$1,010,137	161.2%
Utility	AT&T	$360,500	AT&T	$ 894,400	148.1%
Office Equipment	IBM	$394,331	IBM	$ 940,000	138.4%
Commercial Banking	Bankamerica	$171,543	Bankamerica	$ 390,325	127.5%
Petroleum Refining	Standard Oil (N.J.)	$505,100	Exxon	$1,105,412	118.9%
Brokerage	Merrill Lynch	$296,501	Merrill Lynch	$ 642,524	116.7%
Advertising	J. Walter Thompson	$191,587	JWT Group	$ 372,881	94.6%
Mutual Life Insurance	Prudential	$300,000	Prudential	$ 582,744	94.2%
Conglomerates	General Electric	$500,000	General Electric	$ 853,976	70.8%
Automotive	General Motors	$838,750	General Motors	$ 489,250	(41.7%)
. . . AS COMPARED WITH					
		Compensation		**Compensation**	**Increase**
Major-League Baseball Player (average)		$ 31,543		$ 196,500	523.0%
Starting Lawyer in a Wall Street Law Firm		$ 15,500		$ 43,300	179.4%
Harvard MBA Graduate Entering Consulting (median)		$ 18,000 (1972 data)		$ 46,100	156.1%
Auto Worker (average hourly wage)		$ 4.72		$ 11.01	133.3%
Airline Pilot (average for union members)		$ 28,390		$ 60,280 (1980 data)	112.3%
President of AFL-CIO		$ 70,000		$ 110,000	57.1%
U.S. Senator		$ 42,500		$ 60,663	42.7%
President of the U.S.		$200,000		$ 200,000	0.0%
Consumer Price Index (1967 = 100)		121.3		272.4	124.6%
Minimum Wage		$ 1.60		$ 3.35	109.4%
Standard & Poor's 500 Stock Index (year-end)		102.09		122.55	20.0%

Source: Fortune, July 12, 1982, p. 45. Reprinted with permission.

Phase 1:   Breaking Away (Ages 16–22)

A job initially is viewed as a means of self-support.

During the phase of **breaking away,** the person begins to establish independence and autonomy from the parents. The person strives to demonstrate that he or she is capable of managing in life. Most people finish their schooling during this period and take their first full-time job. Far from being interested in a career, at this stage most people view their job basically as a means of income and self-support. It helps them accomplish their objective of breaking away.

Phase 2:   Initial Adulthood (Ages 22–29)

Then a career plan begins to emerge . . .

During the phase of **initial adulthood,** individuals begin to become adults in the truest sense of the word. One of the primary objectives during this phase is the development of social and intimate relationships with members of the opposite sex. Many people marry during this age period. They also begin to develop organizational and professional ties. A career plan now begins to emerge. This is true for both women and men. In fact, recent research reveals that both groups go into management for the same reasons and the profiles of both are similar, as seen in Table 20–3.

Phase 3:   Transition Period (Ages 29–32)

followed by a personal evaluation period.

During the **transition period,** people often become uneasy about their career progress. Key questions people ask themselves include: Am I moving ahead fast enough? Should I change jobs or move to another organization? Many people do move to another firm during this period. They know they will not always be mobile, and they decide to take advantage of the situation while they can.

Phase 4:   Settling Down (Ages 32–39)

Next comes a drive to succeed . . .

During the phase of **settling down,** individuals are likely to have chosen a career and to be spending their time trying to get ahead. Social contacts are greatly reduced, for most people now have little time for cultivating friendships. Most of their energies are devoted to career-oriented objectives and to their immediate family. During this time they establish the groundwork for career advancement. If a person is not labeled "a winner" or "up-and-coming" by the time he or she is 40, the executive suite may be out of bounds.

Phase 5:   Possible Mid-Life Crisis (Ages 39–43)

followed by another in-depth evaluation period.

During the period of **mid-life crisis,** people realize that some youthful ambitions will never be fulfilled. It becomes clear that the social or financial position once dreamed of will not materialize. The person may never get to be the CEO. He or she may have to settle for being a good, but not the best, salesperson in the firm. For many people, the recognition that many of their dreams will go unrealized comes as a crushing blow. If they are unable to cope with this situation, they face mid-life crisis. This term refers to a psychological state in which individuals feel that they have

Table 20–3
Young Women and Men
in the Management Ranks

	Women	Men
Married	68%	72%
Childless	87	64
Career Motivation		
(1 = highest; 8 = lowest)		
Sense of achievement	1.68	2.10
Challenge	2.91	2.55
Money	3.45	4.04
Independence	3.48	3.96
Power	5.53	5.71
Security	5.58	5.38
Opportunity to meet interesting people	5.80	5.24
Opportunity to travel	7.00	7.00

Source: Reported in Benson Rosen, Mary Ellen Templeton, and Karen Kichline, "The First Few Years on the Job: Women in Management," *Business Horizons,* November–December 1981, p. 27.

failed and that there is no way for them to bounce back. These feelings are typical when individuals review their careers and conclude that they are too old to change careers but do not want to continue with things the way they are. During this phase it is not uncommon to find people quitting their jobs or doing foolish things such as wearing outlandish clothes to a conservative job or going out and buying a boat that is beyond their means and trying to live a different lifestyle. Still others turn to excessive drinking or make a spectacular break with the past, one that hurts their careers. Of course, not everyone behaves this way. In fact, the more realistic people are about their careers, where they are going, how they are going to get there, and what they are willing to settle for, the more likely it is that they will not suffer mid-life crisis.

Phase 6:   Establishment of Equilibrium (Ages 43–50)

Then things often return to normal.

During the phase of **establishment of equilibrium,** things return to normal. The person is likely to review career progress, find that things are going along pretty well, and be basically pleased with the results. There is a large degree of contentment, optimism, and stability. If the person is not going to become an executive vice president, he or she has come to realize and accept this fact. If the person is not able to afford a million-dollar house in the suburbs, he or she finds comfort in a more modest residence.

As you can see, as an individual moves through these phases, his or her attitudes, values, opinions, and even lifestyles change. The person matures and grows in different ways. The important thing to draw from an understanding of these career phases is the different types of changes that people confront during their careers. By having an idea of what you are likely to encounter, you are in a better position to deal with career problems, and there are many of them. The next section examines some of the most typical ones.

Career Problems

It will not always be smooth sailing for you. You will occasionally find yourself facing career problems. Two crucial periods come when you first start out and again later on when you may face a career plateau.

Starting Out

When you begin your career, you are likely to have a great deal of drive and determination. You will want to do well and succeed. Unfortunately, in many cases you will find that your initial view of work is quite different from reality.

Simple and Boring

Initial jobs are usually routine.

One of the first things you will learn is that, except in rarc cases, the work will be simple and perhaps even boring. You will be eager to apply the specific tools and techniques that you learned in college. You will be seeking opportunity and challenge, but there will be little of either. Most of your time will be spent on routine, basic assignments. You may find yourself asking, "Is this it? Doesn't this job have any meaningful aspects? Do I really want to do this for the next year or two?" If you stay with the organization, things should get better. At first, however, you are just going to have to suffer through.

Organizational Politics

You may not know the power relationships that exist . . .

A second early problem relates to organizational politics. When you are new to the enterprise, you are unaware of the power relationships that exist. You do not know whom to cultivate, what to say, or with which groups to associate. You are likely to believe that if you do a good job, everything else will take care of itself. However, if you and your boss have a good relationship but your boss is considered to be a maverick or good in his present position but not promotable, you and your boss may both find yourself eventually having to look for jobs elsewhere. Or, if you write a report showing how the enterprise can cut its workforce by 5 percent and save $500,000 and the cuts are to come from the department of a powerful manager, your promotion path to the top may be blocked. There are many mistakes you can make because you do not know the politics of the organization.

Knowing What Counts

or how your performance will be measured.

Perhaps the basic rule of success for young managers is, "Keep your boss pleased with your performance." Unfortunately, the way to do this is not always clear. Some young people believe they should be as efficient and businesslike as possible. Such behavior sometimes results in their being labeled as lacking in human relations skills, however. Others are extremely personable but are viewed as lacking drive or determination to succeed. Whatever the reason, early evaluations count; and if you are rated as average or below average by your first boss, regardless of how tough an evaluator he or she is, this is likely to hurt your future with the organization. For this reason, you have to learn early on how you are going to be evaluated and then act accordingly.

Loyalty Issues

Loyalty means different things to different people.

Loyalty means different things to different people. Some managers view it in terms of obedience: Do as I tell you to do. Others view it in terms of effort: Come early, stay late, work hard. Other common interpretations relate to (1) success, as found among managers who want their subordinates to do whatever it takes to get the job done, even if the activities are shady; (2) protection, as found among managers who want their people to shield them from ridicule and remember that it is "us against them"; and (3) honesty, as found among managers who want their subordinates to convey to them both good and bad news. The first challenge for the young manager is to determine which of these interpretations is expected. The second challenge is to decide whether the conduct it calls for is personally acceptable.

Ethical Problems

Ethics may prove to be an issue for you.

Sometimes, loyalty problems are also ethical problems. **Ethics,** however, which can be defined as principles that determine right and wrong conduct—extend far beyond simple loyalty. Many members of the general public believe businesspeople are willing to carry out unethical practices in order to succeed. When viewed from a broad perspective, ethics apply to a number of a different subjects, ranging from legal issues to economic self-interest to the impact of one person's actions on other people. Young managers have to decide how far they are prepared to go in order to succeed in their careers. For some, the pressure to conform to less than personally acceptable levels of conduct can be quite great. In some organizations failure to cross this line can cost you a promotion; in other organizations you will be fired if you do. The real issue is finding out what particular ethical problem will confront you, deciding whether your values and those of the organization are in agreement, and being willing to move on to another enterprise if ethical dilemmas cannot be resolved to your satisfaction.

Later On

As your career progresses, you will face still other problems. One of these, discussed earlier, is mid-life crisis. Another more common problem is the career plateau.

The Career Plateau

Upward progress may be halted.

Few individuals find their career to be a continuous climb to the top. Most discover that there is a **career plateau** after which further promotions come either infrequently or not at all. Some people reach their career plateau more quickly than others, but it is a problem for just about everyone. Janet Near, after studying the career plateau's causes and effects, reports that:

The career plateau would be largely an individual problem if it were not for its magnitude; a recent survey of 72 functional and human resource managers produced the estimate that over 70 percent of managers (in their firms) were plateaued. In the next decade, it seems likely that this proportion will increase, at which point it will become an issue of some concern to organizations as well as to individuals. In fact, it has been suggested that organizations will have to find alternative rewards to offer their members, since advancement opportunities will be so drastically reduced.[3]

Personal and organizational factors are the causes.

What causes the career plateau? In Near's survey, 80 percent of the managers partially attributed it to personal factors such as motivation, effort, and ability. These managers plateaued because they lacked sufficient desire, drive, or talent. She also found that 60 percent of the managers partially attributed their plateau to organizational factors such as the competition for promotions and a belief on the part of the enterprise that the person was too valuable in his or her present position to be moved to a higher level.

Some people are terminated.

Whatever the reason, the plateau takes three typical patterns. Some people continue up the line until they reach a position where they are unable to progress any further because they lack the ability to go on. These individuals tend to stay in their jobs either until retirement or until they are forced out because the organization labels them as deadwood and terminates their employment. A second pattern is that in which people become obsolete after they plateau because they are unwilling to keep up with the latest developments in their field. They, too, are eventually terminated. The typical pattern is one in which the individual maintains a successful plateau status. Whether this plateau occurs for organizational or personal reasons, the employee's performance remains high and the organization keeps the person on.

There are ways to overcome the plateau.

Early in your career you are not likely to be very concerned with career plateauing. It will become a concern as you move into middle management, however, or reach your mid-30s. Will you be able to deal with it? Will the organization be willing to help out? The first question can be answered only by you. If you maintain a strong desire to succeed and are determined to keep moving up the ladder, the chance of overcoming personal plateau causes is fairly good. In answering the second question, you need to look at the career development programs offered by the firm. There are numerous ways in which management can avoid practices leading to ineffective plateauing and the need to fire deadwood. Some of these are discussed in the next section.

Career Strategies

Before you begin a career in management, you need to evaluate your own needs, desires, and ambitions.[4] What type of career do you want? You

---

3. Janet P. Near, "The Career Plateau: Causes and Effects," *Business Horizons,* October 1980, p. 54.

4. For another view of this process see: William L. Mihal, Patricia A. Sorce, and Thomas M. Conte, "A Process Model of Individual Career Decision Making," *Academy of Management Review,* January 1984, pp. 95–103.

also need to understand career tactics that can help you sidestep problems and take advantage of opportunities. Finally, you must be aware that career development can help you formulate a long-term plan that will take you to retirement. These three areas constitute career strategy.

Self-Evaluation

The best way to begin a career strategy plan is with a self-examination. What do you do well? What do you do poorly? What would you like to do in terms of a career? The answers to questions like these will help you balance ability (what you do well) with interests (what you would like to do) while sidestepping areas where you are not likely to succeed (what you do poorly). One of the most effective ways to obtain a profile of your work personality is to formulate a series of questions such as those presented in Figure 20–1. These are not designed to be comprehensive, but they do indicate what we are talking about. The purpose of such questions is to help you describe yourself. There are no right and wrong answers; the questions are designed for descriptive purposes only. As you begin to formulate in your mind the type of work you would like to do, you will not find any job that is perfect in terms of demands, pressures, hours, financial reimbursements, and so forth. You will be able to use this type of self-evaluation checklist, however, as a guide in identifying the type of career or job that is best for you.

A supplemental way to obtain personal insights is through the use of time continua. Your life consists of three time periods: past, present, and future. Most people concentrate their attention only on the present. If they do look in any other direction, it is usually to the past for the purpose of reminiscing. The future is where you will spend your career, however, and you should devote your attention to this time period when examining who you are and what you want to do.

Focus on the future.

There are two popular ways of focusing on the future. The easiest, although sometimes most threatening, way is for you to write your own obituary. What do you want people to write about you after you are gone? As you write this obituary, you are actually identifying things you have done (or would like to do) before you die.

Note meaningful job-related events you want to have happen.

A second way is to go back into the past and identify and describe important or meaningful events that have happened to you in your life. Perhaps you remember winning a special prize at school. Or perhaps there was a big birthday party for you and you received a very special present from your favorite aunt and uncle. Whatever these events were, write them down. The reason for this is to get you thinking about what important things have already happened to you. Now continue your list into the future and write down all of the important or meaningful job-related events you would like to experience during your career. By examining this list, you can obtain an idea of what you want to do. You have, albeit indirectly, set some objectives for yourself. Now you need to determine how you can achieve them, and career tactics can help.

Career Tactics

Regardless of the career you choose, you should know some of the ways to increase your chances of success. Every organization has its own set

Read each pair of statements and put an "X" above the appropriate value on the respective continuum. Do not regard the minus signs as good or bad; the only purpose of these mathematical signs is to help establish degree of personal preference.

Do you like to
work by yourself?   Or as a member
                                                         of a team?

```
|----+----+----+----+----+----+----+----+----+----|
5    4    3    2    1    0   -1   -2   -3   -4   -5
Great Deal              Indifferent            Great Deal
```

Do you like to work
under pressure?   Or feel that you are more
                                         effective when there is little, if
                                         any, pressure?

```
|----+----+----+----+----+----+----+----+----+----|
5    4    3    2    1    0   -1   -2   -3   -4   -5
```

Do you like to plan
things out in advance?   Or prefer to act on impulse,
                                         intuition, or gut feeling?

```
|----+----+----+----+----+----+----+----+----+----|
5    4    3    2    1    0   -1   -2   -3   -4   -5
```

Do you have a strong
desire to succeed?   Or could you be happy if you
                                         were just better than average?

```
|----+----+----+----+----+----+----+----+----+----|
5    4    3    2    1    0   -1   -2   -3   -4   -5
```

Do you like to see
results immediately?   Or can you wait to see how
                                         things come out?

```
|----+----+----+----+----+----+----+----+----+----|
5    4    3    2    1    0   -1   -2   -3   -4   -5
```

Are you basically a risk taker?   Or do you prefer to avoid risk?

```
|----+----+----+----+----+----+----+----+----+----|
5    4    3    2    1    0   -1   -2   -3   -4   -5
```

Would you rather work
in a small organization?   Or would you be more
                                         comfortable in a large one?

```
|----+----+----+----+----+----+----+----+----+----|
5    4    3    2    1    0   -1   -2   -3   -4   -5
```

Do you like to work mostly
with figures, data, and reports?   Or do you prefer to work with
                                         people?

```
|----+----+----+----+----+----+----+----+----+----|
5    4    3    2    1    0   -1   -2   -3   -4   -5
```

Are you basically an
analytical person?   Or a perceptive, insightful
                                         individual?

```
|----+----+----+----+----+----+----+----+----+----|
5    4    3    2    1    0   -1   -2   -3   -4   -5
```

Do you like change and
ambiguity?   Or do you prefer routine,
                                         regular, and systematic work?

```
|----+----+----+----+----+----+----+----+----+----|
5    4    3    2    1    0   -1   -2   -3   -4   -5
```

of rules, but there are some general guidelines that are helpful in virtually every enterprise.

Strive for high performance.

One of these is: Be a high performer. Nothing will help you succeed faster than proving you are competent. In fact, when you are first starting out, there will usually be very little management can use to differentiate you from others at your level. All of you may be in your early- to mid-20s, have college degrees, and exude a great amount of enthusiasm and company loyalty. Since all of you cannot be promoted at the same time, management will look for the highest performers. Who does the best job? This is the individual who will be promoted, and that is why it is so important for you to choose a job at which you can succeed. First results really do count!

Be prepared to blow your own horn.

A second rule is: Keep a hero file. When you do something well and the boss sends you a memo telling you about your success, save the memo. If you are charged with writing a special report or preparing a document, keep a copy of it. If you are given an award, make a note of it. In this way, if you ever decide to change jobs you have a file of evidence that shows how effective you have been. This is as useful within the firm as it will be if you should be interviewing for a position with another organization.

Start managing others as soon as possible.

A third rule is: Get into a management position as quickly as possible. The sooner you are managing people, the more likely it is you will be given the chance to increase your responsibility and manage even larger groups and departments. Remember that when it is time to choose someone for a management opening, the person who currently has the next greatest amount of managerial responsibility and scope of authority is often given the nod. All things considered, a manager of a 15-person unit is more likely to be promoted head of a department of 25 people than is a manager of a 10-person unit.

Get yourself a sponsor.

A fourth rule is: Find a sponsor. A sponsor is someone who will help move you along in the organization. This individual will note your accomplishments to the right people, see that you are given a fair shake when it comes to promotion and salary, and ensure that your career is not sidetracked. The most common sponsor is one's boss, although it sometimes is an individual higher up the ranks who becomes aware of your work and decides to look after you because you are a talent the organization needs. For example, you may serve on a management committee with people from all levels of the hierarchy, and one of these individuals may take a liking to you. Or you may write an industry analysis that is read by a senior vice president who concludes that you have real talent. Whoever they are, sponsors are important people and in career planning it is very helpful to develop one. This is particularly true for women, many of whom admit that sponsors have been very helpful to them in their careers.

Help your boss get ahead.

A fifth rule is: Help your boss succeed. Remember that unless you move to another department or unit, your only way up the ranks is by assuming the position of your boss. You cannot do this if the boss remains. So by helping this person, you help yourself at the same time. There are a number of useful approaches in following this rule. One is to help your boss overcome any weaknesses he or she might have; for example, if the person is poor at report writing, help out by offering to write or rewrite these reports. A second way is to help the boss become better at things he or she likes. For example, if your superior likes to spend time visiting with the staff and building a public image in the community, work to free up the individual from desk routine. Help the boss become what he or she wants to become. Remember that when someone is promoted (or moves to another organization), that person will have to recommend a replacement. If you are out to help the boss succeed, you may well be tapped for that promotion.

A sixth rule is: Seek opportunity before money. Many young people will change jobs if more money is offered to them. This is a mistake. In your early years on the job, you should be interested in building a track record for good performance. Very few young managers, except for sales managers or others whose compensation package is tied directly to performance, receive bonuses or other financial incentives. During your first two to three years on the job, you are going to be making about what everyone else does who started with you. Anyone who makes more does so for a reason. The most common reason is that the person has agreed to take a difficult, technical, time-consuming or dead-end job. In any event, such people often find that after they have been in this job for a couple of years, they are unable to move back into the mainstream quickly. There are no openings or the salaries are too low to entice them back. What they fail to realize is that they have accepted a staff or highly technical position that has taken them out of the running for line positions and top executive jobs. They have opted for money, but in the process have given up promotion opportunities. A second part of this picture is that as managers begin to move up the line, two values vie with each other. One is economic (money) and the other is power (authority). We know from research that managers whose highest value is political do the best of all. Research findings show that when confronted with the choice, a person is better off opting for power (promotion, authority, responsibility) because this is the best way to get ahead. Moreover, if you do succeed in moving up, the money will follow. (Again see Table 20–2.)

A seventh rule is: Keep yourself mobile. It is possible that you will not be able to succeed in your first (or second or third) organization. You may find your route blocked by a manager who does not like you. Or your boss may be someone who is out of favor with the upper-level management, with the result that everyone who works for this person is considered in the same light. How do you know when to stay and when to move? Here are some helpful guidelines:

Put opportunity ahead of money.

Maintain your mobility.

1. If your boss is not considered promotable, move to another department or organization; there is no way you are going to overcome this problem unless he or she is fired—an uncommon event in many firms.

2. Look over the people at the same level of the hierarchy as yourself and estimate when they are most likely to be promoted; if you are not promoted at about the same time, consider going elsewhere.

3. By the time you are 30, you should be in a managerial position. If you are not, the firm may have designated you as lacking management timber. It may be time for you to move on.

4. Set some financial goals for yourself, such as earning $30,000 annually by the time you are 30 years old. Check to be sure that this figure is competitive in the industry. Then, if you have not made it, ask yourself why. If the answer is that the firm simply does not pay competitively at your level, look into your opportunities with other companies.

5. If you do exercise your mobility and go to another firm, never say anything bad about your old organization. Leave on good terms and give the impression that your decision was strictly a career move, nothing personal. If you do talk down your old employer, this can hurt you with your new one. Remember that people may smile when they hear you rip up the other firm, but they will be thinking, "I wonder what this person will say about us when he (or she) leaves here." You will get an image as someone who is quick to tear down others, and this reputation can hurt you.

Career Development Plan

A self-examination can help you formulate a short-range career plan. An understanding of career tactics can help you develop an intermediate-range plan. Consideration of career development can help you with long-range planning; but career development does not always depend exclusively on you. Over the last decade organizations have come to realize that career development is a problem not only for the manager but for the organization as well. Why do some enterprises have a great deal of deadwood (ineffective plateauees)? Part of the answer is found in some of the organization's potentially harmful career development failures such as

Career development failures

1. Failure to accurately appraise marginal or poor performance and to initiate corrective action. Long-run problems can be fostered by avoiding the short-run unpleasantness of negative appraisal, thus allowing possibly correctable behavior to become entrenched habit, which later becomes "someone else's problems."

2. Failure to provide training, skill upgrading, and development of [high performers]. This tends to assure that performance will slip as the requirements of a given position change, even if the incumbent's motivation remains high.

3. Failure to appraise, counsel, and develop career paths in the context of an individual's total life situation, and the parallel tendency to promote people beyond their current ability, leading to ineffectiveness and psychological stress.

4. Failure to monitor the attitudes and aspirations of individual managers. Many organizations depend upon informal observations and interpretations of superiors. Conditions maintaining individual performance vary among individuals as a function of particular goals and values.[5]

How can people ensure that these failures do not exist in their firm? One way is to find out the career programs that are currently in use. Some of the most common include career counseling, career pathing, human resources planning, career information systems, management or supervisor development, training, and programs for special groups. Table 20–4 spells out each of these activities in more detail.

5. Thomas P. Ference, James A. F. Stoner, and E. Kirby Warren, "Managing the Career Plateau," *Academy of Management Review*, October 1977, p. 608.

Table 20–4
Specific Career Activities

Career Counseling

Career counseling during the employment interview.
Career counseling during the performance appraisal session.
Psychological assessment and career alternative planning.
Career counseling as part of the day-to-day supervisor/subordinate relationship.
Special career counseling for high-potential employees.
Counseling for downward transfers.

Career Pathing

Planned job progression for new employees.
Career pathing to help managers acquire the necessary experience for future jobs.
Committee performs an annual review of management personnel's strengths and weaknesses and then develops a five-year career plan for each.
Plan job moves for high-potential employees to place them in a particular target job.
Rotate first-level supervisors through various departments to prepare them for upper-management positions.

Human Resources

Computerized inventory of backgrounds and skills to help identify replacements.
Succession planning or replacement charts at all levels of management.

Career Information Systems

Job posting for all nonofficer positions; individual can bid to be considered.
Job posting for hourly employees and career counseling for salaried employees.

Management or Supervisory Development

Special program for those moving from hourly employment to management.
Responsibility of the department head to develop managers.
Management development committee to look after the career development of management groups.
In-house advanced management program.

Training

In-house supervisory training.
Technical skills training for lower levels.
Outside management seminars.
Formalized job rotation programs.
Intern programs.
Responsibility of manager for on-the-job training.
Tuition reimbursement program.

Special Groups

Outplacement programs.
Minority indoctrination training program.
Career management seminar for women.
Preretirement counseling.
Career counseling and job rotation for women and minorities.
Refresher courses for midcareer managers.
Presupervisory training program for women and minorities.

Source: Marilyn A. Morgan, Douglas T. Hall, and Alison Martier, "Career Development Strategies in Industry—Where Are We and Where Should We Be?" *Personnel,* March–April 1979, p. 16. Reprinted, by permission of the publisher, from *Personnel,* March–April 1979. Copyright © 1979 by AMACOM, a division of American Management Associations. All rights reserved.

In addition to investigating career development programs, you must learn how to negotiate for yourself. Using the tactics described in the previous section, as well as your own experience and judgment, you must work out an arrangement that is as beneficial to you as it is to the enterprise. These negotiations can take numerous forms. Table 20–5 illustrates five typical career negotiation scenarios. Remember that these negotiations are designed to supplement the organization's career development programs.

Negotiate for yourself.

Table 20–5
Career Negotiation Scenarios

Organizational Position	Nature of Transaction	Individual Position
"You stay with us now and in return we can offer some exciting challenges in the future." →	1. Both parties agree to increase career options within organization. ←	"I can accept the current job for a while longer if you can help me get into an executive career track."
"We will provide options for outside professional opportunities such as a sabbatical or study, or travel to professional conferences." →	2. Side payments are made. ←	"I'll remain in this organization if you provide outside professional opportunities to offset lack of career opportunities in the organization."
"We can only offer long-term benefits as compensation for lack of work challenge or on chances of increased responsibility. We will give a good vacation and retirement package." →	3. Side payments are made (career is not a negotiating issue). ←	"I will accept limited job projects if I can get an early retirement package."
"If you stay with us for the short term, we will help place you in another attractive organization." →	4. Compromises are made to make use of individual's current talents and to facilitate a future move to another organization. ←	"My career in this organization will not last long, so why don't you agree to help me move into another organization in a few years or so."
"Let's get what we can until he or she is no longer useful." →	5. Both parties engage in cynical manipulation. ←	"I'm going to get mine and get out."

Source: James F. Wolf and Robert N. Bacher, "Career Negotiation: Trading Off Employee and Organizational Needs," *Personnel,* March–April 1981, p. 53. Reprinted, by permission of the publisher, from *Personnel,* March–April 1981. Copyright © 1981 by AMACOM, a division of the American Management Associations. All rights reserved.

The enterprise may offer you assistance in pathing out your career, but you have a responsibility to look out for your own interests. This responsibility is vital to every career development plan.

The other important step in career development planning is to bring together your job-related needs and personal needs and align them with your career stages. Table 20–6 shows how this can be done. Notice from the table that as you move through your career, your strategies have to change. You must match your work life with your personal life. If either is out of step with the other, your career can suffer. Remember that your career success depends, to a large extent, on your ability to formulate a well-designed strategy that meets your particular needs.[6]

Formulate a long-range plan for yourself.

Table 20–6
Career Planning
and Career Stages

Career Stage	Job-Related Needs	Personal Needs
Just starting out	A variety of job activities. An examination of abilities, desires, and goals.	Determination of preliminary job choices. Settling down to work.
Early career	Development of competence in specialty areas. Development of creativity and innovation. Job rotation into new areas for purpose of increased job experience.	Dealing with rivalry and competition at work. Dealing with work-family conflicts. Obtaining support for career choices. Establishment of autonomy.
Mid-career	Updating of technical knowledge and skills. Development of skills in training and coaching younger employees. Rotation into new jobs for acquiring new skills. Development of a broader view of work and personal roles in the organization.	Dealing with mid-life crisis. Reorganizing thinking about oneself in regard to work, family, and the community. Reducing self-indulgence and competitiveness.
Late career	Planning for retirement. Shifting from a power role to one of guidance and consultation. Identification and development of successors. Starting of activities outside the organization.	Support and counseling of others in the organization. Development of a sense of identity in extraorganizational activities.

6. For more on careers see: Harry Levinson, "A Second Career: The Possible Dream," *Harvard Business Review*, May–June 1983, pp. 122–129.

Executive Health

Before concluding our discussion of management as a career, we need to consider the topic of executive health. In the last 10 years this has become a very important issue in modern organizations. After all, every time an executive dies the organization loses one of its most important assets. Who will replace this person? Will the new executive have the same degree of judgment, skill, intelligence, and insight? If not, the organization will have suffered a tremendous blow because of the executive's death.

If you want to make it to the top and become a key executive, you have to know more than just how to manage your career. You have to know something about managing your health. This subject has a number of important dimensions including (1) organizational stress and its effect on the executive's well-being; (2) managerial personality and the differences between those most likely to have heart attacks and those least likely to suffer this fate; (3) excessive stress, namely burnout; and (4) ways to cope with stress and lead a long and fruitful management life.

Organizational Stress

Every year more than 650,000 Americans die from heart attacks. Another 29 million have some form of heart and blood vessel disease.[7] One of the most important causes of coronary heart disease (CHD) is stress. In organizational settings there are many factors or stressors that can cause CHD. Figure 20–2 provides a model for understanding the relationship between stress and CHD.

Stressors are both intra- and extraorganizational.

Notice from the figure that **stressors** can be categorized as intraorganizational and extraorganizational. Intraorganizational stressors occur at three levels: individual, group, and the organization at large, while extraorganizational stressors are heavily influenced by personal factors. When stress is examined as a composite, three major types are perceived: job, career, and life. How serious are the outcomes of such stress? The answer is that it depends on the person. Some people are better able to adjust to stress because of such things as heredity (their bodies can withstand more stress), education (better educated people tend to be able to take more stressful situations than less well-educated people), exercise (they work it off by playing tennis or jogging), and vacation (they get away from the stress by going on a five-day cruise). Other people cannot deal with stress very well. These people are becoming the focus of attention.

What implications does the study of organizational stressors have for modern management? Michael T. Matteson and John M. Ivancevich, well known for their studies on stress and executive health, have noted the following management and organizational implications:

1. Accumulated evidence places the organization at the center of any discussion of stressors and coronary heart disease.

2. Behavioral factors and organizational stressors should be considered

---

7. American Heart Association, *Heart Facts* (Dallas: American Heart Association, 1977).

Figure 20–2 A Model for Organizational Stress Research

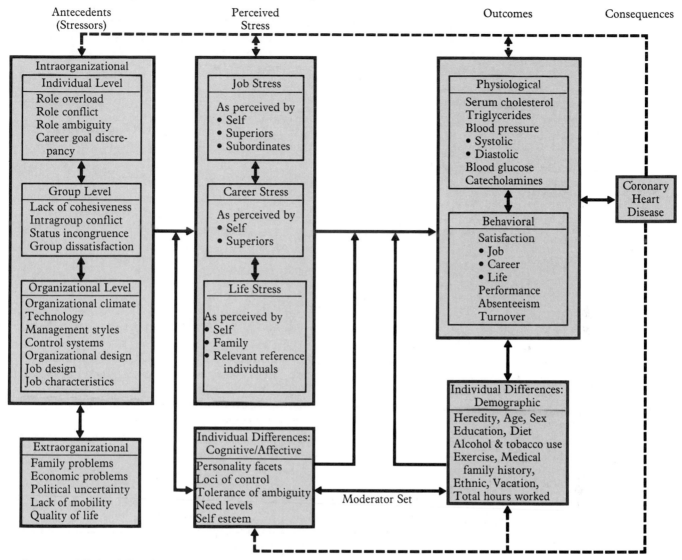

Source: Michael T. Matteson and John M. Ivancevich, "Organizational Stressors and Heart Disease: A Research Model," *Academy of Management Review,* October 1979, p. 350. Reprinted with permission.

Management and organizational implications of stress

in developing coronary preventive medicine programs in much the same way that traditional risk factors such as blood pressure, cigarette smoking, and diet are considered.

3. Available research suggests that three levels of intraorganizational stressors and various or extraorganizational stressors should be viewed as interacting, including family circumstances, organizational climate, intragroup conflict, and role ambiguity.

4. The importance of individual differences in reactions to stressors must not be underestimated because for some people, organizational stressors are not harmful emotionally, physiologically, or psychologically while for others they are.

"Good Night, Henderson—Keep wound up for tomorrow!"

5. Managerial activities are not restricted to improving performance or increasing profitability; in the larger context of managerial accountability it rests in the implicit obligation to improve the quality of organizational life for subordinates.[8]

How can management address this area of stress and its effect on executive CHD? By creating and maintaining a work environment that contributes to the reduction of CHD and increases both general health and longevity. The important thing for you to realize is that in your career there will be times when stress is extremely great and you will have to learn to cope with it, if only for limited periods of time. One of the best ways to prepare yourself is to find out the type of person you are when it comes to stress. There are two basic personality patterns: Type A and Type B.

Type A and Type B Behavior

In 1974, after a decade of medical research, two cardiologists wrote a book that has provided a wealth of information regarding the ability of individuals to cope with stress.[9] In their book they coined two terms that have become

---

8. Michael T. Matteson and John M. Ivancevich, "Organizational Stressors and Heart Disease: A Research Model," *Academy of Management Review*, October 1979, pp. 354–355.

9. Meyer Friedman and Ray Rosenman, *Type A Behavior and Your Heart* (New York: Knopf, 1974).

part of the literature of stress management: Type A and Type B behavior. Of the two, Type A has received the greatest amount of attention because it is characteristic of individuals who suffer from CHD. Friedman and Rosenman described **Type A behavior** as an action-emotion complex that can be observed in any person who is aggressively involved in a chronic, incessant struggle to achieve more and more in less and less time and, if required to do so, against the opposing efforts of other things or other persons. In contrast, the Type B person is rarely harried by desires to obtain a wildly increasing number of things or participate in an endlessly growing series of events in an ever-decreasing amount of time. In particular, the main characteristics of Type A individuals include (1) a sense of time urgency, (they try to get more and more done in less and less time), (2) a quest for numbers (they try to quantify things in terms of dollars or other measurable terms), (3) insecurity of status (they are outwardly confident and self-assured but are often insecure underneath and constantly struggling for recognition through the number of achievements and the rate at which their current status improves) and (4) aggression and hostility (they are extremely competitive and tend always to challenge other people in sports, games, work, and general discussions).[10]

> **Type A people are always in a hurry.**

Are you a Type A person? Or do you have some of the main characteristics of such people? The quiz in Table 20–7 provides some insights into this question. The important thing to remember is that if you are a Type A person (or have fairly similar characteristics), you are more prone to CHD than the average person. Additionally, even if you avoid coronary problems, you are still subject to burnout.

Stress and Burnout

Individuals subjected to prolonged degrees of stress can suffer what is called **burnout.** In the beginning the person may actually increase performance and efficiency. This fact is sometimes referred to as the **Yerkes-Dodson** law, first described by Drs. Robert M. Yerkes and John D. Dodson of the Harvard Physiologic Laboratory. They showed that as stress increases, efficiency and performance also go up to a certain level. If the stress continues, however, performance and efficiency decrease.[11] The result of excessive stress is burnout.

> **There are numerous symptoms of burnout.**

There are many symptoms of burnout. Some of the most common include chronic fatigue, job boredom, cynicism, impatience, irritability, and an unfulfilled need for recognition. How can you tell if you are a potential burnout victim? One way is to answer questions like those in Table 20–7, since Type A persons are most likely to suffer burnout. Another way is to realize that burnout candidates have three distinguishing characteristics. One characteristic is that their problem is predominantly job related. Oliver Niehouse, a personnel development advisor, explains the idea this way:

> In many respects, individual worker problems . . . can contribute to a stressful environment. Some people thrive on stress; but even for them, there

10. Philip Goldberg, *Executive Health* (New York: McGraw-Hill, 1978), p. 103.

11. Herbert Benson and Robert L. Allen, "How Much Stress Is Too Much?" *Harvard Business Review,* September–October 1980, p. 88.

Table 20–7
Are You a Type A Person?

Read each of the following descriptions and ask yourself, in each case, if the statement is descriptive of you. Note the number of times you answer yes.

1. Think of doing two or more things at the same time.
2. Schedule more and more activities into less and less time.
3. Fail to notice or be interested in your environment or things of beauty.
4. Hurry the speech of others.
5. Become unduly irritated when forced to wait in line.
6. Become unduly irritated when driving behind a car you think is moving too slowly.
7. Believe that if you want something done well, you have to do it yourself.
8. Gesticulate when you talk.
9. Frequently jiggle your knee or rapidly tap your fingers.
10. Use explosive speech patterns or frequent use of obscenities.
11. Have a fetish of always being on time.
12. Have difficulty sitting quietly or doing nothing.
13. Play nearly every game to win—even when you are playing against children.
14. Measure your own, and others' successes in quantitative terms (number of sales made, patients seen, books read)
15. Use head nodding, fist-clenching, table pounding or sucking in of air when speaking.
16. Become impatient when watching others do things you feel you can do better yourself.
17. Use rapid eye-blinking or tic-like eyebrow lifting.
18. Feel guilty when relaxing.
19. Have a tendency to dominate conversations and change the subject to topics that interest you.
20. Constantly find yourself having to move, walk, and eat rapidly.
21. Have great difficult finding time to improve yourself or explore new and interesting things.
22. Evidence a great fear of slowing down because you feel your success is due to your ability to do things faster than others.
23. Create deadlines even if none exist currently.
24. Have few hobbies or diversions outside of your work.
25. Often try to do two things at the same time such as drive your car and read the morning newspaper.

If your answer to more than 15 of these is yes, you have Type A characteristics. If your answer to 20 or more is yes, you are undoubtedly a Type A person.

is a limit. . . . The potential to exceed that limit can occur whenever a significant change in job responsibility takes place. For example, your organization absorbs another company and suddenly your human resources have doubled; you're trying to ferret out the human resources problems underlying a drop in productivity on an assembly line; or, like a manager at one computer firm who was given an opportunity, you dive into a heavy schedule of organization and management development programs and workshops that tax your own resources.[12]

Idealists are subject to burnout . . .

A second distinguishing characteristic is excessive idealism or extremely high self-motivation or both. It is often the maverick executive with the "I've got to succeed" attitude who suffers the ill effects of burnout. Another typical victim of burnout is the manager whose entire objective is to win and who never looks closely at the end result. Upon reaching the goal the person asks, "Is this all there is?" Unsatisfied with the objective, the individual pushes on to new goals, never satisfied with current accomplishments and always looking toward new ones.

as are those who never slow down.

A third distinguishing characteristic of burnout candidates is that they set goals that are often too difficult to reach. As a result, they are in a continual battle that can never be won. No matter how long or hard the person works, the goal is beyond his or her abilities. Should it become possible, the individual will revise the objective so that it again becomes unattainable. No wonder, then, that some experts define burnout as the "total depletion of one's physical and mental resources caused by excessive striving to reach some unrealistic, job-related goal(s)."[13]

Learning to Cope

How can you manage stress, avoid burnout, and assure yourself a long, healthy career? The answer is by combining a moderate amount of work-related stress with a good diet and a regular schedule of exercise and relaxation. Primary in this prescription is your diet. What nutritional experts say is true—you are what you eat. Americans typically consume unhealthy amounts of cholesterol, white flour, sugar, and salt. The U.S. Senate Select Committee on Nutrition and Human Needs has recommended the following dietary goals:

1. Increase consumption of fruits and vegetables and whole grains.

2. Decrease consumption of meat.

3. Increase consumption of poultry and fish.

4. Decrease consumption of foods high in fat.

5. Partially substitute polyunsaturated fat for saturated fat.

Set dietary goals.

6. Substitute nonfat milk for whole milk.

7. Decrease consumption of butterfat, eggs, and other high-cholesterol sources.

12. Oliver L. Niehouse, "Burnout: A Real Threat to Human Resources Managers," *Personnel*, September–October 1981, p. 28.

13. *Ibid.*, p. 29.

8. Decrease consumption of sugar and foods high in sugar content.

9. Decrease consumption of salt and foods high in salt content.[14]

Start a physical fitness program.

A second important way to cope is to develop a physical fitness program. By exercising regularly (jogging, playing tennis or racquetball, swimming, lifting weights, or doing calisthenics two to three times a week) you can keep yourself in good physical shape. Robert Kreitner, a management researcher, has noted that these physical fitness programs are now taking on organizational dimensions.

> Company-sponsored fitness programs have sprung up by the hundreds in recent years and represent a tremendous wellness resource. They can help counter the unhealthy side effects of the typical sedentary life/workstyle. Recent studies have begun to document the long-proclaimed administrative and economic benefits of company fitness programs. Among the documented benefits are lower absenteeism and turnover and a positive impact on productivity. Employees who are encouraged in their pursuit of fitness by convenient access to quality facilities and a supportive organizational climate will much more likely stick with a workout program than those with less supportive circumstances.[15]

How can you bring together the three important aspects of executive health: coping with stress, proper diet, and regular exercise? By making them a part of your own daily routine. You must systematically formulate a program that incorporates them into your daily life. Some of the key parts of such a program should be the following:

Coping with Stress

a. Avoid unrealistic deadlines.

b. Pace yourself.

c. Determine when you work best during the day and schedule the most difficult or complex work for those time periods; during the rest of the day carry out assignments requiring average or less-than-average demands.

d. Plan your work day in advance so you know what is supposed to be happening and you can get mentally prepared to meet these challenges.

Diet

a. Do not eat too much.

Develop an overall strategy for maintaining your health.

b. If you have to lose some weight, cut down on supper because there is less time to burn off these calories before you go to bed.

c. Keep your alcohol intake to one to two drinks a day maximum.

---

14. U.S. Senate, Report of the Select Committee on Nutrition and Human Needs, *Eating in America: Dietary Goals for the United States* (Cambridge, Mass.: MIT Press, 1977), p. 13.

15. Robert Kreitner, "Personal Wellness: It's Just Good Business," *Business Horizons,* May–June 1982, p. 34.

d.   In addition to the earlier suggestions on diet, stay away from desserts and other fattening foods unless you are on a regular exercise program and can work off these calories.

Exercise

a.   Engage in a regular physical activity every day and, if you can have the time (and ability) look into semi-rigorous activity such as swimming, jogging, handball, or racquetball on a regular basis (two to three times a week). Be sure to have a physical exam before starting any of these programs.

b.   When you exercise, work on relaxing your mind by thinking about something that makes you happy and helps you develop a positive mental attitude.

c.   If you find yourself getting nervous or tense during the day, sit comfortably in a quiet location and with your eyes closed, and work to calm yourself mentally. Examine what is bothering you and gently try to reestablish a psychological equilibrium.

Summary

1. Successful executives have very similar profiles. Perhaps the most important profile characteristic is their competence. They know their jobs. These individuals also tend to be long-time employees of the firms they head. Recent research shows that these executives come from many different functional areas and that they are well compensated for their efforts.

2. Most people go through a series of career phases or stages. The six most common are breaking away, initial adulthood, a transition period, settling down, possible mid-life crisis, and an establishment of equilibrium.

3. Many people encounter career problems. Some of the most common for people just starting out include simple and boring work, organizational politics, knowing what counts, loyalty issues, and ethical problems. Later on the most common problem is the career plateau.

4. Numerous career strategies can help you succeed. One of these is a sound self-evaluation. By determining what you are good at and what you like, you can help identify an initial career path. A complementary approach is to write an obituary or describe meaningful job events you would like to have happen to you during your career.

5. A second career strategy is the effective use of career tactics. You should be a high performer, keep a hero file, get into a management position as quickly as possible, find a sponsor, help your boss succeed, seek opportunity before money, and keep yourself mobile.

6. A third career strategy is to formulate a career development plan. This involves investigating organizational efforts designed to assist in career pathing, learning to negotiate for yourself, and aligning your job-related and personal needs with your career stages.

7. Another important part of career planning is executive health. Millions of Americans suffer from heart and blood vessel disease, which is partially attributable to stress. Type A people are most likely to suffer coronary heart disease. Three interdependent steps people can take to deal with this problem are to cope with stress, follow a proper diet, and exercise regularly.

Key Terms

Breaking away   The first career phase. During this period individuals begin establishing independence and autonomy from their parents.

Burnout   A total depletion of one's physical and mental resources caused by excessive striving to reach some unrealistic, job-related goals.

Career plateau   A period during which individuals find that their upward progress is halted and, in many cases, their climb to the top is over.

Establishment of equilibrium   A career phase during which individuals reevaluate their progress, find that things are going along pretty well, and feel a large degree of contentment, optimism, and stability.

Ethics   Principles that determine right and wrong conduct.

Initial adulthood   The second career phase. During this period many people begin developing organizational and professional ties and formulating a career plan.

Mid-life crisis   A career phase during which individuals evaluate their work progress, determine that things are not going well for them, and encounter strong psychological stress which can result in their doing foolish or bizarre things.

Settling down   The fourth career phase. During this period most people begin working hard to establish the groundwork for their career advancement.

Stressor   A factor, intraorganizational or extraorganizational in nature, that results in tension, anxiety, nervousness, or other forms of stress.

Transition period   The third career phase. During this period people evaluate their career progress and sometimes, if things are not going according to their plan, move to another organization.

Type A behavior   Behavior that is characterized by an action-emotion complex that can be observed in any person who is aggressively involved in a chronic, incessant struggle to achieve more and more in less and less time.

Yerkes-Dodson law   A law of physiology that holds that as stress increases, efficiency and performance initially increase and then decrease.

Questions for Analysis and Discussion

1. If the current president of a firm is a finance person, how likely is it that the next president will also be a finance person? Explain.

2. How well are executives compensated? Cite some data to support your conclusion.

3. What is the major factor that accounts for executive success? Be complete in your answer.

4. In general terms, most people go through a series of career phases or stages. What are these phases or stages? Identify and describe each in detail.

5. Do the career motivations of young men differ from those of young women? Explain, being sure to cite statistics to back up your answer.

6. Are there any particular problems that you are likely to encounter when starting out your career? Identify and describe three.

7. What is a career plateau? What causes such a plateau? How can such a problem be overcome? Explain.

8. In making a self-evaluation, what are some of the most important questions you should ask? State and describe four.

9. Of what value is writing an obituary to an individual interested in career planning? How can writing down a list of important or meaningful job-related

events that you would like to have happen to you during your career help your plan for the future? Explain.

10. Are there any career tactics that can help you increase your chances of success? Identify and describe four.

11. Of what value is a career development plan? What would be included in such a plan? Be as complete as possible in your description.

12. In what way is stress related to coronary heart disease? Explain, being sure to include information from Figure 20–2 in your answer.

13. How does a Type A person act? In what way is this kind of behavior likely to lead to coronary heart disease?

14. How are stress and burnout related? If a person suffers from stress, will he or she also suffer burnout? Explain.

15. How can you manage stress, avoid burnout, and assure yourself a long, healthy career? Be sure to include in your answer a discussion of diet and physical fitness.

Case

While the Quitting's Good

Sally Cabrera is not happy. For the last year, ever since she was graduated from college, she has worked for a utility firm in the Midwest. During this time she has found herself disillusioned, frustrated, angry, and exhausted.

When Sally first started her job, she had a great amount of enthusiasm and drive. She was looking forward to using all of the tools and techniques she had studied in college. That is not what happened, however. Within a few weeks it was obvious to her that she could do the job with just a high school diploma. Everything was highly routine and simple. Before long Sally found herself becoming bored with the work. Mostly she just read reports, checked data, and kept her boss informed.

In the beginning her boss asked her questions about what the data meant. Sally liked this because it gave her a chance to make a systematic analysis of the information. It soon became evident, however, that the boss was simply trying to get a better personal understanding of the data; it was not to give Sally a chance for analytical experience. In fact, on occasion Sally asked her boss if he would like her to work up some special types of reports or data comparisons, but he always said no.

Sally attributed a great deal of her boss's lack of concern to the fact that rigorous data analysis was not vital to the work. She concluded that the boss had plenty to do without getting into other projects.

Three weeks ago Sally received her annual performance evaluation. She was ranked low/average. Her boss wrote on her evaluation that she had average drive, was only marginally competent in her work, and did not show a great deal of interest or enthusiasm for the job. Sally was shocked. She felt that she had gone out of her way to do a good job. If anything, she thought she would get a superior rating.

After talking with three other people who started at the same time she did, Sally learned that her performance rating was the lowest of all.

Additionally, one of these people told her that he had learned he was going to be promoted within a week. Given her performance evaluation, Sally knows that there is no chance of her being promoted. In fact, she thinks it may be time to start looking around for employment elsewhere. "I might as well move while I'm mobile," she told her mom. "I've only been with this firm for a year and already I've fallen behind those who started when I did. If I wait another year, I might not be able to find anything. After all, if I got a low/average rating when I was really trying, what kind of rating will I get now that I've finally given up? I think I'd better quit while the quitting's good."

1. What typical problems did Sally run into on her first job? Identify and describe them.

2. Drawing upon your understanding of career tactics, what would you recommend that Sally do now? Explain.

3. Before she decides to accept another job offer, what should Sally do to prevent running into the same problem again? Explain.

You Be the Consultant

A Matter of Life or Death

No one ever gave Josh Adams anything for nothing. He earned it all. So when he was elected chief executive officer (CEO) of his corporation at the age of 43, he openly admitted that he got where he was through drive, determination, and hard work. In fact, he loved to recount some of his trials and tribulations to young managers in the firm, urging them to keep their noses to the grindstone. "Maybe someday you'll replace me," he told them. "Remember, you're never too young to succeed."

When he assumed the CEO position, Josh began to work even harder. He increased the number of people in his office by 50 percent, and the amount of work that the office generated more than doubled. At the same time, Josh was gone almost half the time. Four months ago his schedule had him in Saudi Arabia the first week of the month; Paris, London, and Brussels the second week; back at the home office the third week; and in Tokyo the fourth week.

Three months ago he was in Los Angeles to break ground for a new office building the firm was constructing there. As usual his schedule was hectic. As he was heading back to the airport Josh became ill. His assistant ordered the driver to head for the UCLA Medical Center. Josh was lucky. Within an hour he was admitted and initial tests had been run. Josh had suffered a mild heart attack. "If you had been in the air winging your way back to New York," the doctor told him, "you might have wound up in the hospital for three months. As it is, you'll be with us for three weeks."

Josh was relieved, "I'm glad it's not going to be any longer than that," he told the doctor. "I've got a million things to do back at the office." It was then that the doctor pulled his chair up close to Josh's bed and started talking in a hushed, serious tone. The essence of what he said was the following:

> Listen, forget all of this stuff about a lot of work back at the office. You're darned lucky not to have had your entire career terminated. You are a very sick man. Oh sure, I know how hard you work. I've read your comments in the newspaper. You're a national celebrity. And you're also going to be the youngest CEO in the cemetery this month. Who do you think you are? Do you think your body is going to last forever? Look at how far you've come in your short lifetime. You're one of the most famous business-people in the country. But everything has its price. I've heard you quoted as saying just that. So apply your own philosophy to yourself. Look at how fast you work, how fast you live. You've lived more in 43 years than most people have in their entire lifetime. Now it's catching up with you. Do you exercise? Do you watch what you eat? Do you take time to relax? Undoubtedly not. So think about it, Josh. You're going to have to change your lifestyle or you're going to die.

The doctor's words shocked Josh. He had never really thought much about his health. He was always able to get by on four or five hours of sleep a night. Oh sure, he did not eat very healthful foods but he took a vitamin pill every day. And as far as exercise was concerned, while he did not follow any formal program, he felt that he got more than enough exercise running for planes and taxis. Now he thinks that the doctor might be right. Perhaps he has neglected his health in his never-ending quest for the top. Yet he still finds himself caught in a dilemma.

On the one hand, Josh believes he probably should slow down. He needs a better plan for coping with stress. A good diet and a regular exercise program would also help. On the other hand, he has gotten where he is because of his incessant drive. He has developed a lifestyle which, while it is different from that of most other people, has allowed him to succeed where just about everyone else has failed. He has risen far above the crowd. If he changes his habits, he is afraid that he will fall back into the group of "average" individuals found in every organization. How can he protect his unique character and philosophy if he allows himself to adopt a slower lifestyle? The answer to this question still evades him, but Josh knows that he has to do something. At the moment, his doctor's parting words are still ringing inside of his head, "If you don't slow down, you'll kill yourself. Only you can make that decision, Josh. Do you want to live or do you want to die?"

Your Consultation

Assume that you are Josh's closest friend and that he has shared his dilemma with you. What would you advise him to do? Explain, being sure to incorporate into your answer a discussion of executive health, Type A behavior, stress and burnout, diet, and exercise. Phrase your answer so that it will help Josh cope with the stresses of a CEO's job while still helping him lead a long, healthy life.

Name Index

Subject Index